# Scottish Family History

# Scottish Family History

A Guide to Works of Reference on the
History and Genealogy of Scottish Families

BY MARGARET STUART

TO WHICH IS PREFIXED

## AN ESSAY ON HOW TO WRITE THE HISTORY OF A FAMILY

BY

SIR JAMES BALFOUR PAUL, K.C.V.O., LL.D.

EMERITUS LORD LYON KING OF ARMS

*Baltimore*

GENEALOGICAL PUBLISHING CO., INC.

*1983*

Originally published: Edinburgh, Scotland, 1930
Reprinted: Genealogical Publishing Co., Inc.
Baltimore, 1978, 1979, 1983
Reprinted from a volume in the George Peabody Department,
Enoch Pratt Free Library,
Baltimore, Maryland
Library of Congress Catalogue Card Number 77-90813
International Standard Book Number 0-8063-0795-1
*Made in the United States of America*

# PREFACE

My first book was published so long ago as 1875, and from that day to this I have been responsible for a good deal of writing on a variety of subjects—history, heraldry, genealogy, biography, and even to a small extent fiction. But having pled guilty to all this, I think I can promise that the following pages will be my swan song. I trust they may be of some service to those who are interested enough to read them. In the thirty-seven years during which I had the honour to be Lyon King of Arms I was brought so much in contact with persons who were either writing a history of their family or were anxious to do so, but did not know exactly how to begin, that I thought it might be useful to write a little guide for the benefit of the man in the street who might have ambitions that way. I do not pretend to have done more than write a popular sketch of the subject and to have given a few hints to the budding author, which he may expand to the extent of his own ideas on the subject. I have aimed at having a heart-to-heart talk with the prospective chronicler of his family's history. I do not claim that the information I have given is altogether exhaustive, but I hope I may have put the intending writer on the right lines. If he wishes to go further he may consult serious works like Mr Livingstone's *Guide to the Records in the Register House* or Mr Hector Mackechnie's erudite work on *The Pursuit of Pedigree*. Perhaps it is as well to explain that my portion of this book was written some years before Mr Mackechnie can have even thought of his work. I had intended to have added a Bibliography, but other things came in the way and the matter was lost sight of. When my friend Mrs Stuart, who had compiled a remarkably good index to the *Scots Peerage* which I edited, kindly agreed to take up the bibliographical part of the book, I gladly accepted, knowing the work could not be in more competent hands.

I have pleasure in including her in this prefatory bow to our readers. I am asked to state that the origin of this list of family books was the possession of some slips collected for a similar purpose by myself and Mr J. R. Anderson of Glasgow.

Mrs Stuart wishes specially to acknowledge the kindness of Dr Theodore R. F. Thomson in lending her the MS. of his volume on *British Family Histories*, and for supplying the very many references to the thirteenth and fourteenth editions of *Burke's Landed Gentry;* also to express her thanks to the Librarians of the National Library, the Signet Library, and the Free Library in Edinburgh for much useful advice and information.

On my own part I have to acknowledge with gratitude the help given me by Mr H. M. Paton, of the Historical Department in H.M. Register House, who has kindly revised the proofs of my portion of this book, and given me the benefit of his wide knowledge of Scottish records.

J. B. P.

# CONTENTS

## I.—HOW TO WRITE THE HISTORY OF A FAMILY

CHAP.                                                                    PAGE

   I. The Family History in General . . . . 3

  II. The Tabulated Pedigree Chart . . . . . 5

 III. The Small Family History . . . . . 11

 IV. The Anecdotal Family History . . . . . 16

   V. The Historical Method . . . . . . 22

 VI. The Scientific Method . . . . . . 25

 VII. Portraits and Illustrations . . . . . 30

VIII. The Public Records: *A.* The Printed Records . . 34

 IX. The Public Records: *B.* The Unpublished Records . 49

  X. Private Records . . . . . . . 58

 XI. Club Publications . . . . . . . 60

 XII. Chartularies of Religious and other Houses . . . 68

XIII. Miscellanea . . . . . . . 73

## II.—SCOTTISH FAMILY HISTORY

Scottish Families in Alphabetical Order . . . . 77

Miscellaneous Lists of Names of Persons . . . . 379

APPENDIX—

  Bibliography . . . . . . . . 385

  Court of the Lord Lyon . . . . . . 386

  Societies . . . . . . . . 386

# I

# HOW TO WRITE A FAMILY HISTORY

# CHAPTER I

## THE FAMILY HISTORY IN GENERAL

No apology is necessary in the case of anyone who wishes to write a family history. Most well-constituted persons (though there are no doubt exceptions) have an interest in knowing who their ancestors were, and in tracing them back as far as can be done. It is only human nature to feel gratified at being descended from a long line of distinguished ancestry, but this involves a corresponding duty on the part of the individual of to-day to live up to the high standard of his race. It is still no less a matter of interest to trace a pedigree, if the ancestors are not in the least distinguished, or if they have walked in the humbler walks of life. To chase these through musty records to the point when all record disappears is, to many minds, far from being a dry pursuit, one of the most fascinating.

Probably no country of its size has produced more family histories than Scotland, and in some ways this is rather remarkable, because there are comparatively few family names in Scotland, as compared with other countries. The forty or fifty big clans absorb a large proportion of Scottish names, and the big Lowland families account for many more. This occasionally makes the search for a particular individual, who bears a very common name, more difficult than it would otherwise be. But it has not prevented quite a large number of Scottish family histories from being written. They are of all sorts, big and little, good and bad, from Sir William Fraser's sumptuous privately-printed tomes or *The Wedderburn Book* with its wealth of summarised details and carefully marshalled evidence, down to a production like *The Red and White Book of Menzies;* there is ample choice of what to imitate and what to avoid imitating.

There are several ways of setting forth a family history. The shortest and simplest, though not perhaps the least troublesome, is the tabulated pedigree—the "family tree" as it is often popularly called. If the history is only a short one, consisting merely of the names of the different members of the family, their wives and children, and a brief epitome of their career, it may not exceed the dimensions of a pamphlet. Then there is the anecdotal history, which may run to any length, and may vary in character from being first cousin to a novel, as in *By Allan Water*, to a gossipy chat about the family in general, with a good deal of local colour thrown in. There is the more scientific and scholarly method of giving biographical sketches, with the most minute detail in respect of births, deaths, and marriages, or other incidents, giving the authorities for the statements. Lastly, there is the historical method, in which the events of the times are treated in relation to the various personages discussed; Sir William Fraser's works are good examples of this style.

In whatever way the history is written, three things are essential; one, an abstract quality, and the other two, specific entities. The first is absolute accuracy in regard to the statements made, and to names and dates. The second is a good tabulated pedigree, for however cleverly and lucidly arranged the text may be, the tabulated pedigree will always be a great assistance to the reader. The third essential requisite is a good index. If it is an index of the persons mentioned in the work, each name should be identified by a short description. Do not put merely "John Maxwell," but "John Maxwell, 3rd son of 1st Lord Herries of Terregles"; not merely "Marjory Murray," but "Marjory Murray, wife of Sir Alexander Gibson of Durie."

Let us examine the different methods of compiling a genealogical work as mentioned above, somewhat more in detail.

# CHAPTER II

YOU will find this rather a troublesome job, and you will probably spoil a good many sheets of paper, before arriving at a satisfactory result; but it is worth the labour. Of course it must be employed in moderation; in the case of a very large family, it will overflow all bounds and become a monstrosity. In this case it is wise to have separate charts of the various branches, and a key chart, showing the relation of the different cadet branches to each other. Of the key chart we shall speak later. Meanwhile let us make a start on the ordinary pedigree chart.

At the top of the sheet you will put the earliest ancestor you have got, with his wife, if you have been able to find her and the date of their marriage; also the date of both their births and deaths if possible. More than that you will not have room for. It is convenient too to put below the names the pages of the text where the biographical notices of the different persons may be found. So far you have this:—

JOHN SMITH    md. 1 June 1636    AGNES BROUN
b. 18 March 1609                b. 4 May 1616
d. 20 Oct. 1672                 d. 2 Aug. 1680
                                   (pp. 42-44).

You will now draw a vertical line from this couple, and connect it with a horizontal line below, from which you will suspend, from a series of smaller lines, the names of the children.

It is better perhaps to ignore the order of their birth, and to put the sons first and the daughters last; in this

case their order in the family may be indicated by numerals.
Thus :—

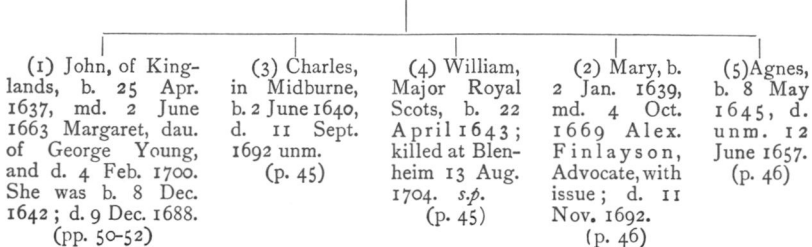

| (1) John, of King-lands, b. 25 Apr. 1637, md. 2 June 1663 Margaret, dau. of George Young, and d. 4 Feb. 1700. She was b. 8 Dec. 1642 ; d. 9 Dec. 1688. (pp. 50–52) | (3) Charles, in Midburne, b. 2 June 1640, d. 11 Sept. 1692 unm. (p. 45) | (4) William, Major Royal Scots, b. 22 April 1643; killed at Blenheim 13 Aug. 1704. s.p. (p. 45) | (2) Mary, b. 2 Jan. 1639, md. 4 Oct. 1669 Alex. Finlayson, Advocate, with issue ; d. 11 Nov. 1692. (p. 46) | (5)Agnes, b. 8 May 1645, d. unm. 12 June 1657. (p. 46) |

You will observe that the eldest son has got an estate.
How he acquired it is not for the chart pedigree to tell; it
will be found in the text to which a reference is given.  You
will also note that the younger brother is styled "in," not
"of," Midburne, which shows that he was not the proprietor
of that place, but merely a tenant.

You may find that your space is all too narrow if any of
the families are large, but space can be economised by writing
the names sideways, and not across the page.  If, however,
the family is a very large one, the details of the various
branches must be given in separate pedigrees, and an index
table supplied, setting forth briefly, without any mention of
wives, etc., the position in which the various members of the
family, who have founded cadet branches, stand to each other
and to their common ancestor, with every information as to
where fuller details of these are to be found.  Good examples
of those index pedigrees may be found in Fraser's *History of
the Carnegies, Earls of Southesk, and of their Kindred.*

It is needless to say that, in a chart pedigree, all members
of the same generation should be put in the same horizontal
line.

### THE COLUMN ARRANGEMENT

Another form of displaying a pedigree may be called the
column system.  It has the advantage of not requiring very
extended space, though it is not perhaps suitable for more
than about seven generations; and any number of female
descents may be traced down without difficulty.  The name
of the common ancestor is put at the head of the page; then

seven (if you are dealing with seven generations) vertical columns are drawn at the left-hand side of the page. Opposite these are put the names, with a numeral corresponding to the generation to which they belong put in the proper column. An example, however, is better than any detailed description, and here is an extract from a Sandeman pedigree which has been done in this way :—

DAVID SANDEMAN md. 1716 Margaret, dr. of David Ramsay of Baldene, Fife. Their descendants are :—

| | | | | | | |
|---|---|---|---|---|---|---|
| I | ... | ... | ... | ... | ... | Catherine Sandeman, b. 1717, d. 1759, m. 1738 John Anderson, Merchant, Perth. |
| ... | I | ... | ... | ... | ... | David Anderson, b. 1739. |
| ... | 2 | ... | ... | ... | ... | Thomas Anderson, b. 1740, m. Sarah Rose. |
| ... | ... | I | ... | ... | ... | Rose Anderson, m. Thos. Hay Marshall. |
| ... | ... | 2 | ... | ... | ... | Catherine Ann Anderson. |
| ... | 3 | ... | ... | ... | ... | Margaret Anderson. |
| ... | 4 | ... | ... | ... | ... | Jane Anderson. |
| ... | 5 | ... | ... | ... | ... | Catherine Anderson, m. David Lindsay. |
| ... | ... | I | ... | ... | ... | Harry Lindsay, m. Jane Sandeman. |
| ... | ... | ... | I | ... | ... | William Sandeman Lindsay. |
| ... | ... | ... | 2 | ... | ... | David Lindsay. |
| ... | ... | ... | 3 | ... | ... | John Lindsay. |
| ... | ... | ... | 4 | ... | ... | Catherine Lindsay. |
| ... | ... | ... | 5 | ... | ... | Mary Lindsay, m. F. H. Ramsbotham, M.D. |

Now supposing you have got to the end of a page, you must, at the head of the next page, put all the couples whose descendants are not yet exhausted, but without putting any numbers against them in the column, thus :—

David Sandeman and Margaret Ramsay.
Catherine Sandeman and John Anderson.
Catherine Anderson and David Lindsay.
Harry Lindsay and Jane Sandeman.

You will then go on to enumerate the Ramsbotham family, remembering to put their numbers in the column after that of their parents, that is to say, in the fifth. In this way you will exhaust all the descendants of Catherine Sandeman and David Anderson, before getting to Catherine's next brother Robert, whose number will be 2 in the first column. All his descendants (if he had any) would then be enumerated, before tackling his younger brother David, whose number would be 3 in the first column.

The advantage of this system is that many more descendants can be introduced than is possible in a tabulated pedigree; a disadvantage is that such a pedigree necessarily requires an index of names in alphabetical order, with references to the pages, so as to indicate where any particular individual may be found.

### THE DROP LINE AND SLIP SYSTEM

There is another very ingenious method of drawing up a pedigree, which may be termed the drop line and slip system. It requires some dexterity and care, but it is an extremely neat way of showing at a glance the direct descent of each branch.

The common ancestor is put at the head of the page, and below him are ranged in one straight line all his children. Below each of these who had issue, you will put a short vertical line; in the case of the eldest son, this vertical line will meet a horizontal line, with the names of his children on the same original page, which will also contain the issue of all the eldest sons in each generation. But to deal with the children of the second son, you will take a fresh sheet, the top of which will only come up to the bottom of the short vertical line which hangs down from his name. Then draw another short line meeting the former one, and connect it with a horizontal line, which will contain the names of all the issue of the second son of the common ancestor. You will treat the remaining children of the latter in exactly the same way, so that all the pages containing the second generation will be cut the same size, the second son's page lying lowest, and those of the younger children being superimposed on it. Then go back to the second son of the eldest son, and treat his issue in exactly the same way, remembering that their pages will be so much the shorter than the former ones. You can then work through the whole family in the same way, always keeping in view that each generation of the different branches will be displayed on the same size of page. By the time you get down to the present generation, they will appear on mere narrow slips. It is a very clever method, but care must be taken in binding it together, to see that the drop lines at the bottom of one generation join accurately the top lines in the next generation. The disadvantage is that, owing to the pages being of different sizes, it does not make a very shapely book. The tabulated pedigree of the Balfours of Pilrig and Mr J. H. Stevenson's Caddell pedigree are good examples of this method.

## THE WHEEL PEDIGREE

This need only be mentioned with a warning to avoid it. Though rather popular at one time, it has nothing to recommend it. The common ancestor is set in the middle of a small circle, and round this are· drawn other circles, each representing a different generation. The various descendants gyrate around their progenitor, being fenced off from each other by the spokes of the wheel. It takes up much room, and the names of the different persons mentioned in it being written at various angles, it requires the sheet to be shifted round and round, before you can catch the name you want. Truly a clumsy and confused method.

## THE FAMILY TREE

The methods mentioned above are pedigree charts, but this one is truly a "tree." It is fortunately obsolete, but flourished vigorously a century ago. In this case a common ancestor was neither put at the top of the page nor in a circle in the middle, but was represented by an aged gentleman, often in armour, lying on his back on a velvety sward. From his stomach grew upwards a portentous trunk, inscribed with the names of his male descendants in the senior line. At intervals along the trunk there issued large branches, from these small branches, and then twigs. They all bore an extraordinary crop of fruit, in the shape of large circular discs, on which were inscribed the names of the various scions of the original stock. Leaves *au naturel* were put in with a free hand, but the result was neither a good botanical specimen, nor a very intelligible pedigree.

Before leaving this part of the subject, it may be well to point out that the somewhat severe lines of a chart pedigree may be lightened up by the insertion, before the names, of coats-of-arms, or in the case of peers of the coronet of their rank. Soldiers may have crossed swords, doctors Æsculapian rods, and many other little appropriate symbols may suggest themselves to the mind of the ingenious compiler. At all events, the family coat-of-arms, if there is one, may be displayed at some size in one of the upper corners of the chart. But take care that it is a genuine and authorised coat, and not merely the suggestion of a silversmith or die-sinker. There is a Swinton pedigree table which admirably displays this style of ornament.

It is an advantage to print the senior line, or the line which you specially wish to be followed, in red; however, this is a counsel of perfection, for it must be remembered that this involves double printing and is proportionately expensive.

# CHAPTER III

## THE SMALL FAMILY HISTORY

LET us leave the mechanical planning - out of charts, and proceed to consider the writing of a family history : and first, as to the small family history or, if you prefer it, the history of a small family; for if you are going back some hundreds of years, and mean to trace all the descendants, you cannot make a very small volume of your history. But you may ask, if the family only goes back for three or four generations before it is lost, if not in the mists of antiquity at least in the crowd of unrecorded lives, what need is there to write a history of it? To which it may be replied, that however undistinguished your ancestors may have been, and however humbly they may have "kept the noiseless tenor of their way," it is not unfitting that for the sake of their and your posterity you should put on permanent record as much information as you can collect about them. How often has it been said to me by persons hunting for their ancestors, "If I had only asked my father or grandmother about all this; but they never spoke about the family to me, and they died when I was too young to take an interest in the matter, and now much information which they must have had is lost for ever."

The writing of a little book, a little pamphlet even, because it need not exceed a few pages, would avoid this loss of information. It is a fairly easy thing to do; you need not make a long story of it, in fact its contents should be as compressed as possible. Go back to the earliest ancestor about whom you can get any information, either from family tradition (not often a safe thing to trust), from private papers, diaries, letters and the like, or from the records to which I shall afterwards refer, and write down his name, date of birth, calling in life, any honours he may have received, and the

11

date of his death. It is more convenient thus to finish him off at once. Then you may mention his wife's name and the names of her father and mother, and the dates of her birth, marriage, and death. You will be careful to prefix to this paragraph the Roman numeral I. Then come the children, and it is a moot point whether it is better to put all the sons first and then all the daughters, or to arrange them in the exact order of their births. Personally I prefer the former, but it may be left to the discretion of the compiler.

Supposing therefore you take the eldest son first, you will put his name in smaller type than the first paragraph and a little indented, that is to say, a little farther in on the page than that of his father, and prefix to him the Arabic numeral 1. You need not in this place do more than mention his name, because he will become the subject of paragraph II., after you have exhausted the other children and their descendants. Then you will take the next son and label him 2. You will, in his case, give all the details as given in the notice of his father. His children will be indented a little further on the page, and will be docketed (1), (2), (3), and so on. The succeeding generations will carry the numbers i., ii., iii., etc., and (i), (ii), (iii), etc. It is possible to go on further and number still younger generations alphabetically A, B, C, etc., (A), (B), (C), etc., a, b, c, and then diverge into the Greek alphabet. But for the practical purpose of a short family history the series (i), (ii), (iii), will be found amply sufficient, and if you push it further you will find your lines getting very short, and the page to consist of more blank paper than letterpress.

But an ounce of example is better than a pound of precept, so here is a short example of a pedigree constructed on the above lines :—

I. Humphrey Cantle (traditionally said to have been a cadet of the Cantells of that ilk; no proof of this has been found, but the fact that Humphrey was a common name in the family of Cantells is suggestive), saddler, burgess of Edinburgh; bailie of that city 1760-66; died 20 August 1777. Married 17 Dec. 1741, Lilias, daughter of Archibald Doughnut,

baker, and Ann Honey his wife. She died 9 July 1778 and
was buried along with her husband in Greyfriars Churchyard.
They had issue:—

1. John, of whom presently.
2. Humphrey, born 8 Feb. 1750; carried on his father's business
   till 1790, when he retired on account of ill-health, and died
   unmarried 11 Sept. 1795.
3. Archibald, born 7 March 1752; apprentice to William Henbane,
   apothecary, Edinburgh, 22 July 1767, and ultimately carried
   on the business under the designation of Henbane and
   Cantle; d. 6 June 1825, having married, first, 9 June 1777
   Sarah, eldest daughter of the Rev. Ephraim Barker, minister
   of Cramond, and Giles M'Corquodale his wife. She died
   11 March 1801, and he married secondly, 2 Jan. 1805,
   Janet, daughter of George Speedwell, farmer, Blinkbonny,
   Midlothian; she died 9 July 1832. By his first wife only
   he had issue:—

   (1) Humphrey, born 1 April 1778; a physician in Edinburgh,
       M.D. Edinr. Univ. 1802, F.R.C.P.E. 1805; d. 28 March
       1850. Married 23 July 1809, Cecilia, second daughter
       of James Hog of Hogpen (Lord Hogpen), a Senator of
       the College of Justice. She died 19 Feb. 1841, leaving
       issue:—

       i. Archibald, b. 7 May 1810; entered the service
          of the H.E.I.C.S. and died at Madras 4 Aug.
          1828, unmarried.
       ii. George, b. 19 March 1812; M.D. Edinr. 1835;
          practised at Knaresborough, Yorks., and died
          there 11 July 1875. Married 9 Nov. 1840,
          Henrietta Susan, third daughter of Horatio
          Deedswell, solicitor, York. They had only
          one daughter.

          (i) Cecilia Hay, b. 6 Aug. 1841; she was
              imbecile and d. 4 May 1862.

II. John, b. 29 Nov. 1742; Advocate 1766, Advocate-Depute
1775-1780, Sheriff of Clackmannanshire 1780 till his death,
which occurred at Edinburgh, 29 Oct. 1802. He married
22 July 1776, Magdalene, daughter and co-heiress of Henry

Foulrig of Blackdub, Fife, and Mary Merrythought his wife. She died 9 June 1810, leaving issue :—

1. Humphrey, of whom presently.
2. Ephraim, b. 3 July 1782 ; went to India in 1796 and engaged in trade there, ultimately founding the firm of Cantle, Green, & Co.  He came home in 1827, having amassed a large fortune, and bought the estate of Tresham Towers, Hants. He died there unmarried 20 May 1842 ; the bulk of his fortune went to his brother's family, but he left £75,000 to found an asylum for decayed cabmen, and he also bequeathed his large collection of pictures to the nation. The Government, however, on the ground that most of them were spurious, declined the bequest.
3. Anna, b. 9 Dec. 1778 ; married in 1796 Jonathan Cutpurse (an elopement).

III.  Humphrey, of Blackdub, to which estate he succeeded on the death of his mother, born 14 June 1779, Ensign 28th Foot 1797, Lieut. 1800, exchanged to 2nd Dragoon Guards 1801, Captain 1803, served in the Peninsular War and received the Portuguese Order of the Tower and Sword.  Retired as Major in 1812, and died at Blackdub, of which he had enlarged the house, and much improved the amenity and value, 2 April 1848.  He married, 15 Jan. 1812, Jessie, daughter of Rev. Thomas Goodenough, minister of Kennaquhair, and Alice Fair his wife.  She d. 2 April 1868, leaving issue :—

1. Thomas.
2. John.

But we need not follow the fortunes of this middle-class family further.  It is enough to have shown in what a succinct way a little family history may be drawn up.  No literary erudition or style is necessary, nothing indeed but ordinary care and absolute accuracy.  If references are to be given, they may be relegated to footnotes, or given in brackets after the event which they are to prove : thus, in the notice of Archibald Cantle the apothecary, after " apprentice to William Henbane, apothecary, Edinburgh," might be put in brackets and italics (*Edinr. Register of Apprentices, Scot. Record Soc.*, p. 23).

Another point must be carefully considered by the compiler either of a pedigree like this or of a family history of a more ambitious kind.  How far is it wise or proper to drag out family skeletons from their closets for the edification (or the reverse) of posterity? No general rule can be laid down; much must be left to the sense and good taste of the compiler. Sir William Fraser, in his series of histories of great Scottish families, carefully avoided giving any disagreeable details, and in consequence much that would have thrown light on personal character and the manners of the time has been omitted. On the other hand, in some other publications of recent years too many scandalous details are given, some based on the merest society gossip, and others calculated to give pain to persons still alive. Now, in the supposed Cantle pedigree, there are two incidents which would require to be carefully weighed before putting them on record. Anna, the only daughter of the most respectable Sheriff John Cantle, is said to have eloped with Jonathan Cutpurse. The story was a sad one and was productive of much grief to the parents. Cutpurse had been introduced to her by Deacon Brodie, whose counsel her father had been in some civil action. The result was that they eloped and went to Glasgow, where they lived as man and wife for some time under an assumed name; they ultimately went to London, and readers of criminal literature will remember the trial of Jonathan for highway robbery, for which he was sentenced to death and was hanged at Tyburn. The family never heard of the unfortunate Anna, though some persons aver that as an old woman she returned to Edinburgh and sold salt on the streets. When such a story occurs in the records of a family, it is perhaps kinder to confine it to the oblivion of the past.

There is another less tragic circumstance connected with the Cantle family which it might or might not be fitting to record. It will be remembered that Ephraim, the Indian merchant, left his pictures, of which he considered himself a great connoisseur, to the nation, but that the gift was not accepted as they were mostly spurious. This does not reflect on the moral character of the worthy nabob in the least degree, but it shows that he was not such a knowing art critic as he fancied himself to be, and that the dealers had got the better of him. Had he left any descendants who might still be alive, they might have felt mildly hurt at this weakness of their ancestor being recorded, but as it is, there seems no reason for the facts not being chronicled.

# CHAPTER IV

## THE ANECDOTAL FAMILY HISTORY

THIS is frequently the work of a lady. It lacks, as a rule, a sufficient number of dates and almost always lacks references. All the same, this kind of history may be made a perfectly good family record. One difference between it and the more serious volumes of the sort is that it is made to be read; the others, though no doubt their authors would like them to be read, are mainly used for purposes of consultation, as books of reference in fact. But the anecdotal history is mostly bright and frequently amusing. The author has generally access to ancestral diaries, old account-books, and drawers full of letters of ancient date. These she may use skilfully and well, and if the author has an orderly mind, and arranges the matter so as to give a clear view of the descent of the main line of the family and of its various branches (if they are to be discussed in detail), it is as good a kind of history as any other, though it is not the sort of book that will satisfy a rigid genealogist.

Now, if you are going to write a work of this sort, there are some points which it may be as well to keep in view.

The "historic present" is no doubt a style which is dear to some writers, but it is unnecessary and out of place in writing a family history, and it is impossible to keep it up throughout a whole book. Alternations between it and the ordinary past tense are irritating to the reader and clumsy in effect. Take for instance this sentence from a typical family history of this kind—a very readable book too—"In 1745 Drummond of Callendar dissents on the part of himself and the other heritors to [? from] the Presbytery dividing and enlarging the Kirk of Crieff, stating that his burial place had been railed off from the choir and requests that this may not, in any alteration made, be encroached upon." Apart from the grammar of this sentence, there seems no apparent gain, either of picturesqueness or force, in putting the statement in the present tense. It would have been equally effective to say that Drummond dissented from the doings of the Presbytery, and that he requested that his burial place might not be encroached upon.

Again, the use of what may be termed local colour is tempting, and, if used with discretion, is not objectionable. However, if you describe an old gentleman sitting below spreading beech-trees in front of his house, surrounded by his family in picturesque costumes, and paint in the view as it appears to you to-day, you had better consider, first, if there were trees there at all in the old gentleman's day, secondly, if you have got your costumes of the right period, and thirdly, if the view from his house was anything like the view as it is seen at present. No doubt the hills and the rivers are the same, but the surface of the earth, which affects a view so largely, may have been very different in his day from what it is in ours.

Avoid, also, too many hypothetical situations: statements of what you think people did or ought to have done, though history remains quite silent on the point. Here is an instance which combines the faults of the historic present and the hypothetical incident:—"The Marquess of Montrose is visiting Black Pate's daughter Lady Nairne. Patrick's old opponent and cousin Lord Rollo dies in June 1669. Remembering the firm friendship with Sir William Rollock, Black Pate would attend what must have been a weird midnight scene, etc." Of course, the picture intended to be conjured up by this passage is the impressive midnight funeral of Lord Rollo, the flambeaux, mourning cloaks, Black Pate looking blacker than ever in the darkness and in his funeral garb. But there is no proof whatever that he was really at the funeral; he may have been or ought to have been, but a hundred things may have prevented him, and though it may be tempting to give rein to imagination, it is perhaps as well not to do it in the limits of a family history.

Having considered what to avoid in an anecdotal family history, let us pay attention for a little to the manner in which the work should be treated. Although anecdotal, or even

B

gossipy, there is no reason why it should not be a reliable history. The danger incurred by the author of a book of this sort is that he, or more frequently she, gets carried away by the subject, introduces a lot of irrelevant matter, and is overwhelmed by the number of children, relatives, and friends, who will keep tumbling over each other in the body of the work, to its detriment as a coherent exposition of the descent of a family. No doubt, more latitude may be allowed than in a history of a more serious and elaborate kind, but it is absolutely necessary to be both clear and accurate; and you must remember that what may be clear to you, who have the ramifications of the family at your fingers' end, may not be clear to the outsider who approaches the subject for the first time. Having therefore duly read and noted all your authorities, and made a rough pedigree-plan for your own reference, as you go along, you will begin of course with the earliest known ancestor; hypothetical progenitors must not be mentioned. If the pedigree goes back to the fifteenth or sixteenth centuries, part of the proof will no doubt depend on charters. In a book of this sort, which is intended, if not for popular reading, at least to be read through with as little difficulty to the reader as possible, it is perhaps better not to give the *ipsissima verba* of the charters, or even a close translation, but to give their general meaning in your own words. Unless you are to a certain extent familiar with charters, if you give them in the original Latin mistakes may creep in. If you give a literal translation, mistakes are still more likely to happen, though you may not perpetrate such a "howler" as a learned author did some time ago in a parish history. In dealing with a sixteenth century charter granted to "Domino Willelmo Sinclare de Rosling, militi," he translated these words as "Sir William Sinclare of the Roslin Militia"!

Having then discussed the first ancestor, you will bring the notice of him to a conclusion probably at the end of the first chapter; but wherever that occurs, give his wife's name (even though you have had occasion to mention it before) after the date of his death, and then the names of his children. If any of the latter died without issue, or with children whose descendants you do not mean to carry further, and whom you can treat of in a summary fashion, you may finish what you have got to say of them here. If any of them require detailed treatment, and if you wish to bring down their families to date, you must not do it here, but reserve the notices for a subsequent chapter. The golden rule in writing a family history is to finish off the main line of the family first, before giving any details about junior branches, unless as has been said above they can be dealt with in two or three lines. If you do not do this, the result will be confusion, and long gaps between the members of the principal family, and the interest of the succession very much lost.

Remember that you have no room to tell long and detailed stories. Such anecdotes as you may give must be to the point, and as condensed as possible. Do not drag in any irrelevant matter; if the book is too short that is a fault on the right side. Anecdotes should always throw some light on the character of the person about whom they are told. They should illustrate his humour, kindliness of heart, eccentricity or habits of life, and even if they illustrate less estimable qualities than these, it does not follow that they should be omitted; they too shed light on character.

Having finished the main line, you can treat any younger branches which are worthy of separate notice, in later chapters, and if any of their offspring are so important as to deserve detailed notices, this also must be done in other chapters. Do not be sparing in cross references; when dealing with those cadets mention the page where their progenitor first appears. Similarly, when their name is mentioned in the list of the children of their father, give the reference where the detailed account of their lives may be found. Sometimes this may be impossible, as when your printer cannot or will not keep up the earlier sheets of the book in type till you have got the later ones set up also. In these circumstances, all you can do is to say after the name "See *post* for detailed account."

While references to the authorities for the various statements made are necessary and obligatory in a scientifically constructed family history, they are not generally found in any great number in the anecdotal history. When they are given, and they are always useful, they should be stated in footnotes, so as to interrupt as little as possible the continuous flow of the narrative.

As in all family histories except the smallest, so in this, a tabulated pedigree of the main family, and other pedigrees of each branch dealt with separately, are indispensable. It is a great advantage to have pedigrees of each of the branches, as it makes the big pedigree-chart so much more simple, and avoids crowding it with a multitude of names. It is most useful, as has been said above, always to give, after each name, the page of the book where that particular person is discussed.

An index is also, it goes without saying, an indispensable adjunct to every family history worthy of the name, and this must not be a mere perfunctory collection of the principal names in the work. You need not necessarily make it an index of matters, but every name mentioned should be included and identified. If the person indexed has a full biography in the volume it is convenient, though not essential, to give the events of his life under his name, with the reference to the pages on which they are mentioned. In many cases, though hardly perhaps in an anecdotal history, a separate index of place-names is most useful. The making of an index is no doubt a piece of rather dull drudgery, but when it is kept in view that the fact of a book's having an index, not having an index, or only an imperfect and perfunctory one, makes all the difference in its usefulness, no pains should be grudged to make the index full and complete. It is a great convenience too, when there are many references after any one name, to put references to the pages where his career is described in detail, in heavier type than the others, thus " Andrew M'Culloch, 51, 72, **103-115**, 128, 205."

If you want to be really generous to your readers, a table of the contents of the various chapters is a very convenient thing. It may either be put by itself at the beginning of the volume, or each chapter may be headed by its own table of contents ; or as is done in many cases, both these plans may be followed, the table at the head of chapters being repeated from the table of contents at the beginning.

A word as to headlines. There is a variety of ways of dealing with these ; the easiest is of course merely to repeat the name of the book, in a condensed form if necessary, at the head of each page. It is difficult to see what object this serves; congenital idiots do not as a rule read family histories, and it is difficult to conceive of any other class of persons who would require to be reminded at every page of the name of the book they were reading. If you are going to devote each chapter to one man alone, then it is proper that his name should appear at the head of each of the pages devoted to him, accompanied, I should recommend, by the dates of his birth and death. Sir William Fraser's practice— and it was not a bad one—was to put a man's name and that of his wife or wives, as the case might be, as headings of the chapters dealing with them. The ideal headline is that which succinctly summarises in four or five words the main incidents in the page below it, but you have to wait till you get your book set up in pages before you can do this, and it is more expensive, because it has to go back to the printer after it has been to you, with the headline inserted, and in consequence charged as a correction.

Many of the matters above mentioned apply to all family histories and not merely to the anecdotal variety. They may seem to many trifling details hardly worth mentioning, and which might well be left to the common sense of the author. But some authors have no common sense, and more have, quite naturally (for a family history is very often the compiler's first attempt at literature), not the requisite knowledge of such details as are necessary to be considered and which, if properly carried out, add so much to the usefulness and value of a book.

# CHAPTER V

## THE HISTORICAL METHOD

IT is obvious that if a family is to be written about from the point of view of the relation which the different members bore to the principal events of their time, it must be a family that had some influence on public affairs. It is not every family that will lend itself to this treatment; the Cantles, for instance, a portion of whose pedigree was given on a previous page, were very honest citizens, but the history of the country would have gone on exactly as it did, had they never existed. Still, it is the "grand manner," and may make an instructive and interesting book. The Fraser cycle of family histories are examples of this method. It must be remembered, however, that all his books were printed privately, at the expense of the families concerned, and form an impressive series of massive tomes, gleaming in scarlet and gold, with all the advantages which a liberal expenditure of money could bestow on them. They are not so practically useful as they might have been, because a large quarto volume of six or seven hundred pages of thick paper is hardly the kind of book which lends itself to comfortable or easy reading. The principle of their arrangement was generally to give the history of the family in one volume, and a selection of the charters and correspondence contained in the muniment room in another. A few, such as the *Carnegie Book* and the work on the Frasers of Philorth, are designed on a more practical and better arranged method, but these were executed under the superintendence of the persons who commissioned the book. Sir William Fraser's volumes are as a whole, though pedestrian in style and not free from occasional error, sound pieces of work. He took his work seriously and always seems afraid of wounding the susceptibilities of his noble employers by narrating any but smooth and pleasant things about the family. In consequence we have no family scandals, even of the lighter sort, and very little anecdote. His selection of charters and other deeds appears often rather arbitrary and there is really little use in taking up space by printing charters at full length, sparing not a word of all their formal clauses of style. A properly calendared charter, such as is given in the printed volumes of the Register of the Great Seal, contains as much information as one transcribed at full length. Of course, if there are any exceptional clauses in a charter, these must be given, as they probably have an important bearing on the subject of the deed. But as a general rule it is sufficient to give the names of the granter and grantee, the land disponed, the series of heirs to whom they are destined, the *reddendo*, that is the yearly payment of money, or other acknowledgment to be made by the grantee to the granter, the names of the persons witnessing the deed, and its date. With regard to the latter, it may be as well to remind an intending compiler of a family history that in Scotland, up to 1st January 1600, the year began on 25th March. So that, previous to 1600, when you see a date like 15th January 1562, it really means the day that we should now call 15th January 1563. It is therefore expedient when such a date occurs, to give the double year and write 1562-63.

Please remember, too, when quoting charters, to see that they are quoted correctly. As regards charters under the Great Seal, there is no excuse for having them incorrect, as the Register is printed down to 1668. A warning as to the care to be taken in translations is given on pp. 18 and 43.

If you have a suitable family as your subject, and have made up your mind to write an account in this historical method, you will find that it will give you a good deal more trouble than if you were writing from a purely genealogical point of view; for you will have to make yourself master of the history of the public events of the times, and to show how they influenced the various individuals with whom you deal, or how on the other hand the latter influenced the times. Given a judicial mind, nothing could be more worthy of being chronicled ; but the worst of it is that a family historian rarely has a judicial mind.  If he is a member of the family about whom he writes, he naturally has a bias in their favour, and if he is not, his subject is still apt to take possession of him in a way that does not tend to strict impartiality.   But whatever he does, he should strive to be as brief as possible, and to avoid entering into irrelevant details.

# CHAPTER VI

## THE SCIENTIFIC METHOD

THIS is family history at its highest point. It may not be picturesque in style, it may not even make lively reading, but it is thorough and accurate. It gives the reader every bit of information about a man, which could be collected; possibly some of these details may not seem of much value, but you cannot tell; what seems insignificant and trifling to one reader, may be the very thing for which another is looking, because though the fact recorded may be in itself insignificant, it may help to fix a date or to elucidate an incident relating to something quite foreign to the history of the individual specified. Let me take as a text on this method, a very good example of this kind of work :—*The Wedderburn Book*, by Alexander Wedderburn, K.C., in two volumes. This was printed privately in 1898, so it is not very accessible. As it is however exceedingly well arranged and executed, a somewhat detailed description of it may not be out of place. Of the two volumes, the first contains the history proper, the second the authorities on which the statements in the history are based, generally given in abbreviated form, but of sufficient length to show the nature of their contents. The first volume begins with a table of contents, set forth in some detail, indicating the titles and contents of the various parts, chapters and sections into which the book is divided. This is followed by a preface explaining the genesis of the work, the manner in which it has been carried out, and acknowledgments of assistance received from various people. We then come to a very valuable feature of the work, the Introduction. This consists of an account of the early notices of the name in Scotland, and of the bearers thereof, though the connection of these with the Dundee family of the name, the subject of the book, cannot now be definitely traced. Then comes a summary of the history itself, written in clear language and without any references to authorities. This is an admirable feature, as it condenses the information about the family into comparatively few pages—some fifty in all, though these are large and closely printed. As the author admits, this no doubt involves some repetition, as the same fact may in consequence be stated three times over, first in the introduction, then in the detailed history, and lastly in the abstract of authorities in the second volume. However, its advantages far outweigh its disadvantages. It provides a succinct and readable account of the family history, and the reader is not distracted by the interpolation of references, or 'detained by unnecessary details. The history proper then commences. It is divided into six parts; the first of the early history of the family in Dundee, with an account of the different branches antecedent and collateral to that of Kingennie; the second part deals with the Wedderburns of Kingennie, Easter Powrie, and that ilk, with some account of the Scrymgeours, progenitors of the Scrymgeour-Wedderburns; the third part has an account of the Blackness branch and its younger lines; the fourth part describes the Wedderburns of Gosford, who became Halketts of Pitfirrane, through a marriage with the heiress of that family; part five is devoted to miscellaneous matter, such as the tombs of the family, their armorial bearings, and the previous histories of the race which have appeared; the volume concludes by treating in part six of various persons of the name in England, the Colonies or America, who are not known to be connected with the Forfarshire family.

These parts are divided into chapters. Each chapter deals with one man and his descendants, till they are either extinct or traced down to the present day. Occasionally, when the number of descendants requires it, the chapters are subdivided into sections, but this is not the general rule. To each chapter is appended, and this is a very important and useful feature in the book, a chart-pedigree tabulating the relationships of the different persons mentioned in it. There is also a good key pedigree to the families mentioned in the first part. Throughout the book too, there are several pedigrees dealing with families connected with the Wedderburns.

Here is part of one paragraph dealing with Alexander Wedderburn, third of Kingennie. It is given as an example of the general style of the book, and of the detailed and verified information contained in it:—

He was for many years an active member of the community in Dundee, of which, on more than one occasion he was chief magistrate. In 1638 (?) May 21, we first find him named as bailie (D. B. R. 407), and 17 Sept. 1639 he is one of the "faithful covenanters" elected to the new Council (D. C. B. 61). He was again elected bailie 22, 27 Sept. 1640 (*ib.* 62) and is often named as so acting 1640-41 (S. W. 280; D. C. B. 450-51; D. B. R. 422a), in the latter of which years 21 Sept., he was again elected on the council (D. C. B. 63). In 1642, March 15, he was kirkmaster (D. C. B. 465) and in this year acts as bailie on the bench, and in giving sasine 6 July, 12, 21 Oct., 17 Nov. (S. W. 285; B. C. B. 468; D. B. R. 428). In 1643, Feb. 13, he and his cousin, the clerk, were appointed commissioners in a proceeding raised by Viscount Dudhope against the town, and as such went to Edinburgh on two occasions (D. C. B. 68). In the same year, Aug. 17, he heard, as bailie, a dispute between two of the family, Alexander, the mariner (*ante*, p. 113) and Elizabeth, relict of Thomas Moncur (*ante*, p. 21) in regard to the claim on the estate of one Patrick Jack (D. A. C. B. 8): 3 Oct. he was elected as Captain of the Overgait, among the officers for the weapon-schawing (D. C. B. 70), while 5 Oct. he was ordained to go to Lord Fodderance (and the clerk to Panmure), the Council having decided to refer to Fodderance and Panmure the still continuing difference between the Town and Lord Dudhope (D. C. B. 71). He is named in the war commission, among those for Angus, 2 Feb. 1646 (A. P. S. 25) and in 1648, April 14, as "sheriff of the shire of Forfar" in that part (*i.e.* on the occasion) when he gives sasine of parts of Blackness to his cousin Sir Alexander (F. S. 17). The references to him in connection with burgh affairs for the next twelve years are not important: perhaps he was less active for a time. In 1660 however he was elected Provost of Dundee and is named as presiding in the Head Court, 1 Oct. in that year (D. B. R. 471): as also 10 July, 7 Oct. 1662 (S. W. 669; D. B. R. vol. 34, title). He also represented the burgh in parliament at this time, 8 May 1662, 18 June 1663 (A. P. S. 40). He is often named as Provost in 1563-66, being re-elected to that office 27-29 Sept. 1664, after which he was sworn in 26-28 Sept. 1665 (D. C. B. 106, 108, 111). At the close of another decade 28 Dec. 1676, he was again elected Provost (B. C. D. 121) and continued to be so elected in the next four years 1677-80 (*ib.* 124, 126, 129-30). In 1678, June 26, he was also again in Parliament for the burgh and a member of a Committee of Supply (A. P. S. 52) and in the next year 28 June 1679, was again nominated by the Council to be their commissioner at the next general convention of the burghs at Edinburgh (D. C. B. 128).   In 1680 Dec. 9, he and the council of the burgh were sued by the Earl of Panmure for letting a debtor to the Earl escape out of the Tolbooth, but were assoilzied by the Court (S. W. 450).

In this paragraph, which occupies about the fifth part of the space devoted to the notice of this Alexander Wedderburn, there are about thirty different facts stated, and each of these is vouched for by a reference to an authority.   These authorities are designated by means of initial letters for the sake of brevity, but of course a table is given in another part of the book explaining the abbreviations.   The references, as you will have noticed, are given within brackets in the text, though personally I prefer footnotes, as these avoid breaking up the continuity of the narrative.   On the other hand, it will be found less expensive to print the references concurrently with the text than to put them in the form of footnotes.

Condensed extracts are given in the second volume from the various records to which reference has been made.   Nor is this all.   There are copious footnotes to the paragraph quoted above, in which various matters are discussed which could not conveniently be treated in the text; and at the end of the notice, there is a postscript giving some eighteen deeds, in which his name is mentioned, but which are not of such outstanding importance as to warrant their being included in the text, such as bonds granted by him, discharges given to him, deeds which he witnessed, etc.

The second volume of this remarkable history contains the evidence.   This is taken in the first place from private records, such as the Scrymgeour-Wedderburn Charter Chest, the Blackness Papers, the Wedderburn Papers at Mounie, the St Andrews University Register; in the second place from the various burgh records of Dundee, the Protocol Books, the Council Minute Book, etc.; in the third place from the various public records, either local records, such as the Sheriff Court Book of the various counties, or the more important archives, preserved in H.M. Register House, Edinburgh, or in the Record Office in London.   These will be discussed in detail in a subsequent chapter.

From this summary of *The Wedderburn Book* which I have attempted to give, you will see how exhaustive its information is, and what meticulous accuracy is aimed at throughout the work. It is also sufficiently embellished with portraits and other illustrations, though the heavy expense connected with the production of a book of this kind, involving the employment of many searchers, has prevented the illustrations from being produced in any very elaborate fashion, but they are sufficient for their purpose.

It is not every one who may find it possible to write a family history on such spacious lines as *The Wedderburn Book*. The ordinary compiler will have to content himself with working, perhaps, on a less extensive scale. But the plan and execution of the book are so good that it is worth a careful study. The continual interpolation of references in the text does not, it must be confessed, tend to easy reading, but this is largely compensated for by the introductory sketch of the family as a whole, to which reference has been made above.

# CHAPTER VII

## PORTRAITS AND ILLUSTRATIONS

THIS is a matter of expense. If you are in funds, or can depend on a sufficient number of subscribers to your book, you may make it a thing of beauty and of value from an art point of view. But the price of the book will be proportionally higher. If you have to study economy, you may have to do without any illustrations at all; this would be unfortunate on many accounts. It adds very much to the interest of a family history to see what manner of men and women are being written about; and the cost of reproductions of portraits and the like is very much less now than it was a comparatively short time ago. Even Sir William Fraser, in his elaborate tomes, had to be content in many cases with very woolly lithographs, and he was extremely proud of them too. But now things can be done better at no greater cost. If you have a series of family portraits, they can be reproduced in permanent photography at a reasonable figure. If you cannot rise even to that, there is the cheap process block, which is sufficient for all practical purposes. You may keep in view, however, that these cannot be reproduced in the text. Portraits done in this way must be printed on sized paper, and as you will not, I trust, have your whole book printed on such a medium, they will require to be on separate pages. Even then it will add to some extent to the weight of the book, and it is advisable to have this in as light and readable form as possible. Fortunately, the old and massive folios, such as Sir Robert Gordon's *History of the House of Sutherland*, are gone for ever. They required a solid table to themselves, whenever you wished to read or consult them. Even the Fraser volumes are rather ponderous for ordinary reading, and *The Wedderburn Book*, referred to in the last chapter, has a page of 11 inches high by $7\frac{1}{2}$ wide, with about nine hundred words on each page. It is of course often impossible to get a family history into the size of an ordinary novel, but an effort should be made to produce it in as light and handy a fashion as possible. A quarto has the advantage of giving a broader page, and so facilitating the display of pedigrees, but an octavo is a more conveniently shaped book, both for the shelves of the library and for practical use. The paper on which it is printed should be of good quality; imitation hand-made papers are seldom lasting, and are apt to gather dust; while real hand-made papers are expensive and unnecessary. Fraser's *Memorial of the Family of Wemyss* was printed on hand-made paper with deckle edges, but though handsome, it is hard and not more suitable for its purpose than an ordinary paper of good quality would have been. Any suspicion of glaze on the paper is to be avoided.

To come back to the illustrations. As to the reproduction of family portraits, the best method no doubt is photogravure; if this should be thought too expensive, the collotype process gives excellent results and is quite permanent. For views of houses or scenery in general the etching on copper is incomparably the finest way of dealing with them; however this is costly, and you may have to fall back on the ordinary photo-zincographic block, which is excellent for reproduction of any line drawing. Lithography has its value too, not for portraits or landscapes, but for the reproduction of coats-of-arms or the like. A lithograph cannot be worked into the letterpress as a process block can, and may have to be printed on a separate page by itself. If, however, room is left for it on the ordinary page, and if it is printed on very thin paper like Japanese vellum, the illustration may be deftly pasted into its proper place.

There is nothing more decorative to a book than to have coats-of-arms interspersed throughout it. But a word of warning is necessary as to this. Do not on any account insert any arms that are without authority, that is, in the case of Scottish arms, those which are not officially recorded at the Lyon Office, or in the case of English and Irish coats at the College of Arms in London, or at the office of Ulster King of Arms in Dublin respectively. Do not think too that because a man's name happens to be Douglas that he is entitled to the arms borne by the old earls of that name; or even, that because another man may be a younger son of somebody who has an undoubted right to arms, that he also is entitled to them; for he is not. The Scottish armorial rule is that when a man records arms, that coat belongs in its undifferenced form only to himself and the eldest son in each generation thereafter. All younger sons, in order to constitute their right to arms, must "matriculate" the arms of the head of their house; that is, must record them in the Lyon Register in their own names with a suitable heraldic "difference." These differences are assigned by Lyon, according to certain definite rules, and serve to indicate the position in the family which the cadet occupies.

It adds to the effect of a heraldic illustration if a coat-of-arms is shown with its proper heraldic colours or "tinctures" as they are technically called. This is easily done in a lithograph, but you should avoid reproducing gold and silver in the actual metals or such substitutes for them as are used in lithography to give the effect. In the first place, it gives a very unpleasant glitter on the surface of the illustration, and in the next place, it is difficult to distinguish gold from silver in artificial light. Again, lithography is not very suitable for the depicting of a whole achievement, by which I mean the shield, crest, helmet, mantling, motto and supporters if there are any; either an etching or a process block is more suitable for that. If you are to have arms lithographed in colour, be content with the shield alone; and take care that it is thoroughly well designed and drawn. There are various shapes of shields, some of which are more suitable than others, but generally it may be said that the plain "heater shape," that is, the shape of the bottom of a flat-iron, is the best. Also, see that the charges in it are well drawn, and that the space within the shield is filled up by them so far as possible. There has been an immense improvement within late years, thanks very much, I am inclined to think, to the influence of the Lyon Office, in heraldic designs in general; it is well worth while to get arms drawn by an artist who has made a speciality of that class of work, and not by the ordinary trade illustrator.

If you have no family portraits, I mean portraits in oils of persons in more or less picturesque costumes, there is no reason why you should not reproduce the humbler family photographs, even if they be of the period of sixty years ago. The gentlemen with long side whiskers, who lean against pillars with a very tall chimney-pot hat in their hands and dressed in what appear to our eyes extremely badly-made clothes—or the ladies in polkas and crinolines, with pork-pie hats and chignons—may look rather ludicrous to us ; but alas, in another sixty years our own portraits may look quite as comical to the eyes of our posterity. The great thing is that they are faithful types of their age, and a very good age too. Therefore do not hesitate to ransack the old family photographic albums and make a selection from them of those whom you wish to commemorate in your book.

It is impossible to do more than to indicate generally, as I have tried to do above, the lines on which you may proceed in the illustrating of a family history. Much depends, it is needless to say, on the amount you are prepared to spend, and the personal taste which will guide you in the choice and arrangement of the pictures.

The same remarks apply to the subject of the binding of your book. Bind it in morocco extra gilt if you like, but eschew calf and the cheaper leathers. It is more probable that you will decide to bind it in cloth ; nothing, if properly done, is better or more lasting. The cloth may be embellished with designs, or be perfectly plain. A family history is a grave book and should, I think, have a correspondingly grave exterior. But even then, it may be tasteful and taking enough. If you are going to embellish the boards, the best and simplest ornament you can have is a coat-of-arms in the centre, or the reproduction of some ancient seal.

If you wish to see how illustrations can be treated in a variety of ways, perhaps the best book on Scottish family history in this respect is *The Family of Seton* by the late Mr George Seton. It is contained in two sumptuous and bulky volumes ; although as a family chronicle it stands somewhat in need of both dates and references, as a beautifully illustrated and printed book it is worthy of all commendation.

C

# CHAPTER VIII

## THE PUBLIC RECORDS

### *A.* **The Printed Records**

BEFORE sitting down to write a family book, it is, of course, necessary to know something about the family whose history you are going to write. This information you will get from various quarters—from published books, from family papers and deeds, or from oral tradition (often wrong with regard to events happening outside the personal experience of the narrator). There is one source to which you will certainly have to resort, even if the pedigree is of quite moderate length, and that is the Public Records. By these I mean not only the parish registers of births, deaths, and marriages, but the vast variety of documents which are stored in the Register House in Edinburgh and in other places throughout the kingdom.

There are two ways of doing this: you may consult them yourself or you may employ a professional searcher to do it for you. If you do it yourself, which is the less expensive method, you will keep in view that the handwriting of the old records is very different from that to which you are usually accustomed, and that it is sometimes difficult to decipher. You must therefore learn to read it. A study of a book like Wright's *Court - Hand Restored*, of which the ninth edition was published in 1879, will perhaps give you some help in the way of deciphering old documents; but you will find that even without this, diligent practice will ultimately lead, if not to perfection, at least to a reasonable facility in reading ancient script. A very good method for the beginner is to take the three volumes of the *Facsimiles of the National Manuscripts of Scotland*, which form one of the official Record Publications, and go over various documents of different periods, which will be found therein, comparing the facsimiles carefully with the renderings of them in ordinary letterpress which will be found beside them. This will soon give you a certain familiarity with the written characters of the various periods, and as your studies proceed, you will find your task get easier and easier. It will be well for you to have at least a rudimentary acquaintance with Latin, as all charters and many other documents are in that language; also they are full of contractions, the scheme of which you will do well to master.

If you are averse from spending your time amongst musty records, and if you can afford it, you can employ a professional searcher. It is impossible to say what this will cost you, as it will all depend on the time taken and the number of records searched. As the cost of searches has a way of mounting up, sometimes to the surprise of the enquirer, it is as well to instruct your searcher that he is not to exceed a certain specified sum, without in the first place reporting his progress to you as his employer. This enables you to see where you are, and helps you to decide whether you will extend your search to further limits. You will do well also to employ a searcher of repute, of whom there are several. They really save money to their employer, as they are familiar with the records, know the most likely sources to consult, and can often make suggestions which are of value. If you employ an unknown man, he will probably consume much time in doing unnecessary work, and may even, to please his employer, produce information which has little or no basis on fact. The genealogy of Coulthart of Coulthart, which was published in Burke's *Landed Gentry* of 1849, is a good instance of this. An able and amusing exposé of it was given by the late Dr Burnett, Lyon King-of-Arms, in a little book called *Popular Genealogists, or the Art of Pedigree-making*, published in 1865. Be careful therefore as to whom you employ to make your searches. In the *Edinburgh Post Office Directory*, names of recognised searchers are to be found at the end of the Law Directory.

It is satisfactory to be able to state that, on the whole, access to the records in H.M. Register House is not difficult. At one period the officials were rather inclined to take the view that the records in their custody were meant to be kept but not to be consulted, and the public in general were not encouraged to make the dust stir from the shelves. But as time went on this restrictive policy was gradually abolished, and all reasonable access is now freely given in the Record Department.   Indeed (but not in the Registrar-General's Department) you can make as many searches as you like, without payment of any fees whatever, provided your purpose is of a purely literary character.   That is to say, if you are writing a family history, even though you may ultimately make a profit on its sale—an extremely unlikely contingency—you will not be required to pay fees.   But if you are searching to establish a pedigree with a view, for instance, of claiming a right to a certain coat-of-arms, this would not be a purely literary purpose, and you would have to pay fees.

If you wish to get a full list of all the records in the Register House, and an exposition of their general contents, you will consult an admirable volume, published officially, called *A Guide to the Public Records of Scotland deposited in H.M. General Register House, Edinburgh*, by M. Livingstone, I.S.O., late Deputy Keeper of the Records.   From the author's preface, it will be seen how the Records grew, and how they came to be in the Register House, together with a graphic account of the vicissitudes through which they have passed, and the many serious losses they have from time to time sustained both through flood and fire.

But what I am going to note in these pages are simply those records which are generally of most service to the pedigree-hunter, and which will more fully reward him for the trouble of his search.   Some of them are either wholly or partially printed and indexed, while others are neither the one nor the other.

### (1) *Acts of Parliament of Scotland.*

These are contained in eleven (or rather twelve, for one volume is now divided into two) huge folio volumes, and there is another still more enormous volume containing the index, one of the most elaborate indexes ever appended to any work. The earlier parliamentary records are but scanty, but from 1466 down to 1706, the minutes are fairly complete, though there are some gaps.   It is needless to say that there is a great deal of information contained in these volumes, and though they no doubt concern the student of constitutional history more than the genealogist, the latter will find much to interest him in the way of appointments of individuals to committees and offices, the forfeiture of estates, and other matters bearing upon the careers of many distinguished and undistinguished persons. The Acts of Parliament were among the first Record Publications, that is, documents printed under authority and at the expense of the Government, having been edited originally by Thomas Thomson, the well-known Scottish archivist, early in the nineteenth century. In 1826, however, four volumes of the MS. Record dealing with the period from 15th May 1639 to 8th March 1650, which were not known to exist, were accidentally discovered in the State Paper Office in London. The records then discovered were not printed till 1870, when, under the editorship of Mr Cosmo Innes, they were incorporated in the old volumes. To carry out this arrangement, Volumes V. and VI. of the original edition were withdrawn and a new issue sent out, with Vol. VI. divided into two parts. In referring to the Acts, therefore, it is well to see that you are referring to an edition which has this new arrangement, and as regards Vol. VI. you will be careful to quote which part you have in view.

## (2) *The Exchequer Rolls.*

These are perhaps the most complete series of ancient records that we possess, extending as they do from 1264 down to 1708. Almost every year is more or less represented, though many rolls are missing. They are a most useful series of records, and mention is frequently made in them of persons who will be found nowhere else. The rolls consist of the accounts of the various sheriffs of the counties and their assistants, whose duty it was to collect the revenues of the Crown, in the shape of the rents of Crown lands, the feudal casualties, and the fines imposed by themselves, by the Justiciars of the King, or by the Chamberlain in his "ayres" or Circuit Courts, which he held from time to time throughout the country. The magistrates and the farmers of the customs in the royal burghs also accounted for moneys coming into their hands. All these officers too paid out considerable sums, so that the balance actually paid into Exchequer was often but small. The accounts of the sheriffs contain on the one side the receipts from the Crown lands in money and farm produce, the annual returns from the casualties of ward, relief, and marriages of vassals, and the fines and escheats of the Sheriffs and Justiciars. On the other side are the miscellaneous household and other expenses of the King and royal family, when resident within the sheriffdom, outlay for the repair of royal castles and manors, and for the defence of the country, pensions, salaries, gifts, and ecclesiastical dues and balances handed over to the different officers of the household for the King's use.[1] You will see, therefore, that while not so genealogical as some other records to be mentioned, there still may be useful information to be obtained by the pedigree-hunter in the Exchequer Rolls. Reference to them is easy, as they have been printed up to the year 1600, and are contained in twenty-three stout octavo volumes; the indexes, like all the indexes of the Record Publications, are very full and good.

### (3) *Retours of Services of Heirs.*

The full and proper title of this publication is *Inquisitionum ad Capellam Domini Regis Retornatorum Abbreviatio*, but it is commonly cited simply as *Retours*, with the name of the county annexed. It was one of the earliest of the Record Publications, being issued 1811-1816. They are contained in three rather slender folio volumes, which are indispensable to the genealogist, as they give what is practically an authentic history of the transmission by inheritance of by far the greater part of the landed property in Scotland, as well as that of the descent of most of its leading families from about 1550 down to 1700.

When a Scottish laird died, his lands did not pass to his heir until the claim of the latter had been formally recognised by certain procedure, under a Brieve of Succession, which was issued from Chancery and directed to the Sheriff of the county in which the lands were situated. The Sheriff empanelled a jury which answered, on production of proof, certain questions which were submitted to them in terms of the Brieve, and the verdict of this assize was transmitted or "retoured" to Chancery. That office then issued to the heir

---

[1] See Exchequer Rolls, I., Preface xlv. *et passim.*

a certified copy of this which was called his "retour," and constituted in some measure his title to the lands, though he had still to be infeft in them by means of sasine. This was done on the lands themselves, and tangible possession was given by the delivery to him of the symbols of earth and stone.

You will see how useful a record such as this is to the genealogist. One great feature in it is that the relationship of the heir serving himself to the ancestor is always mentioned. In the case of an heir to subjects which did not require infeftment, it was sufficient to get a brieve of general service, and the heir in this case became entitled to his rights whenever he got the retour delivered to him from Chancery without any further procedure. These general services are all given in these volumes of retours, but in a much more condensed form than the special services to land.

There are also two other classes of Inquisitions indexed: the Brieves of Tutory had for their object the enquiry as to who was the proper person who ought to be appointed to the office of tutor to a minor below the age of puberty, as being the nearest agnate or paternal relative above the age of twenty-five years. The Brieve of Idiotry or Furiosity was for the purpose of enquiring into the mental capacity of a person alleged to be insane, and for the appointment of his nearest agnate as curator. Both these classes of retour are included together under the designation of *Inquisitiones de Tutela*. There are, of course, not nearly so many of them as of the other classes, but they are often worth consulting.

The arrangement of these volumes of retours and the way in which they should be used may be noticed briefly. In the third volume will be found the various indexes. That to the special services, that is to the services to land, is arranged topographically according to counties, these being arranged alphabetically. In each county there is first the index of persons, the names of the persons mentioned in the various retours belonging to that county being given; that is followed, in the case of each county, by an index of the lands mentioned; the numbers given as references denote the number appended to the abridgment of the retours given in the first two volumes. Then there is an index of personal names relating to the General Services, but of course no index of lands, as these were not dealt with in general services.  After this, there is a similar index to names in connection with the services *de tutela,* after which there are two short indexes, one of both names and land referred to in the Inquisitions of the Extent, or estimated value of the whole of the lands of the county or other district; and the other of the Inquisitions, whose object it was to ascertain the real estate, of which persons forfeited for treason were in possession for five years preceding the dates of their forfeiture.

Having therefore got your reference number from the indexes, you will turn to one of the first two volumes.  If the service for which you are looking is a special service—say Aberdeen, 186—you will find it under that number in the abbreviation of the retours dealing with the county of Aberdeen.  There you will find the following:—"Feb. 11, 1625. Joneta Gordoun sponsa Magistri Thomæ Davidson, clerici commissariatus Aberdonensis, haeres Jacobi Gordoun de Haddo patris, in villa et terris de Braklay, Tarves, Kirktoun de Tarvis et Diracroft ejusdem infra baroniam de Tarves.  E. 14 l. ix. 58."  From this you get the following information, which may perhaps be of much use to you in your work:—that Jonet Gordon was the wife of Mr Thomas Davidson Commissary Clerk of Aberdeen, and that she was the daughter of James Gordon of Haddo; that she succeeded to the lands mentioned as his heir, though this does not necessarily imply that she was an only child, and that the value of these lands was £14 Scots a year.  The numbers ix. 58 at the end of the entry refer to the actual register, where the retour will be found at full length if required.

In the case of the general retours the reference is still simpler.  They are not arranged under counties, but straight on under the order of their date.  Thus, if you are looking for Thomas Strang, you will find him under the reference number 2731, and in turning to the Abbreviate of the General Services in Vol. II., you will see that 12th August 1642 he was served heir-general to his father, John Strang, lieutenant-captain under Colonel John Cochrane in Germany; which may be a very good bit of information for your purpose.

Retours are amongst the oldest records in Scotland; they date certainly from the beginning of the fourteenth century.

Unfortunately none is actually on record of a date earlier than 1544, in which year it is believed that the earlier records of Chancery perished in the burning of Holyrood; and even in the earlier years after 1544, there is no doubt that many retours are missing. There are no retours now in the old sense of the word. Since 1847, services are carried through by petition to a Sheriff, the decree upon which is transmitted to Chancery to be recorded and extracted. From the date 1699, at which the three volumes which have been under consideration stop, their place has been filled by Indexes to Services of Heirs: the period from 1700 to 1859 is in four volumes arranged in decades, and from 1860 downwards the Index is prepared annually. The entries are very condensed, each entry only occupying a line; but the relationships are always given, which from the genealogist's point of view is an important matter.

### (4) Register of the Great Seal.

The valuable record of the *Register of the Great Seal*, or to give the Latin name by which it is usually quoted, *Registrum Magni Sigilli*, is of the utmost use to the family historian. It contains all grants of land by the Crown to its vassals, confirmations of charters by subject superiors to their vassals, patents of nobility and commissions to the greater offices of State, letters of remission (pardons) and letters of legitimation to bastards, charters of incorporation, and a certain number of certificates of descent, or birth-brieves as they were called, as well as other important documents. The earlier portion of the register was published in 1814 in a folio volume, under the direction of the Public Records Commission, but this volume is now obsolete, being superseded by a volume issued in 1912 under the editorship of Dr Maitland Thomson, which includes all its contents, besides those of William Robertson's *Index of Missing Charters*, which was published in 1798, with considerable additions. This volume contains charters from 1306 to 1424. After this date the register has been printed in ten volumes (excluding the one already mentioned), which brings it down to 1668, and the work is still proceeding. The charters are given in a condensed form and in Latin down to 1652, when English was substituted in the original charters. At the

Restoration, however, the use of Latin was again resumed and that language was continued to be employed till 1847, from which time English has again been used.   In the most recently published volume of the register, dealing with the charters since 1660, they have been translated into English, but in all the other volumes the charters are in Latin.   They are given, as has been said above, in a condensed form, and for all practical purposes this is quite sufficient; it is only words of style which have been omitted.   The principal points which are given in charters dealing with land are the names of the granter and the grantee, the lands granted, the series of heirs to which the lands are to descend after the death of the grantee, the reddendum or yearly payment or service to be rendered by the vassal to his superior, and the names of the persons witnessing the charter.   You will see how useful all this information is, as there is hardly a family of any importance in Scotland which does not  occur at some time or other  in this register; and it is most interesting to trace the progress of lands throughout its pages.

The method of quoting this register presents, unfortunately, some little difficulty.   When the first volume of the present issue, dealing with the charters from 1424 to 1513 (of which the present writer was editor) was published, the question arose as to how it should be numbered.   It was thought by the authorities that it could not be called Volume I. for two reasons: first, because there was already in existence the original folio volume of the register, and second, because it was intended to re-issue this in octavo form, at a future date, with additions, a scheme which, as I have said, has since been carried out.   The consequence was that none of the printed volumes of the Great Seal Register were numbered. The charters themselves are numbered in each volume, but they could not be referred to by number, unless the period comprised in the volume in which they occurred was mentioned. Thus, Charter 101 in the first published octavo volume could be referred to as *Reg. Mag. Sig.* 1424-1513, 101.   This is rather clumsy, and it was simpler merely to quote the date of the charter, or in the case of a confirmed charter the date of the confirmation.   The references to the Charter 101 above mentioned would be 2nd October 1427.   But now that the preliminary volume has been issued, there is no reason why it should not be called Vol. I., even though it was not officially so designed. This makes reference much more easy, and the Charter 101 would be quoted as *Reg. Mag. Sig.* ii. 101.

I have said before that a moderate knowledge of Latin is necessary before dealing satisfactorily with charters. If you do not happen to be acquainted with the language, then get somebody who knows, not necessarily classical Latin, but the medieval Latin which is used in charters, to translate them for you. If you are able to do it yourself so much the better ; if you are in any difficulty do not make guesses, but consult a book like Innes's *Legal Antiquities*, where you will find much about charters explained, or the well-known Dictionary of Ducange. Do not attempt to invent a translation which you think ought to be the meaning of the document, though you are not sure. It is certain to be productive of dire results. As an example of what such a practice may lead to, listen to the rendering of a charter, as given by the author of a book dealing with the history of one of the oldest houses in Scotland. In the first place, here is the charter itself, or rather the abridgment of it as it appears in the printed *Register of the Great Seal.*

Rex confirmavit Alexandro Menzeis de eodem, et heredibus ejus masculis quibuscunque cognomen et arma de Menzeis gerentibus,—terras et baroniam de Rannach (viz. terras de Downane, Kinlauchte, 2 Cammy-sirochtis, Ardlarach, Kilquhonane, Larane, Ardlair, Laragane, insulam de Lochrannache, lacus de Rannache et Irochtie et omnes lacus et insulas infra dictas terras, cum silvis, pratis, piscariis tam salmonum quam alborum piscium, tenentibus, &c. extendentes in integro ad 20 libratas terrarum, cum custodia forestarum infra dictas terras jacentium) vic. de Perth :— quas idem Alexander resignavit :—Insuper Rex— informatus existens de dicti Alex. prudentia et de bona affectione ejus predecessorum et ipsius ad propagationem Evangelii, et pro ingentibus summis thesaurario persolutis, — annexuit dicte baronie advocationem rectorie et vicarie ecclesie parochialis de Rannach, cujus dictos Alex. &c. patronos constituit ; et pro bono servitio dicti Alex., dictas terras, advocationem &c. incorporavit in liberam baroniam de Rannach, et voluit quod messuagium in Kilquhonnane esset principale messuagium ejusdem : Solvend. 30 lib. feudifirme :— necnon Rex voluit quod dicta resignatio et hec carta nulla essent causa rupture baronie de Menzeis, &c.

Here is a more or less correct literal translation of the charter :—

The king confirmed to Alexander Menzies of that ilk and his heirs male whomsoever bearing the name and arms of Menzies, the lands and barony of Rannach (viz. the lands of Downane, Kinlauchtie, the two Cammyserochtis, Ardlarach, Kilquhonnane, Larane, Ardlair, Laragane, the island of Lochrannache, the lochs of Rannach and Irochtie and all the lakes and islands within the said lands, with woods, meadows, fishings of salmon as well as of white fish, tenants &c. extending on the whole to twenty pounds of land, with the custodianship of the forests lying within the said lands) in the county of Perth :—which the said Alexander resigned :—the king likewise having been informed of the prudence of the said Alexander and of the good affection of his predecessors and himself towards the propagation of the Gospel, and for large sums paid to the Treasury—annexed to the said barony the right of presentation to the rectory and vicarage of the parish church of Rannach, of which he constituted the said Alexander &c. patrons : and for the good service of the said Alex. he incorporated the said lands, rights of presentation &c. into the free barony of Rannach and ordained that the manor house in Kilquhonnane should be the principal manor of the same : thirty pounds feu-duty to be paid :—the king also ordained that the said resignation and this charter should in no way be the cause of breaking up the barony of Menzies.

Now take the translation as given in the family history above referred to :—

"A.D. 1591.  King James VI. confirms to Alexander Menzies of Menzies and heritably to heirs male, whatsomever of the surname and arms of Menzies by blood, the lands and barony of 'Rannoch' viz. the lands of 'Downane, Kinlauchte' the two 'Cammysirochtis, Ardlarach, Kilquhonane, Larane, Ardlair, Laragane'; the islands of Loch Rannoch; the lochs of Rannoch and 'Trochtie'; and all other lochs and islands of the said lands, with the woods and forests in those parts, and fishings both of salmon and every kind of fish living therein &c., extending in all to 20 lib. land, with castles and fortifications within the same lands and district, in the shire of 'Perth'; which the same Alexander resigned unto the King.  And now regiven wholly to said Alexander for knowledge and good affection to his lamented predecessor and himself, a propogator of the Gospel, and for to plant supreme worship and its expounding within the said barony, the calling or appointing of the rector and vicar to the church of the parish of Rannoch of which Alexander is constituted patron. And for his good learning said Alexander has power of Justiciary &c. all incorporated in the free barony of Rannoch: and spreading thereby the cultivation in Kilquhonnane of grain, chiefly to be cultivated on same :—Discharge 30 lib. in full possession; and also the king gives hereby, with good reason, the country and barony of Menzies."

You will see that this translation does not give a very coherent idea of the contents of the charter : that in fact the translator had very little idea of what it was all about, and has made some very wild shots at the meaning, most of which fall wide of the mark. You will understand, therefore, how essential it is that if translations of charters are given they should be accurate, and that if not given, the transcription of the charter itself should be most carefully made. Here, for instance, is the transcription of a charter which appears in a recently published family history and in other respects a very excellent one too :—

Rex concessit Johanni Dufe filio et heredi Joh. Dufe et heridibus ejus terram que vocatur Tyndachtefield, jacentem ex parte occedentali acquæ de Culane, quam dictus Joh. pater personaliter in castro de Edinburche resignavit. Reddend summatum regi dictus Joh. heredes sui vel assignati i mare et taciend rectum cum bladis dicti tem. ad molendinum burgis de Culane debitam et consuetam . riservato libero tenemento dicta Johe. patri &c.

There are some nine mistakes in this short charter, chiefly misspellings of words, though sometimes the contractions have not been properly understood. They may have arisen either from the bad handwriting of the transcriber, or from their having been copied from a carelessly-compiled inventory and not from the charter itself, or from its abridgment in the printed *Register of the Great Seal.* Whatever their origin they show the necessity of the utmost care being taken in work of this sort.

## (5) *Calendar of Documents relating to Scotland.*

These documents are not to be found in the Register House but in the Public Record Office in London. They are writs connected with Scotland which have found their way, from circumstances which need not be entered into here, to England. As they cover the period from 1108 to 1509, it will be understood that they are most useful for matters of ancient date which will not be found elsewhere. They were entrusted to the editorship of Mr Joseph Bain, and he calendared them in four volumes which appeared between 1881 and 1888. It is needless to say that in the hands of a learned archivist like Mr Bain they have been admirably edited, and they are quite indispensable to the investigator of family history, whose researches lead him to far-back periods. One of the leading features of the series, for instance, is the transcription of the Homage Rolls of King Edward I., when he was in Scotland in 1296. A series of illustrations of the seals of the various Knights subscribing these rolls is also given with verbal blazons of the arms, most useful from a heraldic point of view.

These volumes are quoted as *Cal. of Docs. Scot.* (there is an English publication with the title *Cal. of Docs.*) with the number of volume and number of entry, not of the page. Sometimes, as in the case of the Homage Rolls, which extend over several pages, it is necessary to quote the page and not the entry, and when this is done it should be made clear that it is the page that is being referred to. Sometimes the work is simply quoted as *Bain's Calendar*.

### (6) *Register of the Privy Council.*

It is impossible to summarise the various matters which will be found in this record. It is sufficient to say, that before the institution in 1532 of the Court of Session, the Privy Council had jurisdiction over all manner of cases, civil and criminal: after that date, besides its administrative functions, its jurisdiction was usually limited to appeals from the judges ordinary, in cases of the denial of justice, the punishment of wrongs for which redress could not otherwise be obtained, or of seditious offences against the public peace or special Acts of Parliament, or which the Council were authorised to deal with by commission from the King or Parliament. While not a specially genealogical record, there is an immense number of names to be found in it, particularly in connection with securities given by certain persons that certain other persons would not commit acts of offence or wrongdoing against their

neighbours or the public. Many relationships are thus specified, and it is a record which cannot be overlooked by the
family annalist.

The purely judicial work of the Council, from 1478 to 1501,
is to be found in a folio volume called *Acta Dominorum
Concilii* published so long ago as 1839, and an octavo
volume issued in 1918. After 1545, the Register of the
Privy Council has been printed in octavo form, the first
volume having been published in 1877. The first series consists
of fourteen volumes covering the period from 1545 to 1625:
the second series is in eight volumes and extends from the
last-mentioned date down to 1660: eleven volumes of the third
series have now been published and bring the record down
to 1686.

This record may be quoted as *Privy Council Reg.*, or shorter
still *P. C. Reg.*, and care should be taken to mention the series
to which the volume quoted belongs.

### (7) *Accounts of the Lord High Treasurer.*

This is not a very genealogical record; but as it deals
largely with the officers of the King's household, heralds,
messengers, and persons employed in various capacities by
the Court, it should not be neglected by the diligent investigator.
Eleven volumes have been published dealing with the period
from 1473 to 1566. It may be conveniently referred to as
*Treasurer's Accounts.*

### (8) *Registrum Secreti Sigilli.*

The two volumes of the Register of the Privy Seal
are often of use. The Privy Seal alone was necessary to
the authentication of various classes of Crown letters or
grants, such as gifts of pension, of feudal casualties, of
escheats and other moveable property or rights, tacks of
Crown lands, letters of protection, commissions to minor
offices of Court or State, presentations to benefices and many
others. It was also appended to "precepts," which were
preliminary steps towards the preparation of deeds, which
ultimately passed under the Great Seal. These volumes contain
all the deeds, in a slightly abbreviated form, to which the
Privy Seal only was affixed, from 1488 to 1542: all the precepts,

which were ultimately given effect to in charters or letters-patent recorded in the Register of the Great Seal, are very briefly enumerated.  But many deeds under the Privy Seal, which should afterwards have passed the Great Seal, did not as a matter of fact do so, and these are all given in the text of this volume.  The deeds contained in this record are chiefly in the vernacular, so that they do not impose any difficulty on readers who have any acquaintance with sixteenth century Scots: they are numbered consecutively, and of course their number should be given in any reference.  This series may be quoted either as *Reg. Sec. Sig.* or as *Privy Seal Reg.*

### (9) *Other Printed Records.*

The following, though of more political and historical than genealogical importance, should not be overlooked by the compiler of a family history.  The *Acta Dominorum Auditorum,* or the *Acts of the Lords Auditors of Causes and Complaints,* are decisions of a body which were really a Committee of Parliament appointed to hear and determine all kinds of complaints.  It was in fact the precursor of the Court of Session.  The decisions from 1466 to 1494 were published in a folio volume in 1839, and since then an octavo volume covering the period 1496-1501 has been issued.

The *Calendar of Scottish Papers* preserved in the Public Record Office in London, is a miscellaneous collection of documents which may sometimes be found useful.  Nine volumes have been published, embracing the period from 1547 to 1588, and a tenth volume is in the press, bringing the series down to 1592.

There are two volumes of *Hamilton Papers,* containing letters and other documents illustrating the political relations of England and Scotland in the sixteenth century.  They range from 1532 to 1590.

The *Calendar of Border Papers* is worth consulting for families belonging to that region.  They also are in two volumes, and the period covered extends from 1560 to 1603.

The example set by the learned archivist Thomas Thomson has been diligently followed by subsequent editors.  The volumes have all admirable indexes, so that their consultation presents no difficulty even to the veriest tyro in record research.

# CHAPTER IX

## THE PUBLIC RECORDS

### *B.* The Unpublished Records

THE extracting of information from the printed volumes of the Records is, as has been said, a comparatively easy task. But the greater part of the Records in H.M. Register House have never been printed even in an abbreviated form, and what is more, have never even been indexed. The consequence is that a very difficult task is set before the searcher when he endeavours to master some part of their contents.

### (1) *Register of Deeds.*

This is an enormous register and contains all deeds containing a clause of consent to registration for preservation and execution. Practically anything may be recorded in this register, and the consequence is that it contains information which is of the utmost use to the genealogist, though it has to be got out at the expense of much digging and delving. It is divided into three series: the first contains 621 volumes but is in places imperfect, especially in the earlier volumes; it extends from 1554 to 1657. The second is in three parallel sub-series, as each principal clerk kept his own register. In the case of the first series, these sub-series have been combined and numbered consecutively, but this arrangement has not been carried out in the second series, so that in it we have— (1) 313 volumes in Dalrymple's office. (2) 350 volumes in Durie's office. (3) 296 volumes in Mackenzie's office. The period covered from 1661 to 1811. In referring to them it is necessary to add the office to which the volume quoted belongs, thus—*Reg. of Deeds* (Durie), cclxi. 304. The third series of this colossal register is again numbered consecutively; it comes down to the present time. At the end

D

of 1928 this series consisted of 5259 volumes, and additions are being made at the rate of 80 volumes yearly.

Printed indexes for each year from 1661 to 1671 have been published, containing very full information regarding all parties to the deeds. Material for a continuation of these indexes has been prepared, and will be published in due course.

The official name for this register is the *Books of the Lords of Council and Session*; it is generally quoted simply as the *Register of Deeds*.

### (2) *Register of Acts and Decreets.*

This record contains the judicial decisions of the Court of Session, and extends from the year 1542 to the present date. The first series comprises 609 volumes, and the second series (divided into three offices) extends from 1661 to 1810, embracing 2716 volumes. From 1810 to the end of 1926 the number of volumes amounts to 1224. There is no adequate index.

### (3) *Registers of Hornings, Inhibitions, and Adjudications.*

These registers are often useful to the genealogist. Horning was a process used by a creditor against his debtor, by which, on refusing to obey an order of Court, the latter was denounced a rebel to the king by a messenger-of-arms with three blasts of a horn. After this his goods were held escheat to the Crown under burden of his creditor's claim, and his person liable to imprisonment. The process is now practically in disuse, though occasionally resorted to. The register consists of 1284 volumes, covering the period from 1610 to 1902, but there are a few gaps in it. There is no index, so its consultation is a work of time. There is, however, a Minute Book in 202 volumes from 1661.

Letters of Inhibition had the effect of restraining the debtor from alienating or burdening the heritable property to the prejudice of the creditor's claim. The same effect was secured by the debtor's voluntarily granting a Bond of Interdiction. The register is contained in two series: the first contains hornings as well as inhibitions, and its 44 volumes cover the period from 1602 to 1631; the second has Inhibitions only, from 1610 up to 1924. There are five continuous series in 754 volumes altogether. There is also a Minute Book from 1652 to 1868. From 1869 to date the Minute Books include

Adjudications. By the Conveyancing Act of 1924 the Registers of Inhibitions and Adjudications are combined to form one register.

In addition to these, there were Particular Registers of Hornings and Inhibitions for the various counties in Scotland, all of which are now in the Register House.

The Adjudications, the process by which the lands of a debtor were legally transferred to the creditor in payment of his debt, are contained in a small register, which is unlikely to be consulted by the genealogist.

### (4) *The Commissariot Records.*

The commissaries were originally ecclesiastics, but their duties so far as concerns the confirmation of testaments are now performed by the Sheriffs of the various counties. Formerly they had jurisdiction, not only as regards testaments, but also in actions relating to marriage, divorce, legitimacy, and actions for slander. Fortunately, the records of testaments are kept in an entirely different series of volumes from those connected with the other business of the Court, and it is to the testaments that the pedigree-hunter will most frequently turn his attention. In fact for his purposes there is not a more useful record. It is also doubly fortunate for him, that owing to the public-spirited action of the Scottish Record Society, all the Commissariot Books of the different counties are now indexed and issued in its series of publications. Not only so, but the Society has also issued an index to the Processes and Decreets in the Commissariot of Edinburgh, dealing with actions for divorce, separation and aliment, declarator of marriage, and other matters.

In consulting the indexes to the Testaments, a word of warning may be given to the inexperienced investigator. It does not necessarily follow that because a man's testament is found in the index as having been confirmed, that his will will be found in the relative Commissary Record. It is just as likely that he died intestate, in which case the commissary conferred the office of executor on a person of his own nomination, generally a near relative of the deceased ; this was termed a Testament Dative. When a person died leaving a will, the executor named therein was confirmed by the commissary, that is to say, he formally got power to intromit with and administer the defunct's moveable estate. In this case the will itself, the Testament Testamentar as it is called, is given at length along with the inventory of the goods. The oldest of these records is that of the Edinburgh Commissariot which begins in 1514, but there are several gaps in it. It is also the largest and most complete of any of the registers.

The simplest way of quoting the reference to these records is to give the Commissariot and the date of confirmation—as *Edinburgh Tests.*, 20th April 1602.

### (5) *The Register of Sasines.*

This is one of the most important, as it is certainly the most voluminous, of the Scottish Records. A new proprietor got formal and legal possession of his lands by the delivery to him, on the lands themselves and in presence of witnesses, of certain symbols such as earth and stone; this was called giving him sasine. In this record therefore are preserved the titles to the whole land in Scotland. The record may be divided, for the purpose of explanation, into three parts :—

(a) *The Old General Register of Sasines.*—This is contained in 3779 volumes, commencing 19th August 1617 and ending 31st December 1868. There is also a Minute Book in 234 volumes for this period.

(b) *Particular Registers.* — Concurrent with the General Register there were local registers for each county, in which deeds might be recorded instead of in the General Register. There was also, for a brief period (1599-1609), what is known as the Secretary's Register. These are all now in the custody of the Keeper of Registers and Records in the Register House, Edinburgh. These local registers were all discontinued under the provisions of the Land Registers Act of 1868.

(c) *New General Register.* — The Act just mentioned instituted a New General Register kept in county divisions; this is the current register. When it is mentioned that in 1928 this register alone extended to upwards of 36,000 volumes and that it is being added to at the rate of 45,000 writs, or 500 folio volumes annually, an idea may be obtained of the far-reaching character and great importance of the register.

Indexes for the following periods of the Register of Sasines have been published:—General Register, 1701-1720; Particular Register for Shires of Aberdeen, 1599-1660; Argyll, 1617-1780; Berwick, 1617-1780; Kincardine, 1600-1657. Other indexes are in course of preparation. There is also available in the Record Office an index to General Register of Sasines, 1617-1700. Also from 1781 to date there are abridgments and indexes which facilitate searching.

This register cannot be overlooked by any person engaged in writing the history of a landed family. In quoting the register, add the number of the volume with the page, and the date of instrument, thus: *Gen. Reg. Sas.*, lix. 444, 28th October 1680: or, if it is a Particular Register, insert the county, thus: *Part. Reg. Sas. Ayr.*, vi. 284, 9th November 1698.

### (6) *The Register of Tailzies.*

The Register of Entails will frequently be found useful, as the list of substitute heirs of entail mentioned in the deed often throws a light on relationships which cannot otherwise be had. The register begins in 1688, and is contained in 243 large folio volumes. There is an alphabetical index of the whole series which facilitates consultation.

### (7) *Notarial Protocol Books.*

Notaries, on their admission to office, had blank books delivered to them, in which they were bound to record all their official acts. These were called Protocol Books, and on the death of a notary his Protocol Books were ordered to be delivered to the Lord Clerk Register. As a matter of fact, however, this was often not done, and the consequence is that there are only about 160 such books in the Register House; others may be found in the National Library, and in the possession of Town Clerks of Royal Burghs.

These books contain sasines of lands, bonds, obligations, contracts of marriage and many other memoranda of a miscellaneous character. Deeds are often noted in them, of which there is no other record available. The Scottish Record Society has printed several in its series of publications. As notaries were local officers, the names found in their Protocol Books are generally those of persons who belonged to the district in which they practised.

The above are the principal records in the custody of the Keeper of Registers and Records, which the compiler of a family history will do well to consult. The list now given does not comprise nearly all the records; a complete list of these will be found in Mr Livingstone's *Guide* already referred to. By the time the searcher has mastered the contents of these now given, he will be in a position to judge whether any of the others will yield him further results. He will always find help and guidance from the officials in charge of the Historical Records in the Register House. There are, however, some important records to be found in that building which are not in the custody of the Keeper of Registers and Records.

### (8) *Parish Registers.*

The care of these is entrusted to the Registrar-General. The Parish Registers are among the very first which a family historian is likely to consult. He has one great advantage over the English investigator, in that he will find all the parish registers collected together in the Register House, in absolutely safe keeping, and not entrusted to the tender mercies of incumbents of parishes, who may or may not be interested in them or suitable custodians of them. They are also suitably and safely housed, well bound and carefully repaired if they have at any time become dilapidated. Most of the registers have unfortunately a good many blank years, but a list of these records has been printed and published officially, in which the registers of each parish are gone over in detail. There are over nine hundred parishes represented, and in each case the periods covered by the various registers of births (or rather baptisms, because in general it was these and not the actual births that were recorded), proclamations and/or marriages, deaths and/or burials. In addition, opposite each parish there are remarks on the general condition of its register, giving the years for which there is no record, and any other circumstances of interest connected with it. Few of the registers, except Edinburgh, Dunfermline, and Aberdeen, go back to Reformation times; many commence early in the seventeenth century, and still more are only eighteenth century records. The dates connected with marriages are generally those of the proclamation, not of the marriage itself. The

Scottish Record Society has printed several of the registers, such as the Edinburgh, and Canongate, marriages, and some others which will be found given in detail on another page. Since 1855, when compulsory registration was introduced, every birth, marriage, or death that has taken place in Scotland will be found: the registers are kept in duplicate, one copy being retained by the District Registrar and the other being sent to the Register House. The fees payable for the consultation of these registers at the Register House are 1s. for a particular search for one entry, or 25s. for a general search, which is available on ten consecutive days; at the District Offices the fees are 1s. for a particular, and 2s. for a general search. If an official extract of an entry is required, the charge is 3s. 1d.

There are other records of a similar nature which are not in the custody of the Lord Clerk Register. The register of burials in the Greyfriars Churchyard, Edinburgh, is in possession of the Town Council of Edinburgh. That portion of it relating to the period from 1658 to 1700 has been published by the Scottish Record Society. There is also a Register of the Inscriptions in St Cuthbert's Churchyard, which has been published by the same Society. The Bills of Mortality of the City of Glasgow is an extensive and useful record; it is deposited in the City Chamberlain's Office there. There are other records of this class in different places in Scotland, for which enquiry should be made locally.

### (9) *Lyon Office Records.*

The records of the Lyon Office, or Court of the Lord Lyon as it is officially termed, are in the custody of the Lyon King-of-Arms. The two principal records are the Register of Genealogies and the Register of All Arms and Bearings in Scotland. The first of these begins in 1727, but there is a gap between 1796 and 1827. The early pedigrees must be used with caution, as they are not always accurate in detail. This register is not used nearly so much as it might be, as the charge for registering a pedigree, which was fixed by Act 30 and 31 Victoria cap. 17, amounts to £10 as a duty fee, with 6s. for each member of the pedigree, a charge which compares very unfavourably with those in force either in England or Ireland.

The Lyon Register proper, however, is in a much better condition. It commences in 1672, when the Scottish Parliament ordered every person who claimed a right to arms to record them in the books of the Lyon. From that time onwards it has been kept with perfect regularity. It consists of twenty-four large folio volumes on vellum, and since the beginning of the nineteenth century the arms have not only been blazoned verbally but illuminated in colour. In more recent years, owing to the greater appreciation of and attention paid to heraldic art, these are of a very fine character, and form a noble armorial record. Much pedigree information is to be found in the different entries, especially in those of later times. There is a fee of 5s. for a particular, and 20s. for a general, search in these registers.

There are other interesting and useful MSS. in the Lyon Office. The great Heraldic Register of Sir David Lindsay, Lyon, which was compiled about 1542, and which was in the custody of Sir James Balfour, Lyon 1630-57, is unfortunately, though a public record, not in the Lyon Office, but in the National Library, having been acquired by the Faculty of Advocates along with others of Balfour's papers; but it has been reproduced and published in facsimile. There is, however, a fine armorial manuscript which belonged to Sir Robert Forman of Luthrie, Lyon, compiled about 1566. It contains the arms of the nobility and gentry of Scotland, and quaint portraits of the kings and queens of Scotland in armorial surcoats. These are all indexed in a general index. There is also printed an index to the Lyon Register itself under the form of an "Ordinary of Arms" by the present writer. It is arranged on a method by which, having the arms, you can find out to whom they belong and in the index to the volume itself the names of all the persons who have recorded arms are given.

There are also in this office nine volumes of birth brieves, funeral entries, and funeral escutcheons. These have been indexed and published by the Scottish Record Society. Besides other documents which need not be mentioned in detail, there is here the record of Admissions of Messengers-at-Arms from 1630 onwards, with blanks from 1650 to 1660 and from 1722 to 1754. The Register of Admissions of Heralds and Pursuivants only begins, unfortunately, in 1660, though they are the oldest officers in the King's service known, and even that is blank from 1726 to 1759.

It is useful to know that the Lyon Office contains a large library of books relating to heraldry, genealogy, and topography. Access to this can easily be obtained by any *bona fide* worker in the sphere of family history. It is particularly rich in the department of privately printed books and a fine collection of MS. armorials, either originals or copies, which extend to a period considerably before the commencement of the present official register.

### (10) *Sheriff Court Books.*

These form a valuable series of records, which ought to be, but are not, in the custody of the Keeper of Registers and Records. They contain an immense deal of local information incident to cases tried in the various Sheriff Courts. Their condition and accessibility vary very much. In some Sheriff-doms they are well arranged and taken care of, but in others the reverse of this is the case. It is to be hoped that some day they will all be sent compulsorily to the Register House, the proper place for such valuable records.

The Aberdeenshire Sheriff Court Records have been published in three volumes by the New Spalding Club.

# CHAPTER X

## PRIVATE RECORDS

### (1) The Historical MSS. Commission

MANY Scottish charter chests have been investigated from time to time and their contents made accessible. A great deal of this work has been done by the various literary clubs which have periodically come into existence and some of which still continue an active existence. These publications will be dealt with afterwards. At present, mention must be made of the great national attempt to open to the public the many interesting documents belonging to private families. From 1870 up to 1914, when the labours of the Commission were temporarily suspended, nearly 130 collections bearing on Scottish affairs had been reported on. Some of them had already been partially dealt with by the Clubs, but most of them cover quite fresh ground. A complete list of the families who opened their muniment rooms to the Commissioners is to be found in a very good little book called *An Index to the Papers relating to Scotland, described or calendared in the Historical MSS. Commission's Reports* by Professor Sanford Terry of the University of Aberdeen. In it will be found a short synopsis of each collection, so far as it relates to Scotland, showing in what particular subjects they are specially rich. The genealogist cannot afford to neglect these important publications, but he will do well to remember that the aim of the whole series is historical more than genealogical. The earlier volumes contain many charters which sometimes throw great light on family history, but of late years the transcription of charters has been rather discouraged, unless they are of real historical importance. This is to be regretted, but even without the charters there are many valuable bits of information to be picked up from family letters and other documents which are reported on. A study of Professor Terry's Index will generally indicate to the enquirer whether it is worth while consulting any specified collection with the view of finding family information in it.

## (2) The Laing Charters.

When the eminent antiquary, the late David Laing, LL.D., died in 1878, it was found that he had bequeathed his large collection of MSS. to the University of Edinburgh. Among them was a great quantity of charters and similar documents. These were, to the number of over 3300, calendared in English by the late Mr John Anderson, curator of the Historical Department of the Register House. His work, as might be expected from his intimate knowledge of the subject, was admirably done, and the collection is of the greatest value to the student of family history. Indeed it ranks as a compendium of deeds in relation to persons and places in Scotland, next to the *Register of the Great Seal* itself—I mean, of course, as regards printed volumes. It begins long before the Great Seal, the first deed mentioned being a charter in Anglo-Saxon of the year 854, and it comes down to a date long posterior to the printed volumes of the Great Seal, the last charter given being dated in 1783, and the latest deed 1837.

A Report on the remaining MSS. in this collection has been issued by the Historical MSS. Commission, in two volumes.

## (3) Fasti Ecclesiæ Scoticanæ.

The new edition of Hew Scott's *Fasti*, which has recently been completed in seven volumes, will be found invaluable in its own limited sphere. It contains many thousand biographical notices of all the ministers of the Church of Scotland since the Reformation, with their wives and families. In the lists of the latter may be found many names which afterwards became famous in many ways. It is an admirable compendium of its kind and easily consulted.

A useful companion volume to this will be found in *Sons of the Manse*, by the Rev. A. W. Fergusson of Dundee, which gives notices of many eminent men who have had their origin in Scottish manses.

# CHAPTER XI

## CLUB PUBLICATIONS

A COMPLETE *Catalogue of the Publications of Scottish Historical and Kindred Clubs and Societies* was published in 1909 by Professor Sanford Terry, and a continuation of it was published in 1928 by Cyril Matheson, M.A., Assistant to the Professor of History in the University of Aberdeen. To these the student who wishes to go into the subject in detail must be referred. What is attempted to be given below is a list of the Club Publications which deal more particularly with family history. Professor Terry's work has rendered this task much more easy than it would otherwise have been, and I am under the greatest obligation to it. I have not included Chartularies in this list, but have given them by themselves.

### Abbotsford Club.

1. Miscellany of the Abbotsford Club. 1837.
2. Davidis Humii de familia Humia Wedderburnensi liber. 1839.
3. Memoirs of Sir Ewen Cameron of Lochiel, with an introductory account of the history and antiquities of that family and of the neighbouring clans, 1842.

### Society of Antiquaries of Scotland.

There are not many papers relating to family history to be found in the *Proceedings* of this Society, but there are a few. The first volume of the *Transactions* of the Society appeared in 1792; and under the title of *Archæologia Scotica* further volumes were issued in 1822, 1831, 1857 and 1890. Since 1851 the *Proceedings*, as they are now called, have been issued annually and extend to four series of twelve volumes each. There is a general index to the first two series.

### Ayrshire and Galloway Archæological Association.

This Society flourished from 1877 to 1897, and published fifteen handsome volumes; many of these are of interest to the family historian. Perhaps what will be of most use to him are the Protocol Books of John Mason, Town Clerk of Ayr (1576-1612) and of Robert Broun (1612-1616).

### Banffshire Field Club.

I suppose the annals of a family must be considered as "Natural History," for in the *Transactions* of this Club, which began in 1880 and has been publishing ever since, there are not a few papers on local families. Many of these are from the pen of the late Dr Cramond, an indefatigable worker in this field.

### Bannatyne Club.

Founded in 1823 and dissolved in 1861, this Club did much good work in its day. Few of its volumes, however, have much genealogical interest. But we must not forget the following, though some are only incidentally genealogical :—

1. The History of the House of Seytoun to the year MDLIX, by Sir Richard Maitland of Lethington, knight; with the continuation by Alexander, Viscount Kingston, to MDCLXXXVII. Glasgow, 1829.

2. Ancient Criminal Trials in Scotland, compiled from the original records by Robert Pitcairn, 3 vols. Edinburgh, 1833. This useful and interesting work contains much information for the pedigree-hunter, even though his ancestor may not have been a criminal. The period covered is from 1488 to 1624.

3. A Diary of Public Transactions and other Occurrences chiefly in Scotland, from January 1656 to January 1667, by John Nicoll. Edinburgh, 1836.

4. The Black Book of Taymouth, with other papers from the Breadalbane Charter Room. Edinburgh, 1855.

A quaint account of the Campbells of Glenurquhy, compiled by William Bowie in 1598.

### Berwickshire Naturalists' Club.

The volumes of the *Transactions* of this Club after 1887, and even occasionally before that date, contain many papers relating to local families.

### Buchan Field Club.

The same remark applies to the publications of this Club, which was started in 1887. The volumes were all published at Peterhead.

### Dumfriesshire and Galloway Natural History and Antiquarian Society.

The publications of this Society begin in 1864, but there is little of purely genealogical interest in them. In Vol. XXIV. there is a paper on the Irvings of Hoddom.

### The Gaelic Society of Inverness.

The *Transactions* of this Society, which begin in 1872, contain many contributions relating to Highland families and the Clans of Scotland.

### The Grampian Club.

This Club is almost synonymous with the name of the late Rev. Charles Rogers, LL.D., who was the author or editor of most of their publications. They contain several histories of, or genealogical collections relating to, Scottish families. These will be found in the *Bibliography of Scottish Family Histories.*

### Hawick Archæological Society.

This Society was founded in 1856 and began publishing in 1863. The volumes of its *Transactions* contain a good many papers relating to local families.

### The Iona Club.

This Club had a short career from 1833 to 1838. Its single volume was published at Edinburgh in 1847, and is entitled *Collectanea de Rebus Albanicis.* It contains some interesting papers, including one on the genealogies of the Highland Clans, translated from the ancient Gaelic MSS. by William F. Skene.

### The Maitland Club.

This Club was started in Glasgow in 1828, and published a series of very interesting works down to 1859. The following are those most useful to the genealogist :—

1. History of the House of Seytoun. (This was also published by the Bannatyne Club, *q.v.*)

2. The Diary of Mr John Lamont of Newton, 1649-1671. Edinburgh, 1830. Contains much interesting gossip. This is an enlarged edition of his Diary first published in 1810.

3. Pitcairn's Criminal Trials (which were also published by the Bannatyne Club, *q.v.*).

4. Collections upon the Lives of the Reformers and most eminent Ministers of the Church of Scotland, by the Rev. Robert Wodrow. Glasgow, 1835.

5. The Coltness Collections, 1608-1840. Deals with the families of the Stewarts of Coltness, Allanton and Goodtrees, with relative papers.

6. Analecta: or, Materials for a History of Remarkable Providences, mostly relating to Scottish Ministers and Christians, by the Rev. Robert Wodrow (1701-1731), 4 vols. 1842, 1843.

7. Selections from the Family Papers preserved at Caldwell, 2 vols. 1854.

### New Spalding Club.

This Club was founded in Aberdeen in 1886. The following volumes of its publications deal more particularly with material for family history :—

1. Memorials of the Family of Skene of Skene, edited by William Forbes Skene, D.C.L. Aberdeen, 1887.

2. Selections from Wodrow's Biographical Collections: Divines of the North-East of Scotland; edited by the Rev Robert Lippe. Aberdeen, 1890.

6. Miscellany of the New Spalding Club. Vol. I. contains the Register of Burgesses of Guild and Trade of Aberdeen, 1399-1631 ; and Inventories of Ecclesiastical Records of North-Eastern Scotland, 1890. Vol. II. contains the Register of Burgesses, 1631-1700, and the Register of St Paul's Episcopal Church, Aberdeen, 1720-1793. 1908.

7. Officers and Graduates of King's College, Aberdeen, 1495-1860. Aberdeen, 1893.

8. The Records of Aboyne, 1230-1681. 1894.

9. Fasti Academiæ Mariscallanæ Aberdonensis, 1593-1860. Vol. I., Endowments; Vol. II., Officers, Graduates and Alumni; Vol. III., Index to Vol. II. 1889, 1898.

10. The Family of Burnett of Leys with Collateral Branches. 1901.

11. The House of Gordon, 2 vols. 1903, 1907.

12. Records of the Sheriff Court of Aberdeen, 1503-1660, 3 vols. 1904, 1906, 1907.

13. The Blackhalls of that Ilk and Barra. 1905.

14. Records of the Scots Colleges at Douay, Rome, Madrid, Valladolid and Ratisbon, 1581-1900. Vol. I., 1906.

### Scottish Burgh Record Society.

This Society was founded in 1868 and dissolved in 1908. It published 22 volumes dealing principally with the Burghs of Edinburgh, Glasgow, Aberdeen, and Peebles. Dundee, Stirling, and Lanark published similar volumes on their own account. While not bearing directly on family history, all these volumes are worth consulting for the names of burgesses and burgh officials of the different towns.

### Scottish History Society.

Founded in 1886. The principal publications of this Society likely to be of use to students of family history are the following:—

1. Lists of persons concerned in the Rebellion of 1745. Edinburgh, 1890.

2. Memoirs of the Life of Sir John Clerk of Penicuik, Bart., 1675-1755. Edinburgh, 1892.

3. Miscellany of the Scottish History Society, Vol. I., 1893. Contains, *inter alia*, the Diary of George Turnbull, minister of Alloa and Tyninghame, 1657-1704, and the Masterton Papers, 1660-1719; both useful genealogically.

4. The Account Book of Sir John Foulis of Ravelston, 1671-1707. 1894. Contains pedigrees of the Foulis family.

5. Papers illustrating the History of the Scots Brigade in Holland, 3 vols. Contains the Muster Rolls of the several Regiments, and genealogical notes on many of the persons mentioned. 1899, 1906.

6. Chronicles of the Frasers: The Wardlaw Manuscript, entitled *Polichronicon seu policratica temporum*, or The True Genealogy of the Frasers, 916-1674.

7. Genealogical Collections concerning Families in Scotland, by Walter Macfarlane, 1750-1751. Very useful but must be used with caution.

8. Scottish Forfeited Estates Papers, 1715-1745. Incidentally useful.

9. The Seafield Correspondence from 1685 to 1708. Contains much information as to Ogilvies and allied families.

### Scottish Record Society.

This Society began in 1887, as a section of the British Record Society, but it very soon became a substantive Society. It is perhaps the most useful of all Societies from a genealogical point of view. It has indexed many important records, and has done work which in many cases the Government should have done; and has given the public access to much information which it would have taken much labour and some cost to acquire.

Up to the present time, the Society has issued indexes to the Registers of Testaments in every commissariot in Scotland; and has printed the following Parish Registers:—

Dunfermline, 1561-1700.
Durness, 1764-1814.
Torphichen, 1673-1714.
Kilbarchan, 1649-1772.
Melrose, 1642-1820.
Canisbay, 1652-1666.
Chapel of Birnie and Tillydesk, Baptisms, 1763-1801.
Edinburgh Marriages, 1595-1800.
Canongate Marriages, 1564-1800.
Holyrood Burials, 1706-1900.
Greyfriars Burials, 1656-1700.
Restalrig Burials, 1728-1854.

E

Indexes have been published to :—

Edinburgh Apprentice Register, 1583-1666.
MS. Genealogies, Birth-brieves, etc., in Lyon Office.
Consistorial Processes and Decreets, 1658-1800.
Burgesses and Guild Brethren Roll of Glasgow, 1573-1750.
Roll of Edinburgh Burgesses, 1406-1700 :

and Calendars of the following records :—

Charter Chest of the Earls of Wigtoun, 1214-1681.
Charter Chest of the Earls of Dundonald, 1219-1672.
Inventory of Documents relating to the Scrymgeour Family
Estates, 1328-1636.
Inventory of Lamont Papers, 1231-1897.
Calendar of Writs in Yester House.
Family Papers of the Hunters of Hunterston..
Protocol Book of Gavin Ros, 1512-1532.
Protocol Book of Sir Alex. Gaw, 1540-1558.
Protocol Book of Sir William Corbet, 1529-1555.
Protocol Book of Sir Gilbert Grote, 1552-1573.
Protocol Books of Dominus Thomas Johnsoun.
Protocol Book of James Foulis, 1546-1553.
Protocol Book of Nicol Thounis, 1559-1564.
Argyllshire Inventories, 1693-1702.
Monumental Inscriptions in St Cuthbert's.   Two parts.
Register of Episcopal Church, St Andrews, 1722-1787.
Parish Lists of Wigtownshire and Minnigaff, 1684.

### The Spalding Club.

This Society, founded in 1839, lived till 1870 and published much important and interesting matter.   The following among its publications are of special interest to the investigator of families in the Northern Counties :—

1. The five volumes of the Miscellany of the Club published at intervals from 1841-1852.

2. Collections for a History of the Shires of Aberdeen and Banff.

3. Illustrations of the Topography and Antiquities of the Shires of Aberdeen and Banff.   Vol. I., 1869; Vol. II., 1847; Vol. III., 1857; Vol. IV., 1862.

4. A genealogical deduction of the family of Rose of Kilravock. 1848.

5. Memorials of the Trubles in Scotland and in England, 1624-1645, by John Spalding, 2 vols. 1850, 1851.

6. Fasti Aberdonenses : Selections from the Records of the University and King's College of Aberdeen, 1494-1854.

7. The Book of the Thanes of Cawdor ; a series of papers selected from the charter room at Cawdor, 1236-1742. Edinburgh, 1859.

8. An Account of the Familie of Innes, compiled by Duncan Forbes of Culloden, 1698; with an appendix of charters and notes. Aberdeen, 1864.

### Spottiswoode Society.

This Society was founded in 1843, chiefly for printing works in connection with the Scottish Episcopal Church. Few of these possess much interest for the genealogist, but the two volumes of its Miscellany are worth looking over. In the first there is a genealogy of the family of Spottiswoode.

### Stirling Archæological Society.

Founded in 1868 as the Stirling Field Club, but the name was altered to the Natural History and Archæological Society in 1882. There is not very much genealogical information in its publications. There is a paper on the Napiers of Edinbellie and Culcreuch in Vol. IX., and a note on Sir William de Erthe's family in Vol. XXVI., and there are other papers which might yield some items of interest in relation to families of the district.

# CHAPTER XII

## CHARTULARIES OF RELIGIOUS AND OTHER HOUSES

ONE of the chief values which charters have for the genealogist is that they often go back to a period anterior to the date of any other documents known to us, and give information both as to names and lands which is of much use. Sometimes the earliest ones are not dated, but the date can generally be approximately fixed by the names of the parties mentioned in the deed itself, or by those of the witnesses. The dates of the deaths of the persons witnessing the deed may be already known, so that by a careful winnowing of these names, the date of the charter can often be fixed within a few months. By the same process, the date of death of any of the witnesses not previously known, may be discovered. This is only one of the ways in which charters are useful to the searcher. They are all deserving of close scrutiny by any one engaged in the investigation of the history of a family; but the cautions as to their proper use given on a previous page should not be neglected. The following are the names of the principal chartularies which have been published already; all of them, it will be seen, have been undertaken by literary clubs, as might be expected, for it is unlikely that any chartulary would appeal to a publisher as a remunerative speculation :—

ABERDEEN . . Registrum Episcopatus Abirdonensis, 2 vols. Maitland Club, 1845; Spalding Club, 1845.
Cartularium Ecclesiæ S. Nicholai Aberdonensis, 2 vols. New Spalding Club, 1888, 1892.

ARBROATH . . Liber S. Thome de Aberbrothoc, 2 vols. Bannatyne Club, 1848, 1856.

AYR . . . Charters of the Friars Preachers of Ayr. Ayrshire and Galloway Archæological Society, 1881.

BALMERINO . . Chartulary of Balmerinoch. Abbotsford Club, 1841.

BEAULY . . Charters of the Priory of Beauly. Grampian Club, 1877.

BRECHIN . . Registrum Episcopatus Brechinensis. Bannatyne Club, 1856.

CAMBUSKENNETH Registrum Monasterii S. Marie de Cambuskenneth. Grampian Club, 1872.

COLDSTREAM . Chartulary of the Cistercian Priory of Coldstream. Grampian Club, 1879.

COUPAR-ANGUS . Rental Book of the Abbey of Coupar-Angus, and Breviary of the Register, 2 vols. Grampian Club, 1879, 1880.

CRAIL . . . Register of the Collegiate Church of Crail. Grampian Club, 1877.

CROSSRAGUEL . Charters of Crossraguel Abbey. Ayrshire and Galloway Archæological Society, 1886.

DRYBURGH . . Liber S. Marie de Dryburgh. Bannatyne Club, 1847.

DUNFERMLINE . Registrum de Dunfermelyn. Bannatyne Club, 1842.

EDINBURGH . Registrum Cartarum Ecclesie Sancti Egidii de Edinburgh (charters connected with St Giles Church). Bannatyne Club, 1859.

Liber Cartarum Sancte Crucis (Holyrood Abbey). Bannatyne Club, 1840.

Charters of Trinity College, Edinburgh. Bannatyne Club, 1861.

Charters and Documents relating to the Collegiate Church and Hospital of the Holy Trinity, and the Trinity Hospitals, Edinburgh, 1460-1661. Scottish Burgh Records Society, 1871.

GLASGOW . . Registrum Episcopatus Glasguensis. Bannatyne Club, 1843; Maitland Club, 1843.

Liber Collegii Nostre Domine, and other Registers of Churches and Religious Houses in Glasgow. Maitland Club, 1846.

INCHAFFRAY . Liber Insule Missarum. Bannatyne Club, 1847; Scottish Historical Society, 1908.

KELSO . . . Liber S. Marie de Calchou, 2 vols. Bannatyne Club, 1846.

LENNOX . . Cartularium Comitatus de Levenax. Maitland Club, 1833.

LINDORES . . Chartulary of the Abbey of Lindores, 1195-1474. Abbotsford Club, 1841; Scot. Hist. Soc., 1903.

MELROSE . . Liber Sancte Marie de Melros, 2 vols. Bannatyne Club, 1837.

MORAY. . . Registrum Episcopatus Moraviensis. Bannatyne Club, 1837.

MORTON . . Registrum Honoris de Morton, charters of the Earldom of Morton, 2 vols. Bannatyne Club, 1853.

NEWBATTLE . Registrum S. Marie de Neubotle. Bannatyne Club, 1849.

NORTH BERWICK Carte monialium de Northberwic. Bannatyne Club, 1847.

PAISLEY . . Registrum Monasterii de Passelet. Maitland Club, 1852; New Club, 1877.

PERTH . . . Chartulary of the Black Friars of Perth. Edited by Robert Milne, D.D., the only chartulary of a religious house, which has not been published by a Club. Edinburgh, 1893.

RESTENNET. . Priory of Restennet. Bannatyne Club, 1890.

ST ANDREWS . Liber Cartarum Prioratus S. Andrea, Bannatyne Club, 1841.

SCONE . . . Liber Ecclesie de Scon. Bannatyne Club, 1843; Maitland Club, 1843.

SOLTRA . . Charters of the Hospital of Soltra, Trinity College, and other Collegiate Churches in Midlothian. Bannatyne Club, 1861.

STIRLING . . Registrum Capellæ Regiæ Strivelinensis. Grampian Club, 1882.

### Chronicles.

Chronicle of Lanercost. Bannatyne Club, 1839; Maitland Club, 1839.

Cronica de Mailros. Bannatyne Club, 1835; Maitland Club, 1835.

Scalacronica. Maitland Club, 1836; also edited by Sir Herbert Maxwell.

### University Records.

ABERDEEN.—Fasti Aberdonenses; selections from the Records of the University, and King's College of Aberdeen, 1494-1854. Spalding Club, 1854.

Besides Charters, Papal Bulls and other deeds, this volume contains extracts from the University archives, the register of matriculations from 1601 to 1686, the register of matriculations from 1600 to 1688.

Fasti Academiæ Mariscallanæ Aberdonensis; selections from the records of Marischal College and University, 1593-1860; edited by Peter John Anderson, 3 vols. New Spalding Club.

Vol. I.   Endowments.

Vol. II.   Officers, Graduates, and Alumni.
   The lists in the second volume are annotated and many
   of the names identified.

Vol. III.   Index.
   Officers and Graduates of the University and King's
   College, Aberdeen, 1495-1860; edited by Peter John
   Anderson. New Spalding Club, 1893.
   Names annotated.

Roll of the Graduates of the University of Aberdeen, 1860-1900; edited by Col. William Johnston, C.B., Aberdeen, 1906.

All names annotated.

EDINBURGH.—This, the youngest of the Scottish Universities, has been the least enterprising in the way of publishing lists of its members.   There is only one official publication of the kind:—

A Catalogue of the Graduates in the Faculties of Arts, Divinity, and Law of the University of Edinburgh.   1858.

There are, however, no less than four histories of this University—one by Professor Thomas Craufurd, who died in

1662, and whose MS. was published in 1808; one by Professor Andrew Dalzel, which was edited and published by David Laing in 1862; one by Alexander Bower, a librarian in the University, published in 1817, and which contains much valuable biographical information; and lastly, Sir Alexander Grant's history, which was published in 1884.

GLASGOW.—The Matriculation Albums of the University of Glasgow from 1728 to 1858; transcribed and annotated by W. Innes Addison. Glasgow, 1913.

A Roll of the Graduates of the University of Glasgow from 1728 to 1897, with short biographical notes, by W. Innes Addison. Glasgow, 1898.

Munimenta Alme Universitatis Glasguensis: Records of the University of Glasgow from its foundation till 1727, 4 vols. Maitland Club. Glasgow, 1854.

Vol. I., Privileges and Property. Contains Charters, Rentals of Benefices, and other documents.

Vol. II., Statutes and Annals.

Vol. III., Lists of Chancellors, Principals, Rectors, Deans of Faculty, Professors, Graduates and Undergraduates.

Vol. IV., Index, Preface, etc.

ST ANDREWS. — This, the oldest of all the Scottish Universities, has only issued one volume, dealing with its more modern matriculations:—

The Matriculation Roll of the University of St Andrews, 1747-1897; edited with an introduction and index by James Maitland Anderson, Librarian to the University. Edinburgh, 1905.

The names are not annotated, nor identified.

# CHAPTER XIII

## MISCELLANEA

A GOOD map of the district in which the family of which you are writing lived is a most useful companion for reference. There are several excellent collections of these published, and if any of them omit small details which you require there are always the six inches to the mile Ordnance Survey maps to fall back on ; these can generally be consulted in any large Public Library. For names of places not now in existence Moll's map of the several Scottish Counties will frequently be found useful. It was originally published in 1725 but was reprinted by Shearer & Co., Stirling, in 1896.

Much local information, invaluable for realising our ancestors' surroundings and mode of life, is provided by the ministers of the various parishes in the Old Statistical Account of Scotland. The New Statistical Account published in the middle of last century is not of so much interest to the genealogist.

Many good histories of special parishes and districts have been published and some of these contain valuable pedigree information.

Sir Archibald Dunbar's " Scottish Kings 1005-1625 " is most valuable for putting the facts of a pedigree into their correct historical perspective. It is an admirable chronological work.

There is a large collection of MS. material for family history in the Historical Department of H.M. General Register House, Edinburgh, the Scottish National Library, and in the Lyon Office Library. The main collections in the National Library are detailed in the Catalogue of MSS. relating to Heraldry and Genealogy.

The late Mr Alexander Sinclair made a good many MS. notes about Scottish families, and these he deposited in 1877 in the library at Crawford Priory, where, together with his printed books, they may be consulted on application to the Factor, Crawford Priory, Springfield, Fife.

Besides purely heraldic MSS. the Lyon Office possesses Inventories of Charter Chests belonging to various Scottish families, many MS. notes which have been deposited from time to time by the persons who made them or their representatives, *e.g.* the Cleland Harvey collection which deals chiefly with the Hays of Tweeddale and their branches, and the Gray Buchanan collection which is mainly concerned with Buchanans.

# II
# SCOTTISH FAMILY HISTORY

*Boni venatoris est aliquid capere, non omnia.*

"Hee is held a good Huntsman that can catch some game, though not all."
JOHN SMYTH OF NIBLEY, 16*th cent.*

# SCOTTISH FAMILIES

*An asterisk (\*) indicates a privately printed work.*

**Aberbrothwick**, Hamilton, Lord. The Complete Peerage, by G. E. C[okayne] ; 2nd ed. by Hon. Vicary Gibbs, 1910.

**Abercorn**, Hamilton, Lord of, Earl of, Marquess of, Duke of. Consultation pour James Hamilton, Marquis d'Abercorn (1865). Dictionary of National Biography, *s.v.* The Scots Peerage (1904-1914), i. 37-74. G. E. C.'s Complete Peerage. Burke's and other Annual Peerages.

**Abercrombie** of Abercrombie. Geneal. Collections, by W. Macfarlane, 1750-51. Scot. Hist. Soc., ii. 541 *bis*. East Neuk of Fife, by W. Wood, 2nd ed. (1887), 251-253. Genealogy of the Family of Abercromby, 1456-1895, by the Rev. A. W. C. Hallen. The Tragic History of the Abercrombies, by D. Murray Rose, 24 pp. (Banff, 1902).\*

Aberdeen. Memoir of J. Young, Aberdeen . . . 1861, ed. Lt.-Col. W. Johnston (1894), 24-26, 149-152.\*

of Balcormo. East Neuk of Fife, 2nd ed., 255.

Dunkirk. Complete Baronetage, by G. E. C., v. 8.

Montrose. The Balfours of Pilrig, by Barbara Balfour-Melville, 269.

Sandilands, Lord. History of the Carnegies, by Sir W. Fraser. The Scots Peerage, i. 75-81. G. E. C.'s Complete Peerage.

**Abercromby**. Marriages, 1738-1876, Burials, 1724-1792, *in* Collectanea Genealogica, ed. Joseph Foster (1881), i.

of Airthrey. Logie, by Rev. Dr Menzies Fergusson, ii. 53-58.

of Birkenbog. Nisbet's Heraldry (1742), ii., Appx. 130. Burke's Visitation of Seats and Arms (1853), ii. 38. Complete Baronetage by G. E. C., ii. 417 ; vi., Appx. 63. Burke's and Debrett's Peerage and Baronetage.

of Fetterneir. Nisbet's Heraldry (1722), i. 163.

of Glassaugh. Scottish N. and Q., 2nd S., vii. 143.

of Menstrie. Logie, by Menzies Fergusson, ii. 172-173.

of Pitmeddan. The Scots Peerage, i. 179-180.

of Stirling and Kerse. Rev. A. W. C. Hallen *in* The Scottish Antiquary (1896), x. 68-70, 100.

of Tullibody, Abercromby, Baron. Notes and Queries (1860), 2nd S., x. 190, 319. Memorials of Alloa, by Crawford (1874), 151-163, 174, 180. Logie, by Menzies Fergusson, ii. 58-61. G. E. C.'s Complete Peerage. Burke's and other Annual Peerages.

**Aberdeen**, Gordon, Earl of. Biographical Peerage (1808), 5-6. Case of John Campbell, Earl of Aberdeen (1872). Claim of the Earl of Aberdeen to be Viscount Gordon : (Session Papers, A of 1872). Historical MSS. Commission (1876), 5th Report. Dictionary of National Biography, *s.v.* The Scots Peerage, i. 82-89. G. E. C.'s Complete Peerage (1910). Burke's and other Annual Peerages. The Third Earl of Aberdeen, by J. M. Bulloch *in* Scottish Notes and Queries, 3rd S., ii. 137-139.

**Aberdein** of Keithock. Angus or Forfarshire, by A. J. Warden, iii. 27-28.

**Aberdour**, Douglas, Lord. The Scots Peerage, vi. 375-387. G. E. C.'s Complete Peerage.

**Abernethie** of Corskie. Scottish N. and Q., 2nd S., iii. 30.

**Abernethy.** J. G. Wallace-James *in* Genealogist, N. S., xvii. 150-152. Sir J. Balfour Paul *in* Genealogist, N. S., xviii. 16-25, 73-78, 208.

of Mayen. The Frasers of Philorth, by Wm. Fraser. Scottish N. and Q., xi. 156.

Lord Saltoun. Antiquarian Notes, by C. Fraser-Mackintosh, i. 289-291. The Scots Peerage, vii. 396-407.

**Aboyne**, Gordon, Lord, Viscount of, Earl of. Session Papers, 197 of 1838. The Earls of Aboyne, by J. M. Bulloch (Huntly, 1907). The Scots Peerage, i. 100-102 ; iv. 559-562. G. E. C.'s Complete Peerage, 2nd ed.

**Abrach-Mackay.** Rev. A. Mackay *in* Proc. Soc. Antiq. Scotl. (1904), 520-533. Major Alpin's . . . Descendants, by P. J. Anderson, Aberdeen (1904), 22-25.*

**Acarson** of Glen. Lands and their Owners in Galloway, by M'Kerlie, iii. 33.

**Accarson** of Meikleknox. Lands . . . in Galloway, iii. 247-248.

**Acheson**, Ayrshire. Notes and Queries, 10th S., ix. 91, 215, 392.

**Adair** of Genoch. Lands . . . in Galloway, by M'Kerlie, 2nd ed. (1906), i. 586-587.

of Kinhilt. Lands . . . in Galloway, i. 387-392.

of Portree. Lands . . . in Galloway, i. 376-379.

of Prestwickshaws. Paterson's Ayr and Wigton, i. 674.

**Adam.** Marriages *in* Collectanea Genealogica, ed. Joseph Foster, ii.

of Garpell. Crawfurd's Shire of Renfrew, ed. Robertson, 360.

of Glenboig. Strathendrick, by Guthrie Smith, 241.

of Kershead. Pont's Cuninghame, ed. Dobie (1876), 247-248.

of Lawhill. History of the County of Ayr, by Paterson, ii. 221.

of Maryburgh, *or* Blairadam. Baronage, by Douglas (1784), 255-257. Eminent Men of Fife, by M. F. Conolly (1866), 1-6. Herald and Genealogist, viii. 129-135. Burke's Landed Gentry (1848-1882). Debrett's Baronetage (after 1882).

of Tour. Paterson's Ayr and Wigton, iii. 476.

**Adams.** Scottish N. and Q. (1898), xii. 30.

**Adamson.** System of Heraldry, by Alex. Nisbet (1722), i. 131. Marriages *in* Collectanea Genealogica, ed. J. Foster (1881), i.
of Careston Castle. Angus or Forfarshire, by A. J. Warden, iii. 77. Burke's Landed Gentry (1879-1925).
of Craigcrook. Cramond, by J. P. Wood (1794), 32-34. The Scottish Antiquary (1894), viii. 89.
Perth. Scottish N. and Q., vi. 110, 127.

**Adie.** Zetland Family Histories, by F. J. Grant, 1-3.
Aberdeen. Scottish N. and Q., i. 88-89.
of Smiddiegreen. Geneal. Coll., by W. Macfarlane, 1750-51 ; Scot. Hist. Soc., ii. 192.

**Affleck** of Affleck. Memorials of Angus and the Mearns, by Jervise, ed. Gammack, ii. 111-112. Burke's Peerage and Baronetage. *See also* **Auchinleck.**

**Agnew.** Burials, 1724-1792, and Marriages, *in* Collectanea Genealogica, ed. Joseph Foster (1881), i. ii.
of Galdenoch. The Hereditary Sheriffs of Galloway, by Sir Andrew Agnew. 1 vol. (1864) ; 2 vols. (1893), ii. 434.
of Lochnaw. Lands . . . in Galloway, by M'Kerlie, 2nd ed. (1906), i. 428-474. Complete Baronetage, by G. E. C., ii. 368. Burke's Visitation of Seats and Arms (1853), i. 165. Burke's Peerage and Baronetage. Hereditary Sheriffs of Galloway, i. 213 *et passim* ; ii. 430-433, and Chart Pedigree.
of Lochryan. Lands . . . in Galloway, i. 504. Hereditary Sheriffs, ii. 433.
of Sheuchan. Lands . . . in Galloway, i. 547. Hereditary Sheriffs, ii. 435.
of Wigg. Hereditary Sheriffs, ii. 434.

**Agnew** *or* Agneaux, in England. Hereditary Sheriffs, i. 194-206 ; ii. 430.
in France. Hereditary Sheriffs, i. 180-193 ; ii. 430.

**Aiken,** Ayr. The Dalrymples of Langlands, by J. Shaw, 75, 79-83.*
of Dalmoak. Burke's Landed Gentry (1894 Suppl.-1925).

**Aikin.** Marriages and Burials *in* Collectanea Genealogica, ed. Joseph Foster (1881), i.

**Aikman.** Marriages *in* Collectanea Genealogica, ed. J. Foster (1881), ii.
of Cairny, Rosse and Brambleton. Baronage, by Douglas, 441-442. Nisbet's Heraldic Plates, ed. Ross and Grant, 22. Scottish N. and Q., 2nd S., viii. 191. Burke's Landed Gentry (1879-1894).
of Lordburn and Cairnie. Eminent Arbroathians, by J. M. M'Bain, 171-182.

**Ailesbury,** Bruce, Earl of. Biographical Peerage (London, 1808), 36-37. The Scots Peerage, iii. 466-483. Pedigree of the Marquis of Aylesbury's Descent from Bruce of Scotland ; MS. Tottenham Park Library. G. E. C.'s Complete Peerage, 2nd ed. (1910).

**Ailsa,** Kennedy, Earl of, Marquess of. Paterson's History of Ayr, ii.
272-290. Paterson's Ayr and Wigton, ii. 302-346. Historical MSS.
Commission (1876), 5th Report. Angus or Forfarshire, by Warden,
ii. 6-9. The Scots Peerage, ii. 497-502. G. E. C.'s Complete
Peerage, 2nd ed. (1910). Burke's and other Annual Peerages.

**Ainslie.** Marriages *in* J. Foster's Collectanea Genealogica (1881), ii.
of Blackhill. Nisbet's Heraldic Plates, ed. Ross and Grant, 102.
of Delgaty Castle. Burke's Landed Gentry (1879-1925).
of Dolphington. Baronage, by Douglas, 287-288.
of Overwells. Annals of a Border Club, by G. Tancred, 51.
of Pilton. Baronage, by Douglas, 300-302. Cramond, by J. P. Wood,
21-23. MS. Pedigree in Lyon Office.

**Aird** of Holl. Paterson's History of the County of Ayr, ii. 433. Paterson's
Ayr and Wigton, i. 702.
of Nether Catrine. Paterson's Ayr, ii. 426. Paterson's Ayr and Wigton, i. 689.

**Airlie,** Ogilvy, Earl of. Petition of W. Ogilvie (1813). Historical MSS.
Commission (1871), 2nd Report. Angus or Forfarshire, by Warden,
i. 419-431. The Scots Peerage, i. 106-132. Burke's Peerage.
G. E. C.'s Complete Peerage, 2nd ed. The House of Airlie, by Rev.
Wm. Wilson, 2 vols. (London, 1924).

**Airth,** Graham, Earl of. Case of Robert Barclay Allardice, claiming to
be Earl of Airth, with Pedigree, folio (London, 1838). Appendix to
this Case (1838). Second Appendix. Claim of R. B. Allardice to be
Earl of Airth: (Session Papers, 162 of 1839). Minutes of Evidence
on the Petition of Robert Barclay Allardice (1839). Airth Papers,
in reference to the Claim of R. B. Allardice, by H. Gurney (1839).\*
History of the Earldoms of Strathearn, Menteith and Airth, by Sir
Harris Nicholas (London, 1842). Claim of Mrs Barclay-Allardice
to the Earldom of Airth: (Session Papers, G of 1870 ; E of 1871 ;
F of 1874). The Stirling Antiquary, iv. 171-173. The Scots Peerage,
i. 133-145. G. E. C.'s Complete Peerage, 2nd ed.

**Airthrie,** Hope, Viscount of. The Scots Peerage, iv. 493.

**Aitchison.** Marriages *in* Collectanea Genealogica, ed. J. Foster, ii.
of Gosford. Cockburn-Hood's House of the Cockburns (1888).\*

**Aitken.** Marriages *in* Foster's Collectanea Genealogica (1881), iii.
Historical MSS. Commission (1891), 12th Report, pt. 9. N. and Q.,
9th S., xii. 129, 397.
of Auchengillan. Strathblane, by Guthrie Smith, 39.
of Thornton. The Marquis de Ruvigny *in* Geneal. Mag. (1901), iv.
166-169, 204-209, 256-258, 310-313, 400-403. (Issued separately 1901.)

**Aitkens,** London. Geneal. Mag., iv. 349-351.

**Aiton.** *See* **Aytoun.**

**Albany,** Dukes of. Heraldry, by Nisbet (1742), ii. iii. 83. The Dukes of
Albany and their Castle of Doune, by Sir Wm. Fraser, 4to, illust.
(1881).\* The Scots Peerage (1904-1914), i. 146-155. G. E. C.'s
Complete Peerage, 2nd ed.

**Alexander.** Marriages *in* Collectanea Genealogica, ed. Foster, iii.

Aberdeen. Geneal. Mag. (1904), vii. 416. Scottish N. and Q., 2nd S., vii. 191 ; viii. 85. Tayler's Jacobites of Aberdeenshire, 122-123.

of Ballochmyle. Crawfurd's Shire of Renfrew (1818), 386. Paterson's History of Ayr, ii. 336. Paterson's Ayr and Wigton, i. 553-555. Burke's Landed Gentry (1863-1886). Debrett's Baronetage (after 1886).

Banff. Scottish N. and Q., 2nd S., iv. 143.

of Blackhouse. Paterson's History of the County of Ayr, ii. 509-510. Paterson's Ayr and Wigton, i. 668-671.

of Boydston and Carlung. Ayrshire Families, by G. Robertson (1823), i. 126. Burke's Landed Gentry (1863-1879).

of Drumeldrie. East Neuk of Fife, by W. Wood, 2nd ed., 97-98.

of Glenhowe. Lands . . . in Galloway, by M'Kerlie, v. 386.

of Longkerse. Logie, by Rev. Dr Menzies Fergusson, ii. 116-123.

of Mains of Menstrie. Oliver's History of Antigua, i. 192.

of Menstrie. Logie, by Fergusson, ii. 169-170. Complete Baronetage, by G. E. C., ii. 293. Burke's Extinct Baronetage.

of Coull of Monzie. History of Thomson of Corstorphine, by J. R. Thomson, Appx.

of Newtown. Crawfurd's Shire of Renfrew, ed. Robertson, 88, 386.

of Powis. Burke's Commoners, ii. 170. Burke's Landed Gentry (1848-1858). Herald and Genealogist, iv. 554-556. Pedigree of Mayne of Powis, by H. C. Barnard (1929).*

St Andrews. Geneal. Coll., by W. Macfarlane, 1750-51 ; Scot. Hist. Soc., ii. 201.

Earl of Stirling. The Stirling Peerage, with the Genealogy of the Noble Family of Alexander (1826). Memorials of the Earl of Stirling and of the House of Alexander, by Rev. C. Rogers, 2 vols. (1877). Pedigree by D. E. Davy ; Brit. Mus. Add. MS. 19114. Descent of the Scottish Alexanders, by F. A. Sondley, LL.D., 73 pp. [1912]. *See also* **Stirling**, Earl of.

in Stirling. The Stirling Antiquary, iii. 22-23.

of Westerton. Logie, by Rev. Dr R. M. Fergusson, ii. 73. Burke's Landed Gentry (1848-1914).

**Alexander-Sinclair** of Freswick. Burke's Landed Gentry (1898-1925).

**Alford,** Graeme, Earl of. The Jacobite Peerage, by the Marquis of Ruvigny and Raineval (1904), 6.

**Algoe** of Easter Walkinshaw. Crawfurd's Shire of Renfrew (1818), 92.

**Alison.** Burke's Peerage and Baronetage (after 1852). Dictionary of National Biography, *s.v.*

of Birkhill. Balmerino, by Rev. J. Campbell, D.D., 578, 658.

of Dunjop. Lands and their Owners in Galloway, by M'Kerlie, v. 208.

**Allan** of Easter Crombie. The Allans formerly of Easter Crombie, Banffshire, by P. Rose, 1806, *in* Banffshire Field Club Proc. (1903-4).

of Kilphine. Paterson's Ayr and Wigton, ii. 92.

**Allan**, Kirkcaldy. Memoirs of my Ancestors, by H. B. M'Call (1884).*
Some Old Families, by H. B. M'Call (1890), 3-24.*

of Lauriston Castle. Pedigree *in* Playfair's Notes on the Scottish
Family of Playfair.*

**Allanby** of Balblair. Burke's Landed Gentry (1886-1925).

**Allardice** of Allardice. Case of Robert Barclay Allardice, claiming to be
Earl of Airth, with Pedigree, folio (London, 1838). Appendix to this
Case (1838). Claim of R. B. Allardice to be Earl of Airth : (Session
Papers, 162 of 1839). Case of Mrs Margaret Barclay Allardice, with
Pedigree (1870, 1871, 1874). Minutes of Evidence on above Petition.
Historical MSS. Commission, 5th Report (1876). Geneal. Mag.
(1899), ii. 176 ; iii. 269. Memorials of Angus and Mearns, by
Jervise,\ed. Gammack, ii. 141-147. The Scots Peerage, i. 142-143.

Aberdeen. Memoir of J. Young, Aberdeen . . . 1861, ed. Lt.-Col. W.
Johnston, 144-146.*

of Culquoich. Memoir of J. Young, Aberdeen . . ., 17-19.*

of Dunottar. Scottish N. and Q. (1887), i. 50.

of Memis. The Scottish Antiquary, xiii. 192 ; xiv. 55.

of Scotstoun. Fraser's Laurencekirk, 59-60.

**Allason** of Glasnock. Paterson's Ayr and Wigton, i. 341, 347.

**Allie** of Philiphaugh. Scottish N. and Q., 3rd S., v. 137.

**Alloa**, Erskine, Baron. The Jacobite Peerage, by the Marquis of Ruvigny
and Raineval (1904), 7.

**Alston**, Glasgow. The Scottish Antiquary, xiii. 138 ; xiv. 55.

**Altrie**, Keith, Lord. The Scots Peerage, i. 156-159. G. E. C.'s Complete
Peerage, ed. Hon. V. Gibbs (1910).

**Amos.** Tancred's Rulewater, 312-317.

**Anand.** *See* **Annand.**

**Ancram**, Ker, Earl of. Correspondence of Sir Robert Kerr, First Earl of
Ancram, and William, Third Earl of Lothian, 1616-1667, ed. David
Laing, 2 vols. (Edinr. 1875). The Scots Peerage, v. 466-487.
G. E. C.'s Complete Peerage, 2nd ed.

**Anderson.** The Anderson Family Tree, 1680-1890, compiled by Findlay
B. Anderson (Edinr. 17th April 1891). Obituary *in* Collectanea
Genealogica, ed. Foster, ii. Pedigree of Anderson and Timins *in*
Genealogist, 1st S., v. 205-207.

Aberdeen. Memoir of J. Young, Aberdeen . . . 1861, ed. Lt.-Col.
W. Johnston (1894), 110-111.* Scottish N. and Q., 2nd S., viii. 141.

of Aucharnie. Thanage of Fermartyn, by Temple, 203-204.

of Bourtie. Memoir of J. Young, Aberdeen . . . 130.*

of Candacraig. Scottish N. and Q., 2nd S., vi. 79 : 3rd S. i. 174 ; ii. 15, 46.

of Craigins. Paterson's Ayr and Wigton, ii. 103.

in Bordland of Eddleston. Peeblesshire Localities, by Renwick, 37, 48.

of Dowhill. Memoir of C. Mackintosh of Campsie and Dunchattan,
by his son (Glasgow, 1847).*

Earlston and Selkirk. Annals of a Border Club, by G. Tancred, 54-61.

**Anderson** of Fingland and Carterhope. Buchan and Paton's History of Peeblesshire, iii. 401-402.

Inverkeithing and Pittadro. Inverkeithing and Rosyth, by Rev. Wm. Stephen (Aberdeen, 1921), 498-500.

Inverness. An Inverness Lawyer, and his Sons, 1796-1878, by Isabel Harriet Anderson (Aberdeen, 1903).

of Linkwood. The Thurburns, by Lt.-Col. Thurburn, 33, 37, and Appx. E. F. Annals of Elgin, by Young, 661-663, 674. The Family of King of Newmill, by Young.

of Mudhouse. Scottish N. and Q., 2nd S., viii. 54.

of Montrave. Eminent Men of Fife, by M. F. Conolly, 7. East Neuk of Fife, by W. Wood, 2nd ed. 59.

of Mounie. The Reades of Blackwood Hill, by A. L. Reade (London, 1906).*

Phingask. The Andersons in Phingask and their Descendants, by James M. A. Wood (Aberdeen, 1910).

Rathen. Smith's Genealogies of an Aberdeen Family ; Aberdeen Univ. Studies, 82.

of Roseburn. Agnes Campbell, Lady Roseburn, by J. A. Fairley (1895), 18.

of Stobcross. Glasgow Past and Present, by Senex (1884), iii. 15.

in Sweden. One Year in Sweden, by H. Marryat, ii. 485, 486.

of Tushielaw and Hawkshaw. Craig Brown's Selkirkshire, i. 334-335 Buchan and Paton's History of Peeblesshire, iii. 398.

**Andson** of Friockheim. Baronage of Angus and Mearns, by Peter, 365.

**Angus**, The Celtic Earls of. The Scots Peerage, i. 160-166. Warden's Angus or Forfarshire, i. 264-274.

Aberdeen. Memoir of J. Young, Aberdeen . . . 1861, ed. Lt.-Col. W. Johnston, 227. Scottish N. and Q., ix. 46.

Comyn, Earl of. The Scots Peerage, i. 167.

Douglas, Earl of. The Scots Peerage, i. 172-213. Angus or Forfarshire, i. 275-276. Notes and Queries, 3rd S., vi. 361, 445 : 5th S., vi. 459 ; vii. 37.

Hamilton, Earl of. The Scots Peerage, iv. 393-397.

Stewart, Earl of. The Scots Peerage, i. 169-171. Angus or Forfarshire, i. 274-275.

Umframville, Earl of. The Scots Peerage, i. 167-168. G. H. Watson *in* Genealogist, N. S., xxvi. 193-211.

**Annan**, Murray, Viscount. The Scots Peerage, i. 228-229.

**Annand**, Johnstone, Viscount of. The Scots Peerage, i. 261.

**Annand** of Auchterellon. Burke's Landed Gentry (1848).

of Kinquhery. Memorials of Angus and the Mearns, by A. Jervise, ed. Gammack, ii. 63-64.

of Melgund. Memorials of Angus, ii. 64.

of Sauchie. Heraldry, by Nisbet (1742), ii. Ragman Roll, 35. Some Ancient Scottish Families, by J. B. Brown-Morison, 9-15.

**Annandale**, Johnstone, Earl of, Marquess of. Case for James, Earl of Hopetoun, with Pedigree in Manuscript, 10 pp., with Copy of the Charter of 1662, 15 pp. (1794). Information for Lady Christian Graham, Sir R. B. Johnstone, Bart., and Charles Johnstone, claimants to the Executry of the late George, Marquis of Annandale (1796). Case for John James Hope Johnstone, of Annandale (1825), 7 pp. : Additional Case (1830), 4, 48, 3 pp. : Further Additional Case, with Pedigrees, 15 pp. (1825-30). Case for John Henry Goodinge Johnstone, 12 pp., and Pedigree : Appendix, 4 pp. : Additional Case, 20 pp., with Pedigree : Appendix to same, 6 pp. (1830-34). Case for Sir Frederick George Johnstone, Bart. of Westerhall, with Appendix, 38+vi. pp., with Pedigree of Hay of Linplum : Additional Case, with Proofs of the Pedigree, etc., 83 pp., with Pedigree : Supplemental Case, 15 pp. (1834-1838). Case and further Case of Dougal Campbell, M.D., claiming title, etc., of Earl of Annandale (1834-1844) : Minutes and Evidence on the Claim (1825-1844), including the Speeches of Counsel, 4 vols. Case of Sir Frederic John William Johnstone, of Westerhall, 66 pp., and Pedigree : Additional Cases, 114 pp. [1875]. Case of Edward Johnstone, of Fulford Hall, 14 pp., with Pedigrees : Appendix of Proofs, 39 pp., Pedigree, and Facsimiles (1876-1877). Case for John James Hope Johnstone, of Annandale, 69 pp., with Pedigrees : Additional Case, 29 pp. (1876-1878) : Minutes of Evidence, with Pedigrees, 1202 pp. (1876-1881) : Chronological List of Documents, printed in the above (May 1879), 24 pp. : Names of Petitioners, Session (1877), 4 pp. The Johnstones of Annandale (1853). The Annandale Family Book, by Sir Wm. Fraser, 2 vols. (1894).* Historical MSS. Commission (1897), 15th Report. The Scots Peerage, i. 261-271. G. E. C.'s Complete Peerage. Rev. J. A. D. G. Macdonald *in* Dumfriesshire and Galloway Antiq. Soc. Trans., 3rd S. (1923), viii. 101-117.

**Annandale**, Murray, Earl of. The Scots Peerage, i. 214-229.

**Anstruther.** Obituary *in* Collectanea Genealogica, ed. Foster (1881), ii.
of Airdrie. East Neuk of Fife, by W. Wood, 2nd ed. (1887), 402-403.
of Anstruther. Heraldry, by A. Nisbet (1742), ii. Appx. 65-67. Baronage, by Douglas, 313-316. Eminent Men of Fife, by Conolly, 9-11, 471. East Neuk of Fife, 2nd ed., 347-361. Complete Baronetage, by G. E. C. (1904), iv. 387. History of the Family of Anstruther, by A. W. A[nstruther], 4to, *xvi*+201 pp. (Edinr. 1923).
of Anstrutherfield and Innerkeithing. Baronage, by Douglas, 536. Stephen's Inverkeithing and Rosyth (1921), 80.
of Balcaskie. Eminent Men of Fife, 12-14. East Neuk of Fife, 275-278. Burke's and other Annual Peerages and Baronetages.
of Caiplie. East Neuk of Fife, 391-392.
of Elie. Burke's Visitation of Seats and Arms (1853), i. 204. East Neuk of Fife, 224-232. Complete Baronetage, by G. E. C., iv. 387.
of Newark. East Neuk of Fife, 244-246.
of Wrae. Complete Baronetage, by G. E. C., iv. 387.

**Anstruther-Paterson.** The Complete Baronetage, by G. E. C. (1904), iv. 387 ; (1906), v. 324.

**Anstruther-Thomson** of Charleton. Eminent Men of Fife, 471-472. Visitation of Seats and Arms, by J. B. Burke (1853), i. 70-71. Burke's Landed Gentry (1858-1925).

**Appin,** Stewart, Baron. The Jacobite Peerage, by the Marquis of Ruvigny (1904), 8-13.

**Arbuthnot,** Viscount of Arbuthnot. Heraldry, by Nisbet (1742), ii. Appx. 86-93. J. Foster's Stemmata Britannica (1877), 33. Historical MSS. Commission (1881), 8th Report. Inventory of Arbuthnot Title Deeds, 1206-1488, *in* Nugæ Derelictæ, ed. Maidment and Pitcairn (1888). The Scots Peerage, i. 272-317. G. E. C.'s Complete Peerage, 2nd ed. Burke's Peerage, Lodge's Peerage, etc. Memories of the Arbuthnots of Kincardineshire and Aberdeenshire, by Mrs P. S. M. Arbuthnot ; three gen. Charts, 33 illust. (1920).

of Cairngall. Scottish N. and Q., ii. 111, 125.

Edinburgh. Burke's Peerage and Baronetage. Debrett's Baronetage.

Peterhead. Tayler's Jacobites of Aberdeenshire, 125-126.

of Scotsmill. Scottish N. and Q., ii. 111, 125.

**Arbuthnot-Leslie** of Warthill. Burke's Landed Gentry (1886-1925).

**Arbuthnott.** Obituary *in* Collectanea Genealogica, ed. Foster (1881), ii.

of Findowrie. Angus or Forfarshire, by Warden, iii. 20-23. Scottish N. and Q., 3rd S., i. 23.

**Archer.** Memorials of the Families of the Surname of Archer, by J. H. L. Archer, 4to, 76 pp. (1861).

**Ardrossan** of Ardrossan. Pont's Cuninghame, ed. Dobie, 57-61. Ayrshire Families, by G. Robertson (1823), i. 9-12. Paterson's Ayr and Wigton (1866), iii. 49. Scot. Hist. Soc. No. 56 (1908), *lxxviii.*

**Argyll,** Campbell, Earl of, Marquess of, Duke of. The Scotch Mist cleared up . . . proceedings against Archibald, Earl of Argyle, for High Treason, 45 pp. [Edinburgh, 1681 ?]. Life of John, Duke of Argyll and Greenwich, with History and Genealogy of the Family of Campbell, down to 1740, by Robert Campbell ; geneal. table (London and Belfast, 1745). Biographical Peerage (London, 1808), 19-25. The Marquis of Argyll's Last Will and Testament ; Harl. Misc. viii. (1811). Letters from Archibald, Earl of Argyll, to John, Duke of Lauderdale (Edinr. 1829). The Argyle Papers : Notices relating to the Argyle Family, by Robert Mylne, and other Papers, ed. James Maidment, 57 copies (Edinr. 1834). Some Account of John, Duke of Argyll, and his Family, by his great-niece, Lady Louisa Stuart, 143 pp., and Pedigree (London, 1863)* : *repr. in* Letters of Lady Mary Coke, i. (1889).* The Clan Campbell and the Marquis of Lorne [by J. Hogg], [1871]. The MacCallum-More, a History of the Argyll Family, by Rev. Hely Smith, 8vo ; genealogical table (London, 1871). The House

of Argyll, and collateral branches of the Clan Campbell, from
A.D. 420, Genealogical Tree, 8vo (Glasgow, 1871). Sketches of
the Family of Argyll, by James Maidment (1871).* Stories of Old
Families, by W. Chambers (Edinr. 1878). Hasted's Kent, i. 373.
The MSS. of his Grace the Duke of Argyll, ed. W. Fraser : Royal
Commission on Historical MSS., 4th and 6th Reports (1874-1877).
Great Historic Families, by Jas. Taylor [1887]. Garelochside, by
W. C. Maughan, 138-154, 300. Notices of Portraits, *in* The Scottish
Antiquary (1897), xi. 1-7, 49-58, 97-101. Scottish N. and Q., 2nd S.,
iii. 186-187 ; iv. 14. The Great Marquess : Life and Times of
Archibald, Marquess of Argyll, by J. Willcock, illust. (1903). A
Scots Earl in Covenanting Times ; the Life of 9th Earl of Argyll,
by J. Willcock, illust. (1907). Famous Families in British History :
the Campbells of Argyll, by Hilda T. Skae, 4to, 144 pp., illust.
Burke's, Lodge's, Debrett's Peerages, etc. The Scots Peerage, i.
318-393. G. E. C.'s Complete Peerage, 2nd ed. Dictionary of
National Biography, *s.v.* Abstracts of Entries from Various Sources
relating to the Ducal House of Argyll, and Cadets, collected by
Sir D. Campbell of Barcaldine, ed. by Rev. Henry Paton (1916).

**Arklay** of Ethiebeaton. Angus or Forfarshire, iv. 396.

**Arkley** of Duninald. Angus or Forfarshire, by Warden, iii. 153-154.

**Armstrong.** Border Memories, by W. Riddell Carre (1858), 366-369.
Chronicles of the Armstrongs, by J. L. Armstrong (New York, 1902).

**Arnot** of Arnot. Eminent Men of Fife, 14-17. Brief Notices of the
Families of Arnot, Reid, etc. (1872).* Burke's Extinct Baronetcies.
Complete Baronetage, by G. E. C., ii. 361. The House of Arnot,
and some of its Branches, by James Arnot, M.D., Brigade Surgeon-
Lieut.-Col. I.M.S., 4to, illust. (Edinburgh, 1918). Notes and Queries,
4th S., v. 92, 135 ; 5th S., i. 144.

of Balcormo. East Neuk of Fife, by W. Wood, 2nd ed., 255-257.

of Fenwick. Paterson's Ayr and Wigton, iii. 247.

of Lochrig. Certificates of Birth and Descent of John Arnot of Lochrig ;
Brit. Mus. Eg. Ch., 413, 414. Ayrshire Families, by G. Robertson,
i. 13-21. Paterson's History of Ayr, ii. 457-459. Paterson's Ayr and
Wigton, iii. 247-248, 599-604.

of Woodmiln and Granton. Cramond, by J. P. Wood, 19.

**Arnot-Stewart** of Lochridge. Ayrshire Families, i. 20-21.

*See* The Scots Peerage, ed. Sir J. Balfour Paul, *for*

**Arran**, Boyd, Earl of, v. 147-149.

Douglas, Earl of, iv. 381-382.

Hamilton, Earl of, iv. 355-380, 383-397.

Stewart, Earl of, i. 394-398.

**Arran**, Hamilton, Earl of. R. K. Hannay *in* Scot. Hist. Review, xviii.
258-276.

**Arrat** of Arrat. Angus or Forfarshire, by Warden, iii. 32-33. Memorials of
Angus and the Mearns, by A. Jervise, ed. Gammack (1885), ii. 59-61.

**Arres**, Edinburgh. Proc. Soc. Antiq. Scotl. (1891), 140-141, 151.

**Arrick**, Scottish N. and Q., 3rd S., iv. 62, 103 ; vi. 247.

**Arrott** of Dumbarrow and Almerieclose. Eminent Arbroathians, by J. M. M'Bain (1897), 223-264.

**Arthur** of Ballone. East Neuk of Fife, by W. Wood, 2nd ed., 202-203.
  of Cairnes. Geneal. Coll., by W. Macfarlane, 1750-51 ; Scot. Hist. Soc., ii. 189.
  of Carlung. Debrett's Baronetage (1903-1918). Debrett's, Burke's, and other Annual Peerages (after 1918).
  of Montgomerie Castle. Burke's Landed Gentry (1921-1925).

**Arthurson.** Zetland Family Histories, by F. J. Grant (1907), 227.

**Ashkirk** of Ashkirk. T. Craig Brown's Selkirkshire, i. 438-439.

**Asloan** of Garroch. Lands . . . in Galloway, by M'Kerlie, v. 240.

**Aslois** of Aslois, **Assloss** of Assloss. Ayrshire Families, by G. Robertson, i. 22. Paterson's County of Ayr, ii. 204. Paterson's Ayr and Wigton, iii. 424.

**Aston**, Baron Aston of Forfar. Angus or Forfarshire, by Warden, ii. 41. The Scots Peerage, i. 399-414. G. E. C.'s Complete Peerage, 2nd ed.

**Atholl**, The Celtic Earls of. Genealogy of the Celtic Earls of Atholl, with chart of the descendants of Conan, founder of the De Atholia family, afterwards known as the Robertsons of Strowan, by Sir Noel Paton (1873). Stemmata Robertson et Durdin, by H. Robertson (1893-95), 35-39.* Three Celtic Earldoms, by S. Cowan (1909). The Scots Peerage, i. 415-433. Philippe de Strabolgi, by G. W. Watson *in* Genealogist, N.S., xxix. 1. N. and Q., 4th S., viii. 244 ; xii. 172, 378. Scottish N. and Q., 3rd S., ii. 95.
  Campbell, Earl of. The Scots Peerage, i. 434.
  Douglas, Earl of. The Scots Peerage, i. 435.
  Murray, Earl of, Marquess of, Duke of. Nisbet's Heraldry, ii., Appx. 175-210. The Claim of the Duke of Atholl to the Barony of Strange : (Session Papers, Feb. and March 1726). Case of the Duke of Atholl claiming the Barony of Strange (1736). Memoirs of the Jacobites of 1715 and 1745, by Mrs Katherine Thomson, iii. 1-225. The Earldom of Atholl, by J. A. Robertson (1860).* Notes and Queries, 4th S. x. 161, 235, 303, 363, 402, 525 ; xii. 172, 378 : 8th S., v. 47, 96. Historical MSS. Commission (1879), 7th Report ; (1891), 12th Report. Recreations of an Antiquary, by Fittis, 232. G. E. C.'s Complete Peerage, 2nd ed. The Scots Peerage, i. 449-502. Burke's and other Annual Peerages.
  Stewart, Earl of. The Scots Peerage, i. 436-439, 447-448. Tree of Stewart, Earl of Atholl.

**Atkine** *or* **Atkins**, Culross. J. A. Inglis *in* Scottish Historical Review (1916), xii. 135.

**Aubigny**, Stewart, Lord d'. Some Account of the Stuarts of Aubigny in France, 1422-1672, by Lady E. C. Cust, 4to, Pedigrees (1891).* The Scots Peerage, v. 356-362.

**Auchinleck** of Auchinleck. Heraldry, by Nisbet (1742), ii. Ragman Roll, 39. Angus or Forfarshire, by Warden, iv. 416-419. Memorial of Angus and Mearns, by Jervise, ed. Gammack, ii. 111-112. Paterson's Ayr and Wigton, i. 188-190. Scot. Hist. Review (1912), viii. 321.

of Balmanno. Nisbet's Heraldry, ii., Appx. 252. Genealogical Fragments, by James Maidment (Berwick, 1855), 2 pp.*

West Indies. History of Antigua, by Oliver, i. 14-16. *See also* **Affleck.**

**Auchinloss.** *See* **Aslois, Assloss.**

**Auchmutie.** Leslie, Lord. The Scots Peerage, vii. 301.

**Auchmuty** of Auchmuty and Halhill. Eminent Men of Fife, 18. East Neuk of Fife, by W. Wood, 2nd ed., 99-100.

of Drumeldrie. East Neuk of Fife, 100-101.

St Andrews. Campbell's Balmerino, 651.

**Auchterhouse,** Stewart, Lord. The Scots Peerage, ii. 266.

**Aulay,** The Clan. Capt. F. W. L. Thomas *in* Proc. Soc. Antiq. Scotl., N. S., ii. (1880), 363. *See also* **Macaulay.**

**Auld.** Scottish N. and Q., 3rd S., v. 131-132.

**Avandale,** Stewart, Lord. The Scots Peerage, vi. 509-511.

**Avondale,** Douglas, Earl of. The Scots Peerage, iii. 173-185.

**Ay,** The Clan. Antiquarian Notes, by C. Fraser-Mackintosh, i. 381, 382.

**Ayson.** Scottish N. and Q., xii. 151.

**Ayton, Aytoun, Aiton** of Ayton. An Enquiry into the origin, pedigree and history of the family or clan of Aiton in Scotland, by W. Aiton (Hamilton, 1830). Eminent Men of Fife, by Conolly, 18. The Aytons of Ayton in the Merse . . . by Lt.-Col. A. Aytoun, 63 pp. (Edinburgh, 1887).*

of Inchdairnie. Record of the service of John Aytoun of Inchdairney as nearest heir male to Andrew Aytoun, Governor of Stirling Castle in 1500 (Edinburgh, 1829).* Burke's Landed Gentry (1875-1898).

of Kinnaldie. Geneal. Coll., by W. Macfarlane, 1750-51. Scot. Hist. Soc., ii. 168. Poems by Sir Robert Aytoun of Kinaldie, 1570-1638 ; ed. by Charles Roger; with Family Tree (1844). Eminent Men of Fife, 18-22.

of Kippo. East Neuk of Fife, by W. Wood, 2nd ed. (1887), 465. Monipenny *v.* Aytone ; Case for the Respondent, Appx. (1757).

*See* The Scots Peerage, ed. Sir J. Balfour Paul, *for*

**Badenoch,** Comyn, Lord of, i. 503-510.

Gordon, Lord of, iv. 549-558.

Stewart, Lord of, ii. 170, 262.

**Badenoch-Nicolson** of Glenbervie. Burke's Landed Gentry (1898-1925).

**Baikie** of Tankerness and Isbister. The Frotoft Branch of the Orkney Traills, by T. W. Traill, 20, 22, 23-40, 83. Orkney Armorials, by H. L. Norton Smith, 2-10. Burke's Landed Gentry (1863-1925).

**Baillie.** Lives of the Baillies, by Jas. Wm. Baillie of Culterallers (Edinr. 1872). Obituary *in* Collectanea Genealogica, ed. Foster, ii.

in Callands. Buchan and Paton's History of Peeblesshire, iii. 87.

**Baillie** of Dochfour.  Burke's Landed Gentry (1849-1875).  Antiquarian
  Notes, by C. Fraser-Mackintosh, i. 58, 177 ; ii. 34-38.  The Scottish
  Antiquary, xiii. 183.
of Dunain.  The Family of Baillie of Dunain, Dochfour, and Lamington,
  by J. G. B. Bulloch (Green Bay, Wis., U.S.A., 1898).*  Antiquarian
  Notes, by C. Fraser-Mackintosh, i. 59, 65 ; ii. 32.
of Dunragit.  Lands and their Owners in Galloway, by M'Kerlie, 2nd ed.
  (1906), i. 566-570.
Lord Forrester of Corstorphine.  The Scots Peerage, iv. 93-96.
of Hills.  Peeblesshire Localities, by Renwick, 242-243.
of Jerviswood.  The Household Book of Lady Grisell Baillie, 1692-1733,
  ed. R. Scott Moncrieff (Scot. Hist. Soc., 1911).  Memoirs of the
  Right Hon. George Baillie and of Lady Grisell Baillie, by their
  daughter, Lady Murray of Stanhope (1822).  Upper Ward of
  Lanarkshire, by Irving and Murray, ii. 321-328.  What I have been
  told concerning my great-grandmother, my great-grandfather, and
  also my grandmother, Lady Polwarth, by M. J. Baillie, Selkirk, n.d.
  Burke's Landed Gentry (1848-1858).
of Lamington.  Heraldry, by Nisbet (1742), ii. Appx. 135-140.  Upper
  Ward of Lanarkshire, i. 223-244.  The Scottish Antiquary, viii. 45.
of Leys.  Scottish N. and Q., 3rd S., vi. 104.
of Littlegill.  Upper Ward of Lanarkshire, i. 157-160.
of Lochend.  Complete Baronetage, by G. E. C., ii. 423.
of Monkton.  Ayrshire Families, by G. Robertson, i. 24-36.  History of
  Ayr, by Paterson, ii. 384.  Ayr and Wigton, by Paterson, i. 593.
of Parbroath and Balmudyside.  Nisbet's Heraldic Plates, ed. Ross and
  Grant (1892), 106.
of Polkemmet.  Burke's Peerage and Baronetage.
of Redcastle and Tarradale.  Burke's Landed Gentry (1848-1898).
**Baillie-Cochrane.**  Case of Alexander Dundas Ross Cochrane Wishart
  Baillie on his claim to the title of Baron Wharton (1843).  Historical
  MSS. Commission (1876), 5th Report, pt. 1.
**Baillie-Hamilton,** Earl of Haddington.  The Scots Peerage, iv. 326-329.
**Bain.**  Notes and Queries, 8th S., vi. 507 ; vii. 93.  Genealogical Chart of the
  Family of Bain, co. Haddington, by Rev. C. Rogers (Edinr. 1871).*
**Baird.**  Account of the Surname of Baird—particularly of the Families
  of Auchmeddan, Newbyth, and Sauchtonhall, by W. N. Fraser,
  96 pp. (Edinr. 1857).  Genealogical Collections concerning the
  Sir-name of Baird, and the Families of Auchmedden, Newbyth,
  and Sauchtonhall, from the original MS. of William Baird in the
  Advocates' Library (London, 1870).*  Obituary *in* Foster's Collectanea
  Genealogica, ii.  Notes and Queries, 3rd S., iii. 87 ; 7th S., v. 427.
of Cambusdoon.  Burke's Landed Gentry (1863-1894).
of Cowdam.  Paterson's Ayr and Wigton, i. 737.
of Cullen.  Notes and Queries, 3rd S., vi. 146.
of Elie.  Eminent Men of Fife, by M. F. Conolly, 22-24.  Burke s
  Landed Gentry (1875-1925).

**Baird** of Gartsherrie. The Bairds of Gartsherrie : some Notices of their Origin and History, by A[ndrew] M[acgeorge], (Glasgow Univ. Press, 1875).\* Annals of a Border Club, by G. Tancred (1899), 62-63.

of Muirkirk. Burke's Landed Gentry (1882-1925).

of Newbyth. Complete Baronetage, by G. E. C., iii. 330 ; iv. 310. Burke's Peerage and Baronetage.

of Ordinhnivas. Genealogical Collections concerning the Surname of Baird (1870), Appx.

of Posso. Buchan and Paton's History of Peeblesshire, iii. 559-562.

of Saughton Hall. Complete Baronetage, by G. E. C., iv. 369. Burke's Peerage and Baronetage.

of Urie. Burke's Peerage and Baronetage (after 1897).

**Bairdie** of Salvage. Stephen's Inverkeithing (1921), 331, 475-478.

**Balcarres**, Lindsay, Earl of. Biographical Peerage (London, 1808), 41-42. The Lives of the Lindsays, or a Memoir of the Houses of Crawford and Balcarres, by Lord Lindsay, 3 vols. (London, 1849). Angus or Forfarshire, by A. J. Warden, i. 333-335. The Scots Peerage, i. 511-529. G. E. C.'s Complete Peerage, 2nd ed.

**Balcaskie** of Balcaskie. East Neuk of Fife, by W. Wood, 2nd ed. (1887), 271.

**Bald**, Alloa. Annals of a Border Club, by G. Tancred, 64.

of Culross. The Scottish Antiquary, x. 14.

**Balderston**, Edinburgh. Nisbet's Heraldic Plates, ed. Ross and Grant (1892), 118.

**Balfour.** Balfouriana Memoria, by Sir Robert Sibbald (1699). Heraldry, by A. Nisbet (1722), i. 168-169. Obituary *in* Foster's Collectanea Genealogica, ii. Notes and Queries, 7th S., vii. 188.

of Balbirnie. Nisbet's Heraldry, i. 435. Eminent Men of Fife, by Conolly, 26. Burke's Landed Gentry (1863-1925).

of Balbuthie. East Neuk of Fife, by W. Wood, 2nd ed. (1887), 170.

of Balfour and Trenabie. Eminent Men of Fife, 24-26. Genealogical Sketches : The Frotoft Branch of the Orkney Traills, by T. W. Traill (1902), 16-21, 22, 81.\* Norton Smith's Orkney Armorials, 13-18. Burke's Landed Gentry (1848-1925).

of Balgonie. Kennoway, by A. S. Cunningham (Leven, 1906), 47, 50.

of Balledmonth. Campbell's Balmerino, 504, 646.

of Brockley. MS. pedigree in possession of Lord Kinross.

of Burleigh, Balfour, Lord. Notes and Queries, 3rd S., viii. 149 : 4th S. ii. 270, 281 ; xi. 219. Eminent Men of Fife, 27-28, 31. The Scots Peerage, i. 530-555. G. E. C.'s Complete Peerage (1910). Case and Supplemental Case on behalf of R. Bruce of Kennet (1860, 1864). Claim of Robert Bruce of Kennet to be Lord Balfour of Burley : (Session Papers, 237, 237² of 1861). Case on behalf of Alexander Hugh Bruce of Kennet. Case of F. W. Balfour claiming title of Lord Balfour, 31 pp., n.d. Supplemental Case of same, 26 pp. (1864). Claim of F. W. Balfour to dignity of Lord Balfour of Burley : (Session Papers, G of 1862, A of 1864, D of 1867, C of 1867-8, F of 1868-9).

**Balfour** of Burleigh, Bruce, Lord. Burke's Peerage (after 1869). The Scots
   Peerage, i. 554-555. G. E. C.'s Complete Peerage (1910).
of Dawyck. Pedigree of the Dawyck Branch of the Balfour Family,
   illust. and autographs, sheet 38 × 25 (1911). Buchan and Paton's
   History of Peeblesshire, iii. 444-445. Burke's Landed Gentry
   (1914-1925).
of Denmilne. Eminent Men of Fife, 26, 29, 30. Complete Baronetage,
   by G. E. C., ii. 395. The Denmilne Manuscripts in the National
   Library of Scotland, by J. D. Mackie, 24 pp. (Edinr. 1928).
of Fernie Castle. Burke's Landed Gentry (1875-1925).
of Glenawley. The Scots Peerage, i. 536.
of Grange. Campbell's Balmerino, 568-572, 656.
of Huip. The Frotoft Branch of the Orkney Traills, 22, 81.
of Kinloch. The Genealogist, N. S., v. 207.
of Lalethan. Heraldry, by Nisbet (1722), i. 434.
of Mountquhanie. Eminent Men of Fife, 25, 29.
of Newton Don. Annals of a Border Club, by G. Tancred, 65-69.
   Burke's Landed Gentry (1898-1925).
of Nydie. Geneal. Coll., by W. Macfarlane, 1750-51; Scot. Hist. Soc., ii.200.
of Pharay. Norton Smith's Orkney Armorial, 13-18.
of Pilrig. A Record of Family Grace, by James Balfour, W.S., illust.
   (Edinr. 1877).* Genealogical Table of the Family of Balfour of
   Pilrig, showing the Descendants of Alexander Balfour of Inchrye,
   57 sheets (Edinr. 1890).* The Balfours of Pilrig : a History for the
   Family, by Barbara Balfour-Melville of Pilrig, 17 portraits (Edinr.1907).
of Powis. Notes and Queries, 7th S., xii. 447.
of Randerston. East Neuk of Fife, by W. Wood, 2nd ed., 458.
of Trenaby. Burke's Landed Gentry (1848-1925).
of Whittinghame. Burke's Landed Gentry (1858-1925).
**Balfour-Melville.** Burke's Landed Gentry (1886-1906).
**Balfour-Ogilvy.** Landed Gentry (1875).
**Balfour-Stewart** of Pharay. The Frotoft Branch of the Orkney Traills, by
   Thos. W. Traill (1902), 17.*
**Balgonie,** Leslie, Lord. The Scots Peerage, v. 372-381.
**Baliol, Balliol.** Royal Genealogies, by Anderson (1732), 759. Ayrshire
   Families, by G. Robertson (1823), i. 36-49. Pedigree of the Heirs
   of the Royal House of Baliol, by Alexander Sinclair. Notes and
   Queries, 2nd S., vii. 9, 217 ; 3rd S., ii. 100, 200 ; 4th S., i. 616, ii. 382,
   iii. 492, vii. viii. 487, ix. 130; 5th S., ii. 186, 351 ; 6th S., v. 61-62 ;
   7th S., iii. 496, iv. 50 ; 8th S., viii. 124, 251. The Genealogist, vi. 1.
   The Bailleuls of Flanders, and the Bayleys of Willers Hall, by
   Francis Bayley (London, 1881). The Royal Manor of Hitchin and
   its Lords ; Harold and the Balliols, by W. Wentworth Huyshe (1906).
   Dervorgilla, Lady of Galloway, and her Abbey of the Sweet Heart,
   by Wentworth Huyshe (1913). The Norman Balliols in England,
   compiled in part from Huysche, with additions, etc., and pedigree,
   by Benjamin J. Scott (1914).

**Baliol** le Scot. Genealogist, N. S., xv. 11.

of Cavers. Genealogist, 1st S., vi. 1-7 ; N. S., iv. 141-143 ; xv. 11, 204.

Lord of Galloway. The Scots Peerage, iv. 143.

**Ballantyne** of Castlehill. Paterson's County of Ayr, i. 208 ; Paterson's Ayr and Wigton, i. 139-140.

of Holylee. Burke's Landed Gentry (1863).

*See also* **Bannatyne.**

**Ballingall.** Kennoway, by A. S. Cunningham, 58.

**Balloch.** Scottish N. and Q., 2nd S., vi. 107 ; vii. 50-51.

**Balmerino,** Elphinstone, Lord. The Scots Magazine (1746). Eminent Men of Fife, by Conolly, 163-164. Notes and Queries, 6th S., ii. 288, 408 ; x. 477. Balmerino and its Abbey, by Rev. Jas. Campbell, D.D. (1899), 526-555, 651-652. The Scots Peerage, i. 556-575. G. E. C.'s Complete Peerage, 2nd ed. (1910). The Scot. Hist. Review, xxv. 85.

**Balvaird,** Murray, Lord. The Scots Peerage, viii. 200-214.

**Banff,** Ogilvy, Lord. The Scots Peerage, ii. 1-26. G. E. C.'s Complete Peerage (1910).

**Bannatyne** of Corehouse. Ayrshire Families, by G. Robertson (1823), i. 52 *n.*, 382. Annals of Lesmahagow, by J. B. Greenshields (1854), 70-76.* Upper Ward of Lanarkshire, by Irving and Murray, ii. 213-216.

of Gardrum. Paterson's Ayr and Wigton, iii. 245.

of Glenmaddy. Folklore and Genealogies of Uppermost Nithsdale, by Wilson, 246.

of Kames. Ayrshire Families, i. 50-69, 381. History of County of Bute, by Reid (1864), 246-250.

of Kelly. Crawfurd's Shire of Renfrew (1818), 129. Ayrshire Families, i. 70-71.

of Kerrylamont. History of County of Bute, 250-253.

**Bannerman.** Heraldry, by Nisbet (1742), ii., Appx. 151-152.

Aberdeen. Memoir of J. Young . . . 1861, ed. Lt.-Col. W. Johnston (1894), 232.

of Elsick. The Family of Bannerman of Elsick, 26 pp. (Aberdeen, 1812). D. Murray Rose *in* Scottish N. and Q., 2nd S., iii. 17-18. Complete Baronetage, by G. E. C., iv. 317. Burke's Peerage and Baronetage.

**Baptie,** Langburnshiels. Tancred's Rulewater, 309.

**Barbour** of Barlay. Lands . . . in Galloway, by M'Kerlie, iii. 98.

**Barclay.** Statement of the Services of Lt.-Col. Robert Barclay ; ed. W. B. D. D. Turnbull, 12 copies (Edinr. 1838).* Brief Memoirs of the Barclay Family, 12mo (London, 1851). Registrum de Panmure : Records of the family of . . . Brechin Barclay (1874).* History of the Scottish Barclays, compiled by Leslie Barclay (Folkestone, 1915). History of the Barclay Family, with full Pedigree 1066-1924, by the Rev. C. W. Barclay, 2 vols. (St Catherine's Press, 1925). Obituary *in* Foster's Collectanea Genealogica (1881), ii.

of Abernyte. Geneal. Mag. (1903), vi. 364.

**Barclay** of Barclay. The Barclays of Barclay, of Grantully, of Garth and of Towie Barclay, by Capt. Douglas Wimberley (Aberdeen, 1903).

of Brechin. The Scottish Antiquary (1893), vii. 82, 169 ; viii. 21. The Genealogist, N. S., ix. 4, 129, 193, 197, 200.

of Burnton. The Parish of Laurencekirk, by Rev. W. R. Fraser (1880), 68.

of Cullairnie. Eminent Men of Fife, by Conolly, 35-36. The Scottish Antiquary, xii. 144. Complete Baronetage, by G. E. C., vi., Appx. 63.

of Gardiesting. Zetland Family Histories, by F. J. Grant, 6-9.

of Innergellie. East Neuk of Fife, by W. Wood, 2nd ed., 382-383.

of Johnston. Fraser's Laurencekirk, 106-112.

of Kilbirnie. History of Ayr, by Paterson, ii. 113. Ayr and Wigton, by Paterson, iii. 293.

of Kippo and Arngask. Heraldry, by Nisbet (1742), ii., Appx. 211.

of Ladyland. Pont's Cuninghame, ed. Dobie, 308-311. Robertson's Ayrshire Families, i. 72-74. Paterson's Ayr, ii. 121-122. Paterson's Ayr and Wigton, iii. 296-298.

of Mathers. A Genealogical Account of the Barclays, formerly of Mathers, by R. Barclay (Aberdeen, 1740,* 2nd ed., 1812). Nisbet's Heraldry (1742), ii., Appx. 245-251. Fraser's Laurencekirk, 2-27, 68. Burke's Landed Gentry (1862-1925). Notes and Queries, 9th S., vii. 309, 412.

of the Mearns. Memorials of Angus and Mearns, by Jervise, ed. Gammack, ii. 144-146.

of Piercelon, Pearston, Peirston. Pont's Cuninghame, ed. Dobie, 347-350. Ayrshire Families, i. 74-77. Paterson's Ayr, i. 447-449. Paterson's Ayr and Wigton, iii. 198-201. Burke's Peerage and Baronetage. The Barclays of New York, 398. Complete Baronetage, by G. E. C., iv. 270.

in Sweden. One Year in Sweden, by H. Marryat (1862), ii. 486. Palace of History Catalogue (Glasgow, 1911), 205.

of Tollie. The Barclays of Tollie and their Descendants (Pedigree Chart), (Edinr. 1878). Scottish N. and Q., 3rd S., ii. 191.

of Urie. Genealogical Account of the Barclays of Urie, for upwards of 700 years, by R. Barclay (Aberdeen, 1740 ; 2nd ed., London, 1812).* Nisbet's Heraldry, ii., Appx. 245-251. Court Book of the Barony of Urie, 1604-1747, ed. Rev. D. G. Barron ; (Scot. Hist. Soc., 1892). Burke's Landed Gentry (1862-1925). The Barclays of Ury and other Sketches of the Early Friends . . . by Frances Anne Budge (London, 1881). The Barclays of New York, 66, 222-224, 398.

in U.S.A. The Barclays of New York, and other Barclays, by H. Burnham Moffat (New York, 1904).

of Warrix. Pont's Cuninghame, ed. Dobie, 352. Paterson's Ayr, i. 450. Paterson's Ayr and Wigton, iii. 204.

**Barclay-Allardice.** Burke's Landed Gentry (1848-1894). Historical MSS. Commission (1876), 5th Report. Geneal. Mag. (1904), vii. 294-296. The Scots Peerage, i. 144-145. The Barclays of New York, 224-226.

**Barclay-Steuart** of Collernie. The Stewarts (Stewart Soc. Mag.), iv. 72.

**Barde** of Kilchenzie. Paterson's Ayr, ii. 356. Paterson's Ayr and Wigton, i. 436-437.

**Bargany**, Hamilton, Lord. The Scots Peerage, ii. 27-33.

**Barns** of Kirkhill. Strathblane, by Guthrie Smith, 51.

**Barns-Graham** of Lymekilns. Burke's Landed Gentry (1894-1925).

**Baron** of Preston. Some Old Families, by H. B. M'Call, with Pedigree,53, 117.*
    of Spittlefield. Stephen's Inverkeithing and Rosyth (1921), 311.

**Barr**, Glasgow. Complete Baronetage, by G. E. C., ii. 360.
    of Trearne. Robertson's Ayrshire Families, i. 155, 157. Paterson's Ayr,
        i. 293. Paterson's Ayr and Wigton, iii. 123.
    U.S.A. Memoirs of Mrs Mary Barr with genealogical information relative
        to the Barr family of Scotch origin (Cincinnati, 1863).

**Barret**, Lord Barret of Newburgh. The Scots Peerage, ii. 34-35. G. E. C.'s
    Complete Peerage, 1910.

**Barrie, Barry**. Rulewater, by Tancred, 172-174.

**Barry** of Keiss Castle. Debrett's Baronetage (after 1899).

**Barton** of Ballaird and Kirkhill. Paterson's Ayr, i. 308. Paterson's Ayr
    and Wigton, ii. 141.
    of Over Barnton. Cramond, by J. P. Wood, 52.
    of Bavelaw. The Monros of Auchenbowie, by J. A. Inglis, 174-175.

**Baxter** of Kincaldrum. Angus or Forfarshire, by Warden, iii. 413. Burke's
    Landed Gentry (1886-1925).
    of Lochfeithie. Memorials of Angus and the Mearns, by Jervise, ed.
        Gammack, ii. 64-66.

**Bayne** of Rires. East Neuk of Fife, by W. Wood, 2nd ed., 117-118.
    of Tulloch. Antiquarian Notes, by C. Fraser-Mackintosh, i. 133-136.
        Scottish N. and Q., 3rd S., vii. 18. The Genealogist, N. S., xxxi. 284.

**Bean**, Deskford. Scottish N. and Q., xii. 63.

**Beaton, Beton, Bethune**. Angus or Forfarshire, by Warden, iv. 395.
    Pedigree of the Family of Bethune, by Mrs G. E. Forbes (1881).
    Scottish Antiquary, vi. 45, 112 ; viii. 141 ; ix. 190.
    of Balfour. Histoire Généalogique de la Maison de Béthune, par André
        du Chesne (1639), 382. Nisbet's Heraldry (1742), ii. Ragman
        Roll, 14. Geneal. Coll. by W. Macfarlane, 1750-51 ; Scot. Hist.
        Soc., i. 3-25. W. Wood's East Neuk of Fife, 2nd ed., 368-378.
    of Bandon. East Neuk of Fife, 378-379. J. R. Lyell *in* Scottish
        Antiquary, viii. 188-189.
    of Craigfoodie. Herald and Genealogist, vii. 286, 384. Scottish
        Antiquary, viii. 187-191.
    of Creich and Nether Rires. Geneal. Coll. by W. Macfarlane, i. 25-35.
        East Neuk of Fife, 123-127.
    of Ethiebeaton. Memorials of Angus and the Mearns, by A. Jervise,
        ed. Gammack, ii. 49-53. Monifieth, by Malcolm (1910), 302.
    of Islay. Genealogy of the Macbeths or Beatons of Islay and Mull,
        by Donald Mackinnon *in* Journal of Caledonian Medical Society
        (Glasgow, 1902), 141-153.
    of Kilconquhar. Historical MSS. Commission (1876), 5th Report, pt. 1.
        East Neuk of Fife, 167-169.

**Beaton** of Melgund. Scottish Antiquary, vii. 42, 92, 142. Eminent Arbroathians, by M'Bain, 34-43.

in Skye. An Historical and Genealogical Account of the Bethunes of the Island of Sky [by Rev. Thos. Whyte, Liberton], (1778). Reprinted (London, 1893) by A. A. Bethune-Baker. Wm. Mackenzie *in* Glasgow Herald (14th May 1898).

of Tarvit. East Neuk of Fife, 167.

of Little Tarvit. The Scottish Antiquary, vii. 92.

**Beatson.** Chronological Account of the Beatson Family, Edinburgh, n.d.* Genealogical History of the Beatson Family, by Alex. John Beatson of Rossend (Edinr. 1854 ; 2nd ed. 1860).* Review *in* Herald and Genealogist, ii. 231-236. Story of the Surname of Beatson, by Surgeon-Gen. W. B. Beatson, with genealogies, portraits, and arms.* Reprinted from The Geneal. Mag. (1900), iii.

of Kilrie and Rossend. Burke's Landed Gentry (1858-1863).

of Vicarsgrange. Eminent Men of Fife, by M. F. Conolly, 39.

**Beattie** of Haulkerton. Fraser's Laurencekirk, 169-176, 285.

**Belfrage** in Sweden. One Year in Sweden, by H. Marryat, ii. 486. Palace of History Catalogue (Glasgow, 1911), 202, 210. Scottish Hist. Review, xxv. 85.

**Belhaven**, Douglas, Viscount of. The Scots Peerage, ii. 36-37.

**Belhaven and Stenton**, Hamilton, Lord. The Scots Peerage, ii. 38-60. G. E. C.'s Complete Peerage, 2nd ed. Burke's and other Yearly Peerages. Case of William Hamilton of Wishaw, claiming to be Lord Belhaven and Stenton, 10 pp. (1795). Supplementary Case (1795). Claim of William Hamilton to the Barony of Belhaven and Stenton: (Session Papers, Jan. 1795 to April 1799). State of Evidence produced for proving the Claim of William Hamilton, of Wishaw to be lawful Heir Male of James, last Lord Belhaven (1796). Petition of James Hamilton that he may be allowed to prove he is the lawful heir of James Hamilton, etc., 3 pp. folio (1874). Claim of James Hamilton and R. W. Hamilton to Dignity of Lord Belhaven: (Session Papers, C of 1874, B of 1875). Case for Lt.-Col. R. W. Hamilton. Evidence and Proceedings (1875). The Genealogist, N. S., xx. 77.

**Bell** of Antermony. The Clachan of Campsie, by W. B. Y. D. (Edinr. 1892), 18-20. Notes and Queries, 10th S., ii. 487 ; iii. 12.

of Arkland. Lands . . . in Galloway, by M'Kerlie, iii. 59-60.

of Blacket House. Alexander Cowan, by C. B. Boog Watson, 11.*

Glasgow. Debrett's Baronetage (after 1895).

of Gribdae. Lands . . . in Galloway, iv. 210.

of Hunthill. Annals of a Border Club, by G. Tancred, 71-72.

of Kilduncan. East Neuk of Fife, by W. Wood, 2nd ed., 467.

of Kirkconnel. Bell of Kirkconnel, Blackethouse, etc., by C. D. Bell (Capetown, 1864), pamphlet.

Stirling. The Stirling Antiquary (1904), iii. 202-208.

of Whyteside. Lands . . . in Galloway, iii. 60.

**Bell-Irving** of Whitehill. Burke's Landed Gentry (1914-1925).

**Bellenden** of Auchinoul. Ayrshire Families, by G. Robertson, i. 379-381.
of Auchnolnyshill. East Neuk of Fife, by W. Wood, 2nd ed., 163.
of Broughton, Bellenden, Lord. The Scots Peerage, ii. 61-76. Complete
Peerage, by G. E. C., ed. Gibbs.
Eddleston. Peeblesshire Localities, by Renwick, 50.
of Kilconquhar. East Neuk of Fife, 163-165.

**Bellenden-Ker**, Duke of Roxburghe. The Scots Peerage, vii. 352-354.

**Belsches** of Belsches. Crawfurd's Shire of Renfrew, ed. Robertson, 493.
Baronage of Angus and Mearns, by D. M. Peter (1856), 106-107.

**Belshes-Wishart**. Complete Baronetage, by G. E. C., iv. 435.

**Bennet** of Chesters. The Scottish Antiquary, iii. 59, 112, 159; iv. 95, 188;
vi. 140, 189; Extracts from Ancrum par. reg., 1705-1744, vii. 44-45;
viii. 44; ix. 93-94, with Chart Pedigree. The Genealogist, N. S.,
vi. 192.
of Grubbet. One Year in Sweden, by H. Marryat, ii. 482. Complete
Baronetage, by G. E. C., iv. 279.
of Monsmaynes *or* Marlefield, and Kirk Yetholm. Annals of a Border
Club, by G. Tancred, 251-253.
in Sweden. Scottish Antiquary, iii. 59-60, 159; vi. 189.

**Bennett**, Enzie. Scottish N. and Q., 2nd S., iii. 190-191; iv. 45.

**Beresford** of Macbiehill. Buchan and Paton's Peeblesshire, iii. 51.

**Berkeley** of Conveth and Mathers. Fraser's Parish of Laurencekirk, 18-20.
*See* **Barclay**.

**Bernard** of Dunsinnan and Buttergask. Burke's Landed Gentry
(1906-1925).

**Berriedale**, Sinclair, Lord. The Scots Peerage, ii. 343.

**Berry** of Tayfield. Burke's Landed Gentry (1898-1914).

**Bertram** of Duckpool. Peeblesshire Localities, by Renwick, 234 *n.*
Annals of a Tweeddale Parish, by Rev. A. Baird, 76-77. Buchan's
History of Peeblesshire, iii. 296-297.
of Nisbet and Kersewell. Burke's Landed Gentry (1886-1925).

**Bethune**. Histoire Généalogique de la Maison de Béthune, par André du
Chesne, folio (Paris, 1639). Records, Genealogical Charts and
Traditions of the Families of Bethune and Faneuil, by J. A. Weisse
(New York, 1866). History of the Bethune Family, translated from
the French of André du Chesne . . . by John A. Weisse (New
York, 1884). Pedigree of the Family of Bethune, compiled by
Mrs G. E. Forbes (1881).
of Balfour. Histoire Généalogique de la Maison de Béthune (1639), 382.
Heraldry, by Nisbet (1742), ii. Ragman Roll, 14. Geneal. Coll. by
W. Macfarlane, 1750-51; Scot. Hist. Soc., i. 3-25. Burke's Landed
Gentry (1848-1914). One Year in Sweden, by H. Marryat (1862),
ii. 486. Notes and Queries, 3rd S., v. 112, 200, 402; xi. 58. East
Neuk of Fife, by W. Wood, 2nd ed. (1887), 368-378. Kennoway,
by A. S. Cunningham (Leven, 1906), 48-50. Scottish Antiquary,
v. 72.

**Bethune** of Blebo. Landed Gentry (1875-1914).

in Sweden. One Year in Sweden, by H. Marryat, ii. 486.

**Bethune, Beton.** *See also* **Beaton.**

**Bett.** Scottish N. and Q., xi. 134, 156.

**Beveridge.** Notes and Queries, 2nd S., xii. 416, 481. An Account of the Family of Beveridge in Dunfermline, by Rev. A. W. C. Hallen [1890].* The Story of the Beveridge Families of England and Scotland, by S. A. Beveridge (Melbourne, 1923).

**Beveridge-Duncan** of Damflat. Burke's Landed Gentry (1863).

**Biber-Erskine** of Dryburgh. Burke's Landed Gentry (1894 Suppl.-1925).

**Bickerton** of Luffness. East Neuk of Fife, by W. Wood, 2nd ed., 180.

**Biggar.** Genealogical Sketch of the Biggar Family, by W. H. Biggar (Edinr. 1862). The Family of Biggar, Stewartry of Kirkcudbright, 1614-1912, by G. W. Shirley (Dumfries).*

**Biggart** of Bridgend and Baidlawhill. Pont's Cuninghame, ed. Dobie (1876), 78-79.

**Binning, Binnie.** Burke's Landed Gentry (Suppl. 1849), 168.

**Binning** of Carlowriehaugh, Wallyford and Pilmuir. The Monros of Auchenbowie, by J. A. Inglis, 132-157.

of Machriemore. Paterson's Ayr and Wigton, i. 440.

St Monans. Geneal. Coll. by W. Macfarlane, 1750-51 ; Scot. Hist. Soc., ii. 195, 203.

of Wallyford. Article, by J. A. Inglis, *repr. from* Misc. Gen. et Heraldica, 7 pp. (1915).

**Binning,** Hamilton, Lord. The Scots Peerage, iv. 310-329.

**Binning-Home** of Argaty and Softlaw. Burke's Landed Gentry (Suppl. 1849-1879).

**Dirney** of Redcastle. Burke's Landed Gentry (1906-1925).

**Birnie** of Birnie and Broomhill. Heraldry, by Nisbet (1742), ii., Appx. 68. Account of the Family of Birnie and Hamilton of Broomhill, by John Birnie, ed. W. B. D. D. Turnbull, 4to. (Edinr. 1838).* Nisbet's Heraldic Plates, ed. Ross and Grant (1892), 24. Family Notes, by J. M. Browne, 15.

**Bishop,** Edinburgh. The Herald and Genealogist, viii. 7-12.

**Bisset.** Charters of the Priories of Beauly, Pluscarden, etc., with Notices of . . . the Family of the Founder, by E. C. Batten (Grampian Club, London, 1877). Chalmers' Caledonia. History of the Frasers, by Anderson (1825). Recreations of an Antiquary, by Fittis (1881), 233. Antiquarian Notes, by C. Fraser-Mackintosh, i. 383-385. Scottish N. and Q., 1st S., vi. 93 ; 2nd S., v. 141, 160 ; 3rd S., v. 40, 59.

**Bisset,** Balbrogy. Four Perthshire Families, by Rogers, 22.

of Glenelbert. The Scottish Antiquary, vii. 88, 139, 191.

Inchdreuer. The Aberdeenshire Lawrances, by R. Murdoch (1925), 259.

Bisset of Lessindrum. Temple's Thanage of Fermartyn, 241-256. Book of Exmoor, by F. J. Snell (1903), 319-325. Burke's Landed Gentry (1894-1925).

of Lovat. Geneal. Coll. by W. Macfarlane, 1750-51; Scot. Hist. Soc., ii. 85-88.

Montrose. Scottish N. and Q., 2nd S., viii. 141.

**Black,** Aberdeen. Memoir of J. Young, Aberdeen . . . 1861, ed. Lt.-Col. W. Johnston (1894), 21-23, 148.*

of Over Abington. A Note on the Family of Black of Over Abington, 1694-1908, by W. G. Black (Glasgow), portraits.*

of Ardmay. Burke's Landed Gentry (1921-1925).

of Auchentoshan. Burke's Landed Gentry (1906-1925).

of Kailzie. Burke's Landed Gentry (1906-1925).

of Watridgemuir. Temple's Thanage of Fermartyn, 540-542.

**Blackader** of Tulliallan. Genealogical Tree of the Blackaders of Tulialan, by George Begbie, Folio Sheet. Complete Baronetage, by G. E. C., ii. 315. Burke's Extinct Baronetage. Memoirs of Rev. John Blackader, by Andrew Crichton, 1. Life of Col. Blackader, by A. Crichton.

**Blackburn.** Genealogical Memoranda relating to the Family of Blackburn, and its Alliances, by the Rev. F. J. Poynton (1874).*

of Doonholm. Paterson's Ayr and Wigton, i. 146.

of Killearn. History of Stirlingshire, by Nimmo, 3rd ed. (1880), ii. 108.

**Blackburne** of Brownside. Stephen's Inverkeithing and Rosyth (1921), 98-99.

of Templeland. Stephen's Inverkeithing, 331.

**Blackhall.** The Blackhalls of that Ilk and Barra, by Alex. Morison, M.D., New Spalding Club (Aberdeen, 1905).

**Blackie,** Glasgow. The Family of Black, by W. G. Black, 63-68.*

**Blackwood.** William Blackwood and his Sons, by Margaret Oliphant, 2 vols. (1897). The Early House of Blackwood, by J. C. Blackwood, 20 pp. (Edinr. 1900). Account of the Printing-house Family of Blackwood, see The Critic, Nos. 522-528.

**Blair** of Adamton. Baronage, by Douglas, 197-198. Ayrshire Families, by G. Robertson, ii. 73-82, 103. Paterson's Ayr, ii. 382-383. Paterson's Ayr and Wigton, i. 577-581.

of Ardblair. Baronage, by Douglas, 190-192.

of Auchindrane. History of Ayr, by Paterson, ii. 358-365. Ayr and Wigton, by Paterson, ii. 409-411.

of Balgillo. Angus or Forfarshire, by Warden, iii. 294.

of Balthayock. Baronage, by Douglas, 186-189. Die Schottische Abstammung der Lothringer de Blair, von A. J. Baetche, pamphlet (Hamburg). Burke's Landed Gentry (1848-1863).

of Blair. Baronage, by Douglas, 194-197. Ayrshire Families, i. 77-100. Paterson's History of Ayr, i. 413-417. History of the Lairds of Glenfield (Paisley, 1860). Paterson's Ayr and Wigton (1866), iii. 158-170. Burke's Landed Gentry, 1848-1925. Five Generations of the Family of Blair, by A. T. Mitchell (Exeter, 1895).

**Blair** of Blairston. Paterson's Ayr, ii. 358-365. Paterson's Ayr and Wigton, ii. 409-412. Scottish N. and Q., 2nd S., v. 108.

of Bogtoun, Lochwood. Ayrshire Families, i. 87. Scottish N. and Q., 2nd S., v. 61.

of Borgue. Lands . . . in Galloway, by M'Kerlie, iii. 181-182.

of Braidsorrow. Ayrshire Families, i. 91, 375.

of Burrowland. Paterson's Ayr, ii. 255.

of Cookston. Angus or Forfarshire, by Warden, iii. 18.

of Corbs. Scottish N. and Q., 2nd S., vi. 158.

of Dunrod. Lands . . . in Galloway, iii. 217-218.

of Dunskey. Lands . . . in Galloway, 2nd ed. (1906), i. 379-385.

of Finnick. Strathendrick, by Guthrie Smith, 211-212. Scottish N. and Q., 2nd S., v. 108.

of Giffordland. Ayrshire Families, i. 100-102 ; ii. 78-79. Paterson's Ayr, i. 429. Paterson's Ayr and Wigton, iii. 175-176.

of Glasclune. Baronage, by Douglas, 193.

of Hayly. Pont's Cuninghame, ed. Dobie, 188-189.

of Inchyra. Baronage, by Douglas, 442-443.

of Kinfauns. Geneal. Coll. by W. Macfarlane, 1750-51 ; Scot. Hist. Soc., ii. 179. Case at the instance of Anna Carnegy and her Husband, against Margaret and Anna Blairs, daughters to Alex. Blair, of Kinfauns, deceased, 120 pp. Information for M. and A. Blairs, Lawful Children of deceast Alex. Blair of Kinfauns, against Mrs Lyon and her Husband and Declarator of Bastardy against the Children (1725). Complete Baronetage, by G. E. C., iv. 257.

of Ladykirk. Paterson's Ayr, ii. 384. Paterson's Ayr and Wigton, i. 582.

of Penninghame. Burke's Landed Gentry (1863-1898).

Perth. MS. Pedigree in possession of Lord Kinross. ━━━━

of Pittendreich. Douglas's Baronage, 192-193.

of Rusco. Lands . . . in Galloway, iii. 39.

**Blair,** Murray, Marquis of. The Jacobite Peerage, by the Marquis of Ruvigny (1904), 16.

**Blair-Hyndman** of Burrowland and Springside. Ayrshire Families, ii. 344-347.

**Blair-Imrie** of Lunan. Baronage of Angus and Mearns, by D. M. Peter (1856), 168. Angus or Forfarshire, by Warden, iv. 252. Burke's Landed Gentry (1875-1925).

**Blantyre,** Stewart, Lord. Crawfurd's Shire of Renfrew, ed. Robertson (1818), 51-53, 467-468. The Scots Peerage, ii. 77-93. G. E. C.'s Complete Peerage, 2nd ed. Burke's Peerage (before 1906). Scot. Hist. Review, xv. 201.

**Blaw** of Castlehill. The Scottish Antiquary, viii. 64-66 ; xii. 169-170, short chart pedigree ; xiii. 40. John Blaw of Castlehill, Jacobite and Criminal, by C. N. Johnston (Lord Sands), x+154 pp., illust. and two chart pedigrees (Edinr. 1916).

**Bluntach.** Scottish N. and Q., 3rd S., v. 238.

**Blyth** of Craigie. Angus or Forfarshire, by Warden, iv. 133.

**Blythswood,** Campbell, Lord. Debrett's Peerage (after 1892).

**Boddie, Bodie.** Scottish N. and Q., 2nd S., vii. 156 ; viii. 94.

**Bogie** of Kinnestoun. Some Old Families, by H. B. M'Call, 161-162, and Pedigree.*

**Bogle** of Hutchiston. Airth Peerage Evidence, 116.
of Bogle's Hole. Oliver's History of Antigua, i. 272.

**Bonar** of Bonare. Burke's Landed Gentry (Suppl. 1849). [Not to be consulted without reference to] Popular Genealogists . . . [by G. Burnett], (Edinr. 1865), 55-82. Gideon Guthrie, ed. C. E. Guthrie Wright, 158. Notes and Queries, 3rd S., ix. 50, 379.

**Bontein** of Balglas. Strathendrick, by Guthrie Smith, 245-247.

**Bontine-Cunninghame-Grahame** of Ardoch. Irving's Book of Dumbartonshire, ii. 312. Burke's Landed Gentry (1894-1925).

**Boog, Boag,** Burntisland. Traditions of the Watson Family, by C. B. Boog Watson (Perth, 1908).
of Peel. Tancred's Rulewater, 72.
in Sweden. One Year in Sweden, by H. Marryat, ii. 486.

**Borthwick,** Borthwick, Lord. Nisbet's Heraldry, ii., Appx. 111-114, Claim of Henry Borthwick to the title of Lord Borthwick : (Session Papers, Jan. to April, 1762 ; reprinted 1868). Claim of John Borthwick to the Same : (Session Papers, Feb. 1774 to Nov. 1776, reprinted 1868). Additional Case of John Borthwick (1809). Claim of Archibald Borthwick to the Same : (Session Papers, 83 of 1812 ; 26 of 1812-13 ; 77 of 1813-14 ; 49 of 1814-15). Claim of Cunninghame Borthwick to the Same : (Session Papers, C of 1868-9 ; B of 1870). Petition praying that the Roll of Peers of Scotland may be Amended. Case of C. Lord Borthwick on his claim to precedency, 1871. Burke's Peerage (before 1906). G. E. C.'s Complete Peerage, 2nd ed. The Scots Peerage, ii. 94-119. Notes and Queries, 4th S., iv. 192, 280, 535, 564 ; v. 343 ; xi. 521.

**Borthwick** of Balhouffie. Geneal. Coll. by W. Macfarlane, 1750-51 ; Scots Hist. Soc., ii. 202. East Neuk of Fife, by Wood, 2nd ed., 337.
of Crookston. Case of John Borthwick of Crookston claiming the title of Lord Borthwick (1762, 1868). Burke's Landed Gentry (1848-1925).
of Leny. Cramond, by J. P. Wood, 69.
of Lingo. East Neuk of Fife, 287-288.
of Lochhill and Balcarres. East Neuk of Fife, 129.

**Boston.** A General Account of my Life, by the Rev. Thos. Boston, minister of Simprin, 1699-1707, and at Ettrick, 1707-1732 ; ed. Rev. G. D. Low (Edinr. 1908). Appendix with Account of the Boston Family.

**Boswell.** Brief Notices of the Families of Arnot, Reid, Boswell (1872).*

of Auchinleck. Douglas's Baronage, 458-460. Paterson's History of Ayr, i. 237-241. Paterson's Ayr and Wigton, i. 190-197. Poetical Works of Sir Alexander Boswell, with Memoir, by R. H. Smith (Glasgow, 1871), *xxi-lxviii*. Burke's Peerage and Baronetage (before 1857). The Stewarts Magazine, v. 113, and Chart Pedigree.

of Balmuto. Douglas's Baronage, 307-312. Auchterderran, a Parish History, by Rev. A. M'Neill Houston (Paisley, 1924), 140-144. Burke's Landed Gentry (1863-1925).

of Duncanziemuir and Craigston. Paterson's Ayr, i. 241. Paterson's Ayr and Wigton, i. 197-198.

of Garrallan. Landed Gentry (1886).

of Knockroon. Paterson's Ayr, i. 241. Ayr and Wigton, i. 198.

of Oxmuir. Douglas's Baronage, 307.

*See* The Scots Peerage, ed. Sir J. Balfour Paul, *for*

**Bothwell,** Douglas, Lord, i. 206.

Hepburn, Earl of, ii. 135-167.

Moray, Lord of, ii. 120-131.

Ramsay, Lord, ii. 132-134.

Stewart, Earl of, ii. 168-173.

**Bothwell.** Nisbet's Heraldry (1722), i. 401. Notices of James Hepburn, Earl of Bothwell, *in* A Lost Chapter in the History of Queen Mary. Notes and Queries, 3rd S., i. 323 ; x. 445.

Lord Holyroodhouse. Nisbet's Heraldry, ii., Appx. 242-245. The Scots Peerage, iv. 425-429.

**Bourdon** of Feddal. *See* **Burden.**

**Bower** of Kincaldrum. Angus or Forfarshire, by A. J. Warden, iii. 410-413. Scottish N. and Q., 2nd S., vii. 122, 140 ; 3rd S., iii. 66.

of Kinnettles. Angus or Forfarshire, iv. 64.

**Bowes-Lyon,** Earl of Strathmore and Kinghorne. The Scots Peerage, viii. 310-317.

**Bowman** of Ashinyards, *or* Ashgrove. Ayrshire Families, by G. Robertson, i. 265-266. Paterson's History of Ayr, ii. 249. Paterson's Ayr and Wigton, iii. 487.

**Boy,** in Sweden. One Year in Sweden, by H. Marryat, 1862, ii. 486, 489.

**Boyd** of Badinheath. Paterson's Ayr, ii. 420.

Lord Boyd, Earl of Kilmarnock. Selection from Papers of the Family of Boyd of Kilmarnock, 1468-1590, ed. J. Maidment (Abbotsford Club, Edinr. 1837). The Scottish Antiquary (1893), vii. 158-161, with Chart Pedigree. Paterson's History of Ayr (1852), ii. 171-182, 511-515. The Scots Peerage, v. 136-182. Family Papers *in* Archæol. and Hist. Coll. of Ayr and Wigton (1882), iii. 122-211. History of the Boyd Family, and Descendants, by William P. Boyd (Conesus, New York, 1884).

of Bonshaw. Ayrshire Families, by G. Robertson, i. 187. Pont's Cuninghame, ed. Dobie (1876), 103.

**Boyd** of Carlung. Ayrshire Families, i. 124-125. Paterson's History of County of Ayr, ii. 144. Paterson's Ayr and Wigton, iii. 327.

of Cherrytrees. Annals of a Border Club, by G. Tancred, 73.

of Dykehead. Pont's Cuninghame, ed. Dobie, 313.

of Gavan and Rysk. Crawfurd's Shire of Renfrew (1818), 79-80. Inverness-shire. Scottish N. and Q., 2nd S., i. 188.

of Kipps. The Monros of Auchenbowie, by J. A. Inglis, 194-206.

of Merton Hall. Burke's Landed Gentry (1848-1886).

of Orchard. Ayrshire Families, i. 126.

of Penkill and Trochrig. Paterson's History of Ayr, i. 394-395 ; ii. 79-81. Paterson's Ayr and Wigton, ii. 234-238, 255-261. The History of Kilmarnock, by M'Kay (Kilmarnock, 1864), 37. The Boyds of Penkill and Trochrig . . . by Major Seymour Clarke, 4to, illus., 51 pp., 4 Chart Pedigrees (Edinr. 1919). The Scots Peerage, v. 151-152.

of Pitcon, Potconnell. Ayrshire Families, i. 121-124. Paterson's Ayr, i. 420-422. Paterson's Ayr and Wigton, iii. 186-189.

of Portincross. Ayrshire Families, i. 112-116. Paterson's Ayr, ii. 135-137. Paterson's Ayr and Wigton, iii. 317-319. Pont's Cuninghame, ed. Dobie (1876), 357-359.

of Temple. The Monros of Auchenbowie, 207-210.

of Townend. Paterson's Ayr and Wigton, i. 748.

**Boyd-Kinnear** of Kinnear and Kinloch. Burke's Landed Gentry (1886-1925).

**Boyle,** Earl of Glasgow. Paterson's History of Ayr, ii. 303-305. The Scots Peerage, iv. 183-221.

of Hawkhill. Ayrshire Families, by G. Robertson, i. 131.

of Kelburne. Nisbet's Heraldry, i. 337. Ayrshire Families, i. 127-135. Paterson's Ayr and Wigton, iii. 530-532. J. B. Burke's Visitation of Seats and Arms (1853), i. 164. Genealogical Account of the Boyles of Kelburne, by Col. the Honble. Robert E. Boyle, 27 pp. (Edinr. 1904).* The Scots Peerage, iv. 184-198.

of Montgomerieston. Ayrshire Families, i. 135.

of Shewalton. Burke's Landed Gentry (1848-1886). Paterson's History of Ayr, ii. 36. Paterson's Ayr and Wigton, i. 495.

**Brack-Boyd** of Faldonside. Annals of a Border Club, by G. Tancred, 74.

**Brady** of Easter Kennet. The Stirling Antiquary (1908), iv. 85, 88.

**Brand** of Redhall *or* Castlebrand. The Family of Inglis of Auchindinny and Redhall, by J. A. Inglis, 126-128.

**Brander-Dunbar** of Pitgavenny. Burke's Landed Gentry (1848-1925).

**Brandon,** Hamilton, Duke of. English Peerage, by Rev. A. Jacob (1766), i. 312-322. Case of the Most Noble Douglas, Duke of Hamilton and Brandon, touching the Peerage of Brandon (1782). The Complete Peerage, by G. E. C., 2nd ed. The Scots Peerage, iv. 384-397.

**Breadalbane,** Campbell, Baron, Viscount of, Earl of, Marquess of. Nisbet's Heraldry (1742), ii., Appx. 221-229. Genealogy of the Breadalbane Family, by Joseph M'Intyre (1752). Biographical Peerage (London,

1808), 78-81. Life of Willielma, Viscountess Glenorchy, by T. S. Jones, D.D. (1822, 2nd ed., 1824). The Black Book of Taymouth, ed. Cosmo Innes, illust., 4to (Bannatyne Club, Edinr. 1855). The Breadalbane Case, by James Paterson, 36 pp., Pedigree (Edinr. 1863). Statement of the Breadalbane Case, by Alex. Sinclair, 32 pp., Pedigree (Glasgow, 1866). Herald and Genealogist (1867), iv. 242-257. Genealogist, N. S., xi. 68-69. Case of William Campbell, claiming to be Earl of Breadalbane, 4to (1864). Claim of John Campbell to be Earl of Breadalbane: (Session Papers, C of 1867 ; A of 1867-8). Claim of Gavin Campbell to be Earl of Breadalbane : (Session Papers, B of 1872 ; F of 1877). Petition of J. A. G. Campbell of Glenfalloch (1867). Petition of Gavin Campbell and John Maccallum (1872), and corrected case of J. Maccallum (1872). Historical MSS. Commission (1873), 4th Report. Great Historic Families, by James Taylor [1887]. Lord A. Campbell's Records of Argyll, 101-109. Burke's Peerage, Debrett's Peerage, etc. The Scots Peerage, ii. 174-214. G. E. C.'s Complete Peerage, ed. Vicary Gibbs.

**Brechin.** Nisbet's Heraldry, II. iii. 79-81. J. Bain *in* Genealogist, N. S. v. 22-25. Registrum de Panmure : Records of the Families of Maule, de Valoniis, Brechin, and Brechin-Barclay, compiled by the Hon. Harry Maule of Kelly, 1733, ed. Dr John Stuart, 2 vols., 4to, illust. (Edinr. 1874).* Angus or Forfarshire, by Warden (1880), iii. 2-5.

*See* The Scots Peerage *for*

**Brechin,** Brechin, Lord of, ii. 215-224.
Stewart, Lord of, vii. 246.
and Navar, Maule, Lord, vii. 19-27.

**Brentford,** Ruthven, Earl of. G. E. C.'s Complete Peerage, 2nd ed. (1910). The Scots Peerage, iv. 104-106.

**Brewster,** Botriphnie. Angus or Forfarshire, by Warden, iii. 163.

**Briene,** Ker, Viscount of. The Scots Peerage, v. 477-487.

**Briggs** of Strathairly. East Neuk of Fife, by Wood, 2nd ed., 96. Annals of a Border Club, by G. Tancred (1899), 74. Burke's Landed Gentry (1898-1925).

**Brisbane** of Bishoptoun. Crawfurd's Shire of Renfrew, ed. Robertson, 113, 390-391. Fraser's Genealogical Table (1840).
of Brisbane. Ayrshire Families, by G. Robertson, i. 136-147. Paterson's History of Ayr, ii. 305-308. Paterson's Ayr and Wigton, iii. 525, 527. Genealogical Table of Lt.-Gen. Sir T. M. Brisbane of Brisbane and Makerstoun, Bart., Pedigree Chart, by Sir W. Fraser (Edinr. 1840). Memoirs of Sir Thomas Brisbane. Notes and Queries, 5th S., viii. 516 ; ix. 136. Scottish N. and Q., 3rd S., i. 126. Burke's Landed Gentry (1875-1925).
of Quhitslaid. Peeblesshire Localities, by Renwick, 238.

**Brodie** of Backies. Scottish N. and Q., 2nd S., viii. 66.
Banff. Scottish N. and Q., 3rd S., i. 4.

**Brodie** of Brodie. Burke's Landed Gentry (1849-1925). Notes and Queries, 2nd S., xi. 449, 518 ; 3rd S., xii. 346. Genealogy of the Brodie Family, 1249-1862, by W. Brodie (Eastbourne, 1862).* Diary of Alexander Brodie of Brodie, and of his son, James Brodie of Brodie, 1652-1685, ed. Dr David Laing (Old Spalding Club, Aberdeen, 1863). Scottish N. and Q., 2nd S., viii. 103, 107 ; 3rd S., 14. History of the Family of Brodie of Brodie, 4to (c. 1881).

Cullen. Scottish N. and Q., 2nd S., vii. 108.

in Glassaugh. Scottish N. and Q., 1898-9, xii. 61. Burke's Peerage and Baronetage, s.v. Brodie of Boxford.

Glenbucket. Scottish N. and Q., 2nd S., vi. 111.

of Idvies. Angus or Forfarshire, by Warden, iv. 77.

Latheron and Carnbee. Caithness Family History, by Henderson, 305-31.

of Lethen and Coulmony. Notes and Queries, 3rd S., iv. 209. Burke's Landed Gentry (1849-1925).

of Mayne. Annals of Elgin, by Young, 660. Scottish N. and Q., 3rd S., iii. 122.

New York. Alexander Cowan, by C. B. Boog Watson, 38-41.*

of Easter Polder and Glenboig. Strathendrick, by Guthrie Smith, 242.

Thurso. Scottish N. and Q., 3rd S., ii. 152.

**Brodie-Innes** of Milton Brodie and Windyhills. Annals of Elgin, 610-621. Burke's Landed Gentry (1875 Suppl.-1925).

**Brodie-Wood** of Keithick. Burke's Landed Gentry (1921-1925).

**Brooke** of Fairley. Burke's Landed Gentry (1906-1925).

**Broun** of Carsleuch, Carsluith. Some Ancient Scottish Families, 51-56. Lands . . . in Galloway, by M'Kerlie, iv. 245-247.

of Colstoun. MS. by John Riddell and Robert Riddell in possession of the Library of the Writers to the Signet. Notes and Queries, 3rd S., iii. 466, v. 258, 311 ; 5th S., vi. 383, 440. Landed Gentry (1886-1894). Monograph on the Notice of the Family of Broun of Colstoun in Crawford's MS. Baronage, by J. H. Brown-Morison (1881).* Genealogical Notes anent some Ancient Scottish Families, by J. H. Brown-Morison (Perth, 1884), 59-97 *et passim.** The Scottish Antiquary, i. 94 ; xiii. 139, 193. Complete Baronetage, by G. E. C., iv. 338. Burke's Peerage and Baronetage. Debrett's Baronetage. Papers of An Old Scots Family (Broun of Colstoun), by J. G. A. Baird *in* Blackwood's Magazine (July 1907). *See also* Scot. Hist. Review, vi. 140.

in France. The Scottish Antiquary, i. 94.

of Sauchie. Broun of Sauchie, Balquharne and Finderlie, 1395-1884, by J. H. Brown-Morison (1884). Genealogical Notes anent some Ancient Scottish Families, 2, 19-41.*

**Broun-Morison** of Finderlie and Murie. The Progress of Titles of Finderlie during the 16th Century, 4to, n.d. Burke's Landed Gentry (1894-1925).

**Brown.** Nisbet's Heraldry, i. 386-387. Complete Baronetage, by G. E. C., v. 10.

of Auchlochan. Annals of Lesmahagow, by Greenshields (1854), 98.*

**Brown** of Bagbie and Nuntown. Lands . . . in Galloway, by M'Kerlie,
v. 268-270.

of Balloch. Four Perthshire Families, by Rev. Dr C. Rogers (1887).*

of Capelrig. Crawfurd's Shire of Renfrew (1818), 296.

of Carlops and Newhall. Buchan and Paton's Peeblesshire, iii. 127.

of Cockairnie. Stephen's Inverkeithing (1921), 168.

of Cultermains. The Browns of Cultermains (Edinr. 1866).*

of Dolphington. Upper Ward of Lanarkshire, by Irving and Murray,
i. 368, 374.

of Finmount. Browns of Fordell, by Stodart, 49-59.

of Fod. Stephen's Inverkeithing and Rosyth, 94-95.

of Fordell. Memorials of the Browns of Fordell, Finmount and Vicarsgrange, by R. R. Stodart (Edinr. 1887), 1-44.*

in Gabrochill. Pont's Cuninghame, ed. Dobie, 99.

of Gate and Barharrow. Lands . . . in Galloway, iii. 221, 224.

of Glanderston. Temple's Thanage of Fermartyn, 19.

Glasgow. Diary, 1745-53, by George Brown, Merchant in Glasgow (1856).

of Golf Hall. The Browns of Fordell, 62-66.

of Greenknowe. The Browns of Fordell, 66-70.

Greystone. Smith's Genealogies of an Aberdeen Family ; Aberdeen
Univ. Studies, 111-112.

of Hartree, Logan, and Mossfennan. Peeblesshire Localities, by Renwick,
244, 266. Annals of a Tweeddale Parish, by Baird, 68, 109-118.
Buchan and Paton's History of Peeblesshire, iii. 311-316.

Kirkwall. Diary of Thomas Brown, Writer in Kirkwall, 1675-1693,
ed. A. F. Steuart, *viii*+72 pp. (Kirkwall, 1898), [largely taken up
with recording the births, marriages, and deaths of local persons.]

of Knockmarloch and Kilmarnock. Paterson's History of Ayr, ii. 412.
Paterson's Ayr and Wigton, i. 653. MS. Pedigree, No. 928.
Society of Genealogists, London.

of Landis. Lands . . . in Galloway, v. 15-17.

of Lanfine. Paterson's Ayr and Wigton, i. 530. Selections from Family
Papers *in* Archæol. and Hist. Coll. of Ayr and Wigton (1880), ii.
185-195.

of Langlands. Lands . . . in Galloway, v. 275-277.

of Langside. Crawfurd's Shire of Renfrew (1818), 271.

of Lochton. Burke's Landed Gentry (1906-1925).

of Mollance. Lands . . . in Galloway, iii. 373.

of Newhall. Landed Gentry (1886-1898). Scot. Hist. Review, xvi. 188-
190. Buchan's History of Peeblesshire, iii. 127.

of Nunland. Lands . . . in Galloway, iv. 348.

of Orchard. Some Ancient Scottish Families, by J. H. Brown-Morison,
42-47.*

of Rawflat. Annals of a Border Club, by G. Tancred, 75. Rulewater,
by Tancred, 71.

St Vigeans. Eminent Arbroathians, by J. M. M'Bain, 416-417.

of Scotstoun. Buchan and Paton's History of Peeblesshire, iii. 91-92.

of Stevenston. History of Peeblesshire, iii. 79-80.

**Brown** of Tardors. Paterson's Ayr and Wigton, i. 609.
of Templeland. Stephen's Inverkeithing and Rosyth, 330.
of Waterhead. Paterson's Ayr and Wigton, i. 609, 612.

*See* The Scots Peerage, ed. Sir James Balfour Paul, *for*
**Bruce**, Earl of Ailesbury, iii. 466-483. Lord Balfour of Burleigh, i. 554-555.
Baron Bruce, ii. 435. Viscount Bruce of Ampthill, iii. 478-483.
Baron Bruce of Kinloss, Skelton, Torry, Tottenham, Whorlton,
iii. 476-483. Earl of Carrick, ii. 428-437. Baron Elgin of Elgin,
Earl of Elgin, iii. 466-497. Lord of Galloway, iv. 144. Earl of
Kincardine, iii. 484-497.

**Bruce.** Tabular Pedigrees *in* Royal Genealogies, by Anderson (1732),
759, 760. Genealogical Descent of the Royal Line of Bruce, by
Alexander Sinclair (pamphlet). Pedigree tables of the family, *in*
Drummond's Noble British Families, I. iii., 28 pp., portraits, coloured
shields, views (1846). Prospectus of The History of the Royal
Scottish House of Bruce, by Gabriel Surenne, 3 vols. (1856). La
Maison de Bruce, par M. Borel d'Hauterive (Paris, 1864). Eminent
Men of Fife, by M. F. Conolly, 83-88. A genealogical view of the
origin and descent of the Bruce Family, in the History of Scotland,
by R. Kerr, i. *xxv-xlix*. Notes and Queries, 5th S., v. 424, viii.
459, x. 67, 114 ; 7th S. viii. 366, ix. 176 ; 8th S., viii. 473, xi. 409, 457,
478, 498, xii. 14. Family Records of the Bruces and Comyns, by
M. E. Cumming Bruce ; Pedigree and illustrations (Edinr. 1870).
Lands and their Owners in Galloway, by M'Kerlie (1878), iv. 384-388.
The Brus Cenotaph at Guisborough, by Wm. Brown *in* Yorks.
Archæol. Journal (1894). Geneal. Mag. (1898), i. 54, 118, 185, 306.
Collectanea Bruceana : two very large MS. volumes compiled by
Major William Bruce Armstrong, 7th Dragoon Guards, and pre-
sented by him to the Lyon Office (1898). The Stirling Antiquary
(1904), iii. 156-158. The Skull of King Robert the Bruce, by Thos.
H. Bryce *in* Scot. Hist. Review, xxiii. 81-91. Le Chateau de Brix,
par Etienne Dupont *in* Scot. Hist. Review (1905), ii. 425-427. The
Book of Bruce : ancestors and descendants of King Robert of
Scotland, by Lyman Horace Weeks (New York, 1907). Dictionary
of National Biography, *s.v.*
of Airth. Notes on the Origin of the Baronial House of Bruce of Airth,
by Major W. B. Armstrong (London, 1887).* The Bruces of Airth
and their Cadets, by Major William Bruce Armstrong (Edinr. 1892).
The Bruces of Airth and their Barony, and the Memorial to Major
Alex. Bruce, by Thomas M'Grouther ; Stirling Nat. Hist. and
Archæological Soc. (1927).
of Annandale. The Scots Peerage, ii. 428.
of Arnot. Burke's Landed Gentry (1886).
of Auchenbowie. The Monros of Auchenbowie, by J. A. Inglis, 45-46.
of Balcaskie. Complete Baronetage, by G. E. C., iv. 269.
of Blairhall. Douglas's Baronage, 243-244. Eminent Men of Fife, 92.
The Scots Peerage, iii. 472-489. Stephen's Inverkeithing, 85.

**Bruce** of Braewick. Zetland Family Histories, by F. J. Grant, 28-29.

of Burravoe. Zetland Family Histories, 36-37.

Brudenell-Bruce, Baron. English Peerage, by Rev. A. Jacob (1767), ii. 566-568. Edmondson's Baronagium Genealogicum, vi. 15.

of Carnock. Stephen's Inverkeithing (1921), 86-88.

Earl of Carrick. Paterson's History of the County of Ayr, ii. 270-272. Some Account of the Ancient Earldom of Carrick, by Andrew Carrick (Edinr. 1857).

of Clackmannan. Douglas's Baronage, 238-239. Burke's Commoners, iv. 618. The Scots Peerage, iii. 466-472.

of Craigie Wallace. Angus or Forfarshire, by Warden, iv. 143.

of Cultmalindie. Zetland Family Histories, 10-13. Major W. B. Armstrong *in* the Genealogist, 1st S., vi. 162-165.

of Earlshall. Douglas's Baronage, 510-513. R. R. Stodart *in* Genealogist, 1st S., vii. 131-142.

of Fingask. Recreations of an Antiquary, by Fittis, 386.

of Grangehill. Eminent Men of Fife, 91.

of Ham. Caithness Family History, by Henderson, 267-269.

of Hastigrow and Seater. Caithness Family History, 273.

of Inverquhomery and Longside. Burke's Landed Gentry (1898-1925).

of Kennet. Douglas's Baronage, 241-243. The Descent of the Lairds of Kennet and the Barony of Burleigh (1860).* Eminent Men of Fife, by Conolly, 88-90. Burke's Commoners, ii. 485. Burke's Landed Gentry (1848-1875). Burke's Peerage (after 1869). The Scots Peerage, i. 547-554.

Baron Bruce of Kinloss. Pedigree of the Bruces, Barons Bruce of Kinloss, showing the heirs of line and the collateral heirs male, sheet [1865]. Scottish Peerages, their limitations, particularly with reference to the Barony of Bruce of Kinloss, by J. E. B. Bruce, 8vo (London, 1867). Petition of Victor Alexander, Earl of Elgin and Kincardine, Baron Bruce of Kinloss, etc., in opposition to the Duke of Buckingham and Chandos (1868). Case of Geo. W. F. Brudenell, Marquis of Ailesbury, on his Claim to the Title of Lord Kinloss, with large folding Pedigree. Supplemental Case of Richard P., Duke of Buckingham and Chandos, with Pedigrees of Bruce, Colville, and Butler (18—). G. E. C.'s Complete Peerage, 2nd ed. The Scots Peerage, iii. 476-483.

of Kinnaird. History of Stirlingshire, by William Nimmo, 2 vols., 3rd ed. (1880): i. 323-325, 341 ; ii. 50-63. Burke's Landed Gentry (1848-1875).

of Kinross and Balcaskie. Baronage, by Douglas (1784), 245-246. East Neuk of Fife, by W. Wood, 2nd ed., 274-275. Burke's Extinct Baronetage.

of Langlee. Annals of a Border Club, by George Tancred of Weens (Jedburgh, 1899), 75-79.

of Lyth. Caithness Family History, 270-272.

of Muness. Zetland Family Histories, 13-16. Major W. B. Armstrong *in* Genealogist, 1st S., vi. 165-167.

**Bruce** of Newtown. An Account of the Bruces of Newtown (pamphlet). W. B. Armstrong *in* The Genealogist, 1st S., iii. 19-26, 38-46.

of Pittarthie. The Genealogist, 1st S., vii. 224.

of Powfoulis. Genealogical Notes anent some Ancient Scottish Families, by J. H. Brown-Morison (Perth, 1884), 143-145.*

of Riddoch. The Monros of Auchenbowie, by J. A. Inglis, 49.

of Stanstill. Caithness Family History, 262-266.

of Stenhouse. Baronage, by Douglas, 240-241. Geneal. Mag. (1903), vi. 372. Complete Baronetage, by G. E. C., ii. 358. Burke's Peerage and Baronetage. Debrett's Baronetage.

of Sumburgh. Major W. B. Armstrong *in* Genealogist, 1st S., vi. 205-211. Zetland Family Histories, 20-27.

in Sweden. One Year in Sweden, by H. Marryat, ii. 486.

of Symbister. Churchyard Monuments of Crail, by Erskine Beveridge, 172-181. Zetland Family Histories, 30-35.

of Urie. Zetland Family Histories, 17-19.

**Bruce-Gardyne** of Middleton. Angus or Forfarshire, by A. J. Warden, iv. 80-81.

**Bruce-Hope** of Craighall. Complete Baronetage, by G. E. C., ii. 343.

**Brudenell-Bruce,** Baron Bruce. English Peerage, by Jacob, ii. 566-568. Edmondson's Baronagium Genealogicum, vi. 15.

**Bruntchels** of Bruntchels. Crawfurd's Shire of Renfrew (1818), 96.

**Bryce** of Blawlowan *or* Pathfoot of Airthrey. Logie, by Rev. Dr Menzies Fergusson, ii. 238-245.

**Buccleuch,** Scott, Earl of, Duke of. Biographical Peerage (1808), 88-90, 108. The Scotts of Buccleuch, by Sir Wm. Fraser, 2 vols. Historical MSS. Commission (1897), 15th Report ; 1899, 1903, vols. i. ii. The Scots Peerage, ii. 225-249. G. E. C.'s Complete Peerage, 2nd ed. Burke's and other Annual Peerages.

**Buchan,** The Ancient Earls of. Scottish N. and Q., 1st S., iii. 90-91 ; ix. 181-183 ; x. 28 ; xii. 156. Historic Earls and Earldoms of Scotland, by Dr John Mackintosh (Aberdeen, 1898). The Scots Peerage, ii. 250-252.

Beaumont, Earl of. Genealogist, N. S., iv. 196. The Scots Peerage, i. 432 ; ii. 259 ; vi. 295 ; viii. 253, 566.

Comyn, Earl of. Joseph Bain *in* Genealogist, N. S., iv. 194-196. The Scots Peerage, ii. 252-261.

Douglas, Earl of. The Scots Peerage, ii. 269-272.

Erskine, Earl of. Annals and Antiquities of Dryburgh, by Sir David Erskine, 2nd ed. (Kelso, 1836), 89, 128-140, 158-164. Eminent Men of Fife, by M. F. Conolly, 170-176. Mackintosh's Historic Earldoms. Burke's and other Annual Peerages. The Scots Peerage, ii. 271-284. G. E. C.'s Complete Peerage, 2nd ed. (1910).

Stewart, Earl of. The Scots Peerage, ii. 262-270.

Van Borssele, Earl of. G. W. Watson *in* Genealogist, N. S., xiv. 10-11. The Scots Peerage, i. 19 ; ii. 265 *n*.

**Buchan.** Case of Sir Colin Mackenzie, Bart., on his Claim to the Title of Earl of Buchan, with Appx. (1832). Sir Colin Mackenzie's Claim to the Title and Dignity of Earl of Buchan and Lord Auchterhouse (c. 1840).

**Buchan** of Auchmacoy. Buchan, by Rev. J. B. Pratt (1858), 415. Historical MSS. Commission (1873), 4th Report, i. 528. The Thanage of Fermartyn, by Temple, 525-537. Scottish N. and Q., 2nd S., i. 88-90 ; 3rd S., v. 74.

of Whitsome. The Scottish Antiquary, iii. 49-50.

**Buchan-Hepburn** of Smeaton. Burke's Peerage and Baronetage.

**Buchan-Sydserf** of Ruchlaw. Burke's Landed Gentry (1898-1925).

**Buchanan.** Pedigrees *in* Notes and Queries, 2nd S., vi. 206, 254 ; viii. 148, 219, 277 : 7th S., viii. 387, 475. Scottish N. and Q., x. 9-12, 42-44. Herald and Genealogist, v. 518-525. The Buchanan Book : The Life of Alexander Buchanan, Q.C., of Montreal, followed by an Account of the Family of Buchanan, by A. W. Patrick Buchanan, portraits, *xiii*+475 pp. (Montreal, 1911).*

*See* Historical and Genealogical Essay upon the Family and Surname of Buchanan, by William Buchanan of Auchmar (Glasgow, 1723 ; Edinburgh, 1775 ; Glasgow, 1793, 1820, 1828), *for*

**Buchanan** in Ardmill, 115, 118 ; of Auchneiven, 108-112 ; of Easter Ballat, 89-90 ; of Wester Ballat, 75 ; of Boturich, 72 ; of Cairnock, 93 ; in Calder, 92, 118 ; in Callander, 105 ; in Campsie, 105 ; of Cashill, 115 ; of Duchless, 90 ; in Drymen, 74 ; of Finnick Tenent, 76 ; of Gartfarrand, 90 ; in Sallochie, 118 ; in Strathallan, 104 ; in Strathyre, 104 ; of Stuckrodger, 74 ; of Torry, 104 ; in Virginia, 92.

*See* Strathendrick, by J. Guthrie Smith (1896), *for*

**Buchanan** of Auchineden, 296-298 ; of Auchlessie, 302 ; of Balfunning and Croy Cunninghame, 340-341 ; of Blairhennachra, 327-330 ; of Blairlusk, 350-353 ; of Bochastel, 299 ; of Bultoune, 255 ; of Camoquhill and Templelands of Letter, 223-224 ; in Campsie and Baldernock, 306-308 ; of Carstoun, 338-339 ; of Cashlie, 366-367 ; of Croy Buchanan, 341-343 ; of Dowanhill, 344-345 ; in Finnick Drummond, 343-344 ; of Gartinstarrie, 366-367 ; of Glenny, 303 ; of Hiltoun, 332-333 ; of Ibert and Ballochruin, 324-326 ; of Ledlewan, 255 ; of Moss and Auchintoshan, 336-338 ; of Shandon, 299 ; of Tulliechewan, 330-332 ; in U.S.A., 333-336, 352 ; of Waldens, 305.

**Buchanan** of Arden. Book of Dumbartonshire, by Joseph Irving, ii. 214. Geneal. Mag., iv. 529.

of Ardoch. The Family Book of the Buchanans of Ardoch, commonly called the Ardoch Register, ed. by John Parkes-Buchanan (1894).* Strathendrick, by Guthrie Smith, 354-357. Burke's Landed Gentry (1848-1879).

of Auchintorlie, Ardenconnal, and Craigend. Burke's Commoners, iii. 654. Burke's Landed Gentry (1848-1925). Old Country Houses, by J. G. Smith. Book of Dumbartonshire, by Irving, ii. 291, 292, 370 ; iii. portrait. Strathendrick, 332-333.

**Buchanan** of Arnprior. Family and Surname of Buchanan, 56-63, 154. Strathendrick, 300-303.

of Auchengillan. Strathblane, by Guthrie Smith, 40.

of Auchmar. Family and Surname of Buchanan, 41-48. Strathendrick, 373-376.

of Ballewan. Strathblane, 158-159.

of Boquhan. Family and Surname of Buchanan, 92. Strathendrick, 357-363.

of Buchanan. Family and Surname of Buchanan, 19-36, 143-152. Strathendrick, 284-289. Geneal. Mag. (1899), ii. 497 ; (1901), iv. 440.

of Cameron. Family and Surname of Buchanan, 76. Strathendrick, 322-324.

of Carbeth. Family and Surname of Buchanan, 84. Strathendrick, 223, 224, 346-349. Strathblane, 90-93.

of Carrick. Lands . . . in Galloway, by M'Kerlie (1906), i. 409.

of Cashlie. The Stirling Antiquary, ii. 73-74.

of Catrine Bank. History of Ayr, by Paterson, ii. 426. Ayr and Wigton, by Paterson, i. 692.

of Catter. Geneal. Mag. (1899), ii. 311-316, 356-361, 500 ; iii. 217.

of Craigend. Strathblane, 58-60.

of Craigievairn. Family and Surname of Buchanan, 78. Strathendrick, 317-319.

of Cuninghamehead. History of Ayr, by Paterson, i. 452. Ayr and Wigton, by Paterson, iii. 210.

of Drumhead. Family and Surname of Buchanan, 73-74. Strathendrick, 327-330. Irving's Book of Dumbartonshire, ii. 308-309.

of Drummikill and Moss. Family and Surname of Buchanan, 64-78, 153. Strathendrick, 309-317, 319-322. The Stirling Antiquary, ii. 73.

of Drumpellier. Burke's Landed Gentry (1862-1914). Strathendrick, 305. Lands . . . in Galloway, by M'Kerlie, 2nd ed. (1906), i. 408.

of Dunburgh. Burke's Peerage and Baronetage (after 1878).

of Gartacharn. Family and Surname of Buchanan, 103-104. Strathendrick, 303-305.

of Gartincaber. Family and Surname of Buchanan, 91. Strathendrick, 318, 350, 353-354.

of Hillington. Crawfurd's Shire of Renfrew (1818). Strathendrick, 305.

in Inveraray. The Scottish Antiquary, vii. 89.

of Kirkhouse. Strathblane, 66. Strathendrick, 77.

of Leny. Family and Surname of Buchanan, 94-107. Strathendrick, 290-296, with family tree.

of Powis. Logie, by Rev. Dr Menzies Fergusson, ii. 98-99. Burke's Landed Gentry (1875 Suppl.-1925).

of Ross. Family and Surname of Buchanan, 76. Strathendrick, 319-322.

of Sound and Shapinshaw. Proc. Soc. Antiquaries of Scotland (1889), 277.

of Spittal. Family and Surname of Buchanan, 49-55, 73, 74. Claim and Amended Claim of Buchanan of Spittal as Chief of the Family of Buchanan of Buchanan, with genealogy, by Francis Hamilton Buchanan (Edinr. 1826-1828).* Strathendrick, by Guthrie Smith, 368-371.

**Buchanan-Hamilton** of Spittal, Bardowie and Leny. Strathendrick, by J. Guthrie Smith, 371-372. Burke's Landed Gentry (1849-1925).

**Buchanan-Baillie-Hamilton** of Arnprior. Burke's Landed Gentry (1879-1925).

**Buchanan-Dunlop** of Drumhead. Burke's Landed Gentry (1898 1925).

**Budge** of Toftingall. Caithness Family History, by Henderson, 181-188.

**Bulloch.** History and Genealogy of the Bulloch Family, by Joseph G. Bulloch, M.D. (Savannah, Georgia, 1894). The Scottish Antiquary (1894), viii. 40-42, with chart pedigree. Scottish N. and Q., 1st S., v. 172 ; 2nd S., vi. 24, 38, 40-41, 54-55, 107-108, 122-123, 136-138, 190 ; vii. 40 ; 3rd S., ii. 161.

of Baldernock. Scottish Historical Review (1904), i. 419-420.

**Bunckill, Bunkle.** Heraldry, by Nisbet (1722), i. 411.

**Buntine** of Airdoch. Paterson's History of County of Ayr, i. 293-294. Paterson's Ayr and Wigton, iii. 124. Irving's Book of Dumbartonshire, ii. 312.

of Kilbride. Paterson's Ayr, ii. 138. Paterson's Ayr and Wigton, iii. 363. *See also* **Bontine.**

**Buntine-Barr** of Trearne. Ayrshire Families, by G. Robertson, i. 155-157. Paterson's Ayr, i. 293. Paterson's Ayr and Wigton, iii. 124-125.

**Bunyan,** Spittal. Tancred's Rulewater, 234.

**Burbon,** Largs. Ayrshire Families, i. 182.

**Burden** of Feddal and Auchingarrich. One Year in Sweden, by H. Marryat, ii. 486. The Genealogist, 1st S., iii. 145-150. Nisbet's Heraldic Plates, ed. Ross and Grant, 156-158. Nisbet MS. in Geneal. Mag. (1899), ii. 351.

**Burn,** St Andrews. Geneal. Coll. by W. Macfarlane, 1750-51 ; Scot. Hist. Soc., ii. 188.

**Burn-Callander** of Westerton. Burke's Landed Gentry (1886-1925).

**Burn-Murdoch** of Gartincaber. Burke's Landed Gentry (1849-1925).

**Burnard,** or **Burnett** of Leys. East Neuk of Fife, by W. Wood, 2nd ed., 213.

**Burnes.** Notes on the Name and Family of James Burnes, K.H., F.R.S. [Edinr. 1851].*

of Bogjordan and Brawliemuir. Memorials of Angus and Mearns, by Jervise, ed. Gammack, i. 153-158 ; ii. 303-305.

**Burnet,** Aberdeen. Memoir of J. Young, Aberdeen . . . 1861 (1894), 233.* Scottish N. and Q., 3rd S., ii. 157-158.

of Campfield. Tayler's Jacobites of Aberdeenshire, 129-131.

of Carlops. Buchan's History of Peeblesshire, iii. 125.

**Burnett.** Heraldry, by Nisbet (1722), i. 404-405. Notes and Queries, 3rd S., v. 376; vi. 47, 333. Pedigree *in* The Family of Cadenhead, by G. Cadenhead (1887).* Herald and Genealogist, iii. 546-551.

**Burnett** of Barns. Burke's Landed Gentry (1849). History of Peeblesshire, by Chambers, 399-401. Peeblesshire Localities, by Renwick, 362-364. Scottish N. and Q., 2nd S., iv. 24. Buchan and Paton's History of Peeblesshire, iii. 571-590.

of Burnetland and Barns. Genealogical Account of the Family of Burnett of Burnetland and Barns, by Montgomery Burnett (1845 ; 2nd ed. 1880). Buchan's History of Peeblesshire, iii. 267-270.*

of Caskieben. The Scottish Antiquary (1898), xii. 91, 139. Scottish N. and Q., 2nd S., vii. 31.

of Craigmyle. The Family of Burnett of Leys (1901), 112-117.

of Crimond. The Family of Burnett, 130-142.

of Cringletie. Peeblesshire Localities, by Renwick, 49-50.

of Elrick. Temple's Thanage of Fermartyn, 296-299. Burke's Landed Gentry (1898-1925).

of Gadgirth. Landed Gentry (1875-1894). History of County of Ayr, by Paterson, i. 327. Ayr and Wigton, by Paterson, i. 238.

of Kemnay. Burke's Landed Gentry (1879-1925). The Family of Burnett of Leys, 118-129.

of Leys. Informations and Answers for Burnet of Leys against A. Burnet, Eldest Son of Kemnay, as to Ruinous Claims on the Estate of £150,000 Scots, etc., 4to (1764). Douglas's Baronage (1784), 41-43. Legends of the Leys, Collected from Oral Traditions of the Burnett Family, by E. M. R. (Aberdeen, 1856). Genealogical Tree of the Family of Burnett of Leys (18—, 1893). East Neuk of Fife, 2nd ed., 213. Scottish N. and Q., vii. 33-34. Historical MSS. Commission (1873), 2nd Report. The Family of Burnett of Leys, with Collateral Branches, by G. Burnett, LL.D., Lyon King of Arms, ed. Col. J. Allardyce, LL.D., 4to, illust., *xxiii* + 368 pp. (Aberdeen, New Spalding Club, 1901), 6-100. Burke's Peerage and Baronetage.

of Monboddo. Historical MSS. Commission (1873), 4th Report ; (1877), 6th Report. Burke's Landed Gentry (1875-1925). The Family of Burnett of Leys, 143-149.

**Burnett-Stuart** of Crichie. Burke's Landed Gentry (1886-1925).

**Burnley-Campbell** of Ormidale. Burke's Landed Gentry (1850-1925).

**Burns.** Robert Burns, Notes on his Name and Family, by Sir James Burnes, K.H. (Edinr. 1854). Genealogical Memoirs of the Family of Robert Burns and of the Scottish House of Burnes, by Rev. C. Rogers (Edinr. 1877). Book of Robert Burns, Genealogical and Historical Memoirs of the Poet, his Associates, etc., by Rev. C. Rogers, 3 vols. (1889-1891). Memorials of Angus and Mearns, by Jervise, ed. Gammack, i. 153-158.

of Kilmahew. Book of Dumbartonshire, by Irving, iii., portrait. Burke's Landed Gentry (1849-1925).

**Burton-Mackenzie** of Kilcoy. Burke's Landed Gentry (1894 Suppl.-1925).

**Bute,** Stewart, Stuart, Earl of, Marquess of. Biographical Peerage (1808), 97-99. Crawfurd's Shire of Renfrew (1818), 455-458. Historical MSS. Commission (1872), 3rd Report; (1876), 5th Report. The Scots Peerage, ii. 299-312. Burke's Peerage. G. E. C.'s Complete Peerage, 2nd ed.

**Butler,** Lord Dingwall. The Scots Peerage, iii. 123.

**Butter** of Fascally. Burke's Landed Gentry (1848-1925).

**Byres,** Lindsay, Lord Lindsay of the. Case of Sir J. T. Bethune on his claim to be Lord Lindsay of the Byres (Edinr. 1877). The Scots Peerage, v. 392. *See also* **Lindsay of the Byres.**

**Byres and Binning,** Hamilton, Lord. The Scots Peerage, iv. 310.

**Byres** of Tonley. The Families of Moir and Byres, by A. J. Mitchell Gill (1885). Burke's Landed Gentry (1849-1925). Tayler's Jacobites of Aberdeenshire, 131-133.

**Byset.** *See* **Bisset.**

**Cadell.** The Cadells of Banton, Grange, Tranent and Cockenzie, etc., 1668-1890, by J. H. Stevenson, tabulated pedigree, folio (1890). The Family of Inglis of Auchindinny, by J. A. Inglis, 24, 43. Burke's Landed Gentry (1879-1925).

**Cadenhead.** The Family of Cadenhead, by George Cadenhead (Aberdeen, 1887).

**Caird** of Cassencary. A History of, or Note upon, the Family of Caird, Scotland, by Rennie A. Caird (1913). Burke's Landed Gentry (1898-1925).

**Cairncross.** Nisbet's Heraldic Plates, ed. Ross and Grant (1892), 122. House of Lords, Hugh Cairncross, Mason in Gallashiels, Appellant, in case *re* the ownership of the Cairncross estate, 28 pp. (1769). History of a Forfarshire Family . . . Cairncross, by A. F. Cairncross (Broughty Ferry, 1922?).

of Balmashanner. Angus or Forfarshire, by Warden, iii. 289.

**Cairns.** A History of the Family of Cairnes or Cairns and its Connections, by H. C. Lawlor (London, 1906).

of Kipp. Lands . . . in Galloway, by M'Kerlie, iii. 355.

Longforgan. The Parish of Longforgan, by Rev. A. Philp, 235, 247, 249.

of Torr. Lands . . . in Galloway, by M'Kerlie, v. 130-131.

*See* The Scots Peerage, ed. Sir James Balfour Paul, *for*

**Caithness,** The Ancient Earls of, ii. 313-320.

Campbell, Earl of, ii. 203.

Crichton, Earl of, ii. 323-331.

Sinclair, Earl of, ii. 332-359.

Stewart, Earl of, ii. 321-322.

**Caithness,** Earldom of. Genealogist, N. S., xv. 67. Scottish N. and Q., iii. 17. Geneal. Mag., vii. 237-245, 286-294. Burke's Peerage. Debrett's Peerage. G. E. C.'s Complete Peerage, 2nd ed., 1910.

**Caldell.** *See* **Calder.**

**Calder** of Achigale and Newton. Caithness Family History, by Henderson, 215.
  of Calder. Nisbet's Heraldry, ii., Appx. 237-238. History of the Province of Moray, by Shaw, ii. 278-282. A Succinct Account of the Family of Calder ; Scot. Hist. Soc., 2nd S., No. 5 (1914), 119-126.
  of Lynegar. Caithness Family History, 209-214.
  of Muirton. Complete Baronetage, by G. E. C., iv. 348.
  of Southwick. J. B. Burke's Extinct Baronetcies (1844).
  of Strath. Caithness Family History, 217.

**Calderwood.** Coltness Collections, 393. Calderwood's History of the Kirk of Scotland ; Wodrow Soc., *vii.*, *xxi.*
  of Polton. Letters and Journals of Mrs Calderwood of Polton, ed. Lt.-Col. A. Fergusson (1884), *xliv*, 372-379.

**Caldom, Cauldhame,** Blackness. MS. notes in possession of Lyon Office, and the Society of Genealogists, London.

**Caldwell** of Annanhill. Paterson's Ayr, ii. 204. Paterson's Ayr and Wigton, iii. 422.

**Caledonian** or Pictish Kings. Royal Genealogies, by James Anderson (1732), 751.

**Callander** of Ardkinglas and Craigforth. Complete Baronetage, by G. E. C., vi., Appx. 79. Burke's Landed Gentry (1849-1925).
  of Manor. Logie, by Rev. Dr Menzies Fergusson, ii. 103-106.
  of Westertoun. J. B. Burke's Extinct Baronetcies, 2nd ed. (1844). Complete Baronetage, by G. E. C., v. 327. *See* **Burn-Callander.**

**Callendar** of Callendar. Heraldry, by A. Nisbet (1722), i. 193-194 ; (1742), ii. Ragman Roll, 17.
  Livingston, Earl of. G. E. C.'s Complete Peerage. The Scots Peerage, ii. 360-364.
  Livingston, Lord Livingston of. The Scots Peerage, v. 430-451.

**Callender-Brodie** of Idvies. Burke's Landed Gentry (1921-1925).

**Cambridge,** Hamilton, Earl of. The Scots Peerage, iv. 374.

**Cameron.** Life of Dr A. Cameron, with a Genealogy of the Camerons, by Archibald Cameron (London, 1752). History of the Clan Cameron, with Genealogies of the Principal Families of the Name, by Alex. Mackenzie, 8vo (Inverness, 1884). The Clan Cameron . . . with short notices of Eminent Clansmen, by John Cameron. 8vo, 95 pp., illust. (Kirkintilloch, 1894).
  of Balclutha. Debrett's Baronetage.
  of Baledgarno. Memorials of Angus and Mearns, by Jervise, ed. Gammack, ii. 67-70.
  of Callard. Campbell's Records of Argyll, 131-135.
  in Doule. Antiquarian Notes, by C. Fraser-Mackintosh, ii. 194.
  of Dungallon. Antiquarian Notes, by C. Fraser-Mackintosh, ii. 224-227.
  Fairfax, Lord Fairfax of. The Scots Peerage, iii. 595-606.

**Cameron** of Fassifern. Memorial for Ffasfern, 1753; Scot. Hist. Soc., iii. (1920), 40-51. Memoir of Col. John Cameron, Fassiefern, K.T.S., Lt.-Col. of the Gordon Highlanders, by Rev. Archibald Clerk. 4to, *iv* + 108 pp., illust. (Glasgow, 1858).* History of the County of Inverness, by Rev. J. Cameron Lees, D.D. (1897).

of Glendessary. Antiquarian Notes, by C. Fraser-Mackintosh, ii. 224, 227-230.

of Lochiel. Ancient Scottish Surnames, by Buchanan of Auchmar (1723), 79-82. Baronage, by Douglas, 328-331. Memoirs of Sir Ewen Cameron of Lochiel [by John Drummond] with an introductory account of the history and antiquities of that family, and of the neighbouring Clans [ed. James Maidment], (Maitland Club, Edinburgh, 1842). Memoirs of the Jacobites of 1715 and 1745, by Mrs Katherine Thomson (1845-46), i. 313-390. History of the County of Inverness, by Dr J. C. Lees (1897). Antiquarian Notes, by C. Fraser-Mackintosh (1897), ii. 207-213, 230. Burke's Landed Gentry (1848-1925).

Baron Lochiel. The Jacobite Peerage, by the Marquis of Ruvigny (1904), 77-80.

Lundavra. Major Alpin's . . . Descendants, by P. J. Anderson, 28-29.*

Saumur. Gaston Bonet Maury *in* Scot. Hist. Review (1916), vii. 325-345.

of Worcester. The Family of Cameron of Worcester, by Alex. Mackenzie, *n.d.* The Family of Cameron of Worcester, by John Cameron. 4to (1919). Burke's Landed Gentry (1848).

**Cameron-Head** of Inverailort. Burke's Landed Gentry (1906-1925).

**Campbell.** The Clan Campbell: Abstracts of Entries relating to Campbells, from the Campbell Collections formed by Sir Duncan Campbell of Barcaldine and Glenure, Bart., C.V.O. ; prepared and edited by Rev. Henry Paton, 8 vols—I. From Sheriff Court Books of Argyll and Inveraray (1913): II. From Sheriff Court Books of Perthshire (1914): III. From Sheriff Court Books of Argyll (1915): IV. The Ducal House of Argyll and Cadets, from various Sources (1916): V. From Early Unprinted Records relating to Ayrshire, 1575-1650 (1917): VI. From Books of Council and Session, Register of Deeds, 1554-1660 (1918): VII. From Parish Registers of Glenorchy, Ardchattan, Kilchrinan, Lochgoilhead, Kilmorich, Inishail, and Killin (1920): VIII. From Books of Council and Session, Acts and Decreets, 1500-1660 (1922). Records of Clan Campbell in the Military Service of the East India Company, 1600-1858, by Sir Duncan Campbell (1925). Lists and Abstracts of Wills and Administrations at Somerset House, 1458-1820, compiled by Sir Duncan Campbell ; 171 MS. sheets, No. 925, Society of Genealogists of London. [*See also* a mass of undigested Campbell material collected by Sir D. Campbell, and deposited in the Lyon Office.] Ancient Scottish Surnames, by Buchanan of Auchmar (1723), 23-31. Accompt of the Genealogie of the Campbells, from a 17th century MS. in Advocates' Library ; Scot. Hist. Soc. (1916), 70-111. Pedigree

of all Branches of Campbell, by James Duncanson (Inveraray, 1777).
Notes and Queries, 2nd S., x. 193, 335 : 3rd S., iv. 242, 427 ; vi. 94,
171 : 6th S., iii. 26, 328 : 7th S., i. 109, 158, 211.   Scottish N. and
Q., 2nd S., iv., v.   The Heraldry of the Campbells, by G. Harvey
Johnston (Edinr. 1921).   [Vol. i. contains 108 pp. letterpress, 49
coats of arms in colours, 10 pedigrees ; vol. ii., 92 pp., 59 coats of
arms, 8 pedigrees.]   The Pronunciation of the Name *in* Notes and
Queries, 10th S., x. 228, 278, 338, 393, 432.   [The Oban Times,
*passim*, contains many articles on the various Argyllshire families of
Campbell.   A General History of the Clan Campbell is being
prepared by Mr Hugh Beaver, Queen Anne's Lodge, Westminster,
London, S.W. 1, who invites correspondence.]

**Campbell** of Aberuchill.   Douglas's Baronage (1784), 57.   Herald and
  Genealogist (1870), v. 266-270.   Complete Baronetage, by G. E. C.,
  iv. 265.   Burke's Baronetage.

of Achalader.   Memorial History of Campbells of Melfort (1882).

of Achanduin.   Burke's Landed Gentry (1906-1925).

of Ardbeg.   History of County of Bute, by J. E. Reid, 240.

of Ardchattan.   Burke's Landed Gentry (1848-1894).   The Scottish
  Antiquary, viii. 3-8, 64, 132.

of Ardeonaig.   Lairds . . . of Loch Tayside, by Christie, 76-77.

of Ardkinglas.   Memoirs of Sir James Campbell of Ardkinglas, 2 vols.
  (1832).   Notes and Queries, 9th S., vii. 187, 293, 353-354 ; viii.
  106-107.   Burke's Extinct Baronetcies.

of Ardlarich.   The Genealogist, N. S., xix. 209-211.

of Ardnamurchan.   Complete Baronetage, by G. E. C., ii. 341.   Burke's
  Peerage and Baronetage.

of Ardneave.   Notes and Queries, 6th S., iv. 448, 494.

of Ardpatrick.   Burke's Landed Gentry (1875-1925).

of Ardslignish.   Lord A. Campbell's Records of Argyll, 120.

of Ardtarich.   The Genealogist, xxix. 211-212.

Earl of, Marquess of, Duke of Argyll.   The Scots Peerage, i. 318-393.
  *See also* **Argyll.**

of Ashfield.   The Genealogist, N. S., xxvii. 127-128.

of Asknish.   Baronage, by Douglas, 537-539.   Observations on a publication by Duncan Campbell-MacIver of Asknish, by W. P. Allardice
  (1870).

of Auchinbreck.   Baronage, by Douglas, 61-63.   Notes and Queries,
  6th S., x. 396 ; xi. 473.   J. A. Campbell *in* Oban Times (27th June
  1908).   Burke's Peerage and Baronetage.   Complete Baronetage,
  by G. E. C., ii. 339.

of Auchmannoch.   Ayrshire Families, by G. Robertson, ii. 215-222.
  History of the County of Ayr, by Paterson, 428.   The Scottish
  Antiquary, viii. 139.   Burke's Landed Gentry (1858-1925).   Pater-
  son's Ayr and Wigton, i. 312, 684-687.

of Auchterharley.   Geneal. Mag. iv. 221.

of Auldhouseburn.   Paterson's History of Ayr, ii. 393.   Paterson's Ayr
  and Wigton, i. 607-608.

**Campbell** of Avisyard.   Paterson's Ayr and Wigton, i. 312.

Ayr.  Notes and Queries, 7th S., i. 87.

of Balloch.  Lairds and Lands of Loch Tayside, by John Christie (Aberfeldy, 1892), 1-24.

of Ballochyle.  Burke's Landed Gentry (1879-1894).

of Baltilly.  Eminent Men of Fife, by M. F. Conolly, 106-107.

of Barbieston.  Paterson's Ayr, i. 444.  Paterson's Ayr and Wigton, i. 415-416.

of Barbreck.  A Letter . . . containing an Account of the Campbells of Barbreck from the First Ancestor to the Present Time, 39 pp. (Ipswich, 1830).  Scottish Antiquary, xvii. 50.  Burke's Landed Gentry (1848-1925).

of Barcaldine.  The Campbells of Melfort, by M. O. Campbell, 2 vols. (1882, 1894).  Trial of James Stewart (The Appin Murder), ed. D. N. Mackay (1907), Appx. vi. 324-325.  Debrett's Baronetage.

of Barnhill.  Book of Dumbartonshire, by Irving, iii., portrait.

of Barquharrie.  Ayrshire Families, ii. 240, 246-248.  Paterson's Ayr, ii. 72.  Paterson's Ayr and Wigton, i. 527.

of Bedlay.  Paterson's Ayr and Wigton, iii. 422.

of Blairhall.  Notes and Queries, 6th S., xii. 269.

of Blythswood.  Crawfurd's Shire of Renfrew (1818), 347.  Glasgow Past and Present, by Senex. (1884), iii. 111-115.  Landed Gentry (1875-1879).  Burke's Peerage and Baronetage (after 1880).

Baron, Viscount, Earl of, Marquess of Breadalbane.  The Scots Peerage, ii.  174-214.  *See also* **Campbell of Inverardine,** *and* **Breadalbane.**

of Brocklerdyke.  Paterson's History of Ayr, ii. 429.  Ayr and Wigton, i. 687.

of Brownside.  Paterson's Ayr and Wigton, i. 569.

of Burnbank.  Argyle Papers : papers relative to the abduction of Miss Wharton by the Hon. Jas. Campbell of Burnbank ; . . . the Burnbank Papers, ed. Jas. Maidment (Edinr. 1834).

of Calder or Cawdor.  Heraldry, by Nisbet (1742), ii. Appx. 240-242.  The Book of the Thanes of Cawdor, 1236-1742, 4to, illust., ed. Cosmo Innes (Spalding Club, Edinr. 1859).  The Great Historic Families of Scotland, by James Taylor [1887], i. Antiquarian Notes, by C. Fraser-Mackintosh, ii. 438-441.  Highland Papers, ed. J. R. N. Macphail, i. ; Scot. Hist. Soc., 2nd S., No. 5 (1914), 127-194.

of Calder, Islay.  Notes and Queries, 3rd S., iv. 242 ; x. 262.

of Camsail.  Book of Dumbartonshire, by Irving, ii. 281.

of Carradale.  Notes and Queries, 6th S. iv. 49, 98, 129, 158 ; v. 335 ; x. 349, 396.

of Carwhin.  Notes and Queries, 3rd S., x. 241, 310.  Lairds . . . of Loch Tayside, by J. Christie, 45-47.

of Castlehill.  Caithness Family History, by J. Henderson, 275, 278.

of Cessnock and Treesbank.  Ayrshire Families, ii. 223-239.  Paterson's Ayr, ii. 68-71.  Paterson's Ayr and Wigton, i. 515-523.  Burke's Landed Gentry (1848-1925).  The Genealogist, N. S., xxvi. 190-191.

**Campbell** of Clewis. History of Ayr, by Paterson, ii. 428. Ayr and Wigton, i. 692.

Lord Clyde. Notes and Queries, 7th S., xii. 128, 355.

of Colgrain. Book of Dumbartonshire, by Irving, ii. 307. Burke's Landed Gentry (1858-1925).

of Cowfauldshaw. Ayrshire Families, ii. 253, 254.

of Craigie. Paterson's Hist. of Ayr, i. 341. Ayr and Wigton, i. 297. Burke's Landed Gentry (1879-1925).

of Craignish and Lagganlochan. Lord A. Campbell's Records of Argyll, 149. Notes and Queries, 7th S., i. 109, 158, 211. The History of Craignish, by Alex. Campbell, c. 1708 ; Scot. Hist. Soc., Misc. iv. (1926), 177-299. A Genealogical Sketch, by Major-Gen. T. Hay Campbell, R.A., 15 pp. n. p. (1890).*

of Cruachan. Four Old Families, by Capt. Wimberley, 27-28.

Dundarave. The Genealogist, N.S., xxvii. 192 ; xxxiv. 178-180, 244.

of Duneaves. The Scottish Antiquary, vii. 43, 88, 94 ; viii. 139.

of Dunoon. Burke's Landed Gentry (1848-1894).

of Dunstaffnage. Memorial History of Campbells of Melfort. Campbell's Records of Argyll, 85-91. J. R. N. Macphail *in* Scot. Hist. Review, xvii. 253-271. Landed Gentry (1894-1914).

of Duntroon. Memorial History of the Campbells of Melfort, by M. O. Campbell, 2 vols. (1882, 1894). Memorial History of the Family of Campbell-Maclachlan (1883). The Campbells of Duntroon and their Cadets, by Herbert Campbell (Exeter, 1913), reprinted from The Genealogist, N. S., xxvii., xxviii., xxix. ; vol. ii., 1921, from The Genealogist, N. S., xxxi., xxxii., xxxvii. [The branches are Ardlarich and Ardtalich : Ashfield *or* Lergnachunzeon, i. 39-48 ; ii. 41-43 : Duntroon, i. 1-8 ; ii. 1-39 : Ellanrie, i. 49-51 : Knap, i. 61-63 : Oib, i. 9-19 ; ii. 44 : Raschoille, i. 21-38 ; ii. 47 : Rudill, i. 52-57 ; ii. 46 : Torobolls, i. 64 : Ulva, i. 59-60 ; ii. 41.]

of Edenwood. Eminent Men of Fife, by Conolly, 107. Landed Gentry (1875-1886).

of Edramucky. Lairds . . . of Loch Tayside, by Christie, 50-51.

of Fairfield. Ayrshire Families, ii. 240, 248-250. History of Ayr, by Paterson, ii. 388. Ayr and Wigton, i. 600-602. Burke's Landed Gentry (1848-1925).

of Finnab. Heraldry, by A. Nisbet (1722), i. 199-201.

of Gargunnock. Geneal. Mag. (1903), vi. 450.

of Garrallan. Paterson's History of Ayr, i. 363. Ayr and Wigton, i. 335-337.

in Garth. The Book of Garth and Fortingall, by Duncan Campbell. 4to, maps (1888).*

of Gibliston. Debrett's Baronetage. Burke's Peerage and Baronetage.

of Glasnock. Paterson's Ayr, i. 364. Paterson's Ayr and Wigton, i. 338-341.

of Glendaruel. Burke's Landed Gentry (1906-1925).

of Glenfalloch. Burke's Landed Gentry (1848-1863). The Scots Peerage, ii. 191-194.

of Glenfcochan. Mrs J. B. Campbell *in* Oban Times (27th June 1908).

**Campbell** of Glenlyon. The Lairds of Glenlyon, by Duncan Campbell. 4to (Perth, 1886).* The Scottish Antiquary, vii. 43, 88, 93, 94. Notes and Queries, 6th S., xi. 248.

of Glenorchy, Glenurchay. Heraldry, by Nisbet (1742), ii. Appx. 221-229. The Black Book of Taymouth, with other papers from the Breadalbane Charter Room ; ed. Cosmo Innes (Bannatyne Club, Edinburgh, 1855). Complete Baronetage, by G. E. C. (1902), ii. 282. The Scots Peerage, ii. 174-205.

of Glenure. The Scottish Antiquary, 1899, xiii. 183. Trial of James Stewart (The Appin Murder), ed. D. N. Mackay (1907).

Baroness, Earl of, Duke of Greenwich. Jacob's Peerage (1766). The Scots Peerage (1904), i. 371-377.

of Greenyards. The Scottish Antiquary, xv. 158.

of Hallyards. Buchan and Paton's History of Peeblesshire, iii. 612.

Herefordshire. The Scottish Antiquary, vii. 66.

of Nether Horsburgh. Buchan's History of Peeblesshire, ii. 407.

of Horsecleuch. Paterson's Ayr and Wigton, i. 354-355.

in Hullerhirst. Paterson's History of Ayr, ii. 448. Ayr and Wigton, iii. 568.

of Hundleshope. Buchan and Paton's Peeblesshire, iii. 605.

in India. MS. Collections in Library of Society of Genealogists.

of Innerchagariney. The Genealogist, N. S., xxxiv. 244.

of Inverardine. Pedigree of James R. Campbell of Inverardine, Cornwall, Canada (the Head of the Canada branch of the Breadalbane Campbell family), compiled by Sir G. D. Gibb (1872).

of Inverawe. Memorials of the Campbells of Kilmartin, by Capt. Douglas Wimberley (Inverness, 1894), 2-19. Herald and Genealogist, vii. 465. Campbell's Records of Argyll, 129.

of Inverliver. Memorials of Four Old Families, by Captain Douglas Wimberley, 26-27.

of Inverneil and Ross. J. B. Burke's Extinct Baronetcies, 2nd ed. Burke's Landed Gentry (1879-1925).

in Ireland. Notes and Queries, 6th S., ix. 88, 372.

Earl of Irvine. The Scots Peerage, v. 21-26.

of Islay. Burke's Landed Gentry (1848-1886).

of Jura. Burke's Landed Gentry (1848-1925).

of Little Keithick. Geneal. Coll., by W. Macfarlane, 1750-51 ; Scot. Hist. Soc., ii. 170.

Kelvinside. Life of Sir H. Campbell-Bannerman, by Spender, i. 1-4.

of Kilberry. Burke's Landed Gentry (1906-1925).

of Killoch. Paterson's Ayr, ii. 331. Paterson's Ayr and Wigton, i. 561-563.

of Kilmartin. Wimberley's Four Old Families, pedigree, 19-24, 29-46. Burke's Landed Gentry (1906-1925).

of Kinloch. Memorial History of Campbells of Melfort. The Story of the Campbells of Kinloch, by E. Dalhousie Login, 2 chart pedigrees (1924). Scottish Notes and Queries, 3rd S., iii. 25.

of Kinzeancleuch. Paterson's Ayr, ii. 332. Ayr and Wigton, i. 563-566.

**Campbell**, Larigs. The Genealogist, N. S., xxxi. 158-159, 284.

of Lagganlochan. The Campbells of Lagganlochan, by Thos. Fraser Campbell, 48 pp. ; Typescript in Lyon Office, and in Historical Dept., H:M. Register House (1929).

of Lawers. Notes and Queries, 2nd S., vi. 96 ; 3rd S., vii. 3 ; 6th S., i. 384, 425. R. R. Stodart *in* Genealogist, v. 132-137, 298-299. The Scots Peerage, v. 499-510.

Lethem. The Genealogist, N. S., xxxi. 45-46.

of Lochdochart. Scottish Surnames, by James Paterson, 52-54. Recreations of an Antiquary, by Fittis, 154-163.

of Lochend. Memorial History of Campbells of Melfort. A Caithness Family History, by John Henderson, 275.

of Lochnell. Burke's Landed Gentry (1848-1925). Records of Argyll, 110-119.

of Lochow. Information anent the Pedigree of the House of Lochow. Brit. Mus. Add. MS. (19,797), 58. Records of Argyll, by Lord Archibald Campbell (1885). The Scots Peerage, i. 319-332.

Marquess of Lorne. The Scots Peerage, i. 369-393.

of Loudoun. Ayrshire Families (1824), ii. 205-215. Paterson's Ayr, ii. 319-323. Paterson's Ayr and Wigton, iii. 542, 545-553. Great Historic Families, by James Taylor [1887], i. The Scots Peerage, v. 490-497.

of Loudoun Hill. Paterson's Ayr and Wigton, iii. 545.

of Lundy. Complete Baronetage, by G. E. C., ii. 333. Burke's Extinct Baronetcies.

of Marchmont. Historical MSS. Commission (1894), 14th Report.

of Mayfield. Paterson's History of Ayr, ii. 72. Ayr and Wigton, i. 527.

of Melfort. A Memorial History of the Campbells of Melfort, by Margaret O. Campbell, 4to, *xx*+124 pp., illust., pedigrees (London, 1882, and Suppl. 1894).* Campbell-Bannerman, by Spender, i. 1-3.

of Menstrie. The Stewarts (Stewart Soc. Magazine), iv. 279.

of Montgarswood. Paterson's Ayr, ii. 334. Ayr and Wigton, i. 569.

of Little Mountgarswood. Paterson's Ayr, ii. 430. Ayr and Wigton, i. 704.

of Monzie. Burke's Landed Gentry (1848-1879).

of Murthly. J. Christie *in* Scottish N. and Q., xii. 81-82. A. W. Gray-Buchanan *in* Scottish Antiquary, xiii. 193-194.

of Netherplace. Ayrshire Families, ii. 254-256. Paterson's Ayr, ii. 333. Paterson's Ayr and Wigton, i. 569-572 ; iii. 503 *n.*

of Ormidale. Burke's Visitation of Seats and Arms, ii. 64. Burke's Landed Gentry (1863-1906).

of Queenshill. Lands . . . in Galloway, by M'Kerlie, v. 203, 382.

of Quoycrook. Caithness Family History, by Henderson, 275-282.

of Rachane. Book of Dumbartonshire, by Joseph Irving, ii. 280. The Scottish Antiquary, xii. 136.

of Rankinston. Paterson's History of Ayr, i. 331.

of Schankistone. Paterson's Ayr, i. 361-363. Ayr and Wigton, i. 347-351.

of Skeldon. Paterson's Ayr, i. 443. Ayr and Wigton, i. 410-413. The Genealogist, N. S., xxvii. 154-157.

**Campbell** of Skerrington. Heraldry, by Nisbet (1742), ii., Appx. 174-175. Burke's Landed Gentry (1848-1925). Paterson's Ayr, i. 359-361. Ayr and Wigton, i. 352-357.

of Skipness. Burke's Landed Gentry (1848-1858).

of Sonachan. Burke's Landed Gentry (1863-1875).

of Sornbeg and Barquharrie. Burke's Landed Gentry (1848-1863).

of Southhall. Burke's Landed Gentry (1879-1925).

of Stevenston and Dowcathall. Ayrshire Families, ii. 251-252.

of Stonefield. One Year in Sweden, by H. Marryat (1862), ii. 493. Book of Dumbartonshire, by Irving, ii. 209. Burke's Landed Gentry (1863-1925).

of Stracathro. Burke's Landed Gentry (1850-1925).

of Strachur. Scottish Historical Review, iv. 233-234.

of Strondour. J. A. Campbell *in* Oban Times (27th June 1908).

of Stronmialachan. The Genealogist, N. S., xxxi. 153-159.

of Succoth. Nisbet's Heraldic Plates, ed. Ross and Grant, 60-63. Book of Dumbartonshire, by Irving, ii. 384-385. Burke's Peerage and Baronetage.

Baron Sundridge. The Scots Peerage, i. 386.

in Sweden. Nisbet's Heraldry, i. 423. Palace of History Catalogue (Glasgow, 1911), 210.

of Torrich. Notes and Queries, 6th S., vii. 347. The Scottish Antiquary, vi. 187.

of Treesbank. Ayrshire Families, ii. 240-245. Paterson's Ayr, ii. 412. Ayr and Wigton, i. 655-657. Burke's Landed Gentry (1848-1925).

of Tullichewan. Book of Dumbartonshire, by Irving, ii. 211-212. Burke's Landed Gentry (1879-1925).

of Middle and Over Wellwood. Paterson's Ayr, ii. 392. Ayr and Wigton, i. 609-612.

*alias* M'Iver. Henderson's Caithness Family History, 275-282.

**Campbell-Colquhoun** of Killermont. Irving's Book of Dumbartonshire, ii. 386. Burke's Landed Gentry (1898-1925).

**Campbell-MacIver** of Asknish. Remarks on the Writings of the Rev. Peter C. Campbell, Principal of King's College, Aberdeen, by Duncan Campbell MacIver of Asknish.* Observations on above, by W. P. Allardice, W.S. (Edinr. 1870).*

**Campbell-Maclachlan.** Memorial History of the Family of Campbell Maclachlan, by Rev. A. N. Campbell-Maclachlan (London, 1883).

**Campbell-Orde** of Kilmory. Complete Baronetage, by G. E. C., v. 264. Burke's Peerage and Baronetage.

**Campbell-Preston** of Ardchattan. Landed Gentry (1886-1925).

**Campbell-Renton** of Lamberton. Burke's Landed Gentry (1875-1925).

**Campbell-Swinton** of Kimmerghame. Burke's Landed Gentry (1858-1925).

**Camperdown,** Haldane-Duncan, Earl of. Angus or Forfarshire, by Warden, i. 437-441. Debrett's and other Annual Peerages. G. E. C.'s Complete Peerage, ed. Gibbs.

**Cannan** of Barlay. Lands . . . in Galloway, by M'Kerlie, iii. 97-98.

**Cannon** of Muirdrochwood and Headmark. Paterson's Ayr and Wigton, i. 370.

**Cant.** Scottish N. and Q., 2nd S., vii. 162 ; viii. 24, 58-59.
   of Duloch. Stephen's Inverkeithing (1921), 99-100.
   of Pittenweem, of Priestfield, of St Giles' Grange. The Scottish Antiquary (1893), vii. 78-80.

**Capel-Carnegie-Arbuthnott** of Balnamoon and Findowrie. Burke's Landed Gentry (1906-1925).

**Cardney** of Foss. Scottish N. and Q., xii. 129.

**Cardno**, Fraserburgh. Smith's Genealogies of an Aberdeen Family ; Aberdeen Univ. Studies, *viii-ix*.

**Cardross**, Erskine, Lord. Annals and Antiquities of Dryburgh, by Sir David Erskine, 2nd ed., 140-158. The Scots Peerage, ii. 365-368 ; v. 618-621. Memoirs of Sir D. Erskine of Cardross (1926).

**Carleton** of Carleton. Scottish N. and Q., 3rd S., v. 5-8, 23.

**Carlisle.** History of the Family of Carlisle, by N. Carlisle (1822).
   Review of the above, by T. J. Carlyle of Templehill (Dumfries, 1881), (pamphlet). History of the Paisley Branch of the Carlisle or Carlile Family, by some of its members (Winchester, 1909).*

**Carlyle** of Carlyle. Historical Families of Dumfriesshire, by C. L. Johnstone, 16-17, Appx. B. The Scots Peerage, ii. 369-377.
   of Locharthur. Heraldry, by Nisbet, ii. Ragman Roll, 43. The Scots Peerage, ii. 389-390.
   of Torthorwald, Carlyle, Lord. Notes and Queries, 3rd S., xi. 278, 460. The Scots Peerage, ii. 369-394.

**Carmichael.** Notes and Queries, 3rd S., xi. 120, 483 ; xii. 53 : 6th S., vii. 77 ; x. 350, 396, 477 ; xi. 12, 58, 133, 212 : 7th S., xi. 47, 133, 233, 332, 458 ; xii. 76, 147.
   of Annat in Appin. The Scottish Antiquary, vii. 55-56, with chart pedigree.
   of Balmblae. The Scots Peerage, iv. 566-567.
   of Balmedie. The Scots Peerage, iv. 564-568. Scottish N. and Q., 3rd S., iv. 202.
   of Bonytoun. Upper Ward of Lanarkshire, by Irving and Murray, ii. 331-332.
   of Carmichael. Upper Ward of Lanarkshire, ii. 8-25. Genealogist, N. S., ii. 15. The Scots Peerage, iv. 573-588. Scottish N. and Q., 3rd S., vi. 36-38, 216-218, 238 ; vii. 11, 36, 49.
   Lord Carmichael. G. E. C.'s Complete Peerage, ed. Gibbs. The Scots Peerage, iv. 585-597.
   of Eastend. Upper Ward of Lanarkshire, ii. 27.
   Earl of Hyndford. Upper Ward of Lanarkshire, ii. 330. The Scots Peerage, iv. 563-597.
   of Mauldslie. Upper Ward, ii. 410-412. The Scots Peerage, iv. 592.

**Carmichael** of Meadowflat. The Scots Peerage, iv. 564. A. O. Curle *in* Scot. Hist. Review, iv. 178-184.
of Skirling. History of Peeblesshire, by Chambers, 455. Peeblesshire Localities, by Renwick, 411, 432. History of Peeblesshire, by Buchan and Paton, iii. 224-232.
of Westraw, Westerhall. Complete Baronetage, by G. E. C., ii. 326. Burke's Extinct Baronetcies.
**Carmichael-Anstruther** of Anstruther. Debrett's Baronetage. Complete Baronetage, iv. 387.
**Carmichael-Baillie.** Complete Baronetage, iv. 303.
**Carmichael-Ferrall.** Landed Gentry (1875).
**Carmichael-Smyth.** The Monros of Auchenbowie, by J. A. Inglis, 120-121 The Scots Peerage, iv. 568-572.
**Carnegie.** Heraldry, by A. Nisbet (1722), i. 347-348.
of Ballindarg. Nisbet's Heraldry (1742), ii., Appx. 252.
of Balmachie. Warden's Angus or Forfarshire, v. 75-76.
of Balnamoon. Geneal. Coll., by W. Macfarlane, 1750-51 ; Scot. Hist. Soc., ii. 181-182. Angus or Forfarshire, by A. J. Warden (1880), iv. 356-358. The Scots Peerage, viii. 61-62. Scottish N. and Q., 3rd S., v. 39.
of Boysack. Landed Gentry (1850-1879). Angus or Forfarshire, by Warden, iii. 434-435. The Scots Peerage, vi. 495-496.
of Carnegie. The Scots Peerage, viii. 46-47.
Lord Carnegie. The Scots Peerage, viii. 65-93.
of Charleton. Fraser's Laurencekirk (1880), 92. The Scots Peerage, viii. 82.
of Mill of Conveth and Redhall. Fraser's Laurencekirk, 163-165.
of Cookston. Angus or Forfarshire, by Warden, iii. 16-18.
of Craig. Angus or Forfarshire, iii. 142.
of Craigo. Angus or Forfarshire, iv. 238-239.
of Ethie. Angus or Forfarshire, iii. 441-444.
of Finavon. The Scots Peerage, vi. 497-498.
Inverkeilor and Collessie. Eminent Arbroathians, by J. M. M'Bain, (Arbroath, 1897), 408.
of Kinfauns. The Scots Peerage, vi. 498-499.
of Kinnaird. Geneal. Coll., by W. Macfarlane, 1750-51 ; Scot. Hist. Soc., ii. 160-180. Angus or Forfarshire, iii. 235. The Scots Peerage, viii. 48-59.
of Kinnoull. The Scots Peerage, vi. 495.
of Leuchland. Angus or Forfarshire, iii. 249.
of Lour and Turin. Angus or Forfarshire, iii. 294-297. The Scots Peerage, vi. 498-499. Burke's Landed Gentry (1875-1925).
of Menmuir. Angus or Forfarshire, iv. 356-358.
Earl of Northesk. Angus or Forfarshire, i. 431-436. The Scots Peerage, vi. 493-508.
of Pittarrow. Complete Baronetage, by G. E. C., iii. 337. The Scots Peerage, viii. 66, 67, 74-82. Fraser's Laurencekirk, 85-91.

**Carnegie** of Stronvar and Torrie. The Scots Peerage, viii. 83. Burke's Landed Gentry (1886-1925).

Earl of Southesk. Pedigree of Sir James Carnegie, Baronet of Southesk, Kinnaird and Pittarrow, in reference to the case on his Claim to the Titles and Honours of Earl of Southesk, Lord Carnegy of Kinnaird and Leuchars (1847). History of the Carnegies, Earls of Southesk, by William Fraser, 2 vols., illust. (Edinr. 1867).* Angus or Forfarshire, i. 357-379 ; iii. 240-241. The Scots Peerage, viii. 46-93.

**Carnegie-Arbuthnott** of Balnamoon. Landed Gentry (1886-1925). The Scots Peerage, viii. 62-63.

**Carnwath**, Dalzell, Earl of. Nisbet's Heraldic Plates, ed. Ross and Grant (1892), 30-32. The Scots Peerage, ii. 395-420. Burke's, Lodge's, Debrett's Peerages. G. E. C.'s Complete Peerage, ed. Gibbs. Article by J. Lemuel Chester *in* Collectanea Genealogica, ed. J. Foster (1881), i. Walford's Tales of our Great Families, 2nd S., i. 68-71. Notes and Queries, 9th S., ii. 515 ; iii. 271, 296.

**Carr** of Greenhead. Complete Baronetage, by G. E. C., ii. 429. *See also* **Ker.**

**Carre** of Cavers Carre. R. R. Stodart *in* The Herald and Genealogist, iii. 110-115. Annals of a Border Club, by G. Tancred (1899), 297-303. Burke's Landed Gentry (1875-1925).

of Nisbet. Border Memories, by Walter Riddell Carre of Cavers Carr (1876), 210.

**Carrick**, The Ancient Earls of. Some Account of the Ancient Earldom of Carrick, by Andrew Carrick, ed. Jas. Maidment (Edinr. 1857). Paterson's History of Ayr, ii. 269. Paterson's Ayr and Wigton, ii. 302, 314, 351-358. The Scots Peerage, ii. 421-427.

Bruce, Earl of. Paterson's Ayr, ii. 270-272. Paterson's Ayr and Wigton, ii. 358-363. Notes and Queries, 1858, 2nd S., v. 236, 264 ; vi. 135, 179, 255. The Scots Peerage, ii. 428-437.

Cunningham, Earl of. The Scots Peerage, iv. 227.

Stewart, Earl of. The Scots Peerage, ii. 438-442. G. E. C.'s Complete Peerage, ed. Gibbs. Historical Sketch of the Family and Surname of Carrick (1824).

Leith. The Scottish Antiquary (1894), viii. 24.

**Carrick-Buchanan** of Drumpellier and Corsewall. Burke's Landed Gentry (1863-1925).

**Carrick-Moore** of Corswall. Burke's Landed Gentry (1848).

**Carruthers** of Craig. Lands . . . in Galloway, by M'Kerlie, iii. 93.

of Dormont. Burke's Landed Gentry (1875-1925).

of Holmains. Inventory of Writs belonging to the Family of Holmains. Historical MSS. Commission, 1877, vol. vi., folio. The Family of Carruthers, sm 4to [1878].

of Mouswald. Historical Families of Dumfriesshire, by C. L. Johnstone (Dumfries, 1888), 9, 16. The Barony of Mouswald and its Barons, by J. J. Reid *in* Proc. Soc. Antiq. Scotl. (1888) 24-65, 78.

**Carse** of Cockpen. Nisbet's Heraldry, i. 448. The Scottish Antiquary, xiv. 90.

**Carson, Carsan.** Scottish N. and Q., 2nd S., iii. 79, 94, 109.
of Auchengassel. Lands . . . in Galloway, by M'Kerlie, v. 283.
of Balmangan. Lands . . . in Galloway, iii. 207.

**Carstairs, Carstares.** Geneal. Coll., by W. Macfarlane, 1750-51 ; Scot. Hist. Soc., ii. 191, 193, 196, 202. Letters, etc., of the Rev. John Carstairs of Glasgow, 1649-68, with Account of his Life, and Genealogy of the Family, by Rev. W. Ferrie (1846). The Origin of the Name *in* Notes and Queries, 10th S., xi. 290, 397, 497 ; xii. 57. Sons of the Manse, by A. W. Fergusson, D.D. (Dundee, 1923).
of Cassingray. East Neuk of Fife, by W. Wood, 2nd ed., 149.
of Newgrange and Kilconquhar. East Neuk of Fife, 165-166. Nisbet's Heraldic Plates, ed. Ross and Grant, 138.

**Carter-Campbell** of Possil. Burke's Landed Gentry (1898-1925).

**Carthew-Yorstoun** of East Tinwald. Burke's Landed Gentry (1875-1925).

**Cary,** Viscount Falkland. Records of the Family of Cary, Viscounts Falkland, by C. J. Robinson (Westminster, 1864). The Scots Peerage, iii. 607-617.

**Cassells.** Records of the Family of Cassells and Connections [by Robert Cassells], 4to (Edinr. 1870).*
of Freshfield. Memorials of the Browns of Fordell, by R. R. Stodart (1887), 70-81.
of Greenknowe. The Browns of Fordell, 62.

**Cassie.** Scottish N. and Q., xi. 157. Smith's Genealogies of an Aberdeen Family ; Aberdeen Univ. Studies, 3-5.
of Kirkhouse. Buchan and Paton's History of Peeblesshire, ii. 534.

**Cassillis,** Kennedy, Earl of. Heraldry, by Nisbet (1742), ii., Appx. 38-39. The Cassillis Peerage, 1760-4, with folding pedigree, by W. B. Turnbull, D.D., ed. James Maidment. Paterson's Ayr, ii. 281-291. Paterson's Ayr and Wigton, ii. 267-272, 302-346. The Scots Peerage, ii. 443-502. Burke's and other Annual Peerages. G. E. C.'s Complete Peerage.

**Cathcart** of Alloway and Ayr. Paterson's History of Ayr, ii. 365. Paterson's Ayr and Wigton, ii. 394-399.
of Carbiston. Paterson's History of Ayr, i. 329-331, 462. Paterson's Ayr and Wigton, i. 218-223. Burke's Landed Gentry (1849-1925).
of Carleton. Paterson's Ayr (1847), i. 304-305. Paterson's Ayr and Wigton, ii. 135-139. Complete Baronetage, by G. E. C., iv. 419. Burke's Peerage and Baronetage. The Scots Peerage, ii. 510, 511. Scottish N. and Q., 3rd S., v. 23-25, 47-49, 64-66, 84-86, 105-106, 126-127, 146-148 with chart.
of Carnehill. Paterson's Ayr, i. 343.

**Cathcart,** Lord, Viscount, Earl Cathcart. Biographical Peerage (London, 1808), 122-123. Burke's Peerage. Debrett's Peerage. G. E. C.'s Complete Peerage. The Scots Peerage, ii. 503-531. The Genealogist, N. S., v. 207. The Beautiful Mrs Graham and the Cathcart Circle, by E. Maxtone Graham (1927).

of Cathcart. Heraldry, by Nisbet (1722), i. 246-247. Crawfurd's Shire of Renfrew (1818), 28-30, 267-269. The Scots Peerage, ii. 504-509.

of Craigengillan. Paterson's Ayr and Wigton, i. 477.

of Duchray. Paterson's Ayr and Wigton, i. 218.

of Genoch. Lands . . . in Galloway, by M'Kerlie, 2nd ed., i. 583-585. Paterson's Ayr and Wigton, ii. 162-164. Scottish N. and Q., 3rd S., vi. 90-91, 110.

of Glenduisk. Paterson's Ayr and Wigton, ii. 155.

of Greenock. Old Greenock, by G. Williamson (1886), i. 98-181.

of Knockdolian. Paterson's Ayr, i. 306-307. Paterson's Ayr and Wigton, ii. 162-164. Burke's Landed Gentry (1849-1879). Scottish N. and Q., 3rd S., vi. 90-91, 110.

**Cathro.** Glamis, by Stirton (1913), 127, 131-132.

**Cattanach.** Scottish N. and Q., 2nd S., i. 173 ; iv. 109.

**Cawdor,** Campbell, Earl of. Historical MSS. Commission (1871), 2nd Report. Great Historic Families, by James Taylor [1887]. G. E. C.'s Complete Peerage. Burke's and other Annual Peerages.

**Chalmer** of Balbithan. Thanage of Fermartyn, by Temple, 348-349.

of Galdgirth, Gadgirth. Heraldry, by A. Nisbet (1742), ii., Appx. 20-22. Paterson's History of Ayr, i. 323-326. Paterson's Ayr and Wigton, i. 228-237. Burke's Visitation of Seats and Arms (1853), i. 224.

of Polquhairn. Paterson's History of the County of Ayr, ii. 402. Paterson's Ayr and Wigton, i. 633.

of Strichen. Thanage of Fermartyn, 83-89.

Warsaw. Papers relating to the Scots in Poland ; Scot. Hist. Soc., No. 59 (1915), 325-334.

**Chalmers.** Ancient Scottish Surnames, by Buchanan of Auchmar (1723), 82.

Aberdeen. Smith's Genealogies of an Aberdeen Family ; Aberdeen Univ. Studies, 7-14, 24.

of Aldbar. Baronage of Angus and Mearns, by D. M. Peter (1856), 52-54. Memorials of Angus and the Mearns, by Jervise, ed. Gammack, ii. 73-79. Burke's Landed Gentry (1848-1925).

Anstruther. Memoirs of Thomas Chalmers, D.D., by Wm. Hanna, LL.D., i. 2. Genealogy of the Descendants of Rev. Thos. Guthrie, D.D., by C. J. Guthrie, K.C. (1902).* Alexander Cowan, by C. B. Boog Watson, 50-53.*

Arbroath. Eminent Arbroathians, by J. M. M'Bain, 276.

of Brockloch. Paterson's Ayr and Wigton, ii. 424.

of Cults and Balnecraig. Nisbet's Heraldry (1722), i. 309 ; (1742), ii., Appx. 121-126. Complete Baronetage, by G. E. C., iii. 348.

Gothenburg. Scottish N. and Q., 3rd S., v. 56, 79.

of Longcroft. Alexander Cowan, by C. B. Boog Watson, 52-53.*

**Chalmers** of Monkshill. Thanage of Fermartyn, 45, 91.
 of Murthill. Scottish N. and Q. (1888), i. 196. Thanage of Fermartyn, 82-83.
 of Pitmeddan. Eminent Men of Fife, by M. F. Conolly (Cupar, 1866), 111-112.
 of Sauchrie. Paterson's History of Ayr, ii. 375. Paterson's Ayr and Wigton, i. 448.
 of Tillery. Scottish N. and Q., 2nd S., iv. 190.
**Chambers.** Heraldry, by Nisbet (1722), i. 308.
**Chambers-Hunter** of Tillery. Thanage of Fermartyn, 578-579. Burke's Landed Gentry (1921-1925).
**Champion.** Scottish N. and Q. (1891-2), v. 19.
**Chancellor** of Shieldhill and Quothquhan. Heraldry, by A. Nisbet, 1722, i. 441 ; 1742, ii., Appx. 84-85. Upper Ward of Lanarkshire, by Irving and Murray, i. 439-442. Burke's Landed Gentry, 1875-1898.
**Charteris** of Amisfield. Heraldry, by Nisbet (1742), ii., Appx. 142-148. Baronage, by Douglas (1784), 150-153. Notes and Queries, 3rd S., viii. 261, 408 ; ix. 70; x. 315, 379. Burke's Landed Gentry (1886-1894).
 of Duchra. Lands . . . in Galloway, by M'Kerlie, iii. 147-150.
 of Kinfauns. The Scots Peerage, iii. 29-32.
 Earl of Wemyss. The Scots Peerage, viii. 513-518.
**Charters,** Inverkeithing. Traditions of the Watsons, by C. B. Boog Watson.*
 of Selvage. Stephen's Inverkeithing and Rosyth, 113-116.
**Châtelherault,** Hamilton, Duke of. Titres et pieces justificatives (1713). Factum of the Earl of Arran, touching the restitution of the Duchy of Châtelherault, 1685, ed. W. B. D. D. Turnbull (1843). Consultation pour James Hamilton, marquis d'Abercorn (1865). Defense de S. A. Mme. Marie Caroline de Bade, duchesse de Hamilton (1865). The Scots Peerage, iv. 367-372. G. E. C.'s Complete Peerage, 2nd ed., i., Appx. B, 465-468. Herald and Genealogist, iv. 97-107 ; v. 92.
**Chattan.** Notes and Queries, 8th S., i. 431 ; ii. 94. The Loyal Dissuasive, and other Papers concerning the Affairs of Clan Chattan, by Sir Æneas MacPherson, Knight of Invereshie, 1691-1705, ed. Rev. A. D. Murdoch ; (Scot. Hist. Soc., 1902). The Clan Chattan, by C. M. Fraser, 4to (Glasgow, 1898). *See also* **Mackintosh.**
**Cheape** of Kippo, Wellfield, and Strathtyrum. Douglas's Baronage (1798), 577. East Neuk of Fife, by W. Wood, 2nd ed., 465. Burke's Landed Gentry (1879-1914).
 of Mawhill. Douglas's Baronage, 575.
 of Rossie. Douglas's Baronage, 575-577.
**Chessor.** Scottish N. and Q., 3rd S., ii. 110.
**Cheyne** of Duffus. The Scots Peerage, vi. 34, 37 *n.*
 of Esslemont. Thanage of Fermartyn, by Temple, 507-511. Zetland Family Histories, by F. J. Grant (1907), 38-43.
 of Inverugie. Buchan, by Rev. J. B. Platt (1858), 342.

**Cheyne,** Viscount of Newhaven. The Scots Peerage, vi. 461-468.
of Straloch. Temple's Thanage of Fermartyn, 318-320.
of Tangwick. Zetland Family Histories, 44-45.
of Vaila. Zetland Family Histories, 47-50.

**Chiene,** Crail. Eminent Men of Fife, by M. F. Conolly, 119-120.
Churchyard Monuments of Crail, by Erskine Beveridge, 183, 186-192.

**Chiesley** of Cresswell. Upper Ward of Lanarkshire, by Irving and Murray,
ii. 525-527.

**Chiesly** of Dalry. Walks near Edinburgh, by Margaret Warrender,
156-157. Scottish N. and Q., 2nd S., vi. 141.

**Chinnery-Haldane** of Gleneagles. Burke's Landed Gentry (1858-1925).

**Chisholm** of Chisholm. Memoirs of Chisholm, by Rev. T. S. M. Anderson
(2nd ed. 1842). Burke's Landed Gentry (1863-1925). Antiquarian
Notes, by C. Fraser-Mackintosh, i. 181-188. History of the
Chisholms, with Genealogies of the principal Families of that name,
by Alex. Mackenzie, 8vo, also a 4to edition of 75 copies, $xv + 232$ pp.
(Inverness, 1891). Geneal. Mag. (1900), iii. 475-478. A Day that is
Dead, by the Rev. John Stirton, D.D., 2nd ed. [1929].*
of Erchless. Sketches of Highland Families, by John Maclean (1848-
1895), 109-118. Burke's Landed Gentry (1848-1925).
of Glassburn. Stirton's A Day that is Dead.
in Glengarry, Upper Canada. Stirton's A Day that is Dead, 67-71.
in Glenholm. Peeblesshire Localities, by Renwick, 244.
of Parkhill. Rulewater, by G. Tancred, 189.

**Chisholme** of Stirches, Stirkshaws. Annals of a Border Club, by G.
Tancred, 83-87. Rulewater, 163-164.

**Christie.** Notes and Queries, 3rd S., iii. 150, 319, 478, 516 ; iv. 57 : 5th S.,
vii. 427 ; viii. 56. Genealogical Memoirs of the Scottish House of
Christie, by Rev. C. Rogers (London, Royal Hist. Soc., 1878). The
Stirling Antiquary (1904), iii. 212.
Aberdeen. Notes and Queries (30th April 1927), 310-311. Scottish
N. and Q., 3rd S., v. 116.
of Middle Carnock. Scottish N. and Q., xi. 175, 192.
of Corntoun. Logie, by Rev. R. Menzies Fergusson, ii., 187, 190, 191,
193-197.
of Durie. Eminent Men of Fife, by M. F. Conolly, 121. East Neuk of
Fife, by W. Wood, 2nd ed., 38. Burke's Landed Gentry (1849-1925).
of Heads. Scottish N. and Q., vii. 46.
Norway. Scottish N. and Q., 2nd S., i. 134.
Stirling. Stirling Journal (28th Oct. 1898).
of Whitehouse. Logie, by Rev. R. Menzies Fergusson, ii. 189.

**Christison,** Edinburgh. Debrett's Baronetage.
of Ledcharry. Scottish N. and Q., vii. 46.

**Christopher-Nisbet-Hamilton.** Burke's Landed Gentry (1858-1879).

**Chrystie** of Balchrystie. East Neuk of Fife, by W. Wood (1887), 109, 212.

**Chrystisone** of Sheriffmuirlands. Logie, by Rev. R. Menzies Fergusson, ii. 187-189, 192, 223. The Stirling Antiquary, ed. W. B. Cook, ii. 71-72.

**Churchill**, Lord Churchill of Eyemouth. The Scots Peerage, ii. 532-533.

**Clanranald**, Macdonald, Baroness, Baron. The Jacobite Peerage, by the Marquis of Ruvigny (1904), 31-37.

**Clark**. Confederacy of Clan Chattan, by C. Fraser-Mackintosh (1898), 112-117.
of Culgruff. Lands . . . in Galloway, by M'Kerlie, iii. 393-394.
Edinburgh. Debrett's Baronetage.
of Speddoch. Landed Gentry (1875-1894).

**Clark-Kennedy** of Knockgray. Lands . . . in Galloway, by M'Kerlie, iii. 309-311. Burke's Landed Gentry (1848-1925).

**Clarke** of Achareidh. Burke's Landed Gentry (1863-1925).
of Comrie Castle. Landed Gentry (1848).

**Clason**. Logie, by Rev. Dr Menzies-Fergusson, i. 220.

**Claverhouse**, Grahame, Lord Grahame of. The Scots Peerage, iii. 324-333. *See also* **Dundee**.

**Clayhills**. Scottish N. and Q., 2nd S., vi. 126, 143.

**Clayhills-Henderson** of Invergowrie. Angus or Forfarshire, by A. J. Warden, iv. 183-185. Burke's Landed Gentry (1875-1925).

**Cleghorn** of Cleghorn. The Barony of Cleghorn from 1203 to the Family of Claghorn, U.S.A., by W. C. Claghorn, 4to (Philadelphia, 1912). Burke's Landed Gentry (1875-1886).
of East Drylaw and Weens. Annals of a Border Club, by G. Tancred (1899), 87-92, 470.
Granton. Cramond, by J. P. Wood, 121-122.
of Stravithie. The Cleghorn Papers ; the Diary, 1795-96, of Hugh Cleghorn of Stravithie, ed. Rev. W. Neil, *xx*+296 pp. (1927).
of Weens. Tancred's Rulewater, 356, 384-394.

**Cleland** of Cleland. Nisbet's Heraldry (1722), i. 338. Memorial for Cleland of that Ilk, MS. (1737). A Midlothian Village, by G. V. Selway (1890), 25-26. Notes and Queries, 3rd S., viii. 210, 519 ; ix. 491 ; x. 12, 192, 299. The Ancient Family of Cleland : being an Account of the Clelands of that Ilk, in County Lanark, of the Branches of Faskine, Monkland, etc., by John B. Cleland, 113 pp. (1905).
of Hillhouse. East Neuk of Fife, by W. Wood, 2nd ed., 334-335.
of Stoneypath. History of Peeblesshire, by Chambers, 464-465. History of Peeblesshire, by Buchan and Paton, iii. 156.

**Clelland** of Nakedfield. Geneal. Mag., vii. 31.

**Clephane** of Carslogie. Baronage, by Douglas, 317-319. Eminent Men of Fife, by Conolly, 123-125.

**Clerich**, The Clan ; *or* Clark. Confederacy of Clan Chattan, by C. Fraser-Mackintosh, 112-117.

I

**Clerk** in Broughtonshiels. Annals of a Tweeddale Parish, by Rev. A. Baird, 34.

of Listonshiels. Baronage, by Douglas, 423-424.

of Penicuik. Baronage, by Douglas, 420-423. Cramond, by J. P. Wood, 65. Wilson's Annals of Penicuik (1891), 150-164.* Debrett's Baronetage. Complete Baronetage, by G. E. C., iv. 306.

in Sweden. One Year in Sweden, by H. Marryat (1862), ii. 480, 484. Palace of History Catalogue (Glasgow, 1911), 202. Eric E. Etzel, Upsala, *in* Scot. Hist. Review (1913), ix. 268-269.

**Clerk-Maxwell** of Glenlairs. Lands . . . in Galloway, by M'Kerlie, v. 53.

**Clifton** of **Leighton-Bromswold**, Stewart, Lord. The Scots Peerage, v. 358-362.

**Clouston.** Records of the Earldom of Orkney, 1299-1614, ed. J. Storer Clouston (Scot. Hist. Soc., 1914), c+515 pp. Review of above, by A. W. Johnston, *in* Year Book of Viking Soc. (London, 1924), 46-50. The Bonnie House of Clouston, by Roland Saint-Clair ; Typescript.

**Clunies-Ross** of Cocos Keeling Islands. Zetland Family Histories, by F. J. Grant, 243.

**Clydesdale**, Douglas, Marquess of. The Scots Peerage, iv. 381-382.

Hamilton, Marquess of. The Scots Peerage, iv. 377-397.

**Coats** of Paisley. Burke's Peerage and Baronetage (after 1894).

**Cochran**, Antigua. Oliver's History of Antigua, i. 139-142.

of Ashkirk. Burke's Landed Gentry (1863-1925).

of Edge. Paterson's Ayr and Wigton, iii. 300.

**Cochrane.** Heraldry, by A. Nisbet (1722), i. 323-324, 326. Crawfurd's Shire of Renfrew, ed. Robertson (1818), 82-86. Account of Dunfermline, by Peter Chalmers, ii., Folding Table, No. 2.

of Barbachlaw. The Scots Peerage, iii. 340 *n.*

of Bridgehouse. Paterson's History of Ayr, i. 211-212 ; ii. 503. Paterson's Ayr and Wigton, i. 136-138.

of Chippens. Notes on Cochrane of Chippens in Kilbarchan. Typescript, 27 pp., in Library of Society of Genealogists.

of Cochrane. Paterson's Ayr, ii. 507-508. Pedigree of the Cochranes of Cochrane, Lord Cochrane of Dundonald, Earls of Dundonald, Lords Cochrane of Paisley and Ochiltree, with a few details of the Branches of Pitfour, Lee and Ascoke, Barbachlaw, Ferguslie, Ochiltree, Waterside, Kilmaronoch, Craigmure and Ashkirk, by Mrs Katherine Parker, Folio Sheet (1908). The Scots Peerage, iii. 334-346. [Mrs Katherine Parker has prepared for publication a History of the Family of Cochrane.]

of Craighlaw. Paterson's Ayr (1852), ii. 124.

of Craigmuir. Crawfurd's Shire of Renfrew, ed. Robertson, 88. Paterson's Ayr, ii. 508.

of Culross. The Scots Peerage, iii. 348, 349, 358.

Earl of Dundonald. Paterson's History of Ayr, ii. 26-31. The Scots Peerage, iii. 334-368.

**Cochrane** of Grange. Buchan's History of Peeblesshire, iii. 60.

of Ladyland. Crawfurd's Shire of Renfrew (1818), 361. Robertson's Ayrshire Families, i. 157-158. Paterson's Ayr and Wigton, iii. 301.

of Lamancha. Buchan's History of Peeblesshire, iii. 62-64.

of Ochiltree. Paterson's History of Ayr, ii. 400. Paterson's Ayr and Wigton, i. 629-631. Complete Baronetage, by G. E. C., iv. 299. The Scots Peerage, iii. 346-359. Walford's Tales of our Great Families, 2nd S., i. 129-134.

U.S.A. The Cochranes of Renfrewshire : The Ancestors of Alexander Cochrane of Bellerica and Malden, U.S.A., by Walter Kendals Wathens (Boston, 1904).

of Waterside. Paterson's Ayr, i. 244 ; ii. 400. Paterson's Ayr and Wigton, i. 208, 634.

**Cockburn.** Heraldry, by Nisbet, i. 355.

of Cockburn. The House of Cockburn of that Ilk, and the Cadets thereof, by T. H. Cockburn-Hood (Edinr. 1888).\* Complete Baronetage, by G. E. C., iv. 282 ; vi., Appx. 69. The Records of the Cockburn Family and its Branches of Langton, East Borthwick and Blackmiln, Cockburn, Henderland, Glen, Skirling, Choicelee, Ryslaw, Newbigging and Clerkington, Newhall, Caldra, Cockpen, Kirklands of Bolton, Rowchester, etc., by Sir Robert Cockburn and Henry Cockburn, 4to, 32 pedigrees, 30 plates (Edinr. 1913.)\* Burke's Landed Gentry (1894 Suppl.).

Baroness Forrester of Corstorphine, The Scots Peerage, iv. 96-97.

in France. Chroniques de Louis XII., par Jean d'Auton ; Société de l'Histoire de France, i. Notes and Queries, 8th S., vi. 205.

of Henderland. Peeblesshire Localities, by Renwick, 385-388. Buchan and Paton's History of Peeblesshire, iii. 528-531.

of Langton. The Scottish Antiquary, xi. 160-166. Complete Baronetage, by G. E. C., ii. 327.

of Ormiston. Notes and Queries, 3rd S., xi. 52, 125.

of Quhitslaid. Peeblesshire Localities, by Renwick, 237, 238.

of Rowchester. Burke's Landed Gentry (1849), 170.

of Ryslaw. Debrett's Baronetage. Complete Baronetage, by G. E. C., ii. 330.

of Skirling. History of Peeblesshire, by Chambers, 453. Peeblesshire Localities, 398-410. History of Peeblesshire, by Buchan and Paton, iii. 214-221.

**Cockburn-Campbell** of Gartsford. Debrett's Baronetage.

**Cockburn-Hood** of Stainrig. Burke's Landed Gentry (1898-1925).

**Coghill.** The Family of Coghill from 1377 to 1879, by Jas. H. Coghill (Cambridge, Mass., 1879). Caithness Family History, by Henderson, 253.

**Collace** of Balnamoon. Angus or Forfarshire, by Warden, iv. 353-355.

**Colquhoun.** Ancient Scottish Surnames, by Buchanan of Auchmar, 90-95. Antigua. History of Antigua, by Oliver, i. 177.

of Barnhill. Book of Dumbartonshire, by Irving, ii. 366-368.

**Colquhoun** of Camstradden. Baronage, by Douglas, 23, 438-439. Book of
   Dumbartonshire, by Irving, ii. 262-263.
   of Colquhoun. Baronage, by Douglas, 23-27. The Chiefs of Colquhoun,
      by Sir William Fraser, 2 vols. 4to (1869).* Historical Sketch of the
      Family of Colquhoun in Scotland.* Cartulary of Colquhoun of
      Colquhoun and Luss (1873).
   of Craigallian and Garscadden. Strathblane, by Guthrie Smith, 49.
   of Glins. Baronage, by Douglas, 24, 440. The Scottish Antiquary,
      iv. 77 ; vii. 158-161, with chart pedigree ; viii. 24.
   of Kenmure. Baronage, by Douglas, 440-441.
   of Killermont. Burke's Landed Gentry (1848-1925).
   of Luss. Douglas's Baronage, 23-27. Chiefs of Grant, by Sir W.
      Fraser. Pedigree of the Colquhoun of Luss, 4to (1877).* Book of
      Dumbartonshire, ii. 244-262. Scottish Antiquary, iv. 77. Herald
      and Genealogist, v. 90-92. Annals of Garelochside, by Maughan,
      32-39. Complete Baronetage, by G. E. C., ii. 293 ; iv. 426 ; v. 249.
      Burke's Peerage and Baronetage.
   in Sweden. One Year in Sweden, by H. Marryat, ii. 486, 489. Scottish
      Hist. Review, xxv. 295.
   of Tillyquhoun, Tullichewan. Douglas's Baronage, 27-28. Book of
      Dumbartonshire, ii. 211-212.
**Colquhoun-Stirling.** Lands . . . in Galloway, by M'Kerlie, v. 48.

**Colt.** Genealogical Memoirs of the Families of Colt and Coutts, by Charles
   Rogers (Cottonian Society, 1879). The Browns of Fordell, by
   Stodart, 206. The Colts of that Ilk and Gartsherrie, and of the
   English and American branches of that Family [by G. F. Russell
   Colt], (Edinburgh, 1887).* Burke's Landed Gentry (1848-1925).
   *See also* **Coutts.**

**Coltart** of Nether Laggan. Lands . . . in Galloway, by M'Kerlie, v. 51.
   *See also* **Coulthart.**

**Colvill** of Lesnesock. Paterson's History of Ayr, ii. 401. Paterson's Ayr
   and Wigton, i. 623-626.

**Colville.** Heraldry, by Nisbet (1742), ii. Ragman Roll, 27. Pedigree in
   Suppl. Case for the Duke of Buckingham and Chandos, in title of
   Lord Kinloss (1868).
   of Cleish. The Scots Peerage, ii. 552-573.
   Lord, Viscount, Colville of Culross. Claim of Charles John Colville,
      Baron Colville of Culross to vote at the elections of Scotch Peers :
      (Session Papers, 36, 84 of 1850). Eminent Men of Fife, by
      Conolly, 125. The Ancestry of Lord Colville of Culross, by
      G. M. Colville (London, 1887). The Scots Peerage, ii. 535-568.
      G. E. C.'s Complete Peerage, 2nd ed. Burke's Peerage. Debrett's
      Peerage.
   Lord Colville of Ochiltree. The Scots Peerage, ii. 569-575.
   of Dunduff and Barnhill. Geneal. Mag., v. 320.
   of Kincardine. The Scots Peerage, ii. 550-552.

**Colville** of Ochiltree.  Paterson's Ayr and Wigton, i. 623-626.  The Scots Peerage, ii. 536-546.
  of Oxnam.  The Scots Peerage, ii. 537-545.
  of East Wemyss.  The Scots Peerage, ii. 546-557.

**Colyear,** Earl of Portmore.  The Scots Peerage, vii. 88-97.  The Scottish Antiquary, xi. 61-63.

**Colyear-Robertson.**  Complete Baronetage, by G. E. C., iv. 81.

**Common,** Bedrule.  Tancred's Rulewater, 223-225.

**Competitors** for the Crown of Scotland.  Royal Genealogies, by Anderson (1732), 758.  Scottish Kings, by Sir A. H. Dunbar (1899), 111-112.

**Compton-Lundie** of Spital.  Burke's Landed Gentry (1898-1925).

**Comyn.**  Family Records of the Bruces and Comyns, by M. E. Cumming Bruce (Edinr. 1870).  Lands and their Owners in Galloway, by M'Kerlie (1878), iv. 465-469.  Stemmata Robertson et Durdin, by H. Robertson (1893-95), 110-112.*  J. H. Round *in* The Ancestor (1904), x. 104-119 ; xi. 129-135.
  Earl of Angus.  The Scots Peerage, i. 167.
  Lord of Badenoch.  The Scots Peerage, i. 503-510.  Scot. Hist. Soc., No. 56, 1908, *lxxix.*  Notes and Queries, 4th S., i. 608 ; ii. 302.
  Earl of Buchan.  Buchan, by Rev. J. B. Pratt (1858), 401-404.  The Scots Peerage, ii. 252-261.

**Congalton** of Congalton.  Baronage, by Douglas, 521-524.  Scottish N. and Q., 2nd S., viii. 67.

**Connal** of Parkhall.  Strathendrick, by Guthrie Smith, 227-228.

**Connell.**  House of Lords : Margaret Grierson, of Edinburgh, appellant and James Connell of Conheath, respondent (186—).

**Connon.**  Scottish N. and Q., 3rd S., iv. 134.

**Constable,** Forfarshire.  Four Perthshire Families, by Rogers, 91-110.*
  Viscount Dunbar.  The Scots Peerage, iii. 290-380.

**Constable-Maxwell,** Lord Herries.  The Scots Peerage, iv. 420-424.
  of Caerlaverock and Everingham.  Burke's Landed Gentry (1848-1858).  Lands and their Owners in Galloway, by M'Kerlie, v. 176.

**Cook,** Elie and Pittenweem.  East Neuk of Fife, by W. Wood, 2nd ed., 105.  Alexander Cowan, by C. B. Boog Watson, 48.*

**Cooke.**  Scottish N. and Q., 2nd S., ii. 107.

**Cooper** of Failford and Solsgirth.  Paterson's History of the County of Ayr, ii. 491-492.  Paterson's Ayr and Wigton, i. 767-773.  Burke's Landed Gentry (1863-1894).  Herald and Genealogist, viii. 193-196.
  *See also* **Couper.**

**Copeland.**  Scottish N. and Q., 2nd S., iii. 107-108, 125 ; iv. 127.

**Copland** of Colliestoun.  Heraldry, by Nisbet (1742), ii., Appx. 111.

**Corbet** of Sprouston.  Notes and Queries, 3rd S., ii. 448 ; iii. 18.

**Cornwall** of Bonhard.  Genealogy of the Family of Cornwall of Bonhard, by R. R. Stodart, 11 pp. (Edinr. 1877).*

**Corrie.** Records of the Corrie Family, 802-1899; by Jessie Elizabeth Corrie, 2 vols., 4to (London, 1899). The Early History of the Corries of Annandale, by Christopher Johnston, *in* Transactions of the Dumfriesshire and Galloway Nat. Hist. and Antiq. Soc. (1912-1913), 86. Further Notes on the Corries, by R. C. Reid, *ibid.* (1914-1915).

of Reidbank. Lands . . . in Galloway, v. 245.

**Corry** of Kelwood. Paterson's Ayr, ii. 291. Paterson's Ayr and Wigton, ii. 352-354.

**Corsane** of Auchengassel. Lands . . . in Galloway, v. 283.

of Meikleknox. Heraldry, by Nisbet (1742), ii., Appx. 119-121. Lands . . . in Galloway, by M'Kerlie, iii. 247-248. Pedigree annexed to Edgar's History of Dumfries, ed. R. C. Reid (Dumfries, 1915).

**Corse** or **Cross**, Glasgow. Some Old Families, by H. B. M'Call, 137.*

**Corser,** Edinburgh. Nisbet's Heraldic Plates, ed. Ross and Grant (1892), 114.

**Corstorphine** of Balcaithlie and Nydie. Geneal. Coll., by W. Macfarlane, 1750-51 ; Scot. Hist. Soc., ii. 201.

Forrester, Lord Forrester of. The Scots Peerage, iv. 80-100.

of Pittowie. Burke's Landed Gentry (1863-1914).

**Coulthart.** Burke's Landed Gentry (1848-1863). A Genealogical and Heraldic Account of the Coultharts of Coulthart and Collyn, Chiefs of the Name, from their first Settlement in Scotland, by George Parker Knowles (London, 1855).* Popular Genealogists, or the Art of Pedigree Making [by George Burnett, Lyon King-of-Arms], (Edinr. 1865). [An exposure of the above book, as is also] A Review, by Oswald Barron *in* The Ancestor (1904), iv. 61-80.

**Coupar,** Elphinstone, Lord. Angus or Forfarshire, by Warden, iii. 131. The Scots Peerage, ii. 576-577. G. E. C.'s Complete Peerage, 2nd ed.

**Couper** of Gogar. Paterson's History of Ayr, ii. 490. Paterson's Ayr and Wigton, i. 768-769. A Midlothian Village, by G. W. Selway, 29-30. W. S. Cooper *in* The Genealogist, 1st S., i. 257-266, 334. St David M. Kemys-Tynte *in* Genealogist, N. S., xxiv. 89-96, 216. Complete Baronetage, by G. E. C., ii. 445 ; vi., Appx. 70.

**Courtenay.** Notes and Queries, 6th S., v. 404.

**Couston,** in Clackmannan. The Scottish Antiquary (1893), vii., 67.

**Coutts,** Edinburgh. Memorials of the Haliburtons, by Sir Walter Scott, Bart. (1824, and 1877), 60-61. Geneal. Memoirs of the Family of Sir W. Scott, by Rogers (Grampian Club, 1877), *xxxvii-xxxix.* Genealogical Memoirs of the Family of Colt and Coutts, by the Rev. Charles Rogers (London, Cottonian Society, 1874). Notes and Queries, 7th S., xi. 84, 352, 397. The Scottish Antiquary, xi. 165. Coutts and Co., Bankers, Edinburgh and London : being the Memoir of a Family distinguished for its Public Services . . . by Ralph Richardson, illust., 166 pp. (1900).

**Coutts** of Grange, Pitteuchar and Bowhill. The Browns of Fordell, by Stodart, 207. Stephen's Inverkeithing and Rosyth (1921), 473-475.
Montrose. Geneal. Memoirs of the Family of Sir W. Scott, *xxxvii-xxxix*. John Coutts, or Notes on an Eminent Montrose Family, by J. G. Low (Montrose, 1892).
of Ochtercoull. The Browns of Fordell, 199-202.
of Reafield and Edinburgh. The Browns of Fordell, 202-206.

**Cowan.** Genealogical Table of the Descendants of Charles Cowan, from 1680 : compiled by Mrs Charles William Cowan, folio sheet (1889).*
Alexander Cowan, his Kinsfolk and Connections, by C. B. Boog Watson (1915, and Appx. 1917).*

**Cowane,** Stirling. The Stirling Antiquary, ed. W. B. Cook, ii. 168-178 ; iii. 23 ; iv. 201.

**Cowie** of Dufftown. Burke's Landed Gentry (1925, Suppl.).
Mains of Haulkerton. Fraser's Laurencekirk, 176-181.

**Cowper,** Lord Dingwall. Claim of F. T. de G., Earl Cowper, to be Lord Dingwall : (Sess. Papers C. of 1870, C. of 1871). The Scots Peerage, iii. 123-124.

**Craig.** Scottish N. and Q., xi. 157.
of Ballewan. Strathblane, by Guthrie Smith, 159-161.
of Colbeg. Strathblane, 66-68.
of Dalnair. Strathendrick, by Guthrie Smith, 220.
in Elgin. Young's Family of King of Newmill.

**Craigie** of Gairsay. Complete Baronetage, by G. E. C., iv. 444. Norton Smith's Orkney Armorials, 33-37.
of Kilgraston. Annals of a Border Club, by G. Tancred, 92.
of Lahill and Dumbarnie. East Neuk of Fife, by W. Wood, 2nd ed., 101-102.
of Stebbingrind. Zetland Family Histories, by F. J. Grant, 51-53.

**Craigie-Halkett** of Cramond. Burke's Landed Gentry (1848-1925).

**Craigingelt** of Craigingelt. The Stirling Antiquary, ii. 150-152.

**Craik** of Arbigland. Lands and their Owners in Galloway, iv. 154-155.
of Duchra. Lands . . . in Galloway, by M'Kerlie, iii. 150-151.
Fife. Kennoway, by A. S. Cunningham, 29-30.

**Cramond** of Cramond. Cramond, by J. P. Wood (1794), 39, 49-51, 59.
of Melgund and Auldbar. Cramond, by Wood, 51. Memorials of Angus and Mearns, by Jervise, ed. Gammack, ii. 71-72.
Beaumont, Baroness of. The Scots Peerage, ii. 578.
Richardson, Lord. The Scots Peerage, ii. 578-584.

**Cranstoun** of Corehouse. Burke's Landed Gentry (1858-1906).
of Cranstoun and Denholm. Nisbet's Heraldry, i. 361. The Scots Peerage, ii. 585-592.
Lord Cranstoun. The Scots Peerage, ii. 585-602.
of Dewar. Burke's Landed Gentry (1906).

**Craufuird** of Drumbeg.  Paterson's Ayr and Wigton, i. 223-227.

of Drumsoy.  Crawfurd's Shire of Renfrew (1818), 366-369.  Ayrshire Families, ii. 190-194.  Paterson's Ayr, i. 327-329.

**Craufurd** of Ardmillan.  The Principal Families in Ayrshire, by George Robertson, 2 vols. (Irvine, 1823), i. 222-226, with small tree.  The History of the County of Ayr, by Paterson, 2 vols. (1847, 1852), ii. 77. Ayr and Wigton, by Paterson, ii. 248-250.  Burke's Landed Gentry (1849-1898).  Scottish N. and Q., 3rd S., iv. 125-128, 143-147, 161-165, 179, 4 portraits ; v. 31.

of Auchenames and Crosbie.  Heraldry, by Nisbet (1742), ii., Appx. 94-96. Crawfurd's Shire of Renfrew, ed. Robertson, 80-82, 367-371.  Ayrshire Families, i. 168-178 ; ii. 194-204, 383-384.  Paterson's Ayr, ii. 139-143. Paterson's Ayr and Wigton, iii. 322-326.  Burke's Landed Gentry (1848-1925).  Herald and Genealogist, v. 172-175.  Some Old Families, by H. B. M'Call (1890), 149-150.

of Balgregan.  Ayrshire Families, ii. 167, 170, 182-183.

of Balshagray and Scotstoun.  Paterson's Ayr, ii. 500-502.

of Barbieston.  Paterson's Ayr and Wigton, i. 416.

of Barquharrie.  Paterson's Ayr, ii. 401.  Paterson's Ayr and Wigton, i. 618.

of Birkheid.  Ayrshire Families, i. 216-217.  Paterson's Ayr, i. 430. Paterson's Ayr and Wigton, iii. 177.

of Camlarg.  Ayrshire Families, ii. 171, 183-189.  Paterson's Ayr, i. 403-404.  Paterson's Ayr and Wigton, i. 378-382.

of Classlochie and Powmill.  Ayrshire Families, i. 187.

of Craufurdland.  Baronage, by Douglas, 431-434.  Cramond, by J. P. Wood, 62.  Ayrshire Families, i. 184-204, 382.  Paterson's Ayr, ii. 175-200.  Paterson's Ayr and Wigton, iii. 426-433.  Burke's Landed Gentry (1848-1925).

of Crosbie.  Paterson's Ayr and Wigton, iii. 311, 321-326.  *See also* **Craufurd** of Auchenames.

of Daleglis.  Paterson's Ayr, i. 365.  Paterson's Ayr and Wigton, i. 322-323.

of Dean.  Ayrshire Families, i. 186.

of Doonside.  Paterson's Ayr and Wigton, ii. 427-428.

of Drongan.  Ayrshire Families, ii. 180-183.  Paterson's History of Ayr, ii. 440.  Paterson's Ayr and Wigton, i. 719-721.

of Fergushill.  Ayrshire Families, i. 209-212.  Paterson's Ayr, ii. 504.

in Germany.  Ayrshire Families, i. 195.

of Giffordland.  Ayrshire Families, i. 212-216.  Paterson's Ayr, i. 428. Paterson's Ayr and Wigton, iii. 176-177.

of Grange.  Scottish N. and Q., 3rd S., iv. 163.

of Kerse.  Ayrshire Families, ii. 167-180.  Paterson's Ayr, i. 437-440. Paterson's Ayr and Wigton, i. 399-405.

of Kilbirnie.  Pont's Cuninghame, ed. Dobie, 230-233.  Ayrshire Families, i. 227-235.  Paterson's Ayr, ii. 114-116.  Paterson's Ayr and Wigton, i. 446 ; iii. 293.  Complete Baronetage, by G. E. C., ii. 348 ; v. 213. Burke's Commoners, iii. 181.  Landed Gentry (1846-1894).  Debrett's Baronetage.  Old Cartsburn, by George Williamson (1894).

**Craufurd** of Lefnoreis, Lochnoris. Paterson's Ayr, i. 355-357. Paterson's Ayr and Wigton, i. 326-331. Warrick's History of New Cumnock, 19-21.

of Loudoun. Heraldry, by Nisbet (1742), ii. Ragman Roll, 10. Ayrshire Families, ii. 158-166. Paterson's Ayr, ii. 318. Ayr and Wigton, iii. 543-545. The Scots Peerage, v. 488-490.

of Newark. Paterson's Ayr, ii. 355. Paterson's Ayr and Wigton, i. 444-445.

of Overton. Landed Gentry (1879).

of Possil. Paterson's Ayr, i. 431. Paterson's Ayr and Wigton, iii. 178.

of Skeldon. Paterson's Ayr, i. 440-441. Ayr and Wigton, i. 406-409.

of Smiddyshaw. Paterson's Ayr, ii. 427. Ayr and Wigton, i. 705.

in Sweden. One Year in Sweden, by H. Marryat, ii. 487.

**Craw** of Haughhead. Nisbet's Heraldic Plates, ed. Ross and Grant, 86.

**Crawford**, Lindsay, Earl of. Geneal. Coll. by W. Macfarlane, 1750-51 ; Scot. Hist. Soc., ii. 399-408. Claim of Mr John Lindsay Crawfurd to the title and estates of Crawfurd and Kilbirny, 4to (Paisley, 1819). The Crawford Peerage, . . . relating to the Illustrious Houses of Crawford and Kilbirnie ; including also a succinct Account of the Persecutions and Abuses to which John Lindsay Crawford . . . has been subjected [by Alexander Maxwell Adams, LL.D.], 4to (Edinr. 1829 ; 2nd ed. 1839). Examination of the Claim of John Lindsay Crawfurd to the Titles and Estates of Crawfurd and Lindsay, containing an Exposure of the Forgeries on which that Claim is founded, and a Refutation of the Statements in the Book entitled "The Crawfurd Peerage," by James Dobie, 4to, plates, $ix + 137 + 3$ pp. (Edinr. 1831). Sketch of the Case of John Lindsay Crawford, by Dr A. M. Adams (Edinr. 1834, and 1853). Case of J. L. Crawfurd, fol. pp. 50 and Appx. pp. 44, reprinted with Additions, 3 vols. 8vo (1849). Lives of the Lindsays, or a Memoir of the Houses of Crawford and Balcares, by Lord Lindsay, 4 vols. 8vo (Wigan, 1840). Peerage Claims, by J. Riddell. Crawford Peerage : Case and Petition of James, Earl of Balcarras, etc., and Petition of Robert Lindsay Crawfurd : (Session Papers, 206 of 1845 ; 47 of 1846 ; 231 of 1847 ; 135 of 1847-8 ; 347 of 1852-3). Report of Speeches of Counsel, etc. upon the Claim of James, Earl of Crawfurd and Balcarres to the Original Dukedom of Montrose, by Lord Lindsay, fol. (London, 1855). [A bibliographical catalogue of the Cases and Papers printed is given at p. ix of the Introduction. G. W. M.] Historical MSS. Commission (1871), 2nd Report. Scottish Antiquary, v. 25, 80. Angus or Forfarshire, i. 310-335. The Scots Peerage, iii. 1-151. Debrett's Peerage. Burke's Peerage. G. E. C.'s Complete Peerage, 2nd ed.

**Crawford**, Antigua. History of Antigua, by Oliver, i. 182-183.

Crail. Churchyard Monuments of Crail, by Erskine Beveridge, 108, 169-171.

of Highholme. The Scottish Antiquary, xvii. 212.

**Crawford** in Russia. Notes and Queries, 6th S., ii. 267.

North Fod. Scottish N. and Q., 3rd S., vii. 17.

of Woodside. Ayrshire Families, i. 241.

**Crawford-Leslie.** Burke's Landed Gentry (1925).

**Crawfuird** of Baidland. Ayrshire Families, i. 217-226. Paterson's Ayr, 418 ; ii. 78. Paterson's Ayr and Wigton, iii. 149-153. Burke's Landed Gentry (1849-1863). Scottish N. and Q., 3rd S., iv. 125.

**Crawfurd.** MS. History of the Crawfurds, by Mr Thomas Crawfurd. G. Crawfurd's Shire of Renfrew, ed. Robertson (1818), 119-124.

of Brownmuir. Paterson's Ayr, i. 277.

of Cartsburn. Crawfurd's Shire of Renfrew (1818), 416-417. Ayrshire Families, i. 240-245. Burke's Landed Gentry (1879-1900). Old Greenock, by G. Williamson, i. 250, 314. Old Cartsburn, a History of the Estate from 1669, by G. Williamson (Paisley, 1894).

of Crawfurd. Burke's Landed Gentry (1848).

of Dalmagregan. Crawfurd's Shire of Renfrew (1818), 365.

of Jordanhill. Douglas's Baronage, 429-431. Crawfurd's Shire of Renfrew (1818), 68-74, 346. Ayrshire Families, i. 236-240. Paterson's Ayr and Wigton, iii. 285. Old Cartsburn, by Williamson.

of Milton. Burke's Landed Gentry (1863-1879).

of Newfield. Ayrshire. Families, i. 180-183. Paterson's Ayr, ii. 39. Paterson's Ayr and Wigton, i. 488-490.

Sussex. Scottish N. and Q., 3rd S., iv. 125, 179-182, 200-202, 217.

of Thirdpart. Robertson's Ayrshire Families, i. 178-180. Archæol. and Hist. Coll. of Ayrshire and Galloway (1889), vi. 56-57.

of Tweeddale. Ayrshire Families, i. 187.

**Crawfurd-Pollok** of Pollok Castle. Complete Baronetage, by G. E. C., ii. 350.

**Crawmont** of Fullerton. Angus or Forfarshire, by Warden, iv. 305.

**Craven.** Genealogical Collections relating to the Family of Cravie or Craven in Scotland . . . by J. B. Craven (Kirkwall, 1910).*

**Crichton, Creichton.** Heraldry, by Nisbet (1722), i. 284-285. Great Historic Families of Scotland, by James Taylor [1887]. Family and Genealogical Sketches, by Rev. Thos. Sinton (Inverness, 1911).*

of Auchenskeoch. Lands . . . in Galloway, by M'Kerlie, iii. 345.

of Auchingoul. Tayler's Jacobites of Aberdeenshire, 135-136.

of Bottomcraig. Campbell's Balmerino, 558-562, 653.

of Carco. Folklore and Genealogies of Uppermost Nithsdale, by Wm. Wilson (Dumfries, 1904), 185-190.

of Cranstoun-Riddell. The Scottish Antiquary, xiv. 170.

Lord Crichton. Warrick's History of New Cumnock, 40. The Scots Peerage, iii. 52-68.

Lord Crichton of Frendraught. The Scots Peerage, iv. 129-134.

Lord Crichton of Sanquhar. The Scots Peerage, iii. 219-238.

of Eliock. Uppermost Nithsdale, 197-202. Douglas Crichton *in* Proc. Soc. Antiq. Scotl. (1909), 296-308.

**Crichton** of Frendraught. Thanage of Fermartyn, by Temple, 141-154.
　of Gairland. Uppermost Nithsdale, 191-193.
　of Libry. Uppermost Nithsdale, 195-196.
　of Lugton and Gilmerton. Notes and Queries, 7th S., viii. 247.
　of Naughton. Campbell's Balmerino, 498-506, 645-646.
　of Newhall. Scot. Hist. Review, xvi. 178-180.
　of Quarter. Buchan and Paton's History of Peeblesshire, iii. 288.
　of Ryehill. Uppermost Nithsdale, 173-183.
　of Sanquhar. The Scottish Antiquary (1898), xiii. 12-16. Uppermost
　　Nithsdale, 161-171. Sanquhar and the Crichtons, by Douglas
　　Crichton, 38 pp. (Dumfries, 1907).

**Crichton-Dalrymple, Crichton-Stuart,** Earls of Dumfries. The Scots
　Peerage, iii. 236-238.

**Croc** of Crocstoun and Neilston. Crawfurd's Shire of Renfrew (1818),
　39, 46.

**Croll,** Hill of Haulkerton. Fraser's Laurencekirk, 185-187.

**Cromartie,** Mackenzie, Earl of. Notes and Queries, 8th S., i. 475 ; ii. 450 ;
　iv. 461 ; vi. 205 ; viii. 55. The Earls of Cromartie, by Sir Wm.
　Fraser, 2 vols. 4to, illust. (Edinr. 1876).* Great Historic Families of
　Scotland, by Jas. Taylor [1887]. Nisbet's Heraldic Plates, ed. Ross
　and Grant (1892), 112-114. G. E. C.'s Complete Peerage, 2nd ed.
　The Scots Peerage, iii. 69-86. Burke's Peerage. Debrett's Peerage.

**Crombie** of Phesdo, Thornton and Conveth. Fraser's Laurencekirk, 93.
　of Thornton and Pittarrow. Memorials of Angus and the Mearns, by
　　Jervise, ed. Gammack, ii. 170, 180.

**Crosbie** of Crosbie Park. MS. by John Riddell, W.S., and Robert Riddell,
　in the possession of the Society of Writers to the Signet.
　of Culcottes and Holm. Pedigree annexed to Edgar's History of
　　Dumfries, ed. R. C. Reid (Dumfries, 1915).
　of Kipp. Notes and Queries, 7th S., ii. 507.

**Cross-Buchanan** of Auchintoshan. Strathendrick, by J. Guthrie Smith, 338.

**Cruden,** Aberdeen. Memoir of J. Young, Aberdeen . . . ed. Johnston, 241.*

**Cruickshank** of Hoy. Orkney Armorials, by Norton Smith, 37-38.
　of Langley Park. Baronage of Angus and Mearns, by D. M. Peter
　　(1856), 62-63. Angus or Forfarshire, by A. J. Warden (1880),
　　184-185. Burke's Landed Gentry (1858-Suppl. 1925)
　of Stracathro. Pedigree of the Cruickshanks of Stracathro ; collected
　　by E. G. G. Cruickshank in 1847. Lith. sheet (Elgin). Scottish
　　N. and Q., 3rd S., v. 209.

**Cruikshank,** Aberdeen. Memoir of James Young, Aberdeen, and Rachel
　Cruikshank his Spouse . . . by Alex. Johnston, 1861, ed. Lt.-Col.
　W. Johnston (1894), 121-128.*

**Crum-Ewing.** Landed Gentry (1863-1906).

**Crumbie.** MS. Collections by Alexander Deuchar, relating to a Crumbie
　land claim of early nineteenth century ; in possession of Society
　of Genealogists of London.

**Cullen**, Aberdeen. Scottish N. and Q., i. 195.

**Cumine** of Auchry. Young's Annals of Elgin (1879), 653-656, 674.
of Kininmonth. Tayler's Jacobites of Aberdeenshire, 137-138.
of Pitullie. Jacobites of Aberdeenshire, 138-140.

**Cuming, Cumming** of Altyre. Douglas's Baronage, 331-335.
of Airdrie. Complete Baronetage, by G. E. C., iv. 371.
of Auchry. Douglas's Baronage, 336-338. The Family of King of Newmill, by R. Young.
of Culter. Nisbet's Heraldry (1742), ii. Appx. 59-60. A Table showing the Families descended from Sir Alexander Cumming of Coulter, created a Scots baronet in 1695, by H. B. Tomkins (1877). Miscellaneous Broadsides, chiefly Scottish, i. B. M. Pressmark, 1891, c. 3. Three items. Scottish N. and Q., 1st S., vi. 61 ; 2nd S., ii. 31 ; 3rd S., i. 14. Complete Baronetage, by G. E. C., iv. 370.
of Cummingwood. Complete Baronetage, by G. E. C., iv. 372.
of Earnside. Paterson's History of Ayr, i. 442.
Georgia. History of the Habersham Family, by Dr J. G. B. Bulloch (Columbia, S. C., 1901), 54-55.
of Lochtervandich. Annals of Elgin, by Young, 653-656, 674. The Thurburns, by Lt.-Col. F. A. V. Thurburn, 36. Scottish N. and Q., 2nd S., iii. 170 ; vii. 91. The Family of King of Newmill, by R. Young (Elgin, 1904).
of Logie. Douglas's Baronage, 336. Annals of Elgin, by Young (1879), 664-665.
of Relugas and Presley. Douglas's Baronage, 338-339. Notes and Queries, 8th S., v. 108, 233. The Scottish Antiquary, xiii. 193.

**Cumyn.** See **Comyn.**

**Cuningham(e, Cunningham(e.** Nisbet's Heraldry (1722), i. 195-198, Crawfurd's Shire of Renfrew (1818), 114-118, 398. Tree of the Families of Cunninghame and Erskine. Notes and Queries, 4th S., iii. 605 ; iv. 179 ; vii. 347 ; xi. 488 : 6th S., iv. 47 ; v. 268, 359 ; viii. 517 ; ix. 417, 496 : 7th S., iv. 196 ; v. 67, 169, 272 ; viii. 104 ; ix. 76. [Robertson, in his "Ayrshire Families," gives this table of variant spellings : Cuningham, by Glengarnock, 2nd family. Cuninghame, by Caddel, Monkredding, etc. Cunningham, by Baidland, Clonbeith, etc. Cunninghame, by Glencairn, Corsehill, etc.]

**Cuningham** of Cayen, St Kitts. Ayrshire Families, i. 316-318.
of Dankeith. Paterson's Ayr, ii. 478. Ayr and Wigton, i. 739-741.
of Enterkine. Paterson's Ayr, ii. 487. Ayr and Wigton, i. 766.

**Cuninghame** of Balgownie. Burke's Landed Gentry (1858-1925).
of Boarland. Paterson's Ayr and Wigton, iii. 234.
of Bridgehouse. Ayrshire Families, i. 318-320. Paterson's Ayr, ii. 455. Ayr and Wigton, iii. 580-589. Scottish Surnames, by James Paterson (1866), 10-19. Lands . . . in Galloway, by M'Kerlie, iii. 151-154.
of Brouneshill. Paterson's Ayr, ii. 474, 492. Ayr and Wigton, i. 471, 763.

**Cuninghame** of Caddell and Thornton. Ayrshire Families, i. 285-289. Burke's Commoners, ii. 349, 526. Burke's Landed Gentry (1848-1879). Paterson's History of Ayr, i. 231-232.

of Cangé in Touraine. MS. Notes by Mrs Margaret Stuart, in possession of the Lyon Office.

of Caprington. Douglas's Baronage, 265-268. Case of Sir Robert Keith Dick Cunyngham of Prestonfield v. Thomas Smith Cuninghame of Caprington, 4to, plates and pedigrees (1848). Paterson's Ayr, ii. 410-412, 497-500. Ayr and Wigton, i. 646-652. Landed Gentry (1875-1925). Complete Baronetage, by G. E. C., ii. 387.

of Collellan or Clolynane. Paterson's Ayr, ii. 37-38. Ayr and Wigton, i. 436-440.

of Craigends. Crawfurd's Shire of Renfrew, ed. Robertson (1818), 37, 97-98. Burke's Landed Gentry (1879-1925).

of Creall. One Year in Sweden, by H. Marryat, ii. 487-488.

of Drumquhassle, Mugdock Mitchell, and Blairquhosh. Strathblane, by Guthrie Smith, 84-90, 193.

of Duchra. Lands . . . in Galloway, by M'Kerlie, iii. 151-154.

of Glengarnock. Ayrshire Families, i. 309-312, 313-318. Strathendrick, by Guthrie Smith, 228-230. Pont's Cuninghame, ed. Dobie (1876), 168-178, 179-181. Paterson's Ayr, ii. 117-120, 120-121. Ayr and Wigton, iii. 289-291, 292. Notes and Queries, 8th S., ii. 429, 451, 498.

of Laigland. Paterson's Ayr, i. 210. Ayr and Wigton, i. 149.

of Lainshaw. Ayrshire Families, i. 318-320. Paterson's Ayr, ii. 455. Scottish Surnames, by James Paterson, 10-19. Lands . . . in Galloway, by M'Kerlie, iii. 154. Burke's Landed Gentry (1858-1925).

of Monkredding. Ayrshire Families, i. 321-322. Paterson's Ayr, ii. 254. Ayr and Wigton, iii. 514, 516.

of Polquhairn. Paterson's Ayr, ii. 401, 522. Ayr and Wigton, i. 631-632.

**Cunningham** of Auchinskeith. Paterson's Ayr, ii. 413. Ayr and Wigton, i. 645.

of Baidland. Ayrshire Families, i. 281-284. Paterson's Ayr, i. 427-428. Ayr and Wigton, iii. 153-157.

of Balbougie. Stephen's Inverkeithing (1921), 156-157.

of Balgair. Strathendrick, by Guthrie Smith, 229-230.

of Balglas. Strathendrick, 246.

of Bandalloch. Nisbet's Heraldry, ii., Appx. 297-298. Landed Gentry (1879).

of (West) Barns. East Neuk of Fife, by W. Wood, 2nd ed., 397-399.

of Bloak. Warrick's History of New Cumnock (1899), 274.

of Bonytoun. Upper Ward of Lanarkshire, by Irving and Murray, ii. 331.

of Broomhill. Caithness Family History, by Henderson, 201-208.

Earl of Carrick. The Scots Peerage, iv. 227.

of Clonbeith. Ayrshire Families, i. 294-295, 321. Paterson's Ayr, ii. 253. Ayr and Wigton, iii. 489.

of Drumquhassill. Nisbet's Heraldry, ii., Appx. 297-298. Scottish N. and Q., 2nd S., viii. 159.

**Cunningham** of Gogar. Delegates' Examinations, xxiii., Nos. 20, 21, 1699, *in* Dramatis Personæ, ed. Sherwood (March 1916).

of Hyndhope. Annals of a Border Club, by G. Tancred, 93-95.

of Kirkland. Paterson's Ayr, ii. 221. Ayr and Wigton, iii. 475-476. Complete Baronetage, by G. E. C., ii. 153.

of Lambrughton. Complete Baronetage, by G. E. C., iv. 273.

of Leithenhopes. Burke's Landed Gentry (1914-1925).

of Mountgreenan. Ayrshire Families, i. 323-325. Paterson's Ayr, ii. 250-252. Ayr and Wigton, iii. 512.

of Okehampton. Notes and Queries, 6th S., i. 61, 285, 359 ; ii. 175.

of Tour. Paterson's Ayr and Wigton, iii. 475-476.

**Cunninghame** of Aiket. Pont's Cuninghame, 1604-8, ed. Dobie (1876), 64-67. The Principal Families in Ayrshire, by George Robertson, 2 vols. (Irvine, 1823), i. 257-261. History of the County of Ayr, by J. Paterson, 2 vols. (1847, 1852), ii. 49-53. History of Ayr and Wigton, by Paterson, iii. 222-226.

of Ashinyards. Ayrshire Families, i. 262-265. Paterson's Ayr, ii. 248-249.

of Auchenharvie. Ayrshire Families, i. 269-281. Paterson's Ayr, ii. 497-500. Ayr and Wigton, iii. 563-567. The Complete Baronetage, by G. E. C., ii. 153, 397 ; iv. 295. Burke's Extinct Baronetcies.

of Carlung. Ayrshire Families, i. 290-293. Paterson's Ayr, ii. 143. Ayr and Wigton, iii. 326.

of Corsehill. Crawfurd's Shire of Renfrew (1818), 400-402. Ayrshire Families, i. 299-303. Paterson's Ayr, ii. 459-460. Ayr and Wigton, iii. 589-593. Archæol. and Hist. Coll. of Ayr and Wigton (1884), iv. 65-66. Complete Baronetage, by G. E. C., iv. 285. The Scots Peerage, iv. 238. Debrett's Baronetage.

of Craigcurran. Crawfurd's Shire of Renfrew (1818), 405-406.

of Cunninghamhead. Ayrshire Families, i. 303-308. Paterson's Ayr, i. 450. Ayr and Wigton, iii. 205-208. Pont's Cuninghame, ed. Dobie (1876), 275-280. Complete Baronetage, by G. E. C., ii. 325. Burke's Extinct Baronetcies.

of Finnick. Strathendrick, by Guthrie Smith, 210-211, 216.

of Glencairn. MS. Genealogy by Robert Mylne. Nisbet's Heraldry (1742), ii., Appx. 43-45.

Earl of Glencairn. The Scots Peerage, iv. 222-252.

of Kilmaurs. Nisbet's Heraldry, ii., Appx. 43-45. Ayrshire Families, i. 246-257. Paterson's Ayr, ii. 210-217. Ayr and Wigton, iii. 466-474. The Scots Peerage, iv. 224, 228.

Lord Kilmaurs. The Scots Peerage, iv. 232-252.

of Robertland. Ayrshire Families, i. 325-329, 387. Paterson's Ayr, ii. 461-462. Ayr and Wigton, iii. 607-610. Complete Baronetage, by G. E. C., ii. 384.

of Wattiestoun. Ayrshire Families, i. 354, 387.

**Cunninghame-Fairlie** of Robertland and Fairlie. Ayrshire Families, i. 329-330 ; ii. 48-50. Paterson's Ayr and Wigton, i. 478-486. Complete Baronetage, by G. E. C., ii. 384.

**Cunninghame-Graham** of Ardoch.   Burke's Landed Gentry (1858-1925).

**Cunyngham** of Polmaise.   Nisbet's Heraldry, ii., Appx. 297-298.   Peebles-shire Localities, by Renwick, 552.

**Cunynghame** of Conheath, Woodhall and Dumfries.   Pedigree annexed to Edgar's History of Dumfries, ed. by R. C. Reid (Dumfries, 1915).

of Gilbertfield.   The Scottish Antiquary, viii. 138.

of Milncraig.   Paterson's Ayr, ii. 504-506.   Ayr and Wigton, i. 239-241.   Debrett's Baronetage.

of Whitehurst.   Ayrshire Families, i. 263, 269.

**Curle** of Priorwood.   Annals of a Border Club, by Tancred, 95-99.

**Currie** in Sweden.   One Year in Sweden, by H. Marryat, ii. 499.

**Cuthbert** of Castlehill.   History of the Habersham Family, by J. G. B. Bulloch, M.D. (Columbia, S.C., 1901), 49.   The Cuthberts of Castlehill and their descendants in South Carolina and Georgia, by J. G. B. Bulloch, M.D. (Washington, 1908).

of Daleglis.   Paterson's History of Ayr, i. 365.   Paterson's Ayr and Wigton, i. 324-325.

of Drakies.   Scottish N. and Q., 3rd S., iii. 176.

Inverness-shire.   The Scottish Antiquary, ix. 93.

**Cutlar** of Orroland.   Lands . . . in Galloway, by M'Kerlie, v. 104-108, 205.

**Cutlar-Fergusson.**   Lands . . . in Galloway, v. 108.

**Daer,** Douglas, Lord.   The Scots Peerage, vii. 516-525.

**Dalgarno.**   Scottish N. and Q., ix. 117-118.

**Dalgleish,** Hobkirk.   Tancred's Rulewater, 149.

of Lauriston.   Cramond, by J. P. Wood, 41, 43.

of Scotscraig.   Debrett's Baronetage (after 1896).   Pedigree *in* Playfair's Notes on the Scottish Family of Playfair.*

of Tinnygask.   The Scottish Antiquary, xii. 91, 138.   Dalgleish of Tinnygask, by the Marquis of Ruvigny.   8 pp. (London. 1901).   Revised, corrected and reprinted from the Geneal. Mag., v. 315-320.

of West Grange.   Burke's Landed Gentry (1875).

**Dalhousie,** Ramsay, Baron, Earl of, Marquess of.   Biographical Peerage (1808), 167.   Historical MSS. Commission (1870), 1st Report (1871), 2nd Report.   Angus and Forfarshire, by A. J. Warden, i. 415-419.   Burke's Peerage.   Debrett's Peerage.   The Scots Peerage, iii. 87-110.   G. E. C.'s Complete Peerage.   The Panmure Papers (1908).

**Dalkeith,** Scott, Earl of.   The Scots Peerage, ii. 237.   G. E. C.'s Complete Peerage.

**Dallas.**   History of the Family of Dallas from the twelfth century, by James Dallas.   4to, illust. and Geneal. Charts, 620 pp. (Edinr. 1921).

of Budzet.   James Dallas *in* Genealogist, 1st S., iv. 121-128.

of Cantray.   Antiquarian Notes, by C. Fraser-Mackintosh (1897), ii. 435-436.

of Little Cantray.   James Dallas *in* Genealogist, 1st S., iii. 406.

**Dalmahoy** of Carnbee.   The Scottish Antiquary, viii. 138.
   of Dalmahoy.   Baronage, by Douglas, 549-551.   Account of the Family
     of Dalmahoy of that Ilk and of the Family of Falconer, by
     T. Falconer (London, 1865).   The Family of Dalmahoy of Dalmahoy,
     by Thos. Falconer, 55 pp. (Aberdare, 1868 ; Edinr. 1870).*   Nisbet's
     Heraldic Plates, ed. Ross and Grant, 92-94.   Notes and Queries,
     3rd S., ix. 389, 423 ; xi. 8, 200, 244, 302 ; xii. 53.   Com-
     plete Baronetage, by G. E. C., iv. 309.   Burke's Extinct
     Baronetcies.
   Eddleston.   Peeblesshire Localities, by Renwick, 37.
**Dalmeny,** Primrose, Lord.   Complete Peerage, by G. E. C., ed. Gibbs
     (1910).   The Scots Peerage, vii. 221-229.
**Dalrymple.**   Notes and Queries, 3rd S., ii. 307 ; iv. 449 ; viii. 175, 461 ;
     ix. 193 ; x. 82.
   of Cousland.   The Scots Peerage, viii. 120-123.
   of Cuning Park.   Paterson's History of Ayr, i. 211 ; ii. 520.   Paterson's
     Ayr and Wigton, i. 140-142.
   Viscount Dalrymple.   The Scots Peerage, viii. 149-164.
   of Hailes.   Historical MSS. Commission (1873), 4th Report, 529.   Burke's
     Extinct Baronetcies.   Burke's Peerage and Baronetage.   The
     Complete Baronetage, by G. E. C., iv. 396.   The Scots Peerage,
     viii. 143-146.
   of Killoch.   The Complete Baronetage, by G. E. C., iv. 379.
   of Langlee.   Annals of a Border Club, by G. Tancred, 99.
   of Newhailes.   Historical MSS. Commission (1873), 4th Report, pt. 1.
     Burke's Peerage and Baronetage.   Debrett's Baronetage.
   of North Berwick.   The Complete Baronetage, by G. E. C., iv. 381.
     The Scots Peerage, vii. 125-129.
   of Orangefield.   Paterson's History of Ayr, ii. 387.   Ayr and Wigton,
     i. 598-600.   The Dalrymples of Langlands, by John Shaw, Bath
     [1868] 6, 22, 37-38.*
   of Stair.   Paterson's Ayr and Wigton, i. 725-733.   Chart Pedigree *in*
     Seton's Memoir of Chancellor Seton (Edinr. 1882).   Lines from
     my Log-books, by Admiral Sir J. C. Dalrymple Hay (Edinr. 1898),
     331-333.   Complete Baronetage, by G. E. C., iii. 346.   Lands . . . in
     Galloway, by M'Kerlie (1906), i. 526-541.
   Earl of Stair.   Genealogical Account of the Dalrymples of Stair,
     Earls of Stair, by the Hon. Hew Hamilton Dalrymple, illust. with
     portraits, etc. (1909).*   G. E. C.'s Complete Peerage, 2nd ed.
     The Scots Peerage, viii. 115-119.   Burke's and other Annual
     Peerages.
   U.S.A.   The name of Dalrymple, with a genealogy of one branch of
     the family in the United States, by W. H. Dalrymple (Haverhill,
     Mass. 1878).
   of Waterside.   Some Old Families, by H. B. M'Call, with chart pedigree,
     27-34, iv. Appx.*
**Dalrymple-Hamilton** of Bargany.   The Scots Peerage, viii. 127, 161.

**Dalrymple-Hamilton-MacGill.** The Complete Baronetage, by G. E. C., iv. 379.

**Dalrymple-Hay.** Lands . . . in Galloway, by M'Kerlie, 2nd ed. (1906), i. 573, 582. Complete Baronetage, by G. E. C., v. 323.

**Dalrymple-Horn-Elphinstone** of Horn and Logie Elphinstone. The Scots Peerage, viii. 133. Burke's Peerage and Baronetage.

**Dalyell** of Binns. Case for Major James Bruce Wilkie Dalyell of Binns, claiming to be placed on the official roll of Baronets (1872). Additional Appx. (1914). Historical MSS. Commission (1884), 9th Report. Complete Baronetage, by G. E. C., iv. 334. Burke's Peerage and Baronetage. Scot. Hist. Review, xxii. 236.

of Lingo. Eminent Men of Fife, by Conolly, 137-139. East Neuk of Fife, by W. Wood, 2nd ed., 288-291. Burke's Landed Gentry (1858-1925).

**Dalzell,** Earl of Carnwath. The Scots Peerage, ii. 395-420.
Lord Dalzell, ii. 407-408.

of Dalzell. Nisbet's Heraldic Plates, ed. Ross and Grant, 30-32. Concerning an Old Scottish Surname (1883). Scottish Antiquary, iii. 5. J. B. Dalzell *in* Scot. Hist. Review (1911), vii. 69-72. The Scots Peerage, ii. 398-405.

of Glenae. Complete Baronetage, by G. E. C., iv. 249. The Scots Peerage, ii. 408-417. Burke's Landed Gentry (1875-1925).

of Straith. Notes and Queries, 6th S., xi. 187.

**Dalziel.** Heraldry, by Nisbet (1722), i. 265.

of Eliock. Folk Lore and Genealogies of Uppermost Nithsdale, by Wilson, 202-205.

of Merryhill. Paterson's Ayr and Wigton, iii. 611.

**Danielston** of Mauldislie. Upper Ward of Lanarkshire, by Irving and Murray, ii. 407-408.

**Darleith** of Darleith. Book of Dumbartonshire, by Irving, ii. 210.

**Darnley,** Lennox, Earl of. The Scots Peerage, v. 363-371.
Stewart, Lord. Notes and Queries, 3rd S., x. 379; xii. 172. The Scots Peerage, ii. 168-170; v. 348-361.

**Darroch** of Gourock. Crawfurd's Shire of Renfrew (1818), 425. Burke's Landed Gentry (1858-1925).

**D'Aubigny,** Stewart, Lord. The Scots Peerage, v. 356-362. Some Account of the Stuarts of Aubigny in France, by Lady E. Cust (1891).*

**Davidson.** Davidson Genealogy, by C. T. M'Cready, Sheet (1867). Antiquarian Notes, by C. Fraser-Mackintosh, i. 175. Confederacy of Clan Chattan, by C. Fraser-Mackintosh, 123-128, 186.

of Achingils and Buckies. Caithness Family History, by Henderson, 301-303.

of Cantray. Dallas's Family of Dallas, 521. Burke's Landed Gentry (Suppl. 1849-1925).

K

**Davidson** of Carnbrogie. Scottish N. and Q., 3rd S., vi. 4.
of Curriehill. Complete Baronetage, by G. E. C. (1903), iii. 334.
of Drumley. Paterson's History of the County of Ayr, ii. 493. Paterson's Ayr and Wigton, i. 765.
of Greenan(e. Paterson's County of Ayr, ii. 353. Ayr and Wigton, i. 434-435.
Hyndlie. Annals of a Border Club, by G. Tancred, 34, 35.
of Inchmarlo. Pedigree of the Davidson and Francis Families (London, 1883). Burke's Landed Gentry (1858-1925).
of Muirhouse. Cramond, by J. P. Wood, 23, 28. The Ancestry of Randall Thomas Davidson, D.D., Archbishop of Canterbury, by Rev. Adam Philip (London, 1903). Burke's Landed Gentry (1894-1925). Burke's Peerage (after 1929).
of Newton. Scottish N. and Q., 2nd S., i. 50. House of Gordon, ed. J. M. Bulloch (1903), i. *lxxiii.*
of Pennyglen. Paterson's Ayr, ii. 353. Ayr and Wigton, i. 439.
of Tulloch. Burke's Landed Gentry (1863-1925).
of Wolflaw. Rogers' Four Perthshire Families, 29-30.*

**Daw,** Crail. Churchyard Monuments of Crail, by Erskine Beveridge, 1893, 76-88, with chart pedigree.

**Dawson,** Aberdeen. Scottish N. and Q., 2nd S., v. 144, 189.
of Manor. Logie, by Rev. Dr Menzies Fergusson, ii. 113-114.

**Delap.** *See* **Dunlop.**

**De l'Ard.** The Scottish Antiquary, viii. 185 ; ix. 45, 190-192.

**De la val** of Dalziel. Heraldry, by Nisbet (1742), ii. Ragman Roll, 45.

**Deloraine,** Scott, Earl of. The Scots Peerage, iii. 111-114.

**Dempster** of Auchterless. Temple's Thanage of Fermartyn, 114-117.
of Balbougie. Stephen's Inverkeithing and Rosyth (1921), 151-156.
of Bothers. Angus or Forfarshire, by Warden, iii. 15.
of Careston. Angus or Forfarshire, iii. 69-70.
of Muiresk, Pitliver, etc. Baronage, by Douglas, 531-533.
of Restenneth and Dunnichen. Angus or Forfarshire, iii. 197-200. Memorials of Angus and the Mearns, by Jervise, ed. Gammack, ii. 216, 335-336. Burke's Landed Gentry (1875).
of Pitforthie. Angus or Forfarshire, iii. 29.
of Skibo. Burke's Landed Gentry (1848-1875).

**Denem, Denham, Denholm** of Westshiels. Cramond, by J. P. Wood, 26. Notice of Denham in the Coltness Collections. Notes and Queries, 7th S., xii. 386. Upper Ward of Lanarkshire, by Irving and Murray, ii. 527-528. Scottish Antiquary, v. 83-86 ; vi. 158 ; viii. 64. G. E. C.'s Complete Baronetage, iv. 363.

**Denham-Steuart** of Coltness and Westshiels. The Stewarts (Stewart Soc. Magazine), iv. 71.

**Denholm** of Muirhouse. Cramond, by J. P. Wood, 26.

**Dennistoun** of Colgrain. Crawfurd's Shire of Renfrew (1818), 406. Some Account of the Family of Dennistoun of Colgrain, 4to, with geneal. chart (Dumbarton, 1859).* Scottish Historical Review (April 1918). Garelochside, by Maughan, 277-281. Book of Dumbartonshire, by Irving, ii. 307, 320-343.

of Dalchurne. Irving's Dumbartonshire, ii. 188, 314.

of Dennistoun, *or* Denzelstoun. Crawfurd's Shire of Renfrew, 94. Burke's Commoners, iii. 222. Burke's Landed Gentry (1848-1925). Scot. Hist. Review, xv. 241-244. Book of Dumbartonshire, ii. 337-343 ; iii., portrait.

of Golfhill. Book of Dumbartonshire, iii., portrait. Burke's Landed Gentry.

**Dennistoun - Brown** of Balloch. Book of Dumbartonshire, ii. 216 ; iii., portrait.

**Denny,** Dumbarton. Book of Dumbartonshire, by Irving, iii., portrait.

**Denune** of Catbole. Baronage, by Douglas, 456-458.

**De Quincy** of Fawside and Leuchars. The Genealogist, N. S., vii. 19-20. W. W. Ireland *in* Proc. Soc. Antiq. Scotl. (1898), 275-294 ; (1900), 241-251 [reprinted as pamphlet]. Joseph Bain *in* Proc. Soc. Antiq. Scotl. (1899), 124-128. Charters . . . relating to the Abbey of Inchaffray ; Scot. Hist. Soc., No. 56 (1908), *lxxxvi-ix.*

**Deskford,** Ogilvy, Lord. The Scots Peerage, iv. 26 41.

**Deuchar** of Deuchar. Baronage of Angus and Mearns, by D. M. Peter (1856), 67. Angus or Forfarshire, by Warden, iii. 274-276.

**De Valoniis.** Registrum de Panmure.

**Dewar,** Antigua. History of Antigua, by Oliver, i. 199-202.

of Vogrie. Burke's Landed Gentry (1898-1925).

**Dick** of Braid. On the Connection of the Earls of Morton and Dick of Braid with the Earldom of Orkney and Lordship of Zetland, by David Marshall, 44 pp. *in* Proc. Soc. Antiq. Scotl. (1889). Douglas's Baronage, 268-271, 274. Complete Baronetage, by G. E. C., ii. 448. Burke's Landed Gentry (1894), 1014. The Herald and Genealogist, viii. 257-269.

of Craighouse. Douglas's Baronage, 271. Complete Baronetage, by G. E. C., vi., Appx. 74.

of Fracafield. The Herald and Genealogist, viii. 267-269. Zetland Family Histories, by F. J. Grant, 54-59.

of Grange. Douglas's Baronage, 271-272. *See also* **Dick-Lauder.**

of Pitkerro. Angus or Forfarshire, by A. J. Warden, iv. 160. Monifieth, by J. Malcolm, 345.

of Prestonfield. Douglas's Baronage, 272-273. Curiosities of a Scots Charta Chest, 1600-1800, with the Travels and Memoranda of Sir Alexander Dick, Baronet ; ed. by Hon. Mrs Atholl Forbes, 4to, portrait and facsimiles (Edinr. 1897). Complete Baronetage, by G. E. C., iv. 306, 445.

**Dick-Cunyngham** of Prestonfield.   Burke's Peerage and Baronetage. Complete Baronetage, by G. E. C., iv. 445.

**Dick-Lauder** of Fountainhall.   The Grange of St Giles, the Bass and other Baronial Homes of the Dick-Lauder Family, by Mrs Stewart Smith, 4to, 123 portraits and illustrations (Edinr. 1898).   Burke's Peerage and Baronetage.   Complete Baronetage, by G. E. C., iv., 360.

**Dickson.**   Dickson Genealogy, by C. T. M'Cready, sheet (Dublin, 1868). The Scotch Border Clan Dickson, etc., by B. Homer Dixon (Toronto, 1884).*   The Border, or Riding Clans, followed by a History of the Clan Dickson, by B. Homer Dixon, 4to, 224 pp. (Albany, N.Y., 1889).*

**Dickson** of Badinsgill.   Buchan's History of Peeblesshire, iii. 155.

of Broughton.   Annals of a Tweeddale Parish, by Rev. A. Baird, 35.

of Chatto.   Burke's Landed Gentry (1894-1906).

of Clocksbrig.   Angus or Forfarshire, by Warden, 290.

of Corstorphine.   Burke's Landed Gentry (1894-1925).

of Hartree and Kilbucho.   History of Peeblesshire, by Chambers, 445. Peeblesshire Localities, by Renwick (1897), 267-268.   Annals of a Tweeddale Parish, 118-129.   Landed Gentry (1886-1906).   History of Peeblesshire, by Buchan and Paton, iii. 316-324, 328.

of Hassendeanburn and Chatto.   Annals of a Border Club, by G. Tancred, 99-104.

of Inveresk.   Analecta Scotica, ii. 56.

of Little Keithock.   Baronage of Angus and Mearns, by Peter, 369.

Montrose.   Eminent Arbroathians, by J. M. M'Bain, 277.

of Monybuie.   Lands . . . in Galloway, by M'Kerlie, iii. 92.   Burke's Landed Gentry (1886-1925).

of Ormiston.   Buchan's History of Peeblesshire, ii. 407-408.

of Smithfield.   Buchan's Peeblesshire, ii. 336.

of Sornbeg.   Complete Baronetage, by G. E. C., iv. 368.   Burke's Extinct Baronetcies.

of Stow.   Burke's Landed Gentry (1921-1925).

of Sydenham.   Border Memories, by W. Riddell Carre, 259.   Memoirs of Susan Sibbald, 1783-1812, ed. Hett (London, 1926), 109, 117.

of Whitslade.   Annals of a Tweeddale Parish, 81-82.   Buchan's Peeblesshire, iii. 293.

**Dingwall,** Lord ; title held by the Families of Butler, Cowper, Herbert, Keith, Nassau d'Auverquerque, Preston.   The Scots Peerage, iii. 115-125.   G. E. C.'s Complete Peerage, ed. Gibbs.   Case of Francis Thomas De Grey, Earl Cowper, on his claim to the title of Dingwall : Supplementary Case and Minutes of Evidence (1870, 1871).

**Dingwall** of Rainieston, *or* Rannieston.   Temple's Thanage of Fermartyn, 546-547.   Smith's Genealogies of an Aberdeen Family ; Aberd. Univ. Studies, 69.

**Dingwall-Fordyce.** Family Record of the Name of Dingwall-Fordyce, including relatives of both Names and Connections, by Alex. D. Dingwall-Fordyce, 2 vols. (Toronto, Can., 1885-88).

of Brucklay. Burke's Landed Gentry (1863-1925).

**Dinsmoore, Dinsmore.** History and Genealogy of the Family of Dinsmoore, of Scotland, Ireland, and America, by L. A. Morison (Lowell, Mass., 1891).

**Dinwiddie.** Notes and Queries, 6th S., viii. 13. Scottish N. and Q., 3rd S., i. 44.

**Dirleton,** Erskine, Lord. The Scots Peerage, ix. 116-117. G. E. C.'s Complete Peerage, ed. Gibbs.

Haliburton, Lord Haliburton of. The Scots Peerage, iv. 330-338.

Maxwell, Earl of. The Scots Peerage, iii. 126-131. Scottish Historical Review, xxii. 268-274.

**Dirom,** Aberdeen. Jacobites of Aberdeenshire, by Tayler, 140-141.

**Dishington** of Ardross. East Neuk of Fife, by W. Wood, 2nd ed., 213-218.

**Divie.** Scottish N. and Q., 3rd S., ii. 111.

**Dobie** of Crummock. Pont's Cuninghame, 1604-8, ed. Dobie (1876), 95-96.

of Stonihill. The Dobie Book, MS.

**Dodd.** Annals of a Border Club, by G. Tancred, 104-106.

**Dog.** J. K. Hewison *in* Stirling Antiquary (1904), iii. 160, 164.

**Doig,** Antigua. Oliver's History of Antigua, i. 204-207.

of Reswallie. Warden's Angus or Forfarshire, v. 99.

**Don,** in Angus. Memoirs of the Don Family in Angus, by Dr W. Gerard Don, *ix*+106 pp. (London, 1897).*

of Newton Don. Berwickshire Naturalists' Club (Alnwick, 1893), xiv. 302. Annals of a Border Club, by G. Tancred (1899), 106-113. Burke's Peerage and Baronetage. Complete Baronetage, by G. E. C., iv. 263

**Don-Wauchope** of Edmonstone. Complete Baronetage, by G. E. C., iv. 263. Burke's Peerage and Baronetage.

**Donald.** The Clan Donald, by the Rev. A. Macdonald, Killearnan, and the Rev. A. Macdonald, Kintarlity, 3 vols. (Inverness, 1896-1909). *See also* **Macdonald.**

**Donaldson,** Aberdeen. Genealogies of an Aberdeen Family, by Smith ; Aberd. Univ. Studies, 15-16.

Antigua. Oliver's History of Antigua, ii. 184.

of Auchairne. History of Ayr, by Paterson, i. 253. Ayr and Wigton, by Paterson, ii. 93.

**Doncaster,** Scott, Earl of. English Peerage, by Rev. A. Jacob (1766), i. 576-581. The Scots Peerage, ii. 237-241.

**Donnachie,** The Clan. Ancient Scottish Surnames, by Buchanan of Auchmar (1723), 66-70. *See also* **Robertson.**

**Donnan,** Wigtownshire. Scottish N. and Q., 3rd S., iii. 192.

**Dougal** of Glenferness. Burke's Landed Gentry (1863-1875).

**Dougall** of Scotscraig. Landed Gentry (1863-1886).

**Douglas.** The Origine and Descent of the most Noble and Illustrious Familie and Name of Douglas [by D. Hume, Edinburgh, *c.* 1633], folio 240 pp. ; printed from the original M.S. in the Advocates' Library. The History of the Houses of Douglas and Angus . . . Written by Master David Hume of Godscroft, folio (Edinr. 1644 ; other edits. 1648, 16—, 1657, 1743, 1748, 1814, 1820). Heraldry, by A. Nisbet (1722), i. 76-80 ; (1742), ii. 85. A Synopsis of the Genealogy of the Most Ancient and Most Noble Family of Brigantes, Douglas or Angus, by Peter Pineda. English and Spanish on Parallel pages, 8vo (London, 1754).* History and Martial Achievements of the Houses of Douglas, Angus and Queensberry, by James Herd, 8vo (Edinr. 1769). The Shire of Renfrew, by G. Crawfurd, ed. Robertson (1818). The Broken Cross, a Legend of Douglas, with Chronicles of the Black Douglas as an appendix (Glasgow, 1859). Drumlanrig Castle and the Douglases . . . by C. T. Ramage, LL.D. (Dumfries, 1876). Border Memories, by W. Riddell Carre (1876), 1-45. A collection of family records and biographical sketches and other memoranda of various families and individuals bearing the name of Douglas, or allied to families of that name, by Charles Henry James Douglas (Providence, U.S.A., 1879). Warden's Angus or Forfarshire, i. 277-305. Notes and Queries, 3rd S., ix. 125, 297, 326, 402, 438-439, 441, 515 ; x. 71 : 4th S., i. 562 ; ii. 93 ; iii. 231 ; vi. 361 ; vii. 310 ; viii. 141 ; x. 169 : 5th S. iv. 487 ; v. 35 ; ix. 145 ; xi. 428 ; xii. 115 : 7th S., vii. 490 ; viii. 410. The Douglas Book: Memoirs of the House of Douglas and Angus, by Sir Wm. Fraser, 4 vols., 4to, illust. (Edinr. 1885). History of the House of Douglas from the Earliest Times . . . by Sir Herbert Maxwell, 2 vols., illust. (London, 1902). Critique on above by Sir George Douglas *in* The Ancestor (1902), i. 203-206. The Heraldry of the Douglases, with notes on all the Males of the Family, by G. Harvey Johnston, illust. (Edinr. 1907.) The Crowned Heart of Douglas, *in* Herald and Genealogist, iii. 503-507 ; iv. 107-109. Dictionary of National Biography, *s.v.*

**Douglas** of Aberdour. The Scots Peerage, iii. 173 ; vi. 344-349.

Antigua. Oliver's History of Antigua, i. 208-215.

of Auchincassil. The Scottish Antiquary, xvii. 112.

of Balveny. The Scottish Antiquary, ix. 5. Sir Bruce Seton *in* Scot. Hist. Review, xxiii. 116-118.

Black Isle. Scottish N. and Q., 2nd S., iv. 189.

of Bonjedworth and Timpendean. Heraldry, by Nisbet (1742), ii. Appx. 57. Landed Gentry (1879-1894).

of Brigton. Angus or Forfarshire, by Warden, iv. 59. Monifieth, by J. Malcolm, 293. Burke's Landed Gentry (1894-1925).

of Carr. Complete Baronetage, by G. E. C. (1906), v. 193.

of Castle Douglas. Burke's Extinct Baronetcies, 2nd ed. (1844). Lands . . . in Galloway, by M'Kerlie, iv. 132-134. R. C. Reid *in* Dumfriesshire and Galloway Antiq. Soc. Trans., 3rd S. (1923), viii. 183-191, chart.

**Douglas** of Cavers. Historical MSS. Commission (1879), 7th Report, ii. Burke's Landed Gentry (1875-1906). Annals of a Border Club, by G. Tancred, 114-124.

of Chesterhouse and Gateshaw. Annals of a Border Club, 139-141.

Crail. Churchyard Monuments of Crail, by Erskine Beveridge, 90-96.

of Comlodden. The Scots Peerage, vii. 136-137.

Lord Daer. The Scots Peerage, vii. 516-525.

of Dalkeith. The Scots Peerage, iii. 55, 56, 152, 175.

of Dervoch. Burke's Landed Gentry (1875-1886).

of Dornock. Notes and Queries, 5th S., vii. 243 ; viii. 292.

of Douglas. Upper Ward of Lanarkshire, by Irving and Murray, ii. 56-138. The Scots Peerage, iii. 132-148.

Earl of Douglas. The Scots Peerage, iii. 132-185. The Hereditary Sheriffs of Galloway, by Sir A. Agnew (1893), i. 230 *et passim*. The Scottish Antiquary, vii. 187 ; viii. 14. The Genealogist, N. S., iii. 126.

Marquess of, Duke of. Douglas. The Scots Peerage, i. 204-211. Complete Peerage, by G. E. C., 2nd ed. Memorial for Archibald Douglas of Douglas ; and for Margaret, Dutchess of Douglas, and Chas., Duke of Queensberry and Dover, his Curators, Defenders ; against Geo. Jas., Duke of Hamilton, Lord Douglas Hamilton, and their Tutors, and Sir Hew Dalrymple, of Northberwick, Baronet, Pursuers.—Proof, with Facsimiles, 2 vols. (1766-67). Memorial for George James, Duke of Hamilton, in Opposition to the above.— Proof, together, 2 vols. (1767). Archibald Jas. Ed. Stewart alias Douglas, son of Lady Jane Douglas, Appellant, and Geo. Jas., Duke of Hamilton, and others, Respondents. Case of the Respondents, the Duke of Hamilton, etc., *iv.*+119, 111 pp. Speeches, Arguments, etc. of Lords of Council in the Douglas Cause, Duke of Hamilton, etc., and a Douglas Defendant, etc., by a Barrister, 8vo. (1767). Speeches and Judgements of the Lords in the Douglas Cause, by Wm. Anderson, 8vo (Edinr. 1768). The Case of Archibald Douglas against the Duke of Hamilton, 4to, pedigrees (1769). A State of the Evidence in the Cause between the Duke of Hamilton and Archibald Douglas of Douglas, with Remarks, by Rt. Richardson (1769). Letters to Lord Mansfield, by Andrew Stewart, 8vo (London, 1773).* The Essence of the Douglas Cause, by James Boswell. The Letters of Lady Jane Douglas, ed. James Boswell. Notes and Queries, 2nd S., iv. 69, 110, 158, 209, 285 ; v. 445 ; vi. 130 ; xii. 222 : 10th S., iv. 85; viii. 3 ; xii. 518. Walford's Tales of our Great Families, 2nd S., ii. 270-284.

Lord Douglas of Douglas. The Scots Peerage, i. 121. Case and Statement of Evidence on the Claim of Archibald, Lord Douglas of Douglas, to bear the Crown at the Coronation, etc., with pedigree. Folio, MS. of 28 pp., N.D.

of Douglas Castle. Biographical Peerage (London, 1808), 200. Annals of a Border Club, by G. Tancred, 124-129.

**Douglas** of Douglas Support. Landed Gentry (1894).

of Drumlanrig. C. T. Ramage *in* Herald and Genealogist, vii. 465-467. The Scots Peerage, vii. 112-134.

of Egilshay. Norton Smith's Orkney Armorials, 40-42.

of Fechil. Tayler's Jacobites of Aberdeenshire, 142.

of Fingland. A History of the Douglas Family of Morton . . . and their Descendants, by P. W. L. Adams (Bedford, 1921).

of Friarshaw. Pedigree of the Family of Douglas of Friarshaw or Springwood Park (1869).

of Garallan. History of Ayr, by Paterson, i. 363.

of Glenbervie. Baronage, by Douglas (1784), 18-21. Abstract of the Evidence taken in the Service of the Rt. Hon. Sylvester Douglas, Lord Glenbervie, with a genealogical table, 4to (Edinr. 1815). Burke's Peerage and Baronetage. Burke's Extinct Baronetcies. Complete Baronetage, by G. E. C., ii. 283. Diaries of Sylvester Douglas, Lord Glenbervie, ed. by Francis Bickley, 2 vols. (London, 1928).

of Glenfinart. The Scots Peerage, ii. 529.

of Glenholm. Annals of a Tweeddale Parish, by Baird, 69.

of Kelhead. Complete Baronetage, by G. E. C., iv. 266. The Scots Peerage, vii. 137, 145-151.

Kelso. Annals of a Border Club, 136-140.

of Kilbucho. Peeblesshire Localities, by Renwick, 258. Annals of a Tweeddale Parish, by Baird, 100.

of Kilspindie. Cramond, by J. P. Wood (1794), 47.

of Kirkness. The Scots Peerage, vi. 373.

of Lochleven. Geneal. Coll. by W. Macfarlane, 1750-51 ; Scot. Hist. Soc., ii. 285-300. Logie, by Menzies Fergusson, i. 139-141, 157. The Scots Peerage, vi. 364-374. Scottish N. and Q., 2nd S., iii. 186.

of Mains. Burke's Landed Gentry (1875-1925). Strathblane, by Guthrie Smith, 74-78.

and Mar. Genealogist, N. S., x. 65, 129, 151.

of Montgreenan. The Scots Peerage, vii. 136-137.

of Morton. Registrum Honoris de Morton ; Bannatyne Club (1853). Geneal. Coll., by W. Macfarlane, 1750-51 ; Scot. Hist. Soc., ii. 285-300. D. Marshall *in* Proc. Soc. Antiq. Scotl., (1888), 125-130 ; (1889), 276, 285-292. A History of the Douglas Family of Morton . . . by Percy W. L. Adams, *xxiii*+925 pp. (Bedford, 1921). *See also* **Morton, Douglas, Earl of.**

of Mouswald. The Barony of Mouswald and its Barons, by J. J. Reid, *in* Proc. Soc. Antiq. Scotl. (1888), 62-68, 72-77, 79.

of Mulderg. Genealogy of the Families of Douglas of Mulderg, and Robertson of Kindeace, 4to, 84 pp. (Dingwall, 1895).

of Orchardton. Lands . . . in Galloway, by M'Kerlie, v. 91. Burke's Landed Gentry.

in Orkney. The Frotoft Branch of the Orkney Traills, by T. W. Traill (1902), 41-43, 85.*

**Douglas** of Parkhead. Upper Ward of Lanarkshire, by Irving and Murray, ii. 140-143.

Pennsylvania. Notes and Queries, 8th S., x. 175, 342.

of Pumpherston. The Scots Peerage, viii. 26, 389.

Marquess of Queensberry. Burke's Peerage. Debrett's Peerage. G. E. C.'s Complete Peerage, 2nd ed. (1910).

of St Germans, etc. Stephen's Inverkeithing (1921), 119.

of Skirling. The Scots Peerage, vii. 136-137. Buchan and Paton's History of Peeblesshire, iii. 223.

of Springwood Park. Pedigree of the Family of Douglas of Friarshaw now of Springwood Park, large sheet (July 1869). Annals of a Border Club, 129-136. The Scots Peerage, iv. 215, 216. Burke's Peerage and Baronetage. Debrett's Baronetage.

in Sweden. One Year in Sweden, by H. Marryat, i. 308 ; ii. 461-463, 488. Palace of History Catalogue (Glasgow, 1911), 202.

of Threave. Lands . . . in Galloway, by M'Kerlie, iii. 114-143.

of Tilquhilly. History of the Family of Douglass of Tilwhilly, or Tilquhillie, with 5 folding genealogical tables, Bath [1874].* Pedigree *in* Genealogist, 1st S., v. 193-203. Memoir of J. Young . . . ed. Johnston (1894), 129-130.* The Scottish Antiquary, viii. 41, with chart pedigree ; 88. Scottish N. and Q., 2nd S., i. 141. Burke's Landed Gentry (1906-1921).

of Waterside. Ayr and Wigton, by Paterson, i. 207.

of Whittinghame. One Year in Sweden, by H. Marryat (1862), ii. 461. The Stewarts (Stewart Soc. Magazine), v. 67.

**Douglas and Mar.** J. H. Round *on* The Earldoms of Douglas and Mar, *in* Genealogist, N. S., x. 65-71, 251. W. A. Lindsay *on the same*, Genealogist, N. S., x. 129-131. The Scots Peerage, v. 585-586.

**Douglas-Boswell** of Garallan. Burke's Landed Gentry (1858-1925).

**Douglas-Hamilton,** Duke of Hamilton. Burke's Peerage. Debrett's Peerage. The Scots Peerage, iv. 381-397.

**Douglas-Home,** Earl of Home. Alexander Nisbet's Heraldic Plates. Burke's Peerage. Debrett's Peerage. The Scots Peerage, iv. 440-484.

**Douglas-Scott,** Duke of Queensberry. The Scots Peerage, ii. 242-244.

**Douglass,** Aberdeen. Life and Ancestry of Francis Douglass, Bookseller and Author, of Aberdeen and Paisley, by W. K. Watkins, 37 pp. (Boston, U.S.A., 1903). Scottish N. and Q., 2nd S., v. 47.

**Doull** of Thuster. Caithness Family History, by Henderson, 324.

**Doune,** Stewart, Lord. The Scots Peerage, iii. 186-190 ; vi. 316-330.

**Dover** and Queensberry, Douglas, Duke of. Jacob's English Peerage (1766), i. 300-311. The Scots Peerage, vii. 141.

**Dow,** Antigua. Oliver's History of Antigua, i. 215-216.

of Arnhall. Family of Buchanan, by Buchanan of Auchmar (1723), 133.

of Tirchardy. Scottish N. and Q., 2nd S., i. 63.

**Dreghorn.** [An account of this family is being compiled by Mr Hugh Beaver, Member of the Society of Genealogists, London.]

**Dreux,** Bogleshole. Scottish N. and Q., 3rd S., iii. 214 ; iv. 132.

**Drumlanrig,** Douglas, Viscount of, Earl of, The Scots Peerage, vii. 134-156.

**Drummond.** Genealogy of the House of Drummond, by a Friend to Virtue and the Family [William Drummond], (1681). Genealogy of the Most Noble and Ancient House of Drummond, by William, 1st Viscount of Strathallan, 1681 ; with an Appendix containing the Historie of the Familie of Perth, by Drummond of Hawthornden ; ed. David Laing, 4to (Edinr. 1831 * ; 2nd edition, Glasgow, 1889).* Heraldry, by Alex. Nisbet (1722), i. 62. Genealogical Memoir of the Most Noble and Ancient House of Drummond, by D. Malcolm (Edinr. 1808). Pedigree of the Drummond Family, two sheets. Drummond's Noble British Families (1846), ii., 39 pp., portraits, coloured shields, chart pedigrees, etc. The Drummond Queens of Scotland, by R. S. Fittis, *in* Recreations of an Antiquary (Perth, 1881), 437-468. Charters . . . relating to the Abbey of Inchaffray ; Scot. Hist. Soc., No. 56 (1908), *xcii-vi.* Dictionary of National Biography, *s.v.*

**Drummond** of Albury Park. Burke's Landed Gentry (1858).

of Balhaldie. The Stirling Antiquary, ii. 209-210. The Jacobite Peerage, by the Marquis of Ruvigny, 96-98.

of Blair Drummond. Visitation of Arms and Seats, by J. B. Burke (1853), i. 76. Burke's Landed Gentry (1848-1906).

of The Boyce. Burke's Landed Gentry (1848).

of Cadland. Burke's Commoners, ii. 560. Burke's Landed Gentry (1846-1906). The Scots Peerage, viii. 229-230.

of Cargill. The Scots Peerage, vii. 35-40.

of Carlowrie. Nisbet's Heraldic Plates, ed. Ross and Grant, 98.

of Colquhalzie. Notes and Queries, 2nd S., v. 191 ; viii. 327 ; ix. 84, 283.

of Concraig. Nisbet's Heraldic Plates, ed. Ross and Grant, 88-90. Landed Gentry (1846-1879).

Baron Concraig. The Jacobite Peerage, 37.

of Drummond. Burke's Visitation of Seats and Arms (1853), i. 238-240. The Scots Peerage, vii. 28-39.

Lord Drummond. The Scots Peerage, vi. 66-74 ; vii. 41-62 ; viii. 220-238. G. E. C.'s Complete Peerage.

of Ermore and Carnock. The Scottish Antiquary, x. 100, chart pedigree. Complete Baronetage, by G. E. C., vi., Appx. 74.

of Finnick. Strathendrick, by Guthrie Smith, 210.

Marquis of Forth. The Jacobite Peerage, by the Marquis of Ruvigny (1904), 53.

of Hawthornden. Douglas's Baronage (1798), 571-574. Burke's Peerage and Baronetage. Complete Baronetage, by G. E. C., iii. 325.

of Machany. The Scots Peerage, viii. 216-224, 228.

Lord Madertie. The Scots Peerage, viii. 216-238.

of Megginch. Burke's Landed Gentry (1849 Suppl.-1925).

Duke of Melfort. The Jacobite Peerage, 116-118.

of Milnenab. Geneal. Mag. (1904), vii. 277.

**Drummond** of Newton Castle. An Eighteenth Century Lord Provost, by Wm. Baird *in* The Book of the Old Edinburgh Club (1911), iv. 1-54.

of New Painshaw. An Interesting Statement of the Claims of Thomas Drummond of New Penshaw, near Houghton-le-Spring in the County of Durham, to the Ancient Honours and Entailed Estates of the Earldom of Perth (Newcastle-on-Tyne, 1831). Sequel to the above work, 8vo, 3 pp. The Scottish Antiquary, xiii. 41.

Earl of Perth. The Scots Peerage, vii. 28-62. The Annual Peerages.

Duke of Perth. The Jacobite Peerage, 145-150.

of Pitkellony. The Browns of Fordell, by Stodart (1887), 189-190.

Portugal. Drummond's Noble British Families, ii.

of Stanmore. Burke's Commoners, iii. 501. Burke's Landed Gentry (1848-1862). The Scots Peerage, viii. 224.

in Sweden. One Year in Sweden, by H. Marryat (1862), ii. 488.

**Drummond-Hay** of Cromlix. The Scots Peerage, v. 232-235.

of Seggieden. Burke's Landed Gentry (1921-1925).

**Drummond-Stewart.** Complete Baronetage, by G. E. C., iv. 323.

**Drysdale** in Dollar. The Scottish Antiquary, viii. 185.

**Dudgeon** of Cargen. Lands . . . in Galloway, by M'Kerlie, v. 236. Burke's Landed Gentry (1875-1921).

**Dudhope**, Scrymgeour, Viscount, Viscount of. The Scots Peerage, iii. 313-315.

**Dudingston**, Crail. Churchyard Monuments of Crail, by Erskine Beveridge, 212-213.

of Kilduncan. East Neuk of Fife, by W. Wood, 2nd ed., 466-467.

of Sandford. Baronage, by Sir Robert Douglas, 477-479. East Neuk of Fife, 175-177. The Genealogist, N. S., xv. 7.

**Dudingstoun** of Southouse. Keith W. Murray *in* Genealogist, N. S., xv, 7-19 ; xvii. 288.

**Dudyn** of Broughton. Peeblesshire Localities, by Renwick, 199. Annals of a Tweeddale Parish, by Rev. A. Baird, 27.

**Duff.** Heraldry, by Nisbet (1722), i. 443-444. Scottish N. and Q., xi. 161-164. Genealogical Memoirs of the Duffs, by Wm. Baird of Auchmeddan, ed. L. D. Gordon-Duff (Aberdeen, 1869).* The Book of the Duffs, by Alastair and Henrietta Tayler, 2 vols., 4to, illust. pedigrees (Edinr. 1914).

**Duff** of Balmakilloch. Scottish N. and Q., 2nd S., viii., 127, 144.

of Balvenie. The Castle and Lords of Balveny, by Dr W. Cramond (Elgin, 1893), 20, 21-31.

of Clunybeg. Scottish N. and Q. (1897-8), x. 190 ; xi. 152.

of Crombie. Burke's Peerage and Baronetage, *s.v.* Duff-Gordon of Halkin.

of Culbin. Antiquarian Notes, by C. Fraser-Mackintosh, i. 337-340, 342.

of Drummuir. Temple's Thanage of Fermartyn, 281-283. Antiq. Notes by C. Fraser-Mackintosh, i. 337-339. Scottish N. and Q., 2nd S., iv. 151. Burke's Landed Gentry (1925).

**Duff** of Fetteresso.   Burke's Landed Gentry (1846-1906).

of Haddo.   Thanage of Fermartyn, 233.

of Hatton, Meldrum and Byth.   Thanage of Fermartyn, 125-128. Burke's Landed Gentry (1858-1925).   Tayler's Jacobites of Aberdeenshire, 143.

of Hempriggs.   Complete Baronetage, by G. E. C., iv. 442.

of Keithmore and Braco.   Thanage of Fermartyn, 118-125.   W. Cramond *in* Genealogist, N. S., iii. 205-210.

of Ladyhill.   Annals of Elgin, by R. Young, 686.

of Maldavit and Braco.   Douglas's Baronage, 136-140.   *See also* **Fife**, Duke of.

of Orton.   Landed Gentry (1863-1875).

of Pitcaish.   Scottish N. and Q., 3rd S., vii. 10.

of Woodcote.   Burke's Landed Gentry (Suppl. 1849, Suppl. 1894), *ix.*

**Duff-Sutherland-Dunbar** of Hempriggs.   Burke's Peerage and Baronetage.

**Duff-Gordon** of Maryculter and Halkin.   Burke's Peerage and Baronetage.

**Duffus**, Sutherland, Lord.   Antiquarian Notes, by C. Fraser-Mackintosh, i. 350-354.   The Scots Peerage, iii. 191-215.

**Duguid** of Auchenhove.   Genealogical Fragments, by James Maidment (Berwick, 1855), 2 pp.*   Scottish N. and Q., 3rd S., iv. 80.   Tayler's Jacobites of Aberdeenshire, 145-147.

**Duke**, Montrose.   Baronage of Angus and Mearns, by D. M. Peter, 81.

**Dumbreck** of Dumbreck.   Temple's Thanage of Fermartyn, 467-469.

**Dumfries**, Crichton, Earl of.   Paterson's Ayr and Wigton, i. 331-335.   The Scots Peerage, iii. 219-238.

Crichton-Dalrymple, Earl of.   G. E. C.'s Complete Peerage, 2nd ed. The Scots Peerage, iii. 236-237.

Macdowall-Crichton, Earl of.   The Scots Peerage, iii. 236-238.

Crichton-Stuart, Earl of.   The Scots Peerage, iii. 237-238.

**Dun**, Aberdeen.   Memoir of J. Young, Aberdeen, . . . 1861, ed. Lt.-Col. W. Johnston (1894), 131.*

of Tarty.   Temple's Thanage of Fermartyn, 538-540.

**Dunbar.**   Heraldry, by Nisbet (1722), i. 274-275.   Histories of the Families of Dunbar, Hume and Dundas, by J. Drummond, folio, illust. (1844). " The Old Dunbars," [Genealogical Sketch of the Earls of Dunbar from 1066 to 1436], (1853).   Legends of the Dunbars, and other poems [by Phoebe Masson], with Notes, 4to, *ix*+347 (Edinr. 1854). Dunbar Pedigrees : a Biographical Chart . . . of the Dunbar Family through Fourteen Centuries, by William Jaggard, sheet, 42+31½ ins. (Stratford-on-Avon, 1910).

**Dunbar** of Baldoon.   Notes and Queries, 7th S., x. 485.   Complete Baronetage, by G. E. C., iii. 348.   Case of Captain Charles Dunbar Hope, claiming the baronetcy of Dunbar of Baldoon (1915).

of Bennetsfield.   Young's Annals of Elgin (1879), 672.

of Blantyre.   Herald and Genealogist, vi. 310.

**Dunbar** of Boath. Burke's Peerage and Baronetage.

of Conzie. Thanage of Fermartyn, by Temple, 165-167.

Cullen. Scottish N. and Q., xi. 184 ; xii. 140.

of Cumnock and Mochrum. Geneal. Coll., by W. Macfarlane, 1750-51 ; Scot. Hist. Soc., ii. 525. Paterson's History of Ayr, i. 353-355. Paterson's Ayr and Wigton, i. 316-327. Warrick's History of New Cumnock, 33-36, 51.

of Dalcross. Antiquarian Notes, by C. Fraser-Mackintosh, i. 148-162.

of Duffus. Petition and Answers, Margt. Dunbar, Sister of Mr J. Dunbar of Duffus and A. A. Dunbar of Newton, in Reference to a Marriage Contract, etc. (1743).

Earl of Dunbar. Notes and Queries, 3rd S., v. 97 ; xii. 129, 231. The Scots Peerage, iii. 239-279. Complete Peerage, by G. E. C., 2nd ed.

of Durn. Baronage, by Douglas (1784), 125. Burke's Peerage and Baronetage. Complete Baronetage, by G. E. C., iv. 377. Tayler's Jacobites of Aberdeenshire, 148-152.

of Durris. Parish and Burgh of Elgin, by Young, 673. Scottish N. and Q., 3rd S., i. 32.

of Enterkine and Blantyre. Paterson's History of the County of Ayr, ii. 487. Ayr and Wigton, i. 761. Lands . . . in Galloway, by M'Kerlie, iv. 435-438. Herald and Genealogist, vi. 310.

Forres. History of Antigua, by Oliver, i. 223-226.

of Grangehill. Baronage, by Douglas, 123-125. Elgin, by Young, 673. Notes and Queries, 9th S., i. 88 ; iii. 6.

of Hempriggs. Baronage, by Douglas, 128. The Scots Peerage, iii. 210-215. Geneal. Mag. iii. 298-301. Scottish N. and Q., 2nd S., i. 93. Caithness Family History, by Henderson, 219-225. Complete Baronetage, by G. E. C., iv. 390, 442.

of Kilconquhar. East Neuk of Fife, by W. Wood, 2nd ed., 161-162, Herald and Genealogist, vi. 297-304. The Scots Peerage, iii. 277-278.

of Knockshinnoch. Paterson's Ayr, i. 366. Paterson's Ayr and Wigton, i. 341-342.

of Machriemore. Heraldry, by Nisbet (1722), i. 147. Lands . . . in Galloway, by M'Kerlie, iv. 435-438. Herald and Genealogist, vi. 311.

Earl of March. Geneal. Coll., by W. Macfarlane, 1750-51 ; Scot. Hist. Soc., ii. 513-520. Herald and Genealogist, v. 243-250. Sketch of the Succession of the Ancient Historical Earldom of March, by A. Sinclair (1870), also *in* Herald and Genealogist, vi. 289-297 ; vii. 36-41. East Neuk of Fife, by W. Wood, 2nd ed., 158-161. The Family of Seton, by G. Seton (1896), 39. The Scots Peerage, iii. 262-279. Complete Peerage, by G. E. C. (1910). A. H. Dunbar *in* Proc. Soc. Antiq. Scotl., 187-192, with pedigree chart.

of Mochrum. Geneal. Coll., by Macfarlane, ii. 528-530. Baronage, by Douglas, 113-118. Herald and Genealogist, vi. 309. Burke's Peerage and Baronetage. Complete Baronetage, by G. E. C., iv. 364.

of Monkshill. Thanage of Fermartyn, by Temple, 79-80.

**Dunbar,** Earl of Moray. Geneal. Coll., by Macfarlane, ii. 520. Herald and Genealogist, vi. 304-308. The Scots Peerage, vi. 298-307.

of Newtoun and Thundertoun. Annals of Elgin, by Young, 648-652. Antiquarian Notes, by C. Fraser-Mackintosh, i. 52.

of Northfield and Bowermadden. Annals of Elgin, by Young, 650-652. Caithness Family History, by Henderson, 226-228. Scottish N. and Q., 3rd S., ii. 152-154. Burke's Peerage and Baronetage.

of Weathersta. Zetland Family Histories, by F. J. Grant, 60-61.

of Westfield. Geneal. Coll., by Macfarlane, ii. 528. Baronage, by Douglas, 118-123. Nisbet's Heraldic Plates, ed. Ross and Grant (1892), 124-126. Warrick's History of New Cumnock, 33-36.

**Dunbar,** Murray, Earl of. The Jacobite Peerage, by the Marquis of Ruvigny (1904), 44-45.

**Dunblane,** Osborne, Viscount. The Scots Peerage, iii. 301-302.

**Duncan,** Aberdeen. Forbes of Forbesfield, by A. Forbes (1905), 97-105.

of Ardounie. Nisbet's Heraldic Plates, ed. Ross and Grant, 32.

of Camperdown, Duncan, Viscount. Biographical Peerage (London, 1808), 207-208. Angus or Forfarshire, by Warden, i. 437-441.

of Damflat. Burke's Landed Gentry (1863-1894).

Edinburgh. The Balfours of Pilrig, by Barbara Balfour-Melville, 272.

of Gleneagles. Angus or Forfarshire, i. 436-441.

of Hillar. History of County of Ayr, by Paterson, ii. 432. Ayr and Wigton, by Paterson, i. 701.

in Inverkeithing. Stephen's Inverkeithing and Rosyth, 94.

in Ledlowan. Strathblane, by Guthrie Smith, 93-95.

of Lundie. Angus or Forfarshire, iv. 269.

of Mary-le-bone. Burke's Extinct Baronetcies, 2nd ed. (1844).

in Orkney. Short Chart Pedigree, by W. M'D. Duncan *in* The Ancestor (1905), xii. 189.

of Tow. Zetland Family Histories, by F. J. Grant, 62-63.

**Duncanson** of Fossachie. Logie, by Rev. Dr Menzies Fergusson, ii. 89-91.

**Dundas.** Heraldry, by A. Nisbet (1722), i. 281.

of Arniston and Harviestoun. Heraldry, by A. Nisbet, i. 281; ii., Appx. 17. Douglas's Baronage, 180-181. Historical MSS. Commission (1872), 3rd Report. Burke's Landed Gentry (1848-1898). Genealogical Chart of the Dundases of Arniston, 1570-1880, by Mrs G. E. Forbes (1881). The Arniston Memoirs, 1571-1838, ed. G. W. T. Omond (1887). Burke's Peerage and Baronetage (after 1898).

of Beechwood. Burke's Peerage and Baronetage.

of Blair Castle. Douglas's Baronage, 182. Burke's Commoners, ii. 368. Burke's Landed Gentry (1848-1858).

of Carron Hall. Burke's Landed Gentry (1863-1886).

of Duddingston. Nisbet's Heraldry, ii., Appx. 16. Douglas's Baronage, 177-178. Burke's Landed Gentry (1848-1863).

**Dundas** of Dundas. Heraldry, by Nisbet (1722), i. 281 ; (1742), ii., Appx. 11-14, 15-16. Baronage, by Douglas, 171-176. Drummond's Noble British Families, coloured portraits, shields, etc., chart pedigrees, (1846), ii. Burke's Commoners, i. 642. Burke's Landed Gentry, (1848-1925). Eminent Men of Fife, by M. F. Conolly, 155. Historical MSS. Commission (1872), 3rd Report. Circular Genealogical Table of the Dundas Family of Scotland, from the earliest period, by Louisa L. Forbes, 2 ft. 11 in. across, lithog. (1880). Walford's Tales of our Great Families, 2nd S. (1880), i. 152-164. Chart pedigree *in* Memoir of Chancellor Seton, by George Seton (Edinr. 1882). Nisbet's Heraldic Plates, ed. Ross and Grant (1892), 36-39. Royal Letters and other Historical Documents, selected from the Family Papers . . . by Rev. W. MacLeod, 4to, illust. (1897).

Lord Dundas. Biographical Peerage (1808), 208-209.

of Fingask. Nisbet's Heraldry, ii., Appx. 269-274. Notes and Queries, 4th S., vi. 145. Recreations of an Antiquary, by R. S. Fittis (1881), 387 *n*. Some Memorials of the Family of Dundas of Fingask, by Mrs Dundas senr. of Carronhall (1891).*

of Kerse. Complete Baronetage, by G. E. C., v. 124.

of Kincavil, Airth and Magdalens. Heraldry, by Nisbet, ii., Appx. 18.

of Manor or King's Powes. Douglas's Baronage, 178-180. Logie, by Rev. Dr Menzies Fergusson, ii. 107-113.

of Newliston, Philpstoun and Briestmiln. Nisbet's Heraldry, ii., Appx. 14. Douglas's Baronage, 176-177.

**Dundee** of Benvie and Balruthrie. Memorials of Angus and the Mearns, by Jervise, ed. Gammack, ii. 80-82.

Scrymgeour, Earl of. The Scots Peerage, iii. 303-315.

Grahame, Viscount of. Notes and Queries, 3rd S., v. 97 ; xii. 129, 231. The Scots Peerage, iii. 316-333. G. E. C.'s Complete Peerage, ed. Gibbs. Michael Barrington *on* Claverhouse's Last Letter, *in* Scot. Hist. Review, 1910, vi. 505-509. Prof. C. Sanford Terry, *ibid.*, vi. 63-65. Rev. J. Anderson, *ibid.*, vi. 65-70. John Graham of Claverhouse, Viscount Dundee, by C. S. Terry (London, 1905).

Gualterio, Earl of. The Jacobite Peerage, by the Marquis of Ruvigny, 46.

**Dundonald**, Cochrane, Earl of. Crawfurd's Shire of Renfrew, ed. Robertson, 322. Paterson's Ayr and Wigton, i. 444-450. Case on behalf of the Earl of Dundonald in support of . . . his succession to be Earl of Dundonald, etc., and folding pedigree, folio (1861). Minutes of Evidence on the Earl of Dundonald's Petition to be Lord Dundonald : (Session Papers, 203 of 1861, A and H of 1862, A of 1863). History of the Lairds of Glenfield (Paisley, 1860). Burke's Peerage. Debrett's Peerage. G. E. C.'s Complete Peerage, ed. Gibbs. The Scots Peerage, iii. 334-368. Walford's Chapters from Family Chests, ii. 71-80. Inventory of the Charter Chest of the Earldom of Dundonald, 1219-1672, ed. F. J. Grant, Rothesay Herald (Scot. Rec. Soc. Edinr. 1910), 34 pp. *See also* **Cochrane**.

**Dunduff** of Dunduff. Paterson's Ayr and Wigton, i. 429.

**Dunfermline,** Seton, Earl of. Life of Lord Chancellor Seton, by G. Seton (Edinr. 1882). Account of his funeral obsequies *in* The Scottish Antiquary, xiii. 160-166. Scottish N. and Q., 2nd S., i. 65-68. A History of the Family of Seton, by G. Seton (1896), 634-670. The Scots Peerage, iii. 369-375.

**Dunkeld,** Galloway, Lord. The Scots Peerage, iii. 376-382.

**Dunlop.** Records of the Dunlop, Reid, and Boyd of Bonshaw Families, compiled by Robert Reid, Irvine.

of Aiket. Paterson's Ayr and Wigton, iii. 239.

of Annanhill and Bonnington. Paterson's History of the County of Ayr, ii. 205. Ayr and Wigton, iii. 423.

of Arthurlee. Burke's Landed Gentry (1898-1925).

of Boarland. Pont's Cuninghame, ed. Dobie, 98. Paterson's History of Ayr, ii. 51. Paterson's Ayr and Wigton, iii. 234-235.

of Corsock. Landed Gentry (1863-1894).

of Craig. Robertson's Ayrshire Families, i. 341. Paterson's Ayr, ii. 222. Ayr and Wigton, iii. 456.

of Craigton. Landed Gentry (1863).

of Doonside. Landed Gentry (1894-1921).

of Drumhead. Landed Gentry (1863-1925). Book of Dumbartonshire, by Irving (1879), ii. 308-309.

of Dunlop. Ayrshire Families, i. 331-340. Paterson's History of Ayr, ii. 46-48. Ayr and Wigton, iii. 226-233. Memorabilia of the Families of Dunlop, by Archibald Dunlop, 8vo, illust. (Glasgow, 1898).* Scottish N. and Q., 2nd S., viii. 71. Lands . . . in Galloway, by M'Kerlie, 2nd ed., i. 506.

of Garnkirk. Crawfurd's Shire of Renfrew (1818), 328.

of Hapland. Ayrshire Families, i. 331, 341-342. Paterson's Ayr, ii. 50. Ayr and Wigton, iii. 233-234.

of Hopkailzie. Peeblesshire Localities, by Renwick, 587.

of Househill. Crawfurd's Shire of Renfrew (1818), 328, 522.

of Hunthall. Paterson's Ayr and Wigton, iii. 227.

of Kirkurd. Peeblesshire Localities, 436-437.

of Loanhead. Paterson's Ayr, ii. 53. Ayr and Wigton, iii. 239.

of Lockerbie House. Burke's Landed Gentry (1906-1925).

of Macnairston. Paterson's Ayr, i. 208. Ayr and Wigton, i. 150.

of Millhall. Ayrshire Families, i. 333.

of Whitmuir Hall. Annals of a Border Club, by G. Tancred, 141-145.

**Dunlop-Agnew-Wallace.** Burke's Royal Families (1851), i. 202. Complete Baronetage, by G. E. C., iv. 276.

**Dunmore,** Murray, Earl of. G. E. C.'s Complete Peerage. Burke's Peerage. Debrett's Peerage. The Scots Peerage, iii. 383-396.

**Dunn** of Craigton. Strathendrick, by Guthrie Smith, 259.

of Duntocher. Book of Dumbartonshire, ii. 374-377 ; iii., portrait.

Paisley. Burke's Peerage and Baronetage (after 1895).

**Dunn Waters** of Culcreuch and Craigton. Strathendrick, 259.

**Dunne** of Conestablestun. Peeblesshire Localities, by Renwick, 33.

**Dupplin,** Hay, Viscount. The Scots Peerage, v. 222-239.

**Durand** of Kirkpatrick-Durham. The Origin of the Name Kirkpatrick-Durham, by Rev. W. A. Stark, *in* Transactions of Dumfries and Galloway Antiq. Soc. (1908-9), 44.

**Durham** of Ashludie. Monifieth, by Malcolm, 351.

of Grange. Baronage, by Douglas, 472-473. Angus or Forfarshire, by A. J. Warden, iii. 452 ; iv. 398-400. Monifieth, by J. Malcolm, 335-338.

of Largo. Baronage, by Douglas, 473-476. Eminent Men of Fife, 156-158. East Neuk of Fife, by W. Wood, 2nd ed., 82-84. Burke's Commoners, i. 287. Burke's Landed Gentry (1848).

of Luffness. Baronage, by Douglas, 476. Monifieth, by Malcolm, 344.

of Mollet. The Stirling Antiquary, ii. 105.

of Pitkerro. Baronage, by Douglas, 473-476. Angus or Forfarshire, iv. 157-159, 397. Monifieth, 341-345, 356.

**Durie,** Crail. Churchyard Monuments of Crail, by Erskine Beveridge, 112-114.

of Durie. Geneal. Coll., by W. Macfarlane, 1750-51 ; Scot. Hist. Soc., i. 23. East Neuk of Fife, 2nd ed., 30-33.

of Grange. The Scots Peerage, vii. 373-374.

**Durward.** The Thanes of Cawdor, by Cosmo Innes. Proc. Essex Archæological Society, iii. 100. The Scottish Antiquary, xi. 159. Scottish N. and Q., 3rd S., v. 158.

**Duthie,** Aberdeen. Scottish N. and Q., 3rd S., ii. 111.

of Cairnbulg. Scottish N. and Q., 3rd S., i. 101.

**Dyce** of Tillygreig. Temple's Thanage of Fermartyn, 458-459.

**Dysart,** Murray, Earl of. Eminent Men of Fife, by Conolly, 158-159. The Scots Peerage, iii. 397-420. G. E. C.'s Complete Peerage.

Tollemache, Earl of. Burke's Peerage. Debrett's Peerage. The Scots Peerage, iii. 406-420. Case of William John Manners, Earl of Dysart (1880). Case of Albert Edwin Tollemache, in opposition to above claim. Minutes of Evidence of W. J. Manners, claiming the titles of Earl of Dysart, and Lord Huntingtower (1880).

**Easton** of Couston. The Monros of Auchenbowie, by J. A. Inglis, 11-14.

**Eccles** of Eccles and Kildonan. Baronage, by Douglas, 436-438. Paterson's History of County of Ayr, i. 313. Paterson's Ayr and Wigton, ii. 155-156.

**Echlin(e.** Memoirs of the Ancient Familie of Echlin of Pittadro, by Geo. Crawfurd (Glasgow, 1747) ; Appendix bringing the pedigree down to 1820, n.d.* Revised and enlarged as Genealogical Memoirs of the Echlin Family . . . by Rev. John R. Echlin, 72 pp., Edinr. [1882.]* Inverkeithing and Rosyth, by Rev. W. Stephen (1921), 122-124, 471.

**Eck** of Hollybush. Paterson's Ayr and Wigton, i. 414.

**Edgar.** Nisbet's Heraldry, i. 286-287. Genealogical Collections concerning the Scottish House of Edgar, ed. Andrew Edgar and C. Rogers (Grampian Club, London, 1873).

of Auchingrammont. Herald and Genealogist, iii. 374-377 ; iv. 182, 376-378.

of Keithock. Baronage of Angus and Mearns, by D. M. Peter (1856), 84. Angus or Forfarshire, by A. J. Warden, iii. 26.

of Wedderlie. The Edgars of Wedderlie, by Rev. J. H. Edgar, *in* Berwickshire Naturalists' Club, xi. (Alnwick, 1887). Nisbet's Heraldic Plates, ed. Ross and Grant, 80-82. Account of the Sirname of Edgar, and particularly of the Family of Wedderlie, by Capt. J. H. Lawrence Archer, 4to, illust., pedigrees (London, 1868 and 1873). Herald and Genealogist, iii. 374 ; iv. 182.

**Edmiston.** Heraldry, by Nisbet (1722), i. 246.

**Edmond** of Coneyhill. Logie, by Rev. Dr R. M. Fergusson, ii. 68, 71.

**Edmondston** of Buness. Zetland Family Histories, by F. J. .Grant, 64-73. Burke's Landed Gentry (1906-1925).

Charleston, S. C. Zetland Family Histories, by F. J. Grant, 74-77.

**Edmonstone** of Broich and Spittal. Strathblane, by Guthrie Smith, 95-100.

of Ednem and Duntreath. Heraldry, by Nisbet (1742), ii., Appx. 163-169, 299-300. Genealogy of the Lairds of Ednem and Duntreth, from 1063 to 1699, 18mo, 15 pp. (Glasgow, 1699), (reprinted, Berwick, 1790 ; Edinr. [1834], ed. James Maidment). History of Stirling-shire, by Nimmo, 3rd ed. (1880) ; ii. 86-92, 117-121. Burke's Peerage and Baronetage. Genealogical Account of the Family of Edmonstone of Duntreath, by Sir Archibald Edmonstone, 4to (Edinr. 1875).* Historical MSS. Commission (1872), 3rd Report ; (1909), vol. v. Strathblane, by Guthrie Smith (1886), 72-74, 79, 102-125. Complete Baronetage, by G. E. C. (1906), v. 170.

**Edmondstone-Cranstoun** of Corehouse. Burke's Landed Gentry (1886-1925).

**Edward** of Longcroft. Nisbet's Heraldic Plates, ed. Ross and Grant (1892), 140.

of Pearsie. Warden's Angus or Forfarshire, iv. 40.

**Eglinton,** Montgomerie, Earl of. Biographical Peerage (1808), 215. Ayr-shire Families, by G. Robertson, i. 295-299 ; ii. 307-325. Account of the Tournament at Eglinton, by James Aikman, 4to (Edinr. 1839). Paterson's History of the County of Ayr (1852), ii. 229-244. Memorials of the Montgomeries, Earls of Eglinton, by Sir W. Fraser, 2 vols., 4to, illust. (Edinr. 1859).* Paterson's Ayr and Wigton, iii. 491-507. Historical Memoir of the House of Eglinton and Winton, by John Fullarton, 176 pp. (Ardrossan, 1864.) Walford's Chapters from Family Chests, i. 301-310 ; ii. 228-240. Notes and Queries, 3rd S., x. 404 ; xi. 162 ; xii. 175. Historical MSS. Com-mission (1885), 10th Report, i. The Family of Seton, by George Seton (1896). Burke's and other Annual Peerages. The Scots Peerage, iii. 421-465. G. E. C.'s Complete Peerage, ed. Gibbs (1910).

**Eglinton,** Seton, Earl of. The Family of Seton, by Geo. Seton, 676-707. History of the County of Bute, by Reid, 217-228.

**Eglintoun** of Eglintoun. Ayrshire Families, i. 342-345. Paterson's Ayr, ii. 228.

**Elcho,** Wemyss, Lord. G. E. C.'s Complete Peerage, 2nd ed. (1910). Burke's Peerage. Debrett's Peerage. The Scots Peerage, viii. 500-518.

**Elder.** Notes and Queries, 7th S., xii. 368.

**Elgin.** Bruce, Earl of. G. E. C.'s Complete Peerage, 2nd ed. Burke's Peerage. Debrett's Peerage, etc. The Scots Peerage, iii. 466-497.

**Elibank,** Murray, Lord. G. E. C.'s Complete Peerage, 2nd ed. Burke's Peerage. Debrett's Peerage, etc. The Scots Peerage, iii. 498-524.

**Eliot.** Genealogy of the Eliot Family, by William K. Eliot, revised and enlarged by William S. Porter (New Haven, Conn., U.S.A., 1854). Tabular Pedigree of the Eliot Family, by W. H. Whitmore (1857). Sketch of the Eliot Family, by Walter Graeme Eliot (New York, 1887).

**Eliott** of Stobs. The Border Eliots, by Hon. G. F. S. Elliot (1892)* Annals of a Border Club, 163-177. Tancred's Rulewater, 18-38. Burke's Peerage and Baronetage. Complete Baronetage, by G. E. C., iv. 258.

**Ellice** of Invergarry. Burke's Landed Gentry (1875-1925).

**Elliot.** [Mr George Tancred of Weens, in his "Annals of a Border Club," gives these lines:

> The double L and single T
> Descend from Minto and Wolfelee.
> The double T and single L
> Marks the old race in Stobs that dwell.
> The single L and single T
> The Eliots of St Germains be.
> But double T and double L,
> Who they are, nobody can tell.]

**Elliot.** Metrical History of the Honourable Families of . . . Scot and Elliot, by Capt. Walter Scot of Satchells (Edinr. 1688, 1776, 1892.)* Border Memories, by W. Riddell Carre (1876), 132-180.

of Arkleton. Annals of a Border Club, by G. Tancred (1899), 229-230. Burke's Landed Gentry (1886-1925).

of Borthwickbrae. Annals of a Border Club, 202. T. Craig Brown's Selkirkshire, i. 432-433.

of Clifton Park. Burke's Landed Gentry (1925).

of Harwood, Harrot. Annals of a Border Club, 192-201. Rulewater, by Tancred, 57-71. Burke's Landed Gentry (1879-1925).

of Headshaw. Annals of a Border Club, 178-191. Complete Baronetage, by G. E. C., iv. 393.

of Lariston. Annals of a Border Club, 152-162.

**Elliot** of Melgund and Kynynmound. Eminent Men of Fife, by M. F. Conolly, 162-163.

of Midlem Mill. Tancred's Rulewater, 39-40.

of Minto. Annals of a Border Club, 178-191. The Border Elliots and the Family of Minto, by Hon. G. F. S. Elliot, 4to (Edinr. 1892.)* The Balfours of Pilrig, by B. Balfour-Melville, 271.

Peebles. Complete Baronetage, by G. E. C., v. 196.

of Redheuch and Larriston. The Scottish Antiquary, xiii. 181-182. Annals of a Border Club, 146-157.

of Stonedge *or* Greenriver. Annals of a Border Club, 168. Rulewater, 41-42.

of Wells. Rulewater, 202-209.

of Wolfelee. Sir Walter Elliot of Wolflee, by R. Sewell (Edinr. 1896).* A Chapter in Mediocrity, by Rev. W. S. Stavert (Skipton, 1896).* Annals of a Border Club, 207-229. The Balfours of Pilrig, 272. Rulewater, 83-107. Burke's Landed Gentry (1886-1925).

**Elliot-Lockhart** of Cleghorn. Annals of a Border Club, 202-206. Account of the Families of Lockhart of Cleghorn and Elliot of Borthwick-brae ; typescript in possession of the family.

**Elliot-Murray-Kynynmond.** Complete Baronetage, by G. E. C., iv. 258.

**Ellis.** Notices of the Ellises of England, Scotland and Ireland, from the Conquest, with four Supplements, by William Smith Ellis (London, 1857-81).*

**Elmslie.** Scottish N. and Q., 2nd S., vii. 100 ; viii. 190. Genealogies of an Aberdeen Family, by Smith ; Aberd. Univ. Studies, 16-17.

**Elphinstone.** Heraldry, by A. Nisbet (1722), i. 154, 160-161 ; (1742) ii. Ragman Roll, 22. Historical and Genealogical Tree of the House of Elphinstone from 1263 to 1808, by John Brown, sheet 32 × 26 inches (Edinr. 1808).

**Elphinstone,** Aberdeen. Tayler's Jacobites of Aberdeenshire, 153.

Lord Balmerino. Balmerino and its Abbey, by Dr J. Campbell (1899), 526-555, 651-652. The Scots Peerage, i. 556-575.

of Barnton. Cramond, by J. P. Wood, 53, 266-289.

of Blythswood. Complete Baronetage, by G. E. C., ii. 357.

Lord Coupar. The Scots Peerage, ii. 576-577.

Lord Elphinstone. Historical MSS. Commission (1884), 9th Report. The Elphinstone Family Book of the Lords Elphinstone, Balmerino and Coupar, by Sir Wm. Fraser, 2 vols., 4to, illust. (Edinr. 1897). Burke's and other Annual Peerages. Complete Peerage, by G. E. C., ed. Gibbs. The Scots Peerage, iii. 525-554.

of Elphinstone in Nova Scotia, and of Lopness. The Case of Lt.-Col. Arthur Percy Archibald Elphinstone, claiming to be placed on the roll of Baronets (1912).

of Glack. Burke's Landed Gentry (1925). *See also* **Elphinstone of Logie.**

of Henderstoun. Buchan's and Paton's History of Peeblesshire, ii. 358.

**Elphinstone** of Logie. The Balfours of Pilrig, by B. Balfour-Melville, 271. Complete Baronetage, by G. E. C., iv. 399. The Case of Alexander Elphinstone of Glack (1927).

of New Glasgow. Debrett's Baronetage (1905).

of Pittendreich. Logie, by Rev. Dr Menzies Fergusson, ii. 78. The Scots Peerage, iii. 527-529.

**Elphinstone-Dalrymple** of Horn and Logie Elphinstone. Burke's Peerage and Baronetage. The Scots Peerage, viii. 134-136.

**Elwald, Elwand, Ellwood.** Annals of a Border Club, by G. Tancred, 147.

**Erroll,** Hay, Earl of. Record of the House of Gournay, by D. Gurney, 576. Buchan, by Rev. J. B. Pratt (1858), 313-326. Historic . . . Earldoms of Scotland, by J. Mackintosh, 224-270. Burke's and other Annual Peerages. The Scots Peerage, iii. 555-587. G. E. C.'s Complete Peerage, ed. Gibbs.

**Erskine.** Crawfurd's Shire of Renfrew (1818), 107-112. A Brief Account of the titled family of Erskine of Scotland, by the Earl of Kellie (pamphlet). Chart pedigree *in* Seton's Memoir of Chancellor Seton (1882). French and Italian pedigree of the Erskines, by Lady E. Cust *in* Fergusson's Henry Erskine and his Kinsfolk (1883), 135. Tree of the Families of Cunninghame and Erskine. Notes and Queries, 4th S., iii. 578 ; v. 236 ; vi. 168. Great Historic Families of Scotland, by Jas. Taylor [1887]. The Origin, Increase etc. of the Family of Erskine ; large tabular pedigree, seven sheets (*c.* 1896). The Stirling Antiquary, ii. 147. Dictionary of National Biography, *s.v.* Complete Baronetage, by G. E. C., ii. 304. Historical MSS. Commission, Alloa House Papers (1904), Cd. 2190.

**Erskine,** Baron Alloa. The Jacobite Peerage, by the Marquis of Ruvigny (1904), 7.

of Alva. Historical MSS. Commission (1873), 4th Report, 521. The Dalrymples of Langlands, by J. Shaw, 21-22, 36.* Scottish Antiquary, i. and ii. 182 ; iii. 27, 139 ; v. 93. Complete Baronetage by G. E. C., iv. 250. Stair A. Gillon *in* The Stewarts Magazine, v. 122-127, and pedigree.

of Balgonie. Scottish Antiquary, v. 97-103, 181 ; vi. 62-66 ; xii. 174. Complete Baronetage, by G. E. C., iv. 301.

of Balhagardy. Notes and Queries, 8th S., iv. 507.

of Balhall. Baronage of Angus and Mearns, by Peter (1856), 89. Landed Gentry (1886).

Earl of Buchan. The Hon. Henry Erskine, Lord Advocate, with notices of certain of his Kinsfolk, by Col. A. Fergusson, illust. (1882). Scottish Antiquary, xii. 62, 123 ; xiii. 46. The Scots Peerage, ii. 272-280.

of Cambo. East Neuk of Fife, by W. Wood, 2nd ed. 462-464. Scottish N. and Q., 3rd S., iii. 14-15, 28. Complete Baronetage, by G. E. C., iv. 255. Burke's Peerage and Baronetage. The Scots Peerage, v. 90-93.

**Erskine** of Carbuddo. Angus or Forfarshire, by Warden, iii. 395-396.

of Cardross. Lake of Menteith, by Hutchison, 193-202. Memoirs of Sir David Erskine of Cardross, ed. Mrs Steuart Erskine (London, 1926), 26-34. Burke's Landed Gentry (1879-1925).

Lord Cardross. The Scots Peerage, ii. 365-368 ; v. 618-621.

of Dryburgh. Burke's Landed Gentry (1894 Suppl.-1925).

of Dun. Genealogical Tree of the Ancient Family of Erskine of Dun, by Alex. Sinclair, sheet (Edinr. n.d.) Papers from the Charter Chest at Dun, 1451-1703; Spalding Club Misc., iv. Angus or Forfarshire, by Warden, iii. 171-183. Burke's Landed Gentry (1894-1925). Historical Castles and Mansions of Scotland, by A. H. Millar (1891). Scottish Antiquary, vi. 49-53, 182-184 ; ix. 19-20 ; xiv. 92, 151.

of Erskine. The Scots Peerage, v. 590-604. Memoirs of Sir David Erskine of Cardross, 17-25. Janet Barclay, by Rev. A. W. C. Hallen, etc., *in* Genealogist, N. S., ix. 4-6, 129-137, 193-201.

Lord Erskine. Biographical Peerage (1808), 229-230. G. E. C.'s Complete Peerage, 2nd ed. Burke's Peerage, etc. The Scots Peerage, v. 601-636.

Viscount Fenton. East Neuk of Fife, by W. Wood, 2nd ed., 261-267.

Viscount Garioch. The Jacobite Peerage, by the Marquis of Ruvigny (1904), 58.

of Inchmahome. Lake of Menteith, by Hutchison, 159-193.

Earl of Kellie. The Scots Peerage, v. 81-97.

of Kinnedar. The Scottish Antiquary (1895), ix. 43.

of Kinnoul. The Scottish Antiquary (1895), ix. 42.

of Kirkbuddo. Landed Gentry (1886-1894).

of Linlathen. Angus or Forfarshire, by Warden, iv. 408-409. Monifieth, by Malcolm, 164-165, 299-301, 375.

Earl of Mar. Historic Earls and Earldoms of Scotland, by John Mackintosh (Aberdeen, 1898), 41-77. The Scots Peerage, v. 589-635.

Duke of Mar. The Jacobite Peerage, 113-116.

of Nova Scotia. Complete Baronetage, by G. E. C., ii. 304.

of Pittodrie. Genealogy, by Alex. Sinclair. Burke's Landed Gentry (1875-1894). Geneal. Mag. (1899), ii. 557.

of Little Sauchie. The Scottish Antiquary, xii. 62, 123, 174.

of Shielfield and Chirnside. Annals . . . of Dryburgh, by Sir D. Erskine, 2nd èd., 37, 44, 84-88, 198. Notes and Queries, 6th S., ix. 168, 197, 238, 253 ; x. 437 : 9th S., xii. 429, 512. Scottish N. and Q. (1889), iii. 78. Scottish Antiquary, vi. 62-66. Annals of a Border Club, by G. Tancred (1899), 232-237.

of Smithfield. Buchan and Paton's History of Peeblesshire, ii. 341-342.

Marquis of Stirling. The Jacobite Peerage, by the Marquis of Ruvigny, 169.

in Sweden. One Year in Sweden, by H. Marryat (1862), ii. 484.

of Torrie. Complete Baronetage, by G. E. C., v. 268. Stephen's Inverkeithing, 81-84.

**Erskine-Halcro.** The Erskine-Halcro Genealogy, by Ebenezer Erskine Scott (London, 1890; 2nd ed. 1895). The Scottish Antiquary, v. 143.

**Erskine-Murray.** Historical MSS. Commission (1873), 4th Report, pt. 1.

**Erskine-Wemyss** of Wemyss. Memorials of the Family of Wemyss of Wemyss, by Sir W. Fraser, 3 vols., illust. (Edinr. 1888).* The Scots Peerage, viii. 511-512.

**Ethessone.** Traditions of the Watsons, by C. B. B. Watson.

**Ethie,** Carnegie, Earl of. The Scots Peerage, vi. 494-495.

**Ettrick of Ettrick,** Napier, Baron. The Scots Peerage, vi. 437-439.

**Evart,** Dumfries. MS. Pedigree of the Evart Family, compiled and written by James Campbell Gracie (Dumfries, 1858).

**Ewan, Ewen.** The Clan Ewan : Some Records of its History, by P. S. T. MacEwen (1904).

**Ewart** of Allershaw. Burke's Landed Gentry (1906-1925).
of Craigcleuch. Burke's Landed Gentry (1886-1925).
of Mulloch. Lands and their Owners in Galloway, by M'Kerlie,v. 115-118.

**Ewing** of Keppoch. Heraldry, by Nisbet (1722), i. 438. Burke's Landed Gentry (1862-1906).

**Eyr** of Mossfennan. Peeblesshire Localities, by R. Renwick, 230.

**Eyre** in Sweden. Palace of History Catalogue (Glasgow, 1911), 204 *bis*.

**Eythin,** King, Lord. Notes and Queries, 4th S., viii. 63 ; xii. 267, 351. G. E. C.'s Complete Peerage, ed. Gibbs. The Scots Peerage, iii. 588-594.

**Faa.** Scottish N. and Q. (1898), xii. 11.

**Fair** of Langlee. Annals of a Border Club, by G. Tancred, 238.

**Fairfax,** Lord Fairfax of Cameron. Burke's and other Annual Peerages. The Scots Peerage, iii. 595-606. G. E. C.'s Complete Peerage. Scottish N. and Q., 2nd S., ii. 70.
of Ravenswood. Annals of a Border Club, 239-240.

**Fairfoul** of Lathallan. East Neuk of Fife, by W. Wood, 2nd ed. (1887), 105-106. Notes and Queries, 6th S., iii. 490 ; iv. 73.
of Wester Lachie. Paterson's Ayr and Wigton, ii. 407-408.

**Fairholme** of Chapel. Burke's Landed Gentry (1863-1879).

**Fairlie** of Braid. Edinburgh Evening Dispatch (Oct. 1890).
of Bruntsfield. Ayrshire Families, by G. Robertson, ii. 39-50. History of Ayr, by Paterson, ii. 24. Ayr and Wigton, by Paterson, i. 475-486.
of Coodham. Paterson's History of the County of Ayr, ii. 519. Ayr and Wigton, i. 738. Burke's Landed Gentry (1863-1875).
of Dreghorn. History of Ayr, by Paterson, ii. 20. Ayr and Wigton, i. 475-486.
of Fairlie. Ayrshire Families, i. 346-348. History of Ayr, by Paterson, ii. 302. Ayr and Wigton, i. 475-486 ; iii. 528-529.

**Fairlie** of Holms.   History of Ayr, by Paterson, ii. 73.   Ayr and Wigton,
    i. 526.   Burke's Landed Gentry (1863-1925).
    of Myres.   Burke's Landed Gentry (1906-1925).

**Fairny.**   *See* **Fernie.**

**Fairweather.**   The Fairweathers of Menmuir Parish . . . and others of the
    Surname, by Alex. Fairweather, ed. W. G. Don (1898).*   Churchyard
    Monuments of Crail, by Erskine Beveridge, 200.

**Falconer.**   Heraldry, by Nisbet (1722), i. 353.   Notes on the Family of
    Falconer, 8 pp. (Aberdare).*   Entail in the Falconer Family, 3 pp.*
    Account of the Family of Dalmahoy of that Ilk, and of the Family
    of Falconer, by J. Falconer (London, 1865).   The Falconer Family,
    with Wills of Dalmahoys and Falconers.   [A few copies only printed ;
    n.p., n.d.]*
    of Dunduff.   Annals of Elgin, by R. Young, 677.   Young's Family of
    King of Newmills.
    of Glenfarquhar.   Complete Baronetage, by G. E. C., iv. 279.   The Scots
    Peerage, v. 246, 247.
    of Halkerton.   Memorials of Angus and the Mearns, by Jervise, ed.
    Gammack, ii. 147-150.   Fraser's Laurencekirk, 36-48.   The Scots
    Peerage, v. 243-246.
    Lord Falconer of Halkerton.   The Scots Peerage, v. 242-255.   G. E. C.'s
    Complete Peerage.
    of Lethen.   The Scots Peerage, v. 243-246.
    of Newton.   Fraser's Laurencekirk, 68-69.   The Scots Peerage, v. 243-250.
    of Phesdo.   The Scots Peerage, v. 245-250.

**Falkland,** Cary, Earl of.   The Jacobite Peerage, by the Marquis of Ruvigny,
    49-51.
    Cary, Viscount.   G. E. C.'s Complete Peerage, ed. Gibbs.   Burke's
    Peerage.   Debrett's Peerage.   The Scots Peerage, iii. 607-617.

**Falkoner** of Linkwood.   The Thurburnes, by Lt.-Col. Thurburne, Appx. F.

**Fall,** Dunbar.   Notes and Queries, 6th S., iv. 248, 331.   The Scottish
    Antiquary, xv. 126-132.

**Farie** of Baronald.   Scottish N. and Q., 3rd S., ii. 80.
    of Farme.   Burke's Landed Gentry (1894-1925).

**Farquhar.**   Scottish N. and Q. (1898), xii. 56-57.
    Aberdeen.   Memoir of J. Young, Aberdeen . . . 1861, ed. Lt.-Col. W.
    Johnston (1894), 87-94, 169-173.*
    of Over Catrine.   Paterson's History of Ayr, ii. 426.   Paterson's Ayr and
    Wigton, i. 690-691.
    of Drumnagesk.   Landed Gentry (1894).
    Baron Farquhar.   Burke's and other Annual Peerages (1899-1926).
    of Gilmilnscroft.   Ayrshire Families, by G. Robertson, ii. 51-59.
    Paterson's History of Ayr, ii. 430-431.   Ayr and Wigton, i. 697-701.
    Burke's Commoners, iii. 22.   Burke's Landed Gentry (1846-1898).
    Burke's Peerage and Baronetage.   Complete Baronetage, by G. E. C.,
    v. 308.

**Farquhar** of Munie. Burke's and other Annual Baronetages.

in New Deer. Genealogies of an Aberdeen Family, by Smith ; Aberd. Univ. Studies, 96-97.

of Pitscandly. Baronage of Angus and Mearns, by D. M. Peter (1856), 94. Scottish N. and Q., 3rd S., iii. 194. Warden's Angus and Forfarshire, v. 96-98.

**Farquharson.** Heraldry, by Nisbet (1742), ii., Appx. 26. Antiquarian Notes, by C. Fraser Mackintosh, i. 380. Pedigrees of the Family of James of Culgarth (Exeter, 1913).*

of Achriachan. Farquharson Genealogies, by A. M. Mackintosh (Nairn, 1913), i. 1-25. Scottish N. and Q., 3rd S., iii. 13, 29. Tayler's Jacobites of Aberdeenshire, 157, 180.

of Alford. Scottish N. and Q., 3rd S., ii. 192.

of Allanquoich. Scottish N. and Q., 3rd S., iv. 200; v. 13; vi. 149-151, 169.

of Allargue and Breda. Confederacy of Clan Chattan, by C. Fraser-Mackintosh, 169. Burke's Landed Gentry (1898-1925). Farquharson Genealogies, i. 26-41. Scottish N. and Q., 3rd S., iii. 70, 71 ; vi. 202. Tayler's Jacobites of Aberdeenshire, 171-178.

of Auchindryne. Farquharson Genealogies, ii. 57-69. Jacobites of Aberdeenshire, 155, 178, 181.

of Baldovie. Burke's Landed Gentry (1848).

of Balmoral. Farquharson Genealogies, ii. 44. Tayler's Jacobites, 169.

of Belnabodach. Farquharson Genealogies, ii. 71.

Boharm. Scottish N. and Q., 2nd S., vii. 44.

of Broughdearg. Scot. Hist. Review, vi. 440 ; vii. 110 ; xiv. 238-248.

in Castleton. Scottish N. and Q., 2nd S., viii. 104 ; 3rd S., 128-130, 145-147.

of Craignytie. Burke's Landed Gentry (1848), ii. 1141.

in Drumnapark. Jacobites of Aberdeenshire, 157.

of Finzean. Baronage, by Douglas, 545-547. Confederacy of Clan Chattan, 170. Burke's Landed Gentry (1886-1925). Scottish N. and Q., 3rd S., v. 200.

of Haughton. Confederacy of Clan Chattan, 167. Burke's Commoners, ii. 261. Burke's Landed Gentry (1848-1906). Scottish N. and Q., 3rd S., iii. 70.

Inverarity. Scottish N. and Q., 3rd S., iii. 163.

of Invercauld. Baronage, by Douglas, 339-341. Nisbet's Heraldic Plates, ed. Ross and Grant (1892), 40-42. Confederacy of Clan Chattan, 147-160. Burke's Landed Gentry (1848-1925). Historical MSS. Commission (1873), 4th Report, pt. i. The Records of Invercauld, 1547-1828, ed. Rev. J. G. Michie, $xi+523$ pp. (New Spalding Club, 1901). Notes on "The Records of Invercauld," *in* Scottish N. and Q., 3rd S., i. 168, 180-181 ; ii. 4-6, 19, 35, 51, 66, 81, 98, 113, 132, 145. Burke's Commoners, ii. 98.

of Inverey. Baronage, by Douglas, 547-549. Confederacy of Clan Chattan, 161. Scottish N. and Q., 2nd S., vii. 85 : 3rd S., iv. 99 ; vi. 164. Farquharson Genealogies, ii. 1-57, with chart. A Day that is Dead, by Rev. J. Stirton, D.D.*

**Farquharson** of Langton. Landed Gentry (1875-1925).
  of Lochtervandich. Scottish N. and Q., 2nd S., iii. 170.
  Longside. Scottish N. and Q., 2nd S., viii. 45.
  of Monaltrie. Confederacy of Clan Chattan, 162. Tayler's Jacobites of
     Aberdeenshire, 158-167.
  in Tombea. Tayler's Jacobites, 168-169.
  of Tullochcoy. Farquharson Genealogies, ii. 69-70.
  in Tullycairn. Tayler's Jacobites, 179.
  of Whitehouse. Burke's Landed Gentry (1848-1914). Confederacy of
     Clan Chattan, 163-166. Scottish N. and Q., 3rd S., iii. 156.
  of Whitehousemill. Tayler's Jacobites, 168.

**Farrell** of Davo. Scottish N. and Q., 2nd S., v. 44, 64.

**Fawsyde** of Fawsyde. C. H. Bedford *in* Proc. Soc. Antiq. Scotl. (1890),
  370-378.

**Fea** of Clestrain. Scottish Historical Review (1912), viii. 110.

**Fellowes-Gordon** of Knockespoch. Burke's Landed Gentry (1921-1925).

**Fenton** of Baikie. Memorials of Angus and the Mearns, by A. Jervise,
  ed. Gammack, ii. 44-47. Pedigree of Osler Family (1924).
  of Ogill. Antiquarian Notes, by C. Fraser-Mackintosh (1897), ii. 18.
     Warden's Angus or Forfarshire, v. 190-192.

**Fenton-Livingstone.** Historical MSS. Commission (1879), 7th Report, pt. ii.

**Fentoun,** Erskine, Viscount of. The Scots Peerage, v. 85-97.

**Fergus** of Inverurie. The Family of Forbes of Forbesfield, by A. Forbes,
  83-95.

**Fergushill** of Burnockstone and Ayr. Paterson's Ayr, ii. 402-404.
  Paterson's Ayr and Wigton, i. 618-622.
  of Fergushill. Ayrshire Families, by Robertson, i. 349-351. History of
     the County of Ayr, by Paterson, ii. 504.

**Fergusson, Ferguson.** Heraldry, by A. Nisbet (1722), i. 411-412. The
  Clan and Name of Ferguson, by James Ferguson, pamphlet (Glasgow,
  1892). Records of the Clan and Name of Fergusson, Ferguson,
  and Fergus, by James Ferguson and Rev. R. Menzies Fergusson,
  8vo, illust. (Edinr. 1895). Supplement to above (Edinr. 1899).

**Fergusson,** Aberdeen. Genealogies of an Aberdeen Family; Aberd.
  Univ. Studies, 85.
  Antigua. Oliver's History of Antigua, i. 249.
  of Auchinsoul. Paterson's History of Ayr, i. 259. Paterson's Ayr and
     Wigton, ii. 116.
  of Badifurrow. The Family of Forbes of Forbesfield, by A. Forbes
     (Aberdeen, 1905), 107-118.
  of Bank and Monkwood. Ayr and Wigton, i. 443.
  of Craig. Paterson's History of Ayr, i. 312. Ayr and Wigton, ii. 150.
  of Craigdarroch. Heraldry, by Nisbet (1742), ii., Appx. 97-98. Burke's
     Landed Gentry (1848-1925).
  of Dalduff. Paterson's History of Ayr, ii. 369. Ayr and Wigton, ii. 426.
  of Doonholm. Ayr and Wigton, i. 143.

**Fergusson** of Finnart. Paterson's History of Ayr, i. 230. Ayr and Wigton, ii. 101-102.

in Inverkeithing. Stephen's Inverkeithing (1921), 326-328.

of Kilkerran. Case of Sir Adam Fergusson of Kilkerran, Bart., claiming the Title of Earl of Glencairn (1797). Paterson's History of Ayr, i. 390-392. Ayr and Wigton, ii. 228-233. Burke's Peerage and Baronetage. Complete Baronetage, by G. E. C., iv. 417.

of Kinmundy. Burke's Landed Gentry (1858-1925).

of Pitfour. Burke's Landed Gentry (1858-1925).

of Raith. The Annals of Gallantry, ed. A. Moore (1813), i. 251-273. Landed Gentry (1863-1914). Conolly's Eminent Men of Fife, 180-182.

in Raplochburn. The Stirling Antiquary, ed. W. B. Cook, ii. 137.

of Spitalhaugh. Burke's Peerage and Baronetage. Buchan and Paton's History of Peeblesshire, iii. 172-173.

Tarland. Genealogies of an Aberdeen Family ; Aberd. Univ. Studies, 37-38.

**Fergusson-Buchanan** of Auchentorlie. Burke's Landed Gentry (1894-1925).

**Fernie** of Fernie Castle. Notes from Searches, by Jas. Paterson, *in* Scottish Surnames (1866), 1-9.

**Ferrier** of Belsyde. Burke's Landed Gentry (1879-1925).

of Chippens. Notes on Ferrier of Chippens in Kilbarchan, typed, 1 p., 4to ; in Library of Society of Genealogists.

of Kintrocket. Baronage of Angus and Mearns, by D. M. Peter, 100.

**Ferry** of Springside. Paterson's Ayr and Wigton, iii. 369.

**Fife**, The Ancient Earls of. East Neuk of Fife, by W. Wood, 2nd ed., 9-10, 111. A Short Account of the Earls of Fife, compiled from documents in the Record Offices in Edinburgh, London, etc., by Wm. Wood (1896). The Scots Peerage, iv. 1-15.

Duff, Earl of, Duke of. Biographical Peerage (1808), 242-246. Eminent Men of Fife, by Conolly, 311. Historical MSS. Commission (1873), 4th Report. Genealogy of the Dukes of Fife, by W. Cramond, *in* The Scotsman (29th July 1889), and *in* the Genealogist, N. S., iii. 205-210 ; iv. 224. Geneal. Mag., iv. 96-99. G. E. C.'s Complete Peerage. Burke's and other Annual Peerages.

Stewart, Earl of. The Scots Peerage, iv. 14-15.

**Filshie.** Notes and Queries, 8th S., iii. 288.

**Findlater**, Ogilvie, Earl of. Genealogical Fragments, by James Maidment, 4 pp. (Berwick, 1855).* Historic Earls and Earldoms of Scotland, by J. Mackintosh (1898), 307-347. Scottish N. and Q., 1st S., xii. 156. The Scots Peerage, iv. 16-41. G. E. C.'s Complete Peerage, ed. Gibbs.

in Sweden. Palace of History Catalogue (Glasgow, 1911), 201, 209.

**Findlay** of Aberlour. Burke's Landed Gentry (1894-1925).

of Boturich and Balloch. Book of Dumbartonshire, by Joseph Irving, ii. 232. Burke's Landed Gentry (1906-1925).

**Findlay** of Easterhill. Burke's Visitation of Seats and Arms (1853), ii. 69. Burke's Landed Gentry (1846-1925).

of Tour. Burke's Landed Gentry (1925).

**Finlay** of Balchrystie. East Neuk of Fife, by W. Wood (1887), 107-108, 120.

of Castle Toward. Burke's Landed Gentry (1862-1925).

of Deanston. Landed Gentry (1875-1886).

of Moss. Strathendrick, by Guthrie Smith, 255, 256.

in Sweden. One Year in Sweden, by H. Marryat, ii. 488.

**Fitz Alan.** Collectanea Topographica et Genealogica, vi. 1-20. Miscell. Geneal. et Heraldica, ii. 161. Dallaway's Sussex, i. *xlv.*; ii. 114. Eyton's Antiquities of Shropshire, vii. 228. Fitzalan and Stuart, by Eyton (1856). The Scots Peerage, i. 10-12. The Origin of the Stewarts, by J. H. Round, *in* The Genealogist, N. S., xviii. 1-13.

**Fitz Gilbert.** The Scots Peerage, iv. 340-342. Genealogist, N. S., ii. 43.

**Fitzmaurice,** Earl of Orkney. The Scots Peerage, vi. 581-584. Burke's Peerage. Debrett's Peerage.

**Fleming,** Antigua. Oliver's History of Antigua, i. 252-256.

of Auchintoul. Tayler's Jacobites of Aberdeenshire, 182.

of Barrochan. Crawfurd's Shire of Renfrew (1818), 162, 381. Burke's Landed Gentry (1848). The Last of the Flemings of Barrochan, *in* Herald and Genealogist, ii. 246-249.

of Biggar. Biggar and the House of Fleming, by William Hunter (Biggar, 1862 ; 2nd ed., Edinr. 1867). Upper Ward of Lanarkshire, by Irving and Murray (1864), i. 298, 306-329. The Scots Peerage, viii. 532-555.

of Boghall. Annals of a Tweeddale Parish, by Rev. Andrew Baird, 132-144. The Scots Peerage, viii. 530, 547.

of Bord. The Scots Peerage, viii. 525-527.

of Cumbernauld. Burke's Landed Gentry (1848-1858). The Scots Peerage, viii. 520-555.

of Farme, Ferne. Nisbet's Heraldic Plates, ed. Ross and Grant, 110. Complete Baronetage, by G. E. C., iii. 331.

Lord Fleming. Heraldry, by A. Nisbet (1722), i. 152-153. Kirkintilloch, by Thos. Watson (1894), 11-45. The Complete Peerage, by G. E. C. (1910). The Scots Peerage, viii. 532-558. The Genealogist, N. S., viii. 185-186.

of Mossfennan. Annals of a Tweeddale Parish, 67.

**Fleming-Hamilton.** Lands . . . in Galloway, by M'Kerlie, 2nd ed. (1906), i. 629.

**Fletcher** of Ballinshoe. Baronage of Angus and Mearns, by D. M. Peter, 102. Angus or Forfarshire, by A. J. Warden, iv. 99.

of Corsock. Burke's Landed Gentry (1848-1875).

of Cranston. Ayrshire Families, by G. Robertson, i. 203.

of Dunans. Landed Gentry (1863-1875).

of Innerpeffer. Warden's Angus or Forfarshire, v. 130-131.

**Fletcher** of Parkhall. Strathendrick, by Guthrie Smith, 226.

of Rosehaugh. Landed Gentry (1894-1925).

of Saltoun. The Collections of the Family of Fletcher of Saltoun, 4to, 8 pp. (Edinr. 1803). Burke's Landed Gentry (1848-1925).

**Fogo** of Killearn. Scottish N. and Q., 3rd S., i. 64.

of Row. Burke's Landed Gentry (1906-1925).

**Folisdaill** of Lambesta. Scot. Hist. Review, xxi. 129.

**Folkarton** of Folkardton. Upper Ward of Lanarkshire, by Irving and Murray, ii. 223, 225-227.

**Foratt** in Sweden. One Year in Sweden, by H. Marryat, ii. 489.

**Forbes.** Genealogy of the Family of Forbes, by Mathew Lumsden of Tulliekerne, 1580, ed. Wm. Forbes, 8vo, *xxii.* + 100 pp. (Inverness, 1819 ; reprinted, 1883). Nisbet's Heraldry (1722), i. 327-329. Geneal. Coll., by W. Macfarlane, 1750-51 ; Scot. Hist. Soc., ii. 207-264, 471-483. Scottish N. and Q., 2nd S., vi. 189. Notes and Queries, 4th S., ii. 33 ; v. 238 ; vi. 527 ; xi. 371 : 6th S., v. 498 ; vi. 476. Forbes of Forbesfield (1905), 1-4.

of Auchernach. Scottish N. and Q., 2nd S., viii. 53.

of Auquhorthies. Temple's Thanage of Fermartyn, 99.

in New Balgonen. Forbes of Forbesfield, 13-16.

of Balgownie. Landed Gentry (1863-1925).

of Ballogie. Scottish N. and Q., 3rd S., v. 217.

of Bercleigh. Landed Gentry (1863).

of Blackford. Temple's Thanage of Fermartyn, 99-101.

of Blackton. Two Scottish Soldiers, and A Jacobite Laird and his Forbears, or the Forbeses of Blackton, by J. Ferguson, 8vo (1888).

in Boghead. Tayler's Jacobites of Aberdeenshire, 185.

of Boyndlie. Narrative of the Last Sickness and Death of Dame Christian Forbes, 1789 (Edinr. 1875). Landed Gentry (1886-1894). Buchan, by Pratt (1858), 424-426. Thanage of Fermartyn, 155.

of Brux. The Scots Peerage, iv. 67. Tayler's Jacobites of Aberdeenshire, 186.

of Callendar. Burke's Landed Gentry (1846-1925).

of Colquhany. Burke's Landed Gentry (1848).

of Corse and Craigievar. Douglas's Baronage (1784), 75-77. Memoirs of the Earls of Granard . . ., by the Honble. John Forbes, ed. the Earl of Granard (London, 1868). Complete Baronetage, by G. E. C., ii. 373. Notes and Queries, 6th S., vi. 95 ; viii. 299. Scottish N. and Q., 3rd S., i. 128. Thanage of Fermartyn, 663-666, 668.

of Corsindae. The Scots Peerage, iv. 50.

of Culloden. Sketches of Highland Families, by John Maclean (1848), 77-102. Burke's Landed Gentry (1848-1925). Burke's Visitation of Seats and Arms (1853), i. 108. The Scottish Antiquary (1894), viii. 87. Large Sheet Pedigree, including the Families of Ross of Kindeace and Goodsir of Pitcruvie.*

in Deskrie. Scottish N. and Q., 3rd S., iv. 147.

**Forbes** of Earlstoun. Lands . . . in Galloway, by M'Kerlie, iii. 431-432.
of Echt. Burke's Landed Gentry (1848-1862). The Echt-Forbes Family
Charters, 1345-1727, ed. Rev. G. F. Browne, D.D., 4to (1923).
Edinbanchory. Scottish N. and Q., 3rd S., i. 45.
Edinburgh. The Scottish Antiquary, viii. 137-138, 186. Tancred's
Annals of a Border Club, 242.
in Edindiach. Tayler's Jacobites of Aberdeenshire, 196.
of Edinglassie. Tayler's Jacobites, 183.
Lord Forbes. Biographical Peerage (1808), 251. Historical MSS.
Commission (1871), 2nd Report. The Scots Peerage, iv. 42-68.
Burke's Peerage. Debrett's Peerage. G. E. C.'s Complete Peerage,
ed. Gibbs.
of Forbesfield. Memorials of the Family of Forbes of Forbesfield, by
Alexander Forbes, 4to, illust. (Aberdeen, 1905), 17-82.*
of Foveran. Complete Baronetage, by G. E. C., iv. 389. Thanage
of Fermartyn, by Temple, 573.
of Greens. Scottish N. and Q., 3rd S., iii. 107.
of Inverernan. Burke's Landed Gentry (1906-1925).
in Kildrummy of Templeton. Scottish N. and Q., 3rd S., iv. 39.
of Kingerloch. Burke's Landed Gentry (1848-1921).
of Knapernay. Thanage of Fermartyn, 464-465. The Scottish Antiquary (1895), ix. 43.
of Ludquharn. Scottish N. and Q. (1892-3), vi. 45.
of Medwyn. History of Peeblesshire, by Chambers, 466. Burke's
Landed Gentry (1894-1925).
of Monymusk. Baronage, by Douglas (1784), 39-41. Narrative of the
last sickness and death of Dame Christian Forbes, by her son
Sir William Forbes, 6th Baronet of Monymusk and Pitsligo, 1789
(Edinr. 1875). Circular Genealogical Table of the Forbes Family
of Monymusk and Pitsligo, from 1460-1880, by Louisa L. Forbes
(Mrs G. E. Forbes). Size 2 ft. 11 in. square (1880). Complete
Baronetage, by G. E. C., ii. 205.
of Newe. The Family of Forbes of Forbesfield, 8-12. Burke's Peerage
and Baronetage. Tayler's Jacobites of Aberdeenshire, 190.
of Newhall. Wilson's Annals of Penicuik (1891), 171-173.* Scottish
Historical Review, xvi. 182-188.
Old Meldrum. Scottish N. and Q., 3rd S., iv. 39.
of Pitnacadle. Scottish N. and Q., 3rd S., iii. 136.
of Pitsligo. Historical MSS. Commission (1876), 5th Report, pt. i.
Forbes of Forbesfield, 5-7. Debrett's Baronetage.
Quebec. Scottish N. and Q., 2nd S., i. 126.
of Rires. East Neuk of Fife, by W. Wood, 2nd ed., 115-117.
of Rothiemay. Burke's Landed Gentry (1894-1925).
in Round Lichnot. Scottish N. and Q., 3rd S., iv. 38.
of Skellater. Scottish N. and Q., 2nd S., iii. 43-44, 60. Ian Roy of
Skellater, by James Neil, M.D., 4to, $x+138$ pp. (Aberdeen, 1902).
Temple's Thanage of Fermartyn, 351. Tayler's Jacobites of
Aberdeenshire, 183.

**Forbes** in Sweden. One Year in Sweden, by H. Marryat (1862), ii. 477-478, 479, 489.

of Tolquhoun. Genealogy of the House of Tolquhon, by J. Davidson, 21 pp. (Aberdeen, 1839). Thanage of Fermartyn, 378-387. Burke's Landed Gentry (1848-1921). Scottish N. and Q., 3rd S., iv. 39.

of Tombeg. Scottish N. and Q., 3rd S., iii. 154.

of Watertoun. Memoranda relating to the Family of Forbes of Waterton by John Forbes, who was served heir to the last Thomas Forbes of Waterton in 1775, 4to, plates and pedigrees, 61 pp. (Aberdeen, 1857).* Buchan, by Pratt, 416. Burke's Landed Gentry, *under* Forbes of Bercleigh. Memoir of J. Young, Aberdeen . . . 1861, ed. Lt.-Col. W. Johnston (1894), 164-167.* Account of Forbes of Watertoun, by Hopton Forbes Forbes, *in* Scottish N. and Q., x. 158.

**Forbes of Pitsligo**, Forbes, Lord. Buchan, by Rev. J. B. Pratt, 386-394. Scottish N. and Q., 2nd S., vi. 135, 153, 169 ; vii. 29. The Scots Peerage, iv. 69-76.

**Forbes-Gordon** of Balbithan. Temple's Thanage of Fermartyn, 350.

of Rayne. Burke's Landed Gentry (1875-1925).

**Forbes-Leith** of Fyvie. Fyvie Castle, by A. M. W. Stirling, 364-410. *See also* **Forbes of Tolquhoun.**

**Forbes-Leslie.** Thanage of Fermartyn, 102.

**Forbes-Mitchell** of Thainstone. Burke's Landed Gentry (1848-1894).

**Forbes-Robertson** of Hazlehead. Memoir of J. Young, Aberdeen . . . 1861, ed. Lt.-Col. W. Johnston (1894), 62-64, 164, 167.* Scottish N. and Q., 3rd S., iii. 123. The Picturesque Ancestry of Sir Johnston Forbes-Robertson, by J. M. Bulloch (Aberdeen, 1926).

**Forbes-Sempill**, Lord Sempill. The Scots Peerage, vii. 566-568.

**Ford** of Findhaven. Baronage of Angus and Mearns, by D. M. Peter, 112.

**Fordyce.** Family Record of the name of Dingwall-Fordyce in Aberdeenshire, with Appendix, etc., by Alexander Dingwall Fordyce (Fergus, Canada, 1885). Burke's Landed Gentry (1858-1925). Scottish N. and Q., 2nd S., i. 173.

Aberdeen. Memoir of J. Young, Aberdeen . . . 1861, ed. Lt.-Col. W. Johnston, 173-175.*

of Ayton. Scottish N. and Q., 2nd S., iii. 171, 188-189.

**Forfar,** Aston, Baron Aston of. Angus or Forfarshire, by A. J. Warden (1880), ii. 41. The Scots Peerage, i. 399-414.

Douglas, Earl of. Angus or Forfarshire, ii. 35. The Scots Peerage, iv. 76-79.

**Forrest.** The Stewarts (Stewart Soc. Magazine), i. 124-125.

of Comiston. Burke's Peerage and Baronetage (1839-1928).

of Easter Ogill. Baronage of Angus and Mearns, by D. M. Peter (1856), 113.

**Forrester.** Heraldry, by Nisbet (1722), i. 432-433. The Stewarts Magazine, i. 124-125.

**Forrester** of Arngibbon. Sheet Pedigree (Edinr. 1880). MS. Pedigree in possession of the family.

of Barnton. Cramond, by J. P. Wood, 56.

of Corstorphine. New Statistical Account, i. 209-212. Short Genealogical Account of the Family of Thomson in Corstorphine, by A[lex.] D[euchar], (1816), 1-2. Registrum Domus de Soltre (Bannatyne Club, 1861), 293-304. Proc. Soc. Antiq. Scotl. (1876 and 1895). A Midlothian Village, by G. Upton Selway (1890), 1-5. The Scots Peerage, iv. 80-100; ix. 91-92. G. E. C.'s Complete Baronetage, ii. 303. G. E. C.'s Peerage, 2nd ed., v. 556-559. Burke's Peerage. History of the Family of Thomson of Corstorphine, by T. R. Thomson, M.D. (Edinr. 1926), Appx. A. Printed and illuminated Pedigree in Advocates' Library, n.d. MS. Pedigree (19th c.) in Library of Society of Genealogists, London.

of Craigannet. The Stirling Antiquary (1904), iii. 208-209.

of Drylaw. Cramond, by J. P. Wood, 28.

of Garden. The Scottish Antiquary (1897), xi. 116.

of Logie. Logie, by Rev. Dr Menzies Fergusson, i. 41 ; ii. 85-87.

of Milnhill. The Parish of Longforgan, by Rev. A. Philp, 177-178, 193.

of Strathendry. East Neuk of Fife, by W. Wood, 2nd ed. (1887), 267-268.

of Torwood. The Stirling Antiquary, iv. 89.

**Forret** of Fingask. Recreations of an Antiquary, by Fittis, 387 *n.*

**Forsyth.** Notes and Queries, 6th S., i. 339 ; x. 98 : 7th S., vii. 315.

of Dykes. The Stirling Antiquary, ed. W. B. Cook, ii. 68-69.

of Nydie. Forsyth of Nydie, by Forsyth de Fronsac (Newmarket, Virginia, 1888).

of Quinish. Burke's Landed Gentry (1898-1925).

**Forsyth-Grant** of Ecclesgreig. Forsyth of Ecclesgreig, Kincardineshire, 4to, 6 pp. (1886). Burke's Landed Gentry (1875-1925).

**Forteath** of Newton. Burke's Landed Gentry (1858-1925).

**Forth,** Drummond, Marquis of. The Jacobite Peerage, by the Marquis of Ruvigny (1904), 53.

Drummond, Viscount of. The Scots Peerage, vi. 66-74.

Ruthven, Earl of. Walford's Chapters from Family Chests, ii. 240-246. The Scots Peerage, iv. 101-106.

**Fortrose,** Mackenzie, Viscount. The Scots Peerage, vii. 512-513.

**Fotheringham** of Broughty. Monifieth, by J. Malcolm (1910), 285-287.

**Fothringham** of Powrie. Angus or Forfarshire, by A. J. Warden (Dundee, 1880), iii. 404.

**Foular,** Perth. The Scottish Antiquary, xi. 64, 137-138.

**Foulis.** Nisbet's Heraldry (1722), i. 402. Scot. Hist. Review, xiv. 97, 249.

of Colinton. Nisbet's Heraldry, ii., Appx. 18-19. Douglas's Baronage, 86-88. The Scottish Antiquary, x. 178. Burke's Peerage and Baronetage. Complete Baronetage, by G. E. C., ii. 410.

**Foulis** of Ravelston. Account Book of Sir John Foulis, 1671-1707, ed. Rev. A. W. Cornelius Hallen ; (Scot. Hist. Soc., 1894). The Scottish Antiquary, ix. 23-24 [tabulates the births, marriages and deaths mentioned in above]. A Midlothian Village, by G. V. Selway, 33-37. Burke's Extinct Baronetcies. Complete Baronetage, by G. E. C., iii. 333. Geneal. Mag. (1904), vii. 415.

**Fouller** of Foullerlaw. Works of William Fowler ; Scot. Text Soc. Scot. Hist. Review, xix. 21.

**Fowler** of Braemore. Landed Gentry (1875-1886).

Inverness. Major Alpin's . . . Descendants, by P. J. Anderson (Aberdeen, 1904), 26-27.*

**Foyer** of Cult. Strathblane, by Guthrie Smith, 81-83.

**Frain**, Easter Wooden. Annals of a Border Club, by G. Tancred, 252 *n.*

**Frances** of Stane. Paterson's Ayr and Wigton, iii. 278.

**Frank.** The Franks of Buchtrig, Berwickshire, 1 p., 8vo (1795).

**Fraser, Frazer.** The True Genealogy of the Frasers, 916 to 1674, by James Fraser, minister of Wardlaw, ed. William Mackay ; (Scot. Hist. Soc., 1905). Nisbet's Heraldry (1722), i. 388-390. Annals of such Patriots of the Distinguished Family of Fraser, Frysell, Simson or Fitz-Simon, as have signalised themselves in the public service of Scotland [by Archibald Simson], 8vo (Edinr. 1795 ; 2nd ed., ed. Col. A. Frazer, 1805). Historical Account of the Family of Frisel or Fraser . . . by J. Anderson, 4to (1825).* Memorial of the Family of the Frasers, 4to, 22 pp. Dictionary of National Biography, *s.v.*

**Fraser**, Ancrum. Scottish Historical Review, xxv. 298.

of Balmakewan. Baronage of Angus and Mearns, by Peter, 370.

of Balnain. Oliver's History of Antigua, i. 259.

in Canada. The Clan Fraser in Canada, by Alex. Fraser (Toronto, 1895).

of Castle Fraser and Inverallochy. Burke's Landed Gentry (1848-1925). Tayler's Jacobites of Aberdeenshire, 196 198.

of Cowie. The Scots Peerage, vii. 426-431.

Dornoch. Scottish N. and Q., 2nd S., vi. 69.

of Dunballoch. Mackenzie's History of Frasers of Lovat (1896).

of Durris, Dores. Geneal. Coll., by W. Macfarlane, 1750-51 ; Scot. Hist. Soc., ii. 316-331. Account of the Family of Fraser . . . of Durris . . . by W. N. Fraser of Tornaveen, 4to.* Complete Baronetage, by G. E. C., iv. 293.

of Findrack. Account of the Family of Fraser . . . of Findrack, by W. N. Fraser, 4to.* Burke's Landed Gentry (1858-1925).

of Ford. Burke's Landed Gentry (1879).

Lord Fraser. The Scots Peerage, iv. 107-122.

Lord Fraser of Lovat. *See* **Fraser of Lovat.**

Duke of Fraser. The Jacobite Peerage, by Ruvigny, 55-58.

of Fraserfield. Notes of Births, Deaths and Marriages, chiefly extracted from the pages of a Family Bible and Prayer Book dated 1717, belonging to the Hon. Wm. Fraser of Fraserfield (1869).* Thanage of Fermartyn, 651-654. The Scots Peerage, vii. 444-445.

M

**Fraser** of Frendraught. Thanage of Fermartyn, 138-141.
of Fruid. Buchan and Paton's History of Peeblesshire, iii. 404.
of Guisachan. Visitation of Seats and Arms, by J. B. Burke (1853), i. 214.
of Hospitalfield. Baronage of Angus and Mearns, by Peter, 118.
Eminent Arbroathians, by J. M. M'Bain (Arbroath, 1897), 394-406.
Burke's Landed Gentry (1863-1894).
Inverness. Major Alpin's . . . Descendants, by P. J. Anderson (1904), 27-28.*
of Kiltarlity. Scottish N. and Q. (1890-1), iv. 161.
of Knock. Pont's Cuninghame, ed. Dobie, 219-221. Ayrshire Families,
by G. Robertson, i. 351-353. History of County of Ayr, by Paterson,
ii. 309. Ayr and Wigton, by Paterson, iii. 533.
of Ledclune and Morar. Burke's Peerage and Baronetage.
of Lochavich. Burke's Landed Gentry (1906-1925).
of Lovat. Nisbet's Heraldry (1742), ii., Appx. 114-116. Geneal. Coll.,
by W. Macfarlane, 1750-51 ; Scot. Hist. Soc., ii. 88-96. Historical
Account of the Family of Frisel or Fraser, particularly Fraser of
Lovat, by John Anderson, 4to (Edinr. 1825). Case of T. Frazer of
Lovat, Esq., claiming the title of Baron Lovat, folio, 11 pp.
Additional Case, folio, 9 pp. and folding pedigree (1854). Claim of
Thos. A. Frazer of Lovat, Esq., to the Barony of Lovat : (Session
Papers, 93, 178 of 1826-7, G of 1854-5, L of 1856, H of 1857.) Notes
and Queries (1858), 2nd S., v. 335, 385 ; vi. 176, 194, 237, 271.
Burke's Commoners, iii. 294. The Lovat Peerage and Estates :
Scheme for raising funds in support of the claim of John Fraser,
Lord Lovat, 4to (London, 1885). Republished as The Lovat
Peerage and Estates ; a Short History of the Case, 4to (London,
1885). History of the Frasers of Lovat, with Genealogies of the
Principal Families . . . also Dunballoch and Phopachy, by Alex.
Mackenzie (Inverness, 1896). The Scots Peerage, v. 519-535.
Geneal. Mag. (1898), i. 434. Scottish N. and Q., 2nd S., v. 61.
Papers from the Collection of Sir Wm. Fraser, K.C.B., LL.D., ed.
J. R. N. MacPhail ; Scot. Hist. Soc. (1924).
of Moniack. Burke's Landed Gentry (1848, 1886, 1894).
of Muchalls, Fraser, Baron. The Jacobite Peerage, by the Marquis of
Ruvigny (1904), 53-55.
of Oliver Castle. The Scots Peerage, vii. 421-422.
of Philorth. The Frasers of Philorth, by Alexander Fraser, 17th Lord
Saltoun, 3 vols. 4to, illust. (Edinr. 1879).* Antiquarian Notes, by
C. Fraser-Mackintosh, i. 290-293. The Scots Peerage, vii. 239,
430-441. Scottish N. and Q., v. 76. The Complete Baronetage,
by G. E. C., ii. 348.
of Phopachy and Torbreck. Scottish N. and Q., vi. 63. Antiquarian
Notes, by C. Fraser-Mackintosh, i. 189-192. Notes and Queries,
10th S., x. 330. Mackenzie's History of Frasers of Lovat.
of Reelick. Burke's Landed Gentry (1898-1925).
Lord Saltoun. The Scots Peerage, vii. 417-453.
of Skipness Castle. Landed Gentry (1862-1875).
of Stoneywood. The Scots Peerage, iv. 108-112.

**Fraser** of Strichen. The Scots Peerage, v. 543-546.

in Sweden. One Year in Sweden, by H. Marryat (1862), ii. 489.

of Tornaveen. Burke's Landed Gentry (1906-1925).

of Touch Fraser. The Scots Peerage, vii. 420-429. Lands and Lairds of Touch, by J. C. Gibson (Stirling, 1829).

of Traquair. Peeblesshire Localities, by Renwick, 105.

**Fraser-Campbell** of Dunmore. Burke's Landed Gentry (1925 Suppl.).

**Fraser-Mackintosh** of Drummond. Antiquarian Notes . . . by C. Fraser-Mackintosh, i. *xiii.* Burke's Landed Gentry (1894-1925).

**Fraser-Tytler** of Aldourie and Belnain. Burke's Landed Gentry (1848-1925). Genealogies of an Aberdeen Family, by Smith ; Aberd. Univ. Studies, 103-105.

of Woodhouselee. Landed Gentry (1848-1925).

**Freebairn.** Scot. Hist. Review, xv. 106.

**Freer.** The Freer Family of Essendie, Innernethy and Woodlands in Perthshire, pedigree with arms, folio.

**French.** Heraldry, by A. Nisbet (1722), i. 322. Index Armorial to an Emblazoned MS. of the Surname of French, Franc, François, Frenc and others, both British and Foreign, by A. D. W. French, 8vo, 200 copies (Boston, 1892).*

of Frenchland. Nisbet's Heraldic Plates, ed. Ross and Grant (1892), 84-86.

of Thornidykes. Notes on the Surnames of Francus, Franceis, French, etc., in Scotland, with an Account of the Frenches of Thornicdykes, by A. D. Weld French, 8vo (Boston, 1893).* Nisbet's Heraldic Plates, 84.

**Frendraught,** Crichton, Viscount. Temple's Thanage of Fermartyn (1894), 144-154. The Scots Peerage, iv. 123-134. Abstract of Evidence of the Claim of David Maitland Makgill to be Heir of Line in general of Viscount Frendraught.

**Freskyn** of Sutherland. Sutherland and Caithness in Saga-Time, or The Jarls and the Freskyns, by James Gray (Edinr. 1922). The Scots Peerage, ii. 121 ; viii. 320.

**Frizel.** *See* **Fraser.**

**Fullarton** of Dreghorn. History of Ayr, by Paterson, ii. 22. Ayr and Wigton, by Paterson, i. 472-475.

of Dudwick. Ayrshire Families, by G. Robertson, ii. 106. Tayler's Jacobites of Aberdeenshire, 198.

of Fullarton. Nisbet's Heraldry, i. 339. Geneal. Coll., by W. Macfarlane, 1750-51 ; Scot. Hist. Soc., ii. 332-356. Ayrshire Families, ii. 83-131, 370-372. Cases before the Court of Session on the Family Dispute regarding the Succession to the Estate of Bargany, Sir Hugh Dalrymple Hamilton of North Berwick *versus* the Fullartons ; with chart pedigrees, 4to (1822-24). Paterson's History of Ayr, ii. 12-21. Ayr and Wigton, i. 410, 450-472. Warden's Angus or Forfarshire, iii. 439-440 ; iv. 318, 338-339. Shaw's Dalrymples of Langlands, 134-136. Nisbet's Heraldic Plates (1892), 116-118. Scottish N. and Q., 3rd S., iv. 175. The Scots Peerage, viii. 108-111.

**Fullarton** of Kerila. Pont's Cuninghame, ed. Dobie, 253. Paterson's
 Ayr, ii. 450. Ayr and Wigton, iii. 574.
 of Kilmichael. Reid's History of the County of Bute, 237-240. Ayrshire
  Families, i. 115 *n.*, 118. Burke's Landed Gentry (1863, 1875, 1894).
 of Kinnaber. Warden's Angus or Forfarshire, iv. 436.
 of Overtoun. Ayrshire Families, i. 118. History of Ayr, by Paterson,
  ii. 138. Ayr and Wigton, iii. 320.
 of Portincross. Paterson's Ayr and Wigton, iii. 319.
 of Rosemount. Paterson's Ayr, ii. 481. Ayr and Wigton, i. 747.
 of Skeldon. Paterson's Ayr, i. 441.

**Fuller-Maitland.** Lands . . . in Galloway, by M'Kerlie, v. 201.

**Fullerton** of Carberry. Herald and Genealogist, viii. 197.
 of Carleton. Lands . . . in Galloway, iii. 189.
 of Craighall. Heraldry, by A. Nisbet (1742), II., iii. 14.

**Fullerton-Elphinstone** of Carberry. The Scots Peerage, iii. 546-548.

**Fulton** of Fulton and Grangevale. Paterson's History of Ayr, ii. 516.
 Paterson's Ayr and Wigton, iii. 95.
 of Grangehill. Paterson's Ayr, i. 279. Ayr and Wigton, iii. 97-98.
 of Hartfield. Crawfurd's Shire of Renfrew (1818), 330-331.
 of Muirtoun. Paterson's Ayr, i. 278. Ayr and Wigton, iii. 96.

**Fyfe** in Sweden. One Year in Sweden, by H. Marryat, ii. 482, 483, 485,
 488.

**Fyffe** of Smithfield. Burke's Landed Gentry (1848-1875). Angus or
 Forfarshire, by A. J. Warden (1880), iv. 428.

**Fyvie,** Seton, Lord. The Thanage of Fermartyn, by Rev. Wm. Temple,
 25-27. The Family of Seton, by George Seton, ii. The Scots
 Peerage, iii. 368-375. Fyvie Castle, by A. M. W. Stirling (1928).

**Gairdner,** Ayr. The Dalrymples of Langlands, by J. Shaw, 140-142.*
 in Sweden. One Year in Sweden, by Marryat (1862), ii. 489.

**Gairnes** of Leyes and Dumbarrow. Geneal. Coll., by W. Macfarlane,
 1750-51 ; Scot. Hist. Soc., i. 11, 24.

**Galbraith** of Balgair, and Hill of Balgair. Notes and Queries, 5th S.,
 xi. 87, 198 ; xii. 15. Strathendrick, by Guthrie Smith, 230-239.
 of Blackhouse. Strathblane, by Guthrie Smith, 79 *n.* Strathendrick,
 239-240.
 of Cameron. Strathendrick, 215, 216.
 of Culcreuch. Strathendrick, 165-174.
 of Dalserf. The Scots Peerage, vi. 29.
 of Greenock. Old Greenock, by G. Williamson, i. 313.

**Galloway,** The Ancient Lords of. The Scots Peerage, iv. 135-144.
 Stewart, Earl of. Biographical Peerage (1808), 255-256. Crawfurd's
  Shire of Renfrew, ed. Robertson (1818), 463-466. J. K. Stewart *in*
  The Stewarts Magazine, i. 82-128, 155-205, 211-216, 304-310, *et passim.*
  G. E. C.'s Complete Peerage, ed. Gibbs. The Scots Peerage,
  iv. 145-173.

**Galloway** of Blervie. Burke's Landed Gentry (1914-1925).
   Lord Dunkeld. The Scots Peerage, iii. 376-382.
   of Todshaugh. Geneal. Mag., vii. 73.
**Galt**, Ayrshire. Scot. Hist. Review, xvi. 257. Scottish N. and Q., 2nd S.,
   viii. 148.
**Gammell** of Drumtochty. Baronage of Angus and Mearns, by Peter, 121.
   Burke's Landed Gentry (1886-1925).
**Garden** of Johnston. Scottish N. and Q. (1891-2), 1st S., v. 94, 111, 142.
   of Lathers. Scottish N. and Q., 3rd S., i. 32.
   of Muirhouse. Warden's Angus or Forfarshire, iii. 439.
   of Troup and Dalgety. Fraser's History of Laurencekirk, 114-118.
   Burke's Landed Gentry (1849-1925).
**Garden-Campbell** of Glenlyon. Baronage of Angus and Mearns (1856),
   373. Landed Gentry (1849-1925), s.v. **Garden** of Troup.
**Gardiner** of Bankton. Life of Colonel James Gardiner, by Doddridge.
   The Scots Peerage, ii. 276.
**Gardner**. Genealogical Fragments, by Jas. Maidment, 2 pp. (Berwick,
   1855).*
**Gardyne**, Aberdeenshire. Scottish N. and Q., ii. 50.
   of Gardyne. Angus or Forfarshire, by Warden, iv. 69-72. Memorials
   of Angus and the Mearns, by Jervise, ed. Gammack, ii. 85-88.
   of Lawton. Angus or Forfarshire, iii. 455-456 ; iv. 79.
   of Leys. Angus or Forfarshire, iii. 457.
   of Middleton. Baronage of Angus and Mearns, by D. M. Peter (1856),
   124. Burke's Landed Gentry (1849-1894).
**Garioch**, The Ancient Lords of. The Scots Peerage, v. 581-589, 637.
   Erskine, Viscount. The Jacobite Peerage, by the Marquis of Ruvigny
   (1904), 58.
   Goodeve-Erskine, Lord. Burke's Peerage. G. E. C.'s Complete Peerage,
   ed. Gibbs. The Scots Peerage, v. 635-636.
   Aberdeen. Tayler's Jacobites of Aberdeenshire, 199.
**Garlies**, Stewart, Lord. Burke's Peerage. The Scots Peerage, iv. 160-173.
**Garmoran**, The Ancient Lords of. The Scots Peerage, v. 30-32, 39.
**Garnock**, Crawfurd, Lindsay, Viscount. Burke's Peerage. The Scots
   Peerage, iv. 174-178.
**Garthshore** of Garthshore, **Gartshore** of Gartshore. Heraldry, by Nisbet
   (1742), ii., Appx. 301. Burke's Landed Gentry (1849-1879). Kirkin-
   tilloch, by Thos. Watson (Glasgow, 1894), 97-104.
**Garviehaugh** of Caskieben. Heraldry, by Nisbet, ii., Appx. 123.
**Garvine**, Ayr. Paterson's Ayr and Wigton, i. 151-152.
**Gauden** of Swinister and Overland. Zetland Family Histories, by F. J.
   Grant, 78-80.
**Gauld**. Scottish N. and Q., 2nd S., viii. 59, 66, 161.
**Gavin**, Lunan. Angus or Forfarshire, by Warden, iv. 51-52. Memorials
   of Angus and the Mearns, by Jervise, ed. Gammack, ii. 270, 271.

**Gavine** of Braikie. Baronage of Angus and Mearns, by D. M. Peter (1856), 127.

**Ged(de.** Geneal. Coll., by W. Macfarlane, 1750-51 ; Scot. Hist. Soc., i. 50.

**Geddes** of Rachan, Kirkurd, and Scotstoun. History of Peeblesshire, by Chambers, 447. Peeblesshire Localities, by Renwick, 235-236, 244, 432, 440. Annals of a Tweeddale Parish, by Baird, 71-75. Buchan and Paton's History of Peeblesshire, iii. 92, 188-193, 199, 281-285.

**Geekie**, Kettins. Angus or Forfarshire, by Warden, iv. 9-11.

**Geils** of Geilston. Irving's Book of Dumbartonshire (1879), ii. 309.

**Gellatly** of Ebrokis. The Scottish Antiquary, xiv. 113.

**Gemmell, Gemmill.** The Scottish Antiquary (1893), vii. 92-93.
of Raithmuir. Notes on the Probable Origin of the Name Gemmell or Gemmell . . . with Genealogical Account of the Family of Gemmill of Raithmuir, Fenwick, by J. Leiper Gemmill, 4to (Glasgow, 1909).*
of Templehouse. History of County of Ayr, by Paterson (1852), ii. 52. Paterson's Ayr and Wigton, iii. 238-239. Notes on the probable origin of the Scottish Surname of Gemmell or Gemmill, with a Genealogical Account of the Family of Gemmell of Templehouse (Ottawa, 1901).

**Gerard**, Midmar and Aberdeen. Genealogies of an Aberdeen Family, by Smith, Aberdeen Univ. Studies (1913), 106-110.
of Rochsoles. Annals of a Border Club, by G. Tancred (1899), 242. Burke's Landed Gentry (1849-1925). Scottish N. and Q., 1st S., x. 59, 61 ; xii. 175.

**Gib** of Auchmilling. Paterson's History of the County of Ayr, ii. 338. Paterson's Ayr and Wigton, i. 549-550.

**Gib, Gibb** of Carriber. The Life and Times of Robert Gib, Lord of Carriber . . . with Notices of his Descendants . . . by Sir George Duncan Gibb, Bart., 2 vols. 8vo (London, 1874). Pedigree of the Family of Gibb of Carriber (1874). Complete Baronetage, by G. E. C., ii. 403. [Material for a History of the Family of Gibb is being collected by Mr Hugh Beaver, Queen Anne's Lodge, Westminster, London, S.W. 1.]

**Gibb** of Falkland. Pedigree of J. R. Campbell of Inverardine . . . and Sir George D. Gibb, compiled by the latter (1872).

**Gibbon**, Aberdeen. Memoir of J. Young, Aberdeen . . . 1861, ed. Lt.-Col. W. Johnston (1894), 175-176.*
of Johnston. Fraser's Laurencekirk, 121. Memoirs of J. Young, Aberdeen, 95.

**Gibson** of Durie. Douglas's Baronage, 568-570. East Neuk of Fife, by W. Wood, 2nd ed. (1887), 33-38. Scottish Antiquary, iv. 81 ; xiii. 180-181, small chart pedigree.
Eddleston. Peeblesshire Localities, by Renwick, 37.
of Glencrosh. Some Notes on the Family of Gibson of Glencrosh, by T. M. Fallow, Dumfries [1905].*
of Keirhill. Complete Baronetage, by G. E. C., iv. 404.

**Gibson**, Morphie.  Scottish N. and Q., v. 174.

Orkney.  Caithness Family History, by Henderson, 304-307.

of Pentland.  Burke's Landed Gentry (1906-1925).

**Gibson-Carmichael** of Durie.  Complete Baronetage, by G. E. C., iv. 404.
The Scottish Antiquary, i. and ii. 88, 107-111, 131-132.

**Gibson-Craig** of Riccarton.  Burke's Peerage and Baronetage.

**Gibsone.**  Norton Smith's Orkney Armorials, 50.

**Gifford** of Busta.  Zetland Family Histories, by F. J. Grant, 84-89.

of Linton.  Buchan and Paton's History of Peeblesshire, iii. 103-104.

of Ollaberry.  Zetland Family Histories, 90-92.

of Weathersta.  Zetland Family Histories, 80-83.

Hay, Earl of.  The Scots Peerage, viii. 453-474.

**Gilbertson.**  The Family and Surname of Buchanan, by Wm. Buchanan of
Auchmar, 118.

**Gilchrist**, Antigua.  Oliver's History of Antigua, ii. 16.

of Ospidale.  Burke's Landed Gentry (1863-1898).

**Gilchrist-Clark** of Speddoch.  Burke's Landed Gentry (1898-1925).

**Giles**, Leith.  Annals of a Border Club, by G. Tancred, 243.

**Gilfillan** of Cowdenknowes.  Annals of a Border Club, 244.

**Gill** of Blairythan and Savock.  Account of the Family of Gill . . . by A. J.
Mitchell-Gill, 8vo, 29 pp. (1882).  The Scottish Antiquary, iii. 153-155.
Temple's Thanage of Fermartyn, 587-590.  Burke's Landed Gentry
(1858-1925).

**Gilleis** of Glenkirk, and Quhitslaid.  Peeblesshire Localities, by Renwick,
237, 244.

**Gillespie.**  Pedigrees of the Family of James of Culgarth, by H. E. M. J.
and W. A. J. (Exeter, 1913).*

of Mountquhanie and Kirkton.  Burke's Landed Gentry (1875-1906).

of Newton Rires and Kirkton.  East Neuk of Fife, by W. Wood, 2nd ed.,
121, 203-204.

**Gillies** of Little Keithock.  Angus or Forfarshire, by Warden, iii. 23-24.

of Kintrocket.  Baronage of Angus and Mearns, by D. M. Peter, 130.

**Gillon** of Wallhouse.  Burke's Landed Gentry (1848-1925).

**Gillon-Fergusson** of Isle.  Burke's Landed Gentry (1898-1925).

**Gilmore** of North Hillhead.  Pont's Cuninghame, ed. Dobie, 115.

**Gilmour** of Craigmillar.  Peeblesshire Localities, by Renwick, 139.  Burke's
Extinct Baronetcies.  Complete Baronetage, by G. E. C., iv. 306.
Burke's Landed Gentry (1871-1925).

of Eaglesham.  Burke's Landed Gentry (1879-1925).

Edinburgh.  Complete Baronetage, by G. E. C., iii. 331.

of Montrave.  Burke's Peerage and Baronetage (after 1897).

**Giustiniani-Bandini**, Earl of Newburgh.  The Scots Peerage, vi. 457-460.

**Gladstanes** of Crocketford.  Lands . . . in Galloway, by M'Kerlie (1878),
iv. 327.

**Gladstone** of Fasque and Balfour. Lodge's Peerage and Baronetage. Foster's Lancashire Pedigrees. Burke's Royal Descents and Pedigrees of Founders' Kin, 70. Biggar and the House of Fleming, by W. Hunter, 2nd ed., 141.

in Sweden. One Year in Sweden, by H. Marryat, ii. 489.

**Glaister** of Glaister. Angus or Forfarshire, by Warden, iii. 98. Memorials of Angus and the Mearns, by Jervise, ed. Gammack, ii. 82.

**Glamis**, Lyon, Lord. The Scots Peerage, viii. 270-317.

Bowes-Lyon, Lord. Burke's Peerage. G. E. C.'s Complete Peerage, ed. Gibbs. The Scots Peerage, viii. 313-317.

**Glas.** Genealogical Chart, by Lt.-Col. John Glas Sandeman, M.V.O.* The Clan Magazine, ed. Lt.-Col. John Glas Sandeman.*

Crail. Churchyard Monuments of Crail, by Erskine Beveridge, 208-211.

Stirling. M.S. Pedigree in Lyon Office.

**Glasfoord**, Abercromby, Lord. The Scots Peerage, iv. 179-182.

**Glasgow**, Boyle, Earl of. Biographical Peerage (1808), 260-261. Crawfurd's Shire of Renfrew (1818), 325-327. History of the County of Ayr, by Paterson, ii. 303-305. History of the County of Bute, by Reid (1864), 229-236. Paterson's Ayr and Wigton (1866), iii. 530-532. Hist. MSS. Commission (1872), 3rd Report ; (1881), 8th Report. G. E. C.'s Complete Peerage, ed. Gibbs. The Scots Peerage, iv. 183-221. Burke's and other Annual Peerages. *See also* **Boyle of Kelburne.**

**Glasgow.** Case of Alexander Glasgow claiming to be heir male of the Lords Gray ; for the opinion of Counsel (1880).

of Mountgreenan and Pudevenholme. Ayrshire Families, by G. Robertson, i. 354-355. Paterson's Ayr, ii. 252. Paterson's Ayr and Wigton, iii. 513. Burke's Landed Gentry (1858-1863).

**Glassarie** of Glassarie. Highland Papers, ii. (Scot. Hist. Soc., 1916), 114.

**Glassford.** Genealogical Chart of the Family of Glassford, by William Glassford, Johnstone, 23 × 19 in. (1834).

**Gledstanes.** Heraldry, by Nisbet (1722), i. 266-267.

of Hundleshope. Buchan and Paton's History of Peeblesshire, iii. 599-601.

of Over Kelwood and Craigs. Pedigree annexed to Edgar's History of Dumfries, ed. Reid (1915).

**Gledstone** of Cocklaw. The Gledstones and the Siege of Cocklaw, by Mrs Oliver of Thornwood (Edinr. 1878). Florence M. Gladstone *in* Genealogist, N. S., ix. 153-157. Peeblesshire Localities, by Renwick, 366-370.

**Glen.** Memorials of the Scottish Families of Glen, by the Rev. Charles Rogers (Edinr. 1888).*

of Barr. Crawfurd's Shire of Renfrew (1818), 74.

in Hercots. Stephen's Inverkeithing, 502.

of Longcroft. The Scottish Antiquary, viii. 41, 88.

**Glen-Coats** of Ferguslie. Burke's Peerage and Baronetage (after 1894).

**Glenarthur**, Arthur, Baron. Burke's and other Annual Peerages (after 1918).

**Glencairn,** Cunningham, Earl of. Claims preferred to the House of Lords in the case of the Glencairn Peerage, by J. Maidment (Edinr. 1840). Paterson's History of the County of Ayr, ii. 210-217. Notes and Queries, 4th S., iii. 505, 607 : 6th S., i. 61, 285, 359. The Scots Peerage, iv. 222-252. G. E. C.'s Complete Peerage, ed. Gibbs.

**Glenconner,** Tennant, Baron. The Annual Peerages (after 1911).

**Glendoning, Glendinning, Glendonwyn** of Glendonwyn. Heraldry, by Nisbet (1722), i. 447. Douglas's Baronage, 223-238. The House of Glendinning, by P. Glendinning, 4to (Edinr. 1879).* [Repr. from The Eskdale and Liddesdale Advertizer.]

of Mochrum. Lands . . . in Galloway, by M'Kerlie, v. 61.

of Parton. Lands . . . in Galloway, v. 33-39, 60. Burke's Landed Gentry (1849-1875).

**Glendyne,** Nivison, Baron. The Annual Peerages (after 1922).

**Glenesk** of Glenesk. Memorials of Angus and the Mearns, by Jervise, ed. Gammack, ii. 88-89.

**Glentanar,** Coats, Baron. The Annual Peerages (after 1916).

**Goldie** of Goldielea. Lands . . . in Galloway, by M'Kerlie, v. 248.

**Goldie-Scot** of Craigmuie. Lands . . . in Galloway, iii. 84-88. Burke's Landed Gentry (1886-1925).

**Goodeve-Erskine,** Earl of Mar and Lord Garioch. Burke's Peerage. The Scots Peerage, v. 635-636.

**Goodsir** of Pitcruvie. Pedigree, including the Families of Ross of Kindeace, Forbes of Culloden and Rose of Kilravock, large sheet.

**Gordon.** Nisbet's Heraldry (1722), i. 315-319. History of the Ancient, Noble and Illustrious Family of Gordon, from their first arrival in Scotland in Malcolm III.'s time to 1690 . . . by William Gordon, of Old Aberdeen, 2 vols. 8vo (Edinr. 1726-27), [cf. Scottish N. and Q., 2nd S., v. 166.] The History of Scotland . . . to 1690 ; and a particular account of the Family of Gordon (c. 1735). Pedigree in the Additional Case of Elizabeth, claiming the Title of Countess of Sutherland (177—). Table of Pedigree of the Family of Gordon, 1056-1748, by Dr William Gordon of Harperfield, 4to n.d. Geneal. Coll., by W. Macfarlane, 1750-51 ; Scot. Hist. Soc., ii. 409-423. Concise History of the Ancient and Illustrious House of Gordon . . . by C. A. Gordon, 12mo (Aberdeen, 1754),* 2nd ed., with additions by A. M. Mackintosh, 8vo (Aberdeen, 1890). Surgundo, a Metrical History of the Feuds of the Gordon Family, by C. K. Sharpe (Edinr. 1837).* Historical MSS. Commission (1870), 1st Report ; (1876), 5th Report, pt. i. The Great Historic Families of Scotland, by Taylor [1887]. The House of Gordon, ed. J. M. Bulloch, 2 vols. 4to, with Bibliography of Gordon Genealogy (New Spalding Club, 1903-7). The Gay Gordons, by J. M. Bulloch (London, 1909). Gordons under Arms, a Biographical Muster Roll of Officers named Gordon in the Navies and Armies of Britain, Europe, and in the Jacobite Risings, by Constance Oliver Skelton and John Malcolm Bulloch (Aberdeen : printed for the University, 1912). Notes and Queries, 5th S., i. 169, 275 ; v. 127 : 6th S., v. 149 ; viii. 346 ; ix. 289 ; x. 327 : 7th S., iii. 268 ; ix. 338 : 8th S., iv. 435 ; vi. 27 ; x. 75 : 9th S., ii. 128, 174, 255, 412 ; iii. 178.  Dictionary of National Biography, *s.v.*  Scottish N. and Q., 1st S., i.-xii. ; 2nd S., i.-viii. ; 3rd S., i.-vi. (Aberdeen, 1887 to date), contains many particulars of local families, with specially detailed notices of innumerable Gordons from duke to cadger.

*See* The Scots Peerage, ed. Sir J. Balfour Paul, *for*
**Gordon**, Earl of Aberdeen, i. 82-99.
    Lord Aboyne, i. 100.
    Viscount Aboyne, iv. 546.
    Earl of Aboyne, i. 102-105, iv. 547.
    Lord Gordon, iv. 522-543.
    Duke of Gordon, iv. 253, 506-558.
    Earl of, Marquess of Huntly, iv. 523-562.
    Lord of Lochinvar, v. 98-135.
    Viscount of Kenmure, v. 98-135.
    Earl of Sutherland, viii. 337-361.

**Gordon**, Aberdeen.  Scottish N. and Q., 2nd S., ii. 140.
    of Aberdour.  The Gordons of Aberdour, by J. M. Bulloch (Peterhead, 1913).
    of Abergeldie.  Pedigree of Gordon of Huntly and Abergeldie, folio sheet.  Historical MSS. Commission (1877), 6th Report, 712.  Scottish N. and Q., 3rd S., ii. 122 ; vii. 52.  The House of Gordon, ed. J. M. Bulloch, 71-116.  Burke's Commoners, ii. 219.  Burke's Landed Gentry (1848-1924).
    of Aikenhead.  The Scots Peerage, ii. 279.
    of Airds.  Lands and their Owners in Galloway, by M'Kerlie (1878), iv. 73-78.
    Antigua.  Oliver's History of Antigua, ii. 22-28.
    of Auchanachy.  Scottish N. and Q., 3rd S., iv. 117.
    of Auchendolly.  Burke's Landed Gentry (1886-1925).
    of Auchenreoch.  Lands . . . in Galloway, v. 309.
    Auchinblae, Scottish N. and Q., 2nd S., iii. 141.
    of Auchindoun.  Scottish N. and Q., 3rd S., ii. 107-109.
    of Auchinreath, Scottish N. and Q., 2nd S., v. 14 ; vi. 61.
    of Auchintoul.  The Scottish Antiquary, viii. 24.  Scottish N. and Q., 3rd S., v. 29.
    of Auchleuchries.  Diary of Gen. Patrick Gordon ; *see* Edinburgh Review (July, 1856).  Temple's Thanage of Fermartyn, 309.
    of Auchterhouse.  Scottish N. and Q., 2nd S., iii. 33.
    of Avochie.  Jacobites of Aberdeenshire and Banffshire in the Forty-Five, by Alistair and Henrietta Tayler (Aberdeen, 1928), 238-246.
    of Badenscoth.  Temple's Thanage of Fermartyn, 104-105.
    of Balmaghie.  Burke's ¡Landed Gentry (1846-1875).  Lands . . . in Galloway, iii. 112.

**Gordon** of Banchory. Scottish N. and Q., 3rd S., iv. 168.

of Barskeoch. Lands . . . in Galloway, iv. 79.

of Beldorney. A Short History of the later Gordons of Beldorney, by D. Wimberley (Banff, 1904). Tayler's Jacobites of Aberdeenshire, 246.

of Binhall. Scottish N. and Q., 2nd S., ii. 113 ; iii. 140, 173 ; iv. 157. Tayler's Jacobites, 246-248.

of Birkenburn. House of Gordon, article by Wimberley, 279-326. Scottish N. and Q., x. 174.

of Birkenbush. Tayler's Jacobites, 222.

of Blelack. Tayler's Jacobites of Aberdeenshire, 209.

Bovaglie. Scottish N. and Q., 2nd S., iv. 41.

of Braco. Scottish N. and Q., 2nd S., i. 28. The Scots Peerage, i. 84.

of Braes. Scottish N. and Q., 3rd S., iii. 193.

of Buckie. Scottish N. and Q., 3rd S., 142. Tayler's Jacobites of Aberdeenshire, 223.

of Buthlaw. Temple's Thanage of Fermartyn, 272-275.

of Cairnbulg. Burke's Landed Gentry (1850-1875).

of Cairnburrow. Thanage of Fermartyn, 221.

of Cairness. Burke's Landed Gentry (1894-1925).

of Cairnfield. Pedigree of the Gordons of Cairnfield, compiled by Major-Gen. W. Gordon, lith. sheet (Elgin, c. 1847). The Gordons of Cairnfield, by J. M. Bulloch (Leith, 1910). Burke's Landed Gentry (1848-1925).

of Cluny. Complete Baronetage, by G. E. C., 297. The Gordons of Cluny, by J. M. Bulloch (Buckie, 1911). Landed Gentry (1863-1879).

of Campbelton. Lands . . . in Galloway, by M'Kerlie, v. 278-280.

of Cardoness. Lands . . . in Galloway, iii. 16-23.

of Carleton. Lands . . . in Galloway, iii. 190-194.

of Carnousie. Scottish N. and Q., 2nd S., viii., 143. Tayler's Jacobites, 204.

of Carroll. Scottish N. and Q., 3rd S., iii. 216.

of Chapeltown. Thanage of Fermartyn, 284.

China and Khartoum. Notes and Queries, 7th S., iii. 452 ; iv. 307. Scottish N. and Q., 1st S., xii. 29-30, 70, 109 ; 2nd S., iv. 103. Geneal. Mag. (1899) ii. 248.

of Clashtirum. Scottish N. and Q., 2nd S., iii. 129-131.

of Cluny. Burke's Extinct Baronetcies. Scottish N. and Q., 3rd S., iv. 213. Landed Gentry (1863-1879).

of Cobairdy. Thanage of Fermartyn, 224-225. Tayler's Jacobites of Aberdeenshire, 232.

of Cochlarachie, and Cadets. Thanage of Fermartyn, 276-279. The House of Gordon, ed. J. M. Bulloch, 119-164.

of Coldwells. The Gordons of Coldwells, . . . by J. M. Bulloch (Peterhead, 1914).

of Craichlaw. Lands . . . in Galloway, i. 624. The Gordons of Craichlaw, by William Macmath, ed. T. Fraser, 4to (Dalbeattie, 1924).

Gordon of Craig. Lands . . . in Galloway, iii. 92, 93. Memorials of the
Family of Gordon of Craig, by D. Wimberley (Banff, 1904).*

of Craigwillie. Tayler's Jacobites of Aberdeenshire, 200.

of Crichie. Thanage of Fermartyn, 70. Account by Wimberley, *in*
Bulloch's House of Gordon, 267.

of Crogo. Lands . . . in Galloway, iii. 94-96.

of Cullendoch. Lands . . . in Galloway, iii. 17 ; iv. 288.

of Culvennan. Burke's Commoners, iii. 610. Landed Gentry (1848-
1879). Lands . . . in Galloway, 2nd ed. (1906), i. 633-634.

The Culvennan Writs, by R. C. Reid, Dumf. and Gall. Antiq. Soc. (1923).

of Daach. Scottish N. and Q., 2nd S., iii. 139.

of Dalpholly and Invergordon. Complete Baronetage, by G. E. C., iv. 423.

of Deebank. Lands . . . in Galloway, v. 205.

of Dorlaithers. Tayler's Jacobites of Aberdeenshire, 201-202.

of Drimnin. Burke's Landed Gentry (1894-1925).

of Drummuir. Thanage of Fermartyn, 281.

of Earlston and Afton. Lands . . . in Galloway, iii. 414-427. Complete
Baronetage, by G. E. C., iv. 439. Burke's Peerage and Baronetage.

Elgin. Scottish N. and Q., 3rd S., iv. 213.

of Ellon. Burke's Landed Gentry (1906-1925).

of Embo. Complete Baronetage, by G. E. C., ii. 392. The Gordons of
Embo, by J. M. Mellish (1907). Burke's Peerage and Baronetage.

of Esslemont. Thanage of Fermartyn, 507-511. Landed Gentry
(1879-1925).

of Fechil. Thanage of Fermartyn, 505.

of Fodderletter. Tayler's Jacobites of Aberdeenshire, 275.

Forfarshire. The Gordons in Forfarshire, by J. M. Bulloch (Brechin,
1909). Scottish N. and Q., 3rd S., v. 58.

of Fyvie. Thanage of Fermartyn, 28-30. Fyvie Castle, by A. M. W.
Stirling (1928), 285-361.

of Garcrogo. Lands . . . in Galloway, iii. 102.

Garmouth. Scottish N. and Q., 2nd S., viii. 93-94.

of Geastirum. Tayler's Jacobites of Aberdeenshire, 234-238.

of Gight. Scottish N. and Q., 1st S., xii. 113-116, 145-148, 161-164,
178-180 : 2nd S., i. 1-4, 17-20, 33-36, 48-52, 81-83, 96-100, 113-116,
130-131, 145-146, 163-165, 176-179; ii. 49-51 : 3rd S., iv. 207.
Thanage of Fermartyn, by Temple, 72-78. The House of Gordon,
ed. J. M. Bulloch (1903), 167-310.

of Glenbuchat. J. M. Bulloch *in* Transactions of the Buchan Club
(1926), xiii. pt. i.

of Glenbucket. Notes and Queries, 8th S., iv. 68. Antiquarian Notes
. . . by C. Fraser-Mackintosh, ii. 351. Scottish N. and Q., 2nd S.,
iii. 139, 155, 169. Tayler's Jacobites of Aberdeenshire, 249-264.

of Gordon. Notes and Queries, 8th S., iv. 287. The Scots Peerage,
iv. 507-518.

Lord Gordon. Claim of Sir Bruce Gordon Seton to the Barony of
Gordon (7th Dec. 1928 to 22nd Jan. 1929). Report and Decision
(2nd May 1929).

Gordon, Duke of Gordon. Biographical Peerage (1808), 266-270. Antiq. Notes, by C. Fraser-Mackintosh, i. 162-165. G. E. C.'s Complete Peerage, ed. Gibbs.

Viscount Gordon of Aberdeen. Case of John Campbell, Earl of Aberdeen, claiming a Writ of Summons to Parliament as Viscount Gordon of Aberdeen, 121 pp. and pedigree. Minutes of Evidence, 81 pp. (1872).

of Gordonbank. Heraldry, by Nisbet (1742), ii., Appx. 230.

of Gordonstoun. Douglas's Baronage, 2-12. Historical MSS. Commission (1877), 6th Report. 681. Complete Baronetage, by G. E. C., ii. 277. Tables *in* House of Gordon, by Bulloch, 111-152.

of Gower. Llwyn-y-Bwch . . . Gordon of Gower, compiled by Rev. J. D. Davies (Swansea, 1903).

of Greenlaw. Lands . . . in Galloway, iii. 366-369 ; v. 387.

in Griamachary. The Family of Gordon in Griamachary in the Parish of Kildonan, by J. M. Bulloch (Dingwall, 1907).

of Haddo. Thanage of Fermartyn, by Temple, 1-16. Complete Baronetage, by G. E. C., ii. 451. The Scots Peerage, i. 83-87.

of Hallhead. Scottish N. and Q., 1st S., xi. 139-140 ; 3rd S., iv. 99. Thanage of Fermartyn, 507-511.

of Halmyre. History of Peeblesshire, by Chambers, 496.

Holland. Scottish N. and Q., 2nd S., ii. 79.

of Holm. Lands . . . in Galloway, iii. 74-76.

of Huntly. The Origin, History and Progress of the Family of the Gordons of Huntly down to 1594, by Robert Gordon of Straloch ; Latin MS. with translation, *in* The House of Gordon, by J. M. Bulloch. Papers *in* Spalding Club Misc., iv. ; Scot. Hist. Soc., No. 56 (1908), *xc*.

Marquess of Huntly. G. E. C.'s Complete Peerage. Burke's and other Annual Peerages.

Inveravon. Scottish N. and Q., 2nd S., v. 81-83, 97.

of Invergordon. The Families of Gordon of Invergordon, Newhall, Ardoch and Carroll, by J. M. Bulloch (Dingwall, 1906).

Jamaica. Scottish N. and Q., 2nd S., iv. 40.

of Keithock's Mill. Scottish N. and Q., 2nd S., ii. 1-3, 17-21.

of Kenmure. Lands . . . in Galloway, iv. 41-70. The Scots Peerage, v. 102-105. Burke's Landed Gentry (1894-1925).

in Kincardine Mill. Tayler's Jacobites of Aberdeenshire, 220.

of Knockespoch. A Genealogical Account of the Family of Gordon of Knockespoch, by D. Wimberley (Banff, 1903). Burke's Landed Gentry (1850-1925). Scottish N. and Q., 3rd S., iii. 209.

of Laggan. The Gordons of Laggan, by J. M. Bulloch (Banff, 1907).

of Lawsie. Scottish N. and Q., 3rd S., vi. 174.

of Leitchestoun. Article by Wimberley *in* House of Gordon, 373-422.

of Lesmoir. Baronage, by Douglas (1784), 30-32. Notes and Queries, 6th S., vii. 349 ; ix. 370, 396 : 9th S., iii. 491. Thanage of Fermartyn, 260-262, 269-271. Memorials of the Family of Gordon of Lesmoir, by D. Wimberley (Inverness, 1893).* The House of Gordon, ed. J. M. Bulloch, 153-265. Complete Baronetage. by G. E. C., ii. 299.

Gordon of Letterfourie. Complete Baronetage, by G. E. C., ii. 279.
Burke's Peerage and Baronetage. Tayler's Jacobites of Aberdeenshire, 203.

Lettoch. Scottish N. and Q., 2nd S., iv. 141.

of Lochinvar. Lands . . . in Galloway, iii. 406. Antiquarian Notes,
by C. Fraser-Mackintosh, i. 80-82. Complete Baronetage, by
G. E. C., ii. 314. The Scots Peerage, v. 99-112.

of Logie. Scottish N. and Q., 3rd S., ii. 168. Tayler's Jacobites of
Aberdeenshire, 274.

of Macartney. Lands . . . in Galloway, iv. 305.

of Manar. Family Records of Dingwall-Fordyce, ii. 24, 25, 38. Scottish
N. and Q., 2nd S., iv. 141, 158. Burke's Landed Gentry (1879-1925).

of Methlic. Thanage of Fermartyn, 1-16. The Scots Peerage, i.
83-86.

of Milrig. Scottish N. and Q., 3rd S., ii. 154.

of Minmore. The Gordons and Smiths at Minmore, Auchorachan, and
Upper Drummin, by J. M. Bulloch (Huntly, 1910). Tayler's
Jacobites of Aberdeenshire, 265.

of Monybuie. Lands . . . in Galloway, iii. 90.

of Mosstown. Temple's Thanage of Fermartyn, 550. The Gordons
of Mosstown, by J. M. Bulloch (Aberdeen, 1923).

of Murrayshall. Buchan and Paton's History of Peeblesshire, iii. 38.

of Nethermuir. Paterson's History of Ayr (1847), i. 221. The Gordons
of Nethermuir, by J. M. Bulloch (Peterhead, 1913).

of Newark-on-Trent. Burke's Extinct Baronetcies, 2nd ed. (1844).

of Newton. Scottish N. and Q., 2nd S., iv. 162. House of Gordon,
by J. M. Bulloch, 423-510. Thanage of Fermartyn, 263-264.

of Noth. Scottish N. and Q., 2nd S., iii. 139, 169.

of Oyne. Burke's Peerage and Baronetage (before 1877).

of Park. Notes and Queries, 6th S., vii. 166, 415. Scottish N. and Q.,
1st S., iii., 126-127, 142 : 3rd S., iii., 183-186. Geneal. Mag., 1899,
ii. 248. Complete Baronetage, iv. 344. Burke's Landed Gentry
(1848-1875). Tayler's Jacobites of Aberdeenshire, 277-284.

of Pavidock, or Polloadock. Lands . . . in Galloway, iii. 444.

of Penninghame. The Scots Peerage, v. 108.

of Pitlurg. Burke's Commoners, iv. 45. Landed Gentry (1846-1894),
Life of John Gordon of Pitlurg and Parkhill, with Account of the
Gordons of Pitlurg, by Mrs Gordon (1885). Scottish N. and Q.,
1st S., ix. 113, 114. Thanage of Fermartyn, 310-317.

in Poland. Scottish N. and Q., 1st S., xi. 174 ; xii. 8-9, 23-25, 90 :
2nd S., iv. 17.

Portsoy. Scottish N. and Q., 2nd S., iv. 188.

in Rothney. Scottish N. and Q., 2nd S., iv. 141, 158.

Russia. Scottish N. and Q., 2nd S., i. 11, 42, 124 ; ii. 111.

in Salterhill. The Gordons of Salterhill and their Irish Descendants,
by J. M. Bulloch (Keith, 1910). Young's Memoir of the Family
of King of Newmill (Elgin, 1904).

of Sheelagreen. Thanage of Fermartyn, 264-265.

Gordon of Shirmers.  Lands . . . in Galloway, iii. 80-83.
    of Stitchell.  Early History of Stichill, by G. Gunn (Alnwick, 1901),
        5, 17-18.  The Scots Peerage, v. 98-112.
    of Straloch.  Scottish N. and Q., 1st S., ix. 114.  Thanage of Fermartyn,
        313-317.
    in Sutherland.  The Gordons in Sutherland, by J. M. Bulloch (Dingwall,
        1907-9).
    of Swiney.  Caithness Family History, by Henderson, 326.
    of Terpersie.  Thanage of Fermartyn, 103.  Notes on the Family of
        Gordon of Terpersie, by D. Wimberley (Inverness, 1900).  Account
        by Wimberley *in* House of Gordon, 327-372.  Scottish N. and Q.,
        2nd S., ii. 66-67.  Tayler's Jacobites of Aberdeenshire, 211-219.
    of Threave.  Burke's Landed Gentry (1894-1925).
    of Troquhain.  Lands . . . in Galloway, iii. 70-71.
    of Wardhouse.  The Gordons of Wardhouse and Beldorney, by J. M.
        Bulloch (Banff, 1909).  Scottish N. and Q., 1st S., xii. 65.  Burke's
        Landed Gentry (1879-1925).
    of Woodhouse.  Scottish N. and Q., 3rd S., ii. 193.

Gordon-Cumming of Altyre.  Historical MSS. Commission (1877), 6th
    Report.  Scottish N. and Q., 1st S., ix. 115.  Burke's Peerage and
    Baronetage.

Gordon-Cumming-Skene of Pitlurg.  Scottish N. and Q., 1st S., ix. 115.
    Burke's Landed Gentry (1846-1925).  Temple's Thanage of Fer-
    martyn, 317.

Gordon-Duff of Park and Drummuir.  Burke's Landed Gentry (1886-
    1925).

Gordon-Lennox, Duke of Gordon, Duke of Lennox.  The Scots Peerage,
    v. 369-371.

Gordon Tartan.  J. M. Bulloch *in* Scot. Hist. Review, xxi. 169-177.

Gorthy of Gorthy.  The Barony of Gorthy, by R. S. Fittis (1878).  Scot.
    Hist. Soc., No. 56 (1908), *lxxxi.*

Goudie of Braefield.  Zetland Family Histories, by F. J. Grant, 93-97.
    of Sand.  Zetland Family Histories, 98.
    of Sottrigarth.  Zetland Family Histories, 99.

Gourlay.  Memorials of the Scottish House of Gourlay, by the Rev.
    Charles Rogers (Edinr. 1888).*
    of Balgillie.  Memorials of Angus and the Mearns, by Jervise, ed.
        Gammack, ii. 91-93.
    of Kincraig.  Baronage, by Douglas, 469-471.  T. H. Cockburn-Hood's
        House of the Cockburns of that Ilk.  East Neuk of Fife, 2nd ed.,
        179-183, 202.  Burke's Landed Gentry (1850-1925).

Govan of Cardrona.  Peeblesshire Localities, by Renwick, 575-579.

Gow.  Confederacy of Clan Chattan, by C. Fraser-Mackintosh (1898),
    118-121.
    Wick.  The Scottish Antiquary, v. 184-188.

**Gowrie**, Ruthven, Earl of. An Historical Account of the Conspiracies by the Earls of Gowrie . . . against King James VI., by the Earl of Cromarty, 8vo (1713). The Earle of Gowrie's Conspiracy, by Lord Hailes, 24 copies, n.d. History of the Life and Death of John, Earl of Gowrie, by Rev. J. Scott, 150 copies (1818). Paper relating to William, first Earl of Gowrie, and to Patrick Ruthven, his fifth and last surviving son, 8vo (London, 1867).* The Great Historic Families of Scotland, by Taylor [1887]. The Gowrie Arms, by Andrew Lang *in* The Ancestor (1902), ii. 54-57. James VI. and the Gowrie Mystery, by Andrew Lang, 8vo, illust. (1902). The Gowrie Conspiracy and its Official Narrative, by Samuel Cowan (1902). The Scots Peerage (1904-1914), iv. 254-268. G. E. C.'s Complete Peerage, ed. Gibbs. *See also* **Ruthven**.

**Gracie.** Genealogy of the Family of Gracie, by Col. James Gracie.

**Graeme**, Earl of Alford. The Jacobite Peerage, by the Marquis of Ruvigny and Raineval (1904), 6.

of Garvock. Burke's Commoners, iii. 125. Burke's Landed Gentry (1848-1925).

of Graemeshall. Burke's Landed Gentry (1849-1925).

of Inchbraikie and Inveruthen. Burke's Landed Gentry (1849-1925).

of Orchill. Landed Gentry (1850-1886).

*See also* **Graham**.

**Graham**(e. Heraldry, by Alex. Nisbet (1722), i. 81-82. Ancient Scottish Surnames, by Buchanan of Auchmar (1723). A Genealogical Tree of the Illustrious Family of Graham, by J. Brown, folio sheet (1820). Crawfurd's Shire of Renfrew, ed. Robertson, 46-51. MS. by John Riddell, W.S., and Robert Riddell, in the possession of the Signet Library. Great Historic Families, by Taylor [1887]. Traditions of the Grahams, *in* The Scottish Antiquary, xv. 109-116, 183-195; xvii. 9-14, 87-89, 176-187. Or and Sable : a Book of the Graemes and Grahams, by Louisa G. Graeme, 4to, 750 pp., illust., pedigrees (Edinr. 1903). Dictionary of National Biography, *s.v.*

*See* The Scots Peerage, ed. Sir J. Balfour Paul, *for*

**Graham**, Viscount of Dundee, iii. 316-333.

Lord Graham of Claverhouse, iii. 324-333.

Marquess of Graham and Buchanan, vi. 263-274.

Earl of Kincardine, vi. 247-274.

Lord Kinpont, i. 135-145.

Earl of Menteith, vi. 138, 142-165.

Earl of, Marquess of, Duke of Montrose, vi. 191-274.

**Graham**(e of Airth. Burke's Landed Gentry (1849-1925).

of Airthrey. Logie, by R. Menzies Fergusson, D.D. (1905), ii. 42-44 ; 61-62. Burke's Landed Gentry (1894-1898).

of Balgowan. Heraldry, by Nisbet (1742), ii. Appx. 26. Burke's Landed Gentry (1849-1858). The Beautiful Mrs Graham and the Cathcart Circle, by E. Maxtone Graham (1927).

of Ballagan. Strathblane, by Guthrie Smith, 154-156.

Graham of Ballargus. Angus or Forfarshire, by Warden, iv. 288, 294. C. Sanford Terry *in* Scot. Hist. Review, ii. 72-76.

of Ballewan. Strathblane, 161-165.

of Balmuir. Angus or Forfarshire, iv. 284.

of Boquhapple. The Scots Peerage, vi. 149-151, 157-159.

on the Borders. The Scottish Antiquary, ix. 160-166. The Grahams or Graemes, of the Debateable Land, by Joseph Bain ; originally published in vol. xliii. of the Archæological Journal (1886).

of Borrowfield and Ald Montrose. Memorials of Angus and the Mearns, by A. Jervise, ed. Gammack, ii. 54-56.

of Braco. Logie, by R. Menzies Fergusson, D.D., ii. 44. Complete Baronetage, by G. E. C., ii. 302. The Scots Peerage, vi. 238.

of Breckness. Norton Smith's Orkney Armorials, 53-57.

of Carfin and Stonebyres. Burke's Landed Gentry (1906-1925).

of Claverhouse. Geneal. Coll., by W. Macfarlane, 1750-1751 ; Scot. Hist. Soc., ii. 178. Memoirs of the Lord Viscount Dundee, the Highland Clans, and the Massacre of Glencoe, with an Account of Dundee's officers after they went to France [17—]. Memorials and Letters of John Graham of Claverhouse, by Mark Napier, 3 vols. (1859-1862). Graham of Claverhouse, by Michael Barrington. Angus or Forfarshire, by Warden, ii. 19-21. John Graham of Claverhouse, Viscount of Dundee, by Prof. C. Sanford Terry (1905). The Scots Peerage, iii. 316-324.

of Craig. Paterson's History of Ayr (1847), i. 312. Paterson's Ayr and Wigton, ii. 150.

of Craigallian. Landed Gentry (1886). Strathblane, by Guthrie Smith, 49.

of Craigcrook. Cramond, by J. P. Wood, 32.

of Dalkeith. The Scots Peerage, vi. 194-196.

of Drumgoon. Landed Gentry (1858).

of Drumquhassil. Strathblane, 31-33.

of Duchray. Notes and Queries, 6th S., xi. 489. The Scots Peerage, vi. 148.

Viscount of Dundee. *See* **Graham of Claverhouse.**

Dundee. Geneal. Mag., vii. 461.

of Duntrune. Landed Gentry (1846-1886.) Angus or Forfarshire, by A. J. Warden, iv. 147-149. The Scots Peerage, iii. 321, 332.

Edinburgh. Scottish N. and Q., 2nd S., viii. 68.

of Esk. The Grahams of Esk, by J. H. B. Graham *in* Transactions of the Cumberland and Westmoreland Antiq. and Archæol. Soc., xi. N. S.

of Fintry. Burke's Commoners, iii. 120. Strathendrick, by Guthrie Smith, 153-164. Angus or Forfarshire, iv. 293. Historical MSS. Commission (1909), v. Burke's Landed Gentry (1846-1925).

of Gallingad. The Scots Peerage, vi. 148-149.

of Gartavertane. The Scottish Antiquary (1899), xiii. 65, 124, 173-178.

of Gartmore. The Grahams of Gartmore, by Alex. C. Macintyre, 4to (Glasgow, 1885).* Burke's Extinct Baronetcies. Notes and Queries, 8th S., viii. 162. Complete Baronetage, by G. E. C., iv. 243. The Scots Peerage, vi. 157, 158. The Stirling Antiquary, ed. W. B. Cook (1900), ii. 87, 94, 106.

N

**Graham** of Gartur.  Notes and Queries, 6th S., viii. 309: 8th S., viii.
    370, 494; ix. 153.  The Scottish Antiquary (1893), vii. 43, 90,
    143.  The Stirling Antiquary, ii. 235-241.  The Scots Peerage, vi.
    152-154.
of Over Glenny.  Burke's Landed Gentry (1914-1925).
Earl Graham.  English Peerage, by Rev. Alex. Jacob (1767), ii. 102-107.
of Grougar and Auchenhowie.  Scottish N. and Q., 3rd S., vi. 38.
of Kilbride.  Notes and Queries, 8th S., i. 394; ii. 11; viii. 301, 389;
    ix. 77.  The Scottish Antiquary, xi. 108-112, 66-68; xii. 33, 129-131,
    180, 181; xiii. 17-20, 64, 65, 123.
of Killearn.  The Scottish Antiquary, xii. 181; xiii. 46, 91.
of Kilpont.  Documents regarding the extinction of Lady Elizabeth
    Graham, daughter of John, Lord Kilpont, and wife of Sir John
    Graham, of Gartmore, and her Descendants.  Large folio, 18 pp.,
    Edinr. [18—].  The Scottish Antiquary, xiii. 68-72.
of Knockdolian.  Paterson's History of Ayr, i. 305.  Paterson's Ayr and
    Wigton, ii. 159-160.  Scottish N. and Q., 3rd S., v. 185-188, 204-206,
    226-228; vi. 8, 31-33, 51-54.
of Larchfield.  Landed Gentry (1886-1894).
of Leitchtown.  The Scottish Antiquary, xiii. 65, 123-126, small
    Chart Pedigree, 172-178.  The Stirling Antiquary, ii. 89-94, 106-110.
    Burke's Commoners, iv. 576.  Burke's Landed Gentry (1846-1925).
of Linlathen.  Angus or Forfarshire, by Warden, iv. 408.  Monifieth, by
    J. Malcolm, 297-299.
Lochgelly.  Recreations of an Antiquary, by Fittis, 514.
of Lymekilns.  Strathblane, by Guthrie Smith, 49-52.  Burke's Landed
    Gentry (1886-1925).
of Meathie.  Angus or Forfarshire, by Warden, iii. 420.
of Morphie.  Scottish N. and Q., 3rd S., ii. 122.  Burke's Landed Gentry
    (1894-1925).
of Mossknow.  Scot. Antiq., viii. 16.  Burke's Landed Gentry (1846-1925).
of Netherby.  Life and Letters of Sir James Graham of Netherby, 1792-
    1861, by C. S. Parker, 2 vols., illust. (1907).  The Scots Peerage,
    vii. 98-107.
in Orkney.  The Frotoft Branch of the Orkney Traills, by T. W. Traill,
    52-57, 87.
of Pickhill.  The Scots Peerage, vii. 104.
of Rednock.  The Scot. Antiq., xiii. 179.
in Shannochhill.  The Stirling Antiquary, ed. W. B. Cook, ii. 235.
of Skipness.  Burke's Landed Gentry (1914-1925).
in Sweden.  Scot. Hist. Rev., xxv. 299.
of Tamrawer.  Historical and Genealogical Account of the Grahams of
    Tamrawer, by John Brown, single sheet, n.d.  Burke's Landed
    Gentry (1849-1879).  The Grahams of Tamrawer, by J. Edward
    Graham (Edinr. 1895.)*  Herald and Geneal., v. 535-538.
of Wallacetown.  The Grahams of Wallacetown, Knockdolian, Grugar,
    Auchenharvie, Tamrawer, Dougalston, Kilmannan and Kilmardinny,
    by James Graham (Glasgow, 1887).

**Graham-Campbell** of Shirvan. Burke's Landed Gentry (1886-1925).

**Graham-Moir** of Leckie. The Stirling Antiquary, iv. 313-317.

**Graham-Stirling** of Strowan. Burke's Landed Gentry (1875-1925).

**Graham-Wigan** of Duntrune. Burke's Landed Gentry (1886-1925).

**Grant.** Geneal. Colls., by W. Macfarlane, 1750-51; Scot. Hist. Soc., i. 103-117. Douglas's Baronage, 341-346. Memoires . . . de la Maison de Grant . . . par Charles Grant, Vicomte de Vaux, 8vo (Londres, 1796). Genealogy of the Honourable Family of Grant of Grant, by J. Grant, 4to, two col. plates, 23 pp. (Elgin, 1826). Ane Account of the Rise and Offspring of the Name of Grant [by Sir A. Grant] (1876).* The Chiefs of Grant, by Wm. Fraser, 3 vols., 4to, illust. (Edinr. 1883).* Dictionary of National Biography, *s.v.* The Rulers of Strathspey, a History of the Lairds of Grant and Earls of Seafield [by the Earl of Cassillis], 8vo, *xii*+211 pp., illust. (Inverness, 1911). Urquhart and Glenmoriston, 2nd ed. (1914). Genealogist, N. S., i. 214. Scottish N. and Q., xi. 25-27. The Scots Peerage, vii. 476-485.

**Grant,** Aberlour. Smith's Genealogies of an Aberdeen Family; Aberd. Univ. Studies, 19-22.

of Achininche. The Scottish Antiquary, viii. 24.

of Arndilly. Burke's Landed Gentry (1875-1894).

of Auchanachy. Scottish N. and Q., 2nd S., viii. 92, 111.

of Auchinroath. Notes and Queries, 3rd S., xii. 375.

of Ballindalloch. Information For and Against Peter Leslie-Grant, eldest Son of Capt. Grant, late of Balindalloch, against Count Leslie, etc., being Naturalised and Heir to Large Estates in Germany, etc., 4to (1761). Letters of Patrick Grant, Lord Elchies, 318-320. Burke's Peerage and Baronetage.

of Beldorney. Scottish N. and Q., 3rd S., vi. 173.

of Blairfindy. Tayler's Jacobites of Aberdeenshire, 286.

of Borlumbeg. Scottish N. and Q., 3rd S., v. 119.

*alias* Colquhoun. Complete Baronetage, by G. E. C., ii. 293.

of Corrimony. The Grants of Corrimony, by Francis J. Grant, 4to (Lerwick, 1895).*

of Cour. Oliver's History of Antigua, ii. 28-29.

of Craskie. Major Alpin's . . . Descendants, 10, 26.* Scottish N. and Q., 3rd S., ii. 96.

of Culbin. Antiquarian Notes, by C. Fraser-Mackintosh, i. 340.

of Cullen. Complete Baronetage, by G. E. C., iv. 433.

of Dalvey. Complete Baronetage, iv. 358. Burke's Peerage and Baronetage.

Detroit. Major Alpin's . . . Descendants, 15-16.

of Druminor. Landed Gentry (1886-1894).

of Drummonie. The Scottish Antiquary, viii. 181.

of Duldreggan. Major Alpin's Ancestors, 11.

of Dulshangie. Urquhart and Glenmoriston, 514.

of Ecclesgreig. Landed Gentry (1894-1925).

Grant of Elchies. Letters of Patrick Grant, Lord Elchies, by H. D. MacWilliam (Aberdeen, 1927), 1-29, 315-317. Burke's Landed Gentry (1906-1925).

of Freuchie. The Chiefs of Grant, by Sir W. Fraser. The Grants of Corrimony, by F. J. Grant. Major Alpin's Ancestors and Descendants, by P. J. Anderson (Aberdeen, 1904), 7-8* Scots Peerage (1904-1914), vii. 455-476.

of Glenmoriston. Reminiscences of the Grants of Glenmoriston, by Rev. A. Sinclair (Edinr. 1887). Urquhart and Glenmoriston, by William Mackay (Inverness, 1893). Major Alpin's Ancestors, 9-20.* Burke's Landed Gentry (1846-1925). Antiq. Notes, by C. Fraser-Mackintosh (1897), ii. 98-106, 111-112.

Baron Grant. The Jacobite Peerage, by the Marquis of Ruvigny (1904), 61-63.

of Kilgraston. Burke's Landed Gentry (1863-1925).

of Kincorth. Scottish N. and Q., 3rd S., iii. 175. Burke's Landed Gentry (1875-1879).

of Lochletter. The Grants of Corrimony.*

of Lochtervandich. Scottish N. and Q., 2nd S., viii. 89.

of Monymusk. Historical MSS. Commission (1883), vol. xxxvii., 9th Report, pt. 2. Burke's Peerage and Baronetage.

of Rothiemurchus. Autobiography of a Highland Lady, Elizabeth Grant of Rothiemurchus, afterwards Mrs Smith of Baltiboys, 1797-1830 (1911). Antiquarian Notes, by C. Fraser-Mackintosh, ii. 412-415.

of Sheuglie. The Grants of Corrimony.*

Suffolk. Scottish N. and Q., 2nd S., i. 173.

of Tanmore. Correspondence. Addit. MSS. Brit. Museum, 7 vols., 25405 to 25412.

Grant-Duff of Eden. Burke's Landed Gentry (1863-1925).

Grant-Suttie of Balgone. Complete Baronetage by G. E. C., iv. 403. Burke's Peerage and Baronetage.

Gray of Balbunno. The Scottish Antiquary, xii. 179.

of Bandirran. The Scots Peerage, iv. 281-282, 284.

of Carntyne. Burke's Visitation of Seats and Arms (1853), ii. 36-37. Burke's Landed Gentry (1848-1863). Autobiography of a Scotch Country Gentleman, the Rev. J. Hamilton Gray of Carntyne, 4to (1868).*

of Carse Gray. Baronage of Angus and Mearns, by D. M. Peter, 142-144. Burke's Landed Gentry (1886-1925). Warden's Angus or Forfarshire, v. 94-95.

of Cliff. Zetland Family Histories, by F. J. Grant, 100-102.

of Dalduff. Paterson's Ayr and Wigton, ii. 427.

of Dalmarnock. Ayrshire Families, by G. Robertson, ii. 61-66. Burke's Landed Gentry (1863). Autobiography of a Scotch Country Gentleman, by Rev. J. H. Gray of Carntyne.*

of Fowlis and Broxmouth. The Parish of Longforgan, by Rev. A. Philp, 100.

Gray, Lord Gray. Angus or Forfarshire, by A. J. Warden, ii. 22-30. The Scottish Antiquary, viii. 139-140. The Descent and Kinship of Patrick, Master of Gray, by Peter Gray of Southfield, Fife (Dundee, 1903). Monifieth, by J. Malcolm, 278-285, 291. The Scots Peerage, iv. 269-296. G. E. C.'s Complete Peerage. Burke's Peerage. Case of Mrs Eveleen Smith, claiming the Barony of Gray ; and evidence with documents (1896).

of Hayston. Heraldry, by Nisbet (1742), ii., Appx. 252.

of Laurenston and Bullionfield. Complete Baronetage, by G. E. C., iv. 445.¹

of Lour. Angus or Forfarshire, by Warden, iii. 294.

of Nunraw. Burke's Landed Gentry (1894-1925).

of Oxgang. The Stirlings of Craigbernard and Glorat (1883).* Kirkintilloch, by Thos. Watson (1894), 105.

of Pittendrum. Complete Baronetage, by G. E. C., vi., Appx. 76. Lady Stair's House, by T. B. Whitson, *in* Book of the Old Edinburgh Club (1910), ii. 243-252.

of Skibo. The Scottish Antiquary (1893), vii. 182-187. Skibo, its Lairds and History, by Peter Gray (Edinr. 1906).

in Clochtow of Slains. Scottish N. and Q., 1st S., vii. 28; 3rd S., iii. 105.

Gray-Buchanan of Scotstoun. Strathendrick, by J. Guthrie Smith, 357. Burke's Landed Gentry (1882-1925).

Grear, Antigua. Oliver's History of Antigua, ii. 36.

Green, Aberdeen. Genealogies of an Aberdeen Family ; Aberd. Univ. Studies (1913), 22.

Greenfield of Fascadale. Burke's Landed Gentry (1846-1863).

Greenhill of Craignathro. Baronage of Angus and Mearns, by D. M. Peter (1856), 144.

of Vane. Angus or Forfarshire, by Warden, iii. 272.

Greenlaw of Greenlaw. Scottish N. and Q. 2nd S., ii. 111.

Greenock, Cathcart, Baron Greenock of. Old Greenock, by Williamson. The Scots Peerage, ii. 525-531.

Greenshields-Leadbetter of Stobieside. Burke's Landed Gentry (1921-1925).

Greenwich, Campbell, Baroness of, Earl of, Duke of. English Peerage, by Rev. A. Jacob, i. 581 ; ii. 226, 706. The Scots Peerage, i. 370-377. G. E. C.'s Complete Peerage.

Greer of Grange-Macgregor. Herald and Genealogist, vi. 137-140.

Gregan-Craufurd. Complete Baronetage, by G. E. C., v. 213.

Gregor. Historical Notices of the Clan Gregor, by Donald Gregory (1831). *See* MacGregor.

Gregory. A Short Account of the Family of Gregorie, from the time they gave up the name of Macgregor, by Georgina Gregory (1873).* Records of the Family of Gregory [by Sir P. St George Gregory] 4to, *viii.* + 93 pp., illust., pedigree (London, 1886).* Notes and Queries, 7th S., iii. 147 ; v. 53. The Academic Gregories, by Agnes Grainger Stewart [1901].

**Greif,** Eddleston.  Peeblesshire Localities, by Renwick, 38.
of Glencarse.  Burke's Landed Gentry (1875-1906).

**Greig** of Hallgreig and Tilliery.  MS. pedigree compiled by Mrs Margaret
Stuart, deposited in the Lyon Office, and with the Society of
Genealogists, London.
in Inverkeithing.  Herald and Genealogist, iii. 111; v. 468-470.  Stephen's
Inverkeithing and Rosyth (1921), 488-497.
Kennoway.  Kennoway, by A. S. Cunningham (Leven, 1906), 24.
of Sandsound.  Zetland Family Histories, by F. J. Grant, 103-108.
of Vassay.  Zetland Family Histories, 109-110.

**Grier, Grierson.**  Pedigree of the Families of MacGregor, Grierson, and
Grier, large sheet (London), [c. 1882].

**Grierson,** Edinburgh.  House of Lords : Margaret Grierson, Edinburgh,
Appellant, and James Connell of Conheath, Respondent ; the
Respondent's Case with pedigree of Hay of Linplum, 4to, 105 pp.
(186—).
of Lag.  The Laird of Lag, by Lt. Col. Fergusson, 8vo., illust. (Edinr.
1868).  Herald and Genealogist, vi. 138.  Complete Baronetage, by
G. E. C., iv. 327.  Burke's Peerage and Baronetage.
of Milnmark.  Lands . . . in Galloway, by M'Kerlie, iv. 93.
of Mouswald.  The Barony of Mouswald and its Barons, by J. J. Reid,
*in* Proc. Soc. Antiq. Scotl.
of Quendale.  Zetland Family Histories, by F. J. Grant, 111-113.

**Grieve.**  Annals of a Border Club, by G. Tancred, 245-247.  Burke's
Landed Gentry (1914-1925).

**Grimston,** Lord Forrester of Corstorphine.  The Scots Peerage, iv. 97-100.
Burke's Peerage.

**Groat** of Newhall.  Norton Smith's Orkney Armorials, 58-61.

**Groit** of Brabsterdorran.  Scottish N. and Q., 3rd S., v. 199.

**Groom.**  Notes on the Pedigree of Her Most Serene Highness Ann
Groom, and of her son, Charles Ottley Groom Napier, Prince
of Mantua, etc., by John Riddell (London, 1879).  *See also*
**Graeme.**

**Grosert** of Logie.  Stephen's Inverkeithing (1921), 204.

**Grosett.**  The Family of Muirhead of Lachop, by W. Grosett.

**Grosiert** of Logie.  Heraldry, by Nisbet (1742), ii., Appx. 268.

**Grot** of Duncansby.  The Scottish Antiquary (1894), viii. 51-52.

**Grundeston** of Bunzeon.  East Neuk of Fife, by W. Wood, 2nd ed.,
154.

**Gunn.**  The Gunns, by Thomas Sinclair (Wick, 1890).
of Braemore.  Caithness Family History, by Henderson, 320-323.
of Killearnan.  The Scots Peerage, vii. 165-169.

**Gunn-Munro** of Poyntzfield. Caithness Family History, by Henderson, 322.

**Guppyld** of Linlathen. Monifieth, by J. Malcolm, 295.

**Guthrie**, Brechin. Eminent Arbroathians, by J. M. M'Bain (1897), 285, 331. Genealogy of the Descendants of Rev. Thomas Guthrie, D.D., and Mrs Anne Burns or Guthrie . . . by C. J. Guthrie, K.C., 4to, 159 pp. (Edinr. 1902).* Review *in* Scot. Antiq., xv. 48.

of Carbeth Guthrie. Strathblane, by Guthrie Smith, 41.

of Craigie. Warden's Angus or Forfarshire, iv. 135. Burke's Landed Gentry (1886-1925).

of Gagie. Warden's Angus or Forfarshire, v. 11.

of Guthrie. Historical MSS. Commission (1871), 2nd Report. The Scottish Antiquary, xiii. 108. Tabular Pedigree, by Rev. J. G. Shaw, Forfar. Angus or Forfarshire, iii. 388-393. Burke's Landed Gentry (1848-1925).

of Halkertoun. Burke's Landed Gentry (1848). Herald and Genealogist, v. 538-541. Angus or Forfarshire, iii. 292. Gideon Guthrie, a monograph written 1712-1730, ed. C. E. Guthrie Wright, Appx. B, two chart pedigrees (1900). Review, *in* Scot. Antiquary, xv. 48.

of Kinblethmont. Angus or Forfarshire, iii. 437.

of Kincaldrum. Angus or Forfarshire, iii. 407-409.

of Kingedward. Complete Baronetage, by G. E. C., ii. 451. Scottish N. and Q., 3rd S., v. 239.

of Ludquharn. Scottish N. and Q., 3rd S., v. 218, 239.

of Menmuir. Angus or Forfarshire, iv. 363.

of Pitforthie. Angus or Forfarshire, iii. 31.

of Pitmuies. Visitation of Seats and Arms, by J. B. Burke (1853), i. 159.

**Gwyne**, Fort Augustus. Antiquarian Notes, by C. Fraser-Mackintosh, ii. 90-91.

**Hacket**, Drachlaw Mill. Tayler's Jacobites of Aberdeenshire, 287-288.

**Hackston**. *See* **Halkerston**.

**Hadden**. Scottish N. and Q., 2nd S., vii. 85.

Aberdeen. A short narrative of the Life . . . of an Aberdonian, to which is added an account of the Hadden Family [by J. D. Tough], (Aberdeen, 1848). Memoir of J. Young, Aberdeen . . . 1861, ed. Lt.-Col. W. Johnston (1894), 50-55, 64-86, 154-157.*

of Brochtoun. Peeblesshire Localities, by Renwick, 199-201. Annals of a Tweeddale Parish, by Baird, 27-30. Buchan and Paton's History of Peeblesshire, iii. 249.

**Haddington**, Hamilton, Earl of. Biographical Peerage (1808), 300-302. Memorials of the Earls of Haddington, by Sir Wm. Fraser, 2 vols., 4to, illust. (Edinr. 1889).* The Scots Peerage, iv. 303-329.

Baillie-Hamilton-Arden, Earl of. G. E. C.'s Complete Peerage, ed. Gibbs. Lodge's, Debrett's and Burke's Peerages.

**Haddington,** Ramsay, Viscount of. The Scots Peerage, iv. 297-302.

**Haddo,** Gordon, Lord. The Scots Peerage, i. 88-99.

**Hagart-Speirs** of Elderslie. Burke's Landed Gentry (1849-1925).

**Haig** of Bemersyde. Douglas's Baronage (1784), 132-136. Annals and Antiquities of Dryburgh, by Sir D. Erskine, 2nd ed., 45, 96-110. The Haigs of Bemersyde, a Family History, by John Russell, illust. (Edinr. 1881). [A revision of this work is being prepared by Lt.-Col. Sir Wolseley Haig, K.C.I.E., and Mrs Margaret Stuart.] Walford's Chapters from Family Chests, i. 1-13. Nisbet's Heraldic Plates, ed. Ross and Grant (1892), 46-48. Burke's Landed Gentry (1875-1925). Notes and Queries, 6th S., v. 19, 106 ; vii. 102, 152-3, 194, 231, 275, 297, 313, 457. Chart Pedigree of the Family of Haig of Bemersyde, Co. Berwick, and Cadets, from 1150 to the Present. Compiled chiefly by Miss Margaret Haig and Charles Edwin Haig (1884) (2nd and enlarged ed., Edinr. 1907).* "Tyde What May," a Haig ·Family Magazine, ed. Mrs Alexander Stuart, 5 pts., 4to (Edinr. 1894, 1895, 1900).*

of Blairhill. Landed Gentry (1879-1925). Pedigrees compiled by Alex. Lonsdale Fell (1907), 19-20.*

of Glenogil. Baronage of Angus and Mearns, by D. M. Peter (1856), 149.

of Pen Ithon. Landed Gentry (1886-1914).

of Ramornie. Landed Gentry (1886-1925).

Stirlingshire. Robert Haig of St Ninians, by C. E. Haig ; repr. from Tyde What May, 10 pp. (1895).

**Hailes,** Hepburn, Lord. The Scots Peerage, ii. 135-167.

**Hair** of Glenwharry. Folklore and Genealogies of Uppermost Nithsdale, by W. Wilson, 235-242.

of Rankinstone. Paterson's Ayr and Wigton, i. 242.

**Hairstanes** of Craigs. Pedigree annexed to Edgar's History of Dumfries, ed. R. C. Reid (Dumfries, 1915).

**Halcro** of Coubister. Petition, Answers and Replies of Joshua Johnstone, Writer in Stromness, and M. Halcro, his Wife, one of the Portioners of Estate of Coubister, in Reference to the Management of the Estate, etc., 4to (1790).

of Halcro. The Erskine-Halcro Genealogy . . . by E. E. Scott (1890, 1895). Norton Smith's Orkney Armorials, 61-65. Scottish N. and Q., 2nd S., viii. 62.

**Haldane** of Airthrey. Geneal. Memoirs of the Family of Sir Walter Scott, Bart., by Rev. C. Rogers, *lix.* Logie, by Rev. Dr Menzies Fergusson, ii. 47-53.

of Barmony. Some Perthshire Families, by the Rev. Charles Rogers (Edinr. 1887).*

of Broughton. Renwick's Peeblesshire Localities, 199-201. Buchan and Paton's History of Peeblesshire, iii. 249.

in Fairnilee. Craig Brown's Selkirkshire, i. 554.

**Haldane** of Gleneagles. Heraldry, by Nisbet (1742), ii. Ragman Roll, 9.
Visitation of Seats and Arms, by J. B. Burke (1853), ii. 19.
Memoranda Relative to the Family of Haldane of Gleneagles
[by Alexander Haldane], folio (London, 1880).* Burke's Landed
Gentry (1899-1925). Memoirs of R. Haldane and J. A. Haldane,
by Alexander Haldane. The Haldanes of Gleneagles, by Gen. Sir
Aylmer L. Haldane (Edinr. 1929).

of Keilor. Memorials of Angus and the Mearns, by Jervise, ed.
Gammack, ii. 101.

of Northroe. Zetland Family Histories, by F. J. Grant, 114-115.

**Haliburton** of Denhead. The Scottish Antiquary, x. 41, 96.

in Dryburgh. Memorials of the Haliburtons, 25-62. Russell's Haigs of
Bemersyde, 116.

of Haliburton. Memorials of the Haliburtons, by Sir W. Scott, Bart.
(Edinr. 1820, 1824)* (1877), 1-70. Scottish N. and Q., xii. 41.
The Scots Peerage, iv. 330-334.

Lord Haliburton of Dirleton. The Scots Peerage, iv. 330-338.

of Muirhouselaw. Memorials of the Haliburtons, 7-10, 34, 45.

of Newmains. Memorials of the Haliburtons, 40-53, 64, 66. Geneal.
Memoirs of the Family of Sir Walter Scott, by Rev. C. Rogers
(Grampian Club, 1877), xxix.-xxxvi., xxxix. Annals and Antiquities
of Dryburgh, by Sir D. Erskine, 2nd ed., 34-44.

*See also* **Halyburton.**

**Halkerston,** Culross. Some Old Families, by H. B. M'Call, *v.-vii.**

of Halkerston. A Genealogical Account of the Family of Halkerston
of that Ilk, 15 pp. (1772).

of Over Grange and Halkerstoun Beath. Some Old Families, by H. B.
M'Call (1890), 39-48, and pedigree.*

of Rathillet. An Appeal to Reason : History of the Entail of the Lands
of Rathillet in Fife, by Helenus Halkerston (1778). Some Old
Families, 37-39.

**Halket-Craigie** of Hall-Hill. Baronage, by Douglas, 287-288.

**Halkett** of Cramond. Burke's Landed Gentry (1848).

of Halkett. Eminent Men of Fife, by M. F. Conolly, 210-211.

of Pitfirrane. Baronage, by Douglas, 284-287. Eminent Men of Fife,
by Conolly, 211-212. Burke's Peerage and Baronetage (before 1905).
Complete Baronetage, by G. E. C., iv. 373.

**Hall,** Crail and Elie. Alexander Cowan, by C. B. Boog Watson, 49.*

of Dargavel. Crawfurd's Shire of Renfrew, ed. Robertson.

of Dunglass. Complete Baronetage, by G. E. C., iv. 353. Burke's
Peerage and Baronetage.

of Fulbar. Crawfurd's Shire of Renfrew, ed. Robertson, 86, 392-
393.

Glasgow. Traditions of the Watson Family, by C. B. Boog Watson.*

**Hall-Dempster** of Dunnichen. Burke's Landed Gentry (1925).

**Halley** of Kinnedar. Scottish N. and Q., 3rd S., vi. 62.

**Halliday** of Tullibole, pedigree annexed to Edgar's History of Dumfries, ed. R. C. Reid (Dumfries, 1915).

**Halyburton**, Aberdalgie. Roger's Four Perthshire Families, 44.*
of Drumblade. Thanage of Fermartyn, by Temple, 258-259.
of Pitcur. Baronage of Angus and Mearns, by Peter, 152-154. Angus or Forfarshire, by Warden, iv. 23-26. Complete Baronetage, by G. E. C. (1902), ii. 337.

*See also* **Haliburton**.

**Hamilton.** Heraldry, by Nisbet (1722), i. 390-396. Royal Genealogies, by Anderson (1732), 766. Crawfurd's Shire of Renfrew (1818), 317-322. Memoirs of the House of Hamilton and its Branches, by John Anderson, 4to (Edinr. 1825 and Supplement, 1827). Memoirs of the House of Hamilton corrected, by Dr Hamilton of Bardowie (Edinr. 1828). Reply to the mis-statements of Dr Hamilton, by John Riddell (Edinr. 1828). Index Tables to the Family of Hamilton, oblong 4to, n.d. Notes and Queries, 1st S., vi. 429, 577; vii. 285, 333; xi. 235; xii. 306, 413, 521. History of County of Bute, by J. E. Reid (1864), 176-193. The Pedigree of the Hamilton Family, by Audi Alteram Partem, 8vo, 32 pp. (1867). [Chiefly relating to its origin in Leicestershire.] Review of above *in* Herald and Genealogist, iv. 450-455. Walter Fitz Gilbert, by Joseph Bain *in* Genealogist, N. S., ii. 43-46. Geneal. Mag., i. 184, 532-536; ii. 532-536. Scottish N. and Q., 3rd S., iv. 194; v. 156. Papal Bulls in Hamilton Papers, by Prof. R. K. Hannay *in* Scot. Hist. Review, xxii. G. H. Johnston, Heraldry of the Hamiltons (1909). [Contains references to pedigrees of all the branches]. Dictionary of National Biography, *s.v.* [Lt.-Colonel G. Hamilton, Castle House, Park Hill, Bexley, is editing and continuing Dr John Anderson's House of Hamilton, and invites information of more recent branches of the family.]

*See* the Scots Peerage, ed. Sir James Balfour Paul, *for*

**Hamilton**, Earl of, Marquess of, Duke of Abercorn, i. 37-74.
Earl of Angus, iv. 393-397.
Earl of Arran, iv. 355-397.
Lord Bargany, ii. 27-33.
Lord Belhaven, ii. 38-60.
Lord Binning, iv. 310-329.
Marquess of Clydesdale, iv. 377-397.
Lord Daer, vii. 516-525.
Baron Dechmont, vi. 578-584.
Marquess of Douglas, iv. 396.
Lord, Marquess of, Duke of, iv. 339-381.
Earl of Haddington, iv. 303-329.
Earl of Melrose, iv. 310-311.
Lord Melros of Tynningham, iv. 325-326.
Earl of Orkney, vi. 578-584.
Lord Paisley, i. 39-74.

**Hamilton,** Earl of Ruglen, vii. 361-363.
Earl of Selkirk, vii. 516-525.
Baron of Strabane, i. 48-74.

**Hamilton** of Aikinhead. Ayrshire Families, by G. Robertson, i. 364-368.
of Airdrie. The Balfours of Pilrig, by Barbara Balfour-Melville, 270
of Ardoch. Paterson's History of Ayr, ii. 247. Peeblesshire Localities,
by Renwick, 430.
of Auldtoun. Zetland Family Histories, by F. J. Grant, 116-121.
of Baldoon. The Scots Peerage, vii. 518-521.
of Bangour. Landed Gentry (1846-1862). The Scottish Antiquary,
v. 86-87 ; viii. 64.
of Bardowie. Memorial and Information for John Hamilton of Barduie,
respecting the Peerage of Belhaven and Stenton, folio, 2 pp.
(April, 1797). Landed Gentry (1863).
of Bargany. The Bargany Cause ; a collection of papers relating to
this important case, 3 vols. 4to (1736-1824). Paterson's History of
County of Ayr, i. 382-384. Paterson's Ayr and Wigton, ii. 199-203.
Selections from Family Papers *in* Archæol. and Hist. Coll. of
Ayrshire and Galloway (1894), vii. 83-92. A Short Account of the
Hamiltons of Bargany, by the Hon. Hew Hamilton Dalrymple, 4to
(1897).* Hamilton, Lord Bargany, by the Hon. Hew H. Dalrymple,
4to (1897).*
of Barns and Cochno. Historical MSS. Commission (1881), 8th Report.
Burke's Landed Gentry (1858-1925).
of Barnton. Nisbet's Heraldic Plates (1892), 126. Complete Baronetage,
by G. E. C., iv. 362.
of Barnweill. Paterson's Ayr and Wigton, i. 269.
of Beechgrove. Paterson's History of Ayr, ii. 340.
of Belleisle and Pinmore. Paterson's History of Ayr, i. 207. Ayr and
Wigton, i. 131-133.
of Boreland. Paterson's Ayr, i. 369. Ayr and Wigton, i. 313-314.
Warrick's History of New Cumnock, 23-24.
of Bothwellhaugh. Ayrshire Families, by G. Robertson (1824), ii. 131.
Notes and Queries, 3rd S., xi. 453, 502 ; xii. 10-11, 69 : 5th S.,
xii. 386, 512. Genealogist, N. S., xx. 4-5.
of Bourtreehill. Paterson's Ayr, ii. 103. Ayr and Wigton, iii. 274.
of Broomhill. Account of the Families of Birnie and Hamilton of
Broomhill, by John Birnie, ed. W. B. D. D. Turnbull (Edinr.
1838).* Complete Baronetage, by G. E. C., ii. 406.
of Brownmoore, Brownmuir. Paterson's Ayr, i. 276-277. Ayr and
Wigton, iii. 83-85. Geneal. Mag., vii. 31.
of Burnside. Scottish N. and Q., 3rd S., v. 217.
of Cadzow. The Scots Peerage, iv. 345-352.
of Cairnhill, Carnell. Paterson's Ayr and Wigton, i. 280.
of Cambuskeith. Ayrshire Families, by G. Robertson, i. 356-359.
History of the County of Ayr, by Paterson, ii. 201-203. Ayr and
Wigton, iii. 433.

**Hamilton** of Cathkin. Scottish N. and Q., 2nd S., ii. 142.

Chelsea. Scottish N. and Q., 3rd S., iv. 41, 68, 82-84, 134.

of Coats. Burke's Peerage and Baronetage.

of Cochno. Irving's Book of Dumbartonshire (1879), ii. 377.

of Coldcoat. Buchan and Paton's History of Peeblesshire, iii. 40-49.

of Craighlaw. Paterson's Ayr, ii. 123. Ayr and Wigton, iii. 299-300. Lands . . . in Galloway, by M'Kerlie (1906), i. 627. Burke's Landed Gentry (1846-1925).

Crail. Churchyard Monuments of Crail, by Erskine Beveridge, 114-119.

Edinburgh. Scot. Hist. Review (1910), vi. 329.

of Evandale. Landed Gentry (1858-1863).

of Fala. A Short Account of the Hamiltons of Fala and of Fala House, by the Hon. H. H. Dalrymple, 4to (1907).*

of Fingalton. Crawfurd's Shire of Renfrew (1818), 293-298.

of Gilkerscleugh. Landed Gentry (1863).

of Grange. Ayrshire Families, by G. Robertson, i. 356-363. Paterson's Ayr, ii. 201-203. Ayr and Wigton, iii. 434, 562. Scottish N. and Q., 3rd S., v. 199, 219. The Intimate Life of Alexander Hamilton by Allan M'Lane Hamilton (London, 1910). Buchan and Paton's History of Peeblesshire, iii. 58-60.

of Haggs. Complete Baronetage, by G. E. C., iv. 276.

of Halcraig *or* Harrage. Upper Ward of Lanarkshire, by Irving and Murray, ii. 418-420. Burke's Landed Gentry (1848), 1155.

Duke of Hamilton. The Manifold Practises and Attempts of the Hamiltons and particularly of the present Duke of Hamilton . . . to get the Crown of Scotland, by Marchamont Needham (1648). The Dukes of Hamilton [James 1st and William 2nd], by Gilbert Burnet (London, 1677). Memoirs of the Life and Family of . . . James, late Duke of Hamilton (London, 1717, 1742). Biographical Peerage (1808), 199, 303-307. Inquiry into the Pedigree, Descent and Public Transactions of the Chiefs of the Hamilton Family, by William Aiton (Glasgow, 1827). Historical MSS. Commission (1870) 1st Report; (1887) 11th Report. The Great Historic Families of Scotland, by Jas. Taylor [1887]. Peerages by Debrett, Burke, Lodge, etc. G. E. C.'s Complete Peerage.

Lord Hamilton of Dalzell. Debrett's and other Annual Peerages. G. E. C.'s Complete Peerage.

of Holmhead. Crawfurd's Shire of Renfrew (1818), 264. Ayrshire Families, by G. Robertson, i. 363, 368. Landed Gentry (1846).

of Hullerhirst. Pont's Cunninghame, ed. Dobie, 212-213. Ayrshire Families, ii. 36-38. Burke's Landed Gentry (1871-1925).

of Innerwick. Baronage, by Douglas, 460-463. The Genealogist, N. S., xx. 4-5, 144. Complete Baronetage, by G. E. C., ii. 361. The Scots Peerage, iv. 304-309. A " Memorie," Historical and Genealogical of my Mother's paternal lineage : the Hamiltons of Innerwick, the Lothian Kerrs and the Earls of Angus, by Mark Napier (1872).*

of Kames. Burke's Landed Gentry (Suppl. 1849).

**Hamilton** of Kynbrachmont. Geneal. Coll., by W. Macfarlane, 1750-51; Scot. Hist. Soc., i. 13, 24. East Neuk of Fife, by W. Wood, 2nd ed. (1887), 151-153.

of Kype. Paterson's History of Ayr, ii. 340. Ayr and Wigton, i. 556.

of Ladyland. Ayrshire Families, i. 369-372, 376. Paterson's History of Ayr, ii. 123. Ayr and Wigton, iii. 298.

London. Complete Baronetage, by G. E. C., ii. 170.

of Monkton Mains. The Genealogist, N. S., xx. 1-6.

of Muirhouse. Cramond, by J. P. Wood, 26.

of Newbottle. Geneal. Mag., vi. 561.

of Newton. Burke's Landed Gentry (1863), 593.

of North Park. Joseph Bain *in* Genealogist, N. S., xvi. 73-75.

of Olivestob. Heraldry, by Nisbet (1742), ii. Appx. 38. The Olivestob Hamiltons, by Rev. A. W. H. Eaton, 4to, 32 pp. (New York, 1893.)* Lt.-Col. Otho Hamilton of Olivestob . . . by Rev. A. W. H. Eaton, 8vo, 24 pp. (Halifax, N. S., 1899).

of Orbieston and Dalziell. Baronage, by Douglas, 463-465. Landed Gentry (1863-1879).

of Pencaitland. The Scots Peerage, ii. 43.

of Pinmore. Burke's Landed Gentry (1906-1925).

of Preston. Crawfurd's Shire of Renfrew (1818), 293-298. Burke's Peerage and Baronetage. Complete Baronetage, by G. E. C., iv. 299.

of Priestfield. The Scots Peerage, iv. 305-313.

of Quotquot and Kirkurd. Peeblesshire Localities, by Renwick, 431.

of Raploch. Paterson's Ayr, ii. 43. Burke's Landed Gentry (1906-1925).

of Rosehall. Baronage, by Douglas, 463-465. Burke's Extinct Baronetcies. Complete Baronetage, by G. E. C., iv. 415. The Scots Peerage, ii. 42.

of Rouchbank. The Genealogist, N. S., xx. 6.

of Rozelle and Carcluie. Paterson's Ayr, i. 205-206. Ayr and Wigton, i. 152-155.

of St Christophers. Oliver's History of Antigua, ii. 50-56.

of Samuelston. The Family of Inglis of Auchindinny, by J. A. Inglis, 221.

of Silvertonhill. Baronage, by Douglas, 424-427. Burke's Peerage and Baronetage. Complete Baronetage, by G. E. C., ii. 453. A. W. Gray-Buchanan *in* Scot. Hist. Review (1910), vi. 408-409.

of Stanehouse. Paterson's County of Ayr, i. 271. Peeblesshire Localities, by Renwick, 202-203. Annals of a Tweeddale Parish, by Baird, 31. Buchan and Paton's History of Peeblesshire, iii. 251.

of Sundrum. Paterson's Ayr, i. 319-322. Ayr and Wigton, i. 245-251. Burke's Landed Gentry (1849-1921).

of Stevenston. The Scots Peerage, ii. 55.

in Sweden. One Year in Sweden, by H. Marryat, ii. 472-474, 501. Palace of History Catalogue (Glasgow, 1911), 201, 202, 205, 207.

of Threipwood. Paterson's Ayr, i. 271. Ayr and Wigton, iii. 116-117.

of Torrance. A. W. Gray-Buchanan *in* Scot. Hist. Review, vi. 440.

of Udston. Baronage, by Douglas, 466-467. Scot. N. and Q., 3rd S., iv. 83, 133, 233. The Scots Peerage, ii. 39-41.

**Hamilton** in Ulster. Hamilton Manuscripts: the Settlement of the Territories of the Upper Clandeboye, Great Ardes and Dufferin, County Down, by Sir James Hamilton, ed. T. K. Lowry (Belfast, 1867). Hamilton Memoirs, being genealogical notices of a branch of that family which settled in Ireland in the reign of James I., by Edward Hamilton (1891).

of Westburn. Landed Gentry (1858-1863).

of Westport. Burke's Landed Gentry (1863-1894). Complete Baronetage, by G. E. C., ii. 322.

of Whitecamp. The Scots Peerage, iv. 348, 351.

of Wishaw. Baronage, by Douglas, 479-480. Crawfurd's Shire of Renfrew, ed. Robertson, 402-404. The Scots Peerage, ii. 48-52.

of Ypres and London. The Genealogist, N.S., xiv. 264-271.

**Hamilton-Buchanan** of Spittal and Leny. Burke's Landed Gentry (1863-1925).

**Hamilton-Campbell.** Landed Gentry (1894).

**Hamilton-Dalrymple** of Bargany. Paterson's Ayr (1847), i. 384.

of North Berwick. Complete Baronetage, by G. E. C., iv. 379. Burke's Peerage and Baronetage.

Earl of Stair. The Scots Peerage, viii. 158-164.

**Hamilton-Dundas** of Duddingston. Landed Gentry (1848-1863).

**Hamilton-Gordon.** The Scots Peerage, i. 95-97.

**Hammil** of Roughwood. Ayrshire Families, by Geo. Robertson (1823), i. 372-374, 377 ; ii. 260.

**Hannay** of Grennan. Visitation of Seats and Arms, by J. B. Burke (1853), ii. 70. Landed Gentry (1863).

of Kingsmuir. Eminent Men of Fife, by Conolly, 213-214. East Neuk of Fife, by W. Wood, 2nd ed. (1887), 341-342. Burke's Landed Gentry (1863-1906).

of Kirkdale. Lands . . . in Galloway, by M'Kerlie, iv. 249-256. Landed Gentry (1858-1906).

of Knock and Garrarie. Conolly's Eminent Men of Fife, 214-215.

of Rusco. M'Kerlie's Lands . . . in Galloway, iii. 47, 48.

of Sorbie. Visitation of Seats and Arms, by J. B. Burke (1853), ii. 70.

**Hardy** of Navity. Memoirs of my Ancestors, by Hardy Bertram M'Call (1884).* Some Old Families, by Hardy Bertram M'Call (Birmingham, 1890), 51-75, and pedigree.*

**Harington-Stuart** of Torrance. The Stewarts Magazine, iii. 20.

**Hartfell,** Johnstone, Earl of. G. E. C.'s Complete Peerage. The Scots Peerage, i. 256-271.

**Hartsyde,** Douglas, Lord. G. E. C.'s Complete Peerage. The Scots Peerage, i. 206 ; iv. 77-79.

**Harvey** of Ardo. Thanage of Fermartyn, by Temple, 644.

of Carnousie. Landed Gentry (1863-1921).

of Castle Semple. Crawfurd's Shire of Renfrew (1818), 358.

Grenada. Oliver's History of Antigua, ii. 23, 68.

**Harvey** of Kinnettles. Thanage of Fermartyn, by Temple, 459-461. Angus or Forfarshire, by Warden, iv. 65.

Monycabock. Thanage of Fermartyn, 642.

of Tillygreig. Thanage of Fermartyn, 459-461.

**Harvie** of Broadlie. Ayrshire Families, by G. Robertson (1824), ii. 340-342. Paterson's History of Ayr, i. 422.

of Mameulaw, Rennieshill and Strypes. Scottish N. and Q., 2nd S., ii. 40.

**Harvie-Brown** of Dunipace. Who's Who (1903). Burke's Landed Gentry (1894-1925).

**Hastie-Robertson** of Gossaburgh. Burke's Landed Gentry (1921-1925).

**Haswell.** Scottish N. and Q., 2nd S., vii. 156.

**Haws.** Burke's British Families. The Haws Family and their Seafaring Kin, by Captain George W. Haws (*in preparation*).

**Hay.** De Nobilissimae Gentis Haiorum origine, seu Danorum, carmen Historicum, by James Ross, 12mo (Edinr. 1700 and 1703). Nisbet's Heraldry (1722), i. 184-188. Genealogical Table of the Hays, from William de Haya, Cupbearer to Malcolm IV., 1170, down to 1840, with all the Branches, compiled by John Hay Allan, *otherwise* John Stolberg Sobieski Stuart ; large sheet, 40 × 36 inches (1840). Dictionary of National Biography, *s.v.*

*See* The Scots Peerage, ed. Sir James Balfour Paul, *for*

**Hay**, Viscount Dupplin, v. 222-239.

Earl of Erroll, iii. 555-587.

Earl of Gifford, viii. 453-474.

Lord Hay of Kinfauns, v. 222-239.

Lord Hay of Yester, viii. 430-474.

Baron Kilmarnock of Kilmarnock, iii. 585-587.

Earl of Kinnoull, v. 217-239.

Earl of, Marquess of Tweeddale, viii. 416-474.

**Hay**, Aberdeen. Genealogies of an Aberdeen Family, by Smith ; Aberd. Univ. Studies, 87-89.

of Alderston. Genealogical Table, by William Fraser (Edinr. 1840). Burke's Extinct Baronetcies. Burke's Peerage and Baronetage. Complete Baronetage, by G. E. C., iv. 407.

of Asleid. Tayler's Jacobites of Aberdeenshire, 296.

of Balcomie. East Neuk of Fife, by W. Wood, 2nd ed., 437.

of Balhousie. The Scots Peerage, v. 230-231.

of Barro. Scot. Hist. Review, xv. 124.

of Belton. The Scots Peerage, viii. 454-455.

of Bonnington. History of Peeblesshire, by Chambers, 340.

of Cardenie. Nisbet's Heraldic Plates, ed. Ross and Grant, 70.

of Cassingray. East Neuk of Fife, by W. Wood, 2nd ed., 148.

of Craignethan. Diary of A. Hay of Craignethan, 1659-60, ed. A. G. Reid (1901).

**Hay** of Cruxlands. Buchan and Paton's History of Peeblesshire, ii. 363.

of Delgaty. James Ferguson, *in* Scot. Hist. Review, vi. 248-259.

of Dronlaw. Memorials of Angus and the Mearns, by Jervise, ed. Gammack, ii. 93-97.

of Drumelzier and Duns Castle. The Family of Seton, by G. Seton, 721-732. Buchan and Paton's History of Peeblesshire, iii. 432-433. The Scots Peerage, viii. 449-450. Burke's Landed Gentry (1863-1925).

of Duns Castle. Historical MSS. Commission (1909), x.

of Erroll. Notes and Queries, 3rd S., vi. 545 ; vii. 84, 191. Admiral Sir John Dalrymple Hay, *in* Scottish Antiquary, i. 40-46, 57-61, 77-82. The Scots Peerage, iii. 555-562.

Baron Hay. English Peerage, by Rev. A. Jacob (1767), ii. 494-499.

of Hayfield. Zetland Family Histories, by F. J. Grant, 122-128.

of Haystoun. History of Peeblesshire, by Chambers, 333-342. Herald and Genealogist, iv. 372. A Pedigree of Hay of Haystoun, 1712-1880, compiled by Mrs G. E. Forbes, large sheet (1881). Buchan and Paton's History of Peeblesshire, ii. 360-370.

of Hopes. Landed Gentry (1846-1875). Visitation of Seats and Arms, by J. B. Burke (1853), ii. 10.

Duke of Inverness. The Jacobite Peerage, by the Marquis of Ruvigny (1904), 68.

of Lawfield. The Scots Peerage, viii. 456.

of Leys. Historical Account of the Family of Hay of Lees, and Genealogical Tree, by Alexander Deuchar, folio (Edinr. 1832). East Neuk of Fife, by W. Wood, 2nd ed., 458. Burke's Commoners, i. 504. Burke's Landed Gentry (1846-1862). The Scots Peerage, v. 217.

of Linplum. Burke's Extinct Baronetcies. Information, Petitions, etc., for Lord Charles Hay of Linplum, against J. and J. Hay and Lady M. Hay as to disposal of Estates of Marquis of Tweedale and Opposition to Same, 4to (1857). House of Lords : Margaret Grierson, of Edinburgh, Appellant, and James Connell of Conheath, Respondent ; the Respondent's Case (with Pedigree illustrative of the Case of Hay of Linplum as in the year 1788) 4to, 105 pp. (186-). Complete Baronetage, by G. E. C., iv. 260. The Scots Peerage, viii. 425, 446.

of Locherworth. The Scots Peerage, viii. 417-430.

of Marlefield. Annals of a Border Club, by G. Tancred, 251.

of Megginch. The Scots Peerage, v. 217-220, 230.

of Menzion. Buchan and Paton's History of Peeblesshire, iii. 409-412.

of Mountblairy. Tayler's Jacobites of Aberdeenshire, 304-308.

of Naughton. Balmerino and its Abbey, by Dr J. Campbell, 487-497, 645 ; 506-521, 647.

of Newhall. The Scots Peerage, viii. 459-461.

of Nunraw. The Scots Peerage, viii. 450-451.

of Paris. Douglas's Baronage (1796), 583.

**Hay** of Park. Lines from my Log-books, by Admiral Sir J. C. Dalrymple Hay (1898), 333-335. Lands . . . in Galloway, by M'Kerlie, 2nd ed. (1906), i. 576-582. Complete Baronetage, by G. E. C., iii. 341. Burke's Peerage and Baronetage.

of Pitfour. Baronage, by Douglas, 481-483. Burke's Commoners, i. 507. Landed Gentry (1846).

of Randerston. East Neuk of Fife, by W. Wood, 2nd ed., 458.

of Ranfield and Inchnoch. Heraldry, by Nisbet (1742), ii., Appx. 140. Crawfurd's Shire of Renfrew (1818), 64, 65.

of Rannes. Tayler's Jacobites of Aberdeenshire, 298-304.

of Rattray. The Scots Peerage, v. 229-230.

of Restalrig. The Jacobite Peerage, by the Marquis of Ruvigny, 64-65.

of Scroggs. Peeblesshire Localities, by Renwick, 168-170.

of Seggieden. Burke's Commoners, i. 509. Landed Gentry (1846-1925).

in Shethin. Temple's Thanage of Fermartyn, 396.

of Smithfield and Haystoun. Genealogical Chart, 1712-1880, by Mrs G. E. Forbes (1881). Peeblesshire Localities, by Renwick (1897), 359. Burke's Peerage and Baronetage. Complete Baronetage, by G. E. C., ii. 412. Buchan and Paton's History of Peeblesshire, ii. 336-340.

of Spott. The Scots Peerage, viii. 455-456.

of Strowie. Douglas's Baronage (1796), 584. Geneal. Mag. (1904), vii. 409.

in Sweden. One Year in Sweden, by Marryat (1862), ii. 484. Palace of History Catalogue (Glasgow, 1911), 210. E. E. Etzel *in* Scot. Hist. Review (1913), ix. 270.

of Talla. Buchan and Paton's History of Peeblesshire, iii. 409-412.

of Tullibody. The Scots Peerage, viii. 420-421.

of Tweeddale. The Genealogie of the Hayes of Tweeddale . . . by Father Richard Augustin Hay, Prior of St Pieremont, ed. by James Maidment, 4to, *xvi.*+127 pp. (Edinr. 1835).

of Yester. The Family of Seton, by George Seton, 41. The Scots Peerage, viii. 422-430. Calendar of Writs preserved at Yester House, 1166-1598, ed. by Charles C. Harvey; 1598- , ed. by John MacLeod; (Scot. Rec. Soc., Edinr. 1916-1919 and 1928- ).

**Hay-Drummond.** Hunter's Deanery of Doncaster, i. 316.

**Hay-Gordon.** Burke's Landed Gentry (1875-1898).

**Hay-Makdougall.** Burke's Commoners, iii. 430. Complete Baronetage, by G. E. C., iv. 407.

**Hay-Mackenzie**, Earl of Cromartie and Viscount Tarbat of Tarbat. The Scots Peerage, iii. 84-86.

**Hay-Newton** of Newton. The Scots Peerage, viii. 461. Burke's Commoners, iii. 26. Burke's Landed Gentry (1846-1925).

**Hebden** of Eday. Norton Smith's Orkney Armorials, 66.

**Heddell** of Helliness. Zetland Family Histories, by F. J. Grant, 129-131.

**Heddle** of Melsetter. Burke's Landed Gentry (1858-1925).

**Heiton** of Darnick. Scottish N. and Q., 2nd S., viii. 62, 80.

**Henderson** of Abbotrule. Annals of a Border Club, by G. Tancred, 253-255.

of Achalibster and Westerdale. Caithness Family History, by Henderson (1884), 288-292.

Alloa. MS. Pedigree in Lyon Office.

of Borrowstounness. Genealogical Chart (1892).

of Buness and Gardie. Zetland Family Histories, by F. J. Grant, 132-136.

of Fordell. Baronage, by Douglas, 518-520. Burke's Landed Gentry (1849). Stephen's Inverkeithing (1921), 128-150.

of Gloup. Zetland Family Histories, 147-148.

Langholm. Burke's Peerage and Baronetage (1905).

of Midgarth, Ollaberry and Bardister. Zetland Family Histories, 139-144.

of Nottingham and Gersay. Caithness Family History, by John Henderson, 293.'

of Pettister. Zetland Family Histories, 137-138.

of Springfield. Zetland Family Histories, 145-146.

of Stemster. Caithness Family History, 282-287. Landed Gentry (1858-1886).

Thurso. Caithness Family History, xi.-xiii.

of Tunnygask. Stephen's Inverkeithing, 471-473.

of Westerton. Landed Gentry (1849-1863). Logie, by Rev. Dr Menzies Fergusson, ii., 64-68, 70, 72, 73, 76.

**Henry, Hendrie** of Bayhall. Zetland Histories, by F. J. Grant, 149-151.

**Henryson-Caird** of Cassencary. Burke's Landed Gentry (1914-1925).

**Hepburn.** Heraldry, by A. Nisbet (1722), i. 155, 165.

of Adiston. The Family of Seton, by G. Seton (1896), 248.

of Athelstaneford. Memoirs and Adventures of Sir J. Hepburn, by James Grant (Edinr. 1857).

of Auldhamstocks. Geneal. Mag. (1898), i. 412-416.

of Beinston. The Scots Peerage, ii. 142.

Earl of Bothwell. The Scots Peerage, ii. 135-167.

of Hailes. The Scots Peerage, ii. 135-141.

Lord Hailes. The Scots Peerage, ii. 135-167.

Duke of Orkney. The Scots Peerage, ii. 161-167.

of Rollandston. The Scots Peerage, ii. 139-140, 154-155.

of Wauchton. Genealogical Notes of the Hepburn Family, by Edward Hepburn (London, 1925).*

of Whitsome. The Scots Peerage, ii. 144-146, 162.

**Hepburn-Murray** of Glendoick. Complete Baronetage, by G. E. C., iv. 305.

**Hepburn-Stuart-Forbes.** Complete Baronetage, by G. E. C., ii. 305.

**Hepburne-Scott** of Harden and Humbie. The Scots Peerage, vii. 84-86.

**Herbert,** Lord Dingwall. The Scots Peerage, iii. 125.

**Hering,** Jamaica. The Family of Inglis of Auchindinny, by J. A. Inglis, 72-76.

**Heriot.** The Case and Genealogy of Miss Elizabeth Heriot, folio (Edinr. 1841).

of Lymphoy. Scot. Hist. Review (1910), vi. 330.

of Trabroun. Memoirs of George Heriot (Edinr. 1822). History of Heriot's Hospital, by F. W. Bedford. Historical and Genealogical Notes and Collections regarding the Family of Heriot of Trabroun (Edinr. 1878).* Selections from old Records, regarding the Heriots of Trabroun, compiled by G. W. B[allingall, Glasgow], 66 pp. (Haddington, 1894).*

**Heron.** Traditions of the Watson Family, by C. B. Boog Watson (Perth, 1908).

of Bargaly. Lands . . . in Galloway, by M'Kerlie, iv. 449-452.

of Kirrouchtrie. Lands . . . in Galloway, iv. 413-431.

**Heron-Maxwell** of Springkell. Complete Baronetage, by G. E. C., iv. 320. Debrett's and Burke's Baronetages.

of Teviotbank. Annals of a Border Club, by G. Tancred, 324-327.

**Herries** of Barnbarroch. Lands . . . in Galloway, by M'Kerlie, iii. 349.

of Halldykes. Some Old Families, by H. B. M'Call, with chart pedigree, 278-9.*

of Mabie. Lands and their Owners in Galloway, by M'Kerlie, v. 226. The Scots Peerage, iv. 402.

of Spottes. Burke's Landed Gentry (1886-1925).

of Terregles. Lands . . . in Galloway, v. 141-148. The Scots Peerage, iv. 398-413.

**Herries of Terregles,** Constable-Maxwell, Lord. Case and Suppl. Case of William Constable-Maxwell. Case and Suppl. Case of William Maxwell of Carruchan (1848). Minutes of Evidence (1849-1853). The Scots Peerage, iv. 420-424. Burke's and other Annual Peerages.

Herries, Lord. The Story and Pedigree of the Lords Herries . . . by H. Herries-Crosbie, folio (Wrexford) [19 ]. The Scots Peerage, iv. 398-413.

Maxwell, Lord. The Scots Peerage, iv. 409-418.

**Herries-Crosbie** of Flowerburn. Burke's Landed Gentry (1914-1925).

**Hervey** of Elrick. Scottish N. and Q., 3rd S., i. 171.

**Hibbert-Ware.** Burke's Landed Gentry (1848).

**Higgins** of Neuck. MS. Pedigree compiled by Hector Burn-Murdoch, advocate.

**Hill.** The Early Records of an Old Glasgow Family, 1520-1791 [by William H. Hill, LL.D], xi.+178 pp., Geneal. Table, etc. (Glasgow, 1902).*

St Cyrus. Smith's Genealogies of an Aberdeen Family, Aberd. Univ. Studies, 23-25.

of Waughton. Complete Baronetage, by G. E. C., iv. 444.

**Hillhouse,** Antigua. Oliver's History of Antigua, ii. 75.

Douglas, Lord. The Scots Peerage, vii. 146-147.

Hamilton, Lord. The Scots Peerage, vii. 361-363.

**Hilson**, Jedburgh.   Annals of a Border Club, by G. Tancred, 16, 256-258.

**Hodge** of Gladsmuir.   Notes and Queries, 3rd S., iii. 130.

**Hog** of Harcarse.   Nisbet's Heraldic Plates, ed. Ross and Grant (1892), 148.
   of Ladykirk and Cammo.   Cramond, by J. P. Wood, 65-66.
   of Newliston.   Nisbet's Heraldic Plates, 148-150.   Burke's Landed Gentry
   (1849-1925).
   Stirling.   The Stirling Antiquary, ii. 135-136.

**Hogg** in Sweden.   One year in Sweden, by Marryat, ii. 490.

**Holburne** of Menstrie and Cowcairny.   Stephen's Inverkeithing and
   Rosyth, 170-177, 485-486.   Logie, by Rev. Dr Menzies Fergusson,
   ii. 171-172.   Complete Baronetage, by G. E. C., iv. 438.   Catalogue
   of Holburne of Menstrie Museum, Bath, by A. I. Collier, 3, 11-12.

**Holdernesse**, Ramsay, Earl of.   The Scots Peerage, iv. 301-302.

**Holyroodhouse**, Bothwell, Lord.   Nisbet's Heraldry (1742), ii., Appx.
   242-245.   The Scots Peerage, iv. 425-439.

**Home.**   Heraldry, by A. Nisbet (1722), i. 276-280.   Drummond's Noble
   British Families (1846), ii.   Dictionary of National Biography, *s.v.*
   of Argaty.   Burke's Landed Gentry (1886) 1286, (1894) 1412.   The
      Monros of Auchenbowie, by J. A. Inglis, 85.   The Scots Peerage,
      vi. 3-4.
   of Bassendean.   Memoirs of Walter Pringle of Greenknow (1847).
      Burke's Landed Gentry (1875-1886).
   of Blackadder.   MS. by John Riddell, W.S., and Robert Riddell, in
      possession of the Society of Writers to the Signet.   Complete
      Baronetage, by G. E. C., iv. 280.
   of Broomhouse.   Landed Gentry (1849-1925).
   of Broxmouth.   The Scots Peerage, iii. 285, 287.
   Lord Coldingham.   The Scots Peerage, iv. 465-484.
   of Cowdenknowes.   Annals and Antiquities of Dryburgh, by Sir D.
      Erskine, 2nd ed., 194-198.   Annals of a Border Club, by Tancred,
      258.
   of Eccles.   The Scots Peerage, iv. 472, 473.
   of Home.   Angus or Forfarshire, by Warden, i. 306-309.   The Scots
      Peerage, iv. 441-452.
   Earl of Dunbar.   The Scots Peerage, iii. 280-289.
   Lord Dunglas.   The Scots Peerage, iv. 464-484.
   Earl of Home.   G. E. C.'s Complete Peerage, ed. Gibbs.   Burke's,
      Debrett's and Lodge's Peerages.   Historical MSS. Commission
      (1891), 12th Report.   Nisbet's Heraldic Plates, ed. Ross and Grant,
      6-9.   The Scots Peerage, iv. 440-484.
   of Huttonhall.   N. and Q., 10th S., vi. 209, 276, 316, 371, 397.   The
      Scots Peerage, iv. 457, 580.
   Lord Jedburgh.   The Scots Peerage, iv. 465-484.
   of Lumsden.   Complete Baronetage, by G. E. C., iv. 375.
   of Manderston.   The Scots Peerage, iii. 282-284.

**Home** of Renton. Burke's Extinct Baronetcies. Notes and Queries, 4th S.,
iv. 31, 183. Hist. MSS. Commission (1876), 5th Report, pt. i., 646.
Complete Baronetage, by G. E. C., iv. 302. The Scots Peerage, iii. 282.

of Wedderburn. De Familia Humia Wedderburnensi Liber, by David
Home [before 1620], 4to, ed. J. Miller (Abbotsford Club, Edinr. 1839).
Genealogical Account of the Family of Home of Wedderburne,
made out from the Public Records, 8vo, 10 pp. (1776).* Complete
Baronetage, by G. E. C., ii. 442. Burke's Landed Gentry (1846-1925).
Nisbet's Heraldic Plates, 48-51.

of Whitfield. Landed Gentry (1875). Nisbet's Heraldic Plates, ed.
Ross and Grant (1892), 94.

of Woollee. Tancred's Rulewater, 79-82.

*See also* **Hume.**

**Home-Ferguson.** Pedigree of the Ferguson Branch of the Home Family,
by Geo. Burnett, Lyon-King, and Capt. Home-Ferguson.

**Home-Spiers** of Blackadder. Burke's Peerage and Baronetage. Complete
Baronetage, by G. E. C., iv. 280.

**Home-Stewart** of Argaty. The Monros of Auchenbowie, by J. A. Inglis, 85.

**Honeyman.** The Honeyman Family, in Scotland and America from 1584-
1908, by A. Van Doren Honeyman, 8vo (Plainfield, New Jersey,
U.S.A., 1909).

of Armadale. The Passing of the Honeymans, by Lord Sands (Scotsman, December 1911).

of Graemesay. Caithness Family History, by Henderson, 285. Norton
Smith's Orkney Armorials, 69-73.

in Orkney. The Frotoft Branch of the Orkney Traills, 70-76.

of Pitlairchney. The Frotoft Branch of the Orkney Traills, by T. W.
Traill, 70.

**Hope.** Chart Pedigree *in* Memoir of Chancellor Seton, by Geo. Seton,
(1882). Dictionary of National Biography, *s.v.*

of Balcomie. Eminent Men of Fife, by M. F. Conolly, 233. East Neuk
of Fife, by W. Wood, 2nd ed. (1887), 446-448.

of Carriden. Burke's Landed Gentry (1846-1879).

of Cowdenknowes. Annals of a Border Club, by G. Tancred (1899), 259.

of Craighall and Pinkie. Heraldry, by A. Nisbet (1722), i. 222 ; (1742),
ii. Appx. 97. Baronage, by Douglas, 58-61. Burke's Peerage and
Baronetage. Eminent Men of Fife, by Conolly, 234. Complete
Baronetage, by G. E. C., ii. 343. The Scots Peerage, iv. 487-490.

of Granton. Cramond, by J. P. Wood, 19, 20, 132-145. The Scots
Peerage, iv. 490-492.

of Hopetoun. Visitation of Seats and Arms, by J. B. Burke (1853),
i. 157. The Family of Sir Walter Scott, by Rev. C. Rogers
(Grampian Club, 1877), *lxix.*

Earl of Hopetoun. The Scots Peerage, iv. 485-505.

of Kerse. Burke's Extinct Baronetcies. The Balfours of Pilrig, by
B. Balfour-Melville, 270.

of Kirkliston. Burke's Extinct Baronetcies.

**Hope**, Marquess of Linlithgow.   Burke's and other Annual Peerages.   The
     Scots Peerage, iv. 485-505.
   of Luffness.   Landed Gentry (1886-1925).
   of Rankeillour.   Eminent Men of Fife, by M. F. Conolly (1866), 228.
   in Woolmet.   A Chapter in Mediocrity, by Rev. W. S. Stavert (Skipton,
     1896).*

**Hope-Johnstone** of Annandale.   Sir Wm. Fraser's Annandale Book.   The
     Scots Peerage, i. 270, 271.   Burke's Landed Gentry (1898-1925).

**Hope-Vere** of Craigiehall.   Burke's Landed Gentry (1848-1925).

**Hope-Weir** of Craigiehall.   Cramond, by J. P. Wood (1794), 67-68, 71, 151.
     Graham *v.* Hope-Weir.   Appellant's Case in House of Lords (1803).

**Hopetoun**, Hope, Earl of.   Cramond, by J. P. Wood (1794), 146-160.
     Burke's Peerage.   The Scots Peerage, iv. 485-505.   G. E. C.'s
     Complete Peerage, ed. Gibbs.

**Hop-Pringle** of Smailholm and Whitson.   Douglas's Baronage, 208, 211.
     *See also* **Pringle**.

**Hore-Ruthven**, Lord Ruthven of Freeland.   The Scots Peerage, vii.
     391-393

**Horn.**   Heraldry, by Nisbet (1742), ii. Appx. 73-78.
   of Westhall.   The Scottish Antiquary, viii. 89, 142, 185.

**Horne** of Langwell.   Annals of a Border Club, by G. Tancred, 261-263.

**Horsbrugh** of Horsbrugh.   History of Peeblesshire, by Chambers, 373-376.
     Peeblesshire Localities, by Renwick, 582-584.   Burke's Landed
     Gentry (1886-1894).   Buchan and Paton's History of Peeblesshire
     (1925), ii. 397-404.
   Pittenweem.   Eminent Men of Fife, by Conolly, 238-240.

**Hose** of Craigie.   History of County of Ayr, by Paterson, i. 335-336.   Ayr
     and Wigton, by Paterson, i. 282-283.   The Lairds of Glenfield
     (Paisley, 1860), 6-8.

**Hoseason** of Aywick.   Zetland Family Histories, by F. J. Grant, 152-157.
   of Dalsetter.   Zetland Family Histories, 158-160.

**Houison-Craufurd** of Craufurdland and Braehead.   Burke's Landed
     Gentry (1898-1925).

**Houston** of Balglas.   Strathendrick, by Guthrie Smith, 244, 246.
   of Clerkington.   Landed Gentry (1875-1925).
   of Coneywarren.   Landed Gentry (1846-1862).
   of Fortrose.   The Scottish Antiquary, iv. 93, 140 ; v. 189 ; vi. 94-96.
   Georgia.   History of the Habersham Family, by J. G. B. Bulloch, M.D.
     (Columbia, S. C., 1901), 179-182.
   of Houston.   Crawfurd's Shire of Renfrew (1818), 99-102.   Burke's
     Extinct and Dormant Baronetcies.   Scottish N. and Q., 3rd S.,
     iv. 76.   The Genealogist, 1st S., v. 22-23.
   of Johnstone.   Crawfurd's Shire of Renfrew (1818), 328.   Burke's Landed
     Gentry (1846-1925).

**Houston** of Mayshiel.  Burke's Landed Gentry (1921-1925).

**Houston-Boswall.**  Case before the House of Lords between Henry Inglis, W.S., Edinburgh, and Dame Euphemia Houston Boswall of Black-adder, with the Consent of Sir James, her Husband, folio (1840). Burke's Peerage and Baronetage.

**How** of Damton.  Crawfurd's Shire of Renfrew, ed. Semple (1782).  The Same, ed. Robertson (1818), 378.

**Howat** of Mabie.  Lands . . . in Galloway, by M'Kerlie, v. 228.

**Howie** in Lochgoin.  Paterson's History of Ayr, ii. 58.  Paterson's Ayr and Wigton, iii. 245-246.

**Howieson** of Braehead.  Cramond, by J. P. Wood, 61-62, chart pedigree. Ayrshire Families, by G. Robertson, i. 204-209, 385.  Burke's Commoners, ii. 234.  A Scottish Royal Tradition, by J. Bain *in* Genealogist, N. S., ii. 121-123.

**Hozier** of Mauldslie and Newlands.  Landed Gentry (1863-1886).  Burke's Peerage and Baronetage, *s.v.* Baron Newlands.

**Hughes** of Mountcharles and Balkissock.  Paterson's History of Ayr (1847), i. 207.  Ayr and Wigton, i. 152.

**Hume.**  Nisbet's Heraldry, i. 278-280.  History of the Families of Dunbar, Hume and Dundas, by Drummond.  Dictionary of National Biography, *s.v.*

of Argaty.  The Stirling Antiquary, ed. W. B. Cook, iii. 163.  The Scots Peerage, vi. 3-4.

of Auchendolly.  Burke's Landed Gentry (1894-1925).

Viscount Blasonberrie.  The Scots Peerage, vi. 14-24.

of Burnley Hall.  Baronage of Angus and Mearns, by D. M. Peter (1856), 163-165.

of Drumkose.  Logie, by Rev. Dr R. M. Fergusson, i. 66 *n.*

of Heuch.  The Scots Peerage, vi. 5-6.

of Johnscleugh.  The Scots Peerage, vi. 6, 8.

of Kimmerghame.  The Scots Peerage, vi. 11.

Logie.  The Stirling Antiquary (1904), iii. 18.

Earl of Marchmont.  The Scots Peerage, vi. 1-24.

of Ninewells.  Douglas's Baronage (1798), 587.  Nisbet's Heraldic Plates, 154.  Burke's Landed Gentry (1846-1925).

of North Berwick.  Complete Baronetage, by G. E. C., ii. 443.  The Scots Peerage, vi. 5-8.

of Polwarth.  Walford's Tales of our Great Families, 2nd S., ii. 193-210. Marchmont, and the Humes of Polwarth, by [Margaret Warrender], 8vo, illust. (Edinr. 1894)  Logie, by Rev. Dr Menzies Fergusson, i. 47, 64.  Complete Baronetage, by G. E. C., ii. 304.  The Scots Peerage, vi. 1-14.

Lord Polwarth.  G. E. C.'s Complete Peerage, ed. Gibbs.  The Scots Peerage, vi. 14-24.

of Tully Castle.  The Scots Peerage, vi. 8-9.

**Hume-Campbell** of Marchmont. Report relative to the Lordship and Estate of Marchmont, the Barony of Hume . . . drawn up by order of Sir Wm. P. Hume Campbell of Marchmont and Purves, Bart., 4to, illust., *iv* + 203 pp. (London, 1819).* The Scots Peerage, vi. 19-23.

**Hunt** of Pittencrief and Logie. Burke's Landed Gentry (1846-1925). Stephen's Inverkeithing (1921), 204-206.

**Huntar** of Balcarres. East Neuk of Fife, by W. Wood, 2nd ed. (1887), 128.

of Drumdow. Paterson's History of the County of Ayr, ii. 441.

of Duddingflat. Peeblesshire Localities, by Renwick, 199. Annals of a Tweeddale Parish, by Baird, 27.

of Kirkland. Paterson's History of Ayr, ii. 145. Paterson's Ayr and Wigton, iii. 354, 365.

**Hunter** of Abbotshill. Paterson's History of Ayr, i. 202-205. Paterson's Ayr and Wigton, i. 144-145 ; iii. 336. Pedigree of Hunter of Abbotshill and Barjarg, by A. A. Hunter, 4to, *iv* + 47 pp., illust. (London, 1905).

of Auchterarder. Pedigree, by Andrew A. Hunter.

of Blackness. Landed Gentry (1858-1879).

of Bonnytoun. Landed Gentry (1846-1862). Pedigree by A. A. Hunter.

of Burnside. Baronage of Angus and Mearns, by D. M. Peter, 166. Landed Gentry (1882). Warden's Angus or Forfarshire, v. 91-93.

Crail. Churchyard Monuments of Crail, by Erskine Beveridge, 100-102.

of Darrahill. Scottish N. and Q., 2nd S., iv. 190.

of Doonholm. Paterson's Ayr and Wigton, i. 145. Pedigree, by A. A. Hunter.

of Glencarse and Seaside. Pedigree *in* Playfair's Notes on the Scottish Family of Playfair.*

of Grange. Monifieth, by Malcolm, 339-340.

of Hunterston. Pont's Cuninghame, ed. Dobie, 190-193. Paterson's History of Ayr, ii. 132-135. Paterson's Ayr and Wigton, iii. 314, 327-359. The Pedigree of Hunter of Hunterston, or of that Ilk, compiled from State Records, etc. . . . for Robert Hunter of Hunterston, 8vo, 43 pp. (1865).* Burke's Commoners, ii. 500. Landed Gentry (1846-1925). The Genealogist, 1st S., vi. 310-315. Some Family Papers, 1374-1911, of the Hunters of that Ilk, or Hunterston, ed. M. S. Shaw ; Scottish Record Society, 90 pp. (Edinr. 1925).

of Long Calderwood. Paterson's Ayr and Wigton, iii. 352.

of Lunna. Zetland Family Histories, by F. J. Grant, 161-165.

of Milnholm. Paterson's Ayr and Wigton, i. 470.

of Polmood. History of Peeblesshire, by Chambers, 426-429. History of Peeblesshire, by Buchan and Paton, iii. 451-461.

of Restenneth, Restinet. Angus or Forfarshine, by Warden, ii. 141.

of Thurston. Pedigree, by Andrew Alex. Hunter (London, 1905). Burke's Landed Gentry (1894-1925).

**Hunter-Arundell** of Barjarg.  Landed Gentry (1846-1914).

**Hunter-Blair** of Blairquhan.  Paterson's History of County of Ayr, ii. 473-
475.  Paterson's History of Ayr and Wigton, i. 472-474 ; ii. 470.
Pedigree, by A. A. Hunter (1905).  Complete Baronetage, by
G. E. C., v. 257.

of Dunskey.  Burke's and Debrett's Baronetages.

of Milnholm.  Paterson's History of County of Ayr, ii. 474.

**Hunter-Weston** of Hunterston.  Burke's Landed Gentry (1846-1925).

**Huntingtower**, Murray, Lord of.  The Scots Peerage, iii. 402-406.

Tollemache, Lord of.  The Scots Peerage, iii. 406-420.

**Huntly**, Gordon, Earl of, Marquess of.  Claim of George, Earl of Aboyne
to the Title of Marquis of Huntley (Session Papers, 197 of
1838).

The Rentaill of the Lordschippe of Huntlye, 1600.  Spalding Club
Misc., iv.  The Herald and Genealogist, vi. 595-597.  The Records
of Aboyne, 1230-1681, ed. Charles, 11th Marquess of Huntly, 4to,
illust. (Aberdeen, 1894).  Historic Earls and Earldoms of Scot-
land, by Dr John Mackintosh, 108-223.  Dictionary of National
Biography, *s.v.*  Historical MSS. Commission (1871), 2nd Report.
Scottish N. and Q., 3rd S., iv. 157.  Burke's Peerage.  Debrett's
Peerage.  The Scots Peerage, iv. 506-562.  Complete Peerage, by
G. E. C., ed. Gibbs.  Notes and Queries, 8th S., iv. 48, 112 ; v. 287 ;
vi. 36.

Seton, Earl of.  The Family of Seton, by George Seton.  The Scots
Peerage, iv. 521-524.

Mary Stuart and the House of Huntly, by Thos. Duncan *in* Scot. Hist.
Review, iv. 365-373.

**Husband** of Hatton and Kilry.  Warden's Angus or Forfarshire, iii. 370.

**Hutcheson**, Glasgow.  Scot. Hist. Review, xvi. 91.

of Hairlaw.  Upper Ward of Lanarkshire, by Irving and Murray,
ii. 457.

of Lambhill.  Volume of Documents, MSS. relating to the families of
Hill and Hutcheson.  In the possession of William H. Hill, LL.D.

**Hutchison** of Monkwood.  Paterson's County of Ayr, ii. 370.  Paterson's
Ayr and Wigton, i. 443.

of Rockend.  Burke's Landed Gentry (1849-1863).

of Underwood.  Paterson's History of Ayr, i. 347.  Ayr and Wigton,
i. 248-249.

**Hyndford**, Carmichael, Earl of.  Notes and Queries, 3rd S., i. 482 ; ii. 25.
G. E. C.'s Complete Peerage, ed. Gibbs.  The Scots Peerage, iv.
563-597.

**Hyndman** of Lunderstoun and Springside.  Crawfurd's Shire of Renfrew
(1818), 425-426.  Robertson's Ayrshire Families, ii. 346-347.  Paterson's Ayr and Wigton, iii. 370.

**Hyslop** of Lochend.  Lands . . . in Galloway, by M'Kerlie, iv. 235.

**Ilay,** Campbell, Earl of, Viscount of. The Scots Peerage, i. 379. G. E. C.'s
  Complete Peerage.

**Imrie** of Lunan. Angus or Forfarshire, by Warden, iv. 250-251. Memorials
  of Angus and the Mearns, by Jervise, ed. Gammack, ii. 269. Burke's
  Landed Gentry (1898-1925).

**Inglis** of Auchendinny and Redhall. Family Tree of the Inglises, by
  John A. Inglis (1903). The Family of Inglis of Auchendinny and
  Redhall, by John A. Inglis (Edinr. 1914). Burke's Landed Gentry
  (1879-1925).

  of Cockairny. Stephen's Inverkeithing (1921), 169.

  of Cramond. Douglas's Baronage, 264-265. Cramond, by J. P. Wood,
    47-48, 265-266, with chart. Burke's Extinct Baronetcies. Complete
    Baronetage, by G. E. C., iv. 349.

  of Eastshiel. Upper Ward of Lanarkshire, by Irving and Murray, ii. 529.

  of Langlawhill. Annals of a Tweeddale Parish, by Rev. A. Baird, 32, 36.

  of Manor and Manorhead. Douglas's Baronage, 198-200. Peeblesshire
    Localities, by Renwick, 123, 467. Buchan and Paton's History of
    Peeblesshire, iii. 551-554.

  of Milton Bryant. Historical and Genealogical Notices of the Family of
    Inglis of Milton Bryant, by C. H. Wilson, 4to (1874).

  of St Leonards. Heraldry, by Nisbet (1742), ii., Appx. 60.

  of Tarvit. Geneal. Coll. by W. Macfarlane, 1750-51 ; Scot. Hist. Soc.,
    ii. 169, 171. East Neuk of Fife, by W. Wood, 2nd ed., 386.

**Inglisberry,** Carmichael, Viscount of. The Scots Peerage, iv. 590-597.

**Ingram,** Lord Ingram, Viscount Irvine. The Scots Peerage, v. 9-20.

  of Hillside. Zetland Family Histories, by F. J. Grant, 166-168.

**Innermeath,** Stewart, Lord. The Scots Peerage, v. 1-8.

**Innerpeffer** of Innerpeffer. Warden's Angus or Forfarshire, v. 129.

**Innes.** Ane Account of the Familie of Innes, compiled by Duncan Forbes
  of Culloden, 1698, with Appendix of Charters from . . . Floors,
  Leuchars and Dunkintie, ed. Cosmo Innes, 4to, $ix+287$ pp.
  (Aberdeen, Spalding Club, 1864). Nisbet's Heraldry, i. 262.
  Douglas's Baronage, 13-18. Nisbet's Heraldic Plates, ed. Ross and
  Grant, 100-102. Historical Account of the Origine and Succession
  of the Family of Innes, from the Original MS. in the possession
  of the Duke of Roxburghe ; and Pedigree, 4to (Edinr. 1820).*
  Genealogy of the Innes Family, by W. Berry, folio, 15 pp., n.d.
  Walford's Tales of our Great Families, 2nd S., ii. 225-236. Temple's
  Thanage of Fermartyn, 322-325. Scottish N. and Q., 2nd S., i. 51.
  Complete Baronetage, by G. E. C., ii. 280. The Scots Peerage,
  vii. 354-356.

**Innes,** Ardcronie. Chronicles of the Ardcronie Children (1893).*

  of Ayton. Burke's Landed Gentry (1875-1894).

  of Balnacraig. Tayler's Jacobites of Aberdeenshire (1928), 317. A Day
    that is Dead, by Rev. J. Stirton, D.D., 2nd ed. [1929], 10-20, 99-104,
    118-121.*

**Innes** of Balvenie.  Baronage, by Douglas, 78-79.  The Castle and Lords of
Balveny, by W. Cramond, LL.D. (Elgin, 1893), 20.  Burke's Peerage
and Baronetage.  Complete Baronetage, by G. E. C., ii. 337.
of Blackhills.  Annals of Elgin, by R. Young (1879), 604-605.
of Cowhill Tower.  Burke's Landed Gentry (1898).
of Cowie and Breda.  Memoir of J. Young, Aberdeen . . . 1861, ed.
Lt.-Col. W. Johnston (1894), 160-162.*  Burke's Landed Gentry.
Tayler's Jacobites, 317 (1921-1925).
of Cowtoun.  Complete Baronetage, by G. E. C., iv. 343.
of Coxton.  The Genealogy of the Family of Innes of Coxtown . . .
now represented by Sir Hugh Innes of Lochalsh and Coxtown,
single sheet (1819).*  History of Moray, by Shaw, ed. Gordon (1882),
i. 127, 342.  Parish and Burgh of Elgin, by R. Young, 606-608.
Tayler's Jacobites, 314-316.
of Cromie.  The Scots Peerage, vii. 354-356.
of Edingight and Balveny.  Chronicles of the Family of Innes of
Edingight and Balveny, by Thomas Innes of Learney, 4to, 40 pp.
(Aberdeen, 1898).*  Thanage of Fermartyn, by Temple, 327-328.
Tayler's Jacobites, 320.
of Fracafield.  Zetland Family Histories, by F. J. Grant, 169-170.
of Inaltrie.  Tayler's Jacobites, 319.
of Innermarkie.  Thanage of Fermartyn, 325.
of Kirkseat.  Tayler's Jacobites, 313.
of Learney.  Burke's Landed Gentry (1906-1925).
Leith.  The Scottish Antiquary (1894), viii. 182.
of Lochalsh.  Burke's Extinct Baronetcies.
of Monellie.  Thanage of Fermartyn, 213.
of Muretoun.  Geneal. Mag., vii. 74.
of Raemoir.  Burke's Landed Gentry (1848-1914).
of Sandside.  Caithness Family History, by Henderson, 245-251.
of Thursatter.  Caithness Family History, 238-244.

**Innes-Ker**, Earl Innes, Duke of Roxburghe.  The Scots Peerage, vii. 356-360.
Burke's Peerage.  Lodge's Peerage.  Debrett's Peerage.

**Inveraray**, Campbell, Lord.  The Scots Peerage, i. 369.

**Inverclyde**, Burns, Lord.  Burke's Peerage (after 1889).

**Inverkeithing**, Primrose, Viscount of.  The Scots Peerage, vii. 221-229.
Scrymgeour, Lord.  The Scots Peerage, iii. 315.

**Inverness**, Gordon, Viscount of.  The Scots Peerage, iv. 549-558.
Hay, Earl of, Duke of.  The Scots Peerage, v. 231.  The Jacobite
Peerage, by the Marquis of Ruvigny (1904), 68.

**Inverpeffer** of Inverpeffer.  Memorials of Angus and the Mearns, by
Jervise, ed. Gammack, ii. 98-100.

**Irvine, Irving**.  Heraldry, by Nisbet (1722), i. 403.  The Original of the
Family of the Irvines, by Dr C. Irvine, 12mo (1678 ?).  The Irvines
and their Kin, by Lucinda J. R. Boyd, 8vo, illust., chart pedigree
(Chicago, 1908).  Scottish N. and Q., 3rd S., v. 130.

**Irvine** of Barra. Burke's Landed Gentry (1914).

of Brucklay. Tayler's Jacobites of Aberdeenshire, 321.

Campbell, Earl of. The Scots Peerage, i. 350 ; v. 21-26. G. E. C.'s Complete Peerage.

of Cornyhaugh. Thanage of Fermartyn, by Temple, 230.

of Cults. History and Genealogy of the Family of Irvine of Cults, by J. G. B. Bulloch, M.D.

of Drum. Heraldry, by Nisbet (1742), ii., Appx. 69-71. Visitation of Seats and Arms, by J. B. Burke (1853), i. 152-154. Historical MSS. Commission (1871), 2nd Report. Scottish N. and Q. (1888), i. 119. A Short Account of the Family of Irvine of Drum, by Capt. Douglas Wimberley (Inverness, 1893). Memorials of Four Old Families, by Capt. Wimberley (1894). The Irvings, by J. B. Irving. The Irvines of Drum and their Collateral Branches, by Lt.-Col. J. Forbes Leslie, 4to (Aberdeen, 1909).* Thanage of Fermartyn, 330-345. Notes and Queries, 8th S., ii. 66, 192. Burke's Landed Gentry (1848-1925). Tayler's Jacobites of Aberdeenshire, 322.

of Greenhill. Burke's Landed Gentry (1848-1886).

Viscount Ingram. The Scots Peerage, v. 9-20.

of Kirkconnel. The Irvings, by J. B. Irving.

of Midbrake. Zetland Family Histories, by F. J. Grant, 303-304.

of Monboddo. Scottish N. and Q., 2nd S., v. 1-4.

of Robgill. The Irvings, by J. B. Irving.

**Irvine-Boswell** of Kincousie. Baronage of Angus and Mearns, by Peter (1856), 173, 367.

**Irvine-Burnett** of Monboddo. Baronage of Angus and Mearns, 174.

**Irvine-Fortescue** of Kingcausie. Burke's Landed Gentry (1921-1925).

**Irvine-Ramsay** of Balmain. Complete Baronetage, by G. E. C., ii. 301.

**Irving** of Barwhinnock. Burke's Landed Gentry (1886).

of Bonshaw. The Irvings, Irwins, Irvines, or Erinveines . . . an Old Scots Border Clan, by its present Chieftain, John Beaufin Irving of Bonshaw, 4to *xi*+295 pp., illust. (Aberdeen, 1907). The Scottish Antiquary, viii. 15-17. Burke's Landed Gentry (1886-1894).

of Brucklay. The Irvings, by J. B. Irving.

of Drumcoltran. Lands . . . in Galloway, by M'Kerlie, iv. 232 ; v. 273.

Dumfries. The Irvings, by J. B. Irving.

of Forglen. Burke's Visitation of Seats and Arms, 1853, i. 187.

of Hoddom. The Irvings, by J. B. Irving. The Irvings of Hoddom, by George Irving, *see* Dumfriesshire and Galloway Nat. Hist. and Antiquarian Society's Trans. (1900-2), 75.

of Inveramsay. Burke's Landed Gentry (1858).

of Logan. Lands . . . in Galloway, iii. 267.

of Newton. The Irvings of Newton, by Miles Irving, I.C.S., 8 pp. Burke's Landed Gentry (1863-1886).

of Skaills. The Scottish Antiquary, viii. 130-131.

of Tulloch. Marryat's One Year in Sweden, ii. 490.

**Isaac, MacKessack.** The Herald and Genealogist, vi. 594.

**Isles,** Macdonald, Lord of the.   History of the Macdonalds and Lords of the
  Isles . . . by A. Mackenzie (Inverness, 1881).   G. E. C.'s Complete
  Peerage.   The Scots Peerage, iv. 27-48.   *See also* **Macdonald.**

**Iver.**   Account of the Clan Iver, by Principal Colin Campbell, D.D.
  (Aberdeen, 1868, 1873, 1878).   Remarks on the Writings of the
  Rev. Peter C. Campbell, by Duncan Campbell MacIver of Asknish.*
  Observations on above, by W. P. Allardice, W.S. (Edinr. 1870).*

**Iverach** in Sordale.   Henderson's Caithness Family Histories, 278.

**Jackson** of Kirkbuddo.   Burke's Landed Gentry (1898-1925).
  of Swordale.   Burke's Landed Gentry (1894-1914).

**Jaffray.**   Diary by Alexander Jaffray, Provost of Aberdeen, 1834, ed.
  John Barclay (1856).

**James** of Samieston.   Annals of a Border Club, by G. Tancred, 264.

**Jameson,** Alloa.   MS. Pedigree deposited in the Lyon Office.
  of Windfield.   Burke's Landed Gentry (1898).

**Jamieson** of Kilmorie.   History of County of Bute, by Reid, 255-256.
  Port-Glasgow.   Logie, by Rev. Dr Menzies Fergusson, ii. 257.

**Japp** of Broomhall.   Angus or Forfarshire, by Warden, iii. 365.

**Jardine** of Applegirth.   Some Old Families, by H. B. M'Call, with chart,
  (1890) 213.*   Complete Baronetage, by G. E. C., iv. 289.   Burke's
  Peerage and Baronetage.
  of Castlemilk.   Burke's Peerage and Baronetage.

**Jedburgh,** Home, Lord.   The Scots Peerage, iv. 465-484.   G. E. C.'s
  Complete Peerage.
  Ker, Lord.   The Scots Peerage, v. 49-80.
  Ker, Lord Ker of.   The Scots Peerage, v. 477-487.

**Jedburgh Forest,** Douglas, Lord of, Viscount of.   The Scots Peerage,
  i. 204, 210.

**Jenkins** of Nivinston.   Folklore and Genealogies of Uppermost Nithsdale,
  by Wilson, 153, 252.

**Jerdon** of Bonjedward.   Annals of a Border Club, by G. Tancred, 264-267.

**Joass** of Colleonard.   Scottish N. and Q., 3rd S., i. 31, 80 ; ii. 174.

**Jobson.**   Genealogical History of the Jobson Family, from the Time of
  their first coming to Scotland in 1651-1860, 8vo (1860).

**Johnson,** Ayr.   The Scottish Antiquary, xiv. 52, 116.

**Johnston.**   Heraldry of the Johnstons, with Notes on the different
  Families, their Arms and Pedigrees, by G. Harvey Johnston (1905).
  Notes and Queries, 7th S., xi. 387, 474.

**Johnston,** Aberdeen.   Memoir of J. Young, Aberdeen . . . 1861, ed.
  Lt. Col. W. Johnston of Newton Dee (1894), 106-111.*
  of Badiefurrow.   Memoir of James Young, 224.

**Johnston** of Carnsalloch. Burke's Landed Gentry (1849-1925).

of Caskieben and that Ilk. Baronage, by Douglas, 35-39. Genealogical Account of the Family of Johnston of that Ilk, formerly of Caskieben, in the Shire of Aberdeen, by Alexander Johnston (Edinr. 1832).* Memoir of J. Young, Aberdeen, 186-203. Complete Baronetage, by G. E. C., ii. 307. Burke's Peerage and Baronetage. Pedigree *in* Alexander Cowan, by C. B. Boog Watson.*

of Edgbaston Manor. Historical Families of Dumfriesshire, by C. L. Johnstone, 63-64.

of Elphinston. The Johnstons in Edinburgh, Elphinston, etc. 4to, 4 pp. (1899). Complete Baronetage, by G. E. C., ii. (1902).

Georgia. History of the Habersham Family, by Dr J. G. B. Bulloch (Columbia, S. C., 1901), 177-178.

of Halmyre. Peeblesshire Localities, by Renwick, 466.

of Hilton. Memoir of James Young, 201-203. Burke's Landed Gentry (1849). Burke's Peerage and Baronetage.

of Kincardine. Burke's Landed Gentry (1858).

Lockerbie. A Record of the Descendants of Peter Johnston who came to America from Lockerby, 1773, by C. E. Johnston (Washington, D. C., 1900).

of Rennyhill. East Neuk of Fife, by W. Wood, 2nd ed, 381.

of Shieldhall. Burke's Landed Gentry (1858-1863).

of Viewfield. Memoir of James Young, 204-206.

of Warriston. Diary of Sir Archibald Johnston of Warriston, 1632-1639, ed. Dr G. M. Paul (Scot. Hist. Soc. 1911), vol. ii. 1650-1654, ed. Dr D. H. Fleming (Scot. Hist. Soc. 1919). Pedigree of Johnston of Warriston, Co. Edinburgh, by Major Algernon Tudor Craig, 8vo. 5 pp.* Notes and Queries, 7th S., x. 453 ; xi. 329, 450 ; xii. 36 : 8th S., i. 337 ; iii. 152.

**Johnston-Stewart** of Physgill. Burke's Landed Gentry (1914-1925).

**Johnstone.** History of the Johnstones, 1191-1909, . . . by C. L. Johnstone, 4to, illust., seven pedigrees (Edinr. 1902 ; Suppl. 1925). Heraldry, by A. Nisbet (1722), i. 146-147. Heraldry of the Johnstons, etc., by G. Harvey Johnston (1905). Moffat, History of the Moffats.*

of Alva. Logie, by Rev. Dr Menzies Fergusson, ii. 183. Burke's Commoners, ii. 302. Burke's Landed Gentry (1846-1925).

Viscount of Annand. The Scots Peerage, i. 261.

Earl of, Marquess of Annandale. The Johnstones of Annandale (London, 1853). The Annandale Family : Book of the Johnstones, Earls and Marquises of Annandale, by Sir William Fraser, 2 vols., 4to, illust. (1894). A Century of Romance of the Annandale Peerages . . . by Sir William Fraser, 4to (1894). The Scots Peerage, i. 230-271. G. E. C.'s Complete Peerage. Historical MSS. Commission (1897), 15th Report. *See also* **Annandale.**

of Corry. Historical Families of Dumfriesshire, by C. L. Johnstone, 35.

of Elschieshields. Notes and Queries, 4th S., x. 524 ; xi. 332. Pedigree annexed to Edgar's History of Dumfries, by R. C. Reid (1915).

Johnstone of Galabank.  Burke's Commoners, iv. 556.  Burke's Landed
    Gentry (1846-1894).  Historical Families of Dumfriesshire, 60-62, 65.
of Gretna and Newbie.  Historical Families of Dumfriesshire, 10-11,
    35-39.
of Halmyre.  Buchan and Paton's History of Peeblesshire, iii. 34.
of the Hangingshaw.  Burke's Visitation of Seats and Arms (1853),
    i. 211.  Craig Brown's Selkirkshire, i. 405.
Earl of Hartfell.  The Scots Peerage, i. 256-261.
of Johnstone.  Historical Families of Dumfriesshire, 7-13 *et passim*.
    The Scots Peerage, i. 234-254.
Lord Johnstone.  The Scots Peerage, i. 255-269.
of Kincardine.  Burke's Landed Gentry (1898).
of Outbrecks.  Norton Smith's Orkney Armorials, 77-78.
of Raehills and Annandale.  Burke's Landed Gentry (1846, 1879, 1886).
of Ryehill.  Historical Families of Dumfriesshire, 52, 54.
of Stapleton.  Claim of John Henry Goodinge to be Heir of Line, and
    Provision in general to John Johnstone of Stapleton, 2 pp. and
    pedigree (1830).  Rev. J. A. D. J. Macdonald *in* Dumfriesshire and
    Galloway Antiq. Soc. Trans., 3rd S., viii. 101-117.  The Scottish
    Antiquary, xii. 179 ; xv. 165.  The Alleged Extinction of Johnstone
    of Stapleton, by Macdonald, 62 pp. [1929].*
of Wamphray.  Baronage, by Douglas, 222-223.  Historical Families of
    Dumfriesshire, 37, 51.  The Scots Peerage, i. 239, 241.  Notes and
    Queries, 8th S., xi. 508 ; xii. 296, 364, 430, 470.
of Westerhall.  Burke's Visitation of Seats and Arms (1853), i. 200-202.
    Burke's Peerage and Baronetage.  Complete Baronetage, by
    G. E. C., iv. 394.
of Westraw.  Upper Ward of Lanarkshire, by Irving and Murray, i. 501.

Johnstone-Hope of Annandale.  The Scots Peerage, iv. 495-501.

Jopp of Cotton.  Memoir of J. Young, Aberdeen . . . 1861, ed. Lt. Col.
    W. Johnston (1894), 152-154.*  Scottish N. and Q., xii. 77.

Jordan in Sweden.  One Year in Sweden, by Marryat (1862), ii. 490.

Justice of East Crichton.  Nisbet's Heraldic Plates, ed. Ross and Grant
    (1892), 152.  Peter Beattie's MS. and Descent of Justice Family of
    Crichton and Prestonhall (1895).

Kay of Broomfield.  Paterson's Ayr and Wigton, i. 280.
of Edinbellie.  Strathendrick, by Guthrie Smith, 263.

Keddie.  Three Generations : the Story of a Middle-Class Scottish Family,
    by Henrietta Keddie [Sarah Tytler], (1911).

Keilor of Keilor, Keiller.  Memorials of Angus and the Mearns, by Jervise,
    ed. Gammack, ii. 100-101.

Keir.  Life of James Keir . . . Genealogy of the Keirs, etc., by Alex.
    Blair, 8vo, 164 pp. (1859).*
of Kindrogan.  Burke's Landed Gentry (1898).

**Keith.** Dictionary of National Biography, *s.v.*

Lord Altrie. The Scots Peerage, i. 156-159 ; vi. 51. G. E. C.'s Complete Peerage., 2nd ed.

of Auquhorsk. Scottish N. and Q., x. 60, 123.

of Benholm. The Scots Peerage, vi. 53-55.

of Craig. Baronage, by Douglas, 443-445. Eminent Men of Fife, by Conolly, 253. Laurencekirk, by Fraser, 60-63, 64.

Lord Dingwall. The Scots Peerage, iii. 115-116.

of Drumtochty. Fraser's Laurencekirk, 64-65.

of Dunottar. Dunottar and its Barons, by J. Crabb Watt *in* Scot. Hist. Review, ii. 389-405.

of Galstoun. Paterson's History of Ayr, ii. 64. Paterson's Ayr and Wigton, i. 523.

of Inverugie. Geneal. Mag. (1903), vi. 467.

Lord Keith. G. E. C.'s Complete Peerage. The Scots Peerage, vi. 39-65.

Lord Keith of Inverugie. The Scots Peerage, v. 240-250.

Earl of Kintore. Heraldry, by Nisbet (1742), ii. Appx. 10. The Scots Peerage, v. 240-255. Burke's Peerage. Debrett's Peerage.

of Ludquhairn. Baronage, by Douglas, 73-75. Burke's Extinct Baronetcies.

Earl Marischal. Nisbet's Heraldry (1742), ii. Appx. 1-10. Account of the Ancient and Noble Family of Keith, earls Marichal of Scotland, by P. Buchan, 12mo, *xii*+156 pp. (Peterhead, 1820). Buchan, by Rev. J. B. Pratt (1858), 354-370. Memoir of Marshal Keith, with a Sketch of the Keith Family, by A Peterheadian, 8vo (1869). Great Historic Families of Scotland, by Jas. Taylor [1887]. Parish of Laurencekirk, by Fraser, 27-35. Tales of our Great Families, by Walford, 2nd S., ii. 312-317. A Midlothian Village, by G. V. Selway (1890), 33-37. Recreations of an Antiquary, by R. S. Fittis, 114-127. Historic Earls and Earldoms of Scotland, by Dr John Mackintosh, 271-306. Scottish N. and Q., vii. 177 ; chart pedigree, x. 161. The Scots Peerage, vi. 25-65: Complete Peerage, by G. E. C. Complete Baronetage, by G. E. C., ii. 280. The Castle of Dunnottar and its History, by Rev. Douglas Gordon Barron, W. Mackay Mackenzie, and G. P. H. Watson (1925).

of Murrayshall. Buchan's History of Peeblesshire, iii. 37.

of Northfield. Scottish N. and Q., 2nd S., viii. 169-171 : 3rd S., i. 192 ; ii. 143.

of Pittendrum. Baronage, by Douglas, 445, 589. The Scots Peerage, vi. 44.

of Powburn. Fraser's Laurencekirk, 60-63. Burke's Extinct Baronetage. Complete Baronetage, by G. E. C. (1903), iii. 339.

of Ravelston. Baronage, by Douglas, 445, 589. Memoirs of the Family of Sir W. Scott, by Rev. C. Rogers (1877), *liv-lv*. Recreations of an Antiquary, by R. S. Fittis, 127. A Midlothian Village, by G. V. Selway, 38-42. Scottish N. and Q., xi. 84.

of Usan. Angus or Forfarshire, by Warden, iii. 162.

of Whiteriggs. Genealogical Fragments, by Jas. Maidment, 3 pp. (Berwick, 1855).*

**Keith of Stonehaven-Marischal,** Elphinstone, Lord. Biographical Peerage (1808), 347-349. G. E. C.'s Complete Peerage. The Scots Peerage, iii. 548-549.

**Keith-Elphinstone.** Eminent Men of Fife, by M. F. Conolly (Cupar, 1866), 246-253. The Elphinstone Book, by Sir W. Fraser.

**Keith-Falconer,** Earl of Kintore. The Scots Peerage, v. 251-255.

**Keith-Murray.** Complete Baronetage, by G. E. C. (1904), iv. 291.

**Kelburne,** Boyle, Viscount. The Scots Peerage, iv. 202-221.

**Kelhead of Kelhead,** Douglas, Baron. The Scots Peerage, vii. 154.

**Kellas.** Scottish N. and Q., 3rd S., v. 116.

**Kellie,** Erskine, Earl of. Biographical Peerage (1808), 349-350. Minutes of Evidence before the Lords' Committees for Privileges : the Earl of Mar claiming the Earldom of Kellie (1832). Eminent Men of Fife, by Conolly, 165-170. Walford's Chapters from Family Chests (1887), ii. 200-207. The Scots Peerage, v. 81-97. G. E. C.'s Complete Peerage.

Gordon, Lord. The Scots Peerage, i. 88-99.

**Kelso of Dankeith.** Ayrshire Families, by G. Robertson, ii. 29. History of Ayr, by J. Paterson, ii. 479. Ayr and Wigton, by Paterson, i. 741-745.

of Hullerhirst. Ayrshire Families, ii. 34-38. Paterson's Ayr, ii. 448. Ayr and Wigton, iii. 568-569.

of Kelsoland. Heraldry, by Nisbet (1722), i. 377 ; (1742), ii. Appx. 108-109. Ayrshire Families, ii. 22-30. Paterson's Ayr, ii. 479-480. Ayr and Wigton, i. 741-745. Burke's Landed Gentry (1906-1914).

of Nether Kelsoland. Ayrshire Families, ii. 31-33.

Ker, Earl of. The Scots Peerage, vii. 350-360.

of Sauchrie. Burke's Landed Gentry (1849-1925).

**Kelvin,** Thomson, Baron. Burke's Peerage, 1893-1907.

**Kemp of Cornton.** Logie, by Rev. R. Menzies Fergusson, ii. 220-222, 226, 231. The Stirling Antiquary, ii. 153, 157.

Coull. Scottish N. and Q., xii. 66.

**Kenmure,** Gordon, Viscount of. Memoirs of the Jacobites of 1715 and of 1745, by Mrs Katherine Thomson, ii. 71-91. Geneal. Mag. (1901), iv. 171-176. G. E. C.'s Complete Peerage. The Scots Peerage, v. 98-135.

**Kennedy.** Heraldry, by A. Nisbet (1722), i. 161-162 ; (1742), ii. Appx. 38-39. Historical Account of the Principal Families of the Name of Kennedy, from an Original MS., with notes, etc., by Robert Pitcairn, 4to, xi+218 pp., illust. (Edinr. 1830). Historical Account of the Noble Family of Kennedy [by David Cowan], 4to (Edinr. 1849).* Anecdotes of the Noble Family of Kennedy, by Hugh Blair, 4to (Edinr. 1849). Paterson's History of Ayr and Wigton, (1864), ii., iii-ix 24-78, 302-346. Historical MSS. Commission (1876), 5th Report. Notes and Queries, 3rd S., i. 246-247, 413 ; ii. 466 ; iii. 190. Dictionary of National Biography, s.v.

P

**Kennedy,** Marquess of Ailsa. G. E. C.'s Complete Peerage, ed. Gibbs. The Scots Peerage, ii. 497-502. Debrett's and other Annual Peerages.

of Ardmillan. Ayrshire Families, i. 222, 226. Paterson's History of Ayr (1852), ii. 77. Paterson's Ayr and Wigton, ii. 246-248.

of Ardstinchar. Paterson's Ayr and Wigton, ii. 319, 323.

of Auchtifardle. Upper Ward of Lanarkshire, by Irving and Murray, ii. 219.

of Balmaclanachan. Heraldry, by Nisbet (1742), ii. Appx. 40. Paterson's Ayr (1847), i. 388. Ayr and Wigton, ii. 177-178.

of Baltersan. Paterson's Ayr, ii. 292-295. Ayr and Wigton, ii. 295-301.

of Bargany. Paterson's Ayr, i. 375-382. Ayr and Wigton, ii. 180-199, 320. The Scots Peerage, ii. 467-488.

of Bellimore. Paterson's Ayr, i. 259. Ayr and Wigton, ii. 119.

of Bennane, Bennen. Heraldry, by Nisbet (1742), ii. Appx. 40. Paterson's Ayr, i. 250-252. Ayr and Wigton, ii. 94-100. The Scottish Antiquary (1897), xi. '43. Burke's Landed Gentry (1848-1898).

of Blairquhan. Paterson's Ayr, ii. 471. Ayr and Wigton, i. 461-464.

of Brockloch. Paterson's Ayr, ii. 373. Ayr and Wigton, ii. 422-423.

of Brounstone. Paterson's Ayr and Wigton, ii. 223.

of Carlock. Ayr and Wigton, ii. 102.

Earl of Cassillis. Paterson's Ayr and Wigton, ii. 327-346. The Scots Peerage, ii. 443-502.

of Clowburn. Burke's Extinct Baronetcies. Complete Baronetage, by G. E. C., iv. 383.

of Coif. Paterson's Ayr and Wigton, ii. 328, 346. The Scots Peerage, ii. 452, 463.

of Craig. Paterson's Ayr, i. 312. Ayr and Wigton, ii. 150-151.

of Craigoch and Kilkenzie. The Scottish Antiquary, x. 142 ; xi. 43-45.

of Crochba. Paterson's Ayr, ii. 371. Ayr and Wigton, ii. 425.

of Culzean. Paterson's Ayr, ii. 288. Ayr and Wigton, ii. 348-351. Complete Baronetage, by G. E. C., iv. 316. The Scots Peerage, ii. 465-492.

of Daljarrock. Paterson's Ayr, i. 313. Ayr and Wigton, ii. 151-152.

of Dalquharran. Paterson's Ayr, i. 385. Ayr and Wigton, ii. 205-207.

of Dalvaird. Ayr and Wigton, ii. 141.

of Drummelane. Paterson's Ayr, i. 387-390. Ayr and Wigton, ii. 209-223, 321, 347.

of Dunene. Paterson's Ayr, ii. 372. Ayr and Wigton, i. 431-432.

of Dunure. Paterson's Ayr, ii. 276-290. Ayr and Wigton, ii. 205-207, 312. Scot. Hist. Review (1912), viii. 53-60. Burke's Landed Gentry (1858-1925).

of Finnarts. Burke's Landed Gentry (1906-1925).

of Garrihorne. Paterson's History of Ayr, ii. 374. Paterson's Ayr and Wigton, i. 433.

of Girvanmains. Paterson's Ayr, i. 386. Ayr and Wigton, ii. 207-209, 326. Complete Baronetage, by G. E. C., iv. 246.

of Glenmuck and Bellimore. Heraldry, by Nisbet (1742), ii., Appx. 41.

**Kennedy** of Glentig. Paterson's Ayr and Wigton, ii. 104, 324.

of Hillfoot. Burke's Landed Gentry (1894).

Lord Kennedy. Ayr and Wigton, ii. 323-327. The Scots Peerage, ii. 453. G. E. C.'s Complete Peerage, 2nd ed.

of Kermuckes. Scottish N. and Q., 2nd S., iii. 174-175; 3rd S., v. 109-111.

of Kilhenzie. Paterson's Ayr, ii. 289-290.

of Kirkhill. Paterson's Ayr, i. 386. Ayr and Wigton, ii. 204.

of Kirkmichael. Paterson's Ayr, ii. 261, 519. Ayr and Wigton, ii. 103, 277-281. Scottish N. and Q., 3rd S., vi. 52-53.

of Knockdaw. Paterson's Ayr, i. 311. Ayr and Wigton, ii. 157-159.

of Knockdolian. Scottish N. and Q., 3rd S., v. 166-167.

of Knockdon. Paterson's Ayr, ii. 372. Ayr and Wigton, i. 437-439.

of Knockgray. Burke's Landed Gentry (1849-1898).

of Knocknalling and Knockreoch. Paterson's Ayr and Wigton, i. 439. Notes from Searches, by Jas. Paterson *in* Scottish Surnames (1866), 75-86. Lands . . . in Galloway, by M'Kerlie, iv. 94-96. Burke's Landed Gentry (1849-1925).

of Leffnol. Paterson's Ayr and Wigton, ii. 322.

of Lochinch. Lands . . . in Galloway, by M'Kerlie, 2nd ed. (1906), i. 521-525.

of Monuncion. Paterson's Ayr, i. 259. Ayr and Wigton, ii. 123.

of Pinmore. Paterson's Ayr, i. 314. Ayr and Wigton, ii. 160.

of Pinwherrie, Pinquhirrie. Paterson's Ayr, i. 311. Ayr and Wigton, ii. 166.

of Romanno. Burke's Landed Gentry (1886-1894). History of Peebles-shire, by Chambers, 488-493. Buchan and Paton's History of Peeblesshire, iii. 24-26.

of Smithstoun. Paterson's Ayr, ii. 371. Ayr and Wigton, i. 449.

of Stroma. Caithness Family History, by Henderson, 328. Scottish N. and Q., 3rd S., v. 110-111.

of Underwood. Paterson's Ayr, i. 347. Burke's Landed Gentry (1894-1906).

**Kennedy-Cochran-Patrick** of Woodside and Ladyland. Burke's Landed Gentry (1914-1925).

**Kennedy-Erskine** of Dun. Historical MSS. Commission (1876), 5th Report, pt. i. Burke's Landed Gentry (1914-1925).

**Ker.** Heraldry, by A. Nisbet (1722), i. 156, 166-168. The Raid of the Kers, by James Hogg, the Ettrick Shepherd. Border Memories, by W. Riddell Carre (1876), 95-131. Notes and Queries, 6th S., iv. 523; v. 218; xii. 229. Documents in the possession of the Marquess of Lothian, Historical MSS. Commission (1870), 1st Report (1905), Cd. 2319. Dictionary of National Biography, *s.v.*

**Ker** of Abbotrule. Tancred's Rulewater, 184-189.

Earl of Ancram. The Scots Peerage, v. 466-487. Correspondence of Sir Robert Kerr, first Earl of Ancram, and William, third Earl of Lothian, 1616-1667; ed. David Laing, 2 vols. (Edinr. 1875).

**Ker** of Ancrum.   The Scots Peerage, v. 460.   The Genealogist, 1st S.,
    ii. 289-294.

Antigua.   Oliver's History of Antigua, ii. 118.

of Auchingree.   Ayrshire Families, by G. Robertson, ii. 304-306.
    History of Ayr, by Paterson, i. 426.   Ayr and Wigton, by Paterson,
    iii. 147-149.

of Auldtounburn.   R. R. Stodart *in* Herald and Genealogist, vii. 117.

of Blackshiells and Knock.   R. R. Stodart *in* Herald and Genealogist,
    vii. 241-245.

Marquess of Bowmont.   The Scots Peerage, vii. 350-360.

of Cavers and West Nisbet.   Annals of a Border Club, by G. Tancred,
    297-300, 318.

of Cavertoun.   Haigs of Bemersyde, by Russell (1881), 132-133.

of Cessford.   R. R. Stodart *in* Herald and Genealogist, vii. 117, 407-416.
    The Scots Peerage, vii. 323-339.   Pedigree of the Family of Ker of
    Cessford, Greenhead, and Prymsideloch, by Christian L. Reid, 4to,
    33 pp., illust., chart pedigree (1914).

of Chatto, Sunlaws and Frogden.   R. R. Stodart *in* Herald and
    Genealogist, vi. 238-240.

of Corbethouse.   Genealogy of the Family of Ker of Corbethouse, by
    R. R. Stodart *in* The Genealogist, 1st S., iii. 249-250.

of Dolphinston and Hirsell.   R. R. Stodart *in* Herald and Genealogist,
    vi. 512-523.

of Fairnilee.   T. Craig Brown's Selkirkshire, i. 547.

of Fawdonside.   R. R. Stodart *in* Herald and Genealogist, vii. 416-419.

of Ferniehurst.   R. R. Stodart *in* Herald and Genealogist, vii. 125-130,
    *and in* The Genealogist, 1st S., ii. 282-289.   Annals of a Border
    Club, by G. Tancred, 268-283.   The Scots Peerage, v. 49-69.

of Gateshaw.   Genealogy of the Family of Ker of Gateshaw, by R. R.
    Stodart *in* The Genealogist, 1st S., iii. 246-249.   Annals of a Border
    Club, 294-297.   Burke's Landed Gentry (1848-1875).

of Graden.   Rev. J. F. Leishman, *in* Scot. Hist. Review, v. 181-190.

of Greenhead.   R. R. Stodart *in* Herald and Genealogist, vi. 231-238.
    T. Craig-Brown's Selkirkshire, ii. 376-377.   Complete Baronetage,
    by G. E. C., ii. 427.

of Halydean.   Annals and Antiquities of Dryburgh, by Sir D. Erskine,
    2nd ed., 200.

Earl Ker.   English Peerage, by Rev. A. Jacob (1767), ii. 108-112.

of Kershaugh.   The Scots Peerage, v. 50, 51 *n.*

of Kersland.   Ayrshire Families, by G. Robertson (1824), ii. 289-299.
    Paterson's Ayr, i. 423-426.   Paterson's Ayr and Wigton, iii. 179-183.
    Notices of the Family of Kerr of Kerrisland [by Robert Malcolm
    Kerr], 50+*v* pp. (1881).*   Marion Kett (*sic*) *in* Genealogist, N. S.,
    xxxvi. 70-74.

Kildrummy.   Genealogies of an Aberdeen Family, by Smith, 37-42.

of Kilmore and Kilbeg.   R. R. Stodart *in* Herald and Genealogist, vii.

of Littledean.   Annals and Antiquities of Dryburgh, 2nd ed., 198-204.
    R. R. Stodart *in* Herald and Genealogist, vi. 512-523.

**Ker** of Lochtour and Cherrytrees.  R. R. Stodart *in* Herald and Genealogist, vii. 220-225.

Earl of, Marquess of, Lothian.  The Scots Peerage, v. 452-487.  Burke's Peerage.  Debrett's Peerage.

of Lynetownhead.  Buchan and Paton's History of Peeblesshire, iii. 522.

of Primside.  R. R. Stodart *in* Herald and Genealogist, vi. 231-238.  The Scots Peerage, vii. 320-321.

Lord, Earl of, Duke of Roxburghe.  The Scots Peerage, vii. 314-360.

of Trearne.  Ayrshire Families, ii. 299-303.  Paterson's Ayr, i. 292.  Ayr and Wigton, iii. 121-122.  The Genealogist, N. S., xxxvi. 70-74.

of Whitmuirhall.  T. Craig-Brown's Selkirkshire (1886), ii. 379.

of Yair.  Selkirkshire, ii. 372.

**Ker-Reid** of Hoselaw.  Pedigree of the Family of Ker-Reid, by C. L. Reid (1914).

**Kerr** of Argrennan.  Lands and their Owners in Galloway, by M'Kerlie, v. 205.

of Cuninghamhead.  Paterson's Ayr and Wigton, iii. 211.

of Grange.  Angus or Forfarshire, by Warden, iv. 410.  Monifieth, by J. Malcolm (1910), 163, 340.

Jamaica.  Scottish N. and Q., 3rd S., iv. 62.

of Kerfield.  History of Peeblesshire, by W. Chambers, 331.

of Kersland.  *See* **Ker.**

of Menie.  Temple's Thanage of Fermartyn, 639.

of Redden.  Sir Thomas Kerr of Redden and his Descendants, by R. R. Stodart, *in* The Genealogist, 1st S., ii. 137-142, 176-180.  Burke's Landed Gentry, *s.v.* Kerr of the Haie.

**Kidston** in Logie.  Logie, by Rev. R. Menzies Fergusson, ii. 248-257.

**Kilconquhar.**  East Neuk of Fife, by W. Wood, 2nd ed., 156-158.

**Kilgour** in Nether Kinmundy.  Scottish N. and Q., 2nd S., iii. 109.

of Tulloch and Balgavenny.  Thanage of Fermartyn, by Temple, 208-211.  Burke's Landed Gentry (1879-1925).

**Kilmarnock,** Boyd, Earl of.  Scots Magazine (1746).  Ayrshire Families, by G. Robertson (1823), i. 102-111.  Paterson's Ayr, ii. 171-182.  Memoirs of the Jacobites of 1715 and 1745, by Mrs Katherine Thomson, iii. 381-479.  Paterson's Ayr and Wigton, iii. 415-432.  The Scots Peerage, v. 136-182.  Notes and Queries, 4th S., iii. 287, 372, 417; x. 200, 451, 502; xi. 45: 7th S., xii. 47: 8th S., ii. 111.  G. E. C.'s Complete Peerage.

**Kilmarnock of Kilmarnock,** Hay, Baron.  G. E. C.'s Complete Peerage.  The Scots Peerage, iii. 585-587.

**Kilmaron,** Fife.  Scot. Hist. Review, xvii. 157-158.

**Kilmaurs,** Cunningham, Lord.  G. E. C.'s Complete Peerage.  The Scots Peerage, iv. 232-252.

**Kilpatrick** of Closeburn.  Heraldry, by Nisbet (1742), ii.  Ragman Roll, 27.

of Dalga and Whitehirst.  Ayrshire Families, by G. Robertson, ii. 275-276.

*See also* **Kirkpatrick.**

**Kilpont,** Graham, Lord. The Scottish Antiquary (1898), xiii. 68-72, small chart pedigree. The Lake of Menteith, by Hutchison, 317-322. The Scots Peerage, i. 133-145.

**Kilsyth,** Livingston, Viscount of. G. E. C.'s Complete Peerage. The Scots Peerage, v. 183-194.

**Kilwinning,** Montgomerie, Lord. Case on behalf of Archibald W. Montgomerie, Earl of Eglinton ; and Remarks (1862). Minutes of Evidence (1861). Evidence and Proceedings (1864-1869). The Scots Peerage, i. 541 ; iii. 444.

**Kincaid.** Heraldry, by Nisbet (1722), i. 420.

of Auchenreoch. Notes and Queries, 7th S., i. 387.

of Warriston. Memorial of the Conversion of Jean Livingston, Lady Waristoun (Edinr. 1827), *vi-vii.*

**Kincardine,** Bruce, Earl of. G. E. C.'s Complete Peerage. The Scots Peerage, iii. 484-497.

Gordon, Lord. The Scots Peerage, iv. 549-558.

Graham, Earl of. The Scots Peerage, vi. 247-274.

**Kinclaven,** Stewart, Lord. G. E. C.'s Complete Peerage. The Scots Peerage, ii. 441.

**Kinfauns,** Hay, Lord Hay of. The Scots Peerage, v. 222-239.

**King** of Bannock. One Year in Sweden, by Marryat, ii. 490-491.

of Barra and Bourtie. The Scots Peerage, iii. 588-590.

of Campsie. Burke's Peerage and Baronetage (after 1888).

of Drums and Millbank. Crawfurd's Shire of Renfrew (1818), 394-395.

Lord Eythin. Notes and Queries, 6th S., viii. 166, 209, 335. The Scots Peerage, iii. 588-594.

of Newmill. Memoir of the Family of Kings of Newmill, by Robert Young (Elgin, 1862), ed. W. Cramond (Banff, 1904). Annals of Elgin, by R. Young, 608-612.

of Newmiln of Auchingown. Paterson's Ayr and Wigton, iii. 116.

of Tertowie. Historical MSS. Commission (1872), 3rd Report. Burke's Landed Gentry (1894-1914).

**Kinghorne,** Lyon, Lord, Earl of. The Parish of Longforgan, by Rev. A. Philip, 111-119. The Scots Peerage, viii. 293-317.

**Kingston,** Maxwell, Lord. The Scots Peerage, iii. 126-131.

Seton, Viscount of. G. E. C.'s Complete Peerage. The Scots Peerage, v. 195-198.

**Kington-Blair-Oliphant** of Ardblair. Burke's Landed Gentry (1906-1925).

**Kinloch** of Blair. Scottish N. and Q., 2nd S., v. 159 ; vi. 15.

of Gilmerton. The Genealogist, N. S., xiv. 200-203, 261-263. Burke's Peerage and Baronetage. Complete Baronetage, by G. E. C., iv. 347.

of Gourdie. Baronage, by Douglas, 525.

of Kair. Baronage of Angus and Mearns, by Peter, 183.

of Kilrie, Kilry. Baronage, by Douglas, 536. Warden's Angus or Forfarshire, iii. 361-363 ; iv. 119.

**Kinloch** of Kinloch.   Nisbet's Heraldry (1742), ii., Appx. 27-28.   Baronage, by Douglas, 533-535.   Angus or Forfarshire, by Warden, iv. 339-343. Burke's Peerage and Baronetage.   Burke's Extinct Baronetcies. Complete Baronetage, by G. E. C., iv. 333.   Scot. Hist. Review, ii. 173-174, 177-179.

**Kinloss**, Bruce, Lord.   The Case and Petition of Richard Plantagenet Campbell, Duke of Buckingham and Chandos, and Minutes of Evidence (1867).   Petition of George William Frederick Brudenell, Marquess of Ailesbury (1867).   Burke's Peerage.   G. E. C.'s Complete Peerage.   The Scots Peerage, iii. 475.

**Kinnaird** of Culbin.   Antiquarian Notes, by C. Fraser-Mackintosh, i. 332-335.   Scottish N. and Q., 3rd S., ii. 193.   Nairnshire Telegraph (3rd Feb. 1925).

of Inchture.   The Scots Peerage, v. 205-209.

of Kinnaird.   Geneal. Coll., by W. Macfarlane, 1750-51 ; Scot. Hist. Soc., i. 52-54.   The Scots Peerage, v. 202-205.

Lord Kinnaird of Inchture and Rossie.   Historical MSS. Commission (1876), 5th Report.   G. E. C.'s Complete Peerage.   Burke's and other Annual Peerages.   The Scots Peerage, v. 202-216.

**Kinnear** of Bothers.   Angus or Forfarshire, by Warden, iii. 15.

Glamis.   Genealogies of an Aberdeen Family, by Smith, 42.

of Kinnear.   Campbell's Balmerino, 649-651.

of Spurness.   Norton Smith's Orkney Armorials, 78.

**Kinneir.**   Pedigree *in* Traditions of the Watsons, by C. B. Boog Watson.*

**Kinninmond** of Kinninmond.   Geneal. Coll., by W. Macfarlane, 1750-51 ; Scot. Hist. Soc., ii. 531-548.   Stephen's Inverkeithing (1921), 206-214.

in Sweden.   Marryat's One Year in Sweden, ii. 491.

**Kinnoull**, Hay, Earl of.   Biographical Peerage (1808), 355-356.   Historical MSS. Commission (1873), 4th Report.   Burke's and other Annual Peerages.   The Scots Peerage, v. 217-239.   G. E. C.'s Complete Peerage.

**Kinpont**, Graham, Lord.   The Scottish Antiquary (1898), xiii. 68-72.   The Scots Peerage, i. 133-145.

**Kinrara**, Gordon-Lennox, Earl of.   The Scots Peerage, v. 369-371.

**Kinross**, Balfour, Baron.   Burke's Peerage (after 1902).

**Kintore**, Keith, Earl of.   Nisbet's Heraldic Plates, ed. Ross and Grant, 64-66.   The Scots Peerage, v. 240-255.

Keith-Falconer, Earl of.   G. E. C.'s Complete Peerage.   Debrett's and other Annual Peerages.   The Scots Peerage, v. 240-255.

**Kintyre**, Campbell, Lord, Marquess of.   The Scots Peerage, i. 369-393 ; v. 23-26.

**Kirk.**   Heraldry, by Nisbet (1722), i. 429-430.   Lands . . . in Galloway, by M'Kerlie, iii. 276, 352.   Scottish N. and Q., 2nd S., viii. 15. History of Moffats, by Moffat (1908).*

Alloa.   MS. Pedigree in Lyon Office, and Library of Society of Genealogists, London.

**Kirkaldy** of Grange. Memoirs and Adventures of Sir Wm. Kirkaldy of Grange (1849). A Short History of the Family of Kircaldy of Grange, Monkwearmouth, and London, by James Kircaldy, 4to (London, 1903).* Burke's Extinct Baronetcies. Complete Baronetage, by G. E. C., iii. 345. Scot. Hist. Review, xiv. 399.

**Kirkcaldy**, Melville, Viscount of. The Scots Peerage, vi. 108-123.

**Kirkconnel** of Kirkconnel. Lands . . . in Galloway, by M'Kerlie, v. 214-216, 223.

**Kirkcudbright**, Maclellan, Lord. Record of the House of Kirkcudbright, by John MacClellan, 40 pp., 2nd ed. (Dumfries, 1906). G. E. C.'s Complete Peerage. The Scots Peerage, v. 256-274.

**Kirko.** The Kirkos of Bogrie, Sundaywell, Chapel and Glenesland, by Sir Philip Hamilton Grierson *in* Transactions of the Dumfriesshire and Galloway Nat. Hist. and Antiq. Soc. (1914-15).

**Kirkpatrick** of Closeburn. Heraldry, by A. Nisbet (1722), i. 147. Nisbet's Heraldic Plates, ed. Ross and Grant, 42-45. Genealogical Tree of the Family of Kirkpatrick. Walford's Tales of our Great Families, 2nd S., ii. 176-182. Burke's Peerage and Baronetage. Memoir respecting the Family of Kirkpatrick of Closeburn (1858). Notes and Queries, 12th S., iii. 399. Historical Families of Dumfriesshire, by C. L. Johnstone, 15. Chronicles of the Kirkpatrick Family, by Alexander de Lapère Kirkpatrick, 4to, 55 pp., illust. [1897].* Complete Baronetage, by G. E. C., iv. 329.

*See also* **Kilpatrick.**

**Kirktoun** of Hartrigge. Annals of a Border Club, by G. Tancred of Weens (Jedburgh, 1899), 82.

Mertoun. Ayrshire Families, by G. Robertson, i. 29-30 *n*.

**Knockdolian.** Scottish N. and Q., 3rd S., v. 165.

**Knowles.** Scottish N. and Q., 2nd S., vi. 173 ; 3rd S., v. 157.

**Knox.** Descendants of William Knox and John Knox the Reformer, by a Lineal Descendant [William Crawford], (Edinr. 1896). Genealogical Memoirs of the Family of John Knox, by the Rev. Charles Rogers (London, 1879). Notes and Queries, 8th S., i. 98 ; vii. 201, 261, 335, 470 ; ix. 278.

of Dungannon. Geneal. Coll., by W. Macfarlane, 1750-51 ; Scot. Hist. Soc., ii. 279, 281-283.

of Kilbirnie. Genealogy of the Family of Knox of Kilbirnie, by Wm. Logan (Kilmarnock, 1856).

of Knoc. Crawfurd's Shire of Renfrew (1818), 61.

of Markhouse, Marcus. Warden's Angus or Forfarshire, v. 200.

of Ranfurly. Geneal. Coll., by Macfarlane, ii. 276-284. Crawfurd's Shire of Renfrew (1818), 95-96. John Knox and Ranfurly, by Horatius Bonar *in* Scot. Hist. Review, v. 370.

of Selvieland. Geneal. Coll., by Macfarlane, ii. 280.

Kyd of Craigie. Baronage of Angus and Mearns, by D. M. Peter, 185.
  Angus or Forfarshire, by Warden, iv. 133-134.
  of Pitcastle. Burke's Landed Gentry (1921-1925).

Laidlaw. Rulewater, by Tancred, 327-334.
  of the Holmes. Annals and Antiquities of Dryburgh, by Sir D. Erskine,
    2nd ed., 95.
Laidlay of Seacliffe. Burke's Landed Gentry (1894-1925).

Laing of Strynzie. Norton Smith's Orkney Armorials, 82.
  of Wester Keir. Annals of a Border Club, by G. Tancred, 246 n.
Laird of Strathmartine. Warden's Angus or Forfarshire, iv. 283.

Lamb, Aberdeen. Genealogies of an Aberdeen Family, by Smith, 90-93.

Lamby of Duncany and Newton. See L'Amy.

Lamington, Cochrane-Baillie, Baron. Burke's Peerage (after 1880).

Lamont. Nisbet MS. in Geneal. Mag. (1899), ii. 349-352. Report of the
  First General Meeting of the Clan Lamont Society (Glasgow, 1897).
  Also Reports of Succeeding Years. The Chiefs of Clan Lamont,
  with pedigree, 12 pp., Lamont Society (1898). Sketches of the
  Clan, being addresses to the Clan Lamont Society, 1897-1899, by
  Norman Lamont, yr. of Knockdow.
  in France. Geneal. Coll., by Macfarlane, ii. 159.
  of Gribton. Burke's Landed Gentry (1914-1925).
  of Lamont. Ancient Scottish Surnames, by Buchanan of Auchmar
    (1723), 95-97. An Inventory of Lamont Papers, 1231-1897 ; ed.
    Sir Norman Lamont of Knockdow, Bart., with Index ; 495 pp.
    (Scottish Rec. Soc., 1914-1918). Burke's Landed Gentry (1862-1925).
  of Newton. The Diary of Mr John Lamont of Newton, 1649-1671.
    (Edinr. 1830). East Ncuk of Fife, by W. Wood, 2nd ed. (1887),
    469, 473-474.
  St Andrews and Scoonie. Geneal. Coll., by W. Macfarlane, 1750-51 ;
    Scot. Hist. Soc., ii. 157-159. East Neuk of Fife, 2nd ed., 469-472.

L'Amy of Dunkenny. Baronage of Angus and Mearns, by Peter, 187.
  Fraser's Laurencekirk, 69. Warden's Angus or Forfarshire, iii. 211-
  212. Burke's Landed Gentry (1848-1925).

Lang of Blackdales. Pont's Cuninghame, ed. Dobie, 252.
  in Selkirk. Annals of a Border Club, by G. Tancred (1899), 320-321.
  The Langs of Selkirk, etc., etc., compiled by Patrick Sellar Lang
  (Melbourne, 1910).

Lauder. Notes on Historical References to the Scottish Family of Lauder,
    ed. James Young, 4to (Glasgow, 1884).* Complete Baronetage,
    by G. E. C. (1904), s.v., Maitland of Ravelrig, iv. 310.
  of the Bass. J. J. Reid in Proc. Soc. Antiq. Scotl. (1885), 54-68. The
    Grange of St Giles, by Mrs J. Stewart Smith, 4to (Edinr. 1898).
  of Belhaven. Heraldry, by Nisbet (1722), i. 443.
  of Blyth. Buchan and Paton's History of Peeblesshire, iii. 166.

**Lauder** of Castlelandhill. Stephen's Inverkeithing (1921), 118.
  of Fountainhall. Heraldry, by Nisbet (1722), i. 352. Nisbet's Heraldic
    Plates, ed. Ross and Grant, 96-98. Complete Baronetage, by
    G. E. C., iv. 360.
  of Halton, Hatton. Peeblesshire Localities, by Renwick, 591. Buchan
    and Paton's Peeblesshire, ii. 467-468.
  of Idington. Complete Baronetage, iv. 357.

**Lauder-Dick.** Complete Baronetage, iv. 360.

**Lauderdale**, Maitland, Viscount of, Earl of, Duke of. Biographical Peerage
    (1808), 361-366. Hatton House, by J. R. Findlay (Edinr. 1875).*
    Historical MSS. Commission (1876), 5th Report. The Lauderdale
    Papers, ed. Osmund Airy, 3 vols. (Camden Soc., 1884). Case of
    Sir Jas. Ramsay-Gibson-Maitland (1885). Case of Major F. H.
    Maitland (1885). Minutes of Evidence in House of Lords (1885),
    and Judgment. Lodge's and other Annual Peerages. G. E. C.'s
    Complete Peerage. The Scots Peerage, v. 276-323.

**Laurie.** The Parish of Longforgan, by Rev. A. Philp, 157-167. Sir Peter
    Laurie : a Family Memoir, by P. G. Laurie, 8vo, illust., pedigrees
    (1901).
  of Maxwelton. Burke's Peerage and Baronetage. Complete Baronetage,
    by G. E. C., iv. 332 ; vi., Appx. 78.
  of Redcastle. Lands . . . in Galloway, by M'Kerlie, v. 297-299.

**Laurin.** History in Memoriam of the Clan Laurin, antecedently, and
    subsequently, to its almost entire destruction in the year A.D. 1558
    [by Daniel Maclaurin], London [c. 1867]. One Year in Sweden, by
    Marryat (1862), ii. 491, 492.

**Lauriston** of Lauriston. Cramond, by J. P. Wood, 41.

**Law** of Brunton. Norton Smith's Orkney Armorials, 85.
  of Lauriston. Cramond, by J. P. Wood (1794), 43-44, 161-264. Popular
    Genealogists . . . by G. Burnett (1865), 85-88. Notes and Queries,
    10th S., x. 367, 434. The Laws of Lauriston, n.d.* Lauriston Castle,
    the Estate and its Owners, by John A. Fairley (Edinr. 1925).
  of Pittilloch. The Scottish Antiquary, ix. 144.
  in Sweden. One Year in Sweden, by Marryat, ii. 491.

**Lawrance.** Scottish N. and Q., 2nd S., v., vi., vii., viii. A Branch of the
    Aberdeenshire Lawrances, by Robert Murdoch, xvi + 327 (Aberdeen,
    1925).

**Lawrie** of Barnsoul. Lands . . . in Galloway, iv. 26.
  of Blackwood. Annals of Lesmahagow, by Greenshields (1854), 85-90.*
  of Urral. Lands . . . in Galloway, 2nd ed. (1906), i. 641.
  of Woodhall. Lands . . . in Galloway, iii. 157.

**Lawson** of Cairnmuir. Heraldry, by Nisbet (1742), ii., Appx. 102-104.
    Douglas's Baronage, 581-583. Fraser's Laurencekirk, 182. Buchan
    and Paton's History of Peeblesshire, iii. 149-156.
  Eddleston. Peeblesshire Localities, by Renwick, 38.

**Lawson** of Heiriggs, Lochtulloch, Boghall, and Cambo. Heraldry, by Nisbet (1742), ii., Appx. 100-101.

of Humbie. Heraldry, by Nisbet, ii., Appx. 98-99.

of Powburn. Fraser's Laurencekirk, 182-184.

**Learmonth** of Balcomie. East Neuk of Fife, by W. Wood, 2nd ed., 439-440, 444-446.

of Birkhill. Campbell's Balmerino, 573, 657.

of Clatto. Geneal. Coll., by W. Macfarlane, 1750-51 ; Scot. Hist. Soc., ii. 185.

of Dairsie. The Scottish Antiquary, xv. 103.

of Dean. Burke's Landed Gentry (1858-1894).

**Leask.** Scottish N. and Q., xii. 116. Genealogy of the Family of Leask, Orkney, by J. T. Smith Leask, 7 pp. (Viking Club, 1909).*

**Leckie** of Leckie. The Stirling Antiquary (1908), iv. 289-308. Leckie of that Ilk, by R. G. E. Leckie (Vancouver, 1913).

of Newlands. Crawfurd's Shire of Renfrew (1818), 31.

**Lee,** Tweedmouth. Eminent Arbroathians, by J. M. M'Bain (Arbroath, 1897), 304-316.

**Legertwood, Ligertwood.** Scottish N. and Q., 2nd S., ii. 112, 127.

of Logierieve. Thanage of Fermartyn, by Temple, 479-481.

of Tillery. Thanage of Fermartyn, 576-577.

**Leighton** of Usan *or* Ulshaven. Memorials of Angus and the Mearns, by A. Jervise, ed. Gammack, ii. 36-42. Angus and Forfarshire, by Warden, iii. 158-160.

**Leishman.** Matthew Leishman of Govan, by Rev. James Fleming Leishman (Paisley, 1921).

Carmoore. Traditions of the Watson Family, by C. B. Boog Watson.*

**Leitch.** Scottish N. and Q., 2nd S., vii. 177.

**Leith** of Barnes. Thanage of Fermartyn, by Rev. W. Temple (Aberdeen, 1894).

of Bucharne. Douglas's Baronage (1784), 230-231.

of Edingarroch. Thanage of Fermartyn, 34.

of Freefield and Glenkindy. Douglas's Baronage, 231-232. Memoir of J. Young, Aberdeen . . . 1861, ed. Lt.-Col. W. Johnston (1894), 137-140.* Burke's Landed Gentry (1875-1914).

of Fyvie. Thanage of Fermartyn, 39.

of Harthill. Douglas's Baronage, 229-230.

of Leith-hall. Douglas's Baronage, 224-227. Thanage of Fermartyn, 36-39. Tayler's Jacobites of Aberdeenshire, 339-342. Burke's Landed Gentry (1875-1925).

of Lickliehead. Thanage of Fermartyn, 35.

of Overhall. Douglas's Baronage, 227-228.

Premnay. Scottish N. and Q. (1888), i. 154.

of Treefield. Douglas's Baronage, 230.

of Whitehaugh. Historical MSS. Commission (1871), vol. xxxiii., 2nd Report. Burke's Landed Gentry (1846-1879).

**Leith-Buchanan** of Drygrange. Annals of a Border Club, by G. Tancred, 79-81.

of Ross. G. E. C.'s Complete Baronetage, v. 185. Burke's Peerage and Baronetage.

**Leith-Hay** of Leith Hall. Burke's Landed Gentry (1875-1925).

**Leith-Ross** of Arnage. Memoir of J. Young, merchant burgess of Aberdeen . . . by Alex. Johnston (1861, 1894), 11-16 *et passim.** Burke's Landed Gentry (1886-1925).

**Lendrish.** History of the Family of Lendrish (*or Clan Gillanders*), *in Manuscript*, 64 pp., 4to (unpublished).

**Le Neym** of Broughton. Peeblesshire Localities, by Renwick, 197-198. Annals of a Tweeddale Parish, by Rev. A. Baird, 26.

**Lennox.** History of the Partition of the Lennox, by Mark Napier (1835) Additional Remarks upon the Question of the Lennox or Rusky Representation in answer to the author of "History of the Partition of the Lennox," by John Riddell (1835). Memoirs and Muniments of the Lennox Family, by W. Fraser, 2 vols., 4to, illust. (Edinr. 1874). "The Lannox of Auld," an Epistolary Review of "The Lennox, by W. Fraser," by Mark Napier, 4to (Edinr. 1880).

The Celtic Earls of. The Scottish Antiquary (1897), xi. 8. The Stirling Antiquary, iv. 286-288. The Scots Peerage, v. 324-343. Origin of the Earls of Lennox, by R. E. E. Leckie (Vancouver, 1911).

Lennox, Duke of. The English Peerage, by Rev. A. Jacob (1766), i. 166-168. Crawfurd's Shire of Renfrew (1818), 453-455. Records of the Dukes of Richmond from 1672 down to 1896, by John Kent, portraits (London, 1880). The Scots Peerage, v. 363-371. G. E. C.'s Complete Peerage.

Stuart, Earl of, Duke of. A Monument of Mortalitie, upon the Death and Funerals of . . . Lodovick, late Duke of Richmond and Lenox, by R. Rounthwaite (1624). Nisbet's Heraldry (1742), ii., pt. iii. 84. Crawfurd's Shire of Renfrew (1818), 452. Geneal. Mag. (1900), iii. 208-211, 249-252. The Scots Peerage, v. 344-362. G. E. C.'s Complete Peerage.

**Lennox** of Balglas. Strathendrick, by Guthrie Smith, 245.

of Branshogle. Strathendrick, 248-251.

of Cally. Lands . . . in Galloway, by M'Kerlie (1877), iii. 486-495, 504.

Muthil. The Scottish Antiquary, vi. 139.

of Plunton. Lands . . . in Galloway, iii. 198-201.

of Woodhead. Case of Margaret Lennox of Woodhead, in relation to the Title, Honours, and Dignity of the Ancient Earls of Lennox, with genealogical tree, 4to (1813).

**Lesley,** Pernegg. Macfarlane's Genealogical Collections, ii. 13-14, 16, 17. *See* **Leslie.**

**Leslie, Lesley.**   Laura Lesleiana explicata, sive clarior enumeratio personarum utriusque sexus cognominis Leslie, by Rev. Wm. Lesly, S.J., folio, genealogical table (Græcii. [Gratz] 1667, 1692). Heraldry, by Alex. Nisbet (1722), i. 96-98, 419-420. Geneal. Coll., by W. Macfarlane, 1750-51; Scot. Hist. Soc., ii. 1-84, 424-470. Historical Records of the Family of Leslie, from 1067-1869, collected from Public Records and Authentic Private Sources by [Rev. Wilson, Fetternear and] Col. C. Leslie, 3 vols., 8vo (Edinr. 1869 ; Aberdeen, 1880). Great Historical Families of Scotland, by Taylor [1887]. The Leslies, Earls of Leven, and the Melvilles, Earls of Melville, by Sir William Fraser, K.C.B., 3 vols. (Edinr. 1890).* Notes and Queries, 3rd S., xi. 354, 498 ; xii. 449: 6th S., v. 251 ; ix. 453. Scottish N. and Q., 3rd S., iii. 1. Dictionary of National Biography, *s.v.*

*See* The Scots Peerage, ed. Sir James Balfour Paul, *for*
**Leslie,** Lord, Earl of Leslie, vii. 273-311.
   Earl of Leven, v. 372-381.
   Lord Lindores, v. 382-390.
   Earl of Melville, vi. 110-118.
   Lord Newark, vi. 440-445.
   Earl of Ross, vii. 241-244.
   Earl of, Duke of, Rothes, vii. 264-311.

**Leslie,** Aberdeen.   Macfarlane's Geneal. Coll., ii. 83.
   of Achorsk.   Macfarlane's Geneal. Coll., ii. 62.
   of Aikenway.   Macfarlane's Geneal. Coll., ii. 69-73.
   of Balcomie.   East Neuk of Fife, by W. Wood, 2nd ed., 438.
   of Balquhain.   Macfarlane's Geneal. Coll., ii. 1-18. Pedigree of the Family of Leslie of Balquhain, by Col. C. Leslie, 8vo, 24 pp. (Bakewell, 1861).* Notes and Queries, 6th S., ii. 310. Burke's Landed Gentry (1849-1925).
   Barbados.   Notes and Queries, 5th S., iii. 469 ; iv. 54 ; viii. 48.
   of Birdsbank.   Scottish N. and Q. (1890-1), iv. 242.
   of Birkhill.   Campbell's Balmerino, 574-576, 657.
   of Bucharn, Bacarn.   Macfarlane's Geneal. Coll., ii. 37, 66.
   of Caldwell.   Macfarlane's Geneal. Coll., ii. 56.
   of Conrake.   Macfarlane's Geneal. Coll., ii. 55.
   of Creichis.   Macfarlane's Geneal. Coll., ii. 65.
   of Cults.   Macfarlane's Geneal. Coll., ii. 3, 63.
   of Drumdollo.   Thanage of Fermartyn, by Temple, 215-216.
   of Drummuir.   Macfarlane's Geneal. Coll., ii. 50.
   of Dyce.   Macfarlane's Geneal. Coll., ii. 39.
   of Findrassie, Findressie.   Heraldry, by Nisbet (1742), ii., Appx. 149-151. Macfarlane's Geneal. Coll., ii. 73-76. Burke's Peerage and Baronetage.
   of Folla.   Burke's Landed Gentry (1914).
   of Little Folla.   Thanage of Fermartyn, by Temple, 94-95.
   in France.   Macfarlane's Geneal. Coll., ii. 38. Notes and Queries, 6th S., vi. 27.
   of Iden.   Macfarlane's Geneal. Coll., ii. 68.

**Leslie of** Kincraigs. Macfarlane's Geneal. Coll., ii. 19.
of Kininvie. Macfarlane's Geneal. Coll., ii. 6, 44. The Scottish
Antiquary, ix. 142. Burke's Landed Gentry (1875-1925).
of Leslie. The Scots Peerage, vii. 265-276.
of Lumquhat. The Scots Peerage, v. 388-389.
of Milton and Tullich. Macfarlane's Geneal. Coll., ii. 57-59.
of New Leslie. Macfarlane's Geneal. Coll., ii. 6, 40-44.
of Newtoun. Macfarlane's Geneal. Coll., ii. 80-82.
of Pitcaple. Macfarlane's Geneal. Coll., ii. 59-62.
of Pitnamoon. Macfarlane's Geneal. Coll., ii. 82.
of Quarter. The Scots Peerage, v. 386, 387.
of Rothes. The Scots Peerage, vii. 268-273.
of the Glen of Rothes. Annals of Elgin, by Young (1879), 663-664.
of Rothie. Temple's Thanage of Fermartyn, 47. Burke's Landed
Gentry (1914).
of Rothienorman. Thanage of Fermartyn, 96-98.
of Ruderie. Macfarlane's Geneal. Coll., ii. 54.
of St Monans and Newark. East Neuk of Fife, 2nd ed., 237-244.
in Sweden. One Year in Sweden, by Marryat, ii. 501.
of Urisland. Zetland Family Histories, by F. J. Grant, 171-172.
of Urquhall. Macfarlane's Geneal. Coll., ii. 51.
of Wardis. Macfarlane's Geneal. Coll., ii. 6, 22-30. Baronage, by
Douglas (1784), 28-30. Burke's Peerage and Baronetage. Complete
Baronetage, by G. E. C., ii. 297.
of Warthill, Wartle. Macfarlane's Geneal. Coll., ii. 30-37. Chart pedigree,
with royal descents.* Burke's Landed Gentry (1848-1914). Churchyard Monuments of Crail, by Erskine Beveridge, 162-169.

**Leslie-Melville,** Earl of Leven, Earl of Melville. Eminent Men of Fife,
by Conolly, 324-326. The Leslies, Earls of Leven, and the Melvilles,
Earls of Melville, by Sir Wm. Fraser, 3 vols. (Edinr. 1890).* The
Scots Peerage, vi. 118-123.

**Lessly,** Antigua. Oliver's History of Antigua, ii. 178-179.

**Leven,** Leslie, Earl of. Macfarlane's Geneal. Coll., ii. 51-54. The Leslies,
Earls of Leven, by Sir W. Fraser, 3 vols. (1890).* The Scots Peerage,
v. 372-381 ; vi. 110-118.
Leslie-Melville, Earl of. The Scots Peerage, vi. 118-123. Burke's and
other Annual Peerages.

**Levington of** Jerviswood. Upper Ward of Lanarkshire, by Irving and
Murray, ii. 320.

**Lichton of** Ulshaven. One Year in Sweden, by Marryat (1862), i. 308,
coat-of-arms ; ii. 463-465. *See* **Leighton.**

**Liddel,** Aberdeen. Scottish N. and Q. (1887), i. 101-102.

**Liddell of** Balbanein and Panlathyn. The Scots Peerage, vii. 6, 10 ; viii. 47.
of Hammer. The Frotoft Branch of the Orkney Traills, by T. W. Traill
(1902),* 57-63. Orkney Armorials, by Norton Smith, 86.

**Lidderdale.** Lands . . . in Galloway, by M'Kerlie (1878), iv. 162, 173, 178, 181-184.

**Lightbody.** [A History of the Lightbody Family is in preparation by Mr William Lightbody, Sefton, Shortheath, Farnham, Surrey.]

**Lin** of Larg. Lands . . . in Galloway, 2nd ed. (1906), i. 549-551.
of Lin. Paterson's History of Ayr, i. 418. Paterson's Ayr and Wigton, iii. 184-186.

**Lind.** The Genealogy of the Family of Lind, by Sir Robert Douglas (Windsor, 1795).* Burke's Landed Gentry (1849-1863).

**Lindesay** of the Glen. Scottish N. and Q., 3rd S., v. 87.
of Wormiston. Patrick Lindesay, the Jacobite, by A. Francis Steuart (1927), 32-35. *See also* **Lindsay.**

**Lindores,** Leslie, Lord. W. Macfarlane's Geneal. Coll., ii. 76-78. G. E. C.'s Complete Peerage. The Scots Peerage, v. 382-390.

**Lindsay.** Lives of the Lindsays, or a Memoir of the Houses of Crawford and Balcarres, by Lord Lindsay, 8vo, 4 vols. (Wigan, 1840); * 2nd ed., 3 vols. (London, 1849); 3rd ed., 3 vols. (London, 1858). The History and Tradition of the Land of the Lindsays . . . by Andrew Jervise (1853), 2nd ed. corrected by James Gammack (1882). The Family of Seton, by G. Seton (1896), 40. A Lindsay Record, being a hand-list of books written by or relating to members of the Clan Lindsay, preserved in the Wigan Public Library, 25 copies [1899]. The Origin of the Lindsays, by Sir George Sitwell, J. H. Round, W. A. Lindsay *in* The Genealogist, N. S., xii. 1-6, 75, 152-153; xiii. 19-20. Publications of the Clan Lindsay Society, ed. W. A. Lindsay, K.C., Windsor Herald, and John Lindsay, M.D., illust. (Edinr. 1901 to date). Dictionary of National Biography, *s.v.*

*See* The Scots Peerage, ed. Sir James Balfour Paul, *for*

**Lindsay,** Earl of Balcarres, i. 511-529.
Earl of Crawford, iii. 1-51.
Viscount Garnock, iv. 174-178.
Earl of Lindsay, iii. 35-51 ; v. 391-420.
Lord Lindsay, iii. 51.
Lord Lindsay of Balcarres, i. 518-519.
Lord Lindsay of Balneil, i. 519-523.
Lord Lindsay of the Byres, v. 392-420.
Duke of Montrose, iii. 22-23.
Lord Parbroath, iii. 35-51 ; v. 402-420.
Lord Spynie, viii. 94.

**Lindsay** of Balcarres. Burke's Visitation of Seats and Arms (1853), i. 182. Eminent Men of Fife, by Conolly, 274-295. East Neuk of Fife, by W. Wood, 2nd ed., 132-144. Burke's Peerage and Baronetage.
of Belstane. Upper Ward of Lanarkshire, by Irving and Murray, ii. 418.
of Blacksolm. Crawfurd's Shire of Renfrew (1818), 92, 128.
of Bonhill. Book of Dumbartonshire, by Irving, ii. 173-174.

**Lindsay** of the Byres. Case of Sir J. T. Bethune on his claim to be Lord Lindsay of the Byres (1877). List of Proofs (1877). Minutes of Evidence in Petition of Sir J. T. Bethune (1877-8).

of Corstoun. Some Ancient Scottish Families, by J. B. Brown-Morison (Perth, 1884), 146.*

of Covington. Upper Ward of Lanarkshire, i. 465-469.

of Craigie. History of the Lairds of Glenfield (Paisley, 1860), 8-9.

Crail. Churchyard Monuments of Crail, by Erskine Beveridge, 162-166.

of Crawford. Scottish Antiquary, v. 48. The Scots Peerage, iii. 2-11.

of Dowhill. Clan Lindsay Soc. Publ. (1920), ii.

of Eaglescairny. Baronage, by Douglas (1784), 261-262.

of Edzell. Geneal. Coll., by W. Macfarlane, 1750-51 ; Scot. Hist. Soc., ii. 399-408. Warden's Angus or Forfarshire, iii. 216-224. The Scots Peerage, i. 511-516 ; iii. 27, 28.

of Ethiebeaton. Monifieth, by Malcolm (1910), 303-309.

of Evelick. Burke's Extinct Baronetcies. Complete Baronetage, by G. E. C., iv. 249. Family and Genealogical Sketches, by Rev. T. Sinton (Inverness, 1911).*

of Glenesk. The Scots Peerage, i. 511-516 ; iii. 13, 19.

of Halbeath. Memoir of J. Young, Aberdeen . . . 1861, ed. Lt.-Col. W. Johnston (1894), 56-61, 162-164.*

of Keithock. Angus or Forfarshire, iii. 24-25.

of Kirkforthar. Baronage, by Douglas, 259-261. The Scots Peerage, v. 396-407.

of Lamberton. The Scots Peerage, iii. 3-5.

of Leuchars. East Neuk of Fife, by W. Wood, 2nd ed., 143-144.

of Logie. Stephen's Inverkeithing and Rosyth (1921), 198-200.

of Luffness. The Scots Peerage, iii. 3-10.

of the Mount. Scot. Hist. Review (1916), xii. 167.

of Overshiells. MS. by John Riddell, W.S., and Robert Riddell, in the possession of the Society of Writers to the Signet.

of Pitairlie. Angus or Forfarshire, by Warden, iv. 425. Pedigree in Clan Lindsay Soc. Publ. (1926).

of Pyotston. The Scots Peerage, v. 411-412.

of Stirkfield. Peeblesshire Localities, by Renwick, 203. Annals of a Tweeddale Parish, by Baird, 31.

of Vane. Angus or Forfarshire, by Warden, iii. 270.

of Wormiston, or Wolmerstoun. Baronage, by Douglas (1784), 257-259. East Neuk of Fife, by W. Wood, 2nd ed., 454-456. Churchyard Monuments of Crail, by Erskine Beveridge, 203-207. Scottish Antiquary, vi. 54. The Scots Peerage, v. 413-417. *See* **Lindesay.**

**Lindsay-Bethune** of Kilconquhar. Burke's Peerage. The Scots Peerage, v. 416.

**Lindsay Carnegie** of Spynie, Boysack, and Kinblethmont. Angus and Forfarshire, iii. 440. Eminent Arbroathians, by J. M. M'Bain (1897), 201-222. Burke's Landed Gentry (1849-1925). The Scots Peerage, vi. 496 ; viii. 111-113.

**Lindsay-Crawfurd** of Kilbirnie. The Scots Peerage, iii. 36, 40.

**Linklater.** Scottish N. and Q., 2nd S., v. 127.

**Linlithgow,** Livingston, Earl of. The Scots Peerage, v. 421-451.
Hope, Marquess of. Burke's Peerage (after 1902). The Scots Peerage, iv. 485-505.

**Linning,** Lesmahagow. Ayrshire Families, by G. Robertson (1824), ii. 294-295.

**Linton,** Stewart, Lord. The Scots Peerage, viii. 403-409.
of Pendreich. Logie, by Rev. Dr Menzies Fergusson, ii. 80.

**Liston,** Newliston. Some Old Families, by H. B. M'Call, with pedigree (1890), 79-117.*

**Liston-Foulis** of Colinton. Burke's Peerage and Baronetage. Complete Baronetage, by G. E. C., ii. 410.

**Lithgow.** New York Geneal. and Biog. Record (1898), xxix., *i.*, 1-13.
of Drygrange. Nisbet's Heraldic Plates, ed. Ross and Grant (1892), 54-57.
Lanark. Thos. Reid *in* Proc. Soc. Antiq. Scotl. (1911), 403-416.
Montrose. MS. Pedigree, 907 ; Society of Genealogists, London.

**Little.** Fragmentary Memories . . . an Account of the Clan Little, and the Ancestry of James Little . . . , 8vo, illust. (1913).*

**Little-Gilmour.** Burke's Landed Gentry (1875-1886).

**Littlejohn** of Invercharron. Burke's Landed Gentry (1898-1914).

**Livingston(e.** Nisbet's Heraldry (1722), i. 397-398. Ancient Scottish Surnames, by Buchanan of Auchmar (1723), 35-36. Notice Généalogique de la Famille de Livingstone, par Mons¹ le Maistre Tonnerre, 8vo (1856). Scot. Hist. Review, xxv. 389-390.

*See* The Scots Peerage, ed. Sir James Balfour Paul, *for*
**Livingston,** Earl of Callendar, ii. 360-364.
Lord Campsie, v. 192-194.
Viscount of Kilsyth, v. 183-194.
Lord of, Viscount of Kinnaird, vi. 452-460.
Earl of Linlithgow, v. 421-451.
Lord Livingston of Almond, ii. 360-364.
Lord Livingston of Callendar, v. 430-451.
Lord Livingston of Flacraig, vi. 453-460.
Lord Livingston of Hyndford, viii. 376.
Viscount of, Earl of, Newburgh, vi. 452-460.
Viscount Teviot, viii. 368-377.

**Livingston,** Antigua. Oliver's History of Antigua, ii. 190-192.
of Belstane. Upper Ward of Lanarkshire, by Irving and Murray, ii. 417.
of Caldhame. Warden's Angus or Forfarshire, iii. 37.
of Callendar. Abstract of the Evidence for proving Sir Thomas Livingstone Heir-male of James, First Earl of Calander, folio (1821). Family Records, relating to the Families of Pearce of Holsworthy . . . Livingstone of Calendar . . . compiled by Sir E. R. Pearce-Edgcumbe, 4to (Exeter, 1895), 89-93. The Livingstons of Callendar and their Principal Cadets, by Edwin B. Livingston, 4to, illust., *xviii*+657 pp. (1887).* 2nd ed., 4to, 34 plates, *xix*+530 pp. (1920). The Scots Peerage, v. 423-429.

**Livingston** of Darnchester.  The Scots Peerage, v. 187, 189, 190.

of Drumry.  The Scots Peerage, viii. 368-369.

of Dunipace.  The Scottish Antiquary, v. 12, 74-75, 140.  Complete Baronetage, by G. E. C., ii. 240.

of Glentirran.  Complete Baronetage, by G. E. C., iv. 333 ; vi., Appx. 79.

of Haining.  Scottish Antiquary, xiv. 166.

of Jerviswood.  The Scots Peerage, viii. 370-373.

of Kilsyth.  Walford's Tales of our Great Families, 2nd S., i. 59-67.  My Lady Dundie, by Mrs Katharine Parker.  The Scots Peerage, v. 183-191.

of Kinnaird.  Burke's Extinct Baronetcies.  Complete Baronetage, by G. E. C., ii. 323.

of Lethington.  The Scots Peerage, viii. 374-376.

of Livingston Manor.  The Livingstons of Livingston Manor, by E. B. Livingston (1910).

of Newbigging.  Upper Ward of Lanarkshire, by Irving and Murray, ii. 524.  Complete Baronetage, by G. E. C., ii. 324.  The Scots Peerage, viii. 369-374.

of Ogleface.  The Scottish Antiquary, iii. 75-85.

of Quintinespie.  Lands . . . in Galloway, by M'Kerlie, iii. 165.

in Sweden.  One Year in Sweden, by Marryat (1862), ii. 492.

of West Quarter.  Scottish Antiquary, iii. 75-85 ; iv. 181-182.  Complete Baronetage, by G. E. C., iv. 384.  Burke's Landed Gentry (1863-1894).

**Loch** of Drylaw and Rachan.  Cramond, by J. P. Wood, 29-30, chart pedigree.  Burke's Peerage (1905).

of Over Carnbee.  East Neuk of Fife, by W. Wood, 2nd ed., 336.

**Lochiel**, Cameron, Baron.  The Jacobite Peerage, by the Marquis of Ruvigny (1904), 77-80.

**Lockhart** of Bar.  Paterson's History of Ayr, ii. 66-67.  Paterson's Ayr and Wigton, i. 511-514.

of Barmagachan.  Lands in Galloway, by M'Kerlie, iii. 196.

of Birkhill.  Memoirs of the Family of Sir Walter Scott, by Rev. C. Rogers (1877), *lxvii-lxviii*.  Upper Ward of Lanarkshire, ii. 227-228.

of Boghall.  Paterson's Ayr and Wigton, i. 671.

of Borthwickbrae.  Burke's Landed Gentry (1858-1886).

of Carstairs.  Crawfurd's Shire of Renfrew (1818), 323.  Upper Ward of Lanarkshire, ii. 455-456.  Complete Baronetage, by G. E. C., iv. 286.

of Carnwath.  Upper Ward of Lanarkshire, ii. 517-523.

of Castlehill.  Upper Ward of Lanarkshire, ii. 313.  Burke's Landed Gentry (1875-1898).

of Cleghorn.  Nisbet's Heraldry (1722), i. 325 ; 1742, ii., Appx. 141.  Douglas's Baronage (1798), 585-587.  Nisbet's Heraldic Plates, ed. Ross and Grant (1892), 18-21.  Upper Ward of Lanarkshire, ii. 314-320.  Scottish Antiquary, vi. 179-182.  Burke's Landed Gentry (1894-1914).

of Kirktoun.  Upper Ward of Lanarkshire, ii. 414-417.

**Lockhart** of Lee and Craiglockhart. Nisbet's Heraldry, 1722, i. 325. Douglas's Baronage, 323-327. Visitation of Seats and Arms, by J. B. Burke (1853), i. 78-79. Burke's Peerage and Baronetage. Walford's Tales of our Great Families, 2nd S., i. 226-246. Historical Families of Dumfriesshire, by Johnstone, 61-62. Upper Ward of Lanarkshire, ii. 287-313.

of Symington. Upper Ward of Lanarkshire, by Irving and Murray, i. 187.

of Wicketshaw. Upper Ward of Lanarkshire, ii. 421-422. Burke's Landed Gentry (1863-1894).

**Lockhart-Denham.** Complete Baronetage, by G. E. C., iv. 363.

**Lockhart-Mure** of Livingston. Lands . . . in Galloway, by M'Kerlie, iii. 161-162. Burke's Landed Gentry (1906-1925).

**Lockhart-Ross** of Lockhart Hall. Complete Baronetage, by G. E. C., iv. 286. *See also* **Ross of Balnagown.**

**Logan.** Notice *in* Moffat's History of Moffats (1908).*

of Balvie. Strathendrick, by Guthrie Smith, 215.

of Cameron. Strathendrick, 215-216.

of Camlarg. Paterson's History of Ayr, i. 404. Paterson's Ayr and Wigton, i. 382.

of Cornton. Logie, by Rev. R. Menzies Fergusson, ii. 207, 211.

of Edrom. Burke's Landed Gentry (1882).

in Lintonroderick. Peeblesshire Localities, by Renwick, 18, 493.

of Lochshinnoch, Knockshinnoch. Paterson's Ayr, i. 367. Paterson's Ayr and Wigton, 342-343. The Logans of Lochshinnoch, 4to (Glasgow, 1869). The Logans of Lochshinnoch, " Hoc Majorum Virtus." Revised and corrected by One of Themselves, J. M. H., 4to (Edinr. 1885).*

of Logan. Paterson's Ayr, i. 368 369. Ayr and Wigton, i. 312, 343-347. Warrick's History of New Cumnock, 279-288.

of Restalrig. Heraldry, by A. Nisbet (1722), i. 205. Recreations of an Antiquary, by Fittis (1881), 321-324. Notes and Queries, xii. 248, 336. Pedigree by Wm. Douglas, *in* Proc. Soc. Antiq. Scotl., 6th S., ii. 27.

**Logan-Home** of Broomhouse. Burke's Landed Gentry (1898-1925).

**Lorain** of Harwood. Annals of a Border Club, by G. Tancred, 192 *n.*

**Lorimer.** Genealogy of the Lorimers of Scotland, by R. R. Stodart, 8vo, 4 pp., n.d.

of Kellyfield. Pedigree *in* Playfair's Notes on the Family of Playfair (1913).*

**Lorn,** Stewart, Lord of. A. Sinclair *in* Herald and Genealogist, vi. 481-495. The Scots Peerage, v. 1. *See also* **Stewart of Lorn.**

**Lorne,** Campbell, Marquess of. The Clan Campbell and the Marquis of Lorne [by J. Hogg, 1871]. Walford's Chapters from Family Chests (1887), ii. 295-299. The Scots Peerage, i. 369-393.

**Lothian**, Ker, Earl of, Marquess of. Memorials of the Marquis of Lothian's Majority, with introductory notice of the family, by Alex. Jeffrey (Jedburgh, 1853). Historical MSS. Commission (1870), 1st Report; (1905), Cd. 2319. Annals of a Border Club, by G. Tancred (1899), 268-283. Burke's Peerage. Debrett's Peerage. The Scots Peerage, v. 452-487. G. E. C.'s Complete Peerage.

**Loudoun**, Campbell, Lord Campbell of, Earl of. Paterson's History of Ayr (1852), ii. 319-323. Claim of the Earl of Loudoun to Vote at Elections of Peers of Scotland : (Session Papers, E of 1877). Great Historic Families of Scotland, by Taylor [1887]. Burke's Peerage. Debrett's Peerage. A. C. Jonas *in* Geneal. Mag. (1898), i. 453-459. The Genealogist, N. S., xxxvii. 183-219. The Scots Peerage, v. 488-517. G. E. C.'s Complete Peerage.

**Lour**, Carnegie, Lord. The Scots Peerage, vi. 494-495.

**Louttit**. Scottish N. and Q., 2nd S., v. 77.

**Lovat**, Fraser, Lord Fraser of. Paper on the Lovat Peerage Case (1727). Memoirs of the Jacobites of 1715 and 1745, by Mrs Katherine Thomson (1845-46), ii. 208-388. Sketches of Highland Families, by John Maclean (1848), 54-74. Case of Thos. Alex. Fraser of Lovat. Case of Rev. A. G. Fraser. Reports and Minutes of Evidence (1826-7). Additional Case of Thomas Alexander, Lord Lovat, 1854. Minutes of Evidence (1855-1857). Case of John Fraser of Carnarvon (1885). Case of Simon, Lord Lovat (1885). Minutes of Evidence (1885). Walford's Chapters from Family Chests (1887), ii. 44-54. Burke's Peerage. Debrett's Peerage. G. E. C.'s Complete Peerage. The Scots Peerage, v. 518-548. Inventory of Lovat Writs *in* Antiquarian Notes . . . by C. Fraser-Mackintosh (1913), i. 101-108 ; ii. 13-16, 113-120, 243. Scot. Hist. Review, xxv. 223-226.

**Love**, **Luiff**, of Threipwood. Paterson's History of Ayr, i. 271-273. Paterson's Ayr and Wigton, iii. 118-120.

**Lovel** of Ballumbie. Memorials of Angus and the Mearns, by Jervise, ed. Gammack, ii. 258-260. Warden's Angus or Forfarshire, v. 5-6.
of Castle Cary and Hawick, and of Enoch. J. Bain *in* Genealogist, N. S., iv. 214-215. R. C. Reid *in* Dumfriesshire and Galloway Antiq. Soc. Trans., 3rd S. (1923), viii. 154, 180-183 ; chart pedigree.

**Low**, Monifieth. Angus or Forfarshire, by Warden, iv. 385.
Montrose. Scottish N. and Q. (1888), ii. 62, 79.

**Lowden** of Auchenskeoch. Lands . . . in Galloway, by M'Kerlie, iii. 354.

**Lowis** of Manor. Peeblesshire Localities, by Renwick, 360-362. Buchan and Paton's History of Peeblesshire, iii. 554-559.
of Plean. History of Stirlingshire by Nimmo, 3rd ed. (1880), ii. 126. The Monros of Auchenbowie, by J. A. Inglis, 86.
of Plora. Craig-Brown's Selkirkshire, i. 414-415.

**Lucklaw** of Newton Rires. East Neuk of Fife, by W. Wood, 2nd ed., 121, 201.

**Lumisdaine, Lumsden,** of Airdrie and Dales. East Neuk of Fife, by W. Wood, 2nd ed., 400. Stephen's Inverkeithing (1921), 160-163. Churchyard Monuments of Crail, by Erskine Beveridge (Edinr. 1893), 132-155, with chart pedigree, 1439 to 1605.

of Innergellie. Eminent Men of Fife, by Conolly, 305. East Neuk of Fife, 2nd ed., 383-385.

of Lathallan. Eminent Men of Fife, 307. East Neuk of Fife, 2nd ed., 147. Burke's Landed Gentry (1858-1894).

of Montquhany. Scottish N. and Q., 3rd S., 97, 159.

of Rennyhill. East Neuk of Fife, 2nd ed., 381.

**Lumisden,** Edinburgh. The Jacobite Peerage (1904), 83.

**Lumsdaine, Lumsden.** Heraldry, by A. Nisbet (1722), i. 412-413. Memorials of the Families of Lumsdaine, Lumisden, or Lumsden, by Lt.-Col. H. W. Lumsden, 4to, $xi$+116 pp., illust., chart pedigree (Edinr. 1889).* Scottish N. and Q., 3rd S., v. 96, 117-118, 140, 177, 178.

**Lumsden** of Arden. Irving's Book of Dumbartonshire, iii. Burke's Landed Gentry (1894-1925).

of Ardhuncart. Scottish N. and Q., 2nd S., iii. 157. Tayler's Jacobites of Aberdeenshire (1928), 343.

of Auchendoir. Burke's Extinct Baronetcies. Scottish N. and Q., 3rd S., iii. 122.

in Auchlossan. Tayler's Jacobites, 342-343.

of Balmedie. Temple's Thanage of Fermartyn, 621-632. Scottish N. and Q., 2nd S., ii. 14.

of Clova. Burke's Landed Gentry (1846-1862).

of Cushnie. Thanage of Fermartyn, 623-628. Burke's Landed Gentry (1845-1862).

Dysart. Eminent Arbroathians, by J. M. M'Bain (Arbroath, 1897), 334.

of Pitcaple. Burke's Landed Gentry (1846-1925).

**Lun,** Crail. Churchyard Monuments of Crail, by Erskine Beveridge, 182-186, 193-199.

**Lunan.** Scottish N. and Q., 2nd S., iv. 26. Pedigree *in* Cadenhead's Family of Cadenhead (1887).

**Lundie, Lundin,** of that Ilk. Heraldry, by A. Nisbet (1722), II., iii. 13. East Neuk of Fife, 45-56. Memoir of J. Young, Aberdeen . . . 1861, ed. Lt.-Col. W. Johnston (1894), 207-217.*

**Lundin** of Auchtermairnie. Eminent Men of Fife, 308. East Neuk of Fife, 2nd ed., 56-58. Burke's Landed Gentry (1849-1875). The Browns of Fordell, by Stodart, 195. Kennoway, by A. S. Cunningham (1906), 24-26.

of Balbuthie and Briery Bank. East Neuk of Fife, 170-171.

of Balgonie and Drums. Heraldry, by Nisbet (1742), ii., Appx. 128-129.

of Strathairly. East Neuk of Fife, 94-96.

**Lyall** in Carcary. Angus or Forfarshire, by Warden, iii. 253.

of Gallery. Baronage of Angus and Mearns, by Peter (1856), 209. Angus or Forfarshire (1880), iv. 113-114, 242.

**Lyell**, Abernethy.   The Scottish Antiquary, viii. 162-163.

in Arbroath.   One Year in Sweden, by Marryat, ii. 491.

of Dysart.   Angus or Forfarshire, iv. 315.

of Gardyne.   Baronage of Angus and Mearns, 210.   Angus or Forfarshire, iv. 74.

of Kinnordy.   Baronage of Angus and Mearns, 210.   Burke's Peerage and Baronetage (after 1894).

of Murthill.   Warden's Angus or Forfarshire, v. 202.

**Lyle.**   Heraldry, by A. Nisbet (1722), i. 219-220.

of Arlehaven and Dunburgh.   Strathblane, by Guthrie Smith, 78-79.

of Duchal.   Crawfurd's Shire of Renfrew (1818), 92-93.   Scottish Antiquary, iv. 23-25.   The Scots Peerage, v. 550-552.

Lord Lyle.   The Scots Peerage, v. 549-558.

of Stanypeth and Bassendean.   The Family of Inglis of Auchindinny, by J. A. Inglis, 220-224.

in Sweden.   Scot. Hist. Review, xxv. 295.

**Lynedoch**, Graham, Lord.   Notes and Queries, 8th S., vi. 225, 277, 378. The Scots Peerage, ii. 523 ; iv. 497 ; vi. 219.

**Lynn** of Larg.   Lands . . . in Galloway, by M'Kerlie (1906), i. 549-551.

**Lyon.**   Heraldry, by Nisbet (1722), i. 444-445.   Scottish N. and Q., 2nd S., vi. 151.   Glamis, by Stirton (1913), 16-34 *et passim.*

of Aldbar.   Burke's Commoners, iv. 592.   Burke's Landed Gentry (1846-1863).

of Ballantore.   Baronage of Angus and Mearns, by D. M. Peter (1856), 213.   Angus or Forfarshire, by A. J. Warden, iv. 214.

of Brigton.   The Scots Peerage, viii. 294-295.

of Cossins.   Baronage of Angus and Mearns, 213.   The Lyons of Cossins and Wester Ogil, by Andrew Ross, Marchmont Herald, 4to, $x+150$ pp. (Edinr. 1901).   Angus or Forfarshire, iii. 326.   The Scots Peerage, viii. 276.   Glamis, by Stirton, 107-109, 118.

of Glamis.   Notes and Queries, 3rd S., viii. 119.   Eminent Men of Fife, by Conolly, 308.   The Scots Peerage, viii. 265-270.

Lord Glamis.   The Scots Peerage, viii. 270-317.

of Hetton House.   The Scots Peerage, viii. 309-310.

Earl of Kinghorne.   The Scots Peerage, viii. 298-317.

of Kirkmichael.   Burke's Landed Gentry (1886-1925).

in Longforgan.   The Parish of Longforgan, by Rev. A. Philp (1895), 205, 211-212.

of Ogil.   Lyon of Ogil, by Wm. Lyon, 10th of Ogil (London, *c.* 1869). The Parish of Longforgan, 206-207.

of Scrogerfield.   The Scots Peerage, viii. 294-296.

Earl of Strathmore.   The Scots Peerage, viii. 261-317.

U.S.A.   A General History of the Lyon Families of New England, by Dr A. B. Lyons (Detroit, Mich., 1905).

of Westhill.   Angus or Forfarshire, iii. 325.

**Lyon-Bowes**, Lord Glamis, Earl of Strathmore and Kinghorne.   The Scots Peerage, viii. 312-313.

**McAdam** of Ballochmorrie and Sauchrie. Paterson's History of Ayr, i. 310. Paterson's Ayr and Wigton, ii. 147. Burke's Landed Gentry (1848).

of Blairoer. Strathendrick, by Guthrie Smith, 256-257.

of Craigengillan. Paterson's Ayr, ii. 475. Ayr and Wigton, i. 475-476. Lands . . . in Galloway, by M'Kerlie, iii. 297-299.

of Grimat. Ayrshire Families, by G. Robertson, i. 375.

of Waterhead. Paterson's Ayr, i. 309. Ayr and Wigton, ii. 142-145. Lands . . . in Galloway, by M'Kerlie, iii. 288-293. Burke's Landed Gentry (1848-1894).

**MacAldonich.** Family of Buchanan, by Buchanan of Auchmar (1723), 106.

**McAlester** of Loup and Kennox. Burke's Landed Gentry (1848-1925).

**McAlexander** of Corseclays and Pinmore. Paterson's History of Ayr, i. 314. Paterson's Ayr and Wigton, ii. 148.

of Dalreoch. Paterson's Ayr, i. 312. Ayr and Wigton, ii. 153.

of Daltupene. Ayr and Wigton, ii. 253.

of Drummochrin. Paterson's Ayr, i. 392-394. Ayr and Wigton, ii. 224-227.

**Macalister.** Narrative pedigree and notes : Typescript, 43 pp. ; in Library of Society of Genealogists, London.

of Glenbarr and Cour. Burke's Visitation of Seats and Arms (1853), i. 189. Burke's Landed Gentry (1848-1925).

**McAlpin(e.** Douglas's Baronage, 491-492. Burke's Landed Gentry (1846).

**McAlpine-Leny** of Dalswinton. Burke's Landed Gentry (1894-1925).

**MacAmeline** *or* Bannatyne. Heraldry, by Nisbet (1742), ii. Ragman Roll, 7. Ayrshire Families, by G. Robertson (1823), i. 50.

**MacAndeoir.** Family of Buchanan, by Buchanan of Auchmar, 146.

**MacAndrew.** Confederacy of Clan Chattan, by C. Fraser-Mackintosh, 142-143.

**Macartney** of Auchinleck. Lands and their Owners in Galloway, by M'Kerlie, v. 100.

**Macaulay.** Ancient Scottish Surnames, by Buchanan of Auchmar, 99-100. Memoirs of the Clan " Aulay " . . . by a Sister of T. B. Macaulay, 4to (Carmarthen, 1881).*

of Ardincaple. Irving's Book of Dumbartonshire, ii. 294-302.

of Lewis. Traditions and Genealogy of the Macaulays of Lewis, by Capt. F. W. L. Thomas *in* Proc. Soc. Antiq. Scotl., ii., N. S. (1880), 363-431.

**MacAuselan.** Family of Buchanan, by Buchanan of Auchmar, 120-123. The Scottish Antiquary (1897), xii. 93.

**McAy** of Black Isle. Confederacy of Clan Chattan, by C. Fraser-Mackintosh, 103.

**MacBean** of Daars. Confederacy of Clan Chattan, by C. Fraser-Mackintosh (1898), 39.

of Drummond. Confederacy of Clan Chattan, 36-39.

**MacBean** of Faillie. Confederacy of Clan Chattan, 42-49.
 Inverness-shire. Scottish N. and Q., 3rd S., ii. 166. Antiquarian Notes,
   by C. Fraser-Mackintosh, i. 380.
 of Kinchyle. Antiquarian Notes, by C. Fraser-Mackintosh, ii. 63-68.
   Confederacy of Clan Chattan, 30-36.
 of Tomatin. Confederacy of Clan Chattan, 49-56.
**Macbeth.** Scottish Historical Review, xviii. 154-155, 236.
 Stirling. The Stirling Antiquary, ii. 135.
**MacBhaxter.** Family of Buchanan, by Buchanan of Auchmar, 128.
**Macbrair** of Almagill. The Macbrairs of Almagill and Netherwood,
   pedigree annexed to Edgar's History of Dumfries, edited by
   R. C. Reid (Dumfries, 1915).
**MacBraire** of Tweedhill and Broadmeadows. Burke's Landed Gentry
   (1848-1867).
**MacBrayne** of Glenbranter. Burke's Landed Gentry (1894-1925).
**McBride** of Baidland. Paterson's Ayr and Wigton, iii. 154.
**McBryde.** Scottish N. and Q., 3rd S., i. 189.
**McCaa** of Barnshalloch. Lands . . . in Galloway, by M'Kerlie, iii. 100, 101.
**McCall.** Some Old Families, by H. B. M'Call, *xxi-xxvii.**
 of Daldowie. Burke's Landed Gentry (1886).
 Dumfriesshire. Inglis of Auchindinny, by J. A. Inglis, 60, 61, 66.
 Glasgow and Philadelphia. Memoirs of my Ancestors, by H. B. M'Call
   (Birmingham, 1864).* Some Old Families, by Hardy Bertram
   M'Call (Birmingham, 1890). Three Pedigrees, 122-141.*
 of Guffockland. Folklore and Genealogies of Uppermost Nithsdale, by
   W. Wilson, 243-244.
**McCartney** of Blaiket. Lands . . . in Galloway, by M'Kerlie, v. 301.
 of Leaths. Lands . . . in Galloway, iii. 254, 256.
**McCaw** of Garrachty. History of County of Bute, by Reid, 241.
**MacChruiter.** Family of Buchanan, by W. Buchanan, 140.
**McClameroch** of Stranfasket. Lands . . . in Galloway, by M'Kerlie,
   iv. 97-98.
**MacClellan(d.** *See* **Maclellan.**
**McClune** of Holmes of Dundonald. Paterson's History of Ayr, ii. 40.
   Paterson's Ayr and Wigton, i. 485.
**McClure**, Colinton. Debrett's Baronetage (1875-1905).
**MacCollae.** Scottish N. and Q., 2nd S., v. 156, 176, 191-192.
**MacColman.** Family of Buchanan, by W. Buchanan, 130-133.
**McCombie.** Memoir of the Family of M'Combie, a branch of the Clan
   M'Intosh, by W. M'C. Smith (1887). Memoir of the Families
   of M'Combie and Thoms . . . by William M'Combie Smith,
   *xiv*+224 pp., portraits (2nd ed., Edinr. 1890). Scottish N. and Q.,
   2nd S., viii. 7.
 of Tillyfour. Scottish N. and Q., 3rd S., i. 59.

**McComie** of Crandart. Warden's Angus or Forfarshire, iii. 381.

**MacConnel.** Facts and Traditions collected for a Family Record, 4to (Edinr. 1861).*

of Knockdolian. Scottish N. and Q., 3rd S., vi. 111.

**McConochie** of Ambrisbeg. History of the County of Bute, by J. E. Reid, 241.

**McCorquodale** of Dalchroy. Burke's Landed Gentry (1886-1925).

of Faintislands. Ancient Scottish Surnames, by W. Buchanan (1723), 97. The Barons of Phantilands, or the MacCorquodales and their Story, by Peter Macintyre, 8vo, n.p., n.d.

**McCrae.** *See* **Macrae.**

**McCririck.** Folk Lore and Genealogies of Uppermost Nithsdale, by W. Wilson, 213-225, 253-254.

**McCubbin** of Knockdolian. Paterson's History of Ayr, i. 306. Paterson's Ayr and Wigton, ii. 161. Scottish N. and Q., 3rd S., vi. 53, 70-71.

of Tradunnock. Scottish N. and Q., 3rd S., vi. 53.

**MacCuffok.** Lands . . . in Galloway, by M'Kerlie, iii. 35.

**McCulloch** of Ardwall. Lands . . . in Galloway, 2nd ed. (1906), i. 357-363 ; (1877), iii. 49-54. The Scottish Antiquary (1896), x. 38-39. Burke's Landed Gentry (1848-1925).

of Auchengool. Lands . . . in Galloway, v. 127.

of Barholm. Lands . . . in Galloway, iv. 259-270.

of Cardoness. Lands . . . in Galloway, iii. 10-14.

of Changue. Paterson's Ayr and Wigton, ii. 120.

of Glastulich and Kindeace. Scottish Antiquary, v. 59-61 ; xii. 170-174.

of Kirkclaugh. Lands . . . in Galloway, iii. 55-56.

of Myrtoun. Lands . . . in Galloway, iii. 14-15. Complete Baronetage, by G. E. C., iii. 347.

of Piltoun. Cramond, by J. P. Wood, 21-22.

of Plaids. Scottish Antiquary, v. 58.

**McCulloch-Jameson** of Ardwall. Burke's Landed Gentry (1848-1925).

**McCurdy.** The Scottish Antiquary, xii. 41.

**McDaniel.** Notes and Queries, 4th S., v. 560 ; vi. 47, 259.

**Macdonald.** History of the Macdonalds, by Donald Gregory ; Scot. Hist. Soc., 2nd S., No. 5 (1914), 4-102. Genealogical Tree of the Families of Macdonald and Macdonell, by John Brown, folio sheet (1792, 1816). Macdonald Family Genealogy to 1876, oblong (1876). The Town of Inverness and the Macdonalds in the 17th Century, by A. Fraser *in* Inverness Scientific Soc. Trans., iii. (1883-1888). Records of Argyll, by Lord Archibald Campbell (1885), 194-202. Scottish N. and Q., 2nd S., vi. History and Genealogy of the Clan Donald, by the Rev. A. Macdonald of Killearnan and the Rev. A. Macdonald of Kiltarlity, illust., 3 vols., 8vo (Inverness, 1896-1904). Macdonald Bards from Mediæval Times, by Keith Norman Macdonald, M.D., 4to (1900).

**Macdonald** of Belfinlay. Antiquarian Notes, by C. Fraser-Mackintosh, ii. 305-310.

of Bohuntin. Antiquarian Notes, by C. Fraser-Mackintosh, ii. 447-448.

of Boisdale. Antiquarian Notes, by C. Fraser-Mackintosh, ii. 322-325.

of Bornish. Antiquarian Notes, by C. Fraser-Mackintosh, ii. 320-322, 449.

of Camuscross. Antiquarian Notes, by C. Fraser-Mackintosh, ii. 272-273.

of Clanranald. Historical and Genealogical Account of the Clan of Macdonald, from Somerlett to the present period, more particularly relating to the senior branch of that family, viz. the Clan Ronald (Edinr. 1819). History of the MacDonalds of Clanranald, by Alex. MacKenzie (Inverness, 1881). Moidart, or Among the Clanranalds, by Rev. Charles MacDonald (Oban, 1889). Antiquarian Notes, by C. Fraser-Mackintosh (1897), i. 12-17, 58 ; ii. 254-256. The Chief of the Clan Donald : Who is He ? by A. R. MacDonald of Clanranald (1905).* The Book of Clan Ranald *in* Reliquæ Celticæ, ii. Burke's Landed Gentry (1848-1925).

Baroness, Baron Clanranald. The Jacobite Peerage, by the Marquis of Ruvigny (1904), 31-37.

of Dalchosnie. Burke's Landed Gentry (1848-1886, 1894).

of Dunaverty. Notes and Queries, 3rd S., xii. 473.

East Sheen. Burke's Peerage and Baronetage. Debrett's Baronetage.

in France. Maurice Supplisson *in* Transactions of Franco-Scottish Soc. (Edinr. 1920), vii. 10, 17-21, 28.

Fraserburgh. Scottish N. and Q., 3rd S., iii. 24.

of Glenaladale. Jonas Howe *in* Acadiensis (St John, N.B., 1901), i. 140-142. Burke's Landed Gentry (1863-1925).

of Glencoe. Notes and Queries, 6th S., x. 28, 154, 212.

of Glengarry. Douglas's Baronage (1798), 563-565. Third Pamphlet and Conclusion of the Raonuillach Controversy, also three letters on same, all from the Inverness Journal (1818), 8vo. Vindication of the Clanronald of Glengary, against the attacks made upon them in the Inverness Journal, by John Riddell (Edinr. 1821). History and Genealogy of the Macdonalds of Glengarry, by Alex. Mackenzie (Inverness, 1881). Burke's Landed Gentry (1848-1858). Antiquarian Notes, by C. Fraser-Mackintosh, ii. 120-152. The Scots Peerage, v. 559-565. The Glengarry MacDonalds of Virginia, by Flora M. Williams (Louisville, 1911). *See also* **Macdonell of Glengarry.**

of Inch Kenneth and Gribune. Burke's Landed Gentry (1848-1875).

of Isla. Historical Account of the Macdonnells of Antrim, including notices of other septs, Irish and Scottish, by George Hill (1873), 1-45. The Last Macdonalds of Isla . . . from original bonds and documents . . . in the possession of Charles Fraser-Mackintosh, 4to, illust. (Glasgow, 1895).

of the Isles. Ancient Scottish Surnames, by Buchanan of Auchmar (1723), 39-50. Douglas's Baronage, 21-23. Genealogical Tree of the Families of Macdonald and Macdonell, by John Brown, folio sheet (1792, 1816). Sketch of the History of the Macdonalds of the Isles ; with four tables, by Alex. Sinclair (Edinr. 1858).* History of the

Macdonalds and Lords of the Isles, with Genealogies, by Alex. MacKenzie, 4to (Inverness, 1881). A Romantic Chapter in Family History, by Alice Bosville Macdonald of the Isles (London, 1911).* Scot. Hist. Review (1912), viii. 249. MacDonald of the Isles, by A. M. W. Stirling (London, 1914). The House of the Isles, by Lady Macdonald of the Isles, 168 pp. [Edinr. 1925].* The Scots Peerage, v. 27-48.

**Macdonald** of Keppoch. A Keppoch Song, a Poem in Five Cantos: being the Origin and History of the Family, alias Donald, Lord of the Isles . . . with a Continuation of the Family of Keppoch ; by John P. Macdonald, Private Teacher in Stonehaven, 8vo, 264 pp. (Montrose, 1815). Family Memoir of the Macdonalds of Keppoch, by Angus Macdonald, M.D., Taunton ; ed. Clements R. Markham, with notes by C. E. Stuart, Comte D'Albanie, 8vo, *xii*+153 pp. (London, 1885).* Antiquarian Notes, by C. Fraser-Mackintosh, i. 197 ; ii. 174-178.

of Kingsburgh. Baronage, by Douglas, 391. Life of Flora Macdonald, by Rev. Alex. Macgregor ; Appendix giving her descendants (1901).

of Largie. Glencreggan, by Cuthbert Bede (1861), ii. 230-241. Burke's Landed Gentry (1886-1925).

of Leeks. Notes and Queries, 4th S., ii. 326, 582.

of Lochgarry. Antiquarian Notes, by C. Fraser-Mackintosh, ii. 191-192.

of Milton. Memoirs of the Jacobites of 1715 and 1745, by Mrs Katherine Thomson, iii. 310. Notes and Queries, 8th S., vi. 6 ; xi. 269 ; xii. 412.

of Moidart. Notes and Queries, 10th S., iv. 30, 84, 376.

of Morar. The Scots Peerage, v. 559-561.

of Murligan. Antiquarian Notes, by C. Fraser-Mackintosh, ii. 164-165.

of Prince Edward Island. Jonas Howe *in* Acadiensis (St John, N.B., 1901), i. *ii., iii.*

of Rammerscales. Burke's Landed Gentry (1848-1925).

Earl of Ross. The Scots Peerage, v. 41-47.

of St Martin's Abbey, and Ranathan. Angus or Forfarshire, by A. J. Warden, iii. 145. Burke's Landed Gentry (1849-1925).

of Sanda. Genealogical and Historical Account of the Family of Macdonald of Sanda (London, 1825). The Genealogist, 1st S., v. 208-210.

of Sandside. Burke's Landed Gentry (1848-1886). Caithness Family History, by Henderson, 251.

of Sleat. Antiquarian Notes, by C. Fraser-Mackintosh, ii. 263-272. The Monros of Auchenbowie, by J. A. Inglis, 78-82. Complete Baronetage, by G. E. C., ii. 291 ; vi., Appx. 79.

Baron Sleat. The Jacobite Peerage, 166-168.

of Stapleton. Rev. J. A. D. J. Macdonald *in* Dumfriesshire and Galloway Antiq. Soc. Trans., 3rd S. (1923), viii. 101.

in U.S.A. Genealogy of the American Branches of the Macdonald Family, by Frank Virgil Macdonald (Newhaven, Conn., 1878, Supplement to above, 1880).

of Vallay. Burke's Landed Gentry (1848-1858).

*See also* The Dictionary of National Biography, *s.v.*

**Macdonald-Lockhart** of Lee and Carnwath.   Burke's Peerage and Baronetage.   Debrett's Baronetage.

**Macdonell.**   Genealogical Tree of the Families of Macdonald and Macdonell, by John Brown, folio sheet (1792, 1816).

of Antrim.   A historical account of the MacDonells of Antrim, including notices of some other septs, Irish and Scottish, by Rev. George Hill, 4to (Belfast and London, 1873 ; London, 1874).

of Barrisdale.   The Scottish Antiquary, vii. 108, 156; viii. 133, 163-164 ; ix. 30-31.   Antiquarian Notes, by C. Fraser-Mackintosh, ii. 152-155, 234.

of Glengarry.   Burke's Landed Gentry (1848-1914).   Antiquarian Notes, by C. Fraser-Mackintosh (1897), ii. 120-152.   Pickle the Spy, by Andrew Lang.   Notes and Queries, 7th S., xii. 9, 135 ; 8th S., iv. 508 ; v. 31.

of Keppoch.   Antiquarian Notes, by C. Fraser-Mackintosh, i. 197 ; ii. 174-178.   The Jacobite Peerage, by the Marquis of Ruvigny, 92-96.

Lord Macdonell and Aros.   The Scots Peerage, v. 559-565.

Baron Macdonell.   The Jacobite Peerage (1904), 85-92.

of Scammadale.   Antiquarian Notes, by C. Fraser-Mackintosh, ii. 152-158.

of Scotus.   Antiquarian Notes, by C. Fraser-Mackintosh, ii. 236.

*See also* **Macdonald.**

**McDouall, McDowall.**   Lands and their Owners in Galloway, by M'Kerlie (1906), i. 280-299.

of Castle Semple.   Crawfurd's Shire of Renfrew (1818).

of Freuch and Balgreggan.   Heraldry, by A. Nisbet (1722), i. 291 ; (1742), ii., Appx. 53-56, 253-258.   Lands . . . in Galloway, 2nd ed. (1906), i. 348-351.   Scottish Antiquary, iii. 155.

of Garthland.   Heraldry, by A. Nisbet, i. 289, 292, 446.   Lands and their Owners in Galloway, by M'Kerlie, 2nd ed. (1906), i. 332-340.   Burke's Landed Gentry (1848-1894).   Notes and Queries, 7th S., i. 169.

of Kingseat.   Buchan and Paton's Peeblesshire, iii. 160.

of Lodvica.   Heraldry, by Nisbet, i. 422-423.   One Year in Sweden, by Marryat, ii. 479-480.

of Logan.   Heraldry, by Nisbet (1722), i. 290, 292 ; (1742), ii. Appx. 104-108.   Historical MSS. Commission (1873), 4th Report, 535.   The Scottish Antiquary (1893), vii. 180-181.   Lands . . . in Galloway (1906), i. 300-310 ; v. 287.   Burke's Landed Gentry (1898-1914).

of Machermoir.   Lands . . . in Galloway (1878), iv. 434-435.

of Stodrig.   Heraldry, by A. Nisbet, i. 291-292.

in U.S.A.   The Ancestry of Benjamin Harrison, President of the U.S.A., by Charles P. Keith (Philadelphia, 1896).

**MacDougal(l.**   Campbell's Records of Argyll (1885), 155-177.   Scottish N. and Q., 2nd S., vi. 130-132.

of Gallanach.   Burke's Landed Gentry (1886-1894).

of Lorn.   Ancient Scottish Surnames, by W. Buchanan (1723), 50-54.   Notes and Queries, 8th S., vii. 168 ; viii. 168, 258.   The Galley of Lorn, publication of the MacDougall Clan, ed. Alex. MacDougall (1899-19   ).

MacDougal(1 of Lunga. Burke's Landed Gentry (1886-1925).
of MacDougal and Dunolly. Burke's Landed Gentry (1848-1925).
of Makerston. Heraldry, by A. Nisbet (1722), i. 291. Genealogical
Table of the Makdougalls of Mackerston, by Sir Wm.
Fraser (Edinr. 1840), with additions by Col. Maitland (1880). One Year in
Sweden, by Marryat, ii. 479. *See also* Scott-Makdougal.
of Raray. Four Old Families, by Capt. Wimberley (1894), 49.

Macdowall-Crichton, Lord Crichton of Sanquhar, Earl of Dumfries.
The Scots Peerage, iii. 236-238.

McDowall-Johnston of Gillespie. Lands . . . in Galloway, by M'Kerlie,
2nd ed. (1906), i. 596. Burke's Landed Gentry (1849-1863).

McDowell of Gillespie. Burke's Landed Gentry (1914).

MacDuff. Memorials of the Family of Macduff (Aberdeen, 1848).
of Bonhard. Burke's Landed Gentry (1886-1925).
of Colonsay. The Book of Colonsay and Oronsay, by Symington
Grieve (Edinr. 1923).

MacEntore. Notes and Queries. 4th S., ii. 487 ; iii. 44, 116, 161,
278, 346.

MacEwan, Macewen. Clan Ewen: some Records of its History, by
R. S. T. Macewen (Glasgow, 1904).

Macfarlan(e. History of the Clan MacFarlan and its Various Branches of
Macfarlane, Macfarlan, Macfarland, Macfarlin, by Mrs C. M. Little,
illust. (Tottenville, N.Y., 1893).* History of Clan MacFarlane, by
James MacFarlane, illust., 171 pp. (Glasgow, 1922).

McFarlan of Ballancleroch. Burke's Landed Gentry (1863-1925).

Macfarlane of Kirkton. Heraldry, by Nisbet (1742), ii., Appx. 85-86.
History of Stirlingshire, by Nimmo, 3rd ed. (1880), ii. 100.
of Macfarlane. Ancient Scottish Surnames, by W. Buchanan (1723),
70-79. Nisbet's Heraldry (1742), ii., Appx. 61-64. Genealogical
Collections, by Walter Macfarlane of that Ilk, 1750-51 ; ed.
J. T. Clark, 2 vols. (Scottish History Soc., Edinr. 1900), i. *v., vi.*
Douglas's Baronage (1784), 93-97. The Scottish Antiquary (1897),
xi. 7-10. Irving's Book of Dumbartonshire, ii. 270-275. Burke's
Landed Gentry (1849), 800.

Macfarlane-Grieve of Penchrise of Edenhall. Burke's Landed Gentry
(1914-1925).

Macfie of Dreghorn. Burke's Landed Gentry (1882-1925).
*See also* Macphee.

McGeorge of Cocklick. Lands . . . in Galloway, v. 317.

MacGeorge of Nether Larg. Burke's Landed Gentry (1863, 1875, 1886).

McGhie of Balmaghie. Lands . . . in Galloway, iii. 107-112.

MacGhillemhuire. *See* Morison.

MacGilbert. Family of Buchanan, by Buchanan of Auchmar, 118.

**McGilchrist** of Tarbart and North Bar. Crawfurd's Shire of Renfrew (1818). *See also* **Gilchrist.**

**MacGill.** Heraldry, by Nisbet (1722), i. 358.
of Cranstoun Riddell and Drylaw. Cramond, by J. P. Wood (1794), 29. Complete Baronetage, by G. E. C., ii. 326 ; iv. 379.

**MacGillean.** Ancient Scottish Surnames, by Buchanan of Auchmar, 56-62.

**Macgillivray.** Confederacy of Clan Chattan, by C. Fraser-Mackintosh (1898), 1-29. Antiquarian Notes, by C. Fraser-Mackintosh, i. 379.
of Dunmaglas. Burke's Landed Gentry (1886). Antiquarian Notes . . . by C. Fraser-Mackintosh (1913), i. *xxxii.*, 4.

**MacGilveil**, Lochaber. Family of Buchanan, by W. Buchanan, 128 *bis*, 129.

**McGoun** of Cameron. Strathendrick, by Guthrie Smith, 218.

**McGowan**, Alloa. MS. Pedigree in the Lyon Office.

**MacGown** of Smithston. Paterson's Ayr, ii. 245.

**MacGregor.** Acts and Orders of the Privy Council of Scotland against the Clan Gregour, 1610-1621 (Maitland Club Misc., 1843). Ancient Scottish Surnames, by Buchanan of Auchmar (1723), 86-89. Historical Memoirs of Rob Roy and the Clan Macgregor, by K. Macleay (Glasgow, 1818, 2nd ed. 1819, 3rd ed. 1881). History of the Clan Macgregor, with details of Rob Roy, by Sir Walter Scott, *Quarterly Review*, 18— (Glasgow and London, 1893). Historical Notices of the Clan Gregor, by Donald Gregory, pt. 1 [all published], 4to (Edinr. 1831).* Memoirs of the Jacobites of 1715 and 1745, by Mrs Katherine Thomson, ii. 155-207. MS. Pedigree of the M'Gregor Family, compiled and written by James Campbell Gracie, Dumfries, 1859 ; and in the Public Library, Dumfries. Pedigree of the Families of MacGregor, Grierson and Greer, folio (Mitchell and Hughes, London, *c.* 1882). History of the Clan Gregor, compiled at the Request of the Clan Gregor Society, by Miss Amelia G. Murray of MacGregor, 2 vols., 4to, with Index (1898-1901). The Dictionary of National Biography, *s.v.*
of Balhaldie. Jacobite Peerage, 96-98.
in Ballimenoch. The Stewarts Magazine, iv. 19.
Balquhidder. History of Stirlingshire, by Nimmo (3rd ed., 1880), ii. 136-151.
of Delavorer. Scottish N. and Q., 2nd S., vi. 13.
of Dunan. Genealogical Tree of the Dunan Family of the Macgregors.
in Gairnlarig. Scottish N. and Q., 2nd S., vi. 13.
of Glengyle. Landed Gentry, by Burke (1849-1879). The Scottish Antiquary (1898), xii. 136, 182 ; xiii. 91-93.
of Glenlyon. Records of the Family of Gregory [by P. S. Gregory], (1886).*
of Glenurquhay. Records of the Family of Gregory.*
Inverness. Scottish N. and Q., iv. 57, 78.
of Leragan. Burke's Landed Gentry (1849).

**MacGregor** of MacGregor. Douglas's Baronage (1784), 493-505. Nisbet's Heraldic Plates, ed. Ross and Grant, 158-161.* Case before the House of Lords in the Dispute between Sir Euan John Murray Macgregor, Bart., of Balquidder, His Eldest Son, and others, against Jas. Brown, Esq., Respondent, regarding the Estates (1840).* Baronage of Angus and Mearns, by D. MacGregor Peter (1856), 377-383. Burke's Peerage and Baronetage. Debrett's Baronetage.

of Roro. Records of the Family of Gregory, 1886.*

of Savile Row. Burke's Peerage and Baronetage. Debrett's Baronetage.

**Macgregor-Murray.** Complete Baronetage, by G. E. C., v. 303.

**Macgregor** *alias* **Skinner,** New Jersey. The Scottish Antiquary, x. 29-30, with cut of arms.

**MacGreusich.** Family of Buchanan, by Buchanan of Auchmar, 140.

**McGrigor** of Cairnoch. Visitation of Seats and Arms, by J. B. Burke (1853), ii. 1. Burke's Landed Gentry (1858-1925).

of Campden Hill. Debrett's Baronetage.

**MacGrouther, MacGruder.** Family of Buchanan, by W. Buchanan, 140. The Macgrouthers of Meiger in Glenartney, by John Macgregor. Repr. from The Genealogist, N. S., xxxv. 65-81 (1919).

**MacGuarie** of MacGuarie. Douglas's Baronage, 506-509.

of Ormaig. Douglas's Baronage, 509-510.

**McGuffie** of Crossmichael. Burke's Landed Gentry (1858-1863).

Dumfriesshire. MS. Pedigree in possession of Mr M'Guffie, Isel, Cumberland.

**MacGuffock** of Rusco. Lands . . . in Galloway, by M'Kerlie, iii. 36-43.

**Macguire,** Ayr. Scot. Hist. Review, xiv. 302-309 ; xv. 88.

of Drumdow. The Dalrymples of Langlands, by John Shaw, 7, 21.* History of the County of Ayr, by Paterson, ii. 386.

of Ochiltree. The Dalrymples of Langlands, 22, 32-35.

of Orangefield. The Dalrymples of Langlands, 22, 37-38.

**MacHardy.** Arms, Crest and Tartan, with a short account of the origin of the name MacHardy, 4to, 4 pp. (London) [1894]. Scottish Notes and Queries, 1st S., vi. 175 ; vii. 143. Confederacy of Clan Chattan, by C. Fraser-Mackintosh, 174.

**MacHeth.** Scot. Hist. Review, xvii. 155, 338 ; xviii. 153-155.

**Machomie.** Scottish N. and Q., 2nd S., viii. 7.

**McIlvaine** of Grimmet. Paterson's History of Ayr, ii. 292. Paterson's Ayr and Wigton, ii. 354-356.

**McIlwraith** of Auchinflower. Paterson's Ayr and Wigton, ii. 93-94.

of Drummurchie. Paterson's History of Ayr, i. 259. Ayr and Wigton, ii. 122.

**MacIndeor.** Munro *v.* Campbell, in House of Lords (1798).

**McIndoe** of Carbeth. Strathblane, by Guthrie Smith, 42, 46, 49 *n*.

**McIntosh.** *See* **Mackintosh.**

**Macintyre** of Badenoch. Confederacy of Clan Chattan, by C. Fraser-Mackintosh, 136-138, 185.

**MacIver.** Account of the Clan Iver, by Principal Campbell, D.D. (Aberdeen, 1868, 1873, 1878) ; genealogical tree. *See also* **Iver.**

of Ashnish. Baronage, by Douglas, 537-539. Burke's Landed Gentry (1899-1925).

*alias* Campbell of Quoycrook. Caithness Family History, by Henderson, 276.

**MacIver - Campbell** of Ballochyle. Burke's Landed Gentry (1894-1925).

**McJarrow** of Barr. Paterson's History of Ayr, i. 258. Ayr and Wigton, ii. 117.

**McKain,** Elgin. The Scottish Antiquary, xi. 93, 94, 138.

**Mackay.** History of the House and Clan of Mackay, . . . with a genealogical table, by Robert Mackay, Thurso, 4to (Edinr. 1829).* The Book of Mackay, by Angus Mackay, illust., 4to (Edinr. and Madoc, Ont., Canada, 1906).

of Achmonie. Urquhart and Glenmoriston, by W. Mackay, Inverness, 2nd ed. (1914), 511-514.

of Bigghouse, Mull. Burke's Landed Gentry (1849-1894).

of Bighouse. Selections from some Family Papers of the Mackays of Bighouse, by D. M. R[ose], (1896-99). The Genealogist, 1st S., v. 20. The Scots Peerage, vii. 165, 174.

of Borley. Life of Lt.-Gen. Hugh Mackay, by John Mackay of Rockfield (new ed., London, 1842), 218-222.

of Farr. Complete Baronetage, by G. E. C., ii. 319. The Scots Peerage, vii. 163-169.

Innis-na-cardoch. Antiquarian Notes, by C. Fraser-Mackintosh, ii. 71, 86-89.

Inverness. Major Alpin's . . . Descendants, by P. J. Anderson (Aberdeen, 1904), 22-25.*

of Melness and Torboll. W. Fowler Carter *in* The Genealogist, 1st S., v. 20-22.

of Ogendale. Ancient Scottish Surnames, by Buchanan (1723), 98.

Lord Reay. The Scots Peerage, vii. 157-179.

of Rhinns. Notes and Queries, 7th S., viii. 129.

of Sandwood. Genealogy of the Family of Mackay, sometime of Sandwood, Kinlochbervie, by Angus Mackay, ed. W. P. W. Phillimore (London, 1904).

of Scoury. Life of Lt.-Gen. Hugh Mackay, by John Mackay of Rockfield (new ed., London, 1842), 217.

Sheuglie. Major Alpin's . . . Descendants, 31-32.

of Strathnaver. The Scots Peerage, vii. 158-169.

in Sweden. Palace of History Catalogue (Glasgow, 1911), 210.

*See also* The Dictionary of National Biography, *s.v.*

**MacKean.** Genealogy of the Family of MacKean of Pennsylvania, by Roberdeau Buchanan (Lancaster, Pa., U.S.A., 1890).

**Mackelcan.** Notes and Queries, 3rd S., i. 49 ; ii, 35.

**MacKelvie.** Scottish N. and Q., 2nd S., viii. 127, 143.

**McKennedy.** Paterson's Ayr and Wigton, ii. 302, 310.

**Mackenzie.** Genealogie of the Mackenzie Family, wreatin in the year 1669, by a Person of Qualitie [Mackenzie of Applecross]; ed. from the original MS. by John W. Mackenzie, with Appx., 4to [Edinr. 1829],* (Dingwall, 1843). [Also as] Collections by John McKenzie of Applecross; Highland Papers, ii. (Scot. Hist. Soc., 1916), 2-68. Genealogical-Historical Account of the Family and Surname of Mackenzie; the Letterfearn MS. in possession of Col. John MacRae-Gilstrap. MS. History of the Mackenzies, by Donald Morrison; in Library of Soc. Antiq. Scotl. History of the Mackenzies from Early Times to the Eighteenth Century; MS. of 477 pp. (c. 1830). Add. MSS. Brit. Mus., 39187-39211. Heraldry, by A. Nisbet (1722), i. 336-337. Thirteen Genealogical Tables containing the Succession of the Various Families of Mackenzie, Kintail, Hilton, Gairloch, Suddee, etc., ed. Major J. D. Mackenzie of Findon (1878-1881). History of the Clan Mackenzie, with Genealogies of the Principal Families, by Alex. Mackenzie (Inverness, 1879 and 1899). The Prophecies of the Brahan Seer, by Alexander Mackenzie (Stirling, 1909). Notes and Queries, 4th S., v. 424 : 5th S., iv. 248 ; v. 88 : 7th S., ix. 148. Dictionary of National Biography, s.v.

**Mackenzie** of Achiltie and Kinnahaird. Geneal. Coll., by Walter Macfarlane, 1750-51 ; Scot. Hist. Soc., i. 82 84.

of Allangrange. Burke's Landed Gentry (1894-1925). The Scots Peerage, vii. 505-506.

Alloa. MS. Pedigree in Lyon Office.

of Applecross. Baronage, by Douglas, 402-403. Burke's Landed Gentry (1848).

of Assynt. The Scots Peerage, vii. 509.

of Balmaduthie. Baronage, by Douglas, 393, 414-415.

Brechin. Scottish N. and Q., 3rd S., iii. 214.

of Caldarvan. Irving's Book of Dumbartonshire, iii., portrait.

of Coigach. Macfarlane's Geneal. Coll., i. 94.

of Coul. Macfarlane's Geneal. Coll., i. 98. Baronage, by Douglas, 400-401. Complete Baronetage, by G. E. C., iv. 296. Burke's Peerage and Baronetage. Debrett's Baronetage.

of Cromarty. The Earls of Cromartie : their Kindred, Country and Correspondence, by William Fraser, 2 vols., illust. (Edinr. 1876).* The Scots Peerage, iii. 69-86. Ancient Deeds and other Writs in the Mackenzie-Wharncliffe Charter Chest, ed. J. W. Barty (Edinr. 1906).*

of Dailuaine. Burke's Landed Gentry (1898-1925).

of Darien. Complete Baronetage, by G. E. C., iv. 413. Debrett's Baronetage.

of Davochmaluak. Macfarlane's Geneal. Coll., i. 78-82. Baronage, by Douglas, 403-404.

of Dundonald. Burke's Landed Gentry (1848).

R

**Mackenzie** of Fairburn. Macfarlane's Geneal. Coll., i. 85-89.

of Farr. Burke's Landed Gentry (1898-1925).

of Findon. Burke's Landed Gentry (1879).

of Finegand. Some Account of the M'Kenzies of Finegand in Glenshee (Blairgowrie, 1889).*

of Flowerburn. Burke's Landed Gentry (1875-1925), *s.v.* Crosbie.

of Gairloch. Macfarlane's Geneal. Coll., i. 60-78. Heraldry, by Nisbet (1742), ii., Appx. 29. Douglas's Baronage, 392-394. Burke's Peerage and Baronetage. Debrett's Baronetage.

of Glack. Scottish N. and Q., 3rd S., vi. 44. Burke's Landed Gentry (1849-1925).

of Glenmuick. Burke's Peerage and Baronetage (after 1890). Debrett's Baronetage (after 1890).

of Grandvale. Complete Baronetage, by G. E. C., ii. 356 ; iv. 427 ; vi., Appx. 80. The Scots Peerage, iii. 75, 76.

of Highfield. Baronage, by Douglas, 418. Burke's Landed Gentry (1921-1925).

of Hiltoun. Baronage, by Douglas, 395. Scottish N. and Q., 3rd S., vi. 44.

of Kilcoy. Macfarlane's Geneal. Coll., i. 97. Baronage, by Douglas, 397-398. Burke's Peerage and Baronetage. Debrett's Baronetage. Burke's Landed Gentry (1898-1925). *See* **Burton-Mackenzie.**

of Killichrist. Macfarlane's Geneal. Coll., i. 89.

Kincardine. Chronicles of the Ardcronie Children, Parish of Kincardine, Ross-shire, 4to, 112 pp. (Toronto, 1893).*

of Kinnock. Macfarlane's Geneal. Coll., i. 96.

of Kintail. Macfarlane's Geneal. Coll., i. 54-78. Burke's Landed Gentry (1879-1886). The Scots Peerage, vii. 496-504.

of Loch Slinn. Macfarlane's Geneal. Coll., i. 100, 102. The Scots Peerage, vii. 504-505.

Lord Mackenzie of Kintail. The Scots Peerage, vii. 504-512.

of MacLeod, in Sweden. One Year in Sweden, by Marryat (1862), ii. 492-493.

Lord Macleod. The Scots Peerage, iii. 75-82.

of Mornish. Burke's Landed Gentry (1879-1925).

of Muirton. Burke's Landed Gentry (1848-1858).

of Newhall. Burke's Landed Gentry (1898-1925).

North Berwick. MS. Pedigree in Lyon Office.

of Ord. Baronage, by Douglas, 417. Burke's Landed Gentry (1848-1925).

in Orkney. The Frotoft Branch of the Orkney Traills, by T. W. Traill (1902), 44-51.*

of Pluscardine. Macfarlane's Geneal. Coll., i. 101. Antiquarian Notes, by C. Fraser-Mackintosh, i. 165-170.

of Portmore. Genealogical Table showing the origin and the direct and collateral descent of the Family of Mackenzie of Portmore, by Colin Mackenzie, 78th Highlanders, 2 folio sheets.* History of Peeblesshire, by Chambers, 355. Buchan and Paton's History of Peeblesshire, ii. 505-507. Burke's Landed Gentry (1848-1925).

**Mackenzie** of Redcastle. Macfarlane's Geneal. Coll., i. 92-93. Baronage, by Douglas, 398-400. Sketches of Highland Families, by J. Maclean (1848, 1895), 119-137.

of Rosehaugh. Ancient Deeds and other Writs in the Mackenzie-Wharncliffe Charter Chest, with short notices of Sir G. Mackenzie of Rosehaugh, etc., ed. by J. W. Barty, 4to, illust. (100 copies) (Edinr. 1906).* The Scots Peerage, vii. 505. A. M. Williams *in* Scot. Hist. Review, xiii. 138-148.

of Roystoun. Complete Baronetage, by G. E. C., iv. 425.

of Scatwell. Baronage, by Douglas, 396-397. Complete Baronetage, by G. E. C., iv. 408. Debrett's Baronetage. Burke's Peerage and Baronetage.

of Seaforth. The Seaforth Papers : Letters from 1796 to 1843.* [Very rare.] Genealogical Tree of the Seaforth Family and those descended from them, preceding 1667 ; large folio MS. The Genealogy of the Stem of the Family of Mackenzie, Marquesses and Earls of Seaforth, mentioning also the Cadet branches of the Family, by Sir E. Mackenzie, Bart. (1904).* The Scots Peerage, vii. 495-515.

Marquis of Seaforth. The Jacobite Peerage, by the Marquis of Ruvigny (1904), 162.

of Strickathrow. Baronage of Angus and Mearns, by D. M. Peter (1856), 221.

of Suddy. Baronage, by Douglas, 415-417.

of Tarbat. Complete Baronetage, by G. E. C., ii. 355.

Viscount Tarbat. The Scots Peerage, iii. 75-80.

**Mackenzie-Gillanders** of Highfield. Burke's Landed Gentry (1914-1925).

**McKerlie**, Wigtownshire. Lands and their Owners in Galloway, by John M'Kerlie (1906), i. 454 ; v. 351. Burke's Landed Gentry (1863).

**McKerrell** of Hillhouse. Paterson's History of the County of Ayr, ii. 32-34. Paterson's Ayr and Wigton, i. 480-485. The Browns of Fordell, by Stodart, 196-199. Herald and Genealogist, vi. 411-414. Burke's Landed Gentry (1848-1925).

**McKessack.** Herald and Genealogist, vi. 594.

**Mackie** of Auchencairn. Lands . . . in Galloway, v. 94. Burke's Landed Gentry (1879-1925).

of Corraith. Burke's Landed Gentry (1906-1914).

of Fulwood. Pont's Cuninghame, ed. Dobie, 138-139.

**McKie** of Bargaly. Lands . . . in Galloway, iv. 453 ; v. 386. Burke's Landed Gentry (1858-1925).

of Larg. Lands . . . in Galloway, iv. 405-410.

of Netherlaw. Lands . . . in Galloway, v. 96.

of Palgown. Lands . . . in Galloway, iv. 458.

**Mackieson**, Crail. Churchyard Monuments of Crail, by Erskine Beveridge, 126-131.

**McKilligan**, Banff. Scottish N. and Q., 2nd S., v. 125.

**McKillop.** Notes and Queries, 7th S., ii. 407, 478 ; iii. 94.

of Westhaugh. Logie, by Rev. R. Menzies Fergusson, ii. 218-219.

**Mackinlay.** Family of Buchanan, by W. Buchanan, 141-142.

The Annie. The Stirling Antiquary, iii. 257-260.

in Auchinribach. The Stirling Antiquary, iii. 260.

**McKinley.** Notes and Queries, 8th S., xi. 427, 518.

**Mackinnon.** Genealogical Account of the Family of Mackinnon, by Sir A. Mackenzie Downie and A. D. Mackinnon, (Plymouth, 1882), republished by Lauchlan Mackinnon of Duisdale, Skye, 14 pp. (London, 1883). Reply to the above by the Author of Memoirs of Clan Fingon (T. Wells) [1884]. Memoirs of the Clan Fingon, with chapter on the Antiqua branch and an account of those settled in Nova Scotia, Australia, etc., by the Rev. Donald D. Mackinnon (Tunbridge Wells [1884] and 1899).* Dictionary of National Biography, *s.v.*

Antigua. Oliver's History of Antigua, ii. 224-230.

of Antiqua. Oban Times (16th July 1927, *et seqq.*).

of Bittacy. Burke's Landed Gentry (1863).

of Corry. Antiquarian Notes, by C. Fraser-Mackintosh, ii. 280-283.

of Mackinnon. Burke's Landed Gentry (1848-1925).

Naples. The Petition of Alexander Mackinnon, late Merchant at Naples, to His Majesty in Council, with Appendix, 4to, $v+218+38+8+15$ pp. (1805-6).

**Mackintosh, MacIntosh.** The Macintosh Muniment, 1442-1820, edited and abridged by Henry Paton, 4to (1903). The Loyall Dissuasive, and other Papers concerning the affairs of Clan Chattan, by Sir Æneas Macpherson, Knight of Invereshie, 1691-1705 ; ed. Rev. A. D. Murdoch (Scot. Hist. Soc., 1902). Ancient Scottish Surnames, by Buchanan of Auchmar, 65-68. Heraldry, by Nisbet (1742), ii., Appx. 46-49. Geneal. Coll., by Walter Macfarlane, 1750-51 ; Scot. Hist. Soc., i. 144-407. Historical Memoirs of the House and Clan of Mackintosh, and of the Clan Chattan, by Alex. Mackintosh Shaw (London, 1880), 2nd ed., by A. M. Mackintosh [the same author] (1903).* The Family of Baillie of Dunain, etc., by J. G. B. Bulloch (1898).* Account of the Minor Septs of the Clan Chattan, by Charles Fraser-Mackintosh, tartans, portraits, etc., 4to (1898).

**Mackintosh** of Aberarder. Antiquarian Notes, by C. Fraser-Mackintosh, ii. 430-433.

of Balnespick. Burke's Landed Gentry (1875-1925).

of Borlum. Historical and Traditional Sketches of Highland Families, by John Maclean (1848, 1895), 1-53. Brigadier Mackintosh of Borlum, by A. M. M[ackintosh], 64 pp. (Nairn, 1918).* Notes and Queries, 7th S., i. 328 ; ii. 30 ; v. 446.

of Campsie. Memoir of C. Mackintosh of Campsie and Dunchattan, by his son (Glasgow, 1847).*

of Connage. Antiquarian Notes, by C. Fraser-Mackintosh, i. 136-147.

of Corrybrough More. The Balfours of Pilrig, by B. Balfour-Melville, 273.

**Mackintosh** of Dalmunzie. Confederacy of Clan Chattan, by C. Fraser-Mackintosh (1898), 177. Scot. Hist. Review (1917), xiii. 421. Burke's Landed Gentry (1858-1925).

of Gellovie. Antiquarian Notes, by C. Fraser-Mackintosh, ii. 336, 340.

Georgia. Scottish N. and Q., 3rd S., iv. 57-58, 209.

in Glenshee. Mackintosh Families in Glenshee and Glenisla, by A. M. Mackintosh (Nairn, 1916), *iv*+86 pp.,* *reviewed in* Scot. Hist. Review, xiv. 29. Scottish N. and Q., 2nd S., viii. 7-8.

Kirkhill. Antiquarian Notes, by C. Fraser-Mackintosh, ii. 17, 19.

of Lamancha. Buchan and Paton's Peeblesshire, iii. 64.

of Mackintosh. Douglas's Baronage, 347-353. Burke's Extinct Baronetcies. Burke's Landed Gentry (1848-1925). Antiquarian Notes, by C. Fraser-Mackintosh (1897, 1913), i. 23-27, 82-85, 173, 378; ii. 158-162, 206, 407.

Baron Mackintosh. The Jacobite Peerage, by the Marquis of Ruvigny (1904), 98-101.

of Raitts. Sketches of Highland Families, by John Maclean (1848), 33, 53.

of Rothiemurchus. Antiquarian Notes, by C. Fraser-Mackintosh, ii. 411.

in Rutherglen. Notes and Queries, 7th S., viii. 473 ; x. 177.

**MacKirdy.** History of County of Bute, by Reid, 254. The Scottish Antiquary, xii. 41.

of Birkwood. Burke's Landed Gentry (1849-1894).

**MacKnight** of Ratho. Ayrshire Families, by G. Robertson, i. 244.

**Mackrabie.** Notes and Queries, 4th S., v. 533 ; vi. 123.

**MacLachlan** of Kilbride. Campbell's Records of Argyll, 181-186.

of Maclachlan. Ancient Scottish Surnames, by Buchanan of Auchmar (1723), 82-84. Burke's Landed Gentry (1849-1925).

**McLae.** Glasgow Past and Present (1856), iii. 550.

**Maclagan.** The Clan of the Bell of St Fillans, by R. C. Maclagan, M.D. (Edinr. 1879).*

of Glenquiech. Baronage of Angus and Mearns, by D. M. Peter, 224.

**MacLaine** of Lochbuie. Baronage, by Douglas, 369-371. Burke's Landed Gentry (1848-1925).

**Maclaren** in Anie. Scottish N. and Q., 3rd S., iii. 192.

in Sweden. Palace of History Catalogue (Glasgow, 1911), 204.

**Maclaurin.** Scottish N. and Q., 2nd S., vi. 163-164. *See also* **Laurin.**

**Maclean.** Ancient Scottish Surnames, by Buchanan (1723), 56-62. Geneal. Coll., by Macfarlane, 1750-51 ; Scot. Hist. Soc., i. 118-143. Historical and Genealogical Account of the Clan of Maclean, from its first Settlement . . . by a Seneachie [John Campbell Sinclair] (London and Edinr., 1838). History of Clan Tarlach o' Bui, by Lt.-Col. Charles M. M'Lean (Aberdeen, 1865). Brief Genealogical Account of the Family of M'Lean [by Alex. M'Lean] (Edinr. 1872).* History of the Clan MacLean . . . by J. P. MacLean, illust. (Cincinnati, 1889). The Clan Maclean, pamphlet (Glasgow, 1893). The Clan Gillean, by Rev. A. Maclean Sinclair (Charlottetown, 1899). Scottish Notes and Queries, 2nd S., vi., vii.

**Maclean** of Ardgour.  Burke's Landed Gentry (1849-1925).

of Borreray.  MS. Pedigree, 934 ; Society of Genealogists, London.

of Coll.  Baronage, by Douglas, 372-373.

of Cuidrach.  Wm. Mackenzie *in* Glasgow Herald (14th May 1898).

of Dochgarroch.  Antiquarian Notes, by C. Fraser-Mackintosh (1897), ii. 38-55.  Confederacy of Clan Chattan, by C. Fraser-Mackintosh (1898), 129-135.

of Duart.  Douglas's Baronage, 365-369.  Memoirs of the Jacobites of 1715 and 1745, by Mrs Katherine Thomson, ii. 124-154.  Papers relating to the Macleans of Duart ; Scot. Hist. Soc., i., 2nd S., 5 (1914), 242-337.  Jacobite Peerage, 101-103.  Burke's and other Annual Baronetages.

Baron Maclean.  The Jacobite Peerage, by the Marquis of Ruvigny (1904), 101-103.

of Mark.  Lands . . . in Galloway, by M'Kerlie, iv. 292 ; v. 375.

of Morven.  Douglas's Baronage, 365-369.  Burke's Peerage and Baronetage.  Debrett's Baronetage.  Complete Baronetage, by G. E. C., ii. 394.

of Penny Cross.  Burke's Landed Gentry (1849-1925).

Peterhead.  Scottish N. and Q., 3rd S., iii. 152.

in Sweden.  One Year in Sweden, by Marryat (1862), ii. 483-484.  Complete Baronetage, by G. E. C., iii. 324.

of Torloisk.  Notes and Queries, 3rd S., i. 329, 395.

of Westfield.  Burke's Landed Gentry (1894-1925).

**Macleare**, Sweden.  Complete Baronetage, by G. E. C. (1903), iii. 324.

**Macleay.**  Scottish N. and Q., 2nd S., v. 156, 176, 191-192.

of Keiss.  Burke's Landed Gentry (1848-1875).

**Maclellan(d.**  Notice *in* Moffat's History of Moffats.*

of Auchlane.  Lands . . . in Galloway, by M'Kerlie, iv. 114-116.

of Auchengool.  Lands . . . in Galloway, v. 126.

of Balmangan.  Lands . . . in Galloway, iii. 203-206.  The Scots Peerage, v. 270-271.

of Barmagachan.  Lands . . . in Galloway, iii. 195-196.

of Barscobe.  Lands . . . in Galloway, iii. 67-68.

of Bombie.  Lands . . . in Galloway, iv. 193-205.  Complete Baronetage, by G. E. C., ii. 392.  The Scots Peerage, v. 257, 258-264.  Maclellan of Kirkcudbright and Bombie, by John Maclellan (1874, 1906).*

of Borness.  The Scots Peerage, v. 271.

Cundry.  Lands . . . in Galloway, v. 101.

of Gelston.  Lands . . . in Galloway, iv. 108-109.

of Kirkcudbright.  Lands and their Owners in Galloway, by M'Kerlie, iv. 194 ; v. 364-371.  Record of the House of Kirkcudbright, by John MacClellan (1874), 2nd ed., 40 pp. (Dumfries, 1906).*

Lord Kirkcudbright.  The Case of Lt. John M'Clellan, claiming the title of Lord Kirkcudbright, with addl. appx. : (Session Papers, Dec. 176– to April 1769).  The Scots Peerage, v. 256-274.

of Nunton.  The Scots Peerage, v. 260-261.

**MacLeod.** History of the MacLeods, with genealogies of the principal families of the name, by Alexander Mackenzie (Edinr. 1888 ; Inverness, 1889). The MacLeods ; a short sketch of their clan history, folk-lore, tales, and biographical notices of some eminent clansmen, by the Rev. R. C. Macleod of Macleod, 120 pp., illust. (Clan Macleod Society, Edinr. 1906). Scottish N. and Q., 2nd S., vii., *passim*.

of Assynt and Geanies. Baronage, by Douglas, 384, 387-388.

of Bernera and Muiravenside. Baronage, by Douglas, 378, 381-383.

of Cadboll. Burke's Commoners, ii. 175. Burke's Landed Gentry (1848-1925).

of Colbecks. Antiquarian Notes, by C. Fraser-Mackintosh, ii. 279.

of Drynoch. Scottish N. and Q., 3rd S., vii. 17-18.

of Dunvegan. History of the Macleods of Dunvegan and Lewis, 463 pp. (Inverness, 18—). The MacLeods of Dunvegan, by Rev. Canon R. C. MacLeod of MacLeod, $xx+220$ pp., 25 illust. (1927).

of Flashadder. History of the Habersham Family, by Dr J. G. B. Bulloch (Columbia, S.C., 1901), 97.

of Glendale and Meidle. The Jacobite Peerage, by the Marquis of Ruvigny (1904), 108-111.

of Grishernish. Baronage, by Douglas, 378, 383.

of Hammer. Baronage, by Douglas, 378, 383.

of Harris. Antiq. Notes, by C. Fraser-Mackintosh (1897), ii. 242-244.

of Lewis. Baronage, by Douglas, 384-385. Highland Papers, ii. ; Scot. Hist. Soc. (1916), 262-288.

of Luskinder. Ayrshire Families, by G. Robertson, i. 67 *n.*

of MacLeod. Ancient Scottish Surnames, by Buchanan of Auchmar (1723), 62-64. Baronage, by Douglas, 374-380. Ayrshire Families, by G. Robertson (1823), i. 66 *n.* Burke's Commoners, iii. 476, 479. Burke's Landed Gentry (1848-1925).

Baron Macleod. The Jacobite Peerage, by the Marquis of Ruvigny (1904), 104-108.

of Rasay. Baronage, by Douglas, 386. Burke's Commoners, iv. 584. Burke's Landed Gentry (1848).

of Talisker. Baronage, by Douglas, 380-381.

**Macleod,** Mackenzie, Lord. The Scots Peerage, iii. 74-82.

**Macleod of Castle Leod,** Hay-Mackenzie, Baron. The Scots Peerage, iii. 84-86.

**McLiver** of Kilchoman. Burke's Landed Gentry (1894).

**McMath** of Dalpeddar. Folklore and Genealogies of Uppermost Nithsdale, by Wilson, 231-233.

**Macmaurice.** Family of Buchanan, by Buchanan, 138-140.

**McMeikin** of Kilsanctniniane. Paterson's Ayr and Wigton, ii. 157. Herald and Genealogist, vi. 140-143.

**McMicking** of Miltonise. Lands . . . in Galloway, by M'Kerlie (2nd ed., 1906), i. 612-614 ; v. 341. Burke's Landed Gentry (1849-1925).

**McMikin Craufuird** of Grange. Scottish N. and Q., 3rd S., iv. 163. Burke's Landed Gentry (1894-1925).

**MacMillan.** The Clan Macmillan, addresses given to the Clan Society, by Hugh Macmillan, D.D. (1901).* The Book of Colonsay and Oronsay, by Symington Grieve (1923).

of Antrim. Family of Buchanan, by W. Buchanan, 129.

of Brockloch. Lands and their Owners in Galloway, by M'Kerlie, iii. 302, 305.

Carsphairn. Lands . . . in Galloway, iii. 286.

of Dalshangan. Lands . . . in Galloway, iii. 316.

in Dumbarton. Irving's Book of Dumbartonshire, iii., portrait.

of Dunmore. Family of Buchanan, 128.

of Holm of Dalquhain. Lands . . . in Galloway, iii. 303-305. Burke's Landed Gentry (1894-1925).

of Knap. Family of Buchanan, 124-128.

of Lamloch and Changue. Paterson's History of Ayr, i. 260. Paterson's Ayr and Wigton, ii. 120-121. Lands . . . in Galloway, iii. 103, 306-307.

Viewforth. The Stirling Antiquary, ii. 220-223.

**Macmillan Scott** of Wauchope and Pinnaclehill. Annals of a Border Club, by G. Tancred, 433-434. Burke's Landed Gentry (1875-1925).

**McMin.** Churchyard Monuments of Crail, by Erskine Beveridge, 156.

**MacMorran** of Newhall. East Neuk of Fife, by W. Wood (1887), 459.

**McMurdo.** Lands . . . in Galloway, by M'Kerlie, v. 251-253.

**Macnab.** The Clan Macnab, by John M'Nab, 8vo, illust. (Clan Macnab Association, Edinr. 1907). Recreations of an Antiquary, by Fittis, 469-498.

in France. Maurice Supplisson *in* Transactions of Franco-Scottish Society (Edinr. 1920), vii. 10, 15, 21-23.

of MacNab. Douglas's Baronage, 389-390. Lairds and Lands of Loch Tayside, by John Christie (Aberfeldy, 1892), 66-70.

of Middleton Kerse. Logie, by Rev. Dr Menzies Fergusson, ii. 174-176.

**McNabb,** Dollar. The Dollar Magazine (1927), xxvi. 122-126, 183-188.

**MacNair.** M'Nair, M'Near, and M'Neir Genealogies, compiled by James Birtley M'Nair, 8vo, *viii*+315 pp., illust. (Chicago, 1923). *See also* Scot. Hist. Review, xxi. 164.

of Aucheneck. Strathendrick, by Guthrie Smith, 218-219.

of Foss. Scottish N. and Q., xii. 129.

**MacNauchtan** of MacNauchtan. Heraldry, by Nisbet (1722), i. 419. Ancient Scottish Surnames, by W. Buchanan (1723), 84-86. Douglas's Baronage, 418-420. Campbell's Records of Argyll (1885), 46-49. Scottish History Society, No. 56 (1908), *lxxxiii.* Highland Papers, i. ; Scot. Hist. Soc., 2nd S., No. 5 (1914), 105-113.

**McNaught** of Kilquhanity. Lands . . . in Galloway, by M'Kerlie, iv. 298-300.

**McNeight** of Barns. Paterson's History of Ayr, i. 209. Paterson's Ayr and Wigton, i. 131.

**MacNeil(l.** Ancient Scottish Surnames, by W. Buchanan, 54-56. The Book of Colonsay and Oronsay, by Symington Grieve (1923). The Clan Macneil, Clann Niall of Scotland, by R. L. Macneil of Barra (New York, 1923).

of Barra. Burke's Landed Gentry (1848-1858). Antiquarian Notes, by C. Fraser-Mackintosh (1897), ii. 331-333.

of Colonsay. Burke's Landed Gentry (1886-1925).

of Gigha. Burke's Landed Gentry (1846-1879).

in Knapdale. The Genealogist, N. S., xxxvi. 121-123.

**MacNeil-Hamilton** of Raploch. Burke's Landed Gentry (1863-1925).

**McNeile** of Kippilaw. Burke's Landed Gentry (1914-1925).

**McNeilie** of Auchairne. Paterson's Ayr and Wigton, ii. 92.

**MacNeish.** The History of the Clan Neish or MacNish of Perthshire and Galloway, by David Macnish and William A. Tod (Edinr. 1925).

**McNish,** Dumfries. Oliver's History of Antigua, ii. 230-232.

**Macolagh.** Scot. Hist. Review, xxiv. 260.

**Maconochie** of Meadowbank and Pitliver. Eminent Men of Fife, by M. F. Conolly (Cupar, 1866), 316-317. Annals of a Border Club, by G. Tancred, 322-324. Burke's Landed Gentry (1848-1925).

**Maconochie-Wellwood** of Kirknewton and Garvock. Burke's Landed Gentry (1848-1925).

**McOran.** Life of Sir H. Campbell-Bannerman, by Spender (1923), i. 1-2.

**MacPhail.** Antiquarian Notes, by C. Fraser-Mackintosh, i. 381. Family and Genealogical Sketches, by Rev. Thomas Sinton (Inverness, 1911).*

of Inverairnie. Confederacy of Clan Chattan, by C. Fraser-Mackintosh, 57-62, 182.

**MacPhee, Macfie.** The Book of Colonsay and Oronsay, by Symington Grieve, 2 vols., illust. (Edinr. 1923).

**Macpherson.** Heraldry, by Nisbet (1722), i. 424. Ancient Scottish Surnames, by Buchanan (1723), 65-68. The Loyall Dissuasive, by Sir Æneas Macpherson; Scot. Hist. Soc., (1902). Dictionary of National Biography, *s.v.*

Aberdeenshire. Scottish N. and Q., 2nd S., vi. 105, 108.

Benchar. Scottish N. and Q., 2nd S., vii. 109, 141.

of Blairgowrie. Baronage of Angus and Mearns, by Peter, 230.

of Breakachie. Baronage, by Douglas, 363-364. Antiquarian Notes, by C. Fraser-Mackintosh, 361-363.

of Brin. Baronage, by Douglas, 362.

Calcutta. Burke's Extinct Baronetcies. Complete Baronetage, by G. E. C., v. 249.

of Cluny Macpherson. Douglas's Baronage, 354-359. Burke's Landed Gentry (1848-1925). Antiquarian Notes . . . by C. Fraser-Mackintosh, i. 40, 379; ii. 306-360. Scottish N. and Q., 3rd S., v. 221.

**Macpherson** of Corries. Notes respecting the Family of M'Pherson or M'William of Corries, etc., Glenlivet, by H. Duff-MacWilliam (1903).* Scottish N. and Q., 2nd S., v. 48.

of Dalraddie. Baronage, by Douglas, 361. Antiquarian Notes, by C. Fraser-Mackintosh, ii. 390-391. Scottish N. and Q., 2nd S., v. 174.

of Essich. Baronage, by Douglas, 365.

of Glentruim. Burke's Landed Gentry (1898-1925).

of Grange. Antiquarian Notes, by C. Fraser-Mackintosh, ii. 346-347.

of Inneressie, Invereshie. Baronage, by Douglas, 361. Antiquarian Notes, by C. Fraser-Mackintosh, 390-394. Burke's Peerage and Baronetage. The Loyall Dissuasive ; Scot. Hist. Soc. (1902)

of Ovie. Antiquarian Notes, by C. Fraser-Mackintosh, ii. 71, 364.

of Phoness. Baronage, by Douglas, 361-362. Antiquarian Notes, by C. Fraser-Mackintosh, ii. 375-380.

of Pitmean. Baronage, by Douglas, 359.

Ruthven. Scottish N. and Q., 3rd S., iii. 124, 140.

of Strathmassie. Baronage, by Douglas, 362-363.

in Sweden, etc. Scot. Hist. Review, ix. 448-450.

**Macpherson-Grant** of Ballindalloch. Burke's Peerage and Baronetage.

**McPhun.** Notes and Queries, 11th S., vii. 470.

**McPike.** Scottish N. and Q., 2nd S., vi. 119 ; 3rd S., vi. 12-16, 38.

**MacQuarie** of Ormaig. Burke's Landed Gentry (1848). *See also* **MacGuarie.**

**Macqueen** of Braxfield. Annals of a Tweeddale Parish, by Rev. A. Baird, 46-50. Some Old Scots Judges, by W. Forbes Gray, 98-122. Buchan and Paton's Peeblesshire, iii. 259-261.

of Corrybrough. Burke's Landed Gentry (1848-1886). Confederacy of Clan Chattan, 63-76, 183.

of Pollochaig. Antiquarian Notes, by C. Fraser-Mackintosh, ii. 427. Confederacy of Clan Chattan, by C. Fraser-Mackintosh, 77.

of Raigmore. Confederacy of Clan Chattan, 78.

**McQuyre** of Drumdow. Paterson's Ayr and Wigton, i. 596-598.

**MacRae.** The Genealogy of the MacRas, by Rev. John MacRa, minister of Dingwall, 1698. [The original MS. is lost, but several copies exist in MS., and one was printed privately by Robin MacRae, of the family of Conchra (Camden, So. Carolina, 1874),* also by] Scot. Hist. Soc., 2nd S. (1914), v. 196-239. Genealogical Account of the MacRaes as written originally by Mr John MacRae, 1704 ; transcribed 1786 ; the Ardintoul MS. in possession of Col. John Macrae-Gilstrap. History of the Clan Macrae, with Genealogies, by Rev. Alex. Macrae (Dingwall, 1899).* The Clan Macrae, with its Rolls of Honour and Service, by E. MacRae-Gilstrap (Aberdeen, 1923).

of Feoirlin. Burke's Landed Gentry (1921-1925).

of Holmains. Paterson's History of Ayr, ii. 386. Sir Herbert Maxwell *in* Scot. Hist. Review, xiv. 301. Burke's Landed Gentry (1858-1863).

**MacRae** of Orangefield, Ochiltree, Houston. Paterson's Ayr, ii. 385.
Paterson's Ayr and Wigton, i. 596-598. The Dalrymples of Langlands, by J. Shaw, 7-32.*
of Wellbank. Monifieth, by J. Malcolm, 355.

**Macrae-Gilstrap** of Ballimore. Burke's Landed Gentry (1898-1925).

**MacRankine.** Paterson's History of Ayr, ii. 375.

**Macredie** of Peirceton. Pont's Cuninghame, ed. Dobie, 350. Ayrshire Families, by G. Robertson (1824), ii. 70-72. Paterson's History of Ayr, i. 449. Paterson's Ayr and Wigton, iii. 201-202. Burke's Landed Gentry (1875-1894).

**MacRob.** Family of Buchanan, by W. Buchanan, 107.
*alias* Stewart. The Stewarts of Appin, 184-185.

**McTaggart** of Ardwall. Lands . . . in Galloway, by M'Kerlie (2nd ed. 1906), i. 364-366.

**McTaggart-Stewart** of Southwick. Burke's Peerage and Baronetage.

**McTavish,** Breadalbane. Scottish N. and Q., vi. 149.
of that Ilk and Dunardrie. Sheet Pedigree ; Society of Genealogists (D. MSS. 832).

**MacThomas.** Family of Buchanan, by Buchanan, 142.

**Mactier** of Durris. Baronage of Angus and Mearns, by D. M. Peter, 230.

**McVean,** Mull. Confederacy of Clan Chattan, by C. Fraser-Mackintosh, 182.

**MacWattie.** Family of Buchanan, by Buchanan of Auchmar, 105-106.

**MacWilliam.** Notes and Queries, 7th S., ii. 468 ; iii. 15, 117. Scottish N. and Q., 2nd S., iii. 189 ; iv. 61, 76 ; vii. 58, 74, 85, 92, 125, 141.
of Corries. Notes respecting the Family of M'Pherson or M'William of Corries, etc., Glenlivet, by H. Duff-MacWilliam (1903).*
in Mortlach. The Stewarts Magazine, ii. 74-83, 117-126.

**MacWillie.** Scottish N. and Q., 2nd S., vii. 58, 64 ; viii. 46.

**Madertie,** Drummond, Lord. The Scots Peerage, viii. 216-238.

**Maitland.** A Short Genealogy of the Family of Maitland [by Professor A. Dalzel] (Edinr. 1785, 1868, 1875).* Historical MSS. Commission (1876), 5th Report. Genealogical and Historical Account of the Maitland Family . . . by G. H. Roger Harrison, Windsor Herald, 4to (London, 1860, 1869).* Genealogical Tree of the Family of Maitland, Earl of Lauderdale, compiled by John Maitland in 1828, enlarged by Col. F. T. Maitland, sheet 4 ft. 3 in. × 3 ft. (1880). Misc. Geneal. et Heraldica, ii. 205-213. Notes and Queries, 7th S., i. 48, v. 334. Pedigrees of the Family of James of Culgarth (Exeter, 1913).*

**Maitland** of Barcaple. Lands . . . in Galloway, by M'Kerlie, v. 198-200.
Bass Rock. The Scottish Antiquary, viii. 43 ; ix. 95-96. Erminois, by Rev. C. Moor (Kendal, 1918), 137-138.

Maitland of Dundrennan. Lands . . . in Galloway, v. 74-75. Pedigrees of the Maitland Family of Dundrennan, N.B., and Otago, New Zealand, by G. H. Roger Harrison, Windsor Herald (1905). Burke's Landed Gentry (1848-1925).

of Eccles. Burke's Landed Gentry (1875-1882).

of Fairgarth. Lands . . . in Galloway, by M'Kerlie, iii. 339-341.

of Freugh. Burke's Landed Gentry (1858-1894). The Scots Peerage, v. 316.

of Gight. Pedigree in Notes and Queries (1861), 2nd S., xi. 249, 337.

of Gimmersmills. The Scottish Antiquary, viii. 93-94.

of Halsington. Peeblesshire Localities, by Renwick, 547.

of Holywich. Burke's Landed Gentry (1848).

Inverkeithing. Tayler's Jacobites of Aberdeenshire, 346.

Earl of, Viscount of, Duke of Lauderdale. Minutes of Evidence, and Judgment in the Lauderdale Peerage Case, folio. The Scottish Antiquary, xv. 221. The Scots Peerage, v. 276-323. G. E. C.'s Complete Peerage.

of Lethington. Maitland of Lethington and the Scotland of Mary Stuart, by John Skelton (Edinr. 1887-88). The House of Seton, by G. Seton (1896), 42. The Scots Peerage, v. 280-299. E. Russell in Scot. Antiq. xvii. 57-71. W. S. M'Kechnie in Scot. Hist. Review, iv. 274-293. Maurice Williamson in Scot. Hist. Review, xxv. 19-29.

London. Scottish N. and Q., 2nd S., i. 94.

Viscount Maitland. The Scots Peerage, v. 302-323.

Marquess of March. The Scots Peerage, v. 305.

Montrose. Pyott or Maitland Pedigree, compiled by Horatius Bonar, W.S. (1914).

of Pittrichie. Heraldry, by Nisbet (1722), i. 441. Burke's Extinct Baronetage. Complete Baronetage, by G. E. C., iv. 288. The Scots Peerage, i. 309. Thanage of Fermartyn, by Temple, 449-454. Scottish N. and Q., 1st S., xi. 31 ; 3rd S., iii. 124.

of Rankeillour. Eminent Men of Fife, by M. F. Conolly, 317-319. The Scots Peerage, v. 315, 316.

of Ravelrig. Complete Baronetage, by G. E. C., iv. 310.

of Soltra. The Scottish Antiquary, viii. 91-95.

Lord Thirlestane. Heraldry, by Nisbet (1722), i. 292-294. Peeblesshire Localities, by Renwick, 42. The Scots Peerage, v. 278-323.

of Tillicoultry. The Scots Peerage, v. 311-312.

of Traquair. Peeblesshire Localities, by Renwick, 546, 547. The Scots Peerage, v. 282.

Maitland-Dougall of Scotscraig. Burke's Landed Gentry (1894-1925).

Maitland-Gordon of Kenmure. Burke's Landed Gentry (1894-1925).

Maitland-Kirwan of Gelston Castle. Burke's Landed Gentry (1898-1925).

Maitland-Makgill-Crichton of Rankeilour. Eminent Men of Fife, by Conolly, 134. Herald and Genealogist, v. 171. Burke's Landed Gentry (1879).

**Makdougal** of Makerston. Nisbet's Heraldry, i. 291. Pedigree, by Sir Wm. Fraser (1840), 2nd ed. (1880).

**Makgill** of Cranston Riddell. The Scots Peerage, vi. 591-598.
of Kemback. The Scots Peerage, vi. 590. Burke's Peerage and Baronetage. Debrett's Baronetage.
Lord Makgill of Cousland, Viscount of Oxfuird. Abstract of . . . the Case of James Makgill, claiming the Title, with pedigree. The Scots Peerage, vi. 587-601.
of Rankeillor. The Scots Peerage, vi. 588-589.

**Makgill-Crichton** of Rankeillor. Burke's Landed Gentry (Suppl. 1849).

**Malcolm**, Aberdeenshire. Scottish N. and Q., 2nd S., v. 169-170; vi. 7-8; vii. 146.
of Balbedie. Complete Baronetage, by G. E. C., iv. 245.
Birse. Scottish N. and Q., 3rd S., vii. 10.
of Burnfoot. Burke's Landed Gentry (1858-1925).
of Grange. East Neuk of Fife, by W. Wood, 2nd ed., 188-192.
Lumphanan. Scottish N. and Q., 3rd S., iii. 52, 71.
of Poltalloch. Burke's Landed Gentry (1848-1925). The Genealogist, N. S., xxxviii. 71-77, 135-145, 183, 193.

**Malcolmson**, Lerwick. Scottish N. and Q., 3rd S., v. 117, 236-238.

**Mansfield**, Murray, Baron, Earl of. English Peerage, by Rev. A. Jacob (London, 1767), ii. 587-591. Biographical Peerage (London, 1808), 402-405. G. E. C.'s Complete Peerage. The Scots Peerage, viii. 206-214.

**Manson**. Scottish N. and Q., 3rd S., iv. 42.
of Oakhill. Scottish N. and Q., 3rd S., iv. 18.
Thurso. Henderson's Caithness Family History, 312-316.

**Manson-Sinclair** of Bridgend. Caithness Family History, 148-150.

*See* The Scots Peerage, ed. Sir J. Balfour Paul, *for*

**Mar**, The Ancient Earls of, v. 566-589.
Douglas, Earl of, v. 585-586.
Erskine, Earl of, v. 589-635.
Goodeve-Erskine, Earl of, v. 635-636.
Stewart, Earl of, v. 587-589, 637-639.

**Mar**, Earl of. Heraldry, by A. Nisbet (1722), i. 129-130. Memoirs of the Jacobites of 1715 and 1745, by Mrs Katherine Thomson (1845-46), i. 1-223. Eminent Men of Fife, by Conolly, 164-165. Memorials of Alloa, by Crawford (1874), 83-92. Curious Specimen of the Connection of the Great Families in Scotland, as exemplified in the Earls of Mar, Douglas and Angus [by Alex. Sinclair]. Observations on the . . . Ancient Earldom of Mar, by Alex. Sinclair, 19 pp. The Question of Precedence as to the Old Earldom of Mar [by Alex. Sinclair], 7 pp. Particulars of the First Restoration of the Earldom of Mar [by A. Sinclair], two impressions, 5 and 6 pp. Essential Points in the Succession to the Earldom of Mar [by A. Sinclair], 4 pp. Further Extracts from Act in Favour of the Erle of Mar [by A. Sinclair], 3 pp. Remarks upon the Petition of the Earl of Kellie [by A. Sinclair], 8 pp. New Position of the Old Earldom of Mar [by A. Sinclair], 8 pp. (1875). Sketch of the Earldom of Mar, by A. S., *in* Herald and Genealogist (1873), vii. 1-18. Memorial of Walter Coningsby Erskine, Earl of Kellie, claiming the Honour and Dignity of Earl of Mar (1867). Case on his behalf, also Minutes of Evidence on his Petition, and on the Petition of John Francis E. Goodeve Erskine (1868). Case for John F. E. G. Erskine, Earl of Mar, in opposition to Walter Coningsby, Earl of Kellie, claiming the dignity of the Earl of Mar ; and Supplementary Case (1873). Case and Additional Case with Supplement of Walter Henry, Earl of Kellie. Proceedings and Speeches (1873-4). Chronological Index to the Documents printed in the Evidence on the Mar Peerage Claims, fol., n.d. Minutes of Evidence before the Lords Committees for privileges, the Earl of Mar claiming the Earldom of Kellie (1882). Report of House of Lords on the Earldom of Mar Restitution Bill, with Proceedings and Minutes of Evidence (1885). The Earldom of Mar, by G. W. Marshall *in* Genealogist, 1878, 1st S., ii. 73-83. A Paper on the Mar Peerage, with Judgment of the Committee of Privileges, Pedigrees, etc., by A. W. Hallen, 21+*xl* pp. (Alloa, 1875). The Mar Peerage Ancient and Modern, with Pedigree (1875).* A Short Account of the Earldom of Mar and of the recent Peerage Case, by W. A. Lindsay (1875). Are there two Earls of Mar ? (1876). The Inheritance and Position of the Ancient Earldom of Mar, by A. Sinclair. Particulars of the first restoration of the Earldom. Sketch of the right of female descent in the Earldom, by A. Sinclair. The Earldom of Mar in Sunshine and Shade, during Five Hundred Years, by Alexander, Lord Lindsay, 2 vols. (Edinr., 1882). The Earldom of Marr, by P. H. M'Kerlie (1883). The Great Historic Families of Scotland, by Jas. Taylor [1887]. Nuda Veritas : Shall Wrong Prevail ? with appendix of illustrative documents (1888). Were there two Earls of Mar ? by J. H. Round *in* Foster's Collectanea Genealogica (1883), 3rd pt., 12. Walford's Tales of our Great Families, 2nd S., ii. 75-90. Are there Two Earls of Mar ? *in* Genealogist, N. S. (1884), i. 60, 122-124, 187. W. A. Lindsay *on* The Mar Restitution *in* Genealogist, N. S. (1885), ii. 308-310. The Earldom of Mar *in* Genealogist, N. S., iii. 1-24. The Early Earls of Mar, by G. Burnett *in* Genealogist, N. S., iv. 177-193. The Early Earls of Mar, by Joseph Bain, *in* Genealogist, N. S., vi. 63-64. The Earldoms of Douglas and Mar, by J. H. Round, *in* Genealogist, N. S., x. 65-71, 251 ; by W. A. Lindsay, x. 129-131. The Scottish Antiquary (1895), ix. 1-3, 63-68. Historical MSS. Commission (1904), Cd. 2190. G. E. C.'s Complete Peerage. Burke's and other Annual Peerages. Historic . . . Earldoms of Scotland, by Dr John Mackintosh (1898), 19-33, 31-41. Scot. Hist. Review, xviii. 64. Notes and Queries, 4th S., i. 189, 471, 616 ; v. 111, 537 ; vi. 168-170 ; viii. 320 ; ix. 501 : 6th S., i. 328 ; v. 405, 452, 493. [George Burnett] *in* Journal of Jurisprudence, xxix. 460.

**Mar**, Erskine, Duke of. The Jacobite Peerage, by the Marquis of Ruvigny (1904), 113-116.

**March**, Douglas, Earl of. The Scots Peerage, vii. 145-147.
　Dunbar, Earl of. The Herald and Genealogist, v. 243-250. Alex. Sinclair *in the same*, vi. 289-297 ; vii. 36-41. Sketch of the Succession of the Ancient Historical Earldom of March, by Alex. Sinclair (Edinr. 1870). G. E. C.'s Complete Peerage. The Scots Peerage, iii. 262-279.
　Lennox, Earl of. The Scots Peerage, v. 363-371.
　Stewart, Earl of. The Scots Peerage, i. 20 ; v. 355, 358-362.
　Maitland, Marquess of. The Scots Peerage, v. 305.

**Marchmont**, Hume, Earl of. A Selection from the Papers of the Earls of Marchmont . . . from 1685 to 1750, 3 vols. (1831). Marchmont and the Humes of Polwarth [by Margaret Warrender], (1894). G. E. C.'s Complete Peerage. The Scots Peerage, vi. 1-24. Case of Alexander Home, claiming to be Earl of Marchmont, fol. (London, 1820 ; and Westminster, 1822). Claim of Alexander Home to the Title of Earl of Marchmont : (Session Papers, 40 of 1822). Case and Additional Case for F. D. Home, claiming the Titles of Earl of Marchmont, etc. (Westminster, 1842). Minutes of Evidence on Claim of Francis Home, Esq., to the Title of Earl of Marchmont : (Session Papers, 113 of 1838 ; 141 of 1839 ; 67 of 1840 ; 33 of 1842 ; 103 of 1843). Sir James Balfour Paul *in* Scot. Hist. Review (1915), xi. 27-38.

**Marischal**, Keith, Earl. The First Earl Marischal, by Thos. Innes *in* Scot. Hist. Review, xxiv. 280-297. G. E. C.'s Complete Peerage. The Scots Peerage, vi. 25-65. *See also* **Keith**, Earl Marischal.

**Marjoribanks**. Foster's Collectanea Genealogica (1882), ii. pts. 8, 9 ; (1883), iii. pt. 10. R. R. Stodart *in* The Genealogist, 1st. S., vi. 294-303. The Lyon Office and the Family of Marjoribanks, a reply to the remarks of the Lyon Clerk Depute, entitled " Mr Joseph Foster on the Return of the Members of Parliament," n.d.
　of Lees. Burke's Landed Gentry (1925).
　of Marjoribanks. Burke's Landed Gentry (1849-1875, 1925).

**Marnie** of Deuchar. Baronage of Angus and Mearns, by D. M. Peter, 230.

**Marr** of Hatton. Thanage of Fermartyn, by Temple, 405.

**Marshall**, Dandaleith. Scottish N. and Q., 3rd S., ii. 105.
　St Ninians. Complete Baronetage, by G. E. C., iii. 325 ; vi., Appx. 81.

**Martin** of Auchindennan. Irving's Book of Dumbartonshire, iii. portrait.
　Galloway. Notes and Queries, 6th S., vi. 89.
　of Gibliston. East Neuk of Fife, by W. Wood, 2nd ed., 268-269.
　Skye. The Martins of Skye ; a short history of a Highland Family, (Glasgow, n.d.).

**Martine** of Grange and Ethiebeaton. Monifieth, by J. Malcolm, 338-339.

**Martine** of Lathans. Geneal. Coll., by Macfarlane, ii. 201.

St Andrews. Geneal. Coll., by W. Macfarlane, 1750-51 ; Scot. Hist. Soc., ii. 183-198.

**Marwick.** Norton Smith's Orkney Armorials, 94.

**Mason.** Scottish N. and Q., xii. 29.

**Masterson.** Family of Buchanan, by Buchanan of Auchmar (1723), 132.

**Masterton** of Masterton, Parkmill and Gogar. Baronage, by Douglas, 320-321. Memorials of Alloa, by Crawford, 93-95. A critical examination of the Genealogy of Masterton of that ilk, Parkmill, etc., published in Douglas' Baronage and Crawfurd's Memorials of Alloa [by R. R. Stodart], 7 pp. (London, 1878).* Masterton Papers, 1660-1719, ed. with pedigree, etc., by V. A. Noël Paton ; Scot. Hist. Soc. (1893). Burke's Landed Gentry (1848), ii. 1126. Logie, a Parish History, by Rev. Dr R. Menzies Fergusson (1905), ii. 30-36.

in Sweden. Palace of History Catalogue (Glasgow, 1911), 202, 205 *bis.* Eric E. Etzel *in* Scot. Hist. Review (1913), ix. 271.

**Mather,** Hallrule. Tancred's Rulewater, 44-47.

of Millhall and Muirhouse. Crawfurd's Shire of Renfrew (1818), 245-246.

**Matheson.** History of the Mathesons, with Genealogies of the various branches, by Alexander Mackenzie (Inverness, 1882, 2nd ed., by Alex. Macbain, Stirling and London, 1900).

of Achany. Burke's Landed Gentry (1849).

of Ardross. Burke's Landed Gentry (1849-1879).

of Cordale. Book of Dumbartonshire, by Irving, iii., portrait.

of Lochalsh. Royal Descent of the Mathesons of Loch Alsh, Shinness, etc., a folio Genealogical Table (1880). Sir James Matheson of the Lewis, and his Descent from the Mathesons of Shinness, by Alex. Mackenzie, 8vo, 20 pp. (Inverness, 1882).* Royal Descent of the Mathesons of Shinness and Lochalsh, by W. E. Foster, 4to, *xxi*+186 pp. (1912).

**Maule.** Heraldry, by A. Nisbet (1722), i. 367 ; (1742), II., iii. 48-52. Registrum de Panmure : Records of the Families of Maule, de Valoniis, Brechin, and Brechin-Barclay, compiled by the Hon. Harry Maule of Kelly, A.D. 1733, ed. John Stuart, LL.D., 2 vols., 4to, illust. (Edinr. 1874).* A Genealogy of the Maules, by Archibald Burn-Murdoch of Gartincaber (before 1898).

**Maule** of Kellie. Eminent Arbroathians, by M'Bain, 113-154. The Scots Peerage, vii. 2, 3, 6.

of Panmure. Geneal. Coll., by W. Macfarlane, 1750-51 ; Scot. Hist. Soc., ii. 125-156. Memorials of Angus and the Mearns, by A. Jervise, ed. Gammack (Edinr. 1885), ii. 1-28. The Panmure Papers . . . ed. by Sir G. Douglas and Sir G. D. Ramsay, 2 vols. (1908). The Scots Peerage, vii. 5-19, 23-24.

Earl of Panmure. The Complete Peerage, by G. E. C. The Scots Peerage, vii. 1-27.

Salem. Genealogy of the Maule Family, with account of Thomas Maule of Salem, the progenitor of the Family in U.S.A. (1872).*

**Maule** in Sweden. One Year in Sweden, by Marryat (1862), ii. 493 *ter*.
Palace of History Catalogue (Glasgow, 1911), 201, 205, 208, 209.
Eric E. Etzel *in* Scot. Hist. Review, ix. 270.

**Maxtone-Graham** of Cultoquhey. Burke's Landed Gentry (1875-1925).
*See* The Scots Peerage, ed. Sir J. Balfour Paul, *for*

**Maxwell**, Lord Carlyle, vi. 482-487.
Earl of Dirleton, iii. 126-131.
Lord Eskdaill, vi. 482-487.
Lord Herries of Terregles, iv. 409-418.
Lord Kingston, iii. 126-131.
Lord Maxwell, vi. 475-492.
Earl of Morton, vi. 388-389, 482-487.
Earl of Nithsdale, vi. 469-492.

**Maxwell.** Heraldry, by A. Nisbet (1722), i. 137-139. MS. by John Riddell,
W.S., and Robert Riddell, in the possession of the Society of Writers
to the Signet. The Book of Carlaverock ; Memoirs of the Maxwells,
Earls of Nithsdale, Lords Maxwell and Herries, by Sir Wm. Fraser,
2 vols., 4to, illust. (Edinr. 1873).* Lands and their Owners in
Galloway, by J. M'Kerlie, v. 149-176. Historical Families of
Dumfriesshire, by Johnston, 7-9 *et passim*. . Moffat's History of the
Family of Moffat.*

**Maxwell** of Aikenhead. Scot. Hist. Review, xix. 81-86.
of Auldhouse. Crawfurd's Shire of Renfrew (1818), 31, 34, 283-284.
of Balmangan. Lands . . . in Galloway, v. 121-123.
of Baltersan. Lands . . . in Galloway, iv. 314.
of Barncleuch. Lands . . . in Galloway, iv. 8-12.
of Blackbelly. Lands . . . in Galloway, iii. 253.
of Breconside. Lands . . . in Galloway, iv. 224-228.
of Bredieland. Crawfurd's Shire of Renfrew (1818), 329. Records of the
Maxwells of Bredieland, Merksworth, Castlehead, etc., in the County
of Renfrew, 8vo, n.d.
of Breoch. Lands . . . in Galloway, iii. 256, 264.
of Caerlaverock. Burke's Landed Gentry (1848). The Scots Peerage,
vi. 470-475.
of Calderwood. Douglas's Baronage, 52-56. The Scottish Antiquary
(1899), xii. 144. Marchmont and the Humes of Polwarth [by M.
Warrender], 172. Complete Baronetage, by G. E. C., ii. 320.
of Cardoness. Lands . . . in Galloway, iii. 24-40.
of Carnsalloch. The Scots Peerage, vi. 474-476.
of Carriden. Oliver's History of Antigua, ii. 260-261.
of Carruchan. Case of William Maxwell of Carruchan claiming to be
Earl of Nithsdale ; and Suppl. Case (1848, 1857). Minutes of
Evidence (1849-1855). Case and Suppl. Case for Wm. Maxwell
of Carruchan, in opposition to the Case of W. C. Maxwell, claiming
the Title of Lord Herries, with pedigree (1853). Lands . . . in
Galloway, v. 238.
of Carswada. Lands . . . in Galloway, iv. 341-346.

**Maxwell** of Cavens. The Scots Peerage, iii. 126-127.

    of Cowhill and Drumpark. Genealogy, by George Burnett, Lyon Depute, folding lithographed pedigree, 23½ × 18 inches (1865). Lands . . . in Galloway, iv. 5-7.

    of Crofts. Lands . . . in Galloway, iv. 312.

    of Dargavel. Crawfurd's Shire of Renfrew, ed. Robertson (1818), 104, 392-394. Burke's Landed Gentry (1863-1925).

    of Drumbeg. Geneal. Mag. (1899), ii. 420, 462.

    of Drumcoltran. Lands . . . in Galloway, iv. 230-232.

    Dundee. MS. Pedigree by C. B. Boog Watson, deposited in the Lyon Office (1922).

    Georgia. History of the Habersham Family, by J. G. B. Bulloch, M.D. (Columbia, S.C., 1901), 11-13.

    Glasgow. Crawfurd's Shire of Renfrew (1818), 384 n.

    of Glenlee. Burke's Landed Gentry (1863).

    of Gribton. Historical Families of Dumfriesshire, by Johnstone, 48, 51. The Scots Peerage, iv. 415.

    of Hazlefield. Lands . . . in Galloway, v. 102.

    of Hillis. Heraldry, by Nisbet (1722), i. 442. Lands . . . in Galloway, iv. 334-336.

    of Kirkconnel. Burke's Landed Gentry (1875-1894). Lands . . . in Galloway, v. 216-222.

    of Kirkhouse. The Scots Peerage, iii. 127.

    of Logan. Lands . . . in Galloway, iii. 265-267.

    of Mauldislie. Upper Ward of Lanarkshire, by Irving and Murray, ii. 408-410.

    of Mearns. Crawfurd's Shire of Renfrew (1818), 35-36.

    of Merksworth. Crawfurd's Shire of Renfrew (1818), 329.

    of Monreith. Complete Baronetage, by G. E. C., iv. 311. Burke's Peerage and Baronetage. Debrett's Baronetage.

    of Munches. Lands . . . in Galloway, iii. 240-245. Burke's Landed Gentry (1863-1925).

    of Newark. Crawfurd's Shire of Renfrew (1818), 118.

    of Newlaw. Lands . . . in Galloway, v. 76-83.

    of Orchardtoun. Lands . . . in Galloway, v. 84-91. Complete Baronetage, by G. E. C., iii. 340 ; vi., Appx. 82.

    of Pollok. Douglas's Baronage, 450-453. Crawfurd's Shire of Renfrew (1818), 31-35, 278-286. The Herald and Genealogist, iii. 545. Memoirs of the Maxwells of Pollok, ed. by Sir W. Fraser, 2 vols., 4to, illust. (1863).* The Pollok-Maxwell Baronetcy, by Sir W. Fraser, 4to (1866). The Cartulary of Pollok Maxwell, ed. Sir W. Fraser, 4to (1875). Complete Baronetage, by G. E. C. (1902), ii. 383 ; (1904), iv. 312, 447. Debrett's Baronetage. Burke's Peerage and Baronetage.

    of Slagnaw. Lands . . . in Galloway, iv. 122.

    of Springkell. Pedigree of the Family of Maxwell of Springkell, by Michael J. Maxwell Shaw Stewart (Worksop, 1890). Annals of a Border Club, by G. Tancred, 324. Complete Baronetage, by G. E. C., iv. 320. Debrett's Baronetage. Burke's Peerage and Baronetage.

**Maxwell** of Stainly. Crawfurd's Shire of Renfrew (1818), 89.
of Stroquhan. Geneal. Mag. (1898), i. 544.
of Tealing. Warden's Angus or Forfarshire, v. 217-218.
of Terrauchty. Burke's Landed Gentry (1863-1886). Lands . . . in
Galloway, v. 230-233.
of Terregles. Notes and Queries, 11th S., xii. 240, 289, 309.
of Threave. Lands . . . in Galloway, iii. 147.
of Williamwood. Crawfurd's Shire of Renfrew (1818), 270. Burke's
Landed Gentry (1848, 1875).

**Maxwell-Graham.** Burke's Landed Gentry (1858-1863).

**Maxwell-Heron.** Burke's Landed Gentry (1875-1914).

**Maxwell-Scott** of Abbotsford. Burke's Landed Gentry (1898-1925).

**Maxwell-Stuart** of Terregles and Traquair. Historical MSS. Commission
(1884), 9th Report. The Scots Peerage, iv. 420.

**Maxwell-Witham** of Kirkconnell. Historical MSS. Commission (1876),
5th Report, i. 650. Burke's Landed Gentry (1871-1925).

**Mayne** of Powis, Powhouse. Baronage, by Douglas, 262-263. Logie, by
Rev. Dr Menzies Fergusson, ii. 88, 95-97. Herald and Genealogist,
iv. 554. The Pedigree of the Family of Mayne of Powis, compiled
by H. C. Barnard, 1922, 18+1 sheets folio (Ipswich, 1929).*

**Mearns** of Disblair. Burke's Landed Gentry (1906-1925).

**Monson** of Moredun. Norton Smith's Orkney Armorials, 97-98.

**Mein** of Craigcrook. Cramond, by J. P. Wood, 34.
of Eildon Hall. Memoirs of Susan Sibbald, 1783-1812, ed. F. J. Hett
(London, 1926).
of Hunthill and Scraesburgh. Annals of a Border Club, by G. Tancred, 327.
of Ormiston. Annals of a Border Club, 327-328.

**Mekfen.** Herald and Genealogist, vii. 423. Charters . . . relating to the
Abbey of Inchaffray ; Scot. Hist. Soc., No. 56 (1908), lxxxiv-v.

**Meldrum** of Auchterless. Thanage of Fermartyn, by Temple, 117.
of Fyvie. Thanage of Fermartyn, 22-24. Fyvie Castle, by A. M. W.
Stirling, 65-78.
of Haltoun. Thanage of Fermartyn, 118.
of Meldrum. Heraldry, by Nisbet (1742), ii., Appx. 131. Burke's
Commoners, ii. 298.
of Scotstoun. Fraser's Laurencekirk, 59.

**Melfort**, Drummond, Viscount of, Earl of. Complete Peerage, by G. E. C.
The Scots Peerage, vi. 66-74.

**Melfort**, Drummond, comte de, duc de. The Scots Peerage, vi. 59-72 ;
vii. 60, 61. The Jacobite Peerage, 116-118.

**Melgum**, Gordon, Viscount. Complete Peerage, by G. E. C. The Scots
Peerage, i. 100 ; iv. 127, 545.

**Melros of Tynningham**, Hamilton, Lord. State Papers, etc., of Thomas,
Earl of Melros, 1599-1650, 2 vols. (Abbotsford Club, 1837). G. E. C.'s
Complete Peerage. The Scots Peerage, iv. 325-326.

**Melrose,** Ramsay, Lord. G. E. C.'s Complete Peerage. The Scots Peerage, iv. 300.

Ramsay, Lord Ramsay of. The Scots Peerage, iii. 98.

**Melville.** Heraldry, by Nisbet (1742), ii., Appx. 29-31. The Melvilles, Earls of Melville, and the Leslies, Earls of Leven, by Sir Wm. Fraser, 3 vols., 4to, illust. (Edinr. 1890).* The Melville Family . . . by E. S. Jobert de la Ferté.

**Melville** of Baldovie. Eminent Men of Fife, by Conolly, 326-328. Angus or Forfarshire, by Warden, iii. 146-150.

of Cairnie, Murdochcairnie. Proc. Soc. Antiq. Scotl. (1897), 94-98.

of Carnbee. Geneal. Coll., by W. Macfarlane, 1750-51 ; Scot. Hist. Soc., i. 12, 24. Cramond, by J. P. Wood, 18. East Neuk of Fife, by W. Wood, 2nd ed., 330-332.

of Dysart. Angus or Forfarshire, by Warden, iv. 312-313. Eminent Arbroathians, by J. M. M'Bain (1897), 54-55. The Balfours of Pilrig, by B. Balfour-Melville, 269.

of Garvock. The Scots Peerage, vi. 93-94, 99.

of Granton. Cramond, by J. P. Wood, 18.

of Halhill. The Scots Peerage, vi. 90-92.

Viscount of Kirkcaldy. The Scots Peerage, vi. 108-123.

Earl of Leven. The Scots Peerage, vi. 75-123.

Earl of Melville. G. E. C.'s Complete Peerage. The Scots Peerage, vi. 75-123.

of Raith. Eminent Men of Fife, by Conolly, 325, 328. The Scots Peerage, vi. 82-105.

Lord Raith, Monimail and Balwearie. The Scots Peerage, vi. 108-123.

of Strathkinness and Craigtoun. Baronage, by Douglas, 527-529. The Balfours of Pilrig, 275. Scot. Hist. Review, xiv. 116-146. Biographical Sketch of Gen. R. Melville of Strathkinness, ed. E. Balfour-Melville, 30 pp. (1917).

**Melville,** Dundas, Viscount. Biographical Peerage (1808), 413-414. Burke's Peerage, Debrett's Peerage, etc. G. E. C.'s Complete Peerage.

**Memes.** Scottish N. and Q., 2nd S., iv. 175.

**Menteith,** The Ancient Earls of. The Scots Peerage, vi. 124-141. Scottish N. and Q., 1st S., xii. 156. Memoir of the History of the Old Earldom of Menteith . . . by John Stuart, 4to, 21 pp. (1866). The Red Book of Menteith, by Sir W. Fraser, 2 vols., 4to, illust. (1880).* The Red Book of Menteith reviewed, by George Burnett (1881). The Great Historic Families of Scotland, by James Taylor [1887]. Notes on the District of Menteith, by R. B. Cunninghame Graham (1895). The Lake of Menteith . . . with Historical Account of the . . . Earldom of Menteith, by A. F. Hutchison (Stirling, 1899).

Graham, Earl of. Geneal. Mag. (1898), i. 67-82, 245, 429 ; ii. 417, 509 ; iii. 33, 301-308, 338-341 ; iv. 252-255, 297-301. Pedigrees by Elizabeth, Baroness Hastings, *in* The Ancestor (1903), iv. 81-87. The Stirling Antiquary, ed. W. B. Cook, ii. 106, 235-241 ; iii. 1-10, 73-76, 250, 319-324. The Scots Peerage, vi. 142-165.

**Menteith,** Hastings, Earl of. The Scots Peerage, vi. 135.

Stewart, Earl of. The Stewarts Magazine, iv. 304-314.

**Menteith** of Rusky. The Lake of Menteith, by Hutchison, 253-267. The Scots Peerage, vi. 132.

**Menteth** of Menteth. The Stewarts Magazine, iv. 325-329.

**Menzies** of Auchinsell. R. C. Reid *in* Dumfriesshire and Galloway Antiq. Soc. Trans., 3rd S. (1923), viii. 177-180.

of Baltoquhan. R. C. Reid, *as above*, 162-169.

of Bolfracks. Scottish N. and Q., 2nd S., ii. 47, 62-63, 76.

of Castlehill. Upper Ward of Lanarkshire, by Irving and Murray, ii. 227. R. C. Reid *in* Dumfriesshire and Galloway Antiq. Soc. Trans., 3rd S., viii. 171-177.

of Chesthill. Burke's Landed Gentry (1848, 1898).

of Comrie. The Stewarts of Forthergill, 29.

of Culdares. State of Process of Reduction of Miss E. Mackenzie Menzies of Culdares against A. Menzies, Clerk of Session, as to Loss, etc., Sustained, on Unwarranted Sale of Lands, etc. (1793). Burke's Landed Gentry (1879-1914).

of Culterallers. Upper Ward of Lanarkshire, i. 278.

of Durisdeer. R. C. Reid *in* Dumfries and Galloway Antiq. Soc. Trans., 3rd S., viii. 145. The Stewarts Magazine, iv. 210-211.

of Durne. The Scots Peerage, ii. 5, 13.

of Enoch. R. C. Reid, *as above*, 155-171.

of Kinmundy. Scottish N. and Q. (1887), i. 45, 52-53.

Lanark. The Lanark Manse Family Book, by E. B. Menzies, ed. Thos. Reid, 54 pp. (Lanark, 1901).* Alexander Cowan, by C. B. Boog Watson.*

of Menzies. Heraldry, by Nisbet (1742), ii., Appx. 245-250. Historical MSS. Commission (1877), 6th Report. Complete Baronetage, by G. E. C., iv. 247. Burke's Peerage and Baronetage (before 1912). The Red and White Book of Menzies, by D. P. Menzies, 4to, illust. (Glasgow, 1894, 2nd ed., Plean, 1908): [Must be used with caution]. The Red and White Book of Menzies, a Review, by C. Poyntz Stewart (1906). *See also* The Genealogist, N. S., xxii. 94-105.

of Pitfodels. Scottish N. and Q., 1st S., i. 195-196: 2nd S., vi. 118; vii. 170. Tayler's Jacobites of Aberdeenshire (1928), 347-352.

of Rotmell. Stephen's Inverkeithing (1921), 305.

of Weem. R. C. Reid, *in* Dumfries and Galloway Antiq. Soc. Trans., 3rd S., viii. 155-162.

**Mercer.** Robert Mercer and Helen Chisholm and their Descendants, 1480-1544, 4to, 14 pp., n.d. Pedigree of the Mercer Family, printed by their descendant, Dr Irvine.* Pedigree of the Family of Mercer, by Sir C. W. Hunt.* The Merchant Princes of Bonnie St Johnston, by R. S. Fittis. The Life of General Hugh Mercer, by J. T. Goolrich (Washington, 1906). Memorial of Miss Margaret Mercer, by Casper Morris, M.D. (Philadelphia, 1848). [Mr Walter Mercer, 2 Rothesay Place, Edinburgh, possesses much material for a family history.]

**Mercer**, Aberdeenshire.  Scottish N. and Q., xii. 158.

of Aldie.  Baronage of Angus and Mearns, by Peter, 238.  Some Account of Lieut-Col. William Mercer, by David Laing.  Pedigree ; Proc. Soc. Antiq. Scotl. (1860).  Our Seven Centuries ; an account of the Mercers of Aldie and Meikleour, by G. R. Mercer, 4to (Perth, 1868). The Mercer Chronicle, by an Irish Seanachy (London, 1866). Complete Baronetage, by G. E. C., iii. 326.  Notes and Queries, 8th S., vii. 48, 257.  Scottish N. and Q., 2nd S., vii. 24, 60.  Family and Genealogical Sketches, by Rev. Thos. Sinton (Inverness, 1911).*

of Auchnacant.  Temple's Thanage of Fermartyn, 603-604.  Tayler's Jacobites of Aberdeenshire, 353.

of Innerpeffray.  The Mercers of Innerpeffray, by R. S. Fittis (Perth, 1877).

of Huntingtower.  Burke's Landed Gentry (1875-1925).

Kinellar.  Scottish N. and Q., 1st S., vii. 152-153, 164-165, 183-184.

**Mercer-Henderson**, Countess of Buckinghamshire.  Burke's Peerage (after 1903).  Stephen's Inverkeithing (1921), 150.

**Merleswein** of Ardross.  East Neuk of Fife, by W. Wood, 2nd ed., 18.

**Methven** of Methven.  Baronage, by Douglas (1784), 141-145.  Herald and Genealogist, vii. 423-430.  R. R. Stodart *in* Genealogist, 1st S., iv. 59-61.  Notes and Queries, 8th S., xii. 88, 175.

**Methven**, Stewart, Lord.  G. E. C.'s Complete Peerage.  The Scots Peerage, vi. 166-169.

**Michie**.  Scottish N. and Q., 2nd S., vii. 61 ; viii. 161.

of Culquharry.  Baronage of Angus and Mearns, by Peter, 240.

**Middlemast** of Grevistoun.  Peeblesshire Localities, by Renwick, 552-553, 555, 556.

**Middleton**, Aberdeen.  The.Scottish Antiquary, i. and ii. 172.  Scottish N. and Q., 1st S., i. 181 : 3rd S., ii. 79 ; iii. 119.

of Birkenbrewel and Gelland.  Scottish N. and Q., 3rd S., ii. 31, 127.

of Cauldhame.  Scottish N. and Q., 1st S., ii. 68.

of Kilhill.  The Scots Peerage, vi. 172-176.

of Middleton.  Memorials of Angus and the Mearns, by Jervise, ed. Gammack, ii. 152-156.  Angus or Forfarshire, by Warden, iv. 327-329.  Laurencekirk, by Fraser, 48-56.  Scottish N. and Q., 1897, xi. 130-131.  The Scots Peerage, vi. 170-172.  [An immense amount of material as to the Middleton Family has been collected by Miss M. R. R. MacGilchrist-Gilchrist, 16 South Learmonth Gardens, Edinburgh.]

Earl of Middleton.  The Earls of Middleton, Lords of Clermont and of Fettercairn, and the Middleton Family, by A. C. Biscoe (London, 1876).  G. E. C.'s Complete Peerage.  The Scots Peerage, vi. 170-190.

of Seaton.  Scottish N. and Q., 3rd S., iii. 32, 51, 71, 91.

of Sheils.  Scottish N. and Q., 3rd S., v. 118.

**Midlothian**, Primrose, Earl of.  The Scots Peerage, ix. 152.

**Mill** of Balwyllo.  Warden's Angus or Forfarshire, iv. 319, 330.

of Fearn.  Baronage of Angus and Mearns, by Peter, 243.

**Millar** of Craighill. Angus or Forfarshire, by Warden, iv. 146.

Crail. Churchyard Monuments of Crail, by Erskine Beveridge, 97-99.

Paisley. Oliver's History of Antigua, ii. 265.

of Temple and Killoch. Heraldry, by Nisbet (1742), ii., Appx. 42.

**Miller** of Collier's Wood. Burke's Landed Gentry (1848-1863).

of Dalnair and Earnock. Strathendrick, by Guthrie Smith, 221.

Denny. MS. Pedigree in possession of the Family at The Boards.

Edinburgh. Memorials of Hope Park, an Account of the Miller Family of Edinburgh, from 1655, 4to, illust. (1886).*

of Glenlee. Paterson's History of the County of Ayr, ii. 440. Paterson's Ayr and Wigton, i. 722-724. Lands . . . in Galloway, by M'Kerlie (1878), iv. 87-90.

Haddington. The Millers of Haddington, Dunbar and Dunfermline : a record of Scottish bookselling : by W. J. Coupar (London, 1914).

of Monkcastle. Ayrshire Families, by G. Robertson, ii. 67-69. History of the County of Ayr, by Paterson, ii. 246. Paterson's Ayr and Wigton, iii. 510, 514. Burke's Landed Gentry (1848).

of Stewartfield. Annals of a Border Club, by G. Tancred, 328-329.

**Miller-Cunningham** of Leithenhopes. Burke's Landed Gentry (1914-1925).

**Milne**, Aberdeen. Memoir of J. Young, Aberdeen . . . 1861, ed. Lt.-Col. W. Johnston (1894), 125-128.*

of Balfarg, Belfarge. System of Heraldry, by A. Nisbet (1722), i. 127. Notes and Queries, 3rd S., vii. 198.

of Banff. The Milnes of Banff, by Dr Cramond (Banff, 1894).

of Barntoun. Cramond, by J. P. Wood, 51, 54.

Mains of Esslemont. Temple's Thanage of Fermartyn, 518-520.

Laurencekirk. Fraser's Laurencekirk, 98-99.

New Deer. Genealogies of an Aberdeenshire Family, by Smith (1913) 43.

**Milne-Home** of Wedderburn and Billie. Historical MSS. Commission (1902), Cd. 931. Biographical Memoranda of the Portraits hanging at Milne-Graden, by D. Milne-Home (1862).* Burke's Landed Gentry (1848-1925).

**Milsington**, Colyear, Viscount of. G. E. C.'s Complete Peerage. The Scots Peerage, vii. 92-97.

**Minto**, Elliot, Baron. Biographical Peerage (1808), 417-419. Angus or Forfarshire, by Warden, ii. 9-13. G. E. C.'s Complete Peerage. Burke's, Lodge's, Debrett's Peerages, etc.

**Mitchel** of Dykes. Paterson's Ayr and Wigton, iii. 60.

**Mitchell.** Genealogical Memoranda relating to the Mitchell and Sykes Families (London, 1878).* A Brief History of two families, the Mitchells of Ayrshire and the Symons of Cornwall, by S. Weir Mitchell, M.D., 42 pp. (Philadelphia, 1912).*

in Bandeath. The Scottish Antiquary, vi. 67-69.

of Braehead. Paterson's History of Ayr, ii. 338. Paterson's Ayr and Wigton, i. 557.

of Burnhead, Bromhead. Paterson's Ayr, ii. 423. Ayr and Wigton, i. 688.

**Mitchell** of Carwood.   Burke's Landed Gentry (1894-1925).

of Dalgain.   Paterson's Ayr, i. 368 ; ii. 422.   Ayr and Wigton, i. 312, 695-697.

of Derry.   Angus or Forfarshire, by Warden, iii. 367.

of Drumeldrie.   East Neuk of Fife, by W. Wood, 2nd ed., 98.

Ellon.   Scottish N. and Q., 3rd S., v. 170.

of Kincraig.   Thanage of Fermartyn, 580-585.

of Mitchell and Bandeath.   Baronage, by Douglas, 427-428.

of Moredale.   Pedigree *in* Minutes of Evidence on the Petition of R. Barclay Allardice.

of Newburn.   East Neuk of Fife, by W. Wood, 2nd ed., 105.

of Polmood.   Burke's Landed Gentry (1894-1925).

of Thainston.   Burke's Landed Gentry (1848).   Burke's Visitation of Seats and Arms (1853), i. 179.

of Tilliegreig.   Scottish N. and Q., 3rd S., v. 176.

of Turnerhill and Nether Hillar.   Paterson's History of Ayr, ii. 423. Ayr and Wigton, i. 707.

of Uresland.   Zetland Family Histories, by F. J. Grant, 183-187.

of Westshore and Berrie.   Douglas's Baronage, 427-428.   Burke's Extinct and Dormant Baronetcies.   Case for Sir Hugh Sykes Mitchell, Baronet of Westshore, claiming to be placed on the official roll of baronets (1911).   Zetland Family Histories, 173-182.   Complete Baronetage, by G. E. C., v. 60.

**Mitchell-Gill** of Savock.   Burke's Landed Gentry (1894-1925).

**Mitchell-Innes** of Ayton.   Temple's Thanage of Fermartyn, 385.

of Whitehall.   Burke's Landed Gentry (1898-1925).

**Mitchell-Thomson** of Polmood.   Burke's Peerage and Baronetage (1925).

**Mitchelson** of Middleton.   Baronage, by Douglas, 321-323.

**Moffat** of Moffat.   Short History of the Family of Moffat of that Ilk, with the Genealogies of various branches . . . by Robert Maxwell Moffat, M.D., 4to, 152 pp. (Jersey, 1908).*

of Knock.   Scottish N. and Q., 2nd S., vi. 72.

of Moorbrock.   Lands . . . in Galloway, by M'Kerlie, iii. 321.

**Moir.**   The Families of Moir and Byres, by A. G. Mitchell Gill, 4to (Edinr. 1885).   Scottish N. and Q., 2nd S., iii. 150 ; 3rd S., iii. 124.   Moir Genealogy, and Collateral Lines, by Alexander L. Moir, 8vo, Index, illust. (Lowell, Mass., 1913).   Pedigrees of the Family of James of Culgarth (Exeter, 1913).*

of Craigarnhall.   The Stirling Antiquary, ed. W. B. Cook, iv. 308.

of Denmore.   Geneal. Mag. (1899), ii. 560.

of Leckie.   The Stirling Antiquary, iv. 309-313.   Burke's Landed Gentry (1898-1925).

of Otterburn.   R. R. Stodart *in* The Genealogist, 1st S., iii. 250 (also in pamphlet form).

of Scotstoun.   Temple's Thanage of Fermartyn, 644-647.

of Stoneywood.   Pedigree *in* Alexander Cowan, by C. B. Boog Watson. Tayler's Jacobites of Aberdeenshire, 356-365.

**Moir-Byres** of Tonley.  Burke's Landed Gentry (1849-1925).

**Monach** of Easter Ballat.  Strathendrick, by Guthrie Smith, 215.

**Monboddo**, Burnett, Lord.  Historical MSS. Commission (1873), 4th Report, 518-521 ; (1877), 6th Report, 673-681.  Forbes Gray's Some Old Scots Judges (1914), 41-74.

**Moncreiff** of Carnbee.  East Neuk of Fife, by W. Wood, 2nd ed., 333-334.
    Crail.  Churchyard Monuments of Crail, by Erskine Beveridge, 111, 120-125.
    Baron Moncreiff of Tullibole.  Burke's and other Annual Peerages.  G. E. C.'s Complete Peerage.
    of Randerston.  East Neuk of Fife, by W. Wood, 2nd ed., 457.
    of Sauchope.  Churchyard Monuments of Crail, by Erskine Beveridge (1893), 73, 103-111, with chart pedigree.

**Moncreiff-Wellwood.**  Complete Baronetage, by G. E. C., ii. 310.  Debrett's Baronetage.  Burke's Peerage and Baronetage.

**Moncreiffe** of Moncreiffe.  Nisbet's Heraldry, ii., Appx. 31-32.  Geneal. Coll., by W. Macfarlane ; Scot. Hist. Soc., i. 40-46.  Douglas's Baronage, 43-48.  The House of Moncrieff, by George Seton, 4to, 72 emblazoned coats-of-arms, Edinr. 1890.*  Complete Baronetage, by G. E. C., ii. 310 ; iv. 336.  Burke's Peerage and Baronetage.  Debrett's Baronetage.  The Moncreiffs and the Moncreiffes, by Frederick Moncreiff and William Moncreiffe, 2 vols. (1929).*

**Moncrieff** of Balcaskie.  Geneal. Coll., by W. Macfarlane, 1750-51 ; Scot. Hist. Soc., i. 44.  East Neuk of Fife, by W. Wood, 2nd ed. (1887), 273-274.
    of Barnhill and Culfargie.  Burke's Landed Gentry (1886-1925).
    of Kintullo.  Geneal. Coll., by W. Macfarlane ; Scot. Hist. Soc., i. 43.
    of Tippermalloch.  Notes and Queries, 2nd S., ii. 371 ; iii. 38.

**Moncur** of Slains.  Fraser's Laurencekirk, 105.

**Monfod(e** of Monfode.  Pont's Cuninghame, ed. Dobie, 326-329.  Notices of the Families of Ker of Kerrisland and Monfode of that Ilk, by Robert Malcolm Kerr (London, 1880).  Paterson's Ayr and Wigton, iii. 52-55.  Account of the Family of Monfode of that Ilk, n.p., n.d.  Notes and Queries, 6th S., ii. 182 ; iv. 14.
    of Skirling.  Peeblesshire Localities, by Renwick, 397.

**Monro.**  [The Milntown Family are the senior cadets of the Clan Munro, and spell their name Monro.]
    of Allan.  Burke's Landed Gentry (1875-1925).
    of Auchinbowie.  The Monros of Auchinbowie and cognate families, by John A. Inglis (Edinr. 1911).  Article *in* Misc. Gen. et Her. (March, 1920).  Burke's Landed Gentry (1875-1925).
    of Bearcrofts.  The Monros of Auchenbowie, 8, 35, 37.
    of Craiglockhart.  Heraldry, by Nisbet (1722), i. 351.  The Scottish Antiquary, viii. 138, 187 ; ix. 44.  The Monros of Auchenbowie, 105, 126-131.  Dictionary of National Biography, *s.v.*

**Monro** of Culcairn. The Bethunes of Skye, by Rev. T. Whyte (1778, repr. 1893), 30.

of Milntown. Six Articles on the Monro Families of Milntown and Culcairn, by Alex. Ross *in* The Celtic Magazine (Inverness, 1885), x. The Monros of Auchenbowie, by J. A. Inglis, 1-7.

**Monro-Binning** of Softlaw. The Monros of Auchenbowie, by J. A. Inglis, 122-125.

**Montagu-Douglas-Scott,** Duke of Buccleuch and Queensberry. The Scots Peerage, ii. 244-249.

**Montalt, Monteath, Mowat** of Fern. Memorials of Angus and the Mearns, by Jervise, ed. Gammack, ii. 104-107. Warden's Angus or Forfarshire, iii. 267-269.

**Monteath** of Cauldhame. Logie, by Rev. Dr Menzies Fergusson, ii. 159-160.

**Monteith.** Heraldry, by Nisbet (1722), i. 413. History of the Earldoms of Strathern, Monteith and Airth, by Sir Harris Nicolas (1842).

of Carstairs. J. B. Burke's Visitation of Seats and Arms (1853), i. 88.

of Cranley. Burke's Landed Gentry (1858-1925).

of Egilshay. Norton Smith's Orkney Armorials, 102.

of Randieford. Geneal. Mag. (1904), vii. 415.

*See also* **Menteith.**

**Montford** of Kinneff. Memorials of Angus and Mearns, by Jervise, ed. Gammack, ii. 157-158.

*See* The Scots Peerage, ed. Sir J. Balfour Paul, *for*

**Montgomerie,** Baron Ardrossan of Ardrossan, iii. 461-465.

Earl of Eglinton, iii. 421-465.

Lord Montgomerie, iii. 431-465.

Viscount Montgomerie of the Great Ards, iii. 433.

Earl of Mount Alexander, iii. 433.

Earl of Winton, iii. 462-465.

**Montgomerie, Montgomery.** Heraldry, by Nisbet (1722), i. 383-386. Memorables of the Montgomeries, a narrative in rhyme, composed before the present [18th] century, 4to (Glasgow, 1770, reprinted 8vo, Edinr. 1822). Genealogical History of the Family of Montgomery; comprising the lines of Eglinton and Braidstane in Scotland, and Mount Alexander and Grey Abbey in Ireland, by E. G. S. Reilly, 4to, 84 pp. (1839-42). Crawfurd's Shire of Renfrew, ed. Robertson (1818), 23-28, 248-262. Robertson's Ayrshire Families, i. 295-299; iii. 307-325. Paterson's History of the County of Ayr, ii. 229-244. Paterson's Ayr and Wigton, ii. 274-275. Pedigree of Archibald Montgomerie Hamilton, [13th] Earl of Eglinton, showing he is the male heir of the Fourth Earl of Winton, etc., sheet, 30 × 20 ins.* Service of the Earl of Eglington, as Heir-Male, etc. to George, the Fourth Earl of Winton, Lord Seaton and Tranent, folio, *iv* + 10 + 67 + 5 pp., with Index and Verdict, 8 pp., and folded pedigree (1840).* Memorials of the Montgomeries, Earls of

Eglinton, by Sir W. Fraser, 2 vols., 4to, illust. (1859).* Genealogical
History of the Family of Montgomery, by J. H. Montgomery, with
pedigree (Philadelphia, 1863).* Historical Memoir of the Family
of Eglinton and Winton, by John Fullarton (Ardrossan, 1864).
Historical MSS. Commission (1885), 10th Report (1). Généalogie
de Montgomery ; Écosse, États Unis, France ; Comtes d'Eglinton ;
Seigneurs de Greenfield, etc., folio, n.d.

**Montgomerie** of Annick Lodge. Paterson's History of the County of Ayr,
i. 453. Paterson's Ayr and Wigton, iii. 212. Burke's Landed Gentry
(1848).

of Ardrossan. The Scots Peerage, iii. 429-430.

of Blackhouse. Paterson's History of Ayr, i. 230-231.

of Boreland. Paterson's History of Ayr, i. 370. Ayr and Wigton,
i. 314-316.

of Bowhouse. Ayr and Wigton, iii. 280.

of Braidlie. Pont's Cuninghame, ed. Dobie, 79. Ayrshire Families, by
Robertson, ii. 342-344. Paterson's History of Ayr, i. 422-423. Ayr
and Wigton, iii. 173-175.

of Braidstane. Paterson's History of Ayr, i. 279-285. Ayr and Wigton,
iii. 71-73. Old Greenock, by G. Williamson (1886), i. 276-277.

of Brigend. Genealogical Account of the Montgomeries of Brigend of
Doon, lineal representatives of the families of Eglintoun and Lyle,
by William Anderson, Marchmont Herald (Edinr. 1859). Paterson's
History of Ayr, ii. 517. Ayr and Wigton, ii. 399-402.

of Cassillis. Paterson's History of Ayr, ii. 261.

of Coilsfield. The Scots Peerage, iii. 447-449.

of Coldcoat. Buchan and Paton's History of Peeblesshire, iii. 49.

of Giffen. Pont's Cuninghame, ed. Dobie, 143-164. Paterson's History
of Ayr, i. 286-289. Ayr and Wigton, iii. 99-105. The Scots Peerage,
iii. 429-446, 453.

of Lainshaw. Paterson's History of Ayr, ii. 153-155. Ayr and Wigton,
iii. 594-598. The Scots Peerage, iii. 436, 439.

of Sevenaikers. Paterson's History of Ayr, ii. 246. Ayr and Wigton,
iii. 509.

of Skelmorlie. Ayrshire Families, by Robertson, ii. 322, 326-335.
Paterson's History of Ayr, ii. 309-312. Ayr and Wigton, iii. 534-535.
Archæol. and Hist. Collections of Ayrshire and Galloway (1889),
vi. 58. The Scottish Antiquary, viii. 109, 166. Burke's Extinct
Baronetage. Complete Baronetage, by G. E. C., ii. 336. The Scots
Peerage, iii. 433, 448.

of Smithton, Smiston. Genealogy of the Montgomeries of Smithton, by
Sir Robert Douglas, 8vo (Windsor, 1795). Paterson's History of
Ayr, ii. 245. Ayr and Wigton, iii. 508.

of Stair. The Scots Peerage, iii. 426.

of Stane. Paterson's Ayr, ii. 100. Ayr and Wigton, iii. 278-280.

of Weitlands. Paterson's Ayr and Wigton, iii. 107.

**Montgomerie-Cuninghame.** Complete Baronetage, by G. E. C., iv. 285.

**Montgomery** of the Ards. The Montgomery Manuscripts, 1603-1706, compiled by Wm. Montgomery of Rosemount, 12mo (Belfast, 1830) ; ed. by Rev. G. Hill, 4to (Belfast, 1869).

of Aslois. Ayrshire Families, by G. Robertson, i. 22-23. Paterson's Ayr and Wigton, iii. 605.

of Bogstoun. Ayrshire Families, ii. 335-337, 342. Paterson's History of Ayr, i. 289. Ayr and Wigton, iii. 81-83.

of Broomlands. Paterson's History of Ayr, ii. 101. Ayr and Wigton, iii. 270-271, 275-279. The Monros of Auchenbowie, by J. A. Inglis, 158-163.

of Craighouse. Ayrshire Families, ii. 335, 338-339. Paterson's History of Ayr, i. 290, 462. Ayr and Wigton, iii. 56.

of Hesilheid. Pont's Cuninghame, ed. Dobie, 194-204. Paterson's History of Ayr, i. 290-292. Ayr and Wigton, iii. 106-107. Paterson's Scottish Surnames (Edinr. 1866), 63-74.

of Macbeth-hill *or* Macbiehill, Magbiehill. Baronage, by Douglas, 525-526. Burke's Extinct Baronetage. History of Peeblesshire, by Chambers, 499-503. Complete Baronetage, by G. E. C., v. 176. Buchan and Paton's History of Peeblesshire, iii. 49-51.

of Stanhope and Stobo. History of Peeblesshire, by W. Chambers, 436-439. Buchan and Paton's History of Peeblesshire, iii. 496-502.

in Sweden. One Year in Sweden, by Marryat, ii. 493. Palace of History Catalogue (Glasgow, 1911), 201, 202. Eric E. Etzel *in* Scot. Hist. Review (1913), ix. 271-278.

**Montrose**, Graham, Earl of, Marquess of, Duke of. The Memoirs of James, Marquis of Montrose, 1639-50, by Rev. Dr Geo. Wishart, Bishop of Edinburgh, 1662-71. The original Latin, with translation, etc., by Rev. A. D. Murdoch and H. F. Morland Simpson, 4to, illust. (London, 1893). Biographical Peerage (1808), 425-429. Memorials of Montrose and his Times, ed. Mark Napier, 2 vols., 8vo, illust. (Maitland Club, 1848-50). Memoirs of the Marquis of Montrose, 1612-50, by Mark Napier, 2 vols., 8vo, illust. (Edinr. 1856). Life of Montrose, by John Buchan (1913, 2nd ed. 1928). W. Cunningham *in* Scot. Hist. Review, xiv. 354. Historical MSS. Commission (1871), 2nd Report ; (1872), 3rd Report. Angus or Forfarshire, by A. J. Warden, ii. 1-5. The Parish of Strathblane, by J. Guthrie Smith, 11-31. Walford's Chapters from Family Chests, i. 251-257. Notes and Queries, 4th S., ii. 500 ; iv. 248, 295, 373, 489, 560 ; xii. 247, 522. Dictionary of National Biography, *s.v.* G. E. C.'s Complete Peerage. The Scots Peerage, iii. 191-274. Burke's and other Annual Peerages.

**Montrose**, Lindsay, Duke of. The Scots Peerage, iii. 22-23. Case of James, Earl of Crawford and Balcarres, claiming the Title, Honour and Dignity of the Original Dukedom of Montrose, created in 1488, folio (1850). Case for the same, with reference to the Petition and Right of James, Duke of Montrose, to be admitted in Opposition to the Claim (1851). Supplemental Case and Addenda (1852). Abstract of the Case for James, Duke of Montrose (1851), by John Riddell. Analysis of "Case for James, Duke of Montrose, by John Riddell" (1851). Minutes of Evidence on the Petitions (1853). Report of the Speeches of Counsel and of the Lord Chancellor and Lord St Leonards (1855).

**Monymusk** of Monymusk. The Scots Peerage, vii. 237, 430.

**Monypenny** in France. Chroniques de Louis XII., par Jean d'Auton ; Société de l'Histoire de France, i.
of Leuchars. The Scots Peerage, vi. 275-278.
Lord Monypenny. G. E. C.'s Complete Peerage. The Scots Peerage, vi. 275-279.
of Pitmilly. Eminent Men of Fife, by M. F. Conolly, 337-338. Burke's Landed Gentry (1848-1886). The Scots Peerage, vi. 275-277. Stephen's Inverkeithing, 126-138.

**Moodie** of Cocklaw. Geneal. Mag. (1901), iv. 204-205.
*See also* **Mudie.**

**Moore** of Corswall. Lands and their Owners in Galloway, by M'Kerlie, 2nd ed. (1906), i. 407. Burke's Landed Gentry (1848-1898). Dictionary of National Biography, *s.v.* John Moore, M.D.
of Monfode. Ayrshire Families, by G. Robertson (1824), ii. 141. Paterson's History of Ayr, i. 229. Paterson's Ayr and Wigton, iii. 62.
*or* Muir, Rothesay. History of the County of Bute, by Reid, 242-243.

**Moravia.** *See* **Moray.**

*See* The Scots Peerage, ed. Sir James Balfour Paul, *for*
**Moray,** The Ancient Lords or Earls of, vi. 280-285.
Beaumont, Earl of, vi. 295.
Crichton, Earl of, iii. 63 ; vi. 309.
Douglas, Earl of, vi. 308-310.
Dunbar, Earl of, vi. 298-307.
Plantagenet, Earl of, iii. 150.
Randolph, Earl of, vi. 286-295.

**Moray,** Dunbar, Earl of. Herald and Genealogist, vi. 304-308.
Stuart, Stewart, Earl of. Biographical Peerage (1808), 429-432. Crawfurd's Shire of Renfrew (1818), 458-460. Eminent Men of Fife, by Conolly, 431-434. Historical MSS. Commission (1877), 6th Report. Scottish N. and Q., 2nd S., ii. 129-131. G. E. C.'s Complete Peerage. The Scots Peerage, vi. 311-312, 313-330. Debrett's Peerage, Burke's Peerage, etc.

**Moray** of Abercairney. Heraldry, by Nisbet (1742), ii., Appx. 117-118. Baronage, by Douglas, 98-104. The Stirling Antiquary, iii. 191. Burke's Landed Gentry (1848-1925).
of Bothwell. Baronage, by Douglas, 98-104. Joseph Bain *in* Proc. Soc. Antiq. Scotl. (1890), 461-469. The Stirling Antiquary, ed. W. B. Cook, iii. 172-195. The Genealogist, N. S., xxi. 287. The Scots Peerage, ii. 125-130.

**Moray** of Culbin. Antiquarian Notes, by C. Fraser-Mackintosh, i. 331.

of Drumsargard. Joseph Bain *in* Proc. Soc. Antiq. Scotl. (1885), 380. Scottish History Society (1908), No. 56, *lxxvi.* J. Bain *in* Genealogist, N. S., xvi. 137-139.

of Duffus. Joseph Bain *in* Proc. Soc. Antiq. Scotl. (1890), 462-469. The Scots Peerage, ii. 120-122.

Earl of Strathearn. The Scots Peerage, viii. 255-258.

**Mordingtoun**, Douglas, Lord. Notes and Queries, 8th S., xi. 157. Complete Peerage, by G. E. C. The Scots Peerage, vi. 331-336.

**More.** Vindication of Elizabeth More from the imputation of being a Concubine, by R. Hay (1723).

**Moreton-Macdonald** of Largie. Burke's Landed Gentry (1906-1925).

**Morgan**, Deeside. Memorials of the Family of Forbes of Forbesfield, by A. Forbes (1905), 83-95.

**Morgan-Grenville**, Baron Kinloss. The Scots Peerage, v. 199-201.

**Morice**, Aberdeen. Memoir of J. Young, Aberdeen . . . 1861, ed. Lt.-Col. W. Johnston (1894), 96-116, 177-186.*

**Morison, Morrison.** Traditions of the Morisons (Clan MacGhillemhuire), Hereditary Judges of Lewis, by Capt. F. W. L. Thomas *in* Proc. Soc. Antiq. Scotl. (1878). J. M. Bulloch *in* Aberdeen Univ. Lib. Bulletin (June, 1925). Scottish N. and Q., 2nd S., i. 54 ; 3rd S., iv. 12-14. The History of the Morison or Morrison Family, by Leonard A. Morrison (Boston, Mass., 1880). The Heraldry of the Clan MacGhillemhuire or Morison, by Alex. Morison, M.D., 4to, illust., 16+8 pp. (1910).

**Morison** of Bognie and Frendraught. Temple's Thanage of Fermartyn, 154-161. Scottish N. and Q., 2nd S., i. 95, 127. Burke's Landed Gentry (1879-1925).

of Naughton. Campbell's Balmerino, 522-525, 648.

of Prestongrange. Peeblesshire Localities, by Renwick, 520. Nisbet's Heraldic Plates, ed. Ross and Grant (1892), 135-136.

**Morow.** The Genealogist, N. S., xii. 217.

**Morrice** of Craig. Paterson's Ayr and Wigton, iii.

**Morrine** of Kirkbush. Lands . . . in Galloway, by M'Kerlie, iv. 24.

**Morrison** of Edingham. Lands . . . in Galloway, v. 294.

**Mortimer.** Notes and Queries, 4th S., xii. 149. Scottish N. and Q., 2nd S., vii. 52.

**Morton**, Douglas, Earl of. Registrum Honoris de Morton : a Series of Ancient Charters of the Earldom of Morton, with other original papers, ed. Thomas Thomson, etc., 2 vols., 4to (Bannatyne Club, 1853). Biographical Peerage (1808), 433-435. Eminent Men of Fife, by M. F. Conolly (1866), 144-146. Historical MSS. Commission (1871), 2nd Report. G. E. C.'s Complete Peerage. The Scots Peerage, vi. 337-389. A History of the Douglas Family of Morton, by P. W. L. Adams, 1921. *See also* **Douglas of Morton.**

Morton, Maxwell, Earl of. The Genealogist, N. S., viii. 94-95. The
Scots Peerage, vi. 388-389, 482-487.

Morton of Belmont. Paterson's Ayr and Wigton, i. 778.

of Dalquharne. Paterson's History of the County of Ayr, i. 259.
*See also* Myrton.

Morven, Campbell, Lord. The Scots Peerage, i. 369-393.

Morville, de. Ayrshire Families, by G. Robertson (1824), ii. 9-21. The
Scots Peerage, v. 276-277.

Mosman, Aberdeen. Scottish N. and Q. (1890), iii. 159. Tayler's Jacobites
of Aberdeenshire, 366.

of Auchtyfardle. Annals of Lesmahagow, by Greenshields, 94.* Burke's
Landed Gentry (1886-1925).
Edinburgh. Proc. Soc. Antiq. Scotl. (1891), 140, 152-154, 161.

Mouart of Garth. Zetland Family Histories, by F. J. Grant, 193-199.

Mouat of Garth. Proc. Soc. Antiq. Scotl. (1893), 226.

of North Hammersland. Zetland Family Histories, 200-205.

of Stennis. Zetland Family Histories, 191.

Moubray of Barnbougle and Kolcairny. Nisbet's Heraldry (1742), ii.,
Appx. 22-23.

of Cammo. Cramond, by J. P. Wood, 64.

of Cockairnie and Otterston. Eminent Men of Fife, by Conolly, 339
Stephen's Inverkeithing, 163-168. Burke's Landed Gentry (1848-1925).

of Inverkeithing. Stephen's Inverkeithing (1921), 51 60.

of Naemoor. Burke's Landed Gentry (1914-1925).

Moultray of Seafield and Roscobie. Notes on the Name of Moutray,
by John Armstrong Moutray *in* Genealogist, 1st S., vii. 24-27. An
Historical and Genealogical Memoir of the Family of Moultray,
by the Marquis de Ruvigny, 4to, 32 pp. (London, 1902), *repr. from*
Geneal. Mag. (1902), v.

Moutray, Moulterar of Markinch. East Neuk of Fife, by W. Wood,
2nd ed. (1887), 271.

Mountstewart, Stewart, Baroness. English Peerage, by Rev. Alex. Jacob
(1767), ii. 626.

Mount Stuart, Stuart, Lord. G. E. C.'s Complete Peerage. The Scots
Peerage, ii. 299-312.

Mow of Mow and Mains. Heraldry, by A. Nisbet (1722), i. 326.

Mowat, Aberdeen. Scottish N. and Q., 1st S., xii. 104.

of Ardo and Logie. Scottish N. and Q., 1st S., xii. 104.

of Balquholly. Scottish N. and Q., 1st S., xi. 193; xii. 16, 91-94.
Zetland Family Histories, by F. J. Grant, 188-190. Caithness
Family History, by Henderson, 173-177.

of Brabstermyre and Swinzie. Caithness Family History, by Henderson,
178-180.

of Busbie. Pont's Cuninghame, ed. Dobie, 280-282. Paterson's
History of the County of Ayr, ii. 217-218. Paterson's Ayr and
Wigton, 458-461.

**Mowat** of Hugoland.   Scottish N. and Q., 1st S., xii. 104.
of Inglistoun.   Complete Baronetage, by G. E. C., iii. 345.
of Knockintibber.   Paterson's County of Ayr, ii. 217-218.
of Stanhouse.   Peeblesshire Localities, by Renwick, 201-202.   Annals of a Tweeddale Parish, by Rev. A. Baird, 30.
**Mudie.**   The Mudie Book, being an account of the families of Melsetter, Muir, Cocklaw, Blawhill, Bryanton, Gilchorn, Pitmuies, Arbekie, Masterton, etc., by the Marquis of Ruvigny (1906).*
of Bryanton.   Angus or Forfarshire, by Warden, iii. 453.
of Gilchorn and Pitmuies.   Angus or Forfarshire, by Warden, iv. 85-86.   Burke's Landed Gentry (1848-1875).
of Melsetter.   Information, Memorials, etc., against Ben. Moodie of Melsetter and against Sir J. Stewart and Lord Garlies, as to Murder of Capt. Moodie (1740).   Norton Smith's Orkney Armorials, 106.
of Sauchtonhall.   Scot. Hist. Review, xiv. 310.
*See also* **Moodie.**
**Muir**, Antigua.   Oliver's History of Antigua, ii. 280.
of Cassencary.   Lands . . . in Galloway, by M'Kerlie, iv. 272.
of Craigskean.   Paterson's History of the County of Ayr, ii. 375.
of Laggan-Millan.   Lands . . . in Galloway, by M'Kerlie, iii. 59.
of Monkwood.   Paterson's Ayr, ii. 370.   Paterson's Ayr and Wigton, i. 440-442.
of Park.   Paterson's Ayr, ii. 361.
*or* Moore, Rothesay.   Reid's History of the County of Bute, 242-243.
Slains.   Scottish N. and Q. (1893-4), vii. 28.
in Sweden.   One Year in Sweden, by Marryat (1862), ii. 494.
of Thorntoun.   Paterson's Ayr, ii. 221.   Ayr and Wigton, iii. 475.
**Muir-Mackenzie.**   Lands . . . in Galloway, by M'Kerlie (1878), iv. 273.
**Muirhead.**   C. C. Harvey *in* Scot. Hist. Review, xiv. 69-74.
of Crochmore.   Lands . . . .in Galloway, by M'Kerlie, iv. 29.
of Drumpark.   Lands . . . in Galloway, iv. 3, 4.
of Lachop and Bredisholm.   Heraldry, by Nisbet (1742), ii., Appx. 258-268.   Account of the Family of the Muirheads of Lachop . . . by Walter Grosett of Logie, n.d.   Burke's Landed Gentry (1863-1898).
**Multer** of Grotthill.   Cramond, by J. P. Wood, 30-32.
**Munro.**   [This spelling is used by the Munros of Foulis and their cadets.]
of Achany.   Circular Chart, by H. G. Mill (1881).
of Foulis.   Nisbet's Heraldry, i. 350.   Life of Colonel James Gardiner, by P. Doddridge (1747), 218, 260.   An Account of some Remarkable Particulars concerning the Ancient Family of the Munros of Fowlis, by P. Doddridge, D.D., 28 pp. (London, 1747, 1753, 1814, 1894).   Geneal. Coll., by W. Macfarlane, 1750-51 ; Scot. Hist. Soc., i. 36-40.   History of the Munros of Fowlis, with Genealogies of the Principal Families of that Name, by Alexander Mackenzie (Inverness, 1898).   The Balfours of Pilrig, by Barbara Balfour-Melville, 274.   Debrett's Baronetage.   Burke's Peerage and Baronetage.   Complete Baronetage, by G. E. C., ii. 399.

**Munro** in France. The Munros in France : A History of a branch of the Family in France, descending from the Chiefs of the Clans, seated at Foulis, Ross-shire.; in French and English (1908).

of Novar. Burke's Landed Gentry (1848-1863). Burke's Peerage and Baronetage. Debrett's Baronetage.

of Obsdale. Foulis Castle and the Monroes of Lower Iveagh, by Canon Horace Monroe, illust. and pedigrees (1929).

of Teaninch. Burke's Visitation of Seats and Arms (1853), i. 218. Burke's Landed Gentry (1848-1925).

U.S.A. Sketch of the Clan Munro, also of William Munro . . . who settled in Massachusetts, and some of his posterity, by J. P. Munroe (Boston, U.S.A., 1900).

**Munro-Spencer** of Teaninch. Burke's Landed Gentry (1848-1925).

**Murchison.** Family of Buchanan, by Buchanan of Auchmar (1723), 132.

**Murdoch.** Scottish N. and Q., 2nd S., vii. 46.

of Cornton. Logie, by Rev. Dr Menzies Fergusson, ii. 222.

of Cumloden. A short history of the Family of Murdoch of Cumloden, by J. M. Fallow, Dumfries [1905].* Pedigree of Patrick Murdoch, Glasgow, and his descendants, from 1605, folio, 8 pp.* Lands . . . in Galloway, by M'Kerlie, iv. 411-416. Scottish N. and Q., 2nd S., v. 124.

Fetteresso. Scottish N. and Q., 3rd S., iv. 174.

**Mure** of Anniston. Upper Ward of Lanarkshire, by Irving and Murray, i. 192.

of Auchindrane. Paterson's History of the County of Ayr, ii. 357-358, 361. Paterson's Ayr and Wigton, ii. 402-406, 417-419. Burke's Visitation of Seats and Arms (1853), i. 128-130. The Scots Peerage, ii. 474, 488-489.

of Blairstoun. Paterson's History of Ayr, ii. 361. Ayr and Wigton, ii. 417-419.

of Caldwell. Crawfurd's Shire of Renfrew (1818), 43, 304-309. Paterson's History of Ayr, i. 297-299. Paterson's Ayr and Wigton, iii. 89-95. Burke's Visitation of Seats and Arms (1853), i. 159. Selections from the Family Papers preserved at Caldwell, ed. Col. Mure of Caldwell, 3 vols. (Maitland Club, Glasgow, 1854) ; 3 vols. (New Club, Paisley, 1883-85). Burke's Landed Gentry (1848-1925).

of Cloncaird. Ayr and Wigton, ii. 276. Paterson's History of Ayr, ii. 262.

of Craigspean. Ayr and Wigton, ii. 424.

of Glanderston. Crawfurd's Shire of Renfrew (1818), 40-41.

of Livingston. Lands . . . in Galloway, by M'Kerlie, iii. 161. Burke's Landed Gentry (1886-1914).

of Monyhagen. Ayr and Wigton, ii. 403.

of Park. Ayr and Wigton, ii. 413-419.

of Perceton. Paterson's Ayr and Wigton, iii. 202-203. Burke's Landed Gentry (1894-1925).

of Polkelly. Paterson's History of Ayr, ii. 57. Ayr and Wigton, iii. 246-247.

T

**Mure** of Rowallan.   The Historie and Descent of the House of Rowallane, by
   Sir William Mure of Rowallan, prior to 1657 (Glasgow, 1825).   Pont's
   Cuninghame, ed. Dobie, Appx. ii.   Paterson's Ayr and Wigton,
   iii. 437-445.   Burke's Extinct Baronetcies.   Complete Baronetage,
   by G. E. C., iii. 336 ; vi., Appx. 84.
   of Warriston.   Paterson's Ayr and Wigton, iii. 202-203.

   *See* The Scots Peerage, ed. Sir J. Balfour Paul, *for*

**Murray**, Earl of Annandale, i. 214-229.
   Earl of, Marquess of, Duke of Atholl, i. 449-502.
   Lord, Viscount of Balquhidder, i. 469, 474, 479 ; viii. 411.
   Lord Balvaird, viii. 200-214.
   Earl of Dunmore, iii. 383-396.
   Earl of Dysart, iii. 397-420.
   Lord Elibank, iii. 498-524.
   Viscount of Fincastle, iii. 384.
   Lord Gask, i. 469, 474, 479 ; viii. 411.
   Viscount of Glenlyon, i. 479-502.
   Lord of Huntingtower, iii. 402-420.
   Sovereign of the Isle of Man, i. 488.
   Earl of Mansfield, viii. 206-214.
   Baron Murray of Elibank, ix. 84.
   Lord Murray of Tullibardine, i. 469.
   Duke of Rannoch, i. 481.
   Lord Scone, viii. 192-214.
   Viscount Stormont, viii. 186-214.
   Earl of Tullibardine, i. 469, 474, 478 ; viii. 410-415.
   Marquess of Tullibardine, i. 479.
   Earl of Westminster, iii. 514.

**Murray.**   Heraldry, by Nisbet (1722), i. 253-259.   The Heraldry of the
   Murrays, by G. Harvey Johnston, emblazoned coats-of-arms, with
   notes on all the males of the family (Edinr. 1910).

**Murray**, Antigua.   Oliver's History of Antigua, ii. 280-284.
   of Arbenie.   Douglas's Baronage, 148.
   of Little Ardit.   The Scots Peerage, viii. 187, 189.
   of Ardownie.   Monifieth, by Malcolm, 347-348.
   of Arngask.   Heraldry, by Nisbet (1742), ii., Appx. 211-213.
   Duke of Atholl, *see* **Atholl.**
   of Ayton.   Douglas's Baronage, 149.
   of Balvaird.   The Scots Peerage, viii. 186-193.
   of Berkhampstead.   The Scots Peerage, iii. 399.
   of Binn.   The Scots Peerage, viii. 188-189.
   of Blackbarony.   Baronage, by Douglas, 68-73.   History of Peeblesshire,
      by W. Chambers (1864), 345-349.   Peeblesshire Localities, by
      Renwick, 43-49, 75, 130, 548.   Buchan and Paton's History of
      Peeblesshire, ii. 474-480.   Complete Baronetage, by G. E. C., ii. 352.
      The Scots Peerage, iii. 502-503.

**Murray**, Marquis of Blair. The Jacobite Peerage, by the Marquis of Ruvigny (1904), 16.

of Blebo. The Scots Peerage, i. 467.

of Bowhill. J. B. Burke's Visitation of Seats and Arms (1853), i. 198. The Outlaw Murray, by Keith W. Murray *in* Genealogist, N. S., xii. 217.

of Broughton. Peeblesshire Localities, 207-210. Annals of a Tweeddale Parish, by Rev. A. Baird, 35, 38-44. Notes and Queries, 7th S., ix. 509 ; x. 493 ; xii. 430. Buchan and Paton's History of Peeblesshire, iii. 253.

of Broughton, Kirkcudbright. Burke's Landed Gentry (1848). The Scots Peerage, i. 221.

of Cally. Lands . . . in Galloway, by M'Kerlie, iii. 495-497.

of Cardon. Buchan and Paton's Peeblesshire, iii. 301.

of Cavens. Lands . . . in Galloway, iv. 144-146.

of Cherrytrees. Annals of a Border Club, by G. Tancred, 330.

of Clairden and Castlehill. Caithness Family History, by Henderson, 196-200.

of Claremont, Clermont. Baronage, by Douglas, 48-49. Complete Baronetage, by G. E. C., ii. 314. The Scots Peerage, i. 466-467.

of Cobairdie. Temple's Thanage of Fermartyn, 219-220.

of Cockpool. Historical Families of Dumfriesshire, by C. L. Johnstone, 17. The Scottish Antiquary, xv. 69. The Scots Peerage, i. 216-226, 229.

of Cringletie. Baronage, by Douglas, 112-113. History of Peeblesshire, by Chambers, 358-361, 363. Buchan and Paton's Peeblesshire, ii. 493-500. Burke's Landed Gentry (1858-1925).

of Darnhall. History of Peeblesshire, by Chambers, 349-354.

of Deuchar. Border Memories, by W. Riddell-Carre, 347. Selkirkshire, by T. Craig Brown, ii. 352.

of Dollerie. Baronage, by Douglas, 147-148. The Genealogist, 1st S., vii. 15-19. The Scots Peerage, iii. 397. Burke's Landed Gentry (1886-1925).

in Drochil. Buchan and Paton's Peeblesshire, iii. 83 *n.*

of Drumcairn. The Scots Peerage, viii. 199-202.

of Drumsargard. Joseph Bain *in* Proc. Soc. Antiq. Scotl. (1885), 380. Scot. Hist. Soc., No. 56 (1908), *lxxvi.*

Earl of Dunbar. The Jacobite Peerage, by the Marquis of Ruvigny (1904), 44-45.

Viscount Dunedin. Burke's Peerage. Debrett's Peerage.

of Dunerne. Complete Baronetage, by G. E. C., ii. 374.

Earl of Dunmore. G. E. C.'s Complete Peerage. Burke's and other Annual Peerages. Lady Augusta de Ameland and Sir Augustus D'Este : *See* Herald and Genealogist, ii. 258-261.

of Elibank. Complete Baronetage, by G. E. C., ii. 354. Craig Brown's Selkirkshire, i. 399-402. Buchan and Paton's Peeblesshire, ii. 480-492. The Scots Peerage, iii. 498-524. Burke's Peerage. Debrett's Peerage.

**Murray** of Falahill and Traquair. Peeblesshire Localities, by R. Renwick, 538. The Outlaw Murray, by K. W. Murray *in* Genealogist, N. S., xii. 217-221. *See also* **Murray of Newark.**

of Geanies. Burke's Landed Gentry (1898-1925).

of Glendoick. Nisbet's Heraldic Plates, ed. Ross and Grant, 146. Complete Baronetage, by G. E. C., iv. 305. Burke's Extinct Baronetcies.

of Glendonwyn. Lands . . . in Galloway, by M'Kerlie, v. 39.

of Halmyre. History of Peeblesshire, by Chambers, 493-496. The Scottish Antiquary (1894), viii. 110, 166. Buchan and Paton's Peeblesshire, iii. 30-36.

of the Hangingshaw. Burke's Visitation of Seats and Arms (1853), i. 211. Craig Brown's Selkirkshire, i. 404.

of North Inveramsay. Burke's Landed Gentry (1894-1925).

of Kilbaberton. The Scots Peerage, iii. 509.

of Kippo. East Neuk of Fife, by W. Wood, 2nd ed., 464.

of Langhermiston. The Scots Peerage, iii. 507-508.

of Lanrick. Complete Baronetage, by G. E. C., v. 303.

of Latium, Jamaica. Notes and Queries, 7th S., iii. 389, 480.

of Letter Banachty. The Scots Peerage, viii. 186-199.

of Lintrose. Burke's Landed Gentry (1848-1886). Angus or Forfarshire, by Warden, iv. 20-21.

of Livingstone. Notes and Queries, 7th S., viii. 28.

London. A Publisher and his Friends : Memoir and Correspondence of John Murray, 1768-1843, by S. Smiles, 2 vols. (1891). Notes and Queries, 7th S., i. 498 ; xi. 474.

Sovereign of the Isle of Man. Walford's Chapters from Family Chests, ii. 18-28.

of Meigle. Angus or Forfarshire, by Warden, iv. 346.

of Melgund, Melgum. The Genealogist, N. S., xi. 1-9. Complete Baronetage, by G. E. C., iv. 420.

Earl *or* comte Murray. The Jacobite Peerage, by the Marquis of Ruvigny (1904), 126.

of Murrayfield. History of Peeblesshire, by Chambers, 361.

of Murrayshall. Buchan and Paton's Peeblesshire, iii. 36.

of Murraythwaite. The Scots Peerage, i. 217-218. Burke's Landed Gentry (1849-1925).

Earl of Nairne. The Jacobite Peerage, by the Marquis of Ruvigny, 126-128.

New Plymouth. Geneal. Mag., v. 326.

of Newark. Craig Brown's Selkirkshire, ii. 355-361.

of Newraw. The Genealogist, N. S., xxviii. 27-28.

of Newton. Baronage, by Douglas, 48-49.

of Ochtertyre. Baronage, by Douglas, 145-147. Historical MSS. Commission (1872), 3rd Report. Recreations of an Antiquary, by R. S. Fittis (1881), 127-153. Complete Baronetage, by G. E. C., iv. 291. The Scots Peerage, iii. 397.

of Odiston. The Stirling Antiquary, ed. W. B. Cook, iii. 189.

**Murray**, Pardewis. The Scots Peerage, i. 464.

of Pennyland. Caithness Family History, by Henderson, 189-195.

of Philiphaugh. Baronage, by Douglas, 104-107. Craig Brown's Selkirkshire, ii. 335-350. The Scots Peerage, iii. 499. Burke's Landed Gentry (1848-1925).

of Pitcaithly and Lintrose. Baronage, by Douglas, 149.

of Pitcullen. Baronage, by Douglas, 148.

of Pitlochie. Douglas's Baronage, 109-112.

of Pittencreiff. The Scots Peerage, iii. 509.

of Polmaise. Burke's Landed Gentry (1848-1925). The Scottish Antiquary (1900), xv. 53-77. The Stirling Antiquary, iii. 185. *See also* **Murray of Touchadam.**

of Pulrossie. D. Murray Rose *in* Northern Chronicle (Inverness, 3rd, 10th, 17th August 1910).

Duke of Rannoch. The Jacobite Peerage, 152-155.

of Romanno. History of Peeblesshire, by W. Chambers, 480-482. Sir J. Balfour Paul *in* Genealogist, N. S., xv. 193-202. Peeblesshire Localities, by Renwick, 468-469. Buchan and Paton's Peeblesshire, iii. 11-21.

of Ryvale. The Stirling Antiquary, ed. W. B. Cook, iii. 187.

of Stanhope. Baronage, by Douglas, 107-109. Pedigree of the Murrays of Stanhope, folio, 73 pp. The Murrays of Stanhope, by Sir James Balfour Paul *in* Genealogist, N. S., xv. 193. Peeblesshire Localities, 133. Buchan and Paton's Peeblesshire, iii. 253, 445-450. Complete Baronetage, by G. E. C., iii. 342.

of Stenton. Burke's and other Annual Peerages (after 1905), *s.v.* Viscount Dunedin.

of Stobo. Buchan and Paton's Peeblesshire, iii. 495.

Spital-on-Rule. Tancred's Rulewater, 230.

of Spitalhaugh. Chambers's Peeblesshire, 471.

of Sundhope. Craig Brown's Selkirkshire, i. 415.

in Sweden. One Year in Sweden, by Marryat, ii. 494. Palace of History Catalogue (Glasgow, 1911), 201, 202, 209, 210. E. E. Etzel *in* Scot. Hist. Review, ix. 273.

of Tibbermuir. Recreations of an Antiquary, by Fittis, 211-214.

of Touchadam. Douglas's Baronage, 109-112. Nisbet's Heraldic Plates, ed. Ross and Grant, 52-54. The Scottish Antiquary (1900), xv. 53-77. Chart Pedigree of Murray of Touchadam and Polmaise, folio (1907). Burke's Landed Gentry (1848-1925).

of Traquair. Peeblesshire Localities, by Renwick, 548-551. Buchan and Paton's Peeblesshire, ii. 524-534. The Scots Peerage, ii. 267, 399.

of Troquhain. Lands . . . in Galloway, by M'Kerlie, iii. 72, 73.

of Tullibardine. Chronicles of the Atholl and Tullibardine Families, 5 vols. (1908).* The Scots Peerage, i. 450, 452-468.

Earl of Westminster. The Jacobite Peerage, 184-186.

of Woodend. The Scots Peerage, iii. 398. John MacGregor *in* Genealogist, N. S., xxviii. 27-28.

**Murray-Aynsley.** Burke's Landed Gentry (1886-1914). The Scots Peerage, i. 494.

**Murray-Dunlop** of Corsock. Lands . . . in Galloway, v. 47. Burke's Landed Gentry (1898-1925).

**Murray-Graham** of Murrayshall and Bertha Park. Burke's Landed Gentry (1849-1925).

**Murray-Keith** of Craig. Baronage, by Douglas, 445.

**Murray MacGregor.** Ayrshire Families, by G. Robertson, i. 68-69. Case before the House of Lords . . . Sir E. J. Murray Macgregor, Bart., of Balquhidder . . . regarding the Estates (1840). Complete Baronetage, by G. E. C., v. 303.

**Murray-Pulteney** of Dunerne. Complete Baronetage, by G. E. C., ii. 374.

**Murray-Stewart.** Burke's Landed Gentry (1848-1879).

**Muschet** of Cargill. Memorials of Angus and the Mearns, by Jervise, ed. Gammack, ii. 108-111.

**Mushat** of Spitteltoune. Geneal. Mag., vii. 117.

**Mutch.** Scottish N. and Q., 3rd S., iii. 105.

**Mylne.** The Mylne Family, by R. W. Mylne, 4to (1877). The Master Masons to the Crown of Scotland, . . . by Rev. R. S. Mylne (Edinr. 1893).

of Barnton. Complete Baronetage, by G. E. C., iv. 342.

of Mylnefield. Burke's Landed Gentry (1858-1863). The Parish of Longforgan, by Rev. Adam Philp, 168-170, 217.

*See also* **Milne.**

**Myreton, Myrton** of Cambo. Geneal. Coll., by W. Macfarlane, 1750-51 ; Scot. Hist. Soc., i. 46-52. East Neuk of Fife, by W. Wood, 2nd ed. (1887), 460-461. Churchyard Monuments of Crail, by Erskine Beveridge, 196.

of Gogar and Myrton. Cramond, by J. P. Wood, 70-71. A Midlothian Village, by G. V. Selway, 30-31. Burke's Extinct Baronetcies. Complete Baronetage, by G. E. C., iv. 398.

of Peitfield. Churchyard Monuments of Crail, 194-195.

of Pittowie. Churchyard Monuments of Crail, 195-196.

of Randalston. East Neuk of Fife, 456-457.

**Naesmith** of Dawyck. Chambers's History of Peeblesshire, 418. G. E. C.'s Complete Baronetage, iv. 441. Buchan and Paton's History of Peeblesshire, iii. 442-444.

**Naesmyth** of Posso, Stirkfield and Cardon. Peeblesshire Localities, by Renwick, 203-204, 243, 359. Annals of a Tweeddale Parish, by Rev. A. Baird, 32, 33. Buchan and Paton's Peeblesshire, iii. 563-571. Burke's Peerage and Baronetage. Debrett's Baronetage.

**Nairn** of Drumkilbo. Warden's Angus or Forfarshire, iii. 211.

of Dunsinane. Complete Baronetage, by G. E. C., iv. 425. Burke's Extinct Baronetcies. Notes and Queries, 7th S., vii. 227, 313. The Trial of Katharine Nairn, ed. Wm. Roughead (Edinr. 1926).

**Nairn** of Newton Rires and Elie. Eminent Men of Fife, by Conolly, 346-349. East Neuk of Fife, by W. Wood, 2nd ed., 119, 200-201. Notes and Pedigree *in* Alexander Cowan, by C. B. Boog Watson, 14.

**Nairne** of Mukkersy. The Scots Peerage, vi. 390-392.

Lord Nairne. Bill entitled An Act for the Restoration of William Nairne, Esq. (1824). Case for Emily Jane Mercer-Elphinstone de Flahault, Dowager Marchioness of Lansdowne (1873). Minutes of Evidence (1873). Recreations of an Antiquary, by R. Fittis (1881), 248-282. Complete Peerage, by G. E. C. The Scots Peerage, vi. 390-401. Maurice Supplisson *in* Franco-Scottish Soc. Trans. (Edinr. 1920), vii. 9-16.

of Sandford. Birth Brieve, 1687, *in* The Scottish Antiquary (1895), ix. 118-124 ; with chart of seize quarterings.

of Strathord. Recreations of an Antiquary, by Fittis, 243-248. Scot. Hist. Review, iv. 11-23.

Murray, Earl of. The Jacobite Peerage, by the Marquis of Ruvigny (1904), 126-128.

**Napier.** Nisbet's Heraldry (1722), i. 139-141. History of the Partition of the Lennox, by Mark Napier, *xvi* pp. Additional Remarks upon the question of the Lennox or Rusky representations, etc., in answer to the preceding, by John Riddell, *xxviii*+151 pp. (1835). Border Memories, by W. Riddell-Carre (1876), 288-295, 297, 313.

**Napier** of Ardmore. Strathendrick, by J. Guthrie Smith (1896), 184-186.

of Auchindennan. Book of Dumbartonshire, by Irving, ii. 213.

of Ballachairn. Strathendrick, 185-186.

of Ballikinrain. Strathendrick, 191-206.

of Blackston. Crawfurd's Shire of Renfrew (1818), 377-378. Strathendrick, 186-187.

of Bowhopple. Strathendrick, 187-188.

Clackmannanshire. The Scottish Antiquary, iv. 137.

of Culcreuch. W. M. Graham Easton *in* Geneal. Mag. (1898), i. 290-295. The Stirling Antiquary, ed. W. B. Cook, ii. 116-121. Strathendrick, 179-182. The Scots Peerage, vi. 420.

of Edinbellie. Strathendrick, 176-178. The Scots Peerage, vi. 410, 411.

Baron Ettrick of Ettrick. The Scots Peerage, vi. 437-439.

of Gilletts. Strathendrick, 184, 189-190.

of Greenhill. Strathendrick, 189.

of Kilmahew. Nugae Antiquae : Genealogical Notices of the Napiers of Kilmahew, in Dumbartonshire [by R. M. Kerr], 4to, 39 pp. (Glasgow, 1847-49).* Notes on the Pedigree of Ann Groom, Duchess of Mantua, heiress of line of Napier of Kilmahew . . . by John Riddell and others, 8vo, 40 pp. (London, 1879). The Napiers of Kilmahew and Merchiston, by R. Assheton Napier. Book of Dumbartonshire, ii. 344-353. The Scottish Antiquary (1893), vii. 139.

of Lauriston. Cramond, by J. P. Wood, 40, 42. The Scots Peerage, vi. 414-416.

**Napier** of Merchiston. Crawfurd's Shire of Renfrew (1818), 372-376. Memoirs of John Napier of Merchiston, his Lineage . . . by Mark Napier, 4to, illust. (1834). Strathendrick, by Guthrie Smith, 175-178. Complete Baronetage, by G. E. C., ii. 318. The Scots Peerage, vi. 403-424. Some Notes on the Napiers of Merchiston and Scotts of Thirlestane, by Lord Napier.* Napier Tercentenary Memorial Volume, ed. Cargill Gilston Knott : (Royal Soc. Edinr. 1915). A History of the Napiers of Merchiston, 4to, illust. (1921).*

of Milliken. Crawfurd's Shire of Renfrew (1818), 375-376.

Lord Napier of Merchiston. Biographical Peerage (1808), 440. G. E. C.'s Complete Peerage. The Scots Peerage, vi. 402-439.

of Napier. Burke's Peerage and Baronetage. Debrett's Baronetage.

of Shandon. Garelochside, by Maughan, 48. Book of Dumbartonshire, iii. portrait.

of Thirlestane. Craig Brown's Selkirkshire, i. 307-325.

of Torrie-Easter. Strathendrick, by Guthrie Smith, 183-184. The Scots Peerage, vi. 420-421.

**Nasmyth.** *See* **Naesmyth.**

**Neaf, Neif, Nevoy,** in Sweden. One Year in Sweden, by Marryat (1862), i. 418-420. Memorials of Angus and the Mearns, by Jervise, ed. Gammack (1885), ii. 124, 324.

**Neave** of Methie. Memorials of Angus and the Mearns, by Jervise, ed. Gammack, ii. 124.

**Neill** of Barnweill. Paterson's History of the County of Ayr, i. 346, 460-464. Paterson's Ayr and Wigton, i. 266. Burke's Landed Gentry (1848-1894).

of Schaw. Paterson's Ayr, i. 346.

**Neilson** of Barncalzie, Barcalzie. Baronage, by Douglas, 434-435. Lands and their Owners in Galloway, by M'Kerlie, iv. 309-311.

of Corsock. Heraldry, by Nisbet (1722), i. 439-440. Lands . . . in Galloway, v. 41-46.

of Craigcaffie. Lands . . . in Galloway, 2nd ed. (1906), i. 500-503.

of Greenlaw. Burke's Landed Gentry (1921-1925).

**Neish.** The History of the Clan Neish or MacNish of Perthshire and Galloway, by David Macnish and William A. Tod (Edinr. 1925).

of Tannadice. Warden's Angus or Forfarshire, v. 185-186.

**Nesbitt.** *See* **Nisbet.**

**Nevay** of Nevay. Warden's Angus or Forfarshire, iii. 208-209.

**Neven** of Luning. Zetland Family Histories, by F. J. Grant, 212.

of Scousburgh and Windhouse. Zetland Family Histories, 206-212. Proceedings of Society of Antiquaries of Scotland (1893), 222-223.

**Nevin** of Monkredding. Paterson's Ayr, ii. 253. Paterson's Ayr and Wigton, iii. 515.

**Newall** of Barskeoch. Lands . . . in Galloway, by M'Kerlie, iv. 80-81.

**Newark,** Leslie, Lord. Macfarlane's Geneal. Coll., 1750-51 ; Scot. Hist. Soc., ii. 78-80. G. E. C.'s Complete Peerage. The Scots Peerage, vi. 440-445.

**Newburgh,** Giustiniani-Bandini, Earl of. Case and Supplementary Case of Cecilia, Princess Giustiniani, Marchioness Dowager Bandini, claiming the title of Countess of Newburgh. Petition of Thomas Eyre (1857). Minutes of Evidence (1857). The Scots Peerage, vi. 457-460. G. E. C.'s Complete Peerage. Burke's, Lodge's, Debrett's Peerages, etc.

Livingston, Earl of. Eminent Men of Fife, by Conolly, 298-299. The Scots Peerage, vi. 446-460.

Radcliffe, Earl of. The Scots Peerage, vi. 456-457.

**Newhaven,** Cheyne, Viscount of. The Scots Peerage, vi. 461-468.

**Nowliston,** Dalrymple, Lord. The Scots Peerage, viii. 149-164.

**Newton** of Castlandhill. Stephen's Inverkeithing, 121-122.

of Wester Drumcross. Stephen's Inverkeithing (1921), 121.

of Mitchelhill. Buchan and Paton's History of Peeblesshire, iii. 329.

of Newton. Genealogical Memoranda relating to the Family of Newton, 4to, 12 pp. (1871).* Complete Baronetage, by G. E. C., iv. 373. Burke's Landed Gentry (1906-1925).

**Nicholson.** The Account Book of Dame Magdalen Nicholson, widow of Sir Gilbert Elliot of Stobs, 1671-1693, by A. O. Curle *in* Trans. Hawick Archæol. Soc. (1905).

of Arisaig. Burke's Landed Gentry (1894-1925).

**Nicol** of Ballogie. The Genealogy of the Nicol Family, the Kincardine-shire Branch, by W. E. Nicol, Balogie, 4to (London, 1919).* Burke's Landed Gentry (1898-1925).

Borlum. Major Alpin's . . . Descendants, by P. J. Anderson, 30-31.*

of Netherurd. Buchan and Paton's History of Peeblesshire, iii. 205-207.

**Nicoll,** Arran. Herald and Genealogist, vi. 93.

**Nicolson.** Notes and Queries, 9th S., iv. 207, 317. The Scottish Antiquary, iii. 51-56, 145-148.

of Balcaskie. Complete Baronetage, by G. E. C., iv. 391.

of Carnock. Complete Baronetage, by G. E. C., ii. 424. The Scots Peerage, vi. 426-427. Burke's Peerage and Baronetage. Debrett's Baronetage.

of Cockburnspeth. Complete Baronetage, by G. E. C. (1902), ii. 304.

of Glenbervie. Burke's Landed Gentry (1886-1914).

of Houll. Zetland Family Histories, 223-225.

of Kiltarlity. Scottish N. and Q., 3rd S., vii. 32-34.

of that Ilk and Lasswade. Complete Baronetage, by G. E. C., ii. 363. Burke's Peerage and Baronetage. Debrett's Baronetage.

of Lochend. Zetland Family Histories, by F. J. Grant (1907), 214-222.

of Nether Inverveddie. Scottish N. and Q., 3rd S., vi. 212.

of Shebster. Caithness Family History, by Henderson, 317-318.

of Tillicoultry. Complete Baronetage, by G. E. C., iv. 328.

**Niddrie** of Cammo. Cramond, by J. P. Wood, 45, 63-64.
  of Cramond. Cramond, by Wood, 45.

**Nimmo.** Scottish N. and Q., 2nd S., iv. 158-159, 174, 191.

**Nisbet.** Heraldry, by Alex. Nisbet (1722), i. 319-322. History of the
  Family of Nisbet or Nesbitt in Scotland and Ireland, by Alex.
  Nesbitt and Cecilia Nesbitt, 4to, 63 pp. (Torquay, 1898).*
  of Carfin, Carphin. The Nisbets of Carfin, by John A. Inglis ; Repr.
  from *Misc. Gen. et Herald*, 9 pp. (1916). The Family of Inglis of
  Auchindinny, by J. A. Inglis, 194-205.
  of Craigentinny. Nisbet's Heraldic Plates, *liv*. Complete Baronetage,
  by G. E. C., iv. 275.
  of Dalzell. Nisbet's Heraldic Plates, *xlix-l*.
  of Dean. Nisbet's Heraldic Plates, *lv-lviii*.
  of Dirleton. Nisbet's Heraldic Plates, *lviii-lx*. The Letters of Mary
  Nisbet of Dirleton, Countess of Elgin (1926).
  Edinburgh. Nisbet's Heraldic Plates, *li-liii*.
  of Greenholm. Paterson's History of Ayr, ii. 232. Paterson's Ayr
  and Wigton, iii. 553-554. Nisbet's Heraldic Plates, ed. Ross and
  Grant, 82.
  of Hardhill. The Scottish Antiquary (1897), xi. 92.
  of Nisbet. Notes and Queries, 6th S., ix. 168, 483 ; x. 55, 154. Nisbet's
  Heraldic Plates, ed. Andrew Ross and F. J. Grant (1892), *ix-xxv*.
  The Scottish Antiquary, vii. 180-181.
  of Rochill. One Year in Sweden, by Marryat, ii. 494.
  St Mary's Isle. William Nisbet, an Autobiography, 1816-1830, 102 pp.
  (Providence, R.I., 1885).
  in Sweden. Notes and Queries, 6th S., ix. 406, 783. Palace of History
  Catalogue (Glasgow, 1911), 201, 203, 206, 211. E. E. Etzel *in* Scot.
  Hist. Review (1913), ix. 274.

**Nisbet-Hamilton-Grant** of Belhaven, Dirleton and Pitkeathly. Burke's
  Landed Gentry (1886-1925).

**Nisbett** of Cairnhill. Burke's Landed Gentry (1848-1925).

**Nisbitt**, Antigua. Oliver's History of Antigua, ii. 305-308.

**Nithsdale**, Maxwell, Earl of. Case of William Maxwell of Carruchan
  claiming the title of Earl of Nithsdale (1857). Inventory of the
  Muniments of the Families of Maxwell, Herries and Nithsdale,
  at Terregles, by Sir W. Fraser (1865). The Book of Carlaverock,
  by Sir W. Fraser, 2 vols. (1873). Chronicles of the English
  Augustinian Canonesses . . . at St Monica's in Louvain, by Dom
  Adam Hamilton (1906). Notes and Queries, 8th S., ii. 24, 364 ;
  ix. 408 ; x. 106, 165. Memoirs of the Jacobites of 1715 and 1745,
  by Mrs Katherine Thomson, ii. 1-70. Walford's Tales of our Great
  Families, 2nd S., ii. 53-74. Geneal. Mag. (1898), i. 262-267.
  Complete Peerage, by G. E. C. The Scots Peerage, vi. 469-492.

**Niven**, Aberdeen. Tayler's Jacobites of Aberdeenshire, 366.
  of Maybole. Burke's Landed Gentry (1848, 1894).

Noble of Ferme and Ardardan-Noble. Irving's Book of Dumbartonshire, ii. 308, 353-360.

Northesk, Carnegie, Earl of. Warden's Angus or Forfarshire, i. 431-436. G. E. C.'s Complete Peerage. The Scots Peerage, vi. 493-508. Burke's, Lodge's, Debrett's Peerages, etc.

Nugent-Dunbar of Machermore. Burke's Landed Gentry (1886-1925).

O'Brien, Countess of Orkney. The Scots Peerage, vi. 580-581.

Ochiltree, Colvill, Lord Colville of. The Scots Peerage, ii. 569-575. Stewart, Lord. The Scots Peerage, vi. 511-520. Paterson's Ayr and Wigton, i. 626-629.

Ochterlony of Ochterlony and the Guynd. Petition of J. Ouchterlony of Gaynd, and Answers of the Duke of Gordon, in reference to Removal of Tomb, and Right of Burial within the Abbey of Arbroath (1823). Angus or Forfarshire, by Warden, iii. 103, 192 ; v. 86-89. Memorials of Angus and the Mearns, by Jervise, ed. Gammack, ii. 117-121. Eminent Arbroathians, by M'Bain, 102-112. Burke's Peerage and Baronetage.
of Pitforthie. Burke's Extinct Baronetage. Angus or Forfarshire, iii. 31.
of Seaton. Warden's Angus or Forfarshire, v. 145.
U.S.A. The Ochterloney Family of Scotland and Boston in New England, by Walter K. Watkins, 11 pp. (Boston, U.S.A., 1902).*
See also Ouchterlony.

Ogilvie of Auchiries. The Scottish Antiquary (1898), xii. 91, 138. Tayler's Jacobites of Aberdeenshire, 367-369.
of Balgay. One Year in Sweden, by Marryat, ii. 494.
of Banff. Complete Baronetage, by G. E. C., ii. 327.
of Barras. Heraldry, by Nisbet (1742), ii., Appx. 230-236. Nisbet's Heraldic Plates, ed. Ross and Grant, 150. Memoir of J. Young, ed. Lt. Col. W. Johnston, 132-137. Complete Baronetage, by G. E. C., iii. 335. In Defence of the Regalia, 1651-52 ; Selections from the Family Papers of the Ogilvies of Barras, by Rev. Douglas Gordon Barron, illust. (1910).
of Chesters. Annals of a Border Club, by G. Tancred, 331-340. Burke's Landed Gentry (1879-1925).
of Hartwoodmyres. Annals of a Border Club, 331-340.
of Inchmartine. Douglas's Baronage, 288-290. The Scottish Antiquary (1896), x. 41. The Scots Peerage, iv. 29-37.
of Inshewan. Burke's Landed Gentry (1848-1925). Warden's Angus or Forfarshire, v. 196-199.
of Kempcairn. The Scottish Antiquary, v. 41-42.

Ogilvie-Forbes of Boyndlie. Burke's Landed Gentry (1921-1925).

Ogilvie-Grant, Baron Strathspey of Strathspey, Viscount of Reidhaven, and Earl of Seafield. The Scots Peerage, vii. 454-494.

**Ogilvy.** Heraldry, by Nisbet (1722), i. 301-304. Early Ogilvy Pedigrees, A.D. 1366-1628, by Sir J. H. Ramsay of Bamff, 14 pp. (1919).

Earl of Airlie. Claim of Walter Ogilvy to the Title of Earl of Airlie, and Lord Ogilvy : (Session Papers 67 of 1812-13, 60 of 1813-14). Case of Walter Ogilvy (1813). Historical MSS. Commission (1871), 2nd Report. Warden's Angus or Forfarshire, i. 419-431. Walford's Chapters from Family Chests, i. 100-108. Burke's Peerage, etc. G. E. C.'s Complete Peerage, ed. Gibbs. The Scots Peerage, i. 106-132. The House of Airlie, by Rev. Wm. Wilson, London (1924), 2 vols., illust.

of Auchlevin. The Scots Peerage, iv. 16-18.

of Auchterhouse. Angus or Forfarshire, by A. J. Warden, iv. 103, 216-221. The Scots Peerage, i. 107-109. The Genealogist, N. S., xxxv. 162-168

of Balfour. Warden's Angus or Forfarshire, iv. 34. The Scots Peerage, i. 295-296.

Lord Banff. Notes and Queries, 3rd S., vii. 53 : 4th S., i. 411 ; vi. 521 ; x. 47. The Scots Peerage, ii. 1-26.

of Birnes. The Scots Peerage, ii. 12, 13.

of Boyne. Baronage, by Douglas, 288-290. Nisbet's Heraldic Plates, ed. Ross and Grant, 128. The Scots Peerage, ii. 26.

of Carnowseis. Notes and Queries, 3rd S., vi. 369, and pedigree. Complete Baronetage, by G. E. C., ii. 313. The Scots Peerage, ii. 4-12.

of Clova. The Genealogist, N. S., xxxv. 170-175. The Scots Peerage, ii. 124, 129.

in Cornton. By Allan Water, the Story of an old House, by Katharine Steuart [Agnes Maciver Logan].

of Deskford. The Scots Peerage, iv. 16-26.

Lord Deskford. The Scots Peerage, iv. 28.

of Dunlugus. The Scots Peerage, ii. 8-16.

of East Mill. Angus or Forfarshire, by Warden, iii. 371. The Trial of Katharine Nairn, ed. Roughead (1906).

Earl of Findlater. The Scots Peerage, iv. 16-41.

of Forglen. Complete Baronetage, by G. E. C., iv. 398. The Scots Peerage, ii. 22, 24.

of Innercarity, Inverquharity. Douglas's Baronage, 49-52. Notes and Queries, 3rd S., x. 474 ; xi. 103. Angus or Forfarshire, iv. 276-278, 103-113. Oliver's History of Antigua, iii. 155-162. The Genealogist, N. S., xxxv. 168-169. Complete Baronetage, by G. E. C., ii. 316. Burke's Peerage and Baronetage. Debrett's Baronetage.

of Inverkeiler. The Scots Peerage, i. 118.

of Knock. The Scots Peerage, ii. 13.

of Lintrathen. The Scots Peerage, i. 111-113.

of Muirton. The Scots Peerage, i. 120-121.

of Newgrange. The Scots Peerage, i. 121.

of Ogilvy. Memorials of Angus and the Mearns, by Jervise, ed. Gammack, ii. 115-116. Angus or Forfarshire, iii. 328. The Scots Peerage, i. 107.

**Ogilvy,** Lord Ogilvy of Airlie. The Scots Peerage, i. 114-132. G. E. C.'s Complete Peerage.
sieur de la Perrière. Scottish N. and Q., 3rd S., iii. 154.
of Powrie. Warden's Angus or Forfarshire, v. 12-14.
at Prague. The Scottish Antiquary, vii. 58-59.
Viscount of Reidhaven. The Scots Peerage, iv. 37-41.
Earl of Seafield. The Scots Peerage, iv. 37-41.
of Shielhill. Angus or Forfarshire, iv. 121.
of Stove, Quarff and Seafield. Zetland Family Histories, by F. J. Grant, 229-232.
of Tannadice. Baronage of Angus and Mearns, by D. M. Peter (1856), 15. Burke's Landed Gentry (1879).
**Ogston** of Ardoe. Temple's Thanage of Fermartyn, 394. Burke's Landed Gentry (1906-1925).
**Ogstoun** of Ogstoun. Genealogical History of the Families of Ogstoun from their first appearance, A.D. 1200 [by Alex. Ogston] (1871, 2nd ed. 1876). Temple's Thanage of Fermartyn, 388-394.
**Olifard.** Scot. Hist. Review, ii. 174-176. The Scots Peerage, vi. 523-529.
**Oliphant.** Geneal. Coll., by W. Macfarlane, 1750-51 ; Scot. Hist. Soc., ii. 97-124. Heraldry, by A. Nisbet (1722), i. 244-245. Notes and Queries, 4th S., vi. 260 ; ix. 393.
of Aberdalgie and Kelly. Cramond, by J. P. Wood, 24-25. East Neuk of Fife, by W. Wood, 2nd ed., 258-261.
of Berriedale. The Scots Peerage, vi. 541-542.
of Condie. Burke's Commoners, i. 493. Burke's Landed Gentry (1848-1914).
of Gask. Burke's Commoners, iv. 258. Burke's Landed Gentry (1848-1898). The Jacobite Lairds of Gask, by T. L. Kington Oliphant (Grampian Club, 1870). The Oliphants in Scotland, with a Selection of Original Documents from the Charter Chest at Gask, ed. Joseph Anderson, 4to, illust. (Edinr. 1879).* The Oliphants of Gask ; Records of a Jacobite Family, by E. Maxtone Graham, 8vo, illust. (London, 1910). The Jacobite Peerage, 138-142.
of Newtoun. Complete Baronetage, by G. E. C. (1902), ii. 367.
Baron Oliphant. The Jacobite Peerage, 138-142.
Lord Oliphant. Angus or Forfarshire, by A. J. Warden, ii. 35-40. G. E. C.'s Complete Peerage. The Scots Peerage, vi. 521-563.
of Rossie. Burke's Landed Gentry (1879-1925).
of Turin. The Scots Peerage, vi. 545.
**Oliphant-Ferguson.** Burke's Landed Gentry (1858-1906).
**Oliver** of Dinlabyre. Scottish N. and Q., 2nd S., iii. 106, 127. Tancred's Annals of a Border Club, 340-345.
Rulewater. Tancred's Rulewater, 264-281.
**Oliver-Rutherford** of Fairnington. Annals of a Border Club, 396.
**Omond** of Carness. Norton Smith's Orkney Armorials, 114.
**Oransay,** Campbell, Lord. The Scots Peerage, i. 379.

**Ord.** Scottish N. and Q., 2nd S., ii. 107, 109.
of Findochty. Dr Cramond *in* Trans. Banff Field Club (30th June, 1888).
Scottish N. and Q., 1st S., i. 201 ; iii. 77, 94 ; 3rd S., i. 61.

*See* The Scots Peerage, ed. Sir J. Balfour Paul, *for*

**Orkney,** The Ancient Earls of, ii. 313-320.
Fitzmaurice, Earl of, vi. 581-584.
Hamilton, Earl of, vi. 578-584.
Hepburn, Duke of, ii. 161-167.
O'Brien, Countess of, vi. 580-581.
Sinclair, Earl of, vi. 564-571.
Stewart, Earl of, vi. 572-577.

**Orkney.** The Orkneyinga Saga, ed. Joseph Anderson, *xxi-lxxi, cxxxii.*
Records of the Earldom of Orkney, 1299-1614, ed. J. Storer Clouston,
25 geneal. tables (Scot. Hist. Soc., 1914). J. Storer Clouston *in*
Scot. Hist Review, xvi. 15-28. David Marshall *on* The Connection
of the Earls of Morton and Dick of Braid with the Earldom of
Orkney *in* Proc. Soc. Antiq. Scotl. (1889). Earl Rognvald and his
Forebears, by C. S. Spence (1896). Orkney and Shetland Folk,
880-1350, by A. W. Johnston ; *in* Saga-Book of Viking Soc.,
ix. 372-404. G. E. C.'s Complete Peerage. Peerages by Burke,
Lodge, etc.

**Orme** of Mugdrum. The Scottish Antiquary (1894), viii. 90-91.

**Ormelie,** Campbell, Lord, Earl of. The Scots Peerage, ii. 203, 210.

**Ormiston** of Glenburnhall. Annals of a Border Club, by G. Tancred (1899),
345-346.
of Ormiston. The Ormistons of that Ilk, by T. L. Ormiston, 8vo,
8 pp., n.d.*

**Ormond,** Boysack Muir. Eminent Arbroathians, by J. M. M'Bain, 386.
Douglas, Earl of. G. E. C.'s Complete Peerage. The Scots Peerage,
i. 206 ; vi. 585-586.
Stewart, Marquess of. The Scots Peerage, i. 155 ; vii. 245-246.

**Orr** of Barrowfield. Glasgow Past and Present (1884), iii. 19-25, 181.
of Bridgeton. Angus or Forfarshire, by Warden, iii. 248.
of Ralston. Crawfurd's Shire of Renfrew (1818), 330.
Selkirk. MS. Pedigree in possession of the Lyon Office, and the Society
of Genealogists, London.
of Waterside and Glasgow. Some Old Families, by H. B. M'Call,
Pedigree, 145-155.*

**Orr-Ewing** of Ballikinrain and Lennoxbank. Burke's Landed Gentry
(1875-1886). Burke's Peerage and Baronetage. Debrett's Baronetage
of Levenfield. Irving's Book of Dumbartonshire (1879), iii. portrait.

**Orrok** of Orrok. Temple's Thanage of Fermartyn, 637. Beatson's Family
of Beatson. Letters of John Orrok, 1801-1816 (Aberdeen, 1927),
1-2, 207, 212, 214.

**Osborne,** Viscount Dunblane. The Scots Peerage, iii. 301-302.

**Osler.** Pedigree of the Osler Family, with notes (1924).*

**Oswald** of Auchincruive. Crawfurd's Shire of Renfrew (1818), 347.
Paterson's History of the County of Ayr, ii. 417. Paterson's Ayr and
Wigton, i. 666-668. Lands . . . in Galloway, by M'Kerlie, iv. 148-152.
Burke's Landed Gentry (1848-1925).
Caithness. Dr John Mowat *in* Northern Ensign (Wick, 19th, 26th April,
1910).
of Dalders and Skirling. Peeblesshire Localities, by Renwick, 410.
of Dunnikier. Memorials of James Oswald of Dunnikier (Edinr. 1825).
Burke's Landed Gentry (1858-1925).
Glasgow. John o' Groat Journal (Wick, 15th July, 12th Aug. 1853).
Kirkwall. Henderson's Caithness Family History, 232-237.
of Shieldhall and Scotstoun. Crawfurd's Shire of Renfrew (1818), 347.
Glasgow Past and Present (1884), iii. 28-33.

**Otterburne** of Redhall. Walks near Edinburgh, by Margaret Warrender,
37-39. The Family of Inglis of Auchindinny, by J. A. Inglis, 114-121.

**Ouchterlony** of Kintrocket. Baronage of Angus and Mearns, by Peter, 271.
of Muirhouse. Scottish N. and Q., 3rd S., iii. 155.
*See also* **Ochterlony.**

**Oudny** of Keithock. Angus or Forfarshire, by Warden, iii. 25.

**Oughton** of Granton. Cramond, by J. P. Wood, 20.

**Outram**, Aberdeen. Scottish N. and Q., 3rd S., v. 217.

**Oxenfoord** of Cousland, Dalrymple, Baron. G. E. C.'s Complete Peerage.
The Scots Peerage, viii. 156-164.

**Oxfuird**, Makgill, Viscount of. G. E. C.'s Complete Peerage. The Scots
Peerage, vi. 587-601.

**Paintland**, Campbell, Viscount of. The Scots Peerage, ii. 203, 204.

**Paisley**, Hamilton, Lord, Baron of. The Scots Peerage, i. 39-74.

**Palmer-Douglas** of Cavers. Burke's Landed Gentry (1914-1925).

**Panmure**, Maule, Earl of. Registrum de Panmure, compiled by H. Maule
of Kelly.* Angus or Forfarshire, by Warden, i. 379-414; v. 57-73. The
Panmure Papers . . . ed. by Sir G. Douglas and Sir G. D. Ramsay,
2 vols. (1908). The Scots Peerage, vii. 1-27. G. E. C.'s Complete
Peerage.

**Panter**, Montrose. Proc. Soc. Antiq. Scotl. (1882), 65.

**Panton** of Pitmethan. Temple's Thanage of Fermartyn, 443-444.

**Park**, East Lothian. A Chapter in Mediocrity, by Rev. W. S. Stavert
(Skipton, 1896), 13.*
of Park. Crawfurd's Shire of Renfrew (1818), 114.
of Parkhall. Strathendrick, by Guthrie Smith, 226.

**Parker** of Assloss. Ayrshire Families, by G. Robertson, i. 23. Paterson's
Ayr and Wigton, iii. 425.
of Barleith. Ayrshire Families, i. 23.

**Paterson.** James Paterson's Scottish Surnames (Edinr. 1866), 43-51.

Aberdeen. Genealogies of an Aberdeen Family, by Smith (1913), 86.

of Bannockburn. The Scottish Antiquary, iv. 95, 141-143 ; v. 45, 142 ; xi. 189. The Complete Baronetage, by G. E. C., iv. 342.

of Carpow. Burke's Landed Gentry (1858-1894).

of Castle Huntly. Visitation of Seats and Arms, by J. B. Burke (1853), i. 32. The Parish of Longforgan (1895), 105. Burke's Landed Gentry (1849-1925).

of Craigton. Crawfurd's Shire of Renfrew (1818), 394.

Darnhall. Peeblesshire Localities, by Renwick, 38.

of Eccles. Burke's Visitation of Seats and Arms (1853), ii. 60. Complete Baronetage, by G. E. C., iv. 351.

of Glentig. Paterson's History of the County of Ayr (1847), i. 253. Paterson's Ayr and Wigton, ii. 104.

of Granton. Cramond, by J. P. Wood, 19-20.

Inverness. Scottish N. and Q., 2nd S., i. 143, 160, 175, 191.

"Old Mortality." Notes and Queries, 4th S., vi. 207, 354 ; vii. 264 : 5th S., ii. 97. The Birthplace and Parentage of Wm. Paterson, by Wm. Pagan (Edinr. 1865).

of Preston Hall. Visitation of Seats and Arms, by J. B. Burke (1853), ii. 61-62.

of Whitslade. Peeblesshire Localities, by Renwick, 237.

**Paterson-Anstruther.** Case of Dame Ann Paterson Anstruther claiming the title of Baroness Polewart or Polwarth (1818). Claim of Dame Ann Paterson Anstruther to the title of Baroness Polewart or Polwarth : (Session Papers, 101 of 1818). The Scots Peerage, vi. 21 ; vii. 71.

**Patison,** Paisley. Notes on Patison, Paisley, typewritten, 4 pp. : in Library of Society of Genealogists.

**Paton** of Crailing. Records of the Paton Family [ed. J. H. Paton], 12 pp. (Edinr. 1889).* Annals of a Border Club, by G. Tancred, 347-353. Burke's Landed Gentry (1906-1925).

of Ferrachie and Grandhouse. Burke's Landed Gentry (1848-1894), p. 2254.

of Grandhome. Temple's Thanage of Fermartyn, 648-649.

of Meadowhead. J. H. Paton *in* Scot. Hist. Review, ii. 335-336.

of Sawerston. Paterson's History of Ayr, ii. 428. Paterson's Ayr and Wigton, i. 704.

**Patrick** of Byres. Ayrshire Families, by G. Robertson, ii. 276-277.

of Dalga and Whitehirst. Ayrshire Families, ii. 268, 274, 277.

of Drumbuie and Shotts. Ayrshire Families, ii. 269, 272-274. Paterson's History of the County of Ayr, i. 296. Paterson's Ayr and Wigton, iii. 87-88.

of Ladyland. Burke's Landed Gentry (1858-1925).

of Overmains and Waterside. Ayrshire Families, ii. 268-270.

**Patrick** of Trearne and Hazlehead. Ayrshire Families, ii. 267-272. Paterson's Ayr, i. 295, 462. Paterson's Ayr and Wigton, iii. 126-129. Burke's Landed Gentry (1848-1925). Pedigree of Patrick of Trearne, Hazlehead, Roughwood and Woodside from King Robert III. (Edinr. 1857).*

of Ward. Ayrshire Families, ii. 277-278.

**Patullo** of Balhouffie. East Neuk of Fife, by W. Wood, 2nd ed., 338-339.

**Paul.** Some Pauls of Glasgow and their Descendants, by Sir James Balfour Paul (Edinr. 1912).*

**Peacock**, Lintonroderick. Peeblesshire Localities, by Renwick, 493.

**Pearson, Peirson, Pierson.** A Condensed Account of the Family of Pe—rson in Scotland from A.D. 1296, by David Ritchie Pearson, M.D. Typescript in Lyon Office (1891).

**Pearson** of Johnston. Burke's Landed Gentry (1906-1925).

of Kippenross. The Stirling Antiquary, ii. 207-208.

Kirkcaldy. Pedigree *in* Alexander Cowan, by C. B. Boog Watson.*

of Lochlands. Memoir of J. Young, Aberdeen . . . 1861, ed. Lt.-Col. W. Johnston (1894), 177.*

**Peden** of Auchinlongford. History of County of Ayr, by Paterson, ii. 427. Ayr and Wigton, i. 683.

U.S.A. The Pedens of America, by Eleanor M. Hewell, n.p. (1900).

**Peebles** of Broomlands. Paterson's Ayr and Wigton, iii. 275.

of Crawfield. Ayrshire Families, by G. Robertson (1824), ii. 338 *n*.

Dewsbury, Yorkshire. The Scottish Antiquary, vii. 128-129.

Douglas, Viscount of. The Scots Peerage, vii. 145-147.

**Peile.** Annals of the Peiles of Strathclyde . . . [by Rev. T. W. Peile] (1899).

**Pennecuik** of Newhall. Chambers's History of Peeblesshire, 482. Scot. Hist. Review, xvi. 180-182. Wilson's Annals of Peebles (1891), 170-171.* Memoir *in* Works of Alexander Pennecuik [by Robert Brown] (1815).

of Romanno. Chambers's History of Peeblesshire, 482-488. Buchan and Paton's Peeblesshire, iii. 21-23, 129.

**Pennie, Penny.** Annals and Antiquities of Dryburgh, by Sir D. Erskine, 2nd ed., 39, 40.

Southessie. Scottish N. and Q., 2nd S., v. 58.

**Perth**, Drummond, Lord, Earl of. The Earldom of Perth, by J. Maidment.* Correspondence of James, Earl of Perth ; Camden Soc., No. 3, 1st S. (1845). Memorial for the Earl of Perth and Melfort, 4to, n.d. Case of Thomas Drummond of New Painshaw, claiming the Honours and Estates of the Earldom of Perth (Newcastle-on-Tyne, 1831). An Interesting Statement of the Claims of Thomas Drummond to the Earldom of Perth, interspersed with copious Memoirs of the Noble House of Drummond, 8vo (Newcastle-on-Tyne, 1831). Sequel to the above work, 8vo, 3 pp. Case of Thomas Drummond claiming the Title of Earl of Perth (1832). Case on behalf of George

Drummond, claiming to be Earl of Perth, folio, 22 pp., n.d. Claim of George Drummond, Duke of Melfort, to the Earldom of Perth : (Session Papers, 233 of 1846, 107 of 1847, 326 of 1847-8, 432 of 1852-3). Memoirs of the Jacobites of 1715 and 1745, by Mrs Katherine Thomson (1845-46), iii. 226-309. Nisbet's Heraldic Plates, ed. Ross and Grant (1892), 14-17. Scottish Antiquary, xiii. 41. G. E. C.'s Complete Peerage. The Scots Peerage, vii. 28-62. Burke's and other Annual Peerages.

**Perth,** Drummond, Duke of. The Jacobite Peerage (1904), 145-150. The Scots Peerage, vii. 52-57.

**Petrie,** Aberdeen. Tayler's Jacobites of Aberdeenshire, 379.

**Philip** of Almerieclose. Eminent Arbroathians, by J. M. M'Bain (1897), 81-102. Warden's Angus or Forfarshire, v. 118.

**Phillip,** Old Meldrum. Scottish N. and Q. (1895), ix. 12.

**Philp** of Fingask and Largo. One Year in Sweden, by Marryat (1862), ii. 494.

of Greenlaw. Cramond, by J. P. Wood, 57 *n.* The Family of Inglis of Auchindinny, by J. A. Inglis, 206-219.

of Kippo. East Neuk of Fife, by W. Wood, 2nd ed., 336, 464.

in Sweden. One Year in Sweden, by Marryat, ii. 494-495. Palace of History Catalogue (Glasgow, 1911), 209.

**Pictish Kings.** Royal Genealogies, by Jas. Anderson (1732), 751.

**Pierson** of Balmadies. Warden's Angus or Forfarshire, v. 87. Familien Cronik der Pierson von Balmadies (Berlin, 1901).

of Lochlands. Eminent Arbroathians, by J. M. M'Bain, 155-170.

*See also* **Pearson.**

**Pike.** Scottish N. and Q., 3rd S., vi. 12-16, 38.

**Piper** in Sweden. One Year in Sweden, by Marryat, ii. 476, 498.

**Pirie,** Aberdeen. William Robinson Pirie : In Memoriam [by Miss Pirie] with Genealogy of the Family (Aberdeen, 1888).*

of Buthlaw. Thanage of Fermartyn, by Temple, 275, 476.

in Orchardtown. Thanage of Fermartyn, 474-475.

**Pirie-Gordon** of Buthlaw. Burke's Landed Gentry (1898-1925).

**Pitcairn.** History of the Fife Pitcairns, by Constance Pitcairn, 8vo, illust. (Edinr. 1905). Alexander Cowan, by C. B. Boog Watson, 42-46.*

of Cordoun. The Scottish Antiquary, ix. 60, 63.

of Innernethy. The Scottish Antiquary, ix. 5-9, 59-63.

of Pitblae. The Scottish Antiquary, ix. 60-62.

of Pitcairns. Burke's Landed Gentry (1848).

**Pitman,** Edinburgh. Erminois, by Rev. C. Moor, 46-47.

**Pitsligo,** Forbes, Lord Forbes of. G. E. C.'s Complete Peerage. The Scots Peerage, iv. 69-76. Tayler's Jacobites of Aberdeenshire (1928), 379-383.

**Pittenweem,** Stewart, Lord. G. E. C.'s Complete Peerage. The Scots Peerage, vii. 63-69.

**Playfair.** Some Account of the Rogers of Coupar Grange, by J. C. Roger, 19 pp. (London, 1877), 34 pp. (1879). Warden's Angus or Forfarshire, iv. 337. Four Perthshire Families, by the Rev. Charles Rogers (1887), 42-88.* Herald and Genealogist, viii. 454-456. Notes on the Scottish Family of Playfair, by the Rev. A. G. Playfair (1913), 3rd ed., Supplement to above (1919).

St Andrews. Eminent Men of Fife, by M. F. Conolly (Cupar, 1866), 360-366.

**Plenderleith.** Heraldry, by Nisbet, i. 401.

of Blyth. Buchan and Paton's History of Peeblesshire, iii. 168.

**Plummer** of Middlestead. Craig Brown's Selkirkshire, ii. 317. Border Memories, by W. Riddell-Carre, 321, 324.

of Sunderland Hall. Burke's Landed Gentry (1849-1894).

**Pole** of Mossbank and Greenbank. Zetland Family Histories, by F. J. Grant, 223-236.

**Pollard-Urquhart** of Craigston. Burke's Landed Gentry (1848-1925).

**Pollok** of Balgray. Crawfurd's Shire of Renfrew (1818), 39.

of Pollok. Crawfurd's Shire of Renfrew (1818), 37-38, 289-293. Nisbet's Heraldic Plates, ed. Ross and Grant (1892), 34-36. Complete Baronetage, by G. E. C., iv. 416.

**Pollok-McCall** of Daldowie. Burke's Landed Gentry (1921-1925).

**Polwarth,** Hepburne-Scott, Lord. Case, and Additional Case of Hugh Scott of Harden, claiming the title of Baron Polewart or Polewarth (1835). G. E. C.'s Complete Peerage. The Scots Peerage, vii. 70-87. Lodge's and other Annual Peerages. *See also* **Paterson Anstruther.**

**Polwarth,** Hume, Lord. Marchmont and the Humes of Polwarth [by M. Warrender] (1894). The Scots Peerage, vi. 14-24 ; vii. 71. Historical MSS. Commission (1911, 1916), 17th Report.

**Porteous** of Glenkirk. Peeblesshire Localities, by Renwick, 240. Annals of a Tweeddale Parish, by Baird, 82-84. Buchan and Paton's Peeblesshire, iii. 302-307.

of Halkshaw. Peeblesshire Localities, by Renwick, 328. Buchan and Paton's Peeblesshire, iii. 396-399.

of Lauriston Castle. Baronage of Angus and Mearns, by D. M. Peter (1856), 275. Burke's Landed Gentry (1879-1914).

**Porter** of Blaiket. Lands . . . in Galloway, by M'Kerlie, v. 300.

Coupar Angus. Memorials of Angus and the Mearns, by Jervise, ed. Gammack, ii. 193.

of Porterfield. Crawfurd's Shire of Renfrew (1818), 62.

**Porterfield** of the Chapeltoun. Geneal. Coll., by W. Macfarlane, 1750-51 ; Scot. Hist. Soc., ii. 538.

of Hapland. Pont's Cunninghame, ed. Dobie, 205-211. Paterson's Ayr, ii. 51-52, 506-507. Paterson's Ayr and Wigton, iii. 235-237.

of Porterfield. Crawfurd's Shire of Renfrew (1818), 63, 402.

**Portmore**, Colyear, Lord, Earl of. G. E. C.'s Complete Peerage. The Scots Peerage, vii. 88-97. Buchan and Paton's Peeblesshire, ii. 501-504.

**Pott** of Dod and Knowesouth. Annals of a Border Club, by G. Tancred, 353-359.
in Sweden. One Year in Sweden, by Marryat, ii. 485.
of Todrig. Burke's Landed Gentry (1848-1914).

**Poyntz-Stewart.** Burke's Landed Gentry (1921-1925).

**Pratt,** Fyvie. Thanage of Fermartyn, by Rev. W. Temple, 48.

**Prendergest.** Recreations of an Antiquary, by R. S. Fittis (1881), 333-334.
**Preston.** M'Call's Some Old Families (Birmingham, 1890).*
of Airdrie. East Neuk of Fife, by W. Wood, 2nd ed., 401-402. Complete Baronetage, by G. E. C., ii. 346.
Baron Dumore, Lord Dingwall, Earl of Desmond. The Scots Peerage, iii. 112-125.
of Fyvie. Fyvie Castle, by A. M. W. Stirling, 47-52, 364.
of Gorton. The Family of Inglis of Auchindinny, by J. A. Inglis, 53-55. The Scots Peerage, v. 406, 408.
of Valleyfield. Baronage, by Douglas, 91-92. MS. Genealogical Tree of the Prestons of Valleyfield and Prestons of Gorton ; Two sheets (1834). Burke's Landed Gentry (1875-1894). Complete Baronetage, by G. E. C., ii. 426. Stephen's Inverkeithing (1921), 74-80, 84. Pedigree attached to Chalmers' History of Dunfermline (1859).
of Whitehill. The Scots Peerage, iii. 118-121.

**Preston,** Graham, Viscount of. G. E. C.'s Complete Peerage. The Scots Peerage, vii. 98-108.

**Primrose.** Heraldry, by Nisbet (1722), i. 380-381. Lands and Lairds of Dunipace, by J. C. Gibson (1903).
of Barnbougle. Cramond, by J. P. Wood, 71.
of Burnbrae. The Scottish Antiquary, x. 47.
of Carrington. Complete Baronetage, by G. E. C., iii. 324. The Scots Peerage, vii. 109-110.
of Culross. Nisbet's Heraldic Plates, ed. Ross and Grant (1892), 9.
of Dalmeny. The Scots Peerage, vii. 218.
Lord Dalmeny. The Scots Peerage, vii. 221-229.
Gellyholm. The Scottish Antiquary, ix. 188 ; x. 46.
Earl of Midlothian. The Scots Peerage, ix. 152.
Viscount of Primrose. The Scots Peerage, vii. 109-111, 221-229.
Earl of Rosebery. The Scots Peerage, vii. 212-229. History of the Primrose - Rosebery Family, 1500-1900, by J. Macbeth Forbes, *viii*+444 pp. (London, 1907).
in Sweden. One Year in Sweden, by Marryat (1862), ii. 495.

**Pringle.** Border Memories, by W. Riddell-Carre (1876), 317-320. Notes and Queries, 7th S., ii. 288, 476.
of Blindlie. T. Craig Brown's Selkirkshire (1886), i. 542-543.
of Borgue. Lands . . . in Galloway, by M'Kerlie, iii. 182.

**Pringle** of Carriber. Annals of a Border Club, by G. Tancred, 371.

of Chapelhill. Peeblesshire Localities, by Renwick, 185 *n.*

of Galashiels. Heraldry, by A. Nisbet (1742), ii., Appx. 71-72. Memoirs of Walter Pringle. Craig Brown's Selkirkshire, i. 527-534. The Scots Peerage, vii. 75.

of Greenknowe. Memoirs of Walter Pringle of Greenknowe, ed. Rev. W. Wood, with notes, 12mo (Edinr. 1847).

of Haining. Craig Brown's Selkirkshire, ii. 309-310. Border Memories, by W. Riddell-Carre, 209, 344. Burke's Landed Gentry (1849-1863).

of Newhall. Craig Brown's Selkirkshire, i. 457-458.

of Smailholm. Baronage, by Douglas (1784), 208-213. Annals and Antiquities of Dryburgh, by Sir D. Erskine (Kelso, 2nd ed.), 92-95, 205-217.

of Stichill. Memoirs of Walter Pringle. Nisbet's Heraldic Plates, ed. Ross and Grant (1892), 68-70. Complete Baronetage, by G. E. C., iv. 318 ; v. 138.

of Torsonce. Craig Brown's Selkirkshire, i. 453-456.

of Torwoodlee. Memoirs of Walter Pringle. Craig Brown's Selkirkshire, i. 459-469. Annals of a Border Club, by G. Tancred, 364-366. Burke's Landed Gentry (1849-1925).

of Tynnes. Craig Brown's Selkirkshire, i. 416.

of Whitson. Baronage, by Douglas, 208-209. Annals and Antiquities of Dryburgh, by Sir D. Erskine, 2nd ed., 210.

of Whytbank and Yair. Baronage, by Douglas, 208-213. Memoirs of Walter Pringle. Annals of a Border Club, 359-363, 366. Craig Brown's Selkirkshire, i. 373, 471-474. Our Forefathers, by Mary Anne Scott Moncrieff (Edinr. 1895).* Burke's Landed Gentry (1848-1914). Visitation of Seats and Arms, by J. B. Burke (1853), i. 131-132.

**Proctor** in Conrack. Scottish N. and Q., 3rd S., iv. 19, 43, 214.

of Halkerton. Angus or Forfarshire, by Warden, iii. 335.

**Provan** of Auchengillan. Strathblane, by Guthrie Smith, 35-39, 40.

of Ledlewan. Strathendrick, by Guthrie Smith, 254-255. Strathblane, 37.

**Pulteney,** *né* Johnstone. Burke's Visitation of Seats and Arms (1853), i. 201. Historical Families of Dumfriesshire, by C. L. Johnstone, 65.

**Purdie** of Lynetownhead. Buchan and Paton's History of Peeblesshire, iii. 522.

**Purdy** in Lintonroderick. Peeblesshire Localities, by Renwick, 19.

**Purves** of Abbeyhill. Douglas's Baronage (1798), 566.

of Mossfennan. Peeblesshire Localities, by Renwick, 228.

of Purves. The Revenue of the Scottish Crown, ed. from original MS. of 1681, by D. Murray Rose ; with Genealogy of the Family of Purves (1897). Douglas's Baronage (1798), 566-567. Nisbet's Heraldic Plates, ed. Ross and Grant (1892), 104-106.

of Purves Hall. Complete Baronetage, by G. E. C., iv. 244.

**Purvis** of Kinaldy.   Burke's Landed Gentry (1894-1925).

**Pyott.**   Notes to Genealogical Chart on Pedigree of the Descendants of James Pyott, Merchant, Montrose, 11 sheets in cloth case (1914).

**Queensberry,** Douglas, Earl of, Marquess of, Duke of.   Biographical Peerage (London, 1808), 489-492.   Nisbet's Heraldic Plates, ed. Ross and Grant, 2-5.   G. E. C.'s Complete Peerage.   The Scots Peerage, vii. 112-156.

   Montagu-Douglas-Scott, Duke of.   G. E. C.'s Complete Peerage.   The Scots Peerage, ii. 244-249.   Burke's, Lodge's, Debrett's Peerages, etc.

**Quhitlaw** of Quhitlaw.   Peeblesshire Localities, by Renwick, 45.

**Quincey.**   The Family of Seton, by G. Seton (1896), 66.   *See also* **De Quincy.**

**Radcliffe,** Earl of Newburgh.   The Scots Peerage, vi. 456-457.

**Rae.**   The Rae Family : An old grave : by A. A. Gibson [Rae], pamphlet, reprinted from The Scotsman (Edinr. 1888).

   of Cargen.   Lands . . . in Galloway, by M'Kerlie, v. 234.

   Dornock.   Proc. Soc. Antiq. Scotl. (1888), 46.

   of Eskgrove.   Notes and Queries, 8th S., vi. 333, 358 ; ix. 136.   Forbes Gray's Some Old Scots Judges (1914), 154-156.

**Rainsford-Hannay** of Kirkdale.   Lands . . . in Galloway, by M'Kerlie, iv. 256.   Burke's Landed Gentry (1906-1925).

**Rainy.**   Scottish N. and Q., 2nd S., viii. 124.

**Rait** of Anniston.   Burke's Landed Gentry (1848-1904).   Angus or Forfarshire, by Warden, iii. 430-432.

   of Cononsyth.   Angus or Forfarshire, iii. 100.

   of Hallgreen.   Scottish N. and Q., 3rd S., ii. 174-175.

**Raith, Monimail, and Balwearie,** Melville, Lord.   The Scots Peerage, vi. 108-123.

**Ralston** of Auchantorlie.   Ayrshire Families, by G. Robertson, ii. 265-266.   Paterson's Ayr and Wigton, iii. 211.

   of Ralston.   Crawfurd's Shire of Renfrew (1818), 58, 330.   Ayrshire Families, ii. 257-264.   Paterson's History of County of Ayr, i. 265-269.   Ayr and Wigton, iii. 129-137.   Geneal. Mag., vii. 119.   Burke's Landed Gentry (1848-1858).

   of Warwickhill.   Ayrshire Families, ii. 265.   Paterson's Ayr, i. 450.   Ayr and Wigton, iii. 212.

   of Woodside.   Paterson's Ayr and Wigton, iii. 132-137.

**Ramsay.**   Heraldry, by Nisbet (1722), i. 348.   Notes on Early Ramsay Pedigrees, 1200-1600, by Sir J. H. Ramsay of Bamff, 22 pp. (1914), reprinted from The Genealogist, N. S., xxxi. (1914).

**Ramsay** of Abbotshall.   Complete Baronetage, by G. E. C., iv. 373 ; vi. 85.   Burke's Extinct Baronetcies.   Scottish N. and Q., 2nd S., viii. 92, 111.

   of Ardownie.   Monifieth, by J. Malcolm (1910), 349-350.

   of Auchterhouse.   Memorials of Angus and the Mearns, by Jervise, ed. Gammack, ii. 122-124.

**Ramsay** of Balbougie. Stephen's Inverkeithing (1921), 150.

of Balmain. Douglas's Baronage (1784), 33-35. Trial of the Issues in the Action of damages at the instance of Lady Ramsay, widow of Sir Thomas Ramsay of Balmain, Bart., against James Nairne, for falsehood and defamation, 4to (Edinr. 1833). The Family of Burnett of Leys, by G. Burnett (Aberdeen, New Spalding Club, 1901), 101-111. Complete Baronetage, by G. E. C., ii. 301. Debrett's Baronetage.

of Bamff. Baronage, by Douglas, 551-553. Burke's Peerage and Baronetage. Debrett's Baronetage. Complete Baronetage, by G. E. C., iv. 259. Bamff Charters, A.D. 1232-1703, ed. by Sir James H. Ramsay, Bart., 392 pp. (Oxford, 1915). Scot. Hist. Review, xiv. 301.

of Barnton. Cramond, by J. P. Wood (1794), 55-58. Burke's Landed Gentry (1849-1863).

of Barra. Thanage of Fermartyn, by Temple, 321. Burke's Landed Gentry (1863-1925).

Lord Bothwell. The Scots Peerage, ii. 132-134.

of Brackmont. The Scottish Antiquary, x. 41.

of Burnturk and Balmounth. East Neuk of Fife, by W. Wood, 2nd ed., 340-341.

of Castlelandhill. Stephen's Inverkeithing, 117-118.

of Clatto. The Scots Peerage, iii. 95.

of Cockpen. The Scots Peerage, iii. 88-96.

of Dalhousie, Dalwolsey. The Scots Peerage, iii. 88-97. Life of Sir Alexander Ramsay, by A. H. M. Ramsay, 46 pp., n.d.

Earl of, Marquess of Dalhousie. The Scots Peerage, iii. 87-110.

Edinburgh. Pedigree of the Family of George Ramsay, 1691-1751, Canongate, to 1890, large sheet (1890).

in France. Heraldry, by Nisbet (1722), i. 349.

Glasgow. The Ancestry of Benjamin Harrison, President of the U.S.A., by Charles P. Keith (Philadelphia, 1896).

Viscount of Haddington. The Scots Peerage, iv. 297-302.

of Hill Lodge. Burke's Landed Gentry (1848-1863).

Earl of Holdernesse. The Scots Peerage, iv. 301-302.

of Keryntoun or Carrington. The Scots Peerage, iii. 90-91.

of Kildalton. Burke's Landed Gentry (1886-1925).

of Laws. Monifieth, by J. Malcolm, 317-318.

of Lethendy, Murthly and Mungall. The Scottish Antiquary, viii. 138-139.

Lord Melrose. The Scots Peerage, iv. 300.

of Melross and Claystyles. Thanage of Fermartyn, 320.

of Pitcruvie. The Scots Peerage, v. 394-395.

Lord Ramsay of Carrington. The Scots Peerage, iii. 99-110.

St Andrews. Geneal. Coll., by W. Macfarlane, 1750-51 ; Scot. Hist. Soc., ii. 190.

in Sweden. One Year in Sweden, by Marryat (1862), ii. 495. Palace of History Catalogue (Glasgow, 1911), 202, 210.

**Ramsay** of Whythill. Peeblesshire Localities, by Renwick, 467. Complete Baronetage, by G. E. C., iv. 242. Burke's Landed Gentry (1858-1925).

of Wyliecleuch. The Scots Peerage, iv. 298.

**Ramsay-Fairfax-Lucy** of the Holmes. Debrett's Baronetage (after 1876).

**Ranald**, The Clan. Pamphlets on the Raonuillach Controversy, from the Inverness Journal (1818). Historical and Genealogical Account . . . of the Clan Ranald (Edinr. 1819). Vindication of the Clanronald of Glengarry [by John Riddell] (1821). The Book of Clanranald *in* Reliquæ Celticæ, ii. *See also* **Macdonald, Macdonell.**

**Randolph**, Earl of Moray. The Scots Peerage, vi. 286-295.

**Ranken** of Colden. Some Old Families, by H. B. M'Call, 159-168, and Pedigree.*

Orchardhead. Pedigree *in* Playfair's History of Playfair.

of Sheill. Paterson's Ayr and Wigton, i. 708.

of Whitehill and Glenlogan. Paterson's History of Ayr, i. 370 ; ii. 424-425. Ayr and Wigton, i. 359, 708-712.

**Rankin.** Scottish N. and Q., 2nd S., vii. 106. The Rankins, Pipers to the MacLeans of Duart and Coll, by Henry White, 15 pp. (MacLean Association, 1907).

in Bridgegate. Glasgow Past and Present (1884), iii. 116-117.

of Garngibbock, Otter and Auchengray. Burke's Landed Gentry (1879-1894).

**Rankine**, Ayr. The Dalrymples of Langlands, by J. Shaw, 143-144.

of Beoch. Paterson's Ayr and Wigton, ii. 430-431.

of Lumquhat. Stephen's Inverkeithing (1921), 329.

of Otterden. Paterson's Ayr, ii. 376. Ayr and Wigton, ii. 447.

**Rannoch**, Murray, Duke of. The Scots Peerage, i. 481-482. The Jacobite Peerage, 152-155.

**Rate** of Arroch. Angus or Forfarshire, by A. J. Warden, iii. 33.

**Rattray** of Kirkhillocks, etc. Baronage of Angus and Mearns, by D. M. Peter, 283.

of Rannagullion. Burke's Landed Gentry (1848).

of Rattray and Craighall. Baronage, by Douglas, 274-278. Historical MSS. Commission (1873), 4th Report, 536. Burke's Landed Gentry (1848-1925).

**Rawdon-Hastings**, Viscount, Earl of Loudoun. The Scots Peerage, v. 512-517.

**Reay**, Mackay, Lord. G. E. C.'s Complete Peerage. Burke's and other Annual Peerages. The Scots Peerage, vii. 157-179.

**Reddick** of Dalbeattie. Lands . . . in Galloway, by M'Kerlie, v. 290.

**Reid.** Brief Notices of the Families of Arnot, Reid, etc. (1872).* Eminent Men of Fife, by M. F. Conolly, 376-377. Scottish N. and Q., 2nd S., vii. 155. Dictionary of National Biography, *s.v.*

**Reid** of Ardmealie. Burke's Landed Gentry (1894).

of Bachlaw. Letters of John Orrok, 1801-1816 (Aberdeen, 1927), 2, 213.

of Ballochmyle. Paterson's History of the County of Ayr, ii. 335. Paterson's Ayr and Wigton, i. 551-553.

of Barra. Complete Baronetage, by G. E. C., iv. 415. Tayler's Jacobites of Aberdeenshire, 387.

of Barskimming. Paterson's Ayr, ii. 439. Ayr and Wigton, i. 716.

Crail. Churchyard Monuments of Crail, by Erskine Beveridge, 182-186.

of Daldelling. Paterson's Ayr, ii. 432. Ayr and Wigton, i. 693-695.

of Drumfork. Paterson's Ayr, ii. 336. Ayr and Wigton, i. 559.

Edinburgh. Scot. Hist. Review, vii. 216.

Ellon. Debrett's Baronetage (after 1897).

Glasgow. Glasgow Past and Present (1884), iii. 491.

of Hailles. Notes and Queries, 9th S., iv. 348, 465.

of Hillar. Paterson's Ayr, ii. 433. Ayr and Wigton, i. 702.

of Merkland. Paterson's Ayr, ii. 432. Ayr and Wigton, i. 703.

Portsoy. Genealogies of an Aberdeen Family, by Smith (1913), 22.

of Starquhyte. Paterson's Ayr, ii. 439.

of Willoxhill. Paterson's Ayr, ii. 336. Ayr and Wigton, i. 572.

**Reid-Robertson.** The Barons Reid-Robertson of Straloch, by Rev. James Robertson (Blairgowrie, 1887). Stemmata Robertson et Durdin, by H. Robertson (London, 1893-95), 24-25.*

**Reidhaven,** Ogilvy, Viscount of. The Scots Peerage, iv. 37-41 ; vii. 487-494.

**Rennie** of Melville Castle. Scottish N. and Q., 2nd S., viii. 26 : 3rd S., viii. 10, 538 ; ix. 481 ; x. 58.

**Renny** of Croft. Lands . . . in Galloway, by M'Kerlie, iii. 376-377.

of Usan. Angus or Forfarshire, by A. J. Warden, iii. 161.

**Renny-Strachan-Carnegie** of Seaton and Tarrie. The Scots Peerage, viii. 87.

**Renny-Tailyour** of Borrowfield and Newmanswalls. Baronage of Angus and Mearns, by Peter, 389. Angus or Forfarshire, by Warden, iv. 432-433. Burke's Landed Gentry (1848-1925).

**Renwick,** Blackleemouth. Tancred's Rulewater, 113-117.

**Reoch.** Alexander Cowan, by C. B. Boog Watson, 12.

**Revan,** The Clan, *or* MacQueen. Confederation of the Clan Chattan, by C. Fraser-Mackintosh, 63-76.

**Rhind,** Banff, etc. Dr Cramond *in* Banffshire Field Club Trans. (1896-97).

**Riccartoun,** Douglas, Viscount of. The Scots Peerage, vii. 146-147.

Hamilton, Viscount of. The Scots Peerage, vii. 361-363. G. E. C.'s Complete Peerage.

**Richardson,** Lord Cramond. The Scots Peerage, ii. 578-584.

of Pencaitland and Smeaton. Steamboat Companion betwix Perth and Dundee (Edinr. 1838) ; Pedigree, Appx. ix.

of Pitfour. Complete Baronetage, by G. E. C., ii. 380 ; vi., Appx. 86.

**Richart** of Barskimming. Paterson's History of the County of Ayr, ii. 439.
Paterson's Ayr and Wigton, i. 718.

**Richmond** of Auchincloigh. Paterson's History of Ayr, ii. 427. Paterson's
Ayr and Wigton, i. 682.

of Carlieth. Paterson's Ayr, ii. 428. Ayr and Wigton, i. 683.

**Richmond,** Lennox, Lenox, Duke of. Biographical Peerage (1808),
496-498. G. E. C.'s Complete Peerage. The Scots Peerage,
v. 363-371.

Stewart, Earl of, Duke of. The Scots Peerage, v. 357, 360-362.

Stuart, Duke of. The Scots Peerage, iv. 203.

**Richmond and Gordon,** Duke of. Historical MSS. Commission (1870),
1st Report. Burke's and other Annual Peerages. G. E. C.'s
Complete Peerage.

**Rickart** of Auchnacant and Arnage. Temple's Thanage of Fermartyn,
602-603.

**Rickart-Hepburn** of Rickarton. Baronage of Angus and Mearns, by
D. M. Peter (1856), 286-287.

**Riddell.** A Genealogical Sketch of the Riddell Family, by W. P. Riddell
(New Orleans, 1852). History of the Ancient Ryedales . . . 860 to
1884 . . . Riddell, Riddle, Ridlon, Ridley, etc., by G. T. Ridlon,
illust. (Manchester, N. H., 1884).*

of Ardnamurchan. Baronage, by Douglas (1784), 203. Pedigree of
Sir James Riddell, Bart., of Ardamurchan, with Abstract of the
Descents (Edinr. 1794). Complete Baronetage, by G. E. C., v. 203.
Burke's Peerage and Baronetage.

of Camieston. Burke's Landed Gentry (1875-1925).

of Glenriddell. Baronage by Douglas, 204. Robert Riddell of Glenriddell, by Hugh S. Gladstone, with pedigree.*

of Granton. Cramond, by J. P. Wood, 20.

of Haining. Craig Brown's Selkirkshire, ii. 304-307.

of Kinglass. Douglas's Baronage, 201-203.

of Muselee. Annals of a Border Club, by G. Tancred, 373-374.

of Riddell. Heraldry, by Nisbet (1742), ii., Appx. 303-308. Baronage,
by Douglas (1784), 63-68. Joseph Bain *in* Genealogist, N. S., vi. 1-3.
Notes and Queries, 5th S., vii. 489 ; viii. 208 ; xii. 102 : 6th S.,
v. 482. Riddell-Carre's Border Memories, 181-205. Burke's Peerage
and Baronetage. Debrett's Baronetage.

**Riddell-Carre** of Cavers Carre. Border Memories, by W. Riddell-Carre
(1876). Annals of a Border Club, by G. Tancred, 303-305. Burke's
Landed Gentry (1863-1925).

**Ridpath.** Scottish N. and Q., 2nd S., viii. 133. Diary of George Ridpath
1755-1761 ; (Scot. Hist. Soc., 1922), *viii.*

**Rig** of Dumfries. Pedigree annexed to Edgar's History of Dumfries, ed.
R. C. Reid (Dumfries, 1915).

**Rigg** of Aithernie. East Neuk of Fife, by W. Wood, 2nd ed., 40-43.

**Rippon,** Douglas, Baron. The Scots Peerage, vii. 141-144.

**Risk.** Family of Buchanan, by Buchanan of Auchmar, 141.

**Ritchie** of Busbie and Craigton. Paterson's County of Ayr, ii. 219. Paterson's Ayr and Wigton, iii. 462-463.

Peeblesshire. Annals of a Border Club, by G. Tancred, 374-375.

in Potterton. Scottish N. and Q., 3rd S., ii., 58-59. The Ritchies in India, by Gerald Ritchie (1920).

in Stirling. The Stirling Antiquary, ii. 135-136, 138.

**Robb** of Pitrichie. Thanage of Fermartyn, by Temple, 455.

**Roberton** of Roberton and Earnock. Heraldry, by Nisbet, ii., Appx. 153-157. Crawfurd's Shire of Renfrew (1818), 89.

**Robertson.** ["Ilka Son's a Carle's Son, but Strowan Robertson's a Gentleman."]

Ancient Scottish Surnames, by Buchanan of Auchmar (1723), 69-70. Stemmata Robertson et Durdin, by Herbert Robertson, 4to (London, 1893-95), 1-29.* A Brief Account of the Clan Donnachaidh, with Notes on its history and traditions, by David Robertson (1894). MS. Collection by the Rev. Charles Moncrieff Robertson, in the Scottish National Library. The Chiefs of Clan Donnachaidh [by J. Robertson], pedigrees, illus., etc. (Perth, 1929).

*See* Comitatus de Atholia : the Earldom of Atholl, by J. A. Robertson (1860),* *for*

**Robertson** of Auchleeks, Blairfettie, Bleaton, Calvine, Cray, Downie, Dulcaben, Edradynate, Faskally, Guay, Killiehangy, Kincraigie, Kindrochit, Lude, Pitnacree, Strathloch, Strowan, Tenendry, Trinafour, Tulliebelton.

**Robertson,** Aberdeen. The Picturesque Ancestry of Sir Johnston Forbes-Robertson, by J. M. Bulloch (Aberdeen, 1926).

of Arnhill. Burke's Landed Gentry (1848).

of Auchleeks. Burke's Landed Gentry (1848-1914).

of Cookston. Angus or Forfarshire, by Warden, iii. 18.

of Drumachine. Baronage, by Douglas, 407, 409-410.

Edinburgh. Scottish N. and Q., 2nd S., vi. 157.

of Fascally. The Jacobite Peerage, 159.

of Foveran. Temple's Thanage of Fermartyn, 574-575.

of Gladney. Douglas's Baronage, 407, 413-414.

of Gossaburgh. Zetland Family Histories, by F. J. Grant, 237-239.

of Groundwater. Stemmata Robertson et Durdin, by Herbert Robertson.*

of Inshes, Inches. Douglas's Baronage, 406, 410-412. Antiquarian Notes, by C. Fraser-Mackintosh, i. 372-375. Burke's Landed Gentry (1848-1875).

of Kindeace. Douglas's Baronage, 411, 412-413. Burke's Landed Gentry (1848-1925). Genealogy of the Families of Douglas of Mulderg and Robertson of Kindeace (Dingwall, A. M. Ross & Co., 1895).

of Kinlochmoidart. Burke's Landed Gentry (1849-1879).

**Robertson** of Ladykirk. Burke's Landed Gentry (1848-1875). Pedigree of Inglis . . . and Robertson of Ladykirk, by C. J. L. Inglis, sheet (1880).*

of Lude. Burke's Landed Gentry (1848).

of Muirtown. Douglas's Baronage, 407, 413-414. Scottish Antiquary, i. and ii., 49, 97, 186.

of Newbigging. Genealogy of the Family of Robertson of Newbigging, Orkney, by A. W. Johnston, 11 pp. (Coventry, 1909).*

of Prenderguest. Burke's Landed Gentry (1858-1863).

St Andrews. Geneal. Coll., by W. Macfarlane, 1750-51 ; Scot. Hist. Soc., ii. 191.

of Straloch. Historical Account of the Barons Reid-Robertson of Straloch, by Rev. J. Robertson (Blairgowrie, 1887).

of Strowan, Struan. Geneal. Coll., by W. Macfarlane, 1750-51 ; Scot. Hist. Soc., ii. 301-315. The History of the Robertsons of Strowan, 12mo (Edinr., *c.* 1771). Baronage, by Douglas, 405-410. The History and Martial Atchievements of the Robertsons of Strowan, with the Poems of the Hon. Alexander Robertson of Strowan (Edinr. 1771-1785). Notes and Queries, 1st S., v. 346 ; vi. 461, 591 : 10th S., xi. 409, 517. Genealogy of the Celtic Earls of Atholl . . . the De Atholia Family, afterwards known as the Robertsons of Strowan, by Sir J. Noël Paton (1873). The Scottish Antiquary, ix. 44 ; xi. 60-63. Scottish N. and Q., 3rd S., iii. 91. Burke's Commoners, iv. 419. Burke's Landed Gentry (1848-1925). The Jacobite Peerage, by the Marquis of Ruvigny (1904), 156-159.

in Sweden. One Year in Sweden, by Marryat (1862), ii. 495.

of Tulliebelton. Burke's Landed Gentry (1875-1879).

**Robertson** *alias* Colyear. The Scots Peerage, vii. 88-90.

**Robertson-Aikman** of the Ross. Burke's Landed Gentry (1921-1925).

**Robertson-Glasgow** of Craigmyle. Burke's Landed Gentry (1858-1925).

of Mountgreenan. Paterson's Ayr and Wigton, iii. 513.

**Robertson-Reid.** Burke's Landed Gentry (1894-1906).

**Robertson-Ross.** Burke's Landed Gentry (1875, 1879, 1894).

**Robertson-Scott** of Benholme and Hedderwick. Scottish N. and Q., 3rd S., ii. 32.

**Robertson-Shersby-Harvie** of Brownlee. Burke's Landed Gentry (1914-1925).

**Robertson-Walker.** Burke's Landed Gentry (1848-1863).

**Robeson** of Coldoch. The Stirling Antiquary, ed. W. B. Cook, ii. 167-168.

**Robinson-Douglas** of Orchardton. Burke's Landed Gentry (1906-1925).

**Robison**, Edinburgh. Gideon Guthrie, ed. C. E. Guthrie Wright, 159 and pedigree.

of Leddriegreen. Strathblane, by Guthrie Smith, 68.

**Robson** of Samieston. Annals of a Border Club, by G. Tancred, 376-377.

in Sweden. One Year in Sweden, by Marryat (1862), ii. 496 *bis*. Palace of History Catalogue (Glasgow, 1911), 201, 209. Scot. Hist. Review, xxv. 294.

**Robson-Scott.** Annals of a Border Club, by G. Tancred, 376-379.

**Roger.** The Scottish Branch of the Norman House of Roger, with a Genealogical Account of the Family of Playfair, by Rev. Charles Rogers (London, 1872, 2nd ed., Edinr. 1875).* Some Account of the Rogers in Coupar Grange, by J. Cruikshank Roger (London, 1877). An Historical Summary of the Roger Tenants of Coupar, by J. C. Roger (London, 1879). Review of Above *in* Herald and Genealogist, viii. 449-456. Four Perthshire Families, Roger, Playfair, Constable, and Haldane of Barmony, by the Rev. C. Rogers, LL.D. (Edinr. 1887), 5-41.* Pedigree *in* A. G. Playfair's Family of Playfair.

of Marywell. Baronage of Angus and Mearns, by D. M. Peter, 291-296.

of Ryehill. Eminent Men of Fife, by M. F. Conolly, 380.

of Westmean. History of Our Family, 1451-1902, by J. C. Roger, 4to (London, 1902).*

**Rogerson** of Gillesbie. Burke's Landed Gentry (1894).

of Wamphray. Historical Families of Dumfriesshire, by C. L. Johnstone (1888), 51.

**Rolland** of Auchmithie. Burke's Commoners, iii. 611. Burke's Landed Gentry (1848).

of Disblair. Disblair, 1634-1884, by Alex. Walker, 8vo, illust. (Aberdeen, 1884).*

**Rollo** of Balbegie. The Scots Peerage, vii. 188-191.

of Bannockburn. Complete Baronetage, by G. E. C., iii. 326. The Scots Peerage, vii. 196-197.

of Bello. The Scots Peerage, vii. 182-184.

of Duncrub. The Scots Peerage, vii. 181-200.

of Findony. The Scots Peerage, vii. 182, 184, 185.

of Menmuir. The Scots Peerage, vii. 183.

of Pitmadie. The Scots Peerage, vii. 187-194.

of Powis. The Scots Peerage, vii. 186, 187, 196, 200.

Lord Rollo of Duncrub. Eminent Men of Fife, by Conolly, 382. Historical MSS. Commission (1872), 3rd Report. G. E. C.'s Complete Peerage. The Scots Peerage, vii. 180-211. Burke's Peerage. Debrett's Peerage.

**Rollock** of Piltoun. Cramond, by J. P. Wood, 21. The Scots Peerage, vii. 188-190.

in Reidie. Memorials of Angus and the Mearns, by A. Jervise, ed. Gammack, ii. 49.

of Woodside. The Scots Peerage, vii. 187, 204.

**Romanes.** Portraits of, and Notes on the Romanes Family ; 70 geneal. trees (Davidson, Berwick-on-Tweed).*

**Romanno** of Romanno. Peeblesshire Localities, by Renwick, 467.

**Rome** of Clouden. Lands . . . in Galloway, by M'Kerlie, iv. 18.

**Roney-Dougal** of Ratho. Burke's Landed Gentry (1898-1925).

**Rorison.** Capt. Gunn's Notes on the Gunns, Hendersons and Rorisons *in* Northern Ensign (Wick, 26th Sept. 1905).

of Ardoch. The Scottish Antiquary (1896), x. 189.

**Rose** in Balvraid. D. Murray Rose *in* Northern Chronicle (Inverness, 22nd March 1911).

of Bellivat. The Scottish Antiquary, iv. 132-134.

of Cullisse. Scottish Antiquary, xiii. 45. Geneal. Mag., i. 490.

of Glastullich. Burke's Landed Gentry (1863-1886).

of Holme Rose. Burke's Landed Gentry (1848-1925).

of Kilravock. Geneal. Coll., by W. Macfarlane, 1750-51 ; Scot. Hist. Soc., ii. 484-512. Douglas's Baronage, 453-456. A Genealogical Deduction of the Family of Rose of Kilravock, written in 1683-4, by Mr Hew Rose, minister of Nairne, continued by the Rev. Lachlan Schaw, minister of Elgin, in 1753: with illustrative documents from the family charter room and notes, ed. Cosmo Innes (Spalding Club, 1848). Burke's Landed Gentry (1848-1925).

of Larachmoir. Temple's Thanage of Fermartyn, 557.

of Montcoffer. Inventory of his MSS. *in* Scottish Antiquary, v. 133-139 ; 173-177 ; vi. 43-45. The Domestic Papers of the Rose Family, ed. Alastair and Henrietta Taylor (Aberdeen, 1926).

of Rosehill. Memoir of J. Young, Aberdeen . . . 1861, ed. Lt.-Col. W. Johnston (1894), 217-218.*

**Rose-Innes** of Netherdale. Burke's Landed Gentry (1898-1925).

**Rose-Robinson** of Almorness. Lands . . . in Galloway, by M'Kerlie, iii. 251.

**Rosebery,** Primrose, Baron, Viscount of, Earl of. Nisbet's Heraldic Plates, ed. Ross and Grant, 1892, 9-13. Walford's Chapters from Family Chests, ii. 171-181. G. E. C.'s Complete Peerage. The Scots Peerage, vii. 212-229. Debrett's Peerage. Burke's Peerage. History of the Primrose-Rosebery Family, 1500-1900, by J. Macbeth Forbes, *viii*+444 pp. (London, 1907).

**Rosehill,** Carnegie, Lord. The Scots Peerage, vi. 495-508.

*See* The Scots Peerage, ed. Sir James Balfour Paul, *for*

**Ross,** The Ancient Earls of, vii. 230-244.

Douglas, Viscount of, vii. 138-156.

Leslie, Earl of, vii. 241-244.

Macdonald, Earl of, v. 41-47.

Stewart, Earl of, i. 155 ; ii. 264.

Stewart, Duke of, vii. 245-246.

**Ross.** Ane breve cronicle of the Earlis of Ross, including notices of the Abbots of Fearn and of the Family of Ross of Balnagown, ed. W. R. B[aillie] (Edinr. 1850).* Heraldry, by Nisbet (1722), i. 416-417, 305-306. Francis Nevile Reid *in* The Scottish Antiquary, iii. 140, with key chart ; iv. 1-14, 51-74, 102-111, 163-173 ; v. 27-36, 56-66, 117-123, 155-161 ; vi. 31-40, 81-86, 169-175 ; vii. 15, 124-127, 182-187 ; viii. 26-32. Republished as : The Earls of Ross and their Descendants, by F. N. Reid, with Folding Table, 8vo (1894). Notes and Queries, 7th S., vii. 328, 492. Scottish N. and Q., 3rd S., v. 139.

Ross, Aberdeen. Scottish N. and Q., 2nd S., vii. 173. Genealogies of an Aberdeen Family, by Smith (1913), 44-45.

of Arnage. Temple's Thanage of Fermartyn, 493-497. Memoir of J. Young, Aberdeen . . . 1861, ed. Lt.-Col. W. Johnston (1894), 140-143.* Burke's Landed Gentry (1886-1894).

of Balkail and Balgreen. Lands . . . in Galloway, by M'Kerlie, 2nd ed., i. 600-601. Annals of a Border Club, by G. Tancred, 379-381.

of Balnagown. Antiquarian Notes, by C. Fraser-Mackintosh, i. 63-76. Burke's Peerage and Baronetage. Debrett's Baronetage.

of Balneil. Lands . . . in Galloway, i. 608-609. The Scottish Antiquary, viii. 44, 95, 142, 186.

of Balsarroch. Lands . . . in Galloway, i. 416, 418. Annals of a Border Club, 379-361.

of Borough Muir. Pedigree *in* Traditions of the Watson Family, by C. B. Boog Watson.* Pedigree *in* The Playfair Family, by A. G. Playfair.*

of Craigie. Heraldry, by A. Nisbet (1742), ii., Appx. 24-25. Burke's Commoners, iii. 644. Burke's Landed Gentry (1848).

of Cromarty. Burke's Landed Gentry (1863-1925).

of Dalton. Genealogical Account of the Rosses of Dalton, Co. Dumfries . . . from the 12th century to 1854, by Geo. P. Knowles, 8 pp. (1855).* The Coultharts of that Ilk, by G. P. Knowles (London, 1885). Burke's Landed Gentry (1849-1863). Cf. p. 134 *supra.*

of Galston. Paterson's History of the County of Ayr, ii. 65. Paterson's Ayr and Wigton, i. 525-526.

of Glenmoidart. Burke's Landed Gentry (1886).

of Hawkhead. The Scots Peerage, vii. 247-248, 262.

of Innernethie. Burke's Landed Gentry (1848).

of Insch. Geneal. Mag. (1903), vi. 507.

of Invercharron. Burke's Landed Gentry (1875-1886).

of Kindeace. Pedigree of Ross of Kindeace, and Connection with Rose of Kilravock, large sheet.

of Kirkland. The Scottish Antiquary (1898), xiii. 11-17.

of Lund. Zetland Family Histories, by F. J. Grant, 240-242.

of Melvill. The Scottish Antiquary (1895), ix. 20. The Scots Peerage, vii. 249-251, 262.

of Millanderdale. The Scots Peerage, vi. 595.

of Netherley. Burke's Landed Gentry (1875-1894).

of Pitcalnie. Historical MSS. Commission (1877), 6th Report, 715. Notes and Queries, x. 307, 455 ; xi. 31, 256 ; xii. 149. Burke's Landed Gentry (1879-1898).

of Rossie Castle. Burke's Landed Gentry (1849). Angus or Forfarshire, by Warden, iii. 144.

of Scarpoe. MS. Genealogy of the Rosses of Scarpoe, 4to.

of Tartraven. The Scottish Antiquary, xiii. 16-17.

Warsaw. Papers relating to the Scots in Poland ; Scot. Hist. Soc., No. 59 (1915), 334-339.

in Wigtownshire. Notes and Queries, 4th S., vi. 569 ; vii. 110.

**Ross of Hawkhead,** Boyle, Baron. The Scots Peerage, iv. 216-219.

Ross, Lord. Crawfurd's Shire of Renfrew (1818), 54-56, 323-325, 513-522. The Scots Peerage, vii. 247-263.

**Ross-Hume** of Ninewells. Burke's Landed Gentry (1914-1925).

**Ross-Lockhart.** Complete Baronetage, by G. E. C., iv. 286.

**Rossie of Rossie,** Kinnaird, Baron. The Scots Peerage, v. 214.

**Rosslyn,** St Clair-Erskine, Earl of. Biographical Peerage (1808), 509-510. Burke's Visitation of Seats and Arms (1853), i. 189. Eminent Men of Fife, by Conolly, 412-413. Historical MSS. Commission (1871), 2nd Report. Complete Peerage, by G. E. C. The Scots Peerage, vii. 588. Burke's, Lodge's, Debrett's Peerages.

**Rosslyn,** Wedderburn, Earl of. The Scots Peerage, vii. 588.

**Rotch** of Drumlongfuird. Paterson's History of Ayr, i. 315. Paterson's Ayr and Wigton, ii. 154.

**Rothes,** Leslie, Earl of, Duke of. Eminent Men of Fife, 270-271. Historical MSS. Commission (1873), 4th Report. Complete Peerage, by G. E. C. The Scots Peerage, vii. 264-311. Burke's Peerage, Debrett's Peerage, etc.

**Rothesay,** Stewart, Duke of. The Scots Peerage, i. 17, 26, 27 ; vii. 312.

**Roule** of Primside. The Scots Peerage, vii. 319, 320, 321, 322.

**Row.** Memorials of the Family of Row with pedigree, ed. James Maidment, 4to (Edinr. 1828).* Nisbet's Heraldic Plates, ed. Ross and Grant (1892), 120-122.

of Inverallan. Logie, by Rev. Dr Menzies Fergusson, ii. 162.

**Roxburgh** in Inverkeithing. Stephen's Inverkeithing (1921), 487.

**Roxburghe,** Ker, Lord, Earl of, Duke of. The Scots Peerage, vii. 314-352.

Bellenden-Ker, Duke of. The Scots Peerage, vii. 352-354. [There are about twenty-five printed folio papers, relating to the Claims to the Roxburghe Title and Estates], the Cases of John B. Ker, Brig.-Gen. Walter Ker, Sir James Innes Ker, Wm. Drummond, and Lady Essex Ker (1806-1811). Minutes of Evidence and Report [1808-1812].

Innes-Ker, Duke of. Historical MSS. Commission (1894), 14th Report. Annals of a Border Club, by G. Tancred (1899), 286-293. The Scots Peerage, vii. 356-360. Burke's Peerage. Debrett's Peerage. G. E. C.'s Complete Peerage.

**Roy** of Nenthorn. Burke's Landed Gentry (1848-1898).

**Rudd** of Thorne. The Scots Peerage, v. 417.

**Ruddiman.** Notes on the Ruddimans, and Genealogical Tables, by George Harvey Johnston, 4to, portraits (Edinr. 1887).* The Ruddimans in Scotland, their History and Works, by G. H. Johnston, 4to, illust., *xvii*+115 pp. (Edinr. 1901).*

**Ruglen**, Douglas, Earl of. The Scots Peerage, vii. 146-147. Claim of William, Earl of Ruglen, to be Earl of Cassillis : (Session Papers, March 1760 to Feb. 1761).

Hamilton, Earl of. The Scots Peerage, vii. 361-363.

**Ruskin.** Notes and Queries, 7th S., iii. 438 ; iv. 233 ; x. 417 ; xi. 152.

**Russell** of Aden. Burke's Landed Gentry (1848-1925).

of Ashestiel. Burke's Landed Gentry (1848 - 1886). Genealogical Memoirs of the Family of Sir Walter Scott, Bart., by Rev. C. Rogers (Grampian Club, 1877), *lvi-lvii.* Border Memories, by W. Riddell-Carre, 287. Craig Brown's Selkirkshire, i. 385.

of Blackbraes, and Dundas Castle. Burke's Landed Gentry (1894-1925).

of Cleveden. Burke's Landed Gentry (1894-1925).

of Kingseat and Slipperfield. Scottish Surnames, by Jas. Paterson, 55-62.* Buchan and Paton's History of Peeblesshire, iii. 159.

Leith. The Scottish Antiquary, viii. 24.

of Maulside. Burke's Landed Gentry (1894-1925).

Stobo. Peeblesshire Localities, by Renwick, 131.

**Rutherfurd.** Heraldry, by A. Nisbet (1722), i. 179-180. Notes and Queries, 2nd S., ix. 403 ; x. 18, 55, 178 ; xii. 376.

of Capehope. The Scots Peerage, vii. 381-383.

of Chatto. The Scots Peerage, vii. 369-370.

of Edgerston. Historical MSS. Commission (1879), 7th Report, pt. 2. Annals of a Border Club, by G. Tancred, 343, 344, 382-390. Burke's Landed Gentry (1848-1925).

of Fairnington. Annals of a Border Club, 390-399. Burke's Landed Gentry (1898-1925).

of Hunthill. Memoirs of the Family of Sir Walter Scott, by Rev. C. Rogers (Grampian Club, 1877), *xlvii-lix.* The Scots Peerage, vii. 370-381.

of Knowesouth. Annals of a Border Club, 396.

of Ladfield. Annals of a Border Club, 396 *n.*

of Quarrelholes. The Scots Peerage, vii. 372-373.

of Rutherfurd. The Rutherfurds of that Ilk and their Cadets, compiled from the public records, etc., by J. Cockburn Hood, 4to, illust., tree (1884).* [A supplementary volume, with corrections by C. H. E. Carmichael and other matter, was printed in 1899 ; a copy is in the Lyon Office Library, but it is doubtful if it were ever put into circulation.] The Scots Peerage, vii. 364-367. Burke's Landed Gentry (1848-1925).

Lord Rutherfurd and Earl of Teviot. Heraldry, by Nisbet (1742), ii., Appx. 219-220. Genealogical chart, engraved sheet (1738). The Genealogist, N. S., iv. 173. The Scots Peerage, vii. 364-384.

Lord. Claim of Alexander Rutherfurd to the title of Lord Rutherfurd : (Session Papers, Dec. 1761 to March 1762). Case of John Rutherford, claiming the title of Baron Rutherford of Rutherford, 12 pp., with pedigree (1839).

of Wells. Rulewater, by G. Tancred, 198-201.

X

**Ruthven.** Notes and Queries, 2nd S., x. 93 ; xii. 288 : 3rd S., i. 363, 414 ; iii. 3, 50 ; v. 188, 210, 294 ; viii. 204. Fittis's Recreations of an Antiquary (1881), 283-315. Small chart pedigree *in* Memoir of Chancellor Seton, by Geo. Seton (1882), 43. Great Historic Families of Scotland, by Taylor [1887]. The Ruthven Family Papers, by Samuel Cowan (London, 1912). The Scots Peerage, iv. 255-257.

of Ballindean *or* Bandon. The Scots Peerage, iv. 101-102.

Earl of Brentford. The Scots Peerage, iv. 104-106.

of Dunglass. The Scots Peerage, iv. 102-103.

of Forteviot. The Scots Peerage, iv. 262 ; ix. 98.

Earl of Forth. The Scots Peerage, iv. 101-106.

of Gardyne. The Scots Peerage, iv. 102.

Earl of Gowrie. Complete Peerage, by G. E. C. The Scots Peerage, iv. 254-268. History of the Life and Death of John, Earl of Gowrie, by Rev. Jas. Scott, Perth, 150 copies (1818).* Paper relating to William, first Earl of Gowrie, and to Patrick Ruthven, his fifth and last surviving son [ed. John Bruce], (London, 1867).*

of Redcastle. Complete Baronetage, by G. E. C., iv. 255.

Lord Ruthven. The Scots Peerage, iv. 254-268.

Lord Ruthven of Ettrick. The Scots Peerage, iv. 104-106.

Lord Ruthven of Freeland. Notes and Queries, 6th S., vii. 470 ; viii. 151 ; xii. 306. Memorial as to the Ruthven (of Freeland) Peerage, by Sir Wm. Fraser. The Barony of Ruthven of Freeland, by J. H. Round, *in* Foster's Collectanea Genealogica (1883), iii., pt. 13. The Ruthven of Freeland Peerage, and its Critics, by J. Horne Stevenson, 4to (Glasgow, 1905). J. H. Round *in* Scottish Historical Review (1906), iii. 194-209, 339-353. J. H. Stevenson *in* Scot. Hist. Review, iii. 475-494. J. Maitland Thomson *in* Scot. Hist. Review, iii. 104-108, 521. The Scots Peerage, iv. 260 ; vii. 385.

**Ruthven of Freeland,** Hore-Ruthven, Lord. G. E. C.'s Complete Peerage. The Scots Peerage, vii. 391-393. Burke's Peerage. Debrett's Peerage.

**Ruxton** in Cairnhill. Temple's Thanage of Fermartyn, 607.

**Rymour.** The Scottish Antiquary (1896), x. 43.

**Rynd.** Scottish N. and Q., 3rd S., i. 57-58.

**Sage** in Creich. Eminent Men of Fife, by M. F. Conolly (1866), 387.

**St Clair.** The Saint Clairs of the Isles, being a History of the Sea Kings of Orkney . . . by Roland W. St Clair (Auckland, N.Z., 1898). Scottish N. and Q., xi. 67-69, 83-84, 97-98, 189-190. The Scottish Antiquary, vi. 187. Extracts from Exchequer Rolls, i. 1264-1359, *in* Scot. Antiquary, x. 94-96, 142-144.

**St Clair,** Earl of Caithness. Caithness Family History, by John Henderson (1884), 1-13.

of Herdmanston, Hermiston. Heraldry, by Nisbet (1742), ii. Ragman Roll, 20, 21. Tancred's Rulewater, 155-162. The Scots Peerage, vii. 577-586.

of Kimmerghame. The Scots Peerage, vii. 579-580.

St Clair of Kinnaird. Complete Baronetage, by G. E. C., iv. 301.
of Roslin, Rosslyn. Heraldry, by Nisbet, ii., Appx. 171-174. Genealogie
of the Sainteclaires of Rosslyn, by Father Richard Augustin Hay,
ed. James Maidment, 4to (Edinr. 1835).* Burke's Landed Gentry
(1858-1863). Eminent Men of Fife, by Conolly, 408-412. Scottish
N. and Q., 2nd S., iv. 65-67, 81-84, 96-99, 122. Geneal. Mag. (1903),
vi. 477-481 ; vii. 101-107. Burke's Peerage, s.v. Rosslyn, Earl of.
Debrett's Peerage, etc. G. E. C.'s Complete Peerage.
of Staverton Court. Burke's Landed Gentry (1848-1914).
St Colme, Stewart, Lord. The Scots Peerage, vii. 394-395.
Salmond. Memoir as to the Surname of Salmond [by George Salmond,
Glasgow], n.d.*
Saltoun, Fraser, Lord. G. E. C.'s Complete Peerage. The Scots Peerage,
vii. 417-453. Burke's and other Annual Peerages.
Saltoun of Abernethy, Abernethy, Lord. G. E. C.'s Complete Peerage,
The Scots Peerage, vii. 396-416. See Fraser of Philorth
Sandeman. The Clan, a Family Magazine of the Sandeman Family, ed.
by Col. J. Glas Sandeman (1894-1901).* The Sandeman Genealogy,
compiled by Col. John Glas Sandeman, 4to, pp. vi+viii+37 (Edinr
1895).* Genealogical Chart, by Col. J. G. Sandeman, showing the
connection between Glas, Sandeman, and Walker Families, sheet,
36 × 15 ins.*
Sanderson of Laggan. Lands . . . in Galloway, by M'Kerlie, v. 56.
Sandilands. Heraldry, by Alex. Nisbet (1722), i. 94-95. Complete
Baronetage, by G. E. C. (1902), ii. 473.
Sandilands, Lord Abercrombie. The Scots Peerage, i. 75-81.
of Calder. The Scots Peerage, viii. 378-389.
of Couston. The Scots Peerage, viii. 392, 396.
of Crabstone. The Sandilands of Crabstone, 4to (1863).* Tayler's
Jacobites of Aberdeenshire, 389-390.
of Cruvie. East Neuk of Fife, by W. Wood, 2nd ed., 234-237. The
Scots Peerage, i. 75-78.
of Hilderstoun. The Scots Peerage, viii. 391, 393.
of St Monans. East Neuk of Fife, 2nd ed., 234-237. The Scots
Peerage, i. 78.
of Sandilands. The Scots Peerage, viii. 378, 382.
of Slamannan. The Scots Peerage, viii. 388-390.
Lord Torphichen. The Scots Peerage, viii. 378-398.
Sandison, Delting. Zetland Family Histories, by F. J. Grant, 245-250.
Sandys-Lumsdaine of Innergellie. Eminent Men of Fife, by M. F. Conolly,
305-307. Burke's Landed Gentry (1848-1925).
Schank of Castlerig and Gleniston. Heraldry, by Nisbet (1742), ii.,
Appx. 229-230. Visitation of Seats and Arms, by J. B. Burke
(1853), ii. 17. Shank of Castlerig, 4to (London, 1885).* Scottish
N. and Q., 3rd S., vi. 63. Burke's Landed Gentry (1875-1914).
Stodart in The Genealogist, 1st S., i. 85-92.

**Schaw** of Goldring. History of the County of Ayr, by Paterson, ii. 481.

of Gospetry. Notes and Queries, 9th S., x. 8, 115, 353.

of Greenock. Old Greenock, by G. Williamson (Paisley, 1886), i. 1-97, 275, 278, 313. Complete Baronetage, by G. E. C., iv. 350.

of Grimmet. Paterson's Ayr, ii. 470. Paterson's Ayr and Wigton, i. 476.

of Haylee and Sornbeg. Heraldry, by Nisbet (1742), ii., Appx. 301-303. Paterson's Ayr, ii. 67, 469. Ayr and Wigton, i. 480, 531-533, 746.

of Keirhill. Paterson's Ayr and Wigton, i. 479.

of Keirs. Paterson's Ayr, ii. 469. Ayr and Wigton, i. 480-481.

of Kelsoland. Paterson's Ayr and Wigton, iii. 535.

of Knockhill. Logie, by Rev. Dr R. M. Fergusson, i. 86.

*See also* **Shaw.**

**Schevez** of Kemback. Geneal. Coll., by Macfarlane, 1750-51 ; Scot. Hist. Soc., ii. 199-204.

**Scobie,** Alloa. MS. Pedigree in Lyon Office.

**Scone,** Murray, Lord, Lord of. G. E. C.'s Complete Peerage. The Scots Peerage, viii. 192-214. Burke's and other Annual Peerages.

**Scot** of Balwearie. Heraldry, by Nisbet (1722), i. 309 ; ii., Appx. 133-135, Ragman Roll, 13. Baronage, by Sir Robert Douglas, 302-306. Life and Legend of Michael Scot, by the Rev. J. Wood Brown (1897).

of Kirkstile. Baronage, by Douglas, 305. Warden's Angus or Forfarshire, iv. 192.

of Knightspottie. East Neuk of Fife, by W. Wood, 2nd ed., 387.

of Murdostoun, Murthockston. English Peerage, by Rev. A. Jacob (1766), i. 576-581. The Scots Peerage, ii. 225-226 ; vii. 71 *n.*

**Scotland,** Ancient Kings in. Royal Genealogies, by Anderson (1732), 751-756. J. H. Stevenson *in* Scot. Hist. Review, xxv. 1-12.

Kings of. Royal Genealogies, 757, 760-762, 767, 768.

Table of Peers of. Royal Genealogies, 803-808.

**Scotland,** Leith. Annals of a Border Club, by G. Tancred, 440.

**Scots, Mary, Queen of.** Bibliography of Works relating to Mary, Queen of Scots, 1544-1700, by John Scott (1896). Living Descendants of Mary, Queen of Scots ; tabular pedigrees and lists of senior and junior lines, by the Marquis of Ruvigny and Raineval, *in* The Legitimist Kalendar (1894 and later).

**Scott.** A True History of several Honourable Families of the Right Honourable name of Scot, by Capt. Walter Scot (1688, repr. Hawick, 1786 ; and, ed. J. G. Winning, Hawick, 1894).* Metrical History of several Honourable Families of the name of Scot and Elliot . . . by Captain Walter Scot of Satchell, 4to (Edinr. 1688, repr. Edinr. 1776 ; 1892).* Heraldry, by A. Nisbet (1722), i. 88, 98-100. Border Memories, by W. Riddell-Carre (1876), 46-94. Lands and their Owners in Galloway, by M'Kerlie, iii. 451-467. Scott, 1118-1923 ; being a Collection of Scott Pedigrees, containing all male descendants from Buccleuch, Sinton, Harden, Balweary, etc., by Keith S. M. Scott, 8vo, illust. (1923).

**Scott**, Aberdeen. Scottish N. and Q., 2nd S., viii. 136.

of Abbotsford. Genealogical Memoirs of the Family of Sir Walter Scott, Bart., by Rev. Dr Rogers (Grampian Club, 1877), *xi-lxxii.* Burke's Landed Gentry (1858-1925). Lockhart's Life of Sir Walter Scott.

of Allanhaugh. The Buccleuch Book : with special reference to Allanhaugh, by Rev. R. Young, *in* Trans. Hawick Archæol. Soc. (1882).

of Ancrum. Baronage, by Douglas, 305-306. Nisbet's Heraldic Plates, ed. Ross and Grant, 108-110. Annals of a Border Club, by G. Tancred, 418-425. Warden's Angus or Forfarshire, iv. 192. Complete Baronetage, by G. E. C., iv. 284.

in Angus. Memorials of Angus and the Mearns, by Jervise, ed. Gammack, ii. 263-264.

of Ardross and Elie. East Neuk of Fife, by W. Wood, 2nd ed. (1887), 218-224.

of Balcomie. Notes and Queries, 11th S., xi. 188, 288, 368, 479.

of Balmounth. East Neuk of Fife, 341.

of Bavelaw. The Monros of Auchenbowie, by J. A. Inglis, 164-169, 187-193.

of Benholm. Scottish N. and Q., 2nd S., iv. 89.

of Nether Bonchester. Tancred's Rulewater, 396-398.

of Bonytoun. Peeblesshire Localities, by R. Renwick (1897), 361.

of Bowhill. T. Craig Brown's Selkirkshire, ii. 235-238.

of Branxholme. Historical Notes relating to Branxholme, by Wm. Eliott Lockhart of Borthwickbrae, plates, plan, etc. The Scots Peerage, ii. 226-232.

of Brotherton. Baronage of Angus and Mearns, by D. M. Peter (1856), 299-301. Burke's Landed Gentry (1849-1925).

of Buccleuch, Earl of, Duke of. A Short Genealogical and Historical Account of the Family of Scott of Buccleuch (Dumfries, 1827). The Two Heiresses of Buccleuch, Ladies Mary and Ann Scott, and their Husbands, 1647-1732, by Sir Wm. Fraser, 4to, illust. (Edinr. 1880).* The Scotts of Buccleuch, by Sir Wm. Fraser, 2 vols., illust.* Upper Teviotdale and the Scotts of Buccleugh, by J. Rutherford Oliver, 4to (Hawick, 1887). Craig Brown's Selkirkshire, ii. 243-279. Annals of a Border Club, by G. Tancred, 400-412. The Genealogist, N. S., viii. 94. The Scots Peerage, ii. 225-249. Buchan and Paton's History of Peeblesshire, iii. 181-186.

of Burnhead. Baronage, by Douglas, 219-220. Annals of a Border Club, 480-481.

Lord Campcastel. The Scots Peerage, ii. 237 ; vii. 80-81.

of Clerkington. Ayrshire Families, by G. Robertson, i. 97. The Monros of Auchendinny, by J. A. Inglis, 183-185.

of Coates. East Neuk of Fife, by W. Wood, 2nd ed., 103.

of Craig. Angus or Forfarshire, by A. J. Warden, iii. 143.

Earl of Dalkeith. The Scots Peerage, ii. 237-249.

of Davinton. Annals of a Border Club, 163.

of Deanshouses. Peeblesshire Localities, by Renwick, 470 *n.*

Earl of Deloraine. The Scots Peerage, iii. 111-114.

Earl of Doncaster. The Scots Peerage, ii. 237, 241.

**Scott** of Dryhope. Craig Brown's Selkirkshire (1886), i. 397-398.

Dundee. MS. Pedigree, 908 ; Society of Genealogists, London.

of Duninald. Baronage of Angus and Mearns, by Peter, 303. Warden's Angus or Forfarshire, iii. 152. Burke's Peerage and Baronetage. Debrett's Baronetage.

of Dunrod. Notes and Queries, 2nd S., iii. 289 ; iv. 439.

East Lothian. Notes and Queries, 7th S., ix. 29, 123.

of Eskdale and Castlelour. Heraldry, by Nisbet (1742), ii., Appx. 297-298.

of Ewesdale. The Scotts of Ewisdale, by T. J. Carlyle (Hawick, 1884).*

of Gala. Baronage, by Douglas, 220-221. Selkirkshire, by T. Craig Brown, i. 534-541. Burke's Landed Gentry (1848-1925).

of Glenrath. Peeblesshire Localities, by R. Renwick, 370.

Lord Goldielands. The Scots Peerage, iii. 111-114.

of Greenwall. Zetland Family Histories, by F. J. Grant, 258.

of Haining. Craig Brown's Selkirkshire, ii. 301-304.

of Harden. Baronage, by Sir Robert Douglas (1784), 213-217. Craig Brown's Selkirkshire, ii. 328-329. Annals of a Border Club, 413-418. The Scots Peerage, vii. 71-84.

of Harlawood. The Scots Peerage, ix. 76.

of Harperrig. The Monros of Auchenbowie, by J. A. Inglis, 170-182. The Scotts of Harperrig, by J. A. Inglis, 4to, 8 pp. (1914).

of Hartwoodmyres. Craig Brown's Selkirkshire, ii. 314-315.

of Highchester. Baronage, by Douglas, 213-217. The Scots Peerage, vii. 79, 82.

of Horsliehill. Heraldry, by Nisbet (1742), ii., Appx. 280.

of Howcleuch. Craig Brown's Selkirkshire, i. 435. Annals of a Border Club, 430-436.

of Hundilshope. Heraldry, by Nisbet (1722), i. 443. Buchan and Paton's Peeblesshire, iii. 601-604.

in Inverurie. Tayler's Jacobites of Aberdeenshire, 390.

of Kirkurd. Annals of a Border Club, 480.

of Langlee. Annals of a Border Club, 430-436.

of Logie. Genealogical Tree of James Scott of Logie and his Wife, Katherine Orick, from 1593, sheet, 32 × 38 ins. (1794). Burke's Landed Gentry (1848-1858). Scottish N. and Q., 2nd S., iv. 89. Angus or Forfarshire, by Warden, iv. 237.

of Malleny, Millenie. Baronage, by Douglas, 217-218. Ayrshire Families, by G. Robertson (1824), i. 91, 98. Burke's Landed Gentry (1849-1925).

of Melby. Zetland Family Histories, by F. J. Grant, 259-263. Burke's Landed Gentry (1863, 1886-1925).

of Milsington. Thomson's Life of James Scott (1879), 6-9.

of Mossfennan. Annals of a Tweeddale Parish, by Rev. A. Baird, 67.

of Orchard. Burke's Landed Gentry (1925).

of Peel. Annals of a Border Club, by G. Tancred, 437-438.

of Pitgormo and Fawside. East Neuk of Fife, by W. Wood, 2nd ed., 287.

Lord Polwarth. G. E. C.'s Complete Peerage. The Scots Peerage, vii. 70-87.

Scott of Raeburn. Genealogical Memoirs of the Family of Sir Walter Scott (Grampian Club, 1877), *xx-xxvi*. Burke's Landed Gentry (1848-1925).

of Raefirth. Zetland Family Histories, by Grant, 251-253.

of Rankilburn. The Scots Peerage, ii. 225-226.

of Saline. Stephen's Inverkeithing, 112.

in Sandyknowe. Genealogical Memoirs of the Family of Sir Walter Scott (1877), *xxvi, xxxix-xlvii.*

of Satchels. The Scots Peerage, vii. 71-72.

of Scalloway. Zetland Family Histories, by Grant, 267-269.

of Scarpoe. Zetland Family Histories, 257.

of Scots-Hall. Memorials of the Family of Scott of Scots-Hall, by James R. Scott (London, 1876).* Zetland Family Histories, 264-266.

of Scotsloch. Ayrshire Families, by G. Robertson, i. 95, 97. The Monros of Auchenbowie, by J. A. Inglis, 164-169.

of Scotstarvit. Heraldry, by Nisbet (1742), ii., Appx. 291-297. Baronage, by Douglas (1784), 221-224. East Neuk of Fife, by Wood, 2nd ed., 387-391.

Lord Scott of Buccleuch, etc. The Scots Peerage, ii. 234, 237, 241.

of Singlee. Border Memories, by W. Riddell-Carre, 328-330.

of Sinton. Baronage, by Douglas, 213-217. Annals of a Border Club, by G. Tancred, 425-427. Craig Brown's Selkirkshire, i. 440-443. The Scots Peerage, vii. 70-78. Burke's Landed Gentry (1894-1925).

of Spencerfield. Stephen's Inverkeithing (1921), 102.

of Stokoe. Pedigree of Scott of Stokoe . . . late of Toderick, Selkirkshire, by Wm. Scott, M.D., 8vo, 24 pp. (Newcastle, 1783, Edinr. 1827), repr. with continuation, by John Gray Bell, 48 pp. (London, 1852, 1882).

in Sweden. One Year in Sweden, by H. Marryat, ii. 495, 496.

Earl of Tarras. The Scots Peerage, ii. 237 ; vii. 80-81.

of Teviotbank. Annals of a Border Club, 429-430.

of Thirlestane. Heraldry, by Nisbet (1742), ii., Appx. 58-59. Memoirs of Scott of Thirlestane, and other Families of the name of Scott, by John Scott of Rodono [MS. in possession of the Society of Antiquaries in Scotland]. Craig Brown's Selkirkshire (1886), i. 304-321. Some Old Families, by H. B. M'Call (1890), several pedigrees, 172-236.* Notes and Queries, 8th S., i. 334, 400, 479. Complete Baronetage, by G. E. C., iv. 256. The Scots Peerage, vi. 428-431.

of Todrig. Pedigree of Scott of Stokoe . . . late of Toderick. Craig Brown's Selkirkshire, ii. 366-367.

of Tushielaw. Craig Brown's Selkirkshire, i. 328-334.

Virginia. Scottish N. and Q., 2nd S., i. 48.

of Voesgarth. Zetland Family Histories, by Grant, 254-256.

of Wauchope and Howcleuch. Annals of a Border Club, 430-436. Tancred's Rulewater, 130-141. Burke's Landed Gentry (1921-1925), *s.v.* Macmillan-Scott.

of Whitehaugh. Annals of a Border Club, 436-437.

of Whitslade. Craig Brown's Selkirkshire, i. 443.

of Winterburgh. Craig Brown's Selkirkshire, i. 295-296.

**Scott** of Wooll. Annals of a Border Club, 427-429. Burke's Landed Gentry. *s.v.* Scott-Plummer.

**Scott-Douglas** of Springwood Park. Complete Baronetage, by G. E. C., v. 251. Debrett's Baronetage. Burke's Peerage and Baronetage.

**Scott Elliot** of Arkleton. Annals of a Border Club, 231. Burke's Landed Gentry (1885-1925).
of Larriston. Annals of a Border Club, 162-163.

**Scott-Kerr** of Chatto and Sunlaws. Annals of a Border Club, 311-318. Burke's Landed Gentry (1849-1925).

**Scott-Mackirdy** of Birkwood. Burke's Landed Gentry (1914-1925).

**Scott-Makdougal** of Makerston. Walford's County Families (after 1900).

**Scott-Moncrieff** of Coates and Fossoway. East Neuk of Fife, by W. Wood, 2nd ed., 103. Scot. Hist. Review, xix. 326. Our Forefathers, by Mary Anne Scott Moncrieff; prefixed by an autobiography of the authoress and supplementary notes (Edinr. 1895).* Burke's Landed Gentry (1886-1925). Seton's House of Moncrieff (1890).*

**Scott-Montagu.** The Scots Peerage, ii. 243-246.

**Scott-Plummer** of Sunderland Hall. Craig Brown's Selkirkshire, ii. 364, Burke's Landed Gentry (1906-1925).

**Scragg** in Sweden. One Year in Sweden, by Marryat (1862), ii. 483, 492, 498.

**Scrymgeour.** History of the Scrymgeours, by A. J. Warden (1886). Inventory of Documents, *c.* 1327-1611, relating to the Scrymgeour Family Estates, 1611; ed. Dr J. Maitland Thomson, 70 pp. (Scot. Rec. Soc., Edinr., 1912).

**Scrymgeour** of Ballagernoch. The Scots Peerage, iii. 307-312.
of Dudhope. Heraldry, by Nisbet (1722), i. 294; (1742), ii., Appx. 49-51. Angus or Forfarshire, by Warden, 13-17. The Scots Peerage, iii. 304-313; ix. 72.
Viscount Dudhope. The Scots Peerage, iii. 313-315.
Earl of Dundee. The Scots Peerage, iii. 303-315.
of Fardill. The Scots Peerage, iii. 306, 308, 315 *n.*
of Glassarie. The Scots Peerage, iii. 305-309. Highland Papers, ii. (Scot. Hist. Soc., 1916), 114-245.
Lord Inverkeithing. The Scots Peerage, iii. 315.
of Inverkeithing. Stephen's Inverkeithing (1921), 61-71.
of Kirkton of Erlestrathichty. Campbell's Balmerino, 579-587, 659. The Scots Peerage, iii. 308-309.
Lord Scrymgeour. The Scots Peerage, iii. 303-315.
of Sonahard. The Scots Peerage, iii. 307, 308.

**Scrymgeour-Wedderburn** of Kingennie. Monifieth, by Malcolm, 331-334.
of Wedderburn. Geneal. Mag. (1904), vii. 386. Burke's Landed Gentry (1894-1925).

**Seafield,** Ogilvie, Viscount of, Earl of. The Scots Peerage, iv. 37-41.

Ogilvie-Grant, Earl of. G. E. C.'s Complete Peerage. The Scots Peerage, vii. 454-494. Burke's Peerage, Debrett's Peerage, etc. Historical MSS. Commission (1872), 3rd Report ; (1894), 14th Report. In Memoriam Ian Charles, 8th Earl of Seafield, 27th Chief of the Clan Grant, 8vo (1884).* Historic Earls and Earldoms of Scotland, by Dr John Mackintosh (1898), 314-347. The Rulers of Strathspey : A History of the Lairds of Grant and Earls of Seafield, by the Earl of Cassillis, 8vo, portraits, *xii*+211 pp. (Inverness, 1911). The Chiefs of Grant, by Sir Wm. Fraser, 3 vols. The Seafield Correspondence from 1685 to 1708, ed. Dr James Grant (Scot. Hist. Soc., 1912).

**Seaforth,** Mackenzie, Lord, Earl of. Biographical Peerage (1808), 536-537. Visitation of Seats and Arms, by J. B. Burke (1853), i. 43-45. Great Historic Families of Scotland, by Taylor [1887]. The Scots Peerage, vii. 495-515. Complete Peerage, by G. E. C.

Mackenzie, Marquis of. The Jacobite Peerage, by the Marquis of Ruvigny, 162.

**Seaton** of Schethin. Thanage of Fermartyn, by Temple, 395
*See also* **Seton.**

**Selkirk,** Douglas, Earl of. Biographical Peerage (1808), 537-539. Lands . . . in Galloway, by M'Kerlie, iv. 185-189. Notes and Queries, 4th S., xi. 219, 264. Historical MSS. Commission (1873), 4th Report. Genealogical Magazine (1898), i. 237. Burke's Dormant Peerages. G. E. C.'s Complete Peerage. The Scots Peerage, vii. 516-525.

**Sellar** of Westfield. Annals of Elgin, by Young (1879), 684.

**Sempill.** Heraldry, by Nisbet (1722), i. 433-434.

of Beltrees. The Poems of the Sempills of Beltrees, with Notes and Biographical Notices . . ., by James Paterson, 8vo (1849). The Scots Peerage, vii. 548-549.

of Bruntscheillis. The Scots Peerage, vii. 544-545.

of Cathcart. Baronage, by Douglas, 467-469. Crawfurd's Shire of Renfrew (1818), 268. The Scots Peerage, vii. 533-535. The Scottish Antiquary, xiii. 91.

of Craigbait. The Scots Peerage, vii. 533-535.

of Eliotstoun. The Scots Peerage, vii. 527-531.

Lord Sempill. Crawfurd's Shire of Renfrew (1818), 75-79, 356-357. MS. Genealogical Tree down to Twelfth Lord Sempill. History of the Lairds of Glenfield (Paisley, 1860). G. E. C.'s Complete Peerage. The Scots Peerage, vii. 526-568. Burke's Peerage. Debrett's Peerage.

Baron Sempill. The Jacobite Peerage, by the Marquis of Ruvigny, 164.

**Semple.** Genealogical History of the Family of Semple : compiled and arranged by William Alexander Semple, of Broad Brook, Conn. (Hartford, Conn., U.S.A., 1888).

of Blackburn. Crawfurd's Shire of Renfrew (1818), 103.

**Semple** of Fulwood. Shire of Renfrew, 103.
  in Middleton. Notes on Semple, in Middleton ; typewritten, 4 pp. ;
    in Library of Society of Genealogists.

**Seton, Seaton, Seytoun.** Heraldry, by A. Nisbet (1722), i. 235-244. The
    History of the House of Seytoun to the year MDLIX., by Sir Richard
    Maitland of Lethington, Knight ; with the continuation, by Alexander
    Viscount Kingston, to MDCLXXXVII., ed. John Fullarton (Glasgow,
    Bannatyne and Maitland Clubs, 1829). The Genealogy of the House
    and Surname of Setoun, by Sir Richard Maitland ; with the Chronicle
    of the House of Setoun, compiled in metre by James Kamington,
    alias Peter Manye, 4to, illust. (1830). Annals of Scotland, 1057-1370 ;
    with Tracts on Seton Genealogy, etc., by Sir David Dalrymple,
    Lord' Hailes, 2 vols. (1776-79) ; 3 vols. (1819). Brief Notices of the
    Families of Arnot . . . Seton, etc. (1872).* Chart Pedigree *in*
    Memoir of Chancellor Seton, by George Seton (1882). A History
    of the Family of Seton during Eight Centuries, by George Seton,
    2 vols. 4to, illust., with 350 coloured shields of arms, and numerous
    etchings, etc. (Edinr. 1896).* An Old Family : or, The Setons of
    Scotland and America, by Monsignor Seton, 8vo. illust. (New York,
    1899). Great Historic Families, by Taylor [1887]. Sir Bruce Seton
    *in* Scottish Historical Review, xvii. 272-286.

**Seton** of Abercorn. The Family of Seton, 355-366. Complete Baronetage,
    by G. E. C., iii. 338. Claim of Sir Bruce Gordon Seton to the
    Barony of Gordon (7th Dec. 1928 to 22nd Jan. 1929). Report and
    Decision (2nd May 1929).
  Abroad. The Family of Seton, 764-769.
  of Barns. The Family of Seton, 621-633. The Scots Peerage, viii. 548,
    566, 588, 589.
  of Caraldstone, Cariston. Douglas's Baronage, 185-186. East Neuk of
    Fife, by W. Wood, 2nd ed. (1887), 29-30. Burke's Landed Gentry
    (1848-1894). The Family of Seton, by George Seton, 577-620. The
    Scots Peerage, v. 406-414.
  of Culbeg. Baronage, by Douglas, 170-171. The Family of Seton,
    355-366.
  Earl of Dunfermline. Memoir of Alexander Seton, Earl of Dunfermline,
    by George Seton (1882). The Family of Seton, 634-670. The Scots
    Peerage, iii. 369-375.
  of Ekolsund and Preston. One Year in Sweden, by Marryat (1862), ii.
    497. The Family of Seton, 367-374. E. E. Etzel *in* Scottish
    Historical Review, ix. 274.
  in England. The Family of Seton, 754-763.
  Lord Fyvie. The Scots Peerage, iii. 368-375. Fyvie Castle, by A. M. W.
    Stirling (1928), 277.
  of Garleton. The Family of Seton, 733-742. Burke's Extinct Baronetage.
    Complete Baronetage, by G. E. C., iii. 350. The Scots Peerage,
    viii. 594, 596-600.
  of Gordon. The Scots Peerage, iv. 253, 518, 521.

Seton, Earl of Huntly. The Scots Peerage, iv. 521-523.

Lord Kilwinning. The Scots Peerage, i. 541.

Viscount of Kingston. Family of Seton, 714-732. The Scots Peerage, v. 195-198.

of Kylesmure. Family of Seton, 671-675.

of Lathrisk. Family of Seton, 283-313.

of Meldrum. Heraldry, by Nisbet (1742), ii., Appx. 131-132. Douglas's Baronage, 158-160. The Family of Seton, 460-470.

of Mounie. The Family of Seton, 489-506. Burke's Landed Gentry, (1848-1925).

of Olivestob and St Germains. The Family of Seton, 708-713. The Scots Peerage, viii. 590-592.

of Parbroath. Genealogy of Seton of Parbroath in Scotland and America, by Monsignor Robert Seton of New Jersey, 8vo (New York, 1890).* The Family of Seton, by George Seton (1897), 281, 769.*

of Pitmedden. Baronage, by Sir Robert Douglas (1784), 182-185. Nisbet's Heraldic Plates, ed. Ross and Grant, 132-135. The Family of Seton, 471-488. Complete Baronetage, by G. E. C., iv. 325. The Scots Peerage, ii. 14-15. Temple's Thanage of Fermartyn, 444-448. Scottish N. and Q. (1887), i. 70.

of Seton. The Scots Peerage, viii. 560-574.

Lord Seton. The Scots Peerage, viii. 576-606.

of Spittaltoun. The Stirling Antiquary, ed. W. B. Cook, iii. 165.

of Touch and Tullibody. Baronage, by Douglas, 166-170. Complete Baronetage, by G. E. C. (1902), ii. 450. The Scots Peerage, iv. 520-526. The Stirling Nat. Hist. and Archæological Soc. (1928).

of Treskerby. Burke's Landed Gentry (1906).

Lord Urquhart. The Scots Peerage, iii. 370.

of Windygoul. The Family of Seton, 733-742. Complete Baronetage, by G. E. C., iv. 280.

Earl of Winton. G. E. C.'s Complete Peerage. The Scots Peerage, viii. 559-606.

Seton-Gordon of Embo. The Family of Seton, 507-511.

of Huntly and Aboyne. The Family of Seton, 375-459.

of Letterfourie. The Family of Seton, 512-515.

Seton-Gordon-Sutherland. The Family of Seton, 516-537.

Seton-Karr of Kippilaw. Annals of a Border Club, by G. Tancred, 305-310. The Family of Seton, 320-334. Burke's Landed Gentry (1898-1925).

Seton-Montgomerie, Earl of Eglinton. The Family of Seton, by G. Seton, 676-707.

Seton-Robertson of Monkmylne. The Family of Seton, 538-545.

Seton-Steuart of Gargunnock. The Family of Seton, 335-352.

of Touch and Allanton. The Family of Seton, 320-334. The Stirling Antiquary, iii. 315-318. Burke's Peerage and Baronetage. Debrett's Baronetage.

**Seton-Tytler** of Aldourie. The Family of Seton, 546-560.
of Woodhouselee. The Family of Seton, 561-568.

**Shairp** of Houston. Burke's Landed Gentry (1848-1925).
of Ballindoch. Warden's Angus or Forfarshire, iv. 132-133.

**Shaklock.** Baronage of Angus and Mearns, by Peter (1856), 307.
Memorials of Angus and the Mearns, by Jervise, ed. Gammack,
ii. 158. Angus or Forfarshire, by Warden, iv. 305.

**Shand.** Some Notices of the Surname of Shand, particularly of the County
of Aberdeen [by Rev. Geo. Shand], (Norwich, 1877).\* Scottish
N. and Q., 2nd S., iv. 112 ; 3rd S., iii. 133. Notes on the Surname
of Shand, by Dr Cramond, *in* Banffshire Field Club Trans. (1896-97).
Aberdeen. Geneal. Mag. (1903), vi. 450 ; vii. 72.
of Templeland. Thanage of Fermartyn, by Temple, 196-199.

**Shand-Harvey** of Castle Semple. Burke's Landed Gentry (1894-1925).

**Shank** of the Villa. Fraser's Laurencekirk, 165-167.
*See also* **Schank.**

**Sharp** of Clyth Lodge. Burke's Landed Gentry (1863-1925).
of Maryfield. Burke's Landed Gentry (1906-1925).
of Scotscraig. Case of Alexander Bethune, claiming the Baronetcy of
Sharp of Scotscraig. Complete Baronetage, by G. E. C., iv. 321.
The Scots Peerage, v. 91, 92.
of Stoneyhill. Geneal. Coll., by W. Macfarlane, 1750-51 ; Scot. Hist.
Soc., ii. 48. The Scottish Antiquary, iii. 160-162 ; iv. 189. Notes
and Queries, 3rd S., xii. 321, 447, 449. Scottish N. and Q., ii. 107,
126, 139-140. Tayler's Jacobites of Aberdeenshire, 392.

**Shaw.** Memorials of the Clan Shaw [by Rev. W. G. Shaw], *xii* + 30 (Dundee,
1868).\* Appendices to above, pp. 1-24, 1-12, 1-14.\* Memorials of
the Clan Shaw, by William G. Shaw, incumbent of St John's Church,
Forfar (Forfar, 1871, 1881).\* A Genealogical Account of the
Highland Families of Shaw, by Alexander Mackintosh Shaw
(1877).\* The Name Shaw, the Coat of Arms and Records of
Various Families, by G. C. Martin, 27 pp. (New Jersey, 1911).

**Shaw** in Abererarder. Scottish N. and Q., 3rd S., iii. 17-20, 33-36, 53, 70,
74-75.
Aberdeen. Confederacy of Clan Chattan, by C. Fraser-Mackintosh
(1898), 104.
Ayr. The Dalrymples of Langlands, by John Shaw, 3, 87-129.\*
Ayrshire. Scottish N. and Q., 3rd S., ii. 165-167.
of Barjarran. Crawfurd's Shire of Renfrew (1818), 113.
Crathie. Scottish N. and Q., 3rd S., ii. 90, 95, 174.
of Daldownie. Tayler's Jacobites of Aberdeenshire, 395-396.
of Dalnavert. Confederacy of Clan Chattan, 101.
of Dell. Confederacy of Clan Chattan, 97-100.
of Drummochrin. Paterson's Ayr and Wigton, ii. 227 *n.*
of Glenmure. Paterson's History of Ayr, i. 242-243.

**Shaw** of Sauchie. Heraldry, by Nisbet (1722), i. 431. Crawfurd's Shire of Renfrew (1818), 124-126. The Scottish Antiquary, x. 42, 54, with cut of arms. Logie, by Rev. Dr Menzies Fergusson, ii. 180, 184. Scottish Historical Review, xiv. 327. Some Ancient Scottish Families, by J. B. Brown-Morison, 101-125.* Notes and Queries, 3rd S., i. 38, 98 ; vi. 272, 497 ; vii. 299. Stephen's Inverkeithing (1921), 106-112.

Irvine. Scot. Hist. Review, xvi. 91, 258.

Kinross-shire. Some Ancient Scottish Families, by J. B. Brown-Morison, 140.

of Muirtown. Confederacy of Clan Chattan, 101.

of Rothiemurchus. Confederacy of Clan Chattan, 85-88. Scottish N. and Q., 2nd S., viii. 157.

in Rothiemurcus. The Dalrymples of Langlands, by J. Shaw, 88.

of Kinrara. Confederacy of Clan Chattan, 102-103.

in Selkirk. Memoirs of the Family of Sir Walter Scott, by Rev. C. Rogers (1877), *xlix-li.*

of Tordarroch. Antiquarian Notes, by C. Fraser-Mackintosh, ii. 381-382. Confederacy of Clan Chattan, 89-95.

of Treesbank. Scot. Hist. Review, xvi. 92.

of Tullochgrue. Confederacy of Clan Chattan, 104.

*See also* **Schaw.**

**Shaw** *or* M'Ay of Black Isle. Confederacy of Clan Chattan, 103.

**Shaw-Kennedy** of Kirkmichael. Burke's Landed Gentry (1914-1925).

**Shaw-Mackenzie** of Newhall. Confederacy of Clan Chattan, 93-97. Burke's Landed Gentry (1898-1925).

**Shaw-Stewart** of Greenock and Blackhall. Crawfurd's Shire of Renfrew (1818), 124-126, 412-416. Historical MSS. Commission (1873), 4th Report. Old Greenock, by G. Williamson, i. 182-249. Complete Baronetage, by G. E. C., iv. 261. Burke's Peerage and Baronetage. Debrett's Baronetage. *See also* **Schaw** of Greenock.

**Shedden** of Knockmarloch. Paterson's Ayr and Wigton, i. 653.

of Morrishill and Broadstone. Ayrshire Families, by G. Robertson (1824), ii. 279, 286-287. Paterson's History of Ayr, i. 275-276. Ayr and Wigton, iii. 110.

of Roughwood. Ayrshire Families, ii. 279-281. Paterson's Ayr, i. 274-275. Ayr and Wigton, iii. 112-114.

of Virginia and Stoudonhall. Ayrshire Families, ii. 282-285. Ayr and Wigton, iii. 112-114.

**Shepherd** of Braco. Thanage of Fermartyn, by Temple, 397.

**Sheppard** of Duchray. Burke's Landed Gentry (1906-1925).

**Shoolbred.** The Scottish Antiquary, vi. 41.

**Shortreed,** Jedburgh. Border Memories, by W. Riddell-Carre, 364. Annals of a Border Club, by G. Tancred, 440-443.

**Shortreed-Fair** of Langlee. Annals of a Border Club, 443.

**Sibbald** of Balgony. Heraldry, by A. Nisbet (1722), i. 127 ; (1742), ii., Appx. 127.
of Burnetland. Annals of a Tweeddale Parish, by Rev. A. Baird, 35.
of Gibliston. East Neuk of Fife, by W. Wood, 2nd ed. (1887), 270.
of Kair. Burke's Landed Gentry (1863), 1324.
of Rankeillour. Burke's Extinct Baronetcies. Complete Baronetage, by G. E. C., ii. 379.
Roxburghshire. Annals of a Border Club, by G. Tancred, 444-447. Memoirs of Susan Sibbald, ed. F. J. Hett (London, 1926).

**Simmons,** Barbados. Buchan and Paton's Peeblesshire, iii. 402 *n*.

**Simpson,** Aberdeen. Smith's Genealogies of an Aberdeen Family (1913), 72-74.
of Ogill Easter. Baronage of Angus and Mearns, by Peter (1856), 311-314.
Strichen. Smith's Genealogies of an Aberdeen Family, 95-98.

**Simson.** Gleanings, with a Genealogical Tree, by Robert Stevenson of Glasgow, 40 pp. (1867). Scottish N. and Q., 3rd S., i. 127.
Bedrule. Tancred's Rulewater, 218-219.
Islay. Scottish Historical Review (1910), vi. 218.
of Kirktounhall. Ayrshire Families, by G. Robertson, ii. 132-150. Paterson's History of the County of Ayr, ii. 144-145. Paterson's Ayr and Wigton, iii. 365-367.
of Udoch. The Genealogist, N. S., vii. 64.

**Sinclair.** Heraldry, by A. Nisbet (1722), i. 120-124. The Saint-Clairs of the Isles, being a History of the Sea Kings of Orkney, and their Scottish Successors of the Surname of Sinclair, by Roland W. St Clair, 4to, illust. (Auckland, N.Z., 1898).

*See* Zetland Family Histories, by F. J. Grant (Lerwick, 1907), *for*

**Sinclair** of Bullister and Swining, 280-282.
of Brew, 270-275.
of Brugh, 276-279.
of Goad, 283-285.
of Houss, Aith and Scalloway, 286-291.
of Quendale, 292-295.
of Toft, 296-297.

**Sinclair** of Achigale and Newton. Caithness Family History, 142. The St Clairs of the Isles, 251.
of Assery. Caithness Family History, 31-35, 256, 335. St Clairs of the Isles, 238.
of Barrock. Baronage, by Douglas, 254-255. St Clairs of the Isles, 238. Henderson's Caithness Family History, 97-102.
Baron Barrogill. The Scots Peerage, ii. 358.
of Borlum, Toftkemp and Thura. Caithness Family History, 255-261. St Clairs of the Isles, 252.
of Brabster. Douglas's Baronage, 253-254. St Clairs of the Isles, 237.

Sinclair of Brabsterdorran. The Sinclairs of Brabsterdorran, Caithness, by Roland St Clair, 9 pp. (Coventry, 1911).*

of Broynach. The Broynach Earls of Caithness, by Thos. Sinclair, *in* The Northern Ensign (2nd Feb. 1896, 2nd May 1897). The Sinclairs of Broynach *in* The Highland Monthly (Dec. 1889).

Earl of Caithness. The Earls of Caithness of the Sinclair Line, by G. M. Sutherland, *in* .The Celtic Magazine (Feb. to May, 1887 ; April to June, 1888). The Scots Peerage, ii. 332-359.

of Canisbay. Complete Baronetage, by G. E. C., ii. 390.

Cornton. The Stirling Antiquary, ed. W. B. Cook, ii. 155.

of Dun. Henderson's Caithness Family History, 107-119. The St Clairs of the Isles, 240. Dunn Ancestors *in* Northern Ensign (3rd, 10th May, 1904). The Scots Peerage, ii. 338, 341, 356.

of Dunbeath. Douglas's Baronage, 253-254. Notes and Queries (1856), 2nd S., i. 210, 279. Henderson's Caithness Family History, 14-23. Complete Baronetage, by G. E. C., ii. 391 ; iv. 431. St Clairs of the Isles, 236, 255. Debrett's Baronetage. Burke's Peerage and Baronetage.

of Durran. Henderson's Caithness Family History, 75-79. The Scottish Antiquary, i. 68. St Clairs of the Isles, 235. The Scots Peerage, ii. 348, 353-354.

in England. The Sinclairs of England, Pre-Norman Records, etc. [by Thomas Sinclair], (1887).

of Forss. Burke's Landed Gentry (1848). Henderson's Caithness Family History, 128-141. The St Clairs of the Isles, 245.

of Freswick. Henderson's Caithness Family History, 51-59. The St Clairs of the Isles, 231. The Scots Peerage, ii. 348.

of Geise. Caithness Family History, 43. St Clairs of the Isles, 230.

of Greenland. Caithness Family History, 44-50.

of Hoy and Oldfield. Caithness Family History, 146. St Clairs of the Isles, 251.

of Kirk and Myrelandhorn. Caithness Family History, 330. St Clairs of the Isles, 250.

of Lathrone, Latheron. Douglas's Baronage, 253-254. St Clairs of the Isles, 236.

of Leny. Cramond, by J. P. Wood, 68-69.

of Longformacus. Baronage, by Douglas, 249-251. Complete Baronetage, by G. E. C., iii. 351.

of Lybster. Caithness Family History, 36-38, 46. Old-Lore Miscellany, iii. 226-229.* St Clairs of the Isles, 238.

of Lybster, Reay. Caithness Family History, 144. St Clairs of the Isles, 250.

of Mey. Case of Sir James Sinclair of Mey, claiming the Earldom of Caithness (1772). Minutes of Evidence (1791). Baronage, by Douglas, 251-253. Caithness Family History, 60-66. St Clairs of the Isles, 233, 254. The Scots Peerage, ii. 351-356. Burke's Landed Gentry (1894-1925).

**Sinclair** of Murchil, Murkle. Douglas's Baronage, 89-91. Caithness Family History, 24-30. The Scots Peerage, ii. 340, 345.

of Olrig. Caithness Family History, 80-82. St Clairs of the Isles, 235.

Earl of Orkney. The Complete Peerage, by G. E. C. The Scots Peerage, vi. 564-571.

of Ratter. Case of William Sinclair of Ratter, claiming the Earldom of Caithness, 6 pp., and folding pedigree (1772). Minutes of Evidence (1791). Caithness Family History, 44-50. St Clairs of the Isles, 230. The Sinclairs of Rattar, by K. MacDonald, *in* The Highland Monthly (July, 1889). The Fortunes of the Rattars, by T. Sinclair, *in* The Highland Monthly (Nov. 1889). The Scots Peerage, ii. 347-349.

of Roslin. Douglas's Baronage, 246-249. Geneal. Mag. (1903), vi. 477-481 ; vii. 101-107. *See* **St Clair** of Rosslyn.

of Scotscalder. Caithness Family History, 39-42. St Clairs of the Isles, 229. The Sinclairs of Scotscalder, by Alex. Gunn, *in* Northern Ensign (27th Aug. to 22nd Oct. 1895).

Lord Sinclair. Case of Charles St Clair, claiming the title of Lord Sinclair, with pedigree (1782). G. E. C.'s Complete Peerage. The Scots Peerage, vii. 569-592. Debrett's Peerage. Burke's Peerage.

of Southdun. Caithness Family History, 120-127. St Clairs of the Isles, 242.

of Stemster. Caithness Family History, 14-23.

of Stevenson. Douglas's Baronage, 89-91.

of Stirkoke. Caithness Family History, by Henderson, 103 - 106. St Clairs of the Isles, 247. Geneal. Mag. (1904), vii. 500.

of Strathhalladale. Rev. A. Maclean Sinclair *in* Northern Ensign (May, 1901).

in Sweden. One Year in Sweden, by H. Marryat (1862), ii. 475-476, 485, 496. Palace of History Catalogue (Glasgow, 1911), 209, 210. E. E. Etzel *in* Scot. Hist. Review (1913), ix. 275-276.

of Ulbster. Genealogy of the Sinclairs of Ulbster, by Sir John Sinclair, Bart. (1810). Visitation of Seats and Arms, by J. B. Burke (1853), i. 99-100. Henderson's Caithness Family History, 67-74. Complete Baronetage, by G. E. C., iv. 248. St Clairs of the Isles, 248, 257. Burke's Peerage and Baronetage. Debrett's Baronetage.

of Woodhouselee. The Genealogist, N. S., xx. 3.

Lord of Zetland. The Scots Peerage, vi. 568-571.

*See also* **Saint Clair.**

**Sinclair-Erskine** of Alva. Complete Baronetage, by G. E. C., iv. 250.

**Sinclair-Lockhart** of Stevenston. Complete Baronetage, by G. E. C., ii. 421.

**Sinclair-Sutherland** of Brabster. Caithness Family History, by John Henderson, 93-96. St Clairs of the Isles, 239.

of Risgill *or* Swinzie. Caithness Family History, 171. St Clairs of the Isles, 239.

**Sinton.** Family and Genealogical Sketches, by Rev. Thomas Sinton, folio, 67 pp. (Inverness, 1911).*

**Sivright** of South House and Meggatland. Burke's Landed Gentry (1849, 1858, 1863, 1886-1925).

**Siward** of Pitcorthie and Kellie. East Neuk of Fife, by W. Wood (1887), 153, 258. The Scots Peerage, vi. 533, 536.

**Skelton.** Scottish N. and Q., 2nd S., iv. 59, 80.

**Skene** of Careston. Baronage of Angus and Mearns, by Peter, 318. Angus or Forfarshire, by Warden, iii. 75-77.
   of Curriehill. Burke's Extinct Baronetcies. Complete Baronetage, by G. E. C., ii. 345.
   of Hallyards. Burke's Landed Gentry (1906-1925).
   of Rubislaw. Burke's Landed Gentry (1848-1894).
   of Skene. Heraldry, by Nisbet (1722), i. 331. Baronage, by Douglas, 555-560. Baronage of Angus and Mearns, by Peter, 315-323. Memorials of the Family of Skene of Skene, by William Forbes Skene, D.C.L., 4to, illust. (New Spalding Club, Aberdeen, 1887). Pedigree Chart of the Family of Skene of Skene, n.d. Nisbet's Heraldic Plates, ed. Ross and Grant (1892), 76-78. The Knightly Skenes, by D. Murray Rose, 16 pp. (1906).* Scottish N. and Q., 1st S. (1890-1), iv. 7-10, 34-36, 67-69, 85-88, 116-117, 138-139, 153-154, 193-195 ; (1891-2), v. 4-6, 26-28, 61, 89-91 ; (1892-3), vi., 24-25, 53-55, 74-75, 105 ; ix. 37 and pedigree chart : 2nd S., i. 21-22.
   of Newtyle. Scottish N. and Q., ix. 158.

**Skene-Tytler.** The Family of Seton, by G. Seton (1896), 569-576.

**Skinner.** Lands . . . in Galloway, by M'Kerlie, iii. 276.
   Aberdeenshire. Scottish N. and Q., 2nd S., i. 37-39.
   *or* Macgregor, of New Jersey. The Scottish Antiquary (1896), x. 29 30, with cut of arms.

**Sleat,** Macdonald, Baron. The Jacobite Peerage, by the Marquis of Ruvigny, 166-168.

**Small** of Kirkhillock. Angus or Forfarshire, by Warden, iii. 374.

**Smart** of Cairnbank and Cononsyth. Baronage of Angus and Mearns, by D. M. Peter (1856), 323.

**Smith.** The Heraldry of the Smith Family in Scotland [by F. M. Smith] (London, 1873). Notes and Queries, 4th S., v. 33, 63, 212, 238, 325 ; x. 290, 326, 348, 456, 527 ; xii. 180. The Smith Family : a Popular Account of Most Branches of the Name, however spelt, from the 14th century downwards, with numerous pedigrees [by Compton Reade], (London, 1902).

**Smith,** Aberdeen. Genealogies of an Aberdeen Family, 1540-1913, by Rev. James Smith, 4to, *x*+148 pp., illust. (Aberdeen, 1913). Scottish N. and Q., 3rd S., viii. 15.
   Archieston. Scottish N. and Q., 3rd S., v. 60.
   of Auchendrane and Westfield. Paterson's Ayr and Wigton, ii. 406-409.

**Smith**, Ayr. The Dalrymples of Langlands, by John Shaw, 3, 84-86.*

of Balgonie. The Scottish Antiquary (1897), xii. 92.

of Barnhill. Baronage of Angus and Mearns, by Peter, 345.

Belhelvie and Aberdeen. Genealogies of an Aberdeen Family, by Rev. J. Smith (Aberdeen University Studies, 1913), 46-60.

of Braco. Burke's Landed Gentry (1848), ii. 1258. Herald and Genealogist, vi. 74-77. Notes and Queries, 3rd S., iii. 51 ; v. 426 ; vi. 116. *See also* **Smyth** of Braco.

of Camno and Glasswall. Douglas's Baronage, 543-545. Warden's Angus or Forfarshire, iv. 6-9.

of Carbeth Guthrie. Strathendrick, by J. Guthrie Smith, *xviii-xxv.*

Clatt. Scottish N. and Q., 2nd S., iv. 46.

of Craigend. Strathblane, by ,Guthrie Smith (1886), 52-58. Strathendrick, by Guthrie Smith (1896), *xvii.*

of Drongan. Paterson's Ayr and Wigton, i. 721.

Falkirk. Logie, by Rev. Dr R. M. Fergusson, ii. 257.

of Forret. The Scottish Antiquary, xii. 135 ; xiii. 135.

of Gibliston. East Neuk of Fife, by W. Wood, 2nd ed., 270.

of Glasswall. Baronage, by Douglas, 543-545.

of Grotthill and Southfield. Cramond, by J. P. Wood, 56.

of Inveramsay. Tayler's Jacobites of Aberdeenshire, 397-398.

of Jordanhill. Crawfurd's Shire of Renfrew (1818), 348. Strathendrick, by J. Guthrie Smith, *xviii.* Burke's Landed Gentry (1848-1925).

of Kelly. Baronage, by Douglas, 543.

Kirkcaldy. Life of Adam Smith, by John Rae (1895). The Scottish Antiquary (1895), ix. 157-158.

of Methven. Baronage, by Douglas, 539-542.

Mill of Tifty. Stirling's Fyvie Castle, 238-252.

Pennsylvania. Scottish N. and Q., x. 106-107.

Rulewater. Tancred's Rulewater, 122-125.

of Smithfield. Baronage, by Douglas, 545. Warden's Angus or Forfarshire, iv. 427-428.

of Swindridgemuir. Paterson's History of Ayr, i. 429. Paterson's Ayr and Wigton, iii. 189-191.

of Templeland. Thanage of Fermartyn, by Temple, 198.

of Touch. The Scottish Antiquary, xi. 189.

*or* Lindsay. Notice of the Family of Smith, etc., formerly Lindsay, by Rev. P. C. Campbell (1869).*

*or* Rosenschmidt in Sweden. One Year in Sweden, by Marryat (1862), ii. 496.

**Smith-Cuninghame** of Caprington. Case of Sir Robert Keith Dick Cunyngham of Prestonfield *versus* Thomas Smith Cuninghame, yr. of Caprington, with Genealogical Tables, etc., 4to (1848). Burke's Landed Gentry (1875-1925).

**Smith-Neill** of Barnwell and Swindridgemuir. Paterson's Ayr and Wigton, i. 267-268. Pont's Cuningham, ed. Dobie, 250-251. Burke's Landed Gentry (1848-1925).

**Smithson** of Inverernie. Burke's Landed Gentry (1906-1925).

**Smitton.** Notes and Queries, 11th S., iii. 209, 316.

**Smollett** of Bonhill. Some Account of the Family of Smollett of Bonhill, ed. Joseph Irving, 4to, 24 pp. (Dumbarton, 1859).* Notes and Queries'(1860), 2nd S., ix. 276. Book of Dumbartonshire, by Irving (1879), ii. 175-208. Garelochside, by Maughan, 270-275. Burke's Landed Gentry (1848-1925). Traditions of the Watson Family, by C. B. Boog Watson. Life and Letters of Tobias Smollett, by Lewis Melville (1926), 4-7.

of Kirkton (*misprinted* Kirklow). Life . . . of T. Smollett, by Melville, 3.

**Smyth** of Balhary. Baronage, by Douglas, 542-543. Baronage of Angus and Mearns, by Peter, 324, 383.

of Braco. Baronage, by Douglas, 539-543. J. A. Inglis *in* Scot. Hist. Review (1917), xiii. 229-230. *See also* **Smith** of Braco.

of Methven Castle. Douglas's Baronage, 539-542. Burke's Landed Gentry (1848-1906).

**Snodgrass** of Broadstone. Paterson's Ayr and Wigton, iii. 209.

Renfrewshire. Ayrshire Families, by G. Robertson, i. 148.

**Snodgrass-Buchanan** of Cunninghamehead. Ayrshire Families, i. 148-154. History of the County of Ayr, by Paterson, i. 452. Ayr and Wigton, iii. 209-210.

**Sobieski-Stuart.** Chapters from Family Chests, by E. Walford, i. 197-206. Geneal. Mag. (1898), i. 21-30, 119, 185. Scottish N. and Q., 3rd S., iv. 59, 75, 137-139, 228. The Sobieski Stuarts, by Archibald Craig (1922).

**Somervell** of Prestwickshaws. Paterson's Ayr, ii. 387.

of Sorn. Paterson's History of Ayr, ii. 422. Paterson's Ayr and Wigton, i. 706. Burke's Landed Gentry (1886 1925).

**Somerville.** Memories of the Somervilles, being a history of the house, by James, 11th Lord Somerville, ed. Sir Walter Scott, 2 vols., 8vo, illust. (Edinr. 1815). The Baronial House of Somerville, by James Somerville (Glasgow).* The Family of Somerville, and the Poet of the Clan, by George William Campbell, pamphlet, 8vo (Exeter, 1897).

**Somerville** of Airhouse. The Browns of Fordell, by Stodart, 192-193.

of Cambusnethan. Heraldry, by Nisbet (1742), ii., Appx. 277-280.

of Carnwath. Heraldry, by Nisbet (1722), i. 260. Upper Ward of Lanarkshire, by Irving and Murray, ii. 485-517. The Scots Peerage, viii. 2-9.

of Dinder House. Burke's Landed Gentry (1848).

of Drum. Nisbet's Heraldic Plates, ed. Ross and Grant (1892), 130-132. The Scots Peerage, viii. 23-32. Drum of the Somervilles, by Hamilton More Nisbett (Edinr. 1928).

Jedburgh. Annals of a Border Club, by G. Tancred, 449-453.

of Kennox. Paterson's History of the County of Ayr, ii. 462. Paterson's Ayr and Wigton, iii. 604-607. Burke's Landed Gentry (1848), 786.

**Somerville** of Linton. The Scots Peerage, viii. 2-6.

of Plean. The Scots Peerage, viii. 10.

of Quothquhan. Upper Ward of Lanarkshire, by Irving and Murray, i. 442-445.

Lord Somerville. Nisbet's Heraldry, ii., Appx. 79-80. The Scots Peerage, viii. 1-45. Burke's Dormant Peerages. Notes and Queries, 3rd S., iv. 129; ix. 158, 247. The Dormant Barony of Somerville, by Joseph Bain, *in* The Genealogist, N. S., ix. 1-4. The Genealogist, N. S., xv. 65 ; xiii. 78-81, 152.

**Soulis.** System of Heraldry, by A. Nisbet (1722), i. 158. Pont's Cuninghame, ed. Dobie, 295-299. The Genealogist, N. S., iv. 223.

of Gilmerton. The Scots Peerage, ii. 212, 220, 256 ; viii. 249-250.

**Souper** of Auchlunies. Scottish N. and Q., 3rd S., iii. 156.

**Souter-Johnston** of Wardmilne. Memoir of J. Young, Aberdeen . . . 1861, ed. Lt.-Col. W. Johnston (1894), 147.*

**Souter-Robertson** of Whitehill. Memoir of J. Young, Aberdeen . . . 19-20, 146.*

**Southesk,** Carnegie, Earl of. Case of Sir James Carnegie of Southesk, Bart., on his claim to be Earl of Southesk, etc., fol. pp. 30 (1848). Supplemental Case of same, Westminster, fol. (1853). Case of Sir James Carnegie on his claim to the title of Earl of Southesk, fol. (1855). Claim of Sir James Carnegie to be Earl of Southesk : (Session Papers, 283 of 1847-8 ; 164 of 1854 ; 164 of 1854-5 ; A of 1854-5). History of the Carnegies, Earls of Southesk, by William Fraser, 2 vols., Edinr. (1867).* Historical MSS. Commission (1879), 7th Report, pt. ii. Angus or Forfarshire, by Warden, i. 357-379. The Scots Peerage, viii. 46-93. G. E. C.'s Peerage. Debrett's, and other Annual Peerages.

**Spalding.** Geschichtliches, Urkunden, Stamm-tafeln der Spalding in Schottland, Deutschland und Schweden, von Eduard Spalding (Glockenhof, kr. Greifswald, 1898).

of Broomhall. Angus or Forfarshire, by Warden, iii. 364.

of Holme. Burke's Landed Gentry (1894-1914). Lands . . . in Galloway, by M'Kerlie, iii. 77-80, 439.

Inverarity. Smith's Genealogies of an Aberdeen Family (1913), 43, 44, 61-64.

in Sweden. One Year in Sweden, by H. Marryat (1862), ii. 498. Scot. Hist. Review, xxv. 291.

**Spang,** Glasgow. Geneal. Coll., by W. Macfarlane, 1750-51 ; Scot. Hist. Soc., ii. 283-284.

**Speid** of Ardovie. Baronage of Angus and Mearns, by D. M. Peter (1856), 326. Angus or Forfarshire, by Warden, iii. 14.

**Speid-Binny** of Forneth. Baronage of Angus and Mearns, 327.

**Speir** of Blackstoun. Burke's Landed Gentry (1858-1875).

of Burnbrae and Culdees. Burke's Landed Gentry (1848-1925).

of Camphill. Pont's Cuninghame, ed. Dobie, 112.

Speirs of Culcreuch. Annals of a Border Club, by G. Tancred, 454.
  of Elderslie. Crawfurd's Shire of Renfrew (1818), 346. Strathendrick,
    by Guthrie Smith, 260. Burke's Landed Gentry (1906).
  *See* Zetland Family Histories, by F. J. Grant, *for*

Spence of Gardie, 305-307.
  of Greenfield, 310-311.
  of Hammer, 308-309.
  of Houland, 298-301.
  of Midbrake, 302-303.
  of Uyea, 312-315.

Spencer, Viscount of Teviot. The Scots Peerage, viii. 366-367.

Spens of Craigsanquhar. Burke's Landed Gentry (1848-1925).
  of Lathallan. Baronage, by Douglas, 290-295. Généalogie des Spens de
    Lathallan, d'origine écossaise, desquels il existe en France deux
    branches (Bordeaux, 1786). East Neuk of Fife, by W. Wood,
    2nd ed. (1887), 145-147. Burke's Landed Gentry (1848-1925).
  in Sweden. One Year in Sweden, by Marryat, ii. 465-468, 501. Palace
    of History Catalogue (Glasgow, 1911), 205, 210. E. E. Etzel *in* Scot.
    Hist. Review (1913), ix. 276.
  of Wormiston. East Neuk of Fife, 2nd ed., 452-454.

Spens-Destignots, in France. Baronage, by Douglas, 295-299.

Spittal of Blairlogie. Logie, by Rev. Dr Menzies Fergusson, ii. 142-149.
    Stephen's Inverkeithing, 480-485.
  of Leuchat. Family of Buchanan, by Buchanan of Auchmar, 134-137.
    Logie, by Rev. Dr R. M. Fergusson, ii. 156. The Scots Peerage,
    v. 387. Stephen's Inverkeithing (1921), 478-480.
  Stirling. The Stirling Antiquary, ed. W. B. Cook, ii. 157-168 ; iv. 195.

Spottiswode of Fowler. Paterson's History of the County of Ayr, ii. 338.
    Paterson's Ayr and Wigton, i. 560.

Spottiswood of Muiresk. Burke's Landed Gentry (1848).

Spottiswoode of Spottiswoode. Baronage, by Douglas, 446-450. The
    Spottiswoode Miscellany, containing a Family Genealogy, ed. James
    Maidment, 2 vols. (Edinr. 1844). Genealogy, from the MS. Collection
    of Father Augustin Hay, with notes (12 copies) (1844).* Burke's
    Visitation of Seats and Arms (1853), i. 177. Burke's Landed Gentry
    (1848-1894). Genealogy of the Family of Spotswood, by Chas.
    Campbell (Albany, U.S.A., 1868).

Spreull of Couden, Coldoun. Heraldry, by Nisbet (1722), i. 437 ; (1742),
    ii., Appx. 25-26. Crawfurd's Shire of Renfrew (1818), 44. Book of
    Dumbartonshire, by Irving, ii. 187-188.
  Glasgow. Old Greenock, by G. Williamson (1886), i. 256-262.

Sprot(t. Annals of a Border Club, by G. Tancred, 455. Lands . . . in
    Galloway, by M'Kerlie, v. 332.

Sprot of Garnkirk. Annals of a Border Club, 457-458. Alexander Cowan,
    by C. B. Boog Watson.*

**Sprot** of Riddell. Annals of a Border Club, 456-465. Alexander Cowan.*
Burke's Landed Gentry (1879-1925).

**Spynie,** Lindsay, Lord. Case of William Fullarton, Esq., claiming the
Title of Lord Spynie (1785). Angus or Forfarshire, by Warden,
ii. 30-34. The Scots Peerage, viii. 94-113.

**Stair,** Dalrymple, Viscount of, Earl of. Case and Claim of James
Dalrymple to the Earldom of Stair: (Session Papers, 1747-1748).
Case of John, Earl of Stair (1748). Historical MSS. Commission
(1871), 2nd Report. Memoir of Sir James Dalrymple, 1st Viscount
Stair, by Sheriff Mackay (1873). Annals and Correspondence of the
Viscount and the first and second Earls of Stair, by J. M. Graham
(1875), 2 vols. 8vo, illust. The Scots Peerage, viii. 114-164. Scottish
N. and Q., 2nd S., v. 61. G. E. C.'s Complete Peerage. Burke's
and other Annual Peerages.

**Stalker** of Easter Drylaw. Cramond, by J. P. Wood, 30.

**Stark** of Ballindean. Campbell's Balmerino, 562-567, 654-655.
Edinburgh. Scottish N. and Q., 2nd S., viii. 6.

**Stark-Christie.** Burke's Landed Gentry (1875-1886).

**Stavert** of Hoscote. Annals of a Border Club, by G. Tancred, 465-467.
A Chapter in Mediocrity, by W. J. Stavert (Skipton, 1896). Burke's
Landed Gentry (1906-1925).

**Steel** of Annathill. The Family of Black, by W. G. Black, 57-63.*
of Philiphaugh. Burke's Landed Gentry (1906-1925).

**Steele.** Gleanings, by Robert Stevenson of Glasgow (1867).

**Steil.** Kerr's Monfode of that Ilk, 89.

**Stein, Stiven,** Clackmannanshire. MS. Genealogy of the Steins and allied
families, in possession of the Lyon Office, and the Society of
Genealogists, London.

**Steinson,** Fordyce. Scottish N. and Q., 2nd S., iv. 155.

**Stenhouse** of Fod. Stephen's Inverkeithing and Rosyth (1921), 95-98.

**Stephen** of Ardendraught. Scottish N. and Q., xi. 168-169.

**Sterndale-McMikin** of Grange. Burke's Landed Gentry (1898-1925).

**Steuart** of Ballechin. Baronage, by Douglas, 488-490. Sinton's Family
and Genealogical Sketches (Inverness, 1911).* Burke's Landed
Gentry (1848-1925).
of Banchrie and Trochrie. Recreations of an Antiquary, by Fittis (1881),
317-320.
of Brownlee and Middlehope. The Stewarts Magazine, iv. 77-94.
of Carfin and Westwood. The Stewarts Magazine, iv. 95-100.
of Coltness. Crawfurd's Shire of Renfrew (1818), 477-481. Complete
Baronetage, by G. E. C., iv. 375.
of Cornton. By Allan Water, the Story of an Old House, by Katharine
Steuart [Agnes Maciver Logan]. Logie, by Rev. R. Menzies
Fergusson, ii. 211.
of Daldowie. Crawfurd's Shire of Renfrew (1818), 469-474.

Steuart of Dalguise. Burke's Landed Gentry (1846-1894).

of Glenormiston. Burke's Landed Gentry (1848-1863).

of Goodtrees. Crawfurd's Shire of Renfrew, ed. Robertson (1818), 481-486. Complete Baronetage, by G. E. C., iv. 435. The Stewarts Magazine, iv. 66.

of Killiechassie. Scottish N. and Q., 2nd S., i. 11.

Mitcham. Crawfurd's Shire of Renfrew, 490. The Stewarts Magazine, iv. 76.

Orkney. The Scottish Antiquary (1897), xi. 189 ; xii. 43.

of Steuarthall. Descent of Lt.-Col. Geo. Mackenzie Steuart, fifth son of David Steuart of Steuarthall from King Robert III., by George Steuart, lithograph (Edinr. 1855).* Burke's Landed Gentry (1849-1925). The Stewarts Magazine, iv. 85.

of Tannachy and Auchlunkart. Burke's Landed Gentry (1849-1925). Tayler's Jacobites of Aberdeenshire, 405.

Steuart. *See also* Stewart, Stuart.

Steuart-Barclay of Collerney. Crawfurd's Shire of Renfrew (1818), 486-487.

Steuart-Denham. Complete Baronetage, by G. E. C., iv. 363.

Steuart-Fothringham of Powrie and Fothringham. Burke's Landed Gentry (1906-1925).

Steuart-Menzies of Culdares. Burke's Landed Gentry (1849-1925).

*See* Strathendrick, by J. Guthrie Smith (1896), *for*

Steven, of Bellahouston, 217 ; of Cameron, 217 ; of Finnick-Tennant, 208-209, 217, 218 ; of Polmadie, 217.

Stevenson, Ayr. Pedigree *in* The Thurburns, by Lt.-Col. F. A. V. Thurburn, Appx. C (1864).

of Braidwood. Burke's Landed Gentry (1894-1925).

Edinburgh. Records of a Family of Engineers, by R. L. Stevenson.

Glasgow. Gleanings, with a Genealogical Tree, by Robert Stevenson of Glasgow, 40 pp. (1867).

Jedburgh. Annals of a Border Club, by G. Tancred (1899), 467-469.

of Spittal. Logie, by Rev. Dr R. Menzies Fergusson (1905), ii. 24.

Stevenson-Hamilton of Fairholm. Burke's Landed Gentry (1886-1925).

The Royal House of Stewart or Stuart. Declaratio Parliamenti ubi Johannes, primogenitus Roberti, habet succedere in Regnum, 1371 ; with facsimile sheet with seals, folio (1795). La Recerche des Singularitez plus Remarquables concernant l'estat d'Escosse, et la douairière de France, by David Chambers of Ormond (Paris, 1579). Histoire abbregée de tous les Roys . . . d'Escosse, by D. Chambers (Paris, 1579). De Titulo e Jure Mariæ Scotorum Reginæ quo regni Angliæ successionem sibi juste vendicat libellus . . . Accessit ad Anglos et Scotos Paraenesis [by John Lesley, Bishop of Ross], 4to (Rheims, 1580). The Right, Title and Interest of the most excellent Princesse Marie, Queene of Scotland, and of the most noble King James, her Grace's sonne, to the succession of the

croune of England, by John Lesley, Bishop of Rosse, 8vo [Rheims],
(1584). A Trewe Description of the Nobill Race of the Stewards
(Amsterdam, 1603). The Genealogy of King James . . . with his
lineal Descent from Noah, by G. O. Harry (London, 1604). The
Genealogies of King James I. and Queen Anne his Wife, from the
Conquest, by Morgan Colman (1608). La Généalogie de la Maison
Royale de Stuart, par M. G. de Novblanche (Paris, 1640). The True
Effigies of our most illustrious Sovereigne Lord King Charles . . .
with an abstract of the most famous genealogies and pedegrees
(1641). The Divine Catastrophe of the Kingly Family of the House
of Stuarts . . . by Sir Edward Peyton, *iv*+68 pp. (1652, and 1731).
*Stemma Sacrum :* The Royal Progeny Delineated, . . . by Giles
Fleming (London, 1660). The Case of the Succession to the Crown
of England stated (1679). The Case Put concerning the Succession
of H.R.H. the Duke of York (1679). A Brief History of the
Succession, collected out of the Records, etc., by Thos. Hunt (1681,
*repr.* 1714). The Great Point of Succession Discussed, by R. Brady
(1681). Memoires of the Family of the Stuarts and the Remarkable
Providences of Cod towards them [by Rev. John Watson], (London
1683). A Defence of the Antiquity of the Royal Line of Scotland,
by Sir George Macke.. ie (London, 1685). Origines Britannicæ, by
Edward Stillingfleet, D..?. (1685), preface. The Antiquity of the
Royal Line of Scotland further cleared and defended, by Sir George
Mackenzie (London, 1686), [Mackenzie's Essays were translated into
Latin, and printed at Utrecht, 1689]. La Race et la Naissance . . .
de Marie Stuart, 18mo (Amsterdam, 1695). The Tragical History
of the Stuarts [by D. Jones], 8vo (1697). The Royal Family
Described : or, the Characters of James I., Charles I., Charles II.,
James II., by Mr Stewart, 4to (London, 1702). A Short and Plain
Description of the Royal Family of Great Britain, shewing who of
their Descendants profess themselves Popish, and who not (Edinr.
1704). An Historical Essay, shewing that the Crown and Kingdom
of Scotland is Imperial and Independent, by Jas. Anderson (Edinr.
1705). Chronological, Genealogical, and Historical Dissertation of
the Royal Family of the Stuarts, . . . beginning with Milesius, . . .
and ending with His Present Majesty King James the 3rd of
England and Ireland, and of Scotland the 8th, by Mathew Kennedy,
LL.D., 8vo (Paris, 1705). General Description of the Shire of
Renfrew, including . . . a Genealogical History of the Royal
House of Stewart, . . . from 1034 to 1710, by George Crawfurd,
folio (Edinr. 1710), 2nd edition, continued by W. Semple, 4to
(Paisley, 1782), 3rd edition, continued to the Present Time, by
George Robertson, 4to, maps and plates, 523 pp. (Paisley, 1818).
The Royal Family of the Stuarts vindicated from the False Imputa-
tion of Illegitimacy (London, 1711). Genealogical and Historical
Account of the Illustrious Name of Stuart . . . being the long
expected Work of that Great Antiquary, David Symson, M.A.,
Historiographer Royal for Scotland, sm. 8vo (Edinr. 1712).

Historical and Genealogical Account of the most Illustrious Family
of Stewart . . . , by David Symson, post 8vo (1713). The Fate of
Majesty, . . . the Royal House of the Stuarts (London, c. 1720).
Essay on the Origine of the Royal Family of the Stewarts, by
R. Hay of Drumboote (Edinr. 1722, another edition, 1793). Vindi-
cation of Elizabeth More from the imputation of being a concubine,
by R. Hay (1723). Ancient Scottish Surnames, by W. Buchanan
(Glasgow, 1723), 19-22. The Right of Succession to the Crown of
England in the Family of Stuarts [by Sir Nicolas Bacon], (1723).
The History of England, during the reigns of the Royal House of
Stuart [by John Oldmixon], (1730). Remarks on a Book called
"The History of the House of Stuart" (1731). Royal Genealogies,
by Dr Jas. Anderson (1732), 760-762. The Royal Progeny of
King James VI. and I. *in* Royal Genealogies, by Anderson,
770. A Vindication of the Royal Family of the Stuarts, by
P. Rapin-Thoyras (1734). A Short Account of the Royal Family
of Scotland and of the Surname of Stewart, by Duncan Stewart,
4to, with chart (Edinr. 1739). Compleat View of the Birth of the
Pretender, in which all the Arguments for and against that Intricate
Birth are impartially stated (1744). The Right of the House of
Stewart to the Crown of Scotland considered [by Alexander Taitt],
(Edinr. 1746). The Advantages of the Succession of the House of
Stewart to the Crown of Great Britain Demonstrated ; with many
curious Particulars relating to that Family, and Anecdotes of the
Pretender and his Son in 1715 and 1745. By a True Briton, 8vo,
74 pp. (1747). Impartial History of the Rebellion in 1745, etc., by
S. Boyse, with a Compendious Account of the Royal House of
Stewart, 172 pp. (Dublin, 1748). Genealogical History of the Royal
Family of Stuart (1755). Defence of the Four Illustrious Stuarts,
Kings of Great Britain (1758). A Dissertation on the Royal Line
and the First Settlers of Scotland, by Andrew Henderson (London,
1771). Letters to the Right Hon. Lord Mansfield from Andrew
Stewart, on the History and Genealogies of the Stewarts (1773).
A Genealogical Chart of the Illustrious House of Stuart, beginning
with James I., King of Great Britain, by Philip Luckombe (London,
1779). La Famille des Stuarts, par E. Dubois (Rouen, 1784).
A Historical Genealogy of the Royal House of Stuarts . . . by the
Rev. Mark Noble, 4to, 312 pp., chart (1795). Engraved Tree of the
House of Stewart, by W. Brown (Edinr. 1792 ; London, 1811).
A Genealogical History of the Stuarts from the Earliest Period of
their Authentic History, by Andrew Stuart, M.P. (1798). A Letter
on a Disputed Point of Genealogy in the Stewart Family, by
Geo. Chalmers, n.d. A Genealogical Account of the Royal House
of Stuart from 1043, by Thomas Waterhouse (Grantham, 1816).
Jacobite Minstrelsy, with Notes containing Historical Details in
Relation to the House of Stuart from 1640 to 1784 (Glasgow, 1829).
Stewartiana, containing the Case of King Robert II. and Elizabeth
Mure, by John Riddell (1843). Royal Families of England, Scotland

and Wales, by Burke (1847). Le Dernier des Stuarts, par J. J. E. Roy
(Tours, 1856). Fitzalan and Stuart, by R. W. Eyton, *in* Archæological Journal, xiii. 333-334 (1856). The Descendants of the
Stuarts, by Wm. Townend, 8vo, portraits and pedigrees (1858 ;
2nd ed. 1858 ; 3rd ed. 1867). Eminent Men of Fife, by M. F.
Conolly (Cupar, 1866), 434-461. Les Derniers Stuarts à Saint-
Germain en Laye, par le marquis Campana de Cavelli, 2 vols., illust.
(1869, 1871). Lands and their Owners in Galloway, by M'Kerlie
(1878), iv. 362-383. Tales of our Great Families, by E. Walford,
2nd S. (1880), ii. 256-269. The Stuart Calendar : A Centenary
Memorial of the Royal House of Stuart (1888). Sidelights on the
Stuarts, with portraits, facsimiles, etc., by F. A. Inderwick (1888).
Catalogue of the Exhibition of the Royal House of Stuart ; pictures,
relics, etc. (London, 1889). The Royal House of Stuart, illustrated
by 40 coloured plates of relics, etc., by William Gibb ; introduction
by Sir John Skelton, and notes by W. H. St John Hope (1890).
The Stuart Dynasty, by Percy M. Thornton, illust. and chart (1890).
Scottish N. and Q. (1890-1), iv. 61-64, 84-85, 107-108, 173. Pedigree
of the House of Stewart, by W. A. Lindsay, chart 49 by 26 in. [1891].
Genealogical Chart of the Royal Family of Great Britain : Scotland,
Anglo-Saxon, etc., with Collateral Branches, by Robert Logan,
12½ feet long, atlas folio (1891). The Royal House of Stewart, by
James Hutton, *in* Gentleman's Magazine (1893), cclxxiv. 281-296,
345-361. Real Stuarts or bogus Stuarts, by Archibald Forbes *in*
New Review (1893), viii. 73-84. Living Descendants of Mary Queen
of Scots ; Tabular Pedigrees and Lists of Senior and Junior Lines,
by the Marquis de Ruvigny et Raineval, *in* The Legitimist Kalendar
(1894 and later), 155-227. The Last Stuart Princess, by A. Shield,
*in* Dublin Review (London, 1899), cxxv. 56-85. The Fallen Stuarts,
by F. W. Head, *in* Cambridge Hist. Essays (1901), *xii*+356 pp.
W. B. Blaikie *on* Descendants of the Stewarts *in* Geneal. Mag.
(1901), iv. 1-13 with chart. D. F. de L'Hoste Ranking *in* Geneal.
Mag., iv. 437-440. Studies on Peerage and Family History, by
J. Horace Round (1901). The Story of the Stewarts [by J. K.
Stewart], with 4 charts (Stewart Soc., Edinr. 1901). Critique *on above*
by J. H. Round *in* The Ancestor (1902), i. 218-219. The Stewarts :
a Historical and General Magazine for the Stewart Society, ed.
J. K. Stewart, 4to, illust. (Edinr. 1902 to date). The Stuarts ;
Illustrations of Personal History of the Family in 16th, 17th and
18th Century Art, by J. J. Foster, 2 vols. folio (1902). Five Stuart
Princesses, by R. S. Rait (1902). The Origin of the Stewarts, by
J. H. Round *in* The Genealogist, N. S. (1902), xviii. 1-13. The
Heraldry of the Stewarts, with notes on all the males of the Family,
descriptions of the arms, 8 pedigrees and 128 coloured coats, by
G. Harvey Johnston (Edinr. 1905). The Last of the Royal Stuarts :
Henry Stuart, Cardinal Duke of York, by Herbert M. Vaughan
[1906]. Bibliography of Works on the Stewart and Stuart Families,
by R. Murdoch *in* Scottish N. and Q. (1907), 2nd S., viii. 113-114,

171. The Royal Stuarts in their connection with Art and Letters, by W. G. Blaikie Murdoch (1908). The Royal Stewarts, by T. F. Henderson (1914). The Stewarts and the Saxon Succession, by Robert Stewart, *in* The Stewarts Magazine, iv. 332-335. The Stewart Accession, by Prof. R. K. Hannay, *in* The Stewarts Magazine, v. 243-248. The Origin of the House of Stewart, by J. T. T. Brown, *in* Scot. Hist. Review, xxiv. 255-279. Scotland's Royal Line : The Tragic House of Stuart, by Grant R. Francis (1928). [There is much need of an authoritative History of the Stewart Family, brought up to date from the many authentic genealogical sources which have been tapped in recent years. In the meantime, Duncan Stewart's book is useful for co-ordinating all Stewart branches before 1720 ; and a general view also is given in G. Harvey Johnston's heraldic work.]

*See* The Scots Peerage, ed. Sir James Balfour Paul, *for*

**Stewart,** Lord Abernethy, vi. 314.
    Duke of Albany, i. 146-155.
    Earl of Angus, i. 169-171.
    Lord of Annandale, i. 151.
    Lord Ardmanoch, i. 155.
    Earl of Ardmannach, vii. 246.
    Earl of Arran, i. 394-398.
    Earl of Athole, i. 436-448.
    Lord d'Aubigny, v. 356-362.
    Lord Auchterhouse, ii. 266.
    Lord Avandale, vi. 509-511.
    Lord Badenoch, ii. 170.
    Lord Blantyre, ii. 77-93.
    Lord of Brechin, vii. 246.
    Earl of Buchan, ii. 262-270.
    Lord Caberston, viii. 403-409.
    Earl of Caithness, ii. 321-322.
    Earl of Carrick, ii. 438-442.
    Lord Clifton of Leighton-Bromswold, v. 358-362.
    Lord Dalkeith, v. 356-362.
    Lord Darnley, ii. 168 ; v. 348-355.
    Earl of Darnley, v. 356-362.
    Lord Doune, iii. 186-190.
    Earl of Fife, iv. 14-15.
    Earl of Galloway, iv. 145-173.
    Earl of Garioch, v. 367.
    Lord Garlies, iv. 160-173.
    Lord Hamilton, i. 394-398.
    Lord Innermeath, v. 1-8.
    Lord Kinclaven, ii. 441.
    Earl of, Duke of Lennox, v. 344-362.
    Lord Linton, viii. 403-409.

**Stewart**, Earl of Litchfield, v. 360-361.
 Earl of Mar, v. 637-639 ; vi. 314.
 Earl of March, i. 151 ; v. 355, 362.
 Lord Methven, vi. 166-169.
 Earl of Moray, vi. 311-312, 313-330.
 Earl of Newcastle-upon-Tyne, v. 357.
 Lord Ochiltree, vii. 511-520.
 Earl of Orkney, vi. 572-577.
 Marquess of Ormond, i. 155 ; vii. 245-246.
 Lord Pittenweem, vii. 63-69.
 Earl of, Duke of Richmond, v. 357-362.
 Earl of, Duke of Ross, i. 155 ; vii. 245, 246.
 Duke of Rothesay, vii. 312-313.
 Lord St Colme, vii. 394-395.
 Baron Settrington, v. 357.
 Lord Stewart of Oycheltree, vi. 511-520.
 Lord Stewart of Traquair, viii. 403-409.
 Lord Strathearn, vi. 314.
 Earl of Strathearn, viii. 259-261.
 Lord Tarboltoun, v. 356-362.
 Earl of Traquair, viii. 399-409.
 Lord of Zetland, vi. 572-577.

**Stewart** in Abergairn. The Stewarts (Stewart Society Magazine), iv. 17-28.
 Abernethy. The Stewarts Magazine, i. 326-328.
 of Achnacone. The Stewarts of Appin, 153-155. Burke's Landed
  Gentry (1906-1925).
 of Allans. The Stewarts Magazine, iii. 41-43.
 of Allanton. Crawfurd's Shire of Renfrew, ed. Robertson (1818), 468-
  477. The Salt-Foot Controversy, by John Riddell (1818). The
  Salt-Foot Controversy as it appeared in Blackwood's Magazine ;
  to which is added A Reply to that Article published in No. XVIII.
  of that Work (100 copies), n.d. Coltness Collections, being Memorials
  of the Stewarts of Allanton, etc., by Sir A. Stewart Denholm (1842).
  Pedigree *in* G. Harvey Johnston's Heraldry of Stewarts, 77. The
  Stewarts Magazine, iv. 42-59.
 of Ambrismore. The Scots Peerage, ii. 290.
 of Annat and Ballachallan. Notes and Queries, 9th S., vi. 289.
 of Annefield. Crawfurd's Shire of Renfrew (1818), 495.
 of Appin. Notes and Queries, 5th S., vi. 490 ; vii. 70 ; x. 408. The
  Stewarts of Appin, by John H. J. Stewart and Lt.-Col. Duncan
  Stewart, 4to (Edinr. 1880).* The Jacobite Peerage, by the Marquis
  of Ruvigny and Raineval (1904), 8-13. Burke's Landed Gentry
  (1906-1925). The Stewarts Magazine, i. 217 ; ii. 27-46.
 of Ardgowan. The Scottish Antiquary, iv. 23-25.
 of Ardsheal. The Stewarts Magazine, i. 235-237. The Stewarts of
  Appin, 130-152. The Jacobite Peerage (1904), 8-13. Burke's
  Landed Gentry (1906-1925).

**Stewart** of Ardvorlich. Heraldry, by Nisbet (1742), ii., Appx. 81-83. Visitation of Seats and Arms (1853), i. 186. The Stewarts Magazine (1908), ii. 13-26. Burke's Landed Gentry (1848-1925).

of Auchingray. The Stewarts Magazine, iii. 43, 46.

of Aucholzie. Tayler's Jacobites of Aberdeenshire, 401.

of Auchterhouse. Peeblesshire Localities, by Renwick, 548 *n.*, 551.

of Badenoch. The Stewarts Magazine, ii. 238-250.

of Ballachtoule. Paterson's Ayr and Wigton, ii. 252.

of Ballachelish. The Stewarts of Appin, 181-182. The Stewarts Magazine, i. 239.

of Ballechin. Baronage, by Douglas, 488-490. Burke's Landed Gentry, (1848-1925). Family and Genealogical Sketches, by Rev. Thos. Sinton (Inverness, 1911).*

of Ballintoy. The Stewarts of Ballintoy, with Notices of Other Families of the District in the Seventeenth Century, by George Hill (Coleraine, 1865).

of Balloan. The Stewarts Magazine, iii. 11-15, 150-170, 171-181, 275-305 ; iv. 132.

of Balnakeilly. Burke's Landed Gentry (1906-1925).

of Banchory. Burke's Landed Gentry (1914-1925).

of Barnsoule. The Stewarts Magazine, iii. 54-56 ; v. 155-157.

of Barskimming. Paterson's History of the County of Ayr, ii. 439. Paterson's Ayr and Wigton, i. 717.

of Belladrum. Burke's Landed Gentry (1848).

of Beltrees. Crawfurd's Shire of Renfrew (1818), 79.

of Bigtoun. Zetland Family Histories, by F. J. Grant, 320-322.

of Binny. Burke's Landed Gentry (1848, 1894).

of Blackhall. Crawfurd's Ayr and Wigton (1818), 58. Complete Baronetage, by G. E. C., iv. 261.

of Blackhouse. Burke's Landed Gentry (1894-1925).

of Blair and Balcaskie. Complete Baronetage, by G. E. C., iv. 323.

of Blairhall. Crawfurd's Shire of Renfrew (1818), 494.

of Bohallie. The Stewarts of Appin, 182-183.

of Bonkyl. Pedigrees of Senior and Junior Lines *in* Johnston's Heraldry of the Stewarts, 46, 55. The Stewarts Magazine, i. 183-187.

of Bonskeid. The Stewarts of Forthergill, 24-28.

of Brugh. Zetland Family Histories, by F. J. Grant, 316-319. Norton Smith's Orkney Armorials, 134-135.

of Burray. Complete Baronetage, by G. E. C., iv. 355. Burke's Extinct Baronetcies. Norton Smith's Orkney Armorials, 142. The Stewarts Magazine, ii. 49-73 ; iii. 346-348.

of Bute. History of the County of Bute, by J. E. Reid (1864), 194-215. Rothesay Castle and the Rothesay Tombs, by J. C. Roger (1896).* Complete Baronetage, by G. E. C., ii. 322. The Scots Peerage, ii. 285-298. Pedigree of the Natural Sons of King Robert II. *in* Johnston's Heraldry of the Stewarts, 42.

of Cairnsmore. Lands in Galloway, by M'Kerlie, iv. 455-457. Burke's Landed Gentry (1848-1895).

**Stewart** of Campsie.   The Stewarts Magazine, iii. 260-261.

of Carabella.   The Stewarts Magazine, iv. 116-121.

of Cardneys.   The Scottish Antiquary (1893), vii. 103-108.

of Castlemilk.   *See* **Stuart** of Castlemilk.

of Castle Stewart.   Genealogy of Stewart *in* The State of Evidence of Andrew Thomas Stewart Moore, in Support of his Claim to the Title of Castle Stewart [1769].   The Scots Peerage, iv. 155, 162.

of Catrine.   Paterson's Ayr and Wigton, i. 690.

of Caverston, Cabriston.   The Stewarts Magazine, iv. 29-41.

of Cloichfoldich.   The Stewarts of Forthergill, 37.

of Cluny.   The Stewarts of Forthergill, 28-31, 42-45.

of Coll.   Burke's Landed Gentry (1879-1925).

of Coltness.   Coltness Collections, 1608-1840 ; being Memorials of the Stewarts of Allanton, Coltness, and Goodtrees, by Sir Archibald Stewart Denholm of Coltness and Westshield, Bart., ed. James Dennistoun (Glasgow, Maitland Club, 1842).   Complete Baronetage, by G. E. C., iv. 375.   Letters and Journals of Mrs Calderwood of Polton, ed. Lt.-Col. A. Fergusson (1884), *xxix-lxix*, 365-371.   The Stewarts Magazine, iv. 59, 60-65.

of Concressault.   The Scots Peerage, v. 346-347.

of Corsewell.   G. E. C.'s Complete Baronetage, ii. 323.

of Craigiehall.   M'Kerlie's Lands . . . in Galloway, iii. 477-479.   The Stewarts Magazine, i. 187.

of Craigtoun.   N. and Q., 7th S., xi. 49.

of Culgruff.   The Stewarts Magazine, iii. 46-48.

of Daldowie.   The Stewarts Magazine, iv. 44-55.

of Dalswinton.   The Scots Peerage, iv. 149-159.

of Darnley.   View of the Evidence for proving that the Paternal Ancestor of the Present Earls of Galloway was the second son of Sir Alexander Stewart of Darnley, by Rev. E. Williams (1801). J. K. Stewart *in* The Stewarts Magazine, i. 186, 190-205.   Notes and Queries, 11th S., iv. 89 ; v. 157.   The Scots Peerage, v. 344-348.

of Derculich.   The Stewarts of Forthergill, 38.

of Drumcharry.   The Stewarts Magazine, iii. 25.

of Drumin.   Burke's Landed Gentry (1848-1863).

Dundee.   History of Thomson of Corstorphine, by T. R. Thomson, Appx. C.

of Dunduff.   Paterson's History of the County of Ayr, ii. 354.   Paterson's Ayr and Wigton, i. 429-431.

of Durisdeer.   Scottish Antiquary, v. 3-7.   R. C. Reid *in* Dumfriesshire and Galloway Antiq. Soc. Trans., 3rd S., viii. 146-153.   The Stewarts Magazine, iv. 207-221, and tree.

of Edravinoch.   The Stewarts of Appin, 183-184.

of Fair Isle.   Zetland Family Histories, by F. J. Grant, 316-319.

of Fasnacloich.   The Stewarts of Appin, 155-165.   The Stewarts Magazine, i. 239.   Haud Immemor, by Charles Stewart (1901).

Stewart of Finnick. Strathendrick, by Guthrie Smith, 212.

of Fintalloch. The Stewarts Magazine, iii. 36-41.

of Forthergill. Historic Memorials of the Stewarts of Forthergill, and their Male Descendants . . . ed. by Charles Poyntz Stewart, 4to, Genealogical Tables, etc. (1879).* The Stewarts Magazine, iii. 301.

of Foss. Scottish N. and Q., xii. 130-131.

Earl of Galloway. The Scots Peerage, iv. 145-173. The Heir-Male of the Stewarts, by J. K. Stewart *in* The Stewarts Magazine, i. 20-59, *et passim.* Pedigree by G. Harvey Johnston *in* The Heraldry of the Stewarts, 69.

of Galston. Paterson's History of Ayr, ii. 65. Paterson's Ayr and Wigton, i. 524. The Scots Peerage, v. 345 ; vii. 63-64.

of Garlies. Lands and their Owners in Galloway, by P. H. M'Kerlie (Edinr. 1878), iv. 388-397. The Scots Peerage, iv. 149-159. The Stewarts Magazine, i. 155-205, 304-310, *et passim.*

of Garloff. The Stewarts Magazine, iii. 46, 53.

of Garth. The Stewarts of Forthergill, by C. Poyntz Stewart. History of Thomson of Corstorphine, by T. R. Thomson (1926), pedigree in Appx. C. The Stewarts Magazine, iii. 3, 6, 25, 280.

of Garvocks. Burke's Landed Gentry (1886).

of Glasserton. The Scots Peerage, iv. 154, 161-166.

of Goodtrees. Coltness Collections (1842). Complete Baronetage, by G. E. C., iv. 435.

of Graemsay. Norton Smith's Orkney Armorials, 138.

of Grandtully. Heraldry, by Nisbet, ii., Appx. 160-163. Baronage, by Douglas, 483-488. The Logiad, a poem, with descriptive notes, by one of the family, 4to, 12 copies (1818).* The Red Book of Grandtully, by William Fraser, 2 vols., illust. (Edinr. 1868).* The Stewarts Magazine, iii. 290-295, and two pedigrees ; iv. 145.

of the Grenan. The Scots Peerage, iv. 152, 155, 156.

at Hambledon. The Stewarts Magazine, v. 155-156.

in Hawthornside. Tancred's Rulewater, 51-52.

of Hesilside. Notes and Queries, 7th S., ii. 49, 68. The Stewarts Magazine, iii. 54.

of Hillhead. The Stewarts of Appin, 162-164.

of Horsburgh. Peeblesshire Localities, by R. Renwick, 584-585.

of Inchgarth. Case between Robert Stewart of Garth and Ann Stewart of Inchgarth (1784).

of Innerhadden and Strathgarry. The Stewarts of Appin, 177-181.

of Innermeath, Invermay. Geneal. Coll., by W. Macfarlane, 1750-51 ; Scot. Hist. Soc., i. 30. M. Stuart *in* the Stewarts Magazine, i. 319-322. The Scots Peerage, v. 1-3. The Plenishing of Holyroodhouse, in 1715, by A. Francis Steuart, *in* Proc. Soc. Antiq. Scotl. (1928).

of Innischaoraich. The Stewarts of Appin, 182-183.

of Invernahyle. The Stewarts of Appin, 165-176.

**Stewart** of Jedworth. A View of the Evidence for proving that the present Earl of Galloway is the lineal Heir male and lawful Representative of Sir William Stuart of Jedworth, so frequently mentioned in History from the year 1385 to the year 1429 ; [by Rev. E. Williams, Chaplain to the Earl of Galloway], 4to (1796).* Abstract of the Evidence adduced to prove that Sir William Stewart of Jedworth, the Paternal Ancestor of the Earl of Galloway, was the second son of Sir Alex. Stewart of Darnley, and the brother of Sir John Stewart, who married one of the co-heiresses of the House of Lennox about the year 1385, and who fell at the Siege of Orleans, A.D. 1429 ; [by Rev. E. Williams], 4to, *xvi*+195+*xlvii* pp., with chart (London, 1801). Sir William Stewart of Jedworth, by Joseph Bain, *in* Genealogist, N. S., ii. 81-84 ; xi. 127. The Stewarts Magazine, i. 82-128, 195-205, 211 ; iv. 223-237.

of Keil. The Stewarts Magazine, i. 365-370.

of Kilcattan. The Scots Peerage, ii. 288-290.

of Killiechassie. Baronage, by Douglas, 490-491. The Stewarts of Forthergill, 34-36. Scottish N. and Q., 2nd S., i. 11.

of Kincardine. The Stewarts Magazine, i. 371-374. The Jacobite Peerage, 168-169.

of Kinlochmoidart. Burke's Landed Gentry (1894-1925).

of Kynachan. Scottish N. and Q., 1st S., xii. 171. Family and Genealogical Sketches, by Rev. Thos. Sinton (Inverness, 1911).* The Stewarts Magazine, iv. 256-268.

of Ladywell. Scottish Antiquary, v. 93 ; vi. 41-42.

of Laithers. Fraser's Laurencekirk, 95-97. Burke's Landed Gentry (1848-1925). The Scots Peerage, v. 5, 6.

of Lassintullich. The Stewarts Magazine, iii. 2. MS. Pedigree in Library of Stewart Society.

of Lennox and Darnley. Royal Genealogies, by Anderson (1732), 763, 764, 765. A Genealogical History of the Stuarts, from the Earliest Period of their Authentic History, by Andrew Stuart, M.P., *xxiii*+468 pp. (1798). Genealogy of the Stewarts refuted [by Sir Henry Steuart], with large chart (1799). Supplement to the Genealogical History of the Stewarts, by Andrew Stuart (1799). The Lennox, by Wm. Fraser, 2 vols. (1868). The Lanox of Auld : an Epistolary Review of "The Lennox" by William Fraser ; by Mark Napier (Edinr. 1880). The Scottish Antiquary, xii. 1-4.

of Lesmurdie. Burke's Landed Gentry (1848). Annals of Elgin, by Young (1879), 657-660.

in Linlithgow. The Stewarts Magazine, iii. 255-262.

of Lochrig. Paterson's Ayr and Wigton, iii. 603.

of Lorn. Notes and Queries, 6th S., vii. 248. Herald and Genealogist, vi. 481-595. The Scots Peerage, v. 1-4. The Stewarts Magazine, iv. 278-286. [A. Francis Steuart, advocate, has a MS. Collection of information on the Stewarts of Lorn and Innermeith.]

of Luthrie. The Stewarts Magazine, iv. 352-367.

**Stewart** of Mains. The Stewarts Magazine, ii. 49-73. Norton Smith's Armorials, 142.

of Massater. Norton Smith's Orkney Armorials, 141. The Stewarts of Massater, by R. A. Clapperton-Stewart of Massater, 9 pp. (Viking Society, 1928).*

of Menteith. The Red Book of Menteith, by Sir William Fraser (1881). The Red Book of Menteith Reviewed, by George Burnett (1881). The Lake of Menteith, by Hutchison, 239-252. The Stewarts Magazine, iv. 304-314. Pedigree *in* G. Harvey Johnston's Heraldry of the Stewarts, 65.

of Minto. The Scottish Antiquary, xii. 144.

of Morphie. The Stewarts Magazine, i. 129.

Mortlach. The Stewarts Magazine, ii. 74-83, 117-128.

of Moyne and Townend. Pont's Cuninghame, ed. Dobie, 166.

of Murdostoun. Burke's Landed Gentry (1863-1925).

of Newton. Crawfurd's Shire of Renfrew (1818), 37. Ayrshire Families, by G. Robertson, i. 19-20.

of Ochiltree. Paterson's History of Ayr, ii. 399. One Year in Sweden, by Marryat, ii. 480. Complete Baronetage, by G. E. C., ii. 373.

of Oizon. The Scots Peerage, v. 348, 350.

of Orkney. The Stewarts in Orkney *in* Scot. Review (Paisley, 1890), xv. 285-315.

of Pardovan. The Stewarts Magazine, iii. 262, and tree.

of Physgill. Heraldry, by Nisbet (1742), ii., Appx. 52. Burke's Landed Gentry (1848-1925).

of Pitcastle. The Stewarts of Forthergill, 33.

of Pittyvaich. The Stewarts Magazine, ii. 120-128.

of Redcastle. The Scots Peerage, v. 3-6.

in Rosarie. Scottish N. and Q. (1889), ii. 190.

of Rosyth, Craigiehall and Durisdeer. The Scottish Antiquary, v. 1-9, 77-78 ; vi. 184. R. C. Reid *in* Dumfriesshire and Galloway Antiq. Soc. Trans., 3rd S. (1923), viii. 146-153. The Stewarts Magazine, iv. 220, and tree. Stephen's Inverkeithing and Rosyth (1921), 182-196.

in Ruscachan. MS. Pedigree in Lyon Office, and in Library of the Stewart Society.

of St Fort. Eminent Men of Fife, by M. F. Conolly, 427. Burke's Landed Gentry (1848-1886).

of Shambellie. M'Kerlie's Lands in Galloway (1879), v. 11-13. The Stewarts Magazine, iii. 33, 42-58, with tree ; v. 147.

of Shillinglaw and Horsburgh. Peeblesshire Localities, by R. Renwick, 585. The Scots Peerage, viii. 399, 401.

of Stair. Paterson's History of the County of Ayr, ii. 438. Paterson's Ayr and Wigton, i. 733.

of Stenton. Notes and Queries, 7th S., viii. 48. The Scottish Antiquary, vii. 105-108.

of Stewartfield. Douglas's Baronage, 490-491. Annals of a Border Club, by G. Tancred, 82.

Z

**Stewart** in the Stewartry. Misc. Entries from Parish Registers *in* The Stewarts Magazine, v. 157-162.

of Sticks. Scottish N. and Q., 3rd S., iv. 215.

of Strath. The Stewarts Magazine, v. 140-146.

of Strathgarry. The Stewarts of Appin, 152-153, 177-181. Scottish N. and Q., 3rd S., i. 57.

of Temper, Lassintullich and Crossmount in Rannoch. MS. Pedigree in possession of the Stewart Society, Edinburgh.

of Tillicoultry. Complete Baronetage, by G. E. C., iv. 447.

of Traquair. Peeblesshire Localities, by R. Renwick, 20-21, 548 *n.*, 551. The Stewarts Magazine, iii. 233-254; iv. 29, 41. Complete Baronetage, by G. E. C., ii. 349. The Scots Peerage, viii. 399-408.

of Tynnes. The Stewarts Magazine, iii. 239-248, 253.

of Urrard. Burke's Landed Gentry (1886). The Stewarts Magazine, iii. 6, 7-19.

of Watten. The Stewarts Magazine, v. 140.

**Stewart.** Notes and Queries, 6th S., x. 517; xi. 52, 235, 353: 7th S., iv. 67, 216, 316; vi. 27, 134, 290, 355, 436; viii. 108, 174; ix. 165.

**Stewart** *alias* **McRob.** The Stewarts of Appin, 184-185.

**Stewart-Flemyng** of Killiechassie. Scottish N. and Q., 2nd S., i. 11.

**Stewart-Fullarton** of Fullarton. Crawfurd's Shire of Renfrew (1818), 495.

**Stewart-Mackenzie** of Seaforth. The Scots Peerage, iv. 166.

**Stewart-Menzies** of Chesthill and Farr. Burke's Landed Gentry (1848-1894).

**Stewart-Murray.** The Scots Peerage, i. 500-501.

**Stewart-Richardson** of Pitfour. Complete Baronetage, by G. E. C., ii. 380; vi., Appx. 86. Burke's Peerage and Baronetage. Debrett's Baronetage.

**Stewart-Robertson** of Edradynate. Burke's Landed Gentry (1879-1925).

**Stewart.** *See also* **Steuart, Stuart.**

**Stillie** of Changue. Paterson's Ayr and Wigton, ii. 120.

**Stirling**, Alexander, Earl of. Claim of William Alexander to the Earldom of Stirling: (Session Papers, May 1760—March 1762). Case of Alexander Humphreys or Alexander (1825); Original Case of the Appellant and Appendix, (repr. London, 1867), and Suppl. Case (London, n.d.). Case of the Respondent, A. W. F. Alexander (repr. Edinr. 1867), and Suppl. Case for the Respondents (Edinr. 1868). Resumption of the Titles by the Present Earl of Stirling (London, 1826). Analytical Statement of the Case of Alexander, Earl of Stirling and Dovan, etc., by Sir Thos. C. Banks, *xlix* + 123 pp., 4 pedigrees (London, 1832). Case of the Rt. Hon. Alexander, Earl of Stirling, by F. J. Burn (London, 1833). Narrative of the Oppressive Law Proceedings resorted to by the British Government and numerous Private Individuals to overpower the Earl of Stirling, written by Himself, also a Genealogical Account of the Family of Alexander, Earls of Stirling, ed. Ephraim Lockhart, 4to (Edinr. 1836). [Also in French.] Report of the Trial of Alex. Humphreys or Alexander, claiming the Title of Earl of Stirling, . . . by Archibald Swinton, $vi+xxiv+356$; *cviii* pp. (Edinr. 1839). The Stirling Peerage; Trial of Alexander Humphreys, or Alexander, styling himself Earl of Stirling, for Forgery, ed. by W. B. D. D. Turnbull (Edinr. 1839). Vindication of the Rights and Titles of Alexander, Earl of Stirling, etc., 2 pp. (Washington, U.S.A., 1853). Notes and Queries, 2nd S., vi. 70; viii. 268, 297, 387, 434: 7th S., xi. 342, 445. Memorials of the Earl of Stirling and of the House of Alexander, by Rev. C. Rogers, 2 vols. (Edinr. 1877). Scottish N. and Q., 2nd S., iv. 13. Pedigree, by D. E. Davy, Brit. Mus. Add. MS. 19114. G. E. C.'s Complete Peerage. The Scots Peerage, viii. 165-185. The Stewarts Magazine, v. 190-194, 224.

**Stirling**, Erskine, Marquis of. The Jacobite Peerage, by the Marquis of Ruvigny, 169.

**Stirling.** Heraldry, by Nisbet (1722), i. 410-411. Notes and Queries, 8th S., iv. 386; viii. 449; x. 295; xi. 83.

of Ardoch. Logie, by R. Menzies Fergusson, D.D., ii. 45. Complete Baronetage, by G. E. C., iv. 253.

of Auchyle and Rednock. Burke's Landed Gentry (1906).

of Ballagan. Strathblane, by Guthrie Smith, 150-154.

of Easter Brakie and Balcaskie. East Neuk of Fife, by W. Wood, 2nd ed., 271.

of Cadder. The Stirlings of Keir, by Wm. Fraser (1858). Comments in Refutation, etc., by John Riddell (1860).* The Stirlings of Craigbernard and Glorat (1883). Herald and Genealogist, viii. 6.

of Craigbarnet, Craigbernard. The Stirlings of Craigbernard and Glorat [by Joseph Bain], $xxxiv+127$ pp. (Edinr. 1883).* Review of above *in* Genealogist, N. S., vii. 219-221. Strathendrick, by Guthrie Smith, 244. Strathblane, by Guthrie Smith, 130-141.

of Cult. Strathblane, by Guthrie Smith, 157-158.

of Drumpellier. Comments, etc. . . . and Exposition of the Rights of the Stirlings of Drumpellier to the Representation of the Ancient Stirlings of Cadder, by John Riddell, 4to (Edinr. 1860).* Pedigree of Andrew Stirling of Drumpellier; in the Public Library, Stirling, M 20633.

Edinburgh and Uphall. Complete Baronetage, by G. E. C. (1906), v. 282.

of Fairburn. Burke's Landed Gentry (1894-1925).

of Garden. Burke's Landed Gentry (1894-1925).

of Gargunnock. Burke's Landed Gentry (1875-1925).

of Glorat. The Stirlings of Craigbernard and Glorat (1883).* Strathblane, by Guthrie Smith, 141-148. Complete Baronetage, by G. E. C., iv. 252. Debrett's Baronetage. Burke's Peerage and Baronetage.

**Stirling** of Keir. The Stirlings of Keir and their Family Papers, by William Fraser, 4to, illust. (Edinr. 1858).* Comments in Refutation of Pretensions advanced . . . and Statements in . . . "The Stirlings of Keir," by John Riddell, 4to (Edinr. 1860).* The Armorial Bearings of the Stirlings of Keir, and others of the Name, by Sir Wm. Stirling-Maxwell, 4to (Glasgow, 1860). Historical MSS. Commission (1885). The Scottish Antiquary, viii. 109-110. Logie, by Rev. Dr Menzies Fergusson, ii. 166-168. Burke's Landed Gentry (1858-1925).

of Kippendavie. The Stirling Antiquary, iii. 287-288. Logie, by R. M. Fergusson, D.D., ii. 37. Burke's Landed Gentry (1858-1925).

of Kirklands. Strathblane, by Guthrie Smith, 130-149.

of Larbert. Burke's Landed Gentry (1875-1925).

of Law and Edenbarnet. Strathblane, by Guthrie Smith, 148-149.

of Mansfield. Private Act to deal with very large Estates belonging to Sir Gilbert Stirling of Mansfield, Baronet in Scotland, 25 pp. (1854).

of Powhouse. Logie, by R. M. Fergusson, D.D., ii. 93-94.

of Strowan. Burke's Landed Gentry (1906-1925).

**Stirling-Crawfurd** of Milton. Burke's Landed Gentry (1863-1879).

**Stirling-Hamilton** of Preston. Complete Baronetage, by G. E. C., iv. 299. Burke's Peerage and Baronetage. Debrett's Baronetage.

**Stirling-Home-Drummond-Moray.** Historical MSS. Commission (1872), 3rd Report ; (1885), 10th Report.

**Stirling-Maxwell.** Burke's Peerage and Baronetage. Debrett's Baronetage. Complete Baronetage, by G. E. C., iv. 312, 447.

**Stirling-Stuart** of Castlemilk. Burke's Landed Gentry (1906-1925).

**Stirton.** Stirton of the Stormont, by Rev. John Stirton, D.D., 5 pp. (1920).* MS. Pedigree in possession of H.M. Lyon Office, Edinburgh, and the Society of Genealogists, London.

**Stobie** of Keiss. Smith's Genealogies of an Aberdeen Family ; Aberdeen Univ. Studies, 114.

**Stobo** of Stobo. The Scots Peerage, vii. 420.

**Stodart.** Some Old Families, by H. B. M'Call ; and chart pedigree, 254, 255. Herald and Genealogist, iii. 552-553.

of Kailzie and Ormiston. Burke's Landed Gentry (1848, 1879, p. 1635).

**Stoddart** of Williamshope. Craig Brown's Selkirkshire, ii. 369.

**Stormont,** Murray, Viscount of. Heraldry, by Nisbet (1742), ii., Appx. 211-218. The Scots Peerage, viii. 186-210.

**Stormonth** of Kinclune and Lednathy. Angus or Forfarshire, by Warden, iv. 116. The Scottish Antiquary (Edinr. 1893), vii. 31.

**Story.** Annals of Garelochside, by W. C. Maughan (Paisley, 1896), 193-229.

**Stothert** of Cargen. Lands . . . in Galloway, by M'Kerlie, v. 235. Burke's Landed Gentry (1848-1863).

**Strabane,** Hamilton, Baron of, Viscount of, Marquess of Hamilton of. The Scots Peerage, i. 48-73.

**Strabolgi, Strathbogie.** Earl of Atholl. Scottish N. and Q., 3rd S., ii. 95. Stemmata Robertson et Durdin, by H. Robertson, 108-109.* The Scots Peerage, i. 424-432. Banks' Dormant and Extinct Baronage, i. 414. Philippe de Strabolgi, by G. W. Watson *in* Genealogist, N. S., xxix. 1.

Kenworthy, Baron. Burke's and other Annual Peerages (after 1916).

**Strachan** of Carmyllie. Angus or Forfarshire, by Warden, iii. 92-95.

of Claypots. Angus or Forfarshire, iv. 137.

of Craigcrook. Cramond, by J. P. Wood, 34-37.

of Glenkindie. The Strachans of Glenkindie, 1357-1726, by Col. James Allardice, LL.D., 4to, 43 pp., Aberdeen [1899].*

of Inchtuthill. Complete Baronetage, by G. E. C., iv. 332.

of Thornton. Geneal. Coll., by W. Macfarlane, 1750-51 ; Scot. Hist. Soc., ii. 265-275. Baronage of Angus and Mearns, by Peter, 329. Memorials of the Strachans, Baronets of Thornton . . . with folding pedigrees and plates of arms in colour, by Rev. C. Rogers [1873].* Memorials of the Scottish Families of Strachan and Wise, by Rev. C. Rogers [1877].* Review *in* Herald ·and Genealogist, viii. 302-307. Sheet Pedigree of the Strachans of Thornton, 4to, n.d.* Memorials of Angus and the Mearns, by Jervise, ed. Gammack, ii. 166-169. Burke's Extinct Baronetcies. Complete Baronetage, by G. E. C., ii. 385. Scottish N. and Q., 3rd S., vi. 23.

**Stradichtie,** Lyon, Lord. The Scots Peerage, viii. 299-317.

**Strahan.** Scottish N. and Q., 2nd S., v. 187.

**Straiton, Straton,** of Kirkside. Baronage of Angus and Mearns, by Peter (1856), 332-334. Geneal. Mag. (1903), vi. 399.

of Lauriston. Epitaphs and Inscriptions, by Jervise, i. 36-43. Memorials of Angus and the Mearns, by Jervise, ed. Gammack, ii. 160-163.

**Strang** of Balcaskie. East Neuk of Fife, by W. Wood, 2nd ed., 271-272.

of Kilrenny. Geneal. Coll., by W. Macfarlane, 1750-51 ; Scot. Hist. Soc., i. 12, 24. East Neuk of Fife, 2nd ed., 380.

of Pitcorthie. East Neuk of Fife, 2nd ed., 154.

in Stockholm. Memorials of Angus and the Mearns, by Jervise, ed. Gammack (1861), i. 50.

of Voisgarth. East Neuk of Fife, 2nd ed., 273.

**Strange,** Kirkwall. Norton Smith's Orkney Armorials, 146.

of Westmanland. One Year in Sweden, by Marryat, i. 421 *n.*

**Strange,** Murray, Lord, Earl. The Scots Peerage, i. 488, 495.

**Stranraer,** Dalrymple, Lord. The Scots Peerage, viii. 119, 149.

**Strathallan,** Drummond, Viscount of. The Scots Peerage, viii. 215-238.

**Strathbogie.** *See* **Strabolgi.**

*See* The Scots Peerage, ed. Sir J. Balfour Paul, *for*

**Strathearn.** The Ancient Earls of, viii. 239-254.

Graham, Earl of, viii. 260.

Moray, Earl of, viii. 255-258.

Stewart, Earl of, viii. 259-261.

Stewart, Lord, vi. 314.

**Strathearn.** History of the Earldom of Strathearn, by Sir Harris Nicolas (London, 1842). Angus or Forfarshire, by A. J. Warden (1880), i. 336-356. Joseph Bain *in* The Genealogist, N. S., v. 105-108. The Abbey of Inchaffray ; Scot. Hist. Soc., No. 56 (1908), *lv-lxxv.* Notes and Queries, 8th S., ii. 487 ; iii. 389 ; iv. 33 ; viii. 301, 389 ; ix. 71.

**Stratheden and Campbell,** Campbell, Baron. Burke's and other Annual Peerages.

*See* The Scots Peerage, ed. Sir J. Balfour Paul, *for*

**Strathmore,** Bowes, Earl of, viii. 310-312.

Bowes-Lyon, Earl of, viii. 313-317.

Lyon, Earl of, viii. 261-310.

Lyon-Bowes, Earl of, viii. 312-313. Biographical Peerage (London, 1808), 572-574. Report on the Deeds *re* Family Claims of the Earl of Strathmore against the Trustees of the late Earl of that Family, by Cosmo Innes, 4to, 182 pp. (1835).* Eminent Men of Fife, by M. F. Conolly (1866), 308-310. Historical MSS. Commission (1871), 2nd Report ; (1894), 14th Report. G. E. C.'s Complete Peerage. Burke's and other Annual Peerages.

**Strathnaver,** Lady of, Lord. The Scots Peerage, ii. 122, 316 ; viii. 350-357.

**Strathspey,** Ogilvie-Grant, Baron. Burke's and other Annual Peerages.

**Straton, Straiton.** Dr C. H. Straton, Hill House, Honiton, Devon, has collected a large quantity of material relating to this family.

**Struthers,** Gallowgate. Glasgow, Past and Present (1884), iii. 182-184.

**Stuardo.** The Scots Peerage, i. 30 *n.* The Neapolitan Stuarts, by A. Francis Steuart *in* English Hist. Review (1903), xviii. 470-471. Philip Sidney *in the same*, 718-719.

*See* The Scots Peerage, ed. Sir J. Balfour Paul, *for*

**Stuart,** Marquis of Angra, ii. 304.

Earl of, Marquess of Bute, ii. 285-312.

Viscount Kingarth, ii. 299.

Lord Mount Stuart, ii. 299, 306.

Baron Stuart de Decies, ii. 307.

Baron Stuart de Rothesay, ii. 304.

Earl of Windsor, ii. 306.

**Stuart** of Allanbank. Crawfurd's Shire of Renfrew (1818), 488-490. Folding pedigree, 1643-1880, compiled by Louisa L. Forbes, 4to (1880).* Complete Baronetage, by G. E. C., iv. 353. The Stewarts Magazine, iv. 73-75.

of Annat. Scot. Hist. Review, xxi. 1.

**Stuart** of Aubigny. Chroniques de Louis XII., par Jean d'Auton; Société de l'Histoire de France, i. Some Account of the Stuarts of Aubigny, in France [1422-1673], by Lady Elizabeth Cust, 4to, front. and Genealogical Table (1891).*

of Aucharnie. Thanage of Fermartyn, by Temple, 201-223.

in Milton of Balgonie. Kennoway, by A. S. Cunningham (Leven, 1906), 41-43. Reminiscences, by James Stuart, M.P., *xvi*+302 pp., pedigree (London, 1911).*

of Ballechin. Douglas's Baronage, 488-490. Burke's Landed Gentry (1848-1925).

Berwick-on-Tweed. Scottish N. and Q., x. 165 ; xi. 164.

of Burray. Heraldry, by Nisbet (1742), ii., Appx. 169-171.

of Bute. History of the County of Bute, by J. E. Reid, 194-215. The Scots Peerage, ii. 285-298.

of Carra Castle. Notes and Queries, 8th S., ix. 467.

of Castlemilk. State of the Evidence for proving that Sir John Stuart of Castlemilk is the Lineal Heir Male of Sir William Stuart of Castlemilk, who lived in the Fourteenth Century, 4to (1794). Baronage, by Douglas, 513-516. Crawfurd's Shire of Renfrew (1818), 127, 491-492. Pedigree of the Family of Stewart (now Stuart) of Castlemilk, by Michael J. M. S. Stewart, size 25½ × 22 in., 17 generations, 4to (Worksop, 1890).* J. K. Stewart *in* The Stewarts Magazine, i. 79-81, 93, 197-205. Complete Baronetage, by G. E. C., iv. 267. Burke's Landed Gentry (1886-1925). *See also* **Stewart of Darnley and Lennox.**

of Castle Stuart. Genealogical Sketch of the Stuarts of Castle Stuart, in Ireland, by the Rev. Andrew A. Stuart, 4to (Edinr. 1854). The Stewarts Magazine, i.

of Colinton. Complete Baronetage, by G. E. C., iv. 436.

of Dalguise. Burke's Landed Gentry (1848).

of Dalness. *See* **Stuart of Kishorn.**

of Dunearn. Crawfurd's Shire of Renfrew (1818), 460-462. Stair A. Gillon *in* The Stewarts Magazine, v. 113-129, with tree.

of Eaglescarnie. Historical MSS. Commission (1881), 8th Report.

of Fettercairn. Crawfurd's Shire of Renfrew (1818), 493.

of Glenormiston. Burke's Landed Gentry (1848).

of Inchbreck and Laithers. Baronage of Angus and Mearns, by Peter, 336. Fraser's Laurencekirk, 95-97. The Stirling Antiquary, iii. 291. Scottish Antiquary, xv. 155. Burke's Landed Gentry (1848-1925). The Scots Peerage, v. 5, 6.

of Kincardine. Antiquarian Notes, by C. Fraser-Mackintosh (1897), ii. 417.

of Kishorn. Burke's Landed Gentry (1906-1925).

of Lennox. Genealogical Account of the Stuarts from 1043, with table of Lennox branch, by T. Waterhouse (Grantham, 1816).

of Lorn. Nisbet's Heraldry (1742), ii., Appx. 157-160.

in Sweden. One Year in Sweden, by H. Marryat (1862), ii. 480-482, 498, 501. Palace of History Catalogue (Glasgow, 1911), 202, 205, 207 *bis*, 208, 210.

**Stuart** of Torrence.  Baronage, by Douglas, 517-518.
of Traquair.  Tales of our Great Families, by Walford, i. 93-115.  The Scots Peerage, viii. 399-409.

**Stuart-Gray** of Kinfauns Castle.  Burke's Landed Gentry (1894).  The Scots Peerage, vi. 327.

**Stuart-Menteth** of Closeburn.  Herald and Genealogist, v. 260-261, 456-468, 526-529.

**Stuart-Wortley-Mackenzie.**  The Scots Peerage, ii. 246, 303.

**Stuart.**  *See also* **Steuart, Stewart.**

**Studd** of Banchor.  Burke's Landed Gentry (1925 Suppl.).

**Sturgeon** of Cowcorse.  Lands . . . in Galloway, by M'Kerlie, iv. 143, 144.

**Suittie** of Horsburgh.  Peeblesshire Localities, by R. Renwick, 585.

**Sundridge of Coombank**, Campbell, Baron.  English Peerage, by Rev. A. Jacob (1767), ii. 698-705.  The Scots Peerage, i. 386-393.

*See* The Scots Peerage, ed. Sir J. Balfour Paul, *for*

**Sutherland**, Gordon, Earl of, viii. 337-361.
Sutherland, Earl of, viii. 318-337.
Sutherland-Leveson-Gower, Duke of, viii. 361-365.

**Sutherland.**  Copies of the Summons, etc., in the Process of Declarator of Precedency at the instance of the Earl of Sutherland against the Earl of Crawfurd (1706, repr. Edinr. 1766).  The Case of George Sutherland of Forse, claiming the title of Earl of Sutherland (1767, 1770).  Claim of Sir Charles Gordon to the Earldom of Sutherland : (Session Papers, Dec. 1767 to Jan. 1768).  Case of Sir Robert Gordon, Bart., claiming the Title of Earl of Sutherland, folio, 15 pp. (1769).  Supplemental Case of same, folio, 40 pp. (1770).  Brief for the Counsel of Sir Robert Gordon (1771), and Appendix.  Case and Additional Case of Elisabeth, claiming the title of Countess of Sutherland (177–).  Report and Judgement of the House of Lords (1771).  Genealogical History of the Earldom of Sutherland, by Sir R. Gordon of Gordonstown, ed. H. Weber, folio (Edinr. 1813).  Dates and Documents relating to the Family of Sutherland, by James Loch (1859).\*  Historical MSS. Commission (1871), 2nd Report.  The Sutherland Book, by Sir Wm. Fraser, 3 vols. 4to, illust. (Edinr. 1892).  Antiquarian Notes, by C. Fraser-Mackintosh (1913), i. 281.

**Sutherland** of Ackergill.  The Northern Ensign (Wick, 24th Nov. 1903).
of Clyne.  The Scots Peerage, iii. 204-205.
of Duffus.  The Scots Peerage, iii. 191-207.
of Evelix.  The Scots Peerage, iii. 202, 207.
of Forse.  Henderson's Caithness Family History, 151-162.  Burke's Landed Gentry (1886-1914).
of Kinminitie.  Scottish N. and Q., 2nd S., iii. 76.  The Scots Peerage, iii. 204, 207.
of Kinsteary.  The Scots Peerage, iii. 201-202.
of Langwell.  Caithness Family History, by Henderson, 163-170.
of Rearquhar.  The Scots Peerage, iii. 202.

**Sutherland** of Skibo Castle. Burke's Landed Gentry (1886-1914).
of Strabrock. The Scots Peerage, iii. 192-195.
of Torboll. The Scots Peerage, iii. 192, 194.
of Wester. Caithness Family History, by Henderson, 332.
of Windbreck. Orkney Armorials, by Norton Smith, 149.

**Sutherland-Graeme.** Burke's Landed Gentry (1886-1914).

**Sutherland-Walker.** Burke's Landed Gentry (1879).

**Suttie** of Balgone. Complete Baronetage, by G. E. C., iv. 403. Burke's Peerage and Baronetage.

**Swanson.** Captain Gunn's Notes on the Gunns, Hendersons, Swansons, etc., *in* Northern Ensign (Wick, 26th Sept. 1905).

**Swinburne** of Marcus. Baronage of Angus and Mearns, by Peter (1856), 337.

**Swinton** of Inverkeithing. Stephen's Inverkeithing (1921), 469-470.
of Kimmerghame. Burke's Landed Gentry (1858-1925). Concerning Swinton Family Records and Portraits at Kimmerghame [by A. C. and J. L. Campbell Swinton], *ix*+245 pp. (Edinr. 1908).*
of Swinton. Douglas's Baronage, 127-132. Notes and Queries, 1859, 2nd S., vii. 46, 158 ; 5th S., v. 25, 49, ix. 24 ; 7th S., x. 76, 190. Burke's Landed Gentry (1848-1925). Genealogical Memoirs of the Family of Sir Walter Scott, by Rev. C. Rogers, *liii.* The Family of Swinton, by Capt. G. S. C. Swinton (Exeter, 1899), repr. from The Genealogist, N. S., xv. 133, 205 ; xvi. 14. The Swintons of that Ilk, and their Cadets [by Archibald C. Swinton of Kimmerghame], Berwick Nat. Club, viii. 328 (Alnwick, 1878). Reprinted with additions, 4to, illust., *xx*+114+*cclii* pp. (Edinr. 1883).* The Origin of the Swintons, by J. H. Round, *in* Genealogist, N. S., xv. 205-209. Sir G. Sitwell *in* Genealogist, N. S., xvi. 14-16. Scot. Hist. Review, ii. 176-180, 476-478. Capt. G. S. C. Swinton *in* Scot. Hist. Review, xvi. 261-279. Large pedigree, by Captain G. S. C. Swinton, Lyon, illuminated by John R. Sutherland ; the property of Mr A. A. C. Swinton.
of Swinton Bank. Burke's Landed Gentry (1906-1925).

**Sword**, Glasgow. Scot. Hist. Review (1912), viii. 150.

**Sydserff** of Ruchlaw. Notes and Queries, 2nd S., ii. 367 ; iii. 97. Haddington Courier (10th February 1905). Burke's Landed Gentry (1906-1914).

**Syme.** Scottish N. and Q., 2nd S., iv. 159.
Alford. Scottish N. and Q., 3rd S., iii. 51.

**Symer** of Eassie and Kettle. Angus or Forfarshire, by Warden, iii. 208.

**Symington.** Genealogy of the Symington Family, compiled by Rev. Henry Paton, 4to (1908).*

**Symmer.** Heraldry, by A. Nisbet (1722), i. 442.
of Balzeordie. Baronage of Angus and Mearns, by Peter, 338. Angus or Forfarshire, by Warden, iv. 360-362. The Scots Peerage, i. 293, 294.

**Symmer** of Brathinch. Angus or Forfarshire, iii. 28.

**Symondton** of Symonton. Irving and Murray's Upper Ward of Lanarkshire (1864), i. 189-191 ; ii. 139.

**Symson.** Scot. Hist. Review, xiii. 48.

**Tailyour** of Borrowfield. Memorials of Angus and the Mearns, by Jervise, ed. Gammack, ii. 131. Burke's Landed Gentry (1848-1925).

**Tait,** Aberdeenshire. Scottish N. and Q., 2nd S., vi. 94, 126, 158.
of Harvieston. Herald and Genealogist, vii. 470. Burke's Landed Gentry (1875-1879).
of Milrig. Burke's Landed Gentry (1858-1925).
of Pirn. One Year in Sweden, by Marryat, ii. 499. Peeblesshire Localities, by Renwick, 86 *n.*, 517 *n.*, 524.

**Tancred** of Weens. Annals of a Border Club, by George Tancred of Weens (Jedburgh, 1899), 90, 470-474. Rulewater, by G. Tancred, 395. Burke's Landed Gentry (1898-1925).

**Tarbat,** Hay-Mackenzie, Viscount of. G. E. C.'s Complete Peerage. The Scots Peerage, iii. 84-86.
Mackenzie, Viscount of. Nisbet's Heraldic Plates, ed. Ross and Grant, 112-114. Cramond, by J. P. Wood (1794), 15-18. The Earls of Cromartie, by Wm. Fraser (1876). The Scots Peerage, iii. 74-80.

**Tarras,** Scott, Earl of. The Scotts of Buccleuch, by Sir W. Fraser. The Scots Peerage, ii. 237 ; vii. 80-81.

**Tarratt** of Ellary. Burke's Landed Gentry (1898-1925).

**Tarrill,** The Clan. Confederacy of Clan Chattan, by C. Fraser-Mackintosh (Glasgow, 1898), 139-141.

**Taylor.** Scottish N. and Q., 2nd S., i. 189.
Aberdeen. Smith's Genealogies of an Aberdeen Family ; Aberd. Univ. Studies, 90-91. Scottish N. and Q., 2nd S., i. 189.
Dunnichen. Scottish N. and Q., 1st S., vii. 188.
Fintray. Scottish N. and Q., 1st S., vi. 44.
of Howahill. Tancred's Rulewater, 170.
of Kirktonhill. Baronage of Angus and Mearns, by Peter, 340.
New Deer. Smith's Genealogies of an Aberdeen Family, 71-75.
of Thura. Henderson's Caithness Family History, 299.
Thurso. The Taylors of Ross, Cromarty, Sutherland and Caithness, by D. W. Kemp (Edinr. 1899).
Wanlockhead. Buchan and Paton's History of Peeblesshire, iii. 459.

**Telfer** of Linkings. Lands . . . in Galloway, by M'Kerlie, v. 124.
of Scotstoun. Chambers' History of Peeblesshire, 475.

**Telfer-Smollett** of Bonhill. Burke's Landed Gentry (1898-1925).

**Tennant,** Ayr. The Dalrymples of Langlands, by J. Shaw, 3, 130-132.*
of the Glen. Burke's Landed Gentry (1879). Burke's Peerage and Baronetage. Debrett's Baronetage (1886-1911).

**Terregles,** Herries, Lord Herries of. The Scots Peerage, iv. 398-424.

**Teviot,** Livingston, Viscount. The Scots Peerage, viii. 368-377.

Rutherfurd, Earl of. Heraldry, by Nisbet (1742), ii., Appx. 219-220.
G. E. C.'s Complete Peerage. The Scots Peerage, vii. 374-375.
Buchan and Paton's Peeblesshire, iii. 119.

Spencer, Viscount of. The Scots Peerage, viii. 366-367.

**Thane** of Spencerfield. Stephen's Inverkeithing (1921), 102.

**Thirlestane,** Maitland, Lord. The Scots Peerage, v. 299-323.

**Thoirs.** Stephen's Inverkeithing and Rosyth, 72-73.

**Thomas** of Noranside. Angus or Forfarshire, by Warden, iii. 273.

**Thoms.** Memoir of the Families of M'Combie and Thoms (Edinr., 2nd ed., 1890).

of Wester Clepington. Angus or Forfarshire, by Warden, iv. 141.

**Thomson,** Aberdeen. Scottish N. and Q., 3rd S., ii. 112.

of Banchory. Baronage of Angus and Mearns, by Peter, 341. Smith's
Genealogies of an Aberdeen Family ; Aberd. Univ. Studies, 77-78.
Burke's Landed Gentry (1848-1879).

of Cannonholme. Scottish N. and Q., 3rd S., i. 46.

of Charleton. East Neuk of Fife, by W. Wood, 2nd ed. (1887), 122.
Burke's Landed Gentry (1858-1925).

of Cornton Vale. Logie, by Rev. Dr Menzies Fergusson, ii. 228.

of Corstorphine. Sermons . . . by the late Rev. Patrick Thomson, M.A.,
. . . with a Memoir by J. Radford Thomson (London, 1872), 1-41.
Centenary Memorials of the First Congregational Church in
Aberdeen, by John M. Bulloch (1898), 65-91. Complete Baronetage,
by G. E. C., ii. 416. Burke's Landed Gentry (1925). Printed
Pedigree in National Library, Edinburgh. MS. Pedigree in Library
of Society of Genealogists, London. A Short Genealogical Account
of the Family of Thomson in Corstorphine, Midlothian, by A[lexander]
D[euchar], (Edinr. 1816, repr. London, 1927), A History of the
Family of Thomson of Corstorphine, by Theodore Radford Thomson
(Edinr. 1926).

of Crawton. Smith's Genealogies of an Aberdeen Family (1913).

Duddingston. G. E. C.'s Complete Baronetage, ii. 416.

of Faichfield. Tayler's Jacobites of Aberdeenshire, 405.

Glasgow. Some Old Families, by H. B. M'Call, 137.

Lord Kelvin. Life of William Thomson, Baron Kelvin of Largs, by
Silvanus P. Thompson, 2 vols. (1909). Lord Kelvin's Early Home,
ed. E. T. King (1909).

of Kenfield. Pedigree of the Family of Thomson of Kenfield in Petham,
4to [185-].

Marquhitter. The Thomson Family and its Pedigree : Descendants and
other Kindred of Alexander Thomson, Greens Marquhitter, Aberdeenshire, and Elizabeth Clark his wife, by H. M. and A. S. Thomson,
folio, Norwich [1896].

of Nether Magask. Some Old Families, by H. B. M'Call, 164.

**Thomson,** Monthellie and Aberdeen. Smith's Genealogies of an Aberdeen Family, 5, 65-76.

Newton of Collessie. Memoir of Thomas Thomson, by David Laing (Bannatyne Club, 1854). Eminent Scotsmen, by Chambers. John Thomson of Duddingston, by W. Baird (Edinr. 1895). John Thomson of Duddingston, by R. W. Napier (Edinr. 1919), 395-398. Dictionary of National Biography, *s.v.*

of Portlethen and Banchory. Memoir of J. Young, Aberdeen . . . 1861, ed. Lt.-Col. W. Johnston (1894), 167-168. Smith's Genealogies of an Aberdeen Family, 77.

in Sweden. One Year in Sweden, by Marryat, ii. 490, 499.

Lord Sydenham of Toronto. History of Thomson of Corstorphine (1926), 38.

**Thomson-Carmichael.** Burke's Landed Gentry (1879).

**Thorburn** in Sweden. Palace of History Catalogue (Glasgow, 1911), 202.

**Threipland** of Fingask. The Threiplands of Fingask : a family memoir, by Dr Robert Chambers (1853, 4to and 8vo, London and Edinr. 1880). Baronage of Angus and Mearns, by Peter, 342. Recreations of an Antiquary in Perthshire History and Genealogy, by Fittis (Perth, 1881), 388-436. Complete Baronetage, by G. E. C., iv. 356.

**Thriepland** of Mitchelhill. Annals of a Tweeddale Parish, by Baird, 129. Buchan and Paton's Peeblesshire, iii. 329.

**Thurburn.** The Thurburns, by Lt.-Col. F. A. V. Thurburn ; with pedigrees of Thurbrand and Thurburn (1864).

**Tibberis,** Douglas, Viscount of. The Scots Peerage, vii. 143-144.

**Tingwall** in Sweden. One Year in Sweden, by Marryat, ii. 485.

**Tod,** Carriden. The Scottish Antiquary (1895), ix. 190.

of Haghill. Glasgow Past and Present (1884), iii. 483.

of Kirklands. The Browns of Fordell, by Stodart, 191.

**Tod-Mercer** of Scotsbank. Burke's Landed Gentry (1898-1925).

**Tollemache,** Lord of Huntingtower, Earl of Dysart. The Scots Peerage, iii. 406-420.

**Torphichen,** Sandilands, Lord. Historical MSS. Commission (1871), 2nd Report. G. E. C.'s Complete Peerage. The Scots Peerage, iii. 378-398. Burke's and other Annual Peerages.

**Torthorald** of Torthorald. J. J. Reid *in* Proc. Soc. Antiq. Scotl. (1888), 70-71.

Douglas, Lord, Viscount of. G. E. C.'s Complete Peerage. The Scots Peerage, ii. 392-394 ; vii. 138-156.

**Tosh, Toshach.** Confederacy of Clan Chattan, by C. Fraser-Mackintosh, 179.

**Touche.** Some Notes on the Scottish Surname of Touch or Touche, by W. P. Phillimore, n.d.

**Touraine,** Douglas, Duke of. The Scots Peerage, iii. 166-172.

**Towers** of Inverleithen. Notes and Queries, 7th S., v. 427, 497 ; ix. 148, 313 ; xi. 508.

**Traill.** Chalmers and Traill Ancestry, by C. J. Guthrie, K.C. (1902).\*

of Blebo. Conolly's Eminent Men of Fife, 474. Genealogical Account of the Traills of Orkney, with a Pedigree Table tracing their descent from the Traills of Blebo in Fifeshire, by Wm. Traill, of Woodwick, M.D., *xxv*+83 pp. (Kirkwall, 1883). Genealogical Sketches ; The Frotoft Branch of the Orkney Traills, by Thos. W. Traill, *x*+156 pp. (1902), 1, 10, 91.\*

of Castlehill and Rattar. Caithness Family History, by Henderson, 229-231.

of Frotoft. The Frotoft Branch of the Orkney Traills, 4-15, 79.

of Hobbister, Rattar, and Woodeve. Burke's Landed Gentry (1875-1925).

of Holland. The Frotoft Branch, 10. Burke's Landed Gentry (1863-1886).

in Ireland. The Frotoft Branch of the Orkney Trails, 91-96.

of Legisland. J. Malcolm's Monifieth, 353.

in Westness. The Frotoft Branch of the Orkney Traills, 2-3, 79. Norton Smith's Orkney Armorials, 154-166.

of Woodwick. Burke's Landed Gentry (1875-1886).

**Traquair**, Stewart, Earl of. Crawfurd's Shire of Renfrew (1818), 466. Nisbet's Heraldic Plates, ed. Ross and Grant (1892), 142. The Complete Peerage, by G. E. C. The Scots Peerage, viii. 399-409. Scot. Hist. Review, xxv. 76-80. Buchan and Paton's Peeblesshire, ii. 526-534. The Stewarts Magazine, iii. 233-254 ; iv. 29, 41.

**Trembley** of Delany. Memorials of Angus and the Mearns, by Jervise, ed. Gammack, ii. 172.

**Trotter** of Ballindean. Burke's Landed Gentry (1848-1914).

of Castlehill and the Bush. Burke's Landed Gentry (1848-1914).

of Cattleshiels. East Neuk of Fife, by W. Wood, 2nd ed., 144.

of Colinton. Burke's Landed Gentry (1906-1925).

of Dreghorn. Burke's Landed Gentry (1848-1898).

of Mortonhall. Baronage, by Douglas (1784), 204-208. Nisbet's Heraldic Plates, ed. Ross and Grant, 58-60. Burke's Landed Gentry (1848-1925).

**Trotter-Cranstoun.** Burke's Landed Gentry (1894-1914).

**Tullibardine**, Murray, Earl of, Marquess of. Memoirs of the Jacobites of 1715 and 1745, by Mrs Katherine Thomson, ii. 92-123. Notes and Queries, 4th S., x. 525 ; 5th S., vii. 448, 519. G. E. C.'s Complete Peerage, i. 469-472, 478, 479-502 ; viii. 410-415. Scot. Hist. Soc., No. 56 (1908), *lxxv*. The Scots Peerage, *s.v.*

**Tullideph**, Edrom. Oliver's History of Antigua, iii. 162.

of Rainieston. Thanage of Fermartyn, by Temple, 543.

of Tullideph. Thanage of Fermartyn, 471.

**Tulloch** of Bonnyton. Warden's Angus or Forfarshire, iv. 306-307.

of Tannachie. Annals of Elgin, by Young (1879), 665-667. Scottish N. and Q., 1st S., xi. 125-126 ; 3rd S., iii. 14.

**Turing** of Foveran. The Lay of the Turings, a Sketch of the Family History, 1316-1849, by H. M'K[enzie], 77 pp., folding pedigree [1850].* Case of Sir Robert Fraser Turing, Baronet. Temple's Thanage of Fermartyn, 565-571. Complete Baronetage, by G. E. C., ii. 451. Debrett's Baronetage. Burke's Peerage and Baronetage.

**Turnbull.** Origin of the Name, *in* Notes and Queries, 9th S., xi. 51, 353, 416, 475.

of Bedrule. Annals of a Border Club, by G. Tancred, 474. The Scots Peerage, iv. 472, 473.

of Bogmil. East Neuk of Fife, by W. Wood, 2nd ed., 199, 205.

in Burnfoot. Tancred's Rulewater, 242-248.

of Chesterhall. Tancred's Rulewater, 251.

of Dalladies. Memorials of Angus and the Mearns, by Jervise, ed. Gammack, ii. 173.

of Fauldshope. Craig Brown's Selkirkshire, ii. 289.

of Fenwick. Annals of a Border Club, 475-476.

of Hartishaugh and Swanshiel. Tancred's Rulewater, 249.

of Minto. Tancred's Rulewater, 237.

of Philiphaugh. Craig Brown's Selkirkshire, ii. 332-335.

Rulewater. Tancred's Rulewater, 237-264, 291.

of Strickathrow, Stracathro. Baronage of Angus and Mearns, by Peter, 347. Memorials of Angus and the Mearns, ii. 173. Warden's Angus or Forfarshire, v. 169-170, 174.

**Turner** of Glentyre. Burke's Landed Gentry (1863-1875).

of Kippen House. Burke's Landed Gentry (1879).

of Menie. Thanage of Fermartyn, 640. Burke's Landed Gentry (1846-1875).

of Turnerhall and Tippertie. Temple's Thanage of Fermartyn, 552-555. Burke's Landed Gentry (1886-1925). Tayler's Jacobites of Aberdeenshire (1928), 407.

**Tweddale** of Laggan. Lands . . . in Galloway, by M'Kerlie, v. 56.

**Tweddell,** Wigton. Lands . . . in Galloway, 2nd ed. (1906), i. 343.

**Tweeddale,** Hay, Earl of, Marquess of. Notes and Queries, 4th S., iii. 218, 298. Eminent Men of Fife, by M. F. Conolly, 220-221. G. E. C.'s Complete Peerage. Calendar of Writs preserved at Yester House, 1166-1598, ed. Charles C. Harvey (Scottish Record Soc., 1916-19), 1598-  , ed. John MacLeod (1928-  ). The Scots Peerage, viii. 416-474. Burke's and other Annual Peerages.

**Tweedie.** History of the Tweedie or Tweedy Family, by Michael Forbes Tweedie, 4to, illust. and pedigrees, *viii*+231 pp. (1902).

of Denys, Deans. Buchan and Paton's Peeblesshire, iii. 68.

of Drumelzier. Geneal. Coll., by W. Macfarlane, 1750-51 ; Scot. Hist. Soc., i. 12, 24. Buchan and Paton's Peeblesshire, iii. 67, 69, 421-431. Peeblesshire Localities, by R. Renwick, 204-205, 231-233, 296-299, 309, 426, 467, 526, 573, 587. Annals of a Tweeddale Parish, by Baird, 33-35, 88-97.

**Tweedie** of Fruid. Buchan and Paton's Peeblesshire, iii. 405-407.

of Halmyre. Buchan and Paton's Peeblesshire, iii. 29-30.

of Kingeldoors. Peeblesshire Localities, 307, 308. Buchan and Paton's Peeblesshire, iii. 466.

of Oliver. Buchan and Paton's Peeblesshire, iii. 383-385. Burke's Landed Gentry (1875-1925).

Peeblesshire. Peeblesshire Localities, 84, 88, 92, 130-133.

of Quarter and Rachan. Buchan and Paton's Peeblesshire, iii. 285-286.

of Quhitslaid. Peeblesshire Localities, 236, 237. Annals of a Tweeddale Parish, 78-80.

of Wrae. Peeblesshire Localities, 206, 237, 239, 243. Annals of a Tweeddale Parish, 34-35, 80, 91. Buchan and Paton's Peeblesshire, iii. 294.

**Tyrie** of Drumkilbo. The Tyries of Drumkilbo, Dunnideer and Lunan, by Andrew Tyrie, 50 pp. (Glasgow, 1893). Angus or Forfarshire, by Warden, iii. 210. Scottish N. and Q., 2nd S., iii. 81-82, 131, 166.

of Dunnichen. Scottish N. and Q., 2nd S., iii. 81-82, 166, 169.

of Dunnydeer. Baronage of Angus and Mearns, by Peter (1856), 349. Tayler's Jacobites of Aberdeenshire, 409.

**Tytler**, Midmar. Smith's Genealogies of an Aberdeen Family; Aberd. Univ. Studies, 98-103.

**Udny** of Auchterwellan. One Year in Sweden, by Marryat (1862), ii. 499.

of Newtyle. Thanage of Fermartyn, 610-611.

of Udny. Eight Cases before the Court of Session . . . as to the Heirship of Udny; with folding geneal. tree (1862-3-4). Appeal to the House of Lords : Case of George Udny v. John H. Allat or Udny and Wm. Skinner ; Supplemental Joint Appx., 13 pp., with folding tree [1867]. Temple's Thanage of Fermartyn, 425-435. Genealogical Tree of the Udny Family, 1407-1884. Burke's Landed Gentry (1879-1925).

**Udwart**, Linlithgow. Nisbet's Heraldic Plates, ed. Ross and Grant (1892), 140.

**Umfraville**, Earl of Angus. Memorials of Angus and the Mearns, by A. Jervise, ed. Gammack (1885), ii. 29-34. The Scots Peerage, i. 167-168.

**Umfreville**. The Umfrevilles : their Ancestors and Descendants, 4to, illust., 45 pp., pedigrees [1852].

**Umphray** of Berrie. Zetland Family Histories, by F. J. Grant (1907), 323-324.

of Sand. Zetland Family Histories, 325-330.

of Whitsness. Zetland Family Histories, 331-333.

**Urquhart** of Burdsyards. Scottish N. and Q., 3rd S., i. 159.

of Byth. Baronage, by Douglas, 166. Tayler's Jacobites of Aberdeenshire, 410-412.

of Craigston. Douglas's Baronage, 165-166. Burke's Landed Gentry (1848-1914).

**Urquhart** of Cromarty. Μαντοχρονοχάνον : Or, A Peculiar Promptuary of
Time : . . . and the true Pedigree and Lineal Descent of . . . the
Urquharts, in the house of Cromartie, since the Creation of the World,
until this present yeer of God 1652 (For Richard Baddely, 1652). The
Urquharts of Cromartie : True Pedigree and Lineal Descent . . .
until 1774, *in* Sir Thomas Urquhart's Tracts, 12mo (Edinr. 1774).
Heraldry, by Nisbet (1742), ii., Appx. 274-277.   Baronage, by
Douglas, 156-165.   Geneal. Coll., by W. Macfarlane, 1750-51 ; Scot.
Hist. Soc., ii. 357-379.   Antiquarian Notes, by C. Fraser-Mackintosh,
i. 202-218.   Notes and Queries, 3rd S., ii. 212 : 6th S., vii. 368 ; viii. 53.
of Dunlugas.   Scottish N. and Q., 3rd S., ii. 31.
Fraserburgh.   Scottish Antiquary, vi. 133-135.
of Meldrum.   Heraldry, by Nisbet (1742), ii., Appx. 132-133, 276-277.
Baronage, by Douglas, 156-165.   Burke's Landed Gentry (1848-1914).
Old Deer.   Scottish Antiquary, iv. 43.
Seton, Lord.   G. E. C.'s Complete Peerage.   The Scots Peerage, iii. 370.
George Seton's Family of Seton, ii. 636-638.
in Sweden.   One Year in Sweden, by Marryat, ii. 500.
**Urrie, Urry** of Pitfichie.   Heraldry, by A. Nisbet (1722), i. 295.
**Usher** of Norton and Wells.   Debrett's Baronetage (after 1899).   Tancred's
Rulewater, 210-213.

**Vachell,** Jedburgh.   Annals of a Border Club, by G. Tancred, 477.
**Vallance, Valoignes, de Valoniis.**   Heraldry, by Nisbet (1722), i. 417.
Banks' Dormant and Extinct Baronage.   The Antiquary (1873),
iv. 312.   Registrum de Panmure : Records of the Families of Maule,
de Valoniis, Brechin and Brechin-Barclay, 2 vols. (1874).   Joseph
Bain *in* Notes and Queries (1882), 6th S., v. 61-62.   J. A. C. Vincent
*in* Notes and Queries (1882), 6th S., v. 142, 290.   J. H. Round *in*
The Ancestor (London, 1904), x. 104-119 ; xi. 129-135.   The Scots
Peerage, vii. 5.   Stephen's Inverkeithing and Rosyth (1921), 179-182.
**Vans** of Barnbarroch.   Heraldry, by Nisbet (1742), ii., Appx. 250-252.
An Account, historical and genealogical of the Family of Vance in
Ireland, Vans in Scotland, anciently Vaux in Scotland and England, ,
and originally de Vaux in France, by W. Balbirnie (Cork, 1860).
**Vans, Vaux.**   *See also* **Waus.**
**Vans-Agnew** of Barnbarroch.   Burke's Landed Gentry (1848-1925).
**Vaus, Vaux, de Vallibus.**   Sketch of a Genealogical and Historical
Account of the Family of Vaux, Vaus, or De Vallibus : now repre-
sented in Scotland by Vans Agnew of Barnbarrow . . . by V. Agnew
(Pembroke, 1800).   A Short Account of the Family De Vaux, Vaux,
or Vans (*latine* De Vallibus) of Barnbarroch (1832).*   Memorials
of the Haliburtons, by Sir W. Scott, Bart. (1824, 1877), 21-23.   Royal
and other original Documents addressed to the Lairds of Barnbarroch,
with a sketch of their Family History, 4to, n.d.   The Hereditary
Sheriffs of Galloway, by Sir A. Agnew (1893), i. 225-226.   Scottish
N. and Q., x. 100-101.   *See also* **Waus.**

**Vaus** of Many. Temple's Thanage of Fermartyn, 638.

**Veitch** of Dawyck. Nisbet's Heraldry, i. 341. History of Peeblesshire, by Chambers, 416-417. Peeblesshire Localities, by Renwick, 278-288, 364-366. Buchan and Paton's History of Peeblesshire, iii. 434-442.
of Eliock and Caponflat. Genealogical Fragments, by James Maidment (Berwick, 1855), 2 pp.* Burke's Landed Gentry (1848-1894). Folk-Lore and Genealogies of Uppermost Nithsdale, by Wilson, 206-212.
in Hamiltoun. Buchan and Paton's Peeblesshire, iii. 519.
Inchbonny. Tancred's Rulewater, 220.
Peebles. Peeblesshire Localities, 67 *n.*, 88.
of Stewarton. Peeblesshire Localities, 50, 286.
Spital on Rule. Tancred's Rulewater, 220.

**Vere** of Blackwood and Craigiehall. Baronage, by Douglas (1784), 153-156. Burke's Commoners, iii. 319. Burke's Landed Gentry (1848-1906). *See also* **Weir.**

**Vernor** of Monybuie. Lands . . . in Galloway, by M'Kerlie, iii. 91.

**Villiers-Stuart.** The Scots Peerage, ii. 306, 307.

**Vipont, Weapont, de Vetereponte.** Heraldry, by A. Nisbet (1722), i. 212. Banks' Dormant and Extinct Baronage, i. 193. Family Records— I. The Viponts ; II. The Ecroyds and Viponts . . . by W. Scruton (Bradford, 1904).* Scottish N. and Q., 2nd S., vii. 52.

**Virtuo.** Memorials of Alloa, by Crawford, 151.

**Volum.** Baronage of Angus and Mearns, by Peter, 350. Scottish N. and Q., 2nd S., v. 126, 143, 189.
Peterhead. Tayler's Jacobites of Aberdeenshire, 413.

**Waddell** of Easter Moffat. Burke's Landed Gentry (1848).
of Thornydykes. Buchan and Paton's Peeblesshire, iii. 157.

**Wahab.** *See* **Wauchope.**

**Walden,** Hay, Viscount of. The Scots Peerage, viii. 453-474.

**Waldie, Waltho** of Marklands of Kelso. Annals of a Border Club, by G. Tancred, 248.

**Waldie-Griffith** of Hendersyde Park. Burke's Landed Gentry (1848-1863). Annals of a Border Club, 248-250. Burke's Peerage and Baronetage (after 1858). Debrett's Baronetage.

**Waldo.** Notes respecting the Family of Waldo [by Morris Charles Jones], *iv* + 35 pp. (Edinr. 1863).*

**Walker,** Aberdeen. Smith's Genealogies of an Aberdeen Family, 111-116.
of Bargour. Paterson's History of the County of Ayr, ii. 337. Paterson's Ayr and Wigton, i. 555.
of Crawfordton. Burke's Landed Gentry (1879-1925).
of Dalry. Burke's Landed Gentry (1848-1914).
of Fawfield. East Neuk of Fife, by W. Wood, 2nd ed. (1887), 150.
of Muirhouselaw. Annals of a Border Club, 478-479.
of St Fort. Baronage, by Douglas, 480-481.

**Walker,** Strathdon. Smith's Genealogies of an Aberdeen Family, 116-120.
in Sweden. One Year in Sweden, by Marryat, ii. 500.
of Wooden. Annals of a Border Club, 477-479.

**Walker-Arnott** of Arlary. Burke's Landed Gentry (1848-1863).

**Walker-Morison** of Falfield. Burke's Landed Gentry (1886-1925).

**Walkinshaw.** Heraldry, by Nisbet (1722), i. 372. Crawfurd's Shire of
Renfrew (1818), 90-91. Notes and Queries, 2nd S., xi. 67, 137. The
Scottish Antiquary, iv. 190-192 ; vii. 133-137, with 2 chart pedigrees.
Scot. Hist. Review, xvii. 249.
of Scotstoun. Crawfurd's Shire of Renfrew (1818), 68.

**Wallace** of Auchans. Paterson's History of the County of Ayr, ii. 24-25.
Paterson's Ayr and Wigton, i. 440-444.
of Auchencruive. Ayr and Wigton, i. 663.
of Bargour. Paterson's History of Ayr, ii. 337. Ayr and Wigton, i. 555.
of Barnweill. Paterson's History of Ayr, i. 346. Ayr and Wigton, i. 269.
of Bathgate. Genealogical Chart of the Wallace Family of Bathgate,
by W. A. Cuthbert, folio (1908).
of Biscany. Ayr and Wigton, iii. 464.
of Bonhill. Ayr and Wigton, i. 490.
of Brighouse. Paterson's History of Ayr, ii. 337. Ayr and Wigton,
i. 558-559.
of Busbie. Paterson's History of Ayr, ii. 203. Ayr and Wigton, iii. 463.
Burke's Landed Gentry (1906-1925).
of Cairnhill, Carnell. Crawfurd's Shire of Renfrew (1818), 425. Paterson's
History of Ayr, i. 341-343, 344-345. Ayr and Wigton, i. 270-280.
Notes and Queries, 4th S., xi. 240, 292.
of Cambuseskane. Paterson's History of Ayr, i. 347. Ayr and Wigton,
i. 281-282.
of Candacraig and Balcairn. Burke's Landed Gentry (1925 Suppl.).
of Carsriggan. History of the Habersham Family, by J. G. B. Bulloch,
M.D. (Columbia, S.C., 1901), 24.
of Craigie. Ayrshire Families, by G. Robertson, ii. 348-369. Paterson's
History of Ayr, i. 336-341. History of the Lairds of Glenfield
(Paisley, 1860). Complete Baronetage, by G. E. C., ii. 441 ; iv. 276.
Paterson's Ayr and Wigton, i. 283-296.
of Dundonald. Paterson's History of Ayr, ii. 24-25. Ayr and Wigton,
i. 440-444.
of Elderslie. Royal Genealogies, by Anderson (1732), 759. Crawfurd's
Shire of Renfrew (1818), ed. Robertson, 86-88, 426-429). Upper
Ward of Lanarkshire, by Irving and Murray (1864), i. 224 ; ii. 351-
354. The Wallaces of Elderslie, by J. O. Mitchell, LL.D., *reprinted
from* Transactions of the Archæological Society of Glasgow (1884).
The two Elderslies, by the same, *reprinted from* "The Glasgow
Herald" of 13th Sept. 1884, 4to, 26 pp. (Glasgow, 1884).* The
Book of Wallace ; History and Genealogy of the Family, by the
Rev. Charles Rogers, LL.D., 2 vols., 4to, illust. (Edinr., Grampian
Club, 1889). The Scottish Antiquary, vii. 188-189 ; viii. 45.

**Wallace**, Forfarshire. Eminent Arbroathians, by J. M. M'Bain (1897), 183-200.

of Galrigs, Garrix. Paterson's History of Ayr, ii. 39. Ayr and Wigton, i. 486-488.

of Holmstone. Paterson's History of Ayr, i. 209-210. Ayr and Wigton, i. 146-148.

of Johnstoun. Crawfurd's Shire of Renfrew (1818), 82.

of Kelly. Crawfurd's Shire of Renfrew (1818), 429. Baronage of Angus and Mearns, by Peter, 351. Burke's Landed Gentry (1848).

of Lochryan. Lands and their Owners in Galloway, by M'Kerlie, 2nd. ed. (1906), i. 505, 506-507.

of Menfuird. Paterson's History of Ayr, ii. 203. Ayr and Wigton, iii. 436.

of Neilstonside. Crawfurd's Shire of Renfrew (1818), 428.

New Deer and Aberdeen. Smith's Genealogies of an Aberdeen Family; Aberd. Univ. Studies, 28, 43, 76, 79-81.

of Newton Castle. Ayr and Wigton, i. 281.

of Prestwickshaws. Paterson's History of Ayr, ii. 416. Ayr and Wigton, i. 673.

of Riccarton. Paterson's History of Ayr, ii. 388. Ayr and Wigton, i. 654.

of Shewalton. Paterson's History of Ayr, ii. 35. Ayr and Wigton, i. 491-494.

of Wallacetoun. Paterson's History of Ayr, i. 243. Ayr and Wigton, i. 207.

**Wallace-Dunlop-Agnew.** Lands . . . in Galloway, 2nd ed., i. 507.

**Walwood of Touch.** *See* **Wellwood-Moncrieff.**

**Wardlaw**, Glasgow. Memoirs of Ralph Wardlaw, D.D., by W. L. Alexander (Edinr. 1856).

of Newlands and Logie. Stephen's Inverkeithing, 201-203.

of Pitreavie. One Year in Sweden, by Marryat, ii. 500. Burke's Peerage and Baronetage. Debrett's Baronetage. Complete Baronetage, by G. E. C., ii. 387.

of Torrie and Wilton. Genealogical Collections, by W. Macfarlane, 1750-51; Scot. Hist. Soc., i. 23. Eminent Men of Fife, by M. F. Conolly, 478-479. The Wardlaws in Scotland: a History of the Wardlaws of Wilton and Torrie and their Cadets, by J. C. Gibson, illust. (Edinr. 1912). Chalmers' Dunfermline, i. 301; ii. 303.

**Wardlaw-Ramsay** of Whitehill and Tillicoultry. Burke's Landed Gentry (1894-1925).

**Warner** of Ardeer. Paterson's History of County of Ayr, ii. 449. Paterson's Ayr and Wigton, iii. 570-573. Burke's Landed Gentry (1848-1925).

**Warrand** of Bught. Burke's Landed Gentry (1882-1925).

**Warrender** of Lochend and Bruntsfield. Autobiography of William Nisbet. Walks near Edinburgh, by Margaret Warrender (1895), 12-16. Complete Baronetage, by G. E. C., iv. 432; v. 26. Burke's and Debrett's Baronetages.

**Waterston** of Waterston. Baronage of Angus and Mearns, by Peter, 352. Angus or Forfarshire, by Warden, iii. 73.

**Watson**, Aberdeen. W. J. Couper *in* Scot. Hist. Review (1911), vii. 244-262.

of Aithernie. East Neuk of Fife, by W. Wood, 2nd ed., 43-44. The Watsons of Aithernie, by J. A. Inglis, 3 pp. *in* Misc. Gen. et Her. Sept. 1927).

of Ayton. Burke's Landed Gentry (1894-1925).

of Burnhead. Annals of a Border Club, by G. Tancred, 481-483. Burke's Landed Gentry (1894-1925).

in Burntisland. Traditions of the Watson Family, by C. B. Boog Watson (Perth, 1908). Alexander Cowan, by C. B. Boog Watson, 36.

of Damhead. Cramond, by J. P. Wood, 27.

of Earnock. John Watson of Bathville and John Watson of Earnock, his son, by the latter, 4to, illust. (Glasgow, 1889).*

Fife. Geneal. Coll., by W. Macfarlane, 1750-51 ; Scot. Hist. Soc., ii. 196.

of Muirhouse. Cramond, by Wood, 27.

of Saughton. Cramond, 63, 66. Selway's Midlothian Village (1890), 38-42. Nisbet's Heraldic Plates, ed. Ross and Grant, 144.

**Watt** of Breckness. The Frotoft Branch of the Orkney Traills, by T. W. Traill, 55, 64-69. Norton Smith's Orkney Armorials, 174-177. Burke's Landed Gentry (1886-1925).

of Fulsheills. Geneal. Mag. (1903), vi. 449.

Greenock. Letters respecting the Watt Family, by George Williamson, 8vo, plates, *viii*+69 pp. (Greenock, 1840).* Memoirs of the Lineage . . . of James Watt, by George Williamson, 4to (Edinr. 1856). Old Greenock, by G. Williamson (Paisley, 1886), i. 262-263.

**Wauchope** of Caikmuir. Scottish Surnames, by Jas. Paterson (1866), 33.

of Culter. Paterson's Scottish Surnames, 25.

Edinburgh. The Scottish Antiquary, xvii. 101. Paterson's Scottish Surnames, 34.

of Edmonstone. Burke's Landed Gentry (1848-1858). Burke's Peerage and Baronetage. Debrett's Baronetage.

of Niddrie-Marischal. History of the Family of Wauchope of Niddrie-Marischal, by Jas. Paterson, 4to (Edinr. 1858).* Paterson's Scottish Surnames, 20-42. Historical MSS. Commission (1873), 4th Report. Burke's Landed Gentry (1848-1925).

of Stottencleuch. Paterson's Scottish Surnames, 33.

*alias* **Wahab**. The Ulster Branch of the Family of Wauchope, ed. Dr Gladys M. Wauchope (1929).

**Waus** of Barnbarroch. Royal Letters and other Documents addressed to the Lairds of Barnbarroch, 1509-1618, ed. Alex. Macdonald and J. Dennistoun (Edinr., Maitland Club, 1834). Correspondence of Sir Patrick Waus of Barnbarroch, 1540-1597, ed. Robert Vans Agnew, Ayrshire and Galloway Archæol. Assoc. (Edinr. 1887). *See also* **Vans, Vaux**.

**Webster** of Ethiebeaton and Balruddery. Pedigree *in* Playfair's Family of Playfair.

**Wedderburn.** A Genealogical Account of the Wedderburn Family, by J. Wedderburn Webster, 8vo (Nantes, 1819).* Genealogical Account of the Wedderburn Family, by John Wedderburn (1824). The Wedderburn Book : a History of the Wedderburns in the Counties of Berwick and Forfar, 1296-1896, by Alexander Wedderburn, 2 vols., illust., *xxxii*+521 ; *xv*+600 pp. (1898).* [Blackness, Balindean, Gosford, Kingennie, Easter Powrie, Wedderburn, etc.]

of Blackness and Ballindean. Baronage, by Douglas, 278-282, 578-580. Warden's Angus or Forfarshire, iv. 195-199. Burke's Peerage and Baronetage. Debrett's Baronetage.

in Dundee. The Compt Buik of David Wedderburn, Merchant, of Dundee, ed. A. H. Millar ; (Scot. Hist. Soc., 1898). The Scottish Antiquary, viii. 161-162, with cut of tombstone. Campbell's Balmerino, 581-590, 659. Monifieth, by Malcolm, 325-329.

of Gosford. Baronage, by Douglas, 282-284. Complete Baronetage, by G. E. C., iv. 373.

of Gourdie. Warden's Angus or Forfarshire, iv. 200.

of Kingennie. Malcolm's Monifieth, 325-329.

of Pearsie. Angus or Forfarshire, iv. 40-42.

of Wedderburn. Burke's Landed Gentry (1848-1925). Warden's Angus or Forfarshire, v. 25-31.

**Wedderburn-Colville.** Burke's Landed Gentry (1849-1879).

**Wedderburn-Maxwell** of Middlebie and Glenlair. Burke's Landed Gentry (1906-1925). Debrett's Baronetage (after 1896).

**Weir** of Auchtyfardle. Annals of Lesmahagow, by J. B. Greenshields (1854), 93.*

of Barrachan and Woodend. Strathblane, by Guthrie Smith, 69.

of Blackwood. Baronage, by Douglas, 153-156. Nisbet's Heraldic Plates, ed. Ross and Grant, 26-29. Upper Ward of Lanarkshire, by Irving and Murray, ii. 205-209. Burke's Extinct Baronetcies. Complete Baronetage, by G. E. C., iv. 367. Annals of Lesmahagow 83-85. *See also* **Vere of Blackwood.**

Elgin. Oliver's History of Antigua, iii. 218-220.

of Kerse. Annals of Lesmahagow, 96.

of Kirkhall. History of the County of Ayr, by Paterson, i. 233. Paterson's Ayr and Wigton, iii. 60-61.

of Stonebyres. Annals of Lesmahagow, 79-83. Upper Ward of Lanarkshire, ii. 209-211.

**Welham.** Scottish N. and Q., 2nd S., v. 126.

**Wellwood-Moncreiff.** G. E. C.'s Complete Baronetage, ii. 310. Pedigree attached to Chalmers' History of Dunfermline, ii. (1859).

**Welsh** of Colliston. Sir P. J. Hamilton Grierson *in* Dumfriesshire and Galloway Antiq. Soc. Trans., 3rd S. (1923), viii. 61-65.

of Cornlee. Lands . . . in Galloway, by M'Kerlie, iv. 23.

Craigenputtock. Sir P. J. Hamilton Grierson *in* Dumfriesshire and Galloway Antiq. Soc. Trans., 3rd S., viii. 63-68.

**Welsh** of Mossfennan. History of Peeblesshire, by Chambers, 449-450. Annals of a Tweeddale Parish, by Baird, 67. Buchan and Paton's Peeblesshire, iii. 279-280.
of Skaar. Lands . . . in Galloway, iv. 16.

**Welwood of Garvock.** Burke's Landed Gentry (1848).

**Wemyss, Weems.** Heraldry, by A. Nisbet (1722), i. 282-283.
of Bogie. Douglas's Baronage, 561-562. Eminent Men of Fife, by M. F. Conolly, 480. Herald and Genealogist, viii. 62. Complete Baronetage, by G. E. C., iv. 429. The Scots Peerage, viii. 493-496. Debrett's Baronetage.
Lord Burntisland. The Scots Peerage, ii. 281-284.
of Cameron. The Scots Peerage, viii. 477.
of Caskieberran. The Scots Peerage, ii. 281.
of Dron. The Scots Peerage, viii. 485, 488, 489.
Lord Elcho. The Scots Peerage, viii. 500-518.
of Lathockar. Baronage, by Douglas, 553-555.
Lord Methil. The Scots Peerage, viii. 500-518.
of Rires. East Neuk of Fife, by W. Wood, 2nd ed., 112-114.
of Wemyss. Eminent Men of Fife, by M. F. Conolly, 146, 479-480. Historical MSS. Commission (1872), 3rd Report. Memorials of the Family of Wemyss of Wemyss, by Sir William Fraser, K.C.B., 3 vols., illust. (1888).* The Scots Peerage, viii. 476-511. Complete Baronetage, by G. E. C., ii. 282.
Earl of Wemyss. Nisbet's Heraldry (1742), ii., Appx. 33-38. The Scots Peerage, viii. 475-518. G. E. C.'s Complete Peerage.
Lord Wemyss of Elcho. The Scots Peerage, viii. 499-518.
of Wemyss Hall. Burke's Landed Gentry (1894-1925).

**Wemyss-Charteris-Douglas,** Earl of Wemyss. G. E. C.'s Complete Peerage. The Scots Peerage, viii. 513-518. Burke's and other Annual Peerages.

**Wemyss-Colchester.** Burke's Landed Gentry (1879-1886).

**Westminster,** Murray, Earl of. The Scots Peerage, iii. 514.

**Whitchester,** Scott, Lord of. The Scots Peerage, ii. 237.

**White** of Ardlawhill. Tayler's Jacobites of Aberdeenshire (1928), 414.
of Kellerstain. Burke's Landed Gentry (1848-1925).
of Overtoun. Irving's Book of Dumbartonshire, iii., portrait.

**Whitefoord** of Balloch. Paterson's Ayr and Wigton, i. 467-468.
of Ballochmyle. Ayr and Wigton, i. 469.
of Blairquhan. Paterson's History of the County of Ayr, ii. 471. Ayr and Wigton, i. 466. Complete Baronetage, by G. E. C., iv. 400.
of Dunduff. Ayr and Wigton, i. 431. Whitefoord Papers : Correspondence of Col. Charles W. Whitefoord and Caleb Whitefoord, 1739-1810 ; ed. W. A. S. Hewins (1898).
of Myltoune. Upper Ward of Lanarkshire, by Irving and Murray, ii. 420-421.

**Whitefoord** of Whitefoord. Heraldry, by A. Nisbet (1722), i. 376. Crawfurd's Shire of Renfrew (1818), 56-57. Paterson's History of Ayr, ii. 471.
  Geneal. Mag., ii. 167 ; iii. 221, 271. S. S. *in* Genealogist, 1st S., iv.
  141-144 ; v. 19-20.

**Whitelaw** of Gartshore. Burke's Landed Gentry (1879-1925).
  of Whitelaw. Heraldry, by Nisbet, i. 326. The House of Whitelaw,
  by H. Vincent Whitelaw (Glasgow, 1928).
  of Woodhall. Book of Dumbartonshire, by Irving, iii., portrait.

**Whiteside,** Ayr. The Dalrymples of Langlands, by J. Shaw, 4, 133-139.*

**Whitson** of Parkhill. Baronage of Angus and Mearns, by Peter, 357.

**Whyte** of Maw. Scottish N. and Q., 2nd S., ii. 48.
  of Stockbriggs. Annals of Lesmahagow, by Greenshields (1854), 99.*

**Whyte-Melville** of Strathkinness and Bennochy. Eminent Men of Fife,
  by M. F. Conolly. Burke's Commoners, ii. 659. Burke's Landed
  Gentry (1848-1879).
  of Strathtyrum and Bennochy. Scottish N. and Q., 2nd S., ii. 48.

**Whytt** of Bennochy. Douglas's Baronage, 529-531. The Balfours of
  Pilrig, by Barbara Balfour-Melville, 272.

**Wight** of Barbeth. Paterson's Ayr and Wigton, 476 *n.*

**Wigtown,** Douglas, Earl of. The Scots Peerage, iii. 168.
  Fleming, Earl of. The Scots Peerage, viii. 519-558. Inventory of the
  Charter Chest of the Earldom of Wigtown, 1214-1681 ; ed. F. J.
  Grant, Rothesay Herald, 133 pp. (Scottish Record Society, 1910).
  Notes and Queries, 4th S., viii. 88 ; x. 237. G. E. C.'s Complete
  Peerage. *See also* **Fleming.**

**Wilkie** of Foulden and Cammo. Cramond, by J. P. Wood, 64-65. Some
  Old Families, by H. B. M'Call, 250-251.
  Kennoway. Kennoway, by A. S. Cunningham, 28.
  of Newbarns. Baronage of Angus and Mearns, by Peter, 358.
  of Ormiston. Some Old Families, 251.
  of Rathobyres. Some Old Families, 240-250, and pedigree.

**Williamson.** Scottish N. and Q., 2nd S., v. 30. Notes on the Gunns,
  Hendersons . . . and Williamsons, by Capt. Gunn, *in* Northern
  Ensign (Wick, 26th Sept. 1905).
  of Banniskirk. Caithness Family History, by Henderson, 295-298.
  of Bonnington and Bridgelands. Buchan and Paton's Peeblesshire, ii.
  365 *n.*, and pedigree, 362.
  of Castle Robert. Folklore and Genealogies of Uppermost Nithsdale,
  by Wilson, 227-229.
  of Cardrona. History of Peeblesshire, by W. Chambers, 393-395. Buchan
  and Paton's Peeblesshire, ii. 548-549.
  Edinburgh, and Foxhall. R. R. Stodart *in* Herald and Genealogist, vii.
  225-229.
  of Foulage and Mailingsland. Buchan and Paton's Peeblesshire, ii.
  325-326.

**Williamson**, Fyvie.   The Thanage of Fermartyn, by Temple, 49.
in Sweden.   One Year in Sweden, by Marryat, ii. 500.

**Willison** of Cornton.   Logie, by Rev. Dr R. M. Fergusson, ii. 210.
of Craigforth.   MS. Pedigree by C. B. Boog Watson, in Lyon Office (1922).
Crawford.   The Family of Black, by W. G. Black (1924), 47-56.*

**Wilson** of Auchaber.   Thanage of Fermartyn, by Temple, 205.
of Aucheneck.   Strathendrick, by Guthrie Smith, 219.
in Blawearie.   Eminent Arbroathians, by J. M. M'Bain, 345.
Fyvie.   Thanage of Fermartyn, 50.
of Haylee.   Ayrshire Families, by G. Robertson, ii. 151-157.   Paterson's History of the County of Ayr, ii. 312.   Paterson's Ayr and Wigton, iii. 529.
Orphir.   Stemmata Robertson et Durdin, by H. Robertson (1893-95), 51.*
of Plewlands.   The Scots Peerage, v. 406.
of Polquhirter.   Folklore and Genealogies of Uppermost Nithsdale, by Wilson, 251.
of Spango.   Uppermost Nithsdale, 245.
of Wanlockhead.   Uppermost Nithsdale, 252.

**Wilson-Farquharson** of Allargue.   Burke's Landed Gentry (1898-1925).

**Wilsone** of Dalnair.   Strathendrick, by Guthrie Smith, 207, 221.

**Winchester** of Kinglassie.   Geneal. Coll., by W. Macfarlane, 1750-51 ; Scot. Hist. Soc., ii. 170, 188, 192.

**Windsor**, Stuart, Earl of.   The Scots Peerage, ii. 306-312.

**Wingate** of Cornton.   Logie, by Rev. Dr Menzies Fergusson, ii. 224.
of Hungry Kerse.   Logie, by Menzies Fergusson, ii. 230, 232.

**Winton** of Andate.   Temple's Thanage of Fermartyn, 413-414.

**Winton**, Montgomerie, Earl of.   The Scots Peerage, iii. 462-465.
Seton, Earl of.   The Scots Peerage, viii. 559-606.   Service of the Earl of Eglinton as Heir to the fourth Earl of Winton, folio, pedigree (1849).   The Family of Seton, by George Seton (1896).   Nisbet's Heraldic Plates, ed. Ross and Grant, 72-75.

**Wise** of Hillbank and Lunan.   Memorials of the Families of Wise of Hillbank . . . by Rev. C. Rogers (1873, 1877).   Angus or Forfarshire, by Warden, iv. 141-142, 249.   Pedigree of the Family of Wysse or Wise, sheet, royal 4to.

**Wiseman** of Rothes.   Scottish N. and Q., 2nd S., v. 135.

**Wishart**.   Life of George Wishart . . . and a Genealogical History of the Family of Wishart, by the Rev. C. Rogers (Grampian Club, 1876).
of Balgillo.   Monifieth, by J. Malcolm, 291.
of Cliftonhall.   G. E. C.'s Complete Baronetage, iv. 435.
of Logie-Wishart.   Memorials of Angus and the Mearns, by Jervise, ed. Gammack, ii. 131-134.   Angus or Forfarshire, by Warden, iv. 117-119.   Genealogical History of the Wisharts of Pittarrow and Logie Wishart, 77 pp. (Perth, 1914).

**Wishart** of Pittarrow.　Laurencekirk, by Fraser, 77.　Memorials of Angus and the Mearns, ii. 174-179.

**Wodrow.**　Paterson's History of Ayr, ii. 339, 509.

of Viewfield.　Paterson's Ayr and Wigton, i. 572.

**Wolrige-Gordon** of Hallhead and Esslemont.　Burke's Landed Gentry (1898-1925).

**Wood** of Bonytoun.　Warden's Angus or Forfarshire, iv. 307-311.　Scottish N. and Q. (1898-9), xii. 72-73.　Complete Baronetage, by G. E. C., iv. 254.

of Davo.　Scottish N. and Q., 2nd S., v. 64, 76, 93.

of Drumnagair.　Fraser's Laurencekirk, 113.

Elie and Earlsferry.　Eminent Men of Fife, by Conolly, 491-492.　East Neuk of Fife, by W. Wood, 2nd ed. (1887), *v-vii.*

of Largo.　Memorials of the Family of Wood of Largo, by Mrs F. M. Montague, 4to (1863).*　Eminent Men of Fife, 482-489.　East Neuk of Fife, 2nd ed., 63-76, 86, 89.

of Grange and Lambieletham.　East Neuk of Fife, 2nd ed., 184-186.　Herald and Genealogist, viii. 200-202.

of Orkie.　Eminent Men of Fife, 489.

of Sauchope.　Churchyard Monuments of Crail, by Erskine Beveridge, 72-75.

in Sweden.　One Year in Sweden, by Marryat, ii. 500.

of Warriston and Currichill.　Cramond, by J. P. Wood, 57 *n.*

**Wright** of Loss.　Logie, by Rev. Dr Menzies Fergusson, ii. 154.

of Phallope.　Gideon Guthrie, ed. C. E. Guthrie-Wright, 158.

of Steps.　Logie, by Rev. Dr Menzies Fergusson, ii. 124-125.

in Sweden.　One Year in Sweden, by Marryat, ii. 500.

**Wylie,** Edinburgh.　Nisbet's Heraldic Plates, ed. Ross and Grant (1892), 66.

**Wysse.**　*See* **Wise.**

**Yeaman,** Dundee.　Angus or Forfarshire, by A. J. Warden, iv. 412.　Geneal. Mag., vii. 461.

**Yester,** Hay, Lord Hay of.　The Scots Peerage, viii. 430-474.

**Young,** Aberdeen.　Memoir of James Young, Merchant Burgess of Aberdeen, and Rachel Cruikshank his Spouse, and of their Descendants . . . by Alex. Johnston, 1861 : ed. Lt.-Col. W. Johnston of Newton Dee (Aberdeen, 1894), 1-10, *et passim.**

of Aldbar.　Memorials of Angus and the Mearns, by Jervise, ed. Gammack, ii. 72-73.　Some Old Families, by H. B. M'Call (1890), 263.*

of Ascreavie.　Angus or Forfarshire, by Warden, iv. 36.

Bedrule.　Tancred's Rulewater, 222.

of Castleyaird.　Geneal. Mag., vi. 447.

of Cleish.　Burke's Landed Gentry (1848-1898).

Crail.　Churchyard Monuments of Crail, by Erskine Beveridge, 158-161.

**Young,** Domenica. Complete Baronetage, by G. E. C., v. 153.
of Fawside. Baronage of Angus and Mearns, by Peter, 363.
of Glendoune. Paterson's Ayr and Wigton, ii. 254.
of Insch and Seton. East Neuk of Fife, by W. Wood, 2nd ed., 284-286.
Kincardineshire. Scottish N. and Q., 2nd S., iv. 142 ; v. 173.
of Kings Cramond. Cramond, by J. P. Wood, 57.
of Leny. Wood's Cramond, 57, 70, 73. Oliver's History of Antigua,
iii. 280-284.
Nithsdale. Some Old Families, 263-281, *xxxv.**
of Ouchterlony. H. W. Young's Sir Peter Young, 6-7.*
of Rosebank. Nisbet's Heraldic Plates, ed. Ross and Grant (1892), 90.
of Seaton. H. W. Young *in* Proc. Soc. Antiq. Scotl. (1889), 262-269.
Eminent Arbroathians, by J. M. M'Bain, 64-80. Sir Peter Young
of Seaton, 1544-1628, by Hugh W. Young (1896),* [translated from
Thomas Smith's *Vitæ Illustrum Scotorum*, London, 1707.] Warden's
Angus or Forfarshire, v. 142-145.
of East Seaton. Notes and Queries, 1st S., ii. 441 ; vii. 549.
in Sweden. One Year in Sweden, by Marryat (1862), ii. 487, 492. Palace
of History Catalogue (Glasgow, 1911), 210.
of Youngfield. Lands . . . in Galloway, by M'Kerlie, v. 62, 184.
**Young-Herries** of Spottes. Some Old Families, by H. B. M'Call, 281-289.*
Lands . . . in Galloway, by M'Kerlie, v. 304.
**Young-Ogilvie** of Ascreavie. Baronage of Angus and Mearns, by Peter,
364.
**Younger,** Alloa. The Scottish Antiquary, iii. 6-10, 35-39, 134-138 ; x. 108.
The Family of Younger, by Rev. A. W. C. Hallen (1889).*
of Auchen Castle. Account of the Family of Younger, Co. Dumfries,
by Rev. A. W. C. Hallen, 4to (1890).* The Scottish Antiquary
(1896), x. 108. Burke's Landed Gentry (1882-1906). Debrett's
Baronetage (after 1911).
Kincardine - on - Forth. The Stirling Antiquary, ed. W. B. Cook,
iv. 317-318.
Viscount Younger of Leckie. The Annual Peerages (after 1923).
[Mr G. W. Younger, 2 Mecklenburgh Square, London, W.C. 1, is
collecting notes on Young and Younger.]
**Youngson,** New Deer. Smith's Genealogies of an Aberdeen Family ;
Aberd. Univ. Studies, 83-85.
**Yuille.** Family of Buchanan, by Buchanan of Auchmar, 142.
of Darleith. Irving's Book of Dumbartonshire, ii. 210-211. Burke's
Landed Gentry (1858-1898).

**Zetland,** Dundas, Earl of, Marquess of. G. E. C.'s Complete Peerage.
Debrett's and other Annual Peerages.
Sinclair, Lord of. The Scots Peerage, vi. 572-577.
Stewart, Lord of. The Scots Peerage, vi. 572-577.

# MISCELLANEOUS LISTS OF NAMES
# OF PERSONS

**1112-1477.** A Catalogue of the Bishops of Orkney, by Professor Münch of Christiania. Bannatyne Miscellany, iii. (Edinr. 1855).

**11— -1590.** The Abbots of Deir. Scottish N. and Q. (1889), iii. 55.

**1184-1615.** The Abbots of the Scottish Monastery at Würzburg. Scottish N. and Q. (1888), ii. 20-21.

**1221-1599 ; 1600-1649 ; 1660-1907.** Notices of the Officials of the Sheriff Court of Aberdeenshire : vols. 28, 31, 32 of New Spalding Club (Aberdeen, 1904-06-07).

**1250-1800.** Knights, Burgesses, Students, etc. Scottish Families in Finland and Sweden, by Otto Donner (Helsingfors, 1884).

**1272-1895.** Memorials of the Aldermen, Provosts and Lord Provosts of Aberdeen, by A. M. Munro (1895).

**1300-1814.** Military Officers, Settlers, etc., and Coats-of-Arms. Les Ecossais en France, par Francisque-Michel, 2 vols., 1862 ; and its English version, The Scots in France.

**1336-1538.** The Scottish Nation in the University of Orleans, ed. John Kirkpatrick (Scot. Hist. Soc. Misc., 1904).

**1357-1880.** Members of Parliament, Scotland, including the Minor Barons, the Commissioners for the Shires, and the Commissioners for the Burghs, by Joseph Foster, *in* Collectanea Genealogica (1881, 2nd ed. 1882), *xviii* + 360 pp.

**1396-1855.** Military Officers, Settlers, Students, etc. at Ratisbon, etc. The Scots in Germany, by Th. A. Fischer (1902).

**1413-1579.** The Graduation Roll of the University of St Andrews, ed. J. Maitland Anderson. Scot. Hist. Soc., 3rd S., viii. (1926).

**1418-1762.** Muster Rolls, etc. The Scots Men-at-Arms, by W. Forbes-Leith, 2 vols., 1883.

**1425-1484.** Scottish Students at Louvain University. Scottish Historical Review, xxv. 329-334.

**1436-1875.** List of the Deans of Guild of Aberdeen, by A. Walker (1875).

**1466-1495.** Marriages recorded in *Acta Dom. Conc.* and *Acta Dom. Aud.* The Scottish Antiquary, iii. 102-109.

**1473-1579.** The Matriculation Roll of the University of St Andrews, ed. J. M. Anderson. Scot. Hist. Soc., 3rd S., viii. (1926).

**1495-1860.** Officers and Graduates of University and King's College, Aberdeen, ed. P. J. Anderson. New Spalding Club (Aberdeen, 1893).

**1509-1603.** Denizations of Scotsmen in England. The Scottish Antiquary (Edinr. 1894), viii. 8-14, 58-61.

**1513.** Roll of the Slain at Flodden. The Scottish Antiquary (1899), xiii. 104-111, 168-172.

**1513.** The Kin, Friends and Dependants of Andrew Forman, Bishop of Moray. Scot. Hist. Review, xiii. 317-318.

**1526.** An Obituary from the Rental Book of the Preceptory of St Anthony, near Leith. Bannatyne Miscellany, ii. (1836).

**1531-1768.** Burgesses and Settlers in Danzig, Posen, etc. The Scots in West and East Prussia, by Th. A. Fischer (1903).

**1544-155—.** The Inhabitants of Stirling. The Scottish Antiquary, vi. 175-178.

**1553.** Muster Roll of the French Garrison at Dunbar. Scot. Hist. Soc. Misc. ii. (1904), 107-110.

**1567.** Register of Ministers, Exhorters and Readers, after the Reformation. Maitland Club (Edinr. 1830).

**1568-1746.** List of those attainted and convicted of High Treason for adherence to their rightful Sovereigns. Legitimist Kalendar, ed. by the Marquis de Ruvigny et Raineval, and Cranstoun Metcalfe (1899).

**1571-1753.** The Martyr Roll of Loyalty. Legitimist Kalendar, v.y.

**1573-1818.** Military Officers, Students, etc. The Scots in Sweden, by Th. A. Fischer (1907).

**1574.** Register of Ministers and Readers in the Kirk of Scotland, from the Book of the Assignation of Stipends. Wodrow Soc. Misc. (Edinr. 1844).

**1575-1791.** Victims of the Barbary Pirates. The Scottish Antiquary (1897), xi. 174-182.

**1575-1875.** Index to English-speaking Students at Leyden University, by Edward Peacock (Index Society, 1884).

**1578-1727.** Matriculated Members and Graduates of the University of Glasgow. Maitland Club, No. 72, vol. iii. (Glasgow, 1854).

**1579-1702.** Scots admitted to the Citizenship of Cracow, with evidence regarding their Parentage. Scot. Hist. Soc., No. 59 (1915), 39-58.

**1581-1900.** Registers of Students in the Scots Colleges at Douai, Rome, Madrid, Valladolid and Ratisbon. New Spalding Club (Aberdeen, 1906).

**1583-1858.** A Catalogue of the Graduates in the Faculties of Arts, Divinity, and Law, of the University of Edinburgh, since its Foundation, by David Laing. Bannatyne Club (Edinr. 1858).

**1585-1612.** Scottish Students at Helmstedt University. Scot. Hist. Review, xxiv. 235-237.

**1594-1890.** History of the Society of Writers to Her Majesty's Signet, with a list of the Members of the Society (1890).

**1596-1860.** Roll of Alumni in Arts of the University and King's College of Aberdeen, ed. P. J. Anderson (Aberdeen, 1900).

**1601-1682.** Early Marischal College Regents, Aberdeen. Scottish N. and Q. (1888), ii. 34-36, 56-58.

**1604-1867.** Scottish Middle Templars. Scot. Hist. Review, xvii. 103-117, 251.

**1609.** Undertakers in Scotland of the Ulster Plantation. Dr David Masson's Introduction to the Register of the Privy Council (1887), 1st S., viii., *lxxxviii-xci.*

**1611.** *Ibid.* Dr Masson's Introduction to the Register of the Privy Council (1889), 1st S., ix., *lxxx-lxxxi.*

**1622.** Contribution of St Cuthbert's, Edinburgh, to the Distressed Church in France, with donors' names. Scot. Hist. Soc. Misc., iii., 2nd S., No. 19, 193-201,

**1622-1878.** Register of Indentures of the Burgh of Aberdeen. Scottish N. and Q., x., xi., xii.

**1628-1853.** Masters and Undermasters at Aberdeen Grammar School. Scottish N. and Q., xi. 38-41.

**1634-1636.** List of Owners of Property in Edinburgh. The Book of the Old Edinburgh Club (1924), xiii. 96-145.

**1636.** The Inhabitants of Old Aberdeen. Scottish N. and Q. (1893), vii. 1-2, 20-22.

**1637-1705.** Birth Brieves from the Registers of the Burgh of Aberdeen. Spalding Club Misc., v. (Aberdeen, 1852).

**1641-1747.** Names of Persons exempted from the Acts of Indemnity. Legitimist Kalendar, v.y.

**1643.** Parchment Muster Roll of the Names and Surnames of the Captain . . . and Officers of the Scots Archer Bodyguard . . . under the command of Monsieur François de Rochechouart, seigneur de Chandenier: in the possession of Robert Kirke, Greenmount, Burntisland, in 1891.

**1645-1658.** Englishmen and Foreigners in Edinburgh, from Register of Baptisms, Canongate. The Scottish Antiquary, viii. 133-137 ; ix. 38-40.

**1647.** Names of the men murdered at Dunaverty in Kintyre. Highland Papers, ii. ; Scot. Hist. Soc. (1916), 255-257.

**1650 - 1880.** Marriages in Westminster Abbey Registers. Foster's Collectanea Genealogica (1881), i.

**1656-1760.** The Scottish College at Douai, with List of Personnel, by J. H. Baxter. Scot. Hist. Review, xxiv. 251-257.

**1660.** Scottish Officers who petitioned King Charles II. in 1660. The Scottish Antiquary, vi. 113-115.

**1661-1688.** Names of Officers serving in the Scots Army in Scotland, with Notes and Memoirs. Charles Dalton's Scots Army (1909).

**1662.** List of Middleton's Fines upon the Ayrshire Gentlemen in 1662. The Principal Families of Ayrshire, by George Robertson, ii. 372-375 (Irvine, 1824).

**1667.** Muster Rolls of Troops of Horsemen. Charles Dalton's Scots Army, 55-80.

**1678-1685.** Persons in Tweeddale abstaining from Conventicles, Peeblesshire. The Scottish Antiquary (1897), xi. 126-130.

**1682-1683.** Muster Rolls of the Earl of Mar's Regiment of Foot. Charles Dalton's Scots Army, 125-134.

**1684.** Parish Lists of Wigtownshire and Minnigaff, ed. with indexes by Wm. Scot. Scottish Record Society (Edinr. 1916), 107 pp.

**1684.** Rolls of Covenanters. J. Wood Brown, The Covenanters of the Merse (1893), 250-259.

**1685.** Ross-shire Heritors who took the Test. The Scottish Antiquary, xiii. 38-40.

**1687.** Members of the Edinburgh Merchants Company. The Scottish Antiquary (1898), xii. 126-129.

**1687-1698.** Register of Catholic Baptisms in Aberdeen and Neighbourhood. Scottish N. and Q., viii. 180-182.

**1690.** Notes on Land Valuation in Banffshire, with a full copy of the Valuation Roll of 1690, by Major F. Grant. Banffshire Field Club, 38 (Banff, 1917-18).

**1690-1854.** Scots in the Russian Navy. Scottish N. and Q., 2nd S., iii. 5.

**1693-1695.** Subscribers to the Company of Scotland trading to Africa and the Indies. Scot. Hist. Review, xxv. 243.

**1696.** Pollable Persons within the Shire of Aberdeen, 2 vols. Spalding Club (1844).

**— -1800.** Obituary of the Nobility, Gentry, etc., of England, Scotland and Ireland prior to 1800, collected by Sir Wm. Musgrave, Bt., *in* Foster's Collectanea Genealogica (1881).

**1704.** Apostates, Popish Priests, Papists and their Children in Aberdeenshire. Appx. to Blakhal's Breiffe Narration, ed. John Stuart. Spalding Club (Aberdeen, 1844).

**1713-1779.** Communion Roll of the Old Scots Regiment in Holland. Scot. Hist. Soc., No. 38 (1901).

**1715.** Rebel Prisoners transported to Virginia. Scottish N. and Q., 3rd S., iv. 187-188, 209.

**1715.** Resolve of the Heritors of Argyllshire. The Scottish Antiquary (1894), xiii. 126-128.

**1717.** Names attached to the Call to Mr John Woodrow from the Inhabitants of Stirling. The Scottish Antiquary, vi. 86-89.

**1727-1847.** The Grammar School Teachers in Greenock. Old Greenock, by G. Williamson (1888), ii. 146-222.

**1727-1897.** Roll of the Graduates of the University of Glasgow, with short biographical notices (1898).

**1727-1898.** Roll of Commissioned Officers in the Medical Service of the British Army, *lxxii*+638 pp. (Aberdeen University, 1917).

**1741.** Places and Offices in Scotland at the Gift and Disposal of the Crown. The Scottish Antiquary (1897), xii. 13-19.

**1745-1746.** The Prisoners of the '45, edited from the State Papers, by Sir Bruce Gordon Seton, Bart., and Jean Gordon Arnot (Scot. Hist. Soc.. 1929), 3 vols.

**1745-1746.** Noblemen, Gentlemen and others, attainted and adjudged to be guilty of High Treason since the 24th Day of June, 1745. Reprinted in The Scottish Antiquary, v. 49-53 ; vi. 27-30.

**1746.** Rebel Prisoners in Edinburgh. The Scottish Antiquary, vi. 127-130.

**1746.** A List of Persons concerned in the Rebellion, ed. Rev. Walter Macleod. Scot. Hist. Soc. (1890).

**1746.** List of Rebels. Brit. Mus. Add. MSS. No. 19, 796.

**1746.** An Exact List and Description of 150 Rebel Prisoners ship'd at Liverpool . . . for the Leeward Islands . . . and carried into Martinico, 30 June 1747, *in* Jacobite Gleanings, by J. Macbeth Forbes (1903), 48-50.

**1747.** List of 68 Rebel Prisoners from York Prison, sailing for America. Jacobite Gleanings, 56.

**1747-1897.** Matriculation Roll of the University of St Andrews, ed. J. Maitland Anderson (Edinr. and London, 1905).

**1748.** The Parishes and Islands within the Earldom of Orkney and Lordship of Zetland . . . and Certificate of the . . . Heads of Familys. Misc. Maitland Club, ii. (Edinr. 1840).

**1776-1876.** Burials in the Snow Churchyard, Old Aberdeen. Scottish N. and Q., vii. 148-151.

**1794.** List of the Loyal Greenock Volunteers. Old Greenock, by G. Williamson (1886), i. 302-303.

**1794-1868.** Macra Bursaries, Aberdeen. Scottish N. and Q., x. 177-179.

**1800-1804.** List of Corps of the Loyal Stirling Volunteers. The Stirling Antiquary, ed. W. B. Cook (1904), iii. 77-146.

**1808.** List of the Strathendrick Yeomanry. The Stirling Antiquary (1908), iv. 101.

**1819-1842.** Aberdeen-American Graduates, entrants at King's College. Scottish N. and Q., 1st S., i., v., vii., viii., ix., x., xi., xii. ; 2nd S., i., ii., iii., iv., v., viii.

**1860-1900.** Roll of Graduates of the University of Aberdeen, by Col. Wm. Johnston (Aberdeen, 1906).

List of Macs in Galloway. Scottish N. and Q., 2nd S., viii. 27-28.

# APPENDIX

## BIBLIOGRAPHY

**The Scots Peerage,** containing an Historical and Genealogical Account of the Nobility of that Kingdom, by Sir James Balfour Paul, C.V.O., LL.D., Lord Lyon King-of-Arms, with numerous Armorial illustrations and full index. 9 vols., roy 8vo, £11, 5s., or separate vols., 30s. each 1904-1914. David Douglas, Edinburgh.

**An Ordinary of Arms,** contained in the Public Register of all Arms and Bearings in Scotland, by James Balfour Paul, Lyon King-of-Arms. 1st edition, 10s. 6d., 1893 ; 2nd edition, 10s. 6d., 1903. William Green and Sons, Edinburgh.

**Heraldry in Relation to Scottish History and Art,** being the Rhind Lectures on Archæology for 1898, by Sir James Balfour Paul, F.S.A. Scot., Lord Lyon King-of-Arms. 10s. 6d. 1900. David Douglas, Castle Street, Edinburgh.

**Heraldry in Scotland,** including a Recension of " The Law and Practice of Heraldry in Scotland," by the late George Seton, Advocate ; second edition by J. H. Stevenson, Advocate, Unicorn Pursuivant. 2 vols. with 37 full-page plates, and 81 coats-of-arms in text. £4, 4s., 1914. James Maclehose and Sons, Glasgow.

**A Manual of Heraldry,** by Francis J. Grant, W.S., Lord Lyon King-of-Arms. 350 illustrations. 4s. 1929. John Grant, Edinburgh.

**Scottish Kings,** a revised Chronology of Scottish History, 1005-1625, with Notices of the Principal Events, Tables of Regnal Years, Pedigrees, Calendars, etc., by Sir Archibald H. Dunbar, Bart. 1st edition, 1899 ; 2nd edition. 12s. 6d., 1907.

**A Short History of Scotland,** by P. Hume Brown, M.A., LL.D. Formerly Fraser Professor of Ancient (Scottish) History and Palæography, University of Edinburgh, and Historiographer-Royal for Scotland, 154 illustrations, and 10 maps and plans. 7s. 6d. Oliver and Boyd, Tweeddale Court, Edinburgh.

**Handy Administrative Atlas of Scotland,** a Series of detailed County Maps, showing the Parishes, edited by George Philip, F.R.G.S. 3s. The London Geographical Institute, 32 Fleet Street, London.

**Fasti Ecclesiæ Scoticanæ.** The Succession of Ministers in the Church of Scotland from the Reformation, by Hew Scott, D.D. New Edition. Revised and continued to the Present Time under the Superintendence of a Committee appointed by the General Assembly.

In Seven Volumes. Roy. 8vo. I. Synod of Lothian and Tweeddale. II. Synods of Merse and Teviotdale, Dumfries and Galloway. III. Synod of Glasgow and Ayr. IV. Synods of Argyll, Perth, and Stirling. V. Synods of Fife, Angus, and Mearns. VI. Synods of Aberdeen and Moray. VII. Synods of Ross, Sutherland and Caithness, Glenelg, Orkney, and Shetland. The Church in England. Ireland, and Overseas. Complete, £9, 5s. net. Vols. I. to VI. may be had separately at £1, 10s. net each and Vol. VII. at £2 net. Oliver and Boyd, Tweeddale Court, Edinburgh.

**Oliver and Boyd's Edinburgh Almanac and National Repository.** Part I. The Kalendar, with Astronomical Ephemeris, and Notes and Tide Tables. Part II. Information in Commerce, Agriculture, Law, Chronology, and Statistics. Part III. General Register for the British Empire. Part IV. National Register, Civil and Ecclesiastical, for Scotland, including list of Peers and Baronets of Scotland. Part V. Register for the City and County of Edinburgh. Carefully revised and brought up to date each year. Published annually. Price 15s. net.

## THE COURT OF THE LORD LYON
### Register House, Edinburgh.

#### Lyon King-of-Arms.
FRANCIS JAMES GRANT, W.S.

#### Heralds.
*Marchmont*—John Horne Stevenson, M.B.E., K.C., F.S.A. Scot.
*Albany*—Lt.-Col. Sir T. Wolseley Haig, K.C.I.E., C.S.I., C.M.G., C.B.E.
*Rothesay*—J. M. Norman Macleod, C.A.

#### Pursuivants.
*Carrick*—Thomas Innes of Learney, Advocate.
*Falkland*—Lt.-Col. J. W. Balfour Paul, D.S.O., of Cakemuir.
*Unicorn*—Harold Andrew Balvaird Lawson.

**Lyon Clerk and Keeper of Records**—Harold Andrew Balvaird Lawson.
**Procurator Fiscal**—John MacGregor, W.S.
**Herald Painter**—A. G. Law Samson.

## SOCIETIES
### The Scottish Record Society.
*Secretary*—JOHN MACGREGOR, Esq., W.S., 3 Coates Crescent, Edinburgh.

### The Society of Genealogists.
5 Bloomsbury Square, London, W.C.